Ancient Christian Texts

Lectures on the Psalms

Didymus the Blind

TRANSLATED AND EDITED BY
JONATHAN DOUGLAS HICKS

InterVarsity Press
P.O. Box 1400 | Downers Grove, IL 60515-1426
ivpress.com | email@ivpress.com

©2024 by Jonathan Douglas Hicks, Gerald Bray, Michael Glerup, and the Institute for Classical Christian Studies

All rights reserved. No part of this book may be reproduced in any form without written permission from InterVarsity Press.

InterVarsity Press® is the publishing division of InterVarsity Christian Fellowship/USA®. For more information, visit intervarsity.org.

All Scripture quotations, unless otherwise indicated, are a translation of Didymus's biblical quotes.

The publisher cannot verify the accuracy or functionality of website URLs used in this book beyond the date of publication.

Cover design: Cindy Kiple
Interior design: Daniel van Loon
Images: Saints Peter and Paul by Carlo Crivelli at Accademia, Venice/Art Resource, NY

ISBN 978-1-5140-0604-7 (print) | ISBN 978-1-5140-0605-4 (digital)

Printed in the United States of America ∞

Library of Congress Cataloging-in-Publication Data
Names: Didymus, the Blind, approximately 313-approximately 398, author. | Hicks, Jonathan (Jonathan Douglas), 1984- editor, translator.
Title: Lectures on the Psalms / Didymus the Blind ; edited and translated by Jonathan Douglas Hicks.
Other titles: Eis Psalmous. English
Description: Downers Grove, IL : IVP Academic, [2024] | Series: Ancient Christian texts | Translation of a Greek manuscript known as Eis Psalmous discovered in 1941 near the ruins of an ancient monastery dedicated to Saint Arsenius the Great. | Includes bibliographical references and indexes.
Identifiers: LCCN 2023037089 (print) | LCCN 2023037090 (ebook) | ISBN 9781514006047 (print) | ISBN 9781514006054 (digital)
Subjects: LCSH: Bible. Psalms–Commentaries–Early works to 1800. | Bible. Psalms–Criticism and interpretation–Early works to 1800.
Classification: LCC BS1429 .D4813 2024 (print) | LCC BS1429 (ebook) | DDC 223/.207–dc23/eng/20230913
LC record available at https://lccn.loc.gov/2023037089
LC ebook record available at https://lccn.loc.gov/2023037090

CONTENTS

ABBREVIATIONS / PAGE IX

GENERAL INTRODUCTION / PAGE XI

VOLUME INTRODUCTION / PAGE XIX

LECTURES ON THE PSALMS / PAGE 1

GENERAL INDEX / PAGE 363

SCRIPTURE INDEX / PAGE 365

ABBREVIATIONS

LES2   Lexham English Septuagint, second edition
LXX   Septuagint
NETS   New English Translation of the Septuagint
NRSV   New Revised Standard Version
PsT   Commentary on the Psalms (found at Turah)
PTA   Papyrologische Texte und Abhandlungen

GENERAL INTRODUCTION

Ancient Christian Texts (hereafter ACT) presents the full text of ancient Christian commentaries on Scripture that have remained so unnoticed that they have not yet been translated into English.

The patristic period (AD 95–750) is the time of the fathers of the church, when the exegesis of Scripture texts was in its primitive formation. This period spans from Clement of Rome to John of Damascus, embracing seven centuries of biblical interpretation, from the end of the New Testament to the mid-eighth century, including the Venerable Bede.

This series extends but does not reduplicate texts of the Ancient Christian Commentary on Scripture (ACCS). It presents full-length translations of texts that appear only as brief extracts in the ACCS. The ACCS began years ago authorizing full-length translations of key patristic texts on Scripture in order to provide fresh sources of valuable commentary that previously were not available in English. It is from these translations that the ACT series has emerged.

A multiyear project such as this requires a well-defined objective. The task is straightforward: *to introduce full-length translations of key texts of early Christian teaching, homilies and commentaries on a particular book of Scripture.* These are seminal documents that have decisively shaped the entire subsequent history of biblical exegesis, but in our time have been largely ignored.

To carry out this mission each volume of the Ancient Christian Texts series has four aspirations:

1. To show the approach of one of the early Christian writers in dealing with the problems of understanding, reading and conveying the meaning of a particular book of Scripture.

2. To make more fully available the whole argument of the ancient Christian interpreter of Scripture to all who wish to think with the early church about a particular canonical text.

3. To broaden the base of the biblical studies, Christian teaching and preaching to include classical Christian exegesis.

4. To stimulate Christian historical, biblical, theological and pastoral scholarship toward deeper inquiry into early classic practitioners of scriptural interpretation.

For Whom Is This Series Designed?

We have selected and translated these texts primarily for general and nonprofessional use by an audience of persons who study the Bible regularly.

In varied cultural settings around the world, contemporary readers are asking how they might grasp the meaning of sacred texts under the instruction of the great minds of the ancient church. They often study books of the Bible verse by verse, book by book, in groups and workshops, sometimes with a modern commentary in hand. But many who study the Bible intensively hunger to have available as well the thoughts of a reliable classic Christian commentator on this same text. This series will give the modern commentators a classical text for comparison and amplification. Readers will judge for themselves as to how valuable or complementary are their insights and guidance.

The classic texts we are translating were originally written for anyone (lay or clergy, believers or seekers) who wished to reflect and meditate with the great minds of the early church. They sought to illuminate the plain sense, theological wisdom, and moral and spiritual meaning of an individual book of Scripture. They were not written for an academic audience, but for a community of faith shaped by the sacred text.

Yet in serving this general audience, the editors remain determined not to neglect the rigorous requirements and needs of academic readers who until recently have had few full translations available to them in the history of exegesis. So this series is designed also to serve public libraries, universities, academic classes, homiletic preparation, and historical interests worldwide in Christian scholarship and interpretation.

Hence our expected audience is not limited to the highly technical and specialized scholarly field of patristic studies, with its strong bent toward detailed word studies and explorations of cultural contexts. Though all of our editors and translators are patristic and linguistic scholars, they also are scholars who search for the meanings and implications of the texts. The audience is not primarily the university scholar concentrating on the study of the history of the transmission of the text or those with highly focused interests in textual morphology or historical-critical issues. If we succeed in serving our wider readers practically and well, we hope to serve as well college and seminary courses in Bible, church history, historical theology, hermeneutics, and homiletics. These texts have not until now been available to these classes.

Readiness for Classic Spiritual Formation

Today global Christians are being steadily drawn toward these biblical and patristic sources for daily meditation and spiritual formation. They are on the outlook for primary classic sources of spiritual formation and biblical interpretation, presented in accessible form and grounded in reliable scholarship.

These crucial texts have had an extended epoch of sustained influence on Scripture interpretation, but virtually no influence in the modern period. They also deserve a hearing among modern readers and scholars. There is a growing awareness of the speculative excesses and spiritual and homiletic limitations of much post-Enlightenment criticism. Meanwhile the motifs, methods, and approaches of ancient exegetes have remained unfamiliar not only to historians but to otherwise highly literate biblical scholars, trained exhaustively in the methods of historical and scientific criticism.

It is ironic that our times, which claim to be so fully furnished with historical insight and research methods, have neglected these texts more than scholars in previous centuries who could read them in their original languages.

This series provides indisputable evidence of the modern neglect of classic Christian exegesis: it remains a fact that extensive and once authoritative classic commentaries on Scripture still remain untranslated into any modern language. Even in China such a high level of neglect has not befallen classic Buddhist, Taoist, and Confucian commentaries.

Ecumenical Scholarship

This series, like its two companion series, the ACCS and Ancient Christian Doctrine (ACD), is an expression of unceasing ecumenical efforts that have enjoyed the wide cooperation of distinguished scholars of many differing academic communities. Under this classic textual umbrella, it has brought together in common spirit Christians who have long distanced themselves from each other by competing church memories. But all of these traditions have an equal right to appeal to the early history of Christian exegesis. All of these traditions can, without a sacrifice of principle or intellect, come together to study texts common to them all. This is its ecumenical significance.

This series of translations is respectful of a distinctively theological reading of Scripture that cannot be reduced to historical, philosophical, scientific, or sociological insights or methods alone. It takes seriously the venerable tradition of ecumenical reflection concerning the premises of revelation, providence, apostolicity, canon, and consensuality. A high respect is here granted, despite modern assumptions, to uniquely Christian theological forms of reasoning, such as classical consensual christological and triune reasoning, as distinguishing premises of classic Christian textual interpretation. These cannot be acquired by empirical methods alone. This approach does not pit theology against critical theory; instead, it incorporates critical historical methods and brings them into coordinate accountability within its larger purpose of listening to Scripture.

The internationally diverse character of our editors and translators corresponds with the global range of our audience, which bridges many major communions of Christianity. We have sought to bring together a distinguished international network of Protestant, Catholic, and Orthodox scholars, editors, and translators of the highest quality and reputation to accomplish this design.

But why just now at this historical moment is this need for patristic wisdom felt particularly by so many readers of Scripture? Part of the reason is that these readers have been longer deprived of significant contact with many of these vital sources of classic Christian exegesis.

The Ancient Commentary Tradition

This series focuses on texts that comment on Scripture and teach its meaning. We define a commentary in its plain-sense definition as a series of illustrative or explanatory notes on any work of enduring significance. The word *commentary* is an Anglicized form of the Latin *commentarius* (or "annotation" or "memoranda" on a subject, text, or series of events). In its theological meaning it is a work that explains, analyzes, or expounds a biblical book or portion of Scripture. Tertullian, Origen, John Chrysostom, Jerome, Augustine, and Clement of Alexandria all revealed their familiarity with both the secular and religious commentators available to them as they unpacked the meanings of the sacred text at hand.

The commentary in ancient times typically began with a general introduction covering such questions as authorship, date, purpose, and audience. It commented as needed on grammatical or lexical problems in the text and provided explanations of difficulties in the text. It typically moved verse by verse through a Scripture text, seeking to make its meaning clear and its import understood.

The general Western literary genre of commentary has been definitively shaped by the history of early Christian commentaries on Scripture. It is from Origen, Hilary, the *Opus imperfectum in Matthaeum*, John Chrysostom, and Cyril of Alexandria that we learn what a commentary is—far more so than in the case of classic medical, philosophical, or poetic commentaries. It leaves too much unsaid simply to assume that the Christian biblical commentary took a previously extant literary genre and reshaped it for Christian texts. Rather it is more accurate to say that *the Western literary genre of the commentary (and especially the biblical commentary) has patristic commentaries as its decisive pattern and prototype.*

It is only in the last two centuries, since the development of modern historicist methods of criticism, that modern writers have sought more strictly to delimit the definition of a commentary so as to include only certain limited interests focusing largely on historical-critical method, philological and grammatical observations, literary analysis, and sociopolitical or economic circumstances impinging on the text. While respecting all these approaches, the ACT editors do not hesitate to use the classic word *commentary* to define more broadly the genre of this series. These are commentaries in their classic sense.

The ACT editors freely take the assumption that the Christian canon is to be respected as the church's sacred text. The reading and preaching of Scripture are vital to religious life. The central hope of this endeavor is that it might contribute in some small way to the revitalization of religious faith and community through a renewed discovery of the earliest readings of the church's Scriptures.

An Appeal to Allow the Text to Speak for Itself

This prompts two appeals:

1. For those who begin by assuming as normative for a commentary only the norms considered typical for modern expressions of what a commentary is, we ask: please allow the ancient commentators to define *commentarius* according to their own lights. Those who assume the preemptive authority and truthfulness of modern critical methods alone will always tend to view the classic Christian exegetes as dated, quaint, premodern, hence inadequate, and in some instances comic or even mean-spirited, prejudiced, unjust, and oppressive. So in the interest of hermeneutical fairness, it is recommended that the modern reader not impose upon ancient Christian exegetes modern assumptions about valid readings of Scripture. The ancient Christian writers constantly challenge these unspoken, hidden, and indeed often camouflaged assumptions that have become commonplace in our time.

We leave it to others to discuss the merits of ancient versus modern methods of exegesis. But even this cannot be done honestly without a serious examination of the texts of ancient exegesis. Ancient commentaries may be disqualified as commentaries by modern standards. But they remain commentaries by the standards of those who anteceded and formed the basis of the modern commentary.

The attempt to read a Scripture text while ruling out all theological and moral assumptions—as well as ecclesial, sacramental, and dogmatic assumptions that have prevailed generally in the community of faith out of which it emerged—is a very thin enterprise indeed. Those who tendentiously may read a single page of patristic exegesis, gasp and toss it away because it does not conform adequately to the canons of modern exegesis and historicist commentary are surely not exhibiting a valid model for critical inquiry today.

2. In ancient Christian exegesis, chains of biblical references were often very important in thinking about the text in relation to the whole testimony of sacred Scripture, by the analogy of faith, comparing text with text, on the premise that *scripturam ex scriptura explicandam esse*. When ancient exegesis weaves many Scripture texts together, it does not limit its focus to a single text as much modern exegesis prefers, but constantly relates them to other texts, by analogy, intensively using typological reasoning, as did the rabbinic tradition.

Since the principle prevails in ancient Christian exegesis that each text is illumined by other texts and by the whole narrative of the history of revelation, we find in patristic comments on a given text many other subtexts interwoven in order to illumine that text. In these ways the models of exegesis often do not correspond with modern commentary assumptions, which tend to resist or rule out chains of scriptural reference. We implore the reader not to force the assumptions of twentieth-century hermeneutics upon the ancient Christian writers, who themselves knew nothing of what we now call hermeneutics.

The Complementarity of Research Methods in This Series

The Ancient Christian Texts series will employ several interrelated methods of research, which the editors and translators seek to bring together in a working integration. Principal among these methods are the following:

1. The editors, translators, and annotators will bring to bear the best resources of *textual criticism* in preparation for their volumes. This series is not intended to produce a new critical edition of the original-language text. The best urtext in the original language will be used. Significant variants in the earliest manuscript sources of the text may be commented upon as needed in the annotations. But it will be assumed that the editors and translators will be familiar with the textual ambiguities of a particular text and be able to state their conclusions about significant differences among scholars. Since we are working with ancient texts that have, in some cases, problematic or ambiguous passages, we are obliged to employ all methods of historical, philological, and textual inquiry appropriate to the study of ancient texts. To that end, we will appeal to the most reliable text-critical scholarship of both biblical and patristic studies. We will assume that our editors and translators have reviewed the international literature of textual critics regarding their text so as to provide the reader with a translation of the most authoritative and reliable form of the ancient text. We will leave it to the volume editors and translators, under the supervision of the general editors, to make these assessments. This will include the challenge of considering which variants within the biblical text itself might impinge upon the patristic text, and which forms or stemma of the biblical text the patristic writer was employing. The annotator will supply explanatory footnotes where these textual challenges may raise potential confusions for the reader.

2. Our editors and translators will seek to understand the *historical context* (including socioeconomic, political, and psychological aspects as needed) of the text. These understandings are often vital to right discernment of the writer's intention. Yet we do not see our primary mission as that of discussing in detail these contexts. They are to be factored into the translation and commented on as needed in the annotations, but are not to become the primary focus of this series. Our central interest is less in the social location of the text or the philological history of particular words than in authorial intent and accurate translation. Assuming a proper social-historical contextualization of the text, the main focus of this series will be upon a dispassionate and fair translation and analysis of the text itself.

3. The main task is to set forth the meaning of the biblical text itself as understood by the patristic writer. The intention of our volume editors and translators is to help the reader see clearly into the meanings that patristic commentators have discovered in the biblical text. *Exegesis* in its classic sense implies an effort to explain, interpret, and comment on a text, its meaning, its sources and its connections with other texts. It implies

a close reading of the text, using whatever linguistic, historical, literary, or theological resources are available to explain the text. It is contrasted with *eisegesis*, which implies that interpreters have imposed their own personal opinions or assumptions on the text. The patristic writers actively practiced intratextual exegesis, which seeks to define and identify the exact wording of the text, its grammatical structure and the interconnectedness of its parts. They also practiced extratextual exegesis, seeking to discern the geographical, historical or cultural context in which the text was written. Our editors and annotators will also be attentive as needed to the ways in which the ancient Christian writer described his own interpreting process or hermeneutic assumptions.

4. The underlying philosophy of translation that we employ in this series is, like the Ancient Christian Commentary on Scripture, termed *dynamic equivalency*. We wish to avoid the pitfalls of either too loose a paraphrase or too rigid a literal translation. We seek language that is literary but not purely literal. Whenever possible we have opted for the metaphors and terms that are normally in use in everyday English-speaking culture. Our purpose is to allow the ancient Christian writers to speak for themselves to ordinary readers in the present generation. We want to make it easier for the Bible reader to gain ready access to the deepest reflection of the ancient Christian community of faith on a particular book of Scripture. We seek a thought-for-thought translation rather than a formal equivalence or word-for-word style. This requires the words to be first translated accurately and then rendered in understandable idiom. We seek to present the same thoughts, feelings, connotations and effects of the original text in everyday English language. We have used vocabulary and language structures commonly used by the average person. We do not leave the quality of translation only to the primary translator, but pass it through several levels of editorial review before confirming it.

The Function of the ACT Introductions, Annotations, and Translations

In writing the introduction for a particular volume of the ACT series, the translator or volume editor will discuss, where possible, the opinion of the writer regarding authorship of the text, the importance of the biblical book for other patristic interpreters, the availability or paucity of patristic comment, any salient points of debate between the Fathers, and any special challenges involved in translating and editing the particular volume. The introduction affords the opportunity to frame the entire commentary in a manner that will help the general reader understand the nature and significance of patristic comment on the biblical text under consideration and to help readers find their critical bearings so as to read and use the commentary in an informed way.

The footnotes will assist the reader with obscurities and potential confusions. In the annotations the volume editors have identified Scripture allusions and historical references embedded within the texts. Their purpose is to help the reader move easily from passage to passage without losing a sense of the whole.

The ACT general editors seek to be circumspect and meticulous in commissioning volume editors and translators. We strive for a high level of consistency and literary quality throughout the course of this series. We have sought out as volume editors and translators those patristic and biblical scholars who are thoroughly familiar with their original language sources, who are informed historically, and who are sympathetic to the needs of ordinary nonprofessional readers who may not have professional language skills.

Thomas C. Oden, Gerald L. Bray, and Michael Glerup, Series Editors

VOLUME INTRODUCTION

A good literary introduction possesses the same elements as a good personal one. Without underinforming or misinforming, it is adequate rather than exhaustive. It leaves the introduced with a sense of the next question that should be asked. It invites further engagement, proposing just enough of the terms of engagement to be helpful but not so many of them so as to get in the way of the engagement itself. It prejudices the reader just a little in the right way and then gets out of the way.

Since these *Lectures on the Psalms* will be, for many, a first foray into the lectures of Didymus the Blind, it is my aim to arm them with answers to the few questions that are most likely to occur to them during this initial engagement. Who was Didymus the Blind? Who was his original audience? What was the shared goal that kept them returning to his daily lectures on the Psalms? And finally, what is to be gained from listening in on these lectures today? If this introduction encourages the reader to gain from Christ the inestimable riches of his contemplative and active virtue, then it will have succeeded in introducing the reader to the real subject of Didymus's *Lectures on the Psalms*.

Didymus's Life and Works

The hard facts of Didymus's life make for a short read. He lived between 313 and 398.[1] Born at the close of the Great Persecution (303–313) and during the year when the Edict of Milan gave Christianity legal protection, Didymus was therefore among the first generation of Christians to enjoy this privilege. Due to an illness at the tender age of four, he lost his sight, a condition that earned him his epithet "the Blind" and kept him in the city of Alexandria throughout his life.[2]

The Egyptian metropolis placed him very much at the center of two of the greatest ecclesial developments of his day. Hardly a young man before the Council of Nicaea met

---

[1] From two of his former students, Saint Jerome and Palladius, we learn that he was born in either 310 or 313 and lived until his eighty-fifth year. See Jerome, *On Illustrious Men*, ed. Thomas P. Halton, Fathers of the Church 100 (Washington, DC: Catholic University of America Press, 2010), 109.3 (p. 142), and Palladius, *The Lausiac History*, trans. Robert T. Meyer, Ancient Christian Writers 34 (Mahwah, NJ: Paulist Press, 1964), 4.1 (p. 35). However, the manuscript tradition varies widely on Jerome's numbers. Hence, Palladius is generally preferred. See Gustave Bardy, *Didyme l'Aveugle* (Paris: Beauchesne, 1910), 3. Grant Bayliss favors Jerome's evidence in *The Vision of Didymus the Blind: A Fourth-Century Virtue-Origenism* (Oxford: Oxford University Press, 2015), 8n3.
[2] Palladius, *Lausiac History* 4.1 (p. 35); Socrates Scholasticus, *The Ecclesiastical History* 4.25, in *Nicene and Post-Nicene Fathers*, ed. Philip Schaff, second series (repr., Peabody, MA: Hendrickson, 1994), 2:110.

xix

in 325, Didymus would support the theological vision of a succession of pro-Nicene bishops in his city—Alexander, Athanasius, and Theophilus. His response to the Arian and Eunomian heresies, which threatened the church for the better part of the fourth century, earned him a reputation as a defender of the orthodox faith. Likewise, when the Egyptian desert began to attract world-weary Christians after it became profitable for Roman citizens to convert to Christianity, Didymus served as a link between the city and the desert. Although he was not a member of an ascetic community, the simplicity of his life and his wisdom attracted many an ascetic to his cell, there to benefit from his labor in interpreting Holy Scripture and to give and receive mutual encouragement. Such great ascetics as Saint Antony the Great and Evagrius Ponticus were among this number.

In spite of his disability, Didymus excelled in learning. Although by most accounts he had not mastered the alphabet by the time he went blind, he compensated for his lack of vision by intense effort at his studies. While his fellow students slept, Didymus used the nocturnal hours to rehearse all that he had heard during the day's lessons, so that he gradually surpassed them all.[3] Relying on the reading of others and on constant repetition, Didymus's memory of Holy Scripture particularly impressed his contemporaries. He eventually earned the approbation of his bishop, Saint Athanasius, to lead a church-sanctioned school within the city of Alexandria. He remained in this position, teaching an ascetically minded circle of scholars, engaging in verbal and written polemic with those who challenged the church's teaching, and publishing a wide array of books until his death just before the turn of the fourth century.

As a scholar, Didymus was prolific. Palladius's remark that "he interpreted the Old and New Testaments word by word" is hardly hyperbolic.[4] We know of about thirty commentaries on the books of the Old and New Testaments. His commentaries *On Genesis*, *On Job*, *On the Psalms*, *On Ecclesiastes*, and *On Zechariah* are all extant. The length of these works and their numerical preponderance within his overall corpus suggests that commentary on Holy Scripture was the mainstay of his school.

Another significant portion of his corpus is dedicated to dogmatic works. Among the twenty or so works that fall into this category are his *Against the Manichees*, *Against Eunomius*, *On Virtues*, *On the Holy Spirit*, and *On the Trinity*. A *Commentary on Origen's First Principles* and a *Dialogue with a Heretic* round out a corpus impressive for its breadth of interest and varied style.[5] They also suggest that Didymus was as much a student of theology as he was a biblical scholar, at a time when these pursuits were not as estranged as they have become in our time.

---

[3]Rufinus, *The History of the Church*, trans. Philip R. Amidon, Fathers of the Church 133 (Washington, DC: Catholic University of America Press, 2016), 11.7 (pp. 442-43).
[4]Palladius, *Lausiac History* 4.2 (p. 35).
[5]For a fuller list, see Bayliss, *Vision of Didymus the Blind*, 54-55.

Finally, a sense of his personality also survives in two of the most frequently repeated anecdotes about his life. Palladius relates that he once refused Didymus's request for him to offer a prayer in his cell. The likeliest motivation behind this refusal was Palladius's sense that he was not up to the task. Didymus, however, read the refusal in a different light, saying:

> The Blessed Antony entered this cell . . . and when I begged him to pray, he knelt down in the cell to pray at once and did not force me to repeat my invitation, thereby giving me an example of obedience by his compliance. Now, if you are going in the footsteps of his way of life, inasmuch as you are living the life of a solitary away from home, put aside your contentious spirit.[6]

The anecdote accords with instances in the *Lectures on the Psalms*, where Didymus also censures his students, quite straightforwardly, for perceived failures in judgment or virtue. In modern classrooms, such directness would likely be interpreted as a pedagogical misstep. Palladius, who would hardly have repeated the anecdote if he thought the rebuke was wide of the mark, thought that it illustrated his host's knowledge of his own personal weakness and his willingness to help him with it by pointing it out.[7]

A second story also features St. Antony. The saint was visiting Alexandria in order to urge the faithful to follow their bishop's teaching on the Son's divinity against the Arian position. On this trip he took the opportunity to say to Didymus, "Do not be troubled, Didymus, because you are deemed deprived of your physical eyes, for what you lack are those eyes which mice, flies, and lizards have; rejoice rather that you have the eyes which angels have, by which God is seen, and through which a great light of knowledge is being kindled for you."[8] This story illustrates the role that Didymus played in the struggle with Arianism throughout the fourth century. Not untroubled by his loss of physical sight, Didymus courageously acknowledged the providence that governs the course of human life. He prayed and studied in order that his spiritual vision might grow stronger by the day, becoming in him a light of knowledge for others. We meet in Didymus a personality whose charisms were laid at the disposal of this goal: that his spiritual vision might become a lighthouse, shedding abroad the knowledge of God.

Original Audience

In 1941, these *Lectures on the Psalms* and several others attributed to Didymus the Blind were discovered near the ruins of an ancient monastery dedicated to Saint Arsenius the Great. It was quickly discovered that this commentary and the *Commentary on Ecclesiastes* contained something unique in Didymus's known corpus, something quite rare in the surviving records of antiquity. Unlike the Alexandrian's other known works, in which

---
[6]Palladius, *Lausiac History* 4.3 (pp. 35–36).
[7]Palladius, *Lausiac History* 4.1-2 (p. 35).
[8]Rufinus, *History of the Church* 11.7 (pp. 443-44).

some level of editing had taken place between the initial dictation of the work and its written publication, these two commentaries were unedited transcriptions of his lectures. In them, we hear the living voice of Didymus, directly addressing his students in the second person. He refers to the passage of time with phrases such as "As I was saying yesterday." The students respond to the lecture with questions. Even the arguments within the classroom are recorded. In brief, we are never closer to Didymus's original audience than we are in his lectures on the Psalms and Ecclesiastes.[9]

Who were these auditors? If the portrait that emerges from the *Lectures on the Psalms* and the *Commentary on Ecclesiastes* tells against identifying them as members of an institutional school—replete with a set curriculum, staff, and building—neither do they appear to be a casual audience attending, say, a series of open lectures.[10] There are indications that the auditors met together with Didymus daily (and perhaps twice daily, morning and evening) for a formal lecture on a predetermined passage of Holy Scripture. This happened with at least some degree of continuity, so that we are permitted to use the word *school* of this circle, though we ought to keep in mind that ancient schools were often less formal than modern ones.

There is internal evidence within the commentaries for a range of intellectual ability within the student body. Of the questions that occur within the commentaries, two are by far the most common.[11] Some ask for clarifications on the meanings of words within the psalm that is being studied. Others simply ask for Didymus to explain a portion of the text that he has appeared to skip over or has delayed in coming to. These occasionally betray inattentiveness on the part of the student. On the other side of the spectrum there appears the occasional student who is confident enough to ask truly probing questions. Such an example occurs during the widely cited argument that occurs between Didymus and his student during his exegesis of Psalm 34:17.[12] Here the student reveals that he has followed large segments of Didymus's teaching, that he is able to wield scriptural examples that successfully challenge his teacher, and that he is aware of the broader metaphysical problems posed by following his teacher's interpretation.

From the side of the teacher, we see a corresponding valuation of his students' abilities. On the one side, topics that occur regularly in his discussion with his students are etymologies, grammar, and logic, topics usually considered elementary to educational formation.[13] On the other hand, more advanced topics also occur: for example, Protagorean

---

[9] See L. Koenen and W. Muller-Wiener, "Zu den Papyri aus dem Arsenioskloster bei Ṭurā," *Zeitschrift für Papyrologie und Epigraphik* 2 (1968): 42-43, and Anne Browning Nelson, "The Classroom of Didymus the Blind" (PhD diss., University of Michigan, 1995), 17.

[10] For more on this, see Bayliss, *Vision of Didymus the Blind*, 12-16.

[11] For a fuller analysis of the questions of Didymus's audience, see Nelson, "Classroom of Didymus," 28-50.

[12] The most insightful discussion of this passage occurs in Richard Layton, *Didymus the Blind and His Circle in Late-Antique Alexandria* (Urbana: University of Illinois Press, 2004), 29-33.

[13] See Lincoln Blumell, *Didymus the Blind's Commentary on Psalms 26:10–29:2 and 36:1-3*, Brigham Young University Papyri 1 (Turnhout: Brepols, 2019), 18.

epistemology, dialectics, and detailed numerological discussion. Additionally, Didymus assumes that his audience will pursue questions raised within the scope of the lectures by reading outside material, whether by referring to his own published works or the works of secular philosophers.

Finally, we have external evidence from Rufinus that the circle around Didymus was both numerically significant and very active.[14] The circle not only took down his lectures with the help of stenographers but also worked with him to revise and publish his lectures in the form of books. Didymus's *Commentary on Zechariah* represents a work one step removed from the lecture hall, revised by Didymus with his students' help in response to Jerome's request for a commentary on the prophet.[15] The community that gathered for daily lectures on the Psalms was active in promoting Didymus's spiritual vision. Though it was composed of ascetics in various degrees of intellectual formation—novice, intermediate, and advanced—all shared alike in Didymus's commitment to pursue formation in virtue through the exposition of Holy Scripture.

A Shared Goal

This shared commitment deserves some attention. The community that was gathered around Didymus the Blind shared with him a doctrinal framework that rendered their pursuit of a common goal tenable. Fundamental to Didymus's understanding of the grand narrative of the world was his commitment to trinitarian orthodoxy. The perfections of God's limitless life, and his immutability in particular, are the beginning sine qua non. Creation, which comes into being at the divine will but differs from the Creator insofar as it does not possess immutability by nature, is sustained by the Creator's goodwill. The intent of God in the creation of souls is that they come to share in his perfections through participation, through communion with the divine life. By the imitation of God, they are to express his way and his thought to such a degree that they become perfected as creatures, at last secure in their resemblance of and proximity to him.

The great sin of humans is that they departed from the contemplation of God, seeking instead the contemplation of vanity. For this reason, humanity is weighed down by the misuse of freedom. Humans are afflicted by the force of habit and by the oppression of the demonic powers that will their rebellion from God. People travel the easy road from the first suggestion of sin (*propatheia*), to its becoming a settled emotion (*pathos*) within the soul, to its becoming within them a disposition or inclination (*diathesis*), to the final flowering of its act. In such a state humanity remains unable to fulfill its creaturely goal, unable to rid itself of the fetters that bind them to the earth and rise to the eternal vision of God.

In response to humanity's plight, God sent his Son, Jesus Christ. Jesus is both the revealer of original righteousness and goodness, and the one who enables its growth within

---

[14] Rufinus, *History of the Church* 11.7 (p. 443).
[15] See Jerome, *On Illustrious Men* 110.2 (p. 142).

the human soul. As the revealer, Jesus Christ is "of one being" (*homoousios*) with God, the co-sharer by nature in divine immutability and the one in whom all virtue is resident from the beginning. As the one who shares in the Father's glory, Christ is the only one capable of revealing its fullness to God's creatures. In the Word-become-flesh, humanity once again beholds the one who is the righteousness of God, the one in whom that same righteousness becomes our own. It becomes our own because, after his descent, the incarnate Son is also "of one being" (*homoousios*) with us. The victory that he wins over sin, death, and the devil is not merely God's victory over the enemy—it is that—but it is our victory as well. In him, the human soul triumphs over sin and is restored to fullness of communion with God.

By baptism, the soul responds to the Christ and the church's invitation to enter into the life of Christ, receiving the grace of the same Spirit who appeared on the Son at his baptism, the Spirit who is "of one being" with the Father and the Son in their divinity. The Spirit bestows on the soul the fullness of the virtues, the fullness of communion with the Son. He awakens the formerly captive and latent powers of the soul to imitate and contemplate the life of God. In this synergy between God and humans, everywhere aided by the grace of God's Spirit, everywhere also humanity's truest work, the Christian ascends toward the goal of becoming so imbued with the divine likeness that he becomes fully deified: so united to God that he is incapable of being parted from him.

This was the great goal (telos) that lay beyond all others in Didymus's interpretation of Scripture. It is this grand narrative, with its overarching metaphysical structure, that forms the frame by which Holy Scripture is read within his school. All of the exegetical movements that Didymus makes—the examination of textual variants, the discernment of the precise meaning of the literal sense, the consistent movement from this sense to the higher anagogical sense—are at the service of this final goal. They are the proverbial trees for which the telos is the forest. The shared commitment to assisting one another in reaching this goal, chiefly through the imitation of the contemplative and active virtues of their Spirit-bearing teacher, was what kept Didymus's students returning to the lectures that he gave day after day.

Advice for Today's Reader

A word of caution before I proceed to commend Didymus's exegesis. Didymus's doctrine of the preexistence of souls and the universal restoration (*apokatastasis*) that follows from it as a necessary corollary were both condemned by the church in the years after his death. The Fifth Ecumenical Council (553) taught that Origen and his followers had erred in teaching these doctrines, although Didymus was not personally anathematized. In these instances, I would advise the reader to listen carefully to the questions of Didymus's students. Although these teachings were not yet formally anathematized, it is interesting to note that the students were the most lively in their opposition to their teacher precisely on these points.

With this caveat in mind, I advise readers to make the central goal of Didymus and his circle their own as they approach the reading of the *Lectures*. Readers who aim merely to inform themselves about the "use that Didymus makes of Scripture" or about any one of the other curiosities that they may find while reading will find themselves out of touch with Didymus's interpretive goal. To be sure, there are many such curiosities in the lectures: the animal stories, especially those about the deer and the rhinoceros, are especially memorable. The incredibly detailed numerology given to the surtitles of some of the Psalms is also fascinating. Likewise are the passages where Didymus applies his speculative theories on the preexistence of the soul and the nature of the resurrection body to the interpretation of a psalm. However interesting such curiosities may prove, they ought not to distract readers from the chief question that needs to be asked: What is of profit here for my soul?

Of course, the answer to this question depends a great deal on the answer to another one that should attend readers throughout: Has Didymus correctly discerned the divine sense of Holy Scripture? For "all Scripture is divinely inspired and profitable" (2 Tim 3:16). All Scripture, that is, yields its profit to those who read it in harmony with the divine inspiration that breathes it into being.

Readers' answers to this question will depend a great deal on what they make of the fundamental movement of Didymus's exegesis: that is, the movement from the literal to the anagogical sense. The charge of allegorism looms large. Jerome, for example, accused Didymus of caring almost nothing for the historical sense of Scripture in his interest to pursue allegory.[16] The charge has sometimes been repeated by modern scholarship. However, thanks in large measure to the welcome renaissance of interest in precritical exegesis, this charge has been revisited. Allegorism, as a tendency to abandon the literal sense, to use it as little more than a cipher for a hidden meaning, is rightly rejected as an interpretive method that contradicts the nature of the biblical texts as historical witnesses.

But this kind of allegorism is nonexistent in Didymus. For him allegory enters in once the literal sense has been explored, and the allegory is developed in a manner consistent with the literal sense. The emerging consensus that he often "extracts maximum utility from the literal meaning" before moving onto an allegorical interpretation ought to allay any suspicion that he develops figural meanings because he finds the literal sense unimportant.[17] Inveighing in his interpretation of Psalm 23:10 against Apollinarian accounts of the crucifixion, Didymus says that the Apollinarian account of the crucifixion is docetic and treats the crucifixion as though it were an allegory. And "if the cross is allegorized, so also will the resurrection be allegorized: all the things that took place are like dreams." He understood that the witness of the Christian faith to a real historical encounter

---

[16]Jerome, *Commentary on Zechariah*, in *Commentaries on the Twelve Prophets*, trans. Thomas P. Scheck, ACT (Downers Grove, IL: InterVarsity Press, 2016), prologue (p. 2).
[17]Justin Rogers, *Didymus the Blind and the Alexandrian Christian Reception of Philo* (Atlanta: SBL Press, 2017), 7.

between God and his people in the history of Israel and the incarnation of the Son of God are indispensable to Christianity. It is one of the great ironies of history that Didymus's charge of allegorizing fits modern historicist readings of the Bible—which treat the crucifixion and the resurrection agnostically—even better!

Spiritual reading, or anagogical reading, proceeds from the conviction that God speaks to us everywhere in Holy Scripture about his Son Jesus Christ. Once a person is able to enter with Didymus into the Old Testament Psalms with the conviction that they speak not only of the historical events of their own time but also consistently of the new and greater David to come, then a whole world of promise opens up. It is Christ who is being spoken of; it is his struggle against sin into which we are invited to enter, in the company of those saints who have gone before us and have gained victory over the world in this way. So, for example, Psalm 22 (23 in English) not only speaks to us of how David regarded the Lord as his shepherd but holds out to us the invitation to become sheep of the Good Shepherd, instructing us where we can find spiritual grass to eat and fresh water to drink. Psalm 23 (24 in English) details not merely the festal procession of Jewish pilgrims through the temple gates but the entrance of Christ into the heavenly sanctuary after his ascension. The present reality of sharing in his glorious victory over death becomes the joyous object of our contemplation.

There is much to commend in Didymus's spiritual wisdom regarding the weighty matter of working together with the mercy of God. He accurately describes the effects of forepassions on one's emotions (see the comments on Ps 21:21), urging self-examination in the early stages of temptation so as to be able to resist. He reminds his students that striving against sin and the attainment of perfection is only something that comes from the mercy of God. Human power, even the renewed humanity that has been restored in the image of God, cannot attain victory on its own (see the comments on Ps 24:6). In his comments on Psalm 30:15-16, he teaches Christians to flee from ambition in the matter of seeking ecclesiastical position. "Such a person" who flees from ambition and merely accepts his lot from the hands of the Lord "is free from intrigues." I trust that the reader will find numerous other gems of this kind.

Final Notes

In the footnotes that follow, I try as much as possible to allow the translation to speak for itself. I do not pursue any parallels within Didymus's corpus. I refer to secondary literature only when necessary to illuminate Didymus's argument (for example, when a numerological argument proved opaque to me without the help of other interpreters who were more mathematically astute). In these footnotes I attempt to inform the reader when I have leaned heavily on a contemporary English translation of the Bible, when there was enough correspondence between it and Didymus's Greek text to warrant this. Unmarked citations follow my own translations.

The modern reader will be more familiar with the Hebrew numbering of the Psalms than with those of the Septuagint (LXX). At the beginning of each psalm, I note in brackets which English psalm corresponds to the one under discussion according to the LXX numbering. In addition, for any other references to the Psalms, I give the typical English Bible's citation of chapter and verse first, followed by the numbering of the LXX in the footnotes. At times, for a half-verse that appears only in the Septuagint, I mark it with "LXX." In the main body of the text, I keep Didymus's numbering of the Psalter, since these are the numbers that appear in the manuscript, and altering them would confuse Didymus's references to the Psalms.

LECTURES ON THE PSALMS
PSALM 20 [21]

[1] From Scripture and from common wisdom, we hold the opinion about God that he is unchangeable, that he is immutable. For the one who is completely free of quality neither undergoes change nor suffers alteration, since alteration is nothing other than qualitative change.[2] Not every kind of change is an alteration, but a change in quality is an alteration. To be sure, there are various kinds of change, since there are various kinds of motion. Something that comes into being changes, but this motion is not an alteration. Something that grows changes, but this is not an alteration, either, for this kind of motion involves an addition and increase of quantity. When someone, however, becomes zealous for virtue after being wicked or becomes wicked after being virtuous, he undergoes a qualitative alteration, as when, again, someone passes from sickness into health, and vice versa.

So then, we understand words in relation to the content of the subject about which they are spoken. God is not composed of members, since he is not composite at all. For this reason, in his case sitting, rising, walking, the turning away of his face, and the manifestation of his face are accessory descriptions. So, in order to preserve the faith by means of these descriptions that are assigned to him, one must receive them in a manner worthy of God.

Some, by their words and their forceful style, debase what is signified. For example, some dare to arrive at such a degree of naivete or impiety as to consider God to be manlike because of things written in a figural sense. And they claim that God has hands, members, feet, a visible appearance, and the rest. But if we understand the following on each occasion: of whom, and again, from whom these things are spoken, we can refer the difficulties back to the thing that is being identified, to the thing being made known.

Unless we comprehend them in a manner that is worthy of God, we cannot have a godly opinion about them, according to one of the Twelve Prophets. In a certain place, he says, "Are not his words good with him, and have they not proceeded upright?"[3] Unless they are "with him," with him in mind, they are not good. Come! When you hear about sleep, wakefulness, and repentance, and you do not understand such things with him in mind, the things said about him have not proceeded uprightly with him! But when you receive such things with him, the words, walking uprightly with him and having been filled with the Spirit, do not contain anything harmful and trifling. In the Gospel the Savior said, "You are wrong, because you know neither the scriptures nor the power of God."[4] You are wrong when you claim that God does not create the universe out of nonbeing. Indeed, some say as

---

[1] Didymus the Blind, *Psalmenkommentar (Tura-Papyrus)*, vol. 1, *Kommentar zu Psalm 20–21*, ed. M. Gronewald, L. Doutreleau, and A. Gesché, PTA 7 (Bonn: Rudolf Habelt, 1969), begins here. Numbers in brackets in the text refer to page numbers in *Psalmenkommentar*.

[2] For an excellent discussion of these key terms and their place in Didymus's interpretation of the Psalms, see Richard Layton, *Didymus the Blind and His Circle in Late-Antique Alexandria* (Urbana: University of Illinois Press, 2004), 43-48.

[3] Mic 2:7 NETS.
[4] Mt 22:29 NRSV.

follows: "Creating follows after being, since some substrate must first exist. The dead are unable to partake of resurrection."[5] Since they do not understand the words together with the power of God, for this reason they crash against them. God can bring things into being out of nonbeing, and he can cause corruptible bodies to change. He is speaking to the Sadducees. One who presumes [**2**] to understand the Scriptures is wrong when he is ignorant of God's meaning, which relates to the one about whom and by whom they are spoken.

However, the one for whose benefit I have said these things, I will mention in an excursus from the following lecture. Our Savior and Lord is God and man at the same time. He is always God, but he was not always man, for before the creation he was God but not man. And he would undertake this for our salvation. On the one hand his becoming man has a cause; on the other his being God has no cause, save only because of his own existence and the essence of his generation. For I understand the saying "I live because of my Father"[6] as follows. He is not saying this: "The Father gives me life," as the Eunomians wish. Rather, he is saying this in the same sense as when someone says, "I am rational for this reason, because I have a rational father," and, "I am mortal for this reason, because I have a mortal father." And that is true. The word *hoti* provides an explanatory principle. Since he lives because of the Father, therefore, he is called "life," not as one derived from life, but as the source of life and the one who causes everyone to participate in it. For we say that the Living One has life. We also call him the life that is not derived from life, for life does not participate in life but *is* life itself. In this way, then, he lives "because of the Father."

He is man, then, because of something, but he is not God because of anything. Both, however, converge at the time of his appearance. By "appearance" I do not always mean the one in the flesh, for he willed many appearances; he is always appearing! At least, that is how I have understood the saying in Micah: "And you, O Bethlehem, house of Ephatha, are the very least. One from you shall come forth for me, and his goings forth are from of old."[7] For in a sense, after coming forth from the Father, he did not appear for the first time when there was need of his saving administration. There is need of his going forth when and where it happens. For this reason, the prophet spoke not of one but of many goings forth. "Therefore he shall give them up until the time when she gives birth."[8] Indeed, Scripture is not exalting women who give birth, but it speaks of one who gives birth: the one who is signified by the passage. Strictly speaking, one who gives birth is not one who receives sperm, becomes pregnant, gives the child form, and contains it; rather, she generates the child herself. For this reason he has come from a woman. None of the rest of us came from a woman, but all came through a woman, and all are from men. For the woman comes from the man, and the man through the woman.

This also must be said, that genealogies are impassively, wisely, and piously produced when they are derived from fathers, for the genealogy that stems from women is discredited. She alone, then, who gives birth without a husband, has truly "given birth." And because of this the Savior has come from a woman, not through a woman, even though many others come who do not say "from Mary" but "through Mary." [**3**] In this way, many proclaim docetism.

Now, he is God from the Father, and without a cause, while he is man from David

---

[5] The Saducean teaching about the impossibility of a resurrection is here related to a "nameless heresy" (PsT 3) against which Didymus warns his audience throughout this introduction.
[6] Cf. Jn 6:57.

[7] Cf. Mic 5:2 (5:1).
[8] Mic 5:3 (5:2).

and Mary and with a cause. He has come for the salvation of the world: to destroy death, to give many things to mortals that they had lost because of their own indolence.

Why, then, am I saying these things? The things said about the Savior manifest his divinity. And all that is proclaimed about his divinity is inapplicable to any other, since he is unique. However, the virtuous actions that concern the Man[9] as a man apply in a certain sense to the righteous also. The virtuous become imitators of the Man. However, they do not imitate the divinity—for this is unholy to say—they imitate the Man.

Therefore, whatever is said about the Man could also be said about angels and perfect men. On the other hand, whatever is said about the divinity will be said neither of angels nor holy men. I am not saying that Wisdom, or the radiance of God's glory, or the exact impression of the divine being, or the only-begotten Son of God is a kind of created being. Rather, whatever is said about the Man could be said about others. For example, "You are trying to kill me," because I am "a man who has told you the truth that I heard from God."[10] Many others also spoke the truth after they learned it from God. He, however, did so more often; he did so more weightily; he did so incomparably. And again, "But because I tell the truth, you do not believe me."[11] Others also speak the truth; for if we grant that no one spoke the truth except Christ himself, we yield ground to the nameless heresy.[12]

There is a certain nameless heresy that seems to be born or to have come into being by means of books. And many people own books and systematic treatises that say the following: that the truth has never appeared among men except during the Savior's appearance. For "grace and truth came through Jesus Christ."[13]

But look where their argument brings them! Since they desire the ancient Scripture and the Prophets not to be from God, they say that the truth had never come to men except when the appearance of Christ had taken place. And when they say these things, they split apart the one divinity, and they claim that the Creator of the world before the appearance is one person, and they seek for another as the Father of Christ.

But we do not say this, that the truth was at one time suppressed. The truth always sends forth testimonies about itself. And it is the province of humans either to perceive it or not to perceive it. In the case of the perceptible sun, just as it happens that the one who closes his eyes does not see it, and we certainly do not conclude that there is no sun, so we do not say that the truth had at one time not come among men, because we do not wish to split the Scripture in two. And I say, if you consider the fruits of a fruit tree—such as the fruits of a fig tree—it is necessary for the fruits to be distinct from each other as soon as you separate them from their stalk. So then, it is impossible for the instruction of the Gospel [4] to have brought the truth to men, and that which is called "old" before Christ's appearance not to have brought illumination in the truth. Clearly they inferred from the different fruits a different quality as well—not that there is a different divinity, but this follows from their absurd first principle.

When, therefore, the Savior says, "I am the truth,"[14] and "shepherd,"[15] and "gate,"[16] and the

---

[9] Didymus does not employ the abstraction "humanity" to speak of what would later be termed Christ's human nature. He refers to the Man assumed by the Word. Throughout I capitalize the word to distinguish the humanity of the Savior from the humanity of others.
[10] Jn 8:40 NRSV.
[11] Jn 8:45 NRSV.
[12] More literally, to "give mortar to" or "build up" the nameless heresy. As described in the next paragraph, the nameless heresy has much in common with forms of Gnosticism, especially the Gnostic system proposed by Marcion.

[13] Jn 1:17 NRSV.
[14] Jn 14:6.
[15] Jn 10:11.
[16] Jn 10:9.

rest, these names and the things signified by them cannot be shared with creatures. But when he says, "I am a man,"[17] when it is said of him that he is righteous—"You killed the righteous one,"[18] says Peter—these names relate both to men and to angels.

In the case of the word *king*, understand it in the same way. Since there is a certain kingdom that is naturally connected with the Word, neither acquired nor able to be lost, he is the "kingdom" in person. And just as he is not called righteous because he possesses righteousness but rather is righteousness itself, so also he is king not by virtue of his coronation, but is in person king from the King, as he is God from God. He also has an acquired kingdom, which he wished to have when he appeared, that he should destroy those who war against the human race and lead them into their lawful dominion so that they might be ruled justly. Therefore, when he says, "But I was established king by him, on Sion, his holy mountain,"[19] he is not speaking about his innate and eternal kingdom, but of the one he has received for our sake.

In God's case, *kingdom* means instruction. There was one instruction before his appearance, which I said that he produces from within himself as God the Word, and there is another instruction that exists for other purposes. This latter one, then, has a beginning and an end. For example, it was said in one of the Twelve Prophets, "And the Lord will reign from Zion from now until the age."[20] The words *from* and *until* designate time. But when it is said of a man that he reigns from this time until that, this implies his deficiency, for before the time from which he began his reign, he was not a king, and when his reign comes to its end, he is no longer a king. We do not say this about the Savior, however; on the contrary, he reigned from the time when he took up his rule by coronation, but he reigns no longer when this rule of his accomplishes its goal. Indeed, that other kingdom of his exists in himself. As divinity does not befit him because of another, so neither does this kingdom, nor does holiness. "God is our King from of old."[21] And the kingdom from of old exists for his own sake. Again, "Your kingdom is a kingdom of all the ages."[22] This is said in reference to God the Word. The Word has a kingdom that neither begins nor ends, for "the Lord is king throughout the age, forever and beyond."[23] The writer was at a loss to signify what was beyond time and the age, and he said, "and beyond." We understand the word *beyond* in this way: even if you assume another age, he still reigns, and if you take another still, he continues to reign, and if you take all the ages, he still reigns. From this it is shown that his rule is without end. For the kingdom that he had in his condescension will be ended [5] at some time and has received a beginning. For it exists because of something, because of the salvation of the world, for the taking away of "the sin of the world."[24] And just as a doctor is continually a doctor from the time when he has the profession and for as long as he practices medicine, yet in relation to his patient he has a beginning and an end of his being the doctor of that person any longer, when the patient is brought into health and into a treatable condition. You can say the same things about instructions as well. A person is a teacher from the time when he has received knowledge. And he becomes an instructor of someone when he dedicates himself to him. And when that other person is instructed and completely receives the knowledge that the teacher has, he is finished being his teacher.

---

[17]Cf. Jn 8:40.
[18]Cf. Acts 3:14-15.
[19]Ps 2:6 (2:6 NETS).
[20]Mic 4:7.
[21]Ps 74:12 (73:12 NETS).
[22]Ps 145:13 (144:13 NETS).
[23]Ex 15:18.
[24]Jn 1:29 NRSV.

And in a way it is a virtue of a teacher to cease at some time from being the teacher of others, for when he has perfected them he teaches them no longer. If, however, a person always remains the teacher of someone, no one is perfected by him in the teaching.

Therefore, when people hear such passages and do not understand the Scriptures in this way—for example, "when he hands over the kingdom to God the Father,"[25] he rules no longer in this way. For it is not that he rules no longer in an absolute sense; rather, he rules no longer in this way.

In our passage a king and his kingdom are named, for *the king will be made glad by your power, O Lord*. If we receive this expression in relation to God the Word, he himself is found to be both king and power, for "Christ is the power of God"[26] and "the power of the Most High"—which is himself—"overshadowed"[27] Mary, in order that she should become pregnant and become the mother of the temple.[28] If instead we wish to understand the power as coming from God the Word, we take the word *king* as indicating the Lord's Man. This one is made glad by God's power. Did his appearance not accomplish things for which one must rejoice and be glad? These accomplishments have not come from the side of the Man toward the power, but rather from the side of the power toward the Man. In any case, so says Paul, insisting that the resurrection of the Savior took place in this way: "He was crucified in weakness, but lives by the power of God."[29] We do not say that life lives from the power of God, nor that power lives from the power of God. "Being put to death," therefore, "in the flesh, he was made alive in the spirit."[30] He is put to death in the flesh; he is not put to death in his divinity.

We therefore understand that the following was said about the Man: *The king will be made glad by your power*. For if he has prevailed over the enemies and subjected them, and has given to others "authority to tread on snakes and scorpions,"[31] this has taken place by power, for power itself empowered him, who is the temple and the king, to become "the author of salvation."[32] "You killed the Author of life."[33] In all things he has the primacy, for it says, "that in everything he might be preeminent."[34] He is second to none, nor is anyone his equal in the common things. I was saying earlier that there are things that are shared in common between the Lord's Man and holy men. Yet none is his equal, nor is he second to anyone, for which reason he is also called "author."

O Lord, by your power the king will be made glad. Now, this may be said about each kingdom that exists in relation to God. Abraham was a commoner, as far as his ordinary life was concerned, and it was said that he was "a king from God."[35] He possessed another kingdom, then: [6] the preservation of the divine and spiritual laws. And the one who rules in this way, even if he does not govern others, rules over himself. First one must govern oneself, then others. Again, "Quite apart from us you have become kings! Indeed, I wish that you had become kings, so that we might be kings with you!"[36] "Do not suppose, O Corinthians," he is saying—and these were haughty people who thought great things about themselves—"do not suppose that we are envious of you when you rule. We ourselves do not rule with respect to you. It is for this very reason that we do not rule: because you do not yet rule. If

---

[25] 1 Cor 15:24 NRSV.
[26] 1 Cor 1:24.
[27] Cf. Lk 1:35.
[28] "Temple" is another of Didymus's favored ways of referring to the humanity assumed by the Word.
[29] 2 Cor 13:4 NRSV.
[30] 1 Pet 3:18.
[31] Lk 10:19 NRSV.
[32] Heb 2:10.
[33] Acts 3:15 NRSV.
[34] Col 1:18 ESV.
[35] Gen 23:6.
[36] 1 Cor 4:8 NRSV.

then you become kings, we are ready to become kings as well."

To illustrate, certain great ones were invited by the king to a banquet. The king's philanthropy also invited some who were inferior to those present. He said, "Let us not eat without them, lest those who come to be fed be neglected in consequence." So, these later ones have those who both preceded them and were invited to the meal as the main guests.

In a psalm it says the following: "The righteous ones wait for me, until you respond to me."[37] No one, upon obtaining things that are expected, is said to "wait for" them, but is one who has already received them and has the intention of using these things.

Each of the saints, then, is a king. And I was saying earlier that the things which are appropriate to the Man of the Savior befit the righteous as well, albeit incompletely and to a lesser degree. He says, therefore, about each saint: O Lord, by your power the king will be made glad. He did not say, "is made glad" but "will be made glad." When the time of joyful serenity arrives, then the saint will be made glad.

This can also be said about David in particular and his human and perceptible kingdom, because he, having governed the kingdom well, will receive a reward for this. For each person, when he fulfills well those things that are entrusted to him, receives a reward for them. When he is faithful in a few things, he enters "into the joy"[38] of his neighbor and his God.

[20:2] O Lord, by your power the king will be made glad.

He calls the Savior the power that gladdens the king, since he is God the Word. I was saying just now that one must receive the words just as their underlying realities are and not drive out these realities by forcing one's way to the sense. The word *power* has been handled by us already. It means many things. I observe that *power* means the same thing as *strength*. But not in this way do I mean that the Savior is the power of God. I observe that *power* means "capability." Someone will think that this signification of the word is not present in Scripture. It is. "God is faithful, and he will not let you be tested beyond your strength, but with the testing he will also provide the way out so that you may be able to endure it."[39] He is speaking of the capability, for both words communicate the same thing. And so the contestant has the capability of enduring and of seizing the victorious way out. You see, this meaning is present.

And again, [7] "The power of sin is the law."[40] The law can be transgressed. It does not have this ability by its own activity. Both well and opportunely has the apostle said in this passage, "The power of sin is the law," for he wishes that we be in the ability of sin and not in its activity. Now, if this were said: "The power of righteousness is the law," we would not be righteous in activity, but only in capability. And though we were capable of righteousness, we would in fact be unrighteous in our activity. Therefore, the apostle set down the propitious word, since the law has the capability of both in equal measure: to be kept and to be transgressed. But he wrote what he did because of its usefulness. The word *power* also means "capability."

And it also signifies the army of the king: "The chariots of Pharaoh and his power he threw into the sea."[41] "A king is not saved because of much power,"[42] because of his mighty hand and his troops.

---

[37] Ps 142:7 (141:8).
[38] Cf. Mt 25:21, 23.
[39] 1 Cor 10:13 NRSV.
[40] 1 Cor 15:56 NRSV.
[41] Ex 15:4.
[42] Ps 33:16 (32:16 LES2).

The Savior, quite apart from these significations, is called the power of God. Indeed, in a similar way that the Father is powerful—not having this from a power, but from his essence, and his essence is that in which he is powerful so that he may be called power itself—it is thus also with the Son. It says therefore, "He was crucified in weakness, but lives by the power of God."[43] Inasmuch as it befits human weakness, he submitted to a cross. God was incapable of enduring this; rather, as a man he was able to suffer this. And indeed he has suffered it but now lives from the power of God. The power of God, therefore, is Christ, since Christ is God.

The king, then, *is made glad by your power*. The word *king* was used in many figural senses. We have mentioned David in the historical sense, the Man who is from Mary in the anagogical sense, by whose imitation and discipleship those who imitate him become kings. And we established from the letter to the Corinthians that there is another kingdom besides the temporal one.

O Lord, then, *by your power the king will be made glad*. This phrase is spoken either by the Spirit-bearing man or by the Holy Spirit himself, who abides in him, for whenever the Holy Spirit says, "O Lord," he does not say this alone and apart from a man, but he says this when he prepares someone to be a bearer of the Spirit. That person, then, is the one who says as follows: "The Lord says to my Lord,"[44] and the Savior says, "If by the Holy Spirit he called him 'Lord,' how is he his Son?"[45] If he is his Son, how is he a servant? And if a servant, how is he his Son? The word *Lord* reveals a kind of relation and disposition. For even when the Savior says, "The Lord created me,"[46] he is speaking suitably, since he did not say, "The Lord begot me." Truly begetting belongs to the Father, and creating to the Lord. Whenever he speaks of his own divinity, he does not say, "Lord," but rather, "I am in the Father and the Father is in me."[47] "My Father and I are one."[48] *Lord* and *Father* are different words.

Often when we talk about a single quality, we join together the attributes of the quality to the condition of something as a whole, and we also join together the attributes of the whole condition [**8**] to a single quality. I say that knowledge knows. And it is a falsehood to say that knowledge is ignorant. The opposites are found to coexist: knowledge and ignorance. And I also say that the knowledgeable person knows. And again, people often say that the physician must not be greedy for money. Then they say that medical science understands how to avoid greed. One names the habit, without excluding the person who has the habit, and the person who has the habit, without excluding the habit. Therefore, such attributes are common both to the one who possesses the quality and to the quality that is possessed.

And we established many times from the teaching of the apostle that he calls the one who has love "love," for when he says, "Love is never rude; it is not boastful,"[49] he calls the one who has the habit by the name of the habit. And I also say about the one who possesses love that he is beneficial. He benefits with that benefit that love bestows.

Therefore, when I say that the saint says this—the psalmist, for example—I am not separating the Holy Spirit from the one who possesses him, nor do I say that the one who possesses the Spirit says these things without the Holy Spirit. If then "David in the Holy Spirit calls him 'Lord,'" it is in this manner so that the one who is partaken of is not sundered from the one who participates,

---

[43]2 Cor 13:4 NRSV.
[44]Ps 110:1 (109:1).
[45]Cf. Mt 22:43-45; Mk 12:35-37.
[46]Prov 8:22 NETS. The Hebrew has "the Lord possessed me."

[47]Jn 14:10 NRSV.
[48]Cf. Jn 10:30.
[49]Cf. 1 Cor 13:4-5.

just as knowledge is not separate from the knowledgeable person.

[20:2] *And at your deliverance he shall rejoice exceedingly.*

Just as the king is gladdened by your power, so he rejoices exceedingly at your deliverance. The deliverance and the power are the same thing, understood in two different conceptions. Power is that which maintains all things and so leads them as seems good to it. So also is deliverance: for what it does, it does for the sake of salvation; what it accomplishes among men, it does for the salvation of men.

[20:3] *You gave him the desire of his soul.*

You know that the word *him* signifies the substance, not the accidents. The desire of the soul is bad when one presupposes a wicked soul. But when I say that the soul itself has a desire, I am speaking of the desire that is essential to it. The one who makes use of this desire loves none of the wicked things but only the good ones, because he received both the appetitive faculty and the desire in order that he might pursue good things, in order that he might reach toward things that profit. Come then! If someone is greedy for wealth, he did not receive the desire of his own soul but the desire of greed. It is then a great thing to obtain the desire of the soul, when the word *wicked* is not adjoined to it. Take, for instance, what it says in another psalm: "who satisfies your desire with good."[50] [9] It is speaking about the soul.

Many times it was said by us in other places that things that are proper to the soul do not create a contradiction. If I say, "The desire of the soul is good," and then I say on the other hand, "The desire of the righteous person is good," that which is added does not create a contradiction. When I say, "The shameful desire, the wicked desire, the desire of the unrighteous," then a contradiction arises. That is not simply the desire of the soul but of such a soul. Therefore, there are times when the accidents agree together with the substance; but when they war against it, they create a contradiction. So, for example, was it said, "The desire of the righteous is completely good."[51] To consider the desire of the righteous soul and the desire of the soul, without further qualification, is one and the same thing.

This appears even in the case of perceptible things. If I say now, "Such and such a father desires for his children to live well," since I have made mention of a "father," I want to say next that his children live well. But if I say, "The wicked father wishes for his children to do such and such," I have annulled fatherly compassion.

"With great desire I have desired to eat this Passover with you."[52] The phrases "with desire" and "I desired" mean the following: "I pursued what was righteous in a righteous way," what is worthy of being desired. However, there are times when someone desires what is unworthy of being desired, as it says: "passion, evil desire."[53] The evil desire is not desirable, since nothing that is falsely called "good" is said to be choice, even if some choose it.

[20:3] *And you did not deprive him of the prayer of his lips.*

If the discourse is about the one who came from Mary, clearly he advances his request on behalf of those he has come to save. You have, for example, "Consequently he is able for all time to save, since he always lives to make intercession for them."[54] He always lives in intercession. And understand the word *always* in this sense: for as long as they have need of

---

[50] Ps 103:5 (102:5 NETS).
[51] Prov 11:23 LES2.
[52] Lk 22:15.
[53] Col 3:5 NRSV.
[54] Cf. Heb 7:25 NRSV.

an advocate and arbiter. "But if anyone does sin, we have an advocate with the Father, Jesus Christ the righteous."[55] And so, since others also eagerly agree with the teacher, they also desire to advocate for those with whom they were entrusted, not arranging for their own consolation as though it were of primary importance but establishing an intercession that follows after the righteousness of the one who summons them to imitate him.

Therefore, in relation to all the definitions of the word *king*, one must understand that he is not deprived of his prayer. When we say, for example, of one who is king in a perceptible way that the prayer of his lips was not taken away but that it has come to fulfillment, we intend his praise. And if we say this about the saints—for they too were called "kings"—their praise is also great when their prayer is received. For "the eyes of the Lord are upon the righteous, and his ears are attentive to their prayer."[56] And "he listens to the prayers of the righteous."[57]

[20:3] *Diapsalma.*

[10] The word *diapsalma* appears nowhere else but in the Hebrew Scriptures, especially in the Psalms. And it appears also in the song of Habakkuk. Those who understand the Hebrew language can say what it means best of all. All the same, we report what has come to us. There are those who say that it signifies a change of person. But this is a fallacious conclusion: we have found a change of persons in the Psalms even without the *diapsalma*.

Again, they say that the *diapsalma* signifies a kind of interval—as though the speaker ceased talking and then resumed on another occasion—and the *diapsalma* signifies this: the temporal interval. We are unable to affirm this, however, for it is never explicitly stated that, having spoken these verses of the psalm, the psalmist spoke again after another period of time.

Those who are slightly familiar with the Hebrew interpretations say this: that it is the rhythm of a musical composition, just as they talk about rhythms and melody in the study of music. These matters are not ours to know; they belong instead to those who are familiar with the language. In any case, it can be appropriate for music in every language. And music is nothing other than a rhythm of sounds, harmoniously composed.

At some point, I hope to understand the Hebrew letters and dedicate myself to their interpretations. But when we see something on a farm, although it is named by a farmer, since we do not understand what it is, we learn it from him. And, so long as we do not reject it as unworthy of our knowledge, we remain ignorant no longer, because we asked him. So also in this case: when we do not understand the Hebrew language, yet we hear that it signifies a musical rhythm in the Hebrew language.

[20:4] *For you went before him with blessings of kindness.*

God went before *the king*, according to every interpretation, with blessings of kindness. The phrase *You went before with blessings* is the equivalent of the phrase "while you are still speaking, I will say, 'See! Here I am!'"[58] Take this as an example: someone sends up a prayer for one who lives well, for one who possesses virtue. God says, "while you are still speaking," though you have not yet finished the words of the prayer, I tell you that I am present by granting it.

We understand *kindness* here to mean "goodness." For often we understand the word

---

[55] 1 Jn 2:1 NRSV.
[56] Ps 34:15 (33:16).
[57] Prov 15:29.

[58] Cf. Is 58:9.

kind as though it were an accusation: "Bad company ruins kind morals,"[59] meaning good morals that are superficial. And the phrase "good character" is indeed understood as a compliment, when someone has good conduct that is more than superficial. Likewise also with the word *innocent*, for "by smooth talk they deceive the hearts of the innocent,"[60] and again, "The innocent believes every word."[61]

[20:4] *You placed on his head a crown made of precious stone.*

If this was said about the Lord's Man, this crown that will be placed on his head is composed of precious stones, which are either the virtues or those who [11] possess the virtues. In the construction of this crown are found those stones that are wrought together with gold and silver on the foundation: Christ.[62] Clearly neither gold, nor silver, nor stones are to be taken in a literal sense.

But if this was said about each king, such as Abraham was, such as the rest of the saints are, we say the following: just as the king of Tyre, when he lived well and was placed with the cherubim on God's holy mountain, when he was "signet of likeness" and "a crown of beauty,"[63] was not encircled with sensible stones, with such stones by which someone is crowned. Come now! Joseph found delight in chastity. Chastity is a precious stone. These virtues crowned him, Susanna, and the martyrs. And since the virtues are interdependent with each other, and the one who has one of them has them all, the crown that is created is not merely one stone.

You placed on his head a crown made of precious stone. The word *precious* is joined to it. The word *precious* belongs among the relative words. These stones here, such as pearls, sapphires, and the rest, we call "precious," since there are also stones that are different from them. Since, therefore, these great stones are also the specific kinds of virtue, see how precious these stones are and how they surpass all the stones that seem to be good in the world!

Now, Paul taught that disciples are the crowns of their teachers, addressing the church that followed his instruction as "my joy and crown."[64]

"On that day the Lord Sabaoth will be the crown of hope."[65] The material of this crown is the Lord of Sabaoth, for "the Lord Sabaoth will be the crown of hope." And since a person in this circumstance is not yet able to possess a perfect participation in God, yet this will happen at that time when "God becomes all in all,"[66] when the final object of desire is in the possession of all. This is why it called him a crown of hope: for if we will know him at the time when we see him as he is,[67] and we see him as he is to appear at the time when we approach the goal, then this crown is a crown of hope. In the meantime, it is a crown of hope; it is being anticipated.

[20:5] *He asked you for life, and you gave it to him.*

We were saying that the Savior as Man—and when I say "as Man," do not separate him from the Word—that the Savior is "an advocate with the Father."[68] The Word is not separated from the Man; neither is the Man separated from the Word, but he, having been composed of both, becomes an advocate and advocates "since he always lives to make intercession for them."[69]

---

[59] 1 Cor 15:33.
[60] Rom 16:18.
[61] Prov 14:15 NETS.
[62] Cf. 1 Cor 3:11-12.
[63] Cf. Ezek 28:12-14.
[64] Phil 4:1 NRSV.
[65] Is 28:5 LES2.
[66] 1 Cor 15:28.
[67] Cf. 1 Jn 3:2.
[68] 1 Jn 2:1 NRSV.
[69] Heb 7:25 NRSV.

He asks for that life, which he wishes to be revived. By him comes vivification, for "he was put to death in the flesh, but made alive in the spirit."[70] **[12]** Now, the soul of Jesus is not life, but he has life from God who assigns and gives it to him. So it is with all other souls as well, so that each says, "My soul lives for him."[71] The soul has the dignity of living in immortality. "To live for God," however, is a fruit that is produced out of our free will, just as to live again for sin is produced out of our free will.

[20:5] *Length of days forever and unto all ages.*

Again, we cannot understand *length of days* literally. It says, *forever and unto all ages.* These days that are given to us and exist because of the sun are spoken of in this age only. It was also said, "When will these things be? And what will be the sign of your coming and of the end of the age?"[72] and, "to the end of this age."[73] And when the Scriptures say, "in these days," they are speaking of the days of this age. But this one who prayed is a great man and was not offering up a prayer about something small and indifferent, so that his prayer is also remembered, and it is not about these days that are limited by sun and moon. Therefore, one must contemplate these words differently. Observe that in the Scriptures such things often fail and seem as though they are impossible. "Honor," they say, "your father and your mother, so that it may be well for you and so that you live for a long time upon the earth."[74] He who honors his parents, however, does not always remain for many years on the earth. Many younger people are carried away. For example, of such people it was said in the Wisdom of Solomon: "He was taken away so that wickedness would not change his understanding or treachery deceive his soul."[75] And it says, "Being perfected in a short time, he fulfilled long years,"[76] and it says that Wisdom is gray-haired and that the unstained life is aged.[77] However, if the spotless life is old-aged, and this is not composed of days but of virtue, one must understand the days differently.

He asked you for life, then, not that he himself might live but those for whom he offers up his prayer. We spoke not of the common life but of the life that accords with virtue. He who knew no sin nor performed it,[78] and had no deceit in his heart,[79] did not experience the state of death that separates us from the blessed life. For this reason, when he asked for life, he did not ask for himself, but he desires that life be given to those for whom he offers up his petition: for he "always lives to make intercession for"[80] those who are going to receive life from him.

He asked you for life, then, *and you gave it to him*. Either the psalmist, or the Holy Spirit in him, says this to God. And great is the testimony when the one who offered up the prayer receives his requests. *You gave it to him*, therefore: *length of days forever and unto all ages.*

In general, the saints do not wish to have their common life prolonged for a long time in this life. Take as an example when he says, "It is better to depart and be with Christ,"[81] and again, "Woe is me, that my sojourning was prolonged."[82] **[13]** "I am a sojourner on the earth."[83] He who is "a sojourner and a

---

[70]1 Pet 3:18 NRSV.
[71]Ps 22:29 (21:30 NETS).
[72]Cf. Mt 24:3 NRSV.
[73]Mt 28:20.
[74]Ex 20:12.
[75]Wis 4:11 LES2.
[76]Wis 4:13 NETS.
[77]Cf. Wis 4:9.
[78]Cf. 2 Cor 5:21; 1 Pet 2:22.
[79]Cf. Is 53:9; Ps 32:2 (31:2).
[80]Heb 7:25.
[81]Phil 1:23.
[82]Ps 120:5 (119:5 LES2). The English translations take *mešek* as a place name, where the Greek translates the verbal form *māšak* (to draw out, prolong).
[83]Ps 39:12 (38:13); 119:19 (118:19).

foreigner"[84] has the desire and goal of removing himself from his exile, in order that he might dwell in his homeland. Therefore, just as it is not a common life that is meant here—the life that both impious men and unreasoning animals live—so neither is he saying that *length of days* is a long-lasting life; rather, *length of days* is meant in the same sense as the one who honored his parents will be long-lived and of many days. In Deuteronomy, it is also said, "This is your life and this is length of days,"[85] that "you love me, the Lord your God, with all your heart and with all your soul."[86] See how *length of days* is to love him with all of one's soul, with all of one's might, and with all of one's desire.

Length of days, then, *forever*. It is possible to take these words about the blessed life in this manner, for this is a life that is identical with the knowledge of God. When the following was said: "And this is eternal life, that they know you, the only true God, and Jesus Christ whom you sent,"[87] this life is the knowledge of the Father and the Son. And again, "whoever believes in me has eternal life."[88] The one who believes in the Savior does not have a common life. The ungodly one often is found to be more long-lived than the virtuous. These people ardently desire this life to be of many days, since they in fact hold that there is no other good but such a condition.

Therefore, just as the present life and the life to come are praiseworthy, so also is *length of days* in the present age, so that someone has great illumination, each doctrine of the truth being understood and giving him light.

Each practical virtue that is successfully performed is also a praiseworthy *day*. Since then, just as perfect and total knowledge will succeed the knowledge that at present is only partial, so also in the case of practical virtue, those who are shown to be righteous in practical virtue from now on will be virtuous in another way—for again, they have righteousness now and in the future—*length of days* referring to the present age, not to this common day, but to the day that can exist, of which they say, "This is the day that the Lord made."[89] For they have spoken in demonstration of it. No one, however, demonstrates something that is to come but that which is already at hand and present. The future, whenever that time arrives in which it comes, is no longer future. Then in its turn it will fall under demonstration.

In whatever way, then, you understand the king—whether the holy man or him who has come forth from Mary—they do not pray about that life or length of perceptible [14] days, but about the days already mentioned. They have in mind a long life and they are sending up a petition about this. Long life is not the life of a single age. Understand the life in correspondence to each age: at first primary and introductory, then intermediate, and then perfect.

Question: What comes after all these days that are mentioned?

Each doctrine that illuminates the soul, being emitted by the Sun of Righteousness,[90] we have called a "day." After these progressive illuminations, there is a kind of perfect state of light. That day is not interrupted by night; a multitude of days does not elapse.

One can also understand it thus: since the virtues have a connection to each other—for each virtue is full of light—a single length of days comes from their interdependence; it is not interrupted.

I say: each theory of knowledge is detached from the others, for the wise man knows many things. For example, just as in the case of

---

[84]Gen 23:4.
[85]Deut 30:20.
[86]Cf. Deut 6:5; 10:12.
[87]Jn 17:3.
[88]Jn 6:47.

[89]Ps 117:24 NETS.
[90]Mal 4:2 (3:20).

medical science, there is surgical theory and dietary theory, in the case of grammatical science, it is the same. Whenever someone becomes perfect, he no longer holds them as though they were different. Indeed, at present it is possible for someone to master surgical theory to a greater degree while mastering dietary theory to a lesser degree. But when you presuppose a perfect physician, someone who possesses all the theories perfectly and without a superior, the theories are no longer disparate, nor do they have any difference in their subject matter. Presuppose a man who has perfect health in his body. He no longer requires a strict diet; he does not require a surgical incision. He has left behind those conditions because of which he had need of these things. At length he has a health that no longer brings something else into being. For his sake all these things are attempted. And the possession of health is pursued with a certain eagerness. In fact, just as there are some things that produce health, so also there are some that preserve it: for example, physical exercise or a particular kind of food.

That long day, then, is uninterrupted; for at some time in the evening there arrives that time when the saying is fulfilled: "The Lord will be to you an everlasting light," when the sun no longer fails, "nor shall the rising of the moon illuminate the night."[91] These words are not spoken about sensible bodies of light, for "immediately after the suffering of those days the sun will be darkened, and the moon will not give its light."[92] These will no longer grant the light that is so dear to the people of this age, for the sun will be seven times brighter and the moon will be like the sun. It was said of the heavens in general that "they will be changed."[93] And when he says that the heavens are changed [15], he means the stars and the luminous bodies in them, just as we say of the earth, "The whole earth worships,"[94] and we mean those who dwell on the earth. "Sing to the Lord, all the earth."[95]

[20:6] *Great is his glory in your salvation.*

If we understand *glory* in a strict sense, we do not mean the glory that is the happiest state. For example, we do not mean the glory that is human authority, nor do we mean reputation; for all these things are the little glories of narrow-minded and foolish men. Physicians, then, who bestow healing on those who recover from sickness seem to earn glory for their patients—for the one who is cured has been glorified rather than the sickness—but this glory is not great. So it is with the pilot of a ship as well.[96]

In the salvation of God, therefore, there is *great glory*. For this salvation reaches intellect and soul. The intellect, however, is superior to all that is in us, and the soul is superior to the body, even if others do not think so.

And it is also possible to call the Savior himself "salvation," as appears in many passages: "All the ends of the earth saw the salvation of our God,"[97] and: "All flesh shall see the salvation of God,"[98] instead of "every man" or "every soul endowed with perception." *In* this *salvation*, then, the *glory* is *great*. If the death that he endured seems to be dishonorable—for according to the law, "cursed is everyone who is hanged on a tree"[99]—yet the apparent dishonor succeeded in obtaining such great glory because of the object of salvation. For salvation was accomplished not for animals, nor simply for men, but for soul, intellect, and spirit, as Paul writes, "your whole

---

[91] Is 60:19.
[92] Mt 24:29 NRSV.
[93] Ps 102:26 (101:27).
[94] Cf. Ps 66:4 (65:4).
[95] Ps 96:1 (95:1 NETS).
[96] That is, the pilot of a ship glorifies his fellow passengers over the trials of the sea when he delivers them safely to the destination of their voyage.
[97] Ps 98:3 (97:3 LES2).
[98] Lk 3:6.
[99] Gal 3:13.

spirit, soul, and body."[100] The apparent dishonor, then, is a surpassing glory.

I want to suggest an idea. When I was speaking about the Gospel, in that passage that says, "The one who believes in me will also do the works that I do, and will do greater works than these,"[101] in addition to other interpretations this one has also been given: when you consider the analogy of the one who does the works, even the great things he does are small, since they are small in comparison with God. The apostles have not performed perceptible works that are greater than those of the Savior. The Savior raised Lazarus even though he was already dead for four days, was near to decaying, and had already begun to stink. The apostles have done nothing like this. Jesus led into sight a man blind from birth. But if you consider these works of the Savior, they are small when compared with the creation of the rational essence, the heavens, and souls. And the works of the apostles, even if they were inferior to those [16] of the Savior, since they are beyond their power they are called greater than those things the Savior has done, for they were not capable of doing things greater than these. Jesus, however, has both done such things and is always doing them.

And the apostle also says: indeed, "we see Jesus, who is made lower because of the suffering of death."[102] He was made lower because of the suffering of death but was crowned "with glory and honor."[103] The diminution brought him glory, and even glory of the greatest kind. "I consider that the sufferings of this present time are not worth comparing with the glory about to be revealed."[104] Now, those are the sufferings of Christ, which those who imitate him have suffered, though he suffered first. *Great*, then *is his glory*. Even though there was a cross, even though there was death, how great is his glory when you contemplate the object of salvation and the Savior! And the glory of all the rest is not great. Most certainly there was a time when they had glory, but the glory of some of them departed even while they were still alive.

So also have I understood what is said in Isaiah: "And there is no boundary to his peace."[105] "In his days righteousness will sprout, and an abundance of peace, until the moon vanishes."[106] Observe the peace that arises, for it prevails until the consummation. For the annihilation of the moon signifies nothing other than the consummation of all things, when "the sun will be darkened and the moon will not give its light."[107] The peace does not prevail in one nation, nor does it prevail over the earth alone, for "he reconciled by the blood of his cross" not only "the things on earth" but also "the things in heaven."[108]

[20:6] *Glory and magnificence you will confer on him.*

The glory and magnificence are conferred on him together with this great glory that began at his salvation. Now, the *magnificence* is the actions and zealous deeds done by those in whom that which is fitting is found. The deeds that stem from virtue are performed fittingly. While many deeds seem to be done fittingly by men, they are not truly fitting. As I have said about glory, the signs of honor and little glories are not so great a thing as men suppose them to be; nonetheless, such honors were welcomed by them.

With the word *magnificence* people also mean the following—first of all understand the meaning from the literal sense—there are organizers of athletic contests, and if they are stingy, they diminish the contests and the

---
[100] 1 Thess 5:23.
[101] Cf. Jn 14:12 NRSV.
[102] Cf. Heb 2:9.
[103] Heb 2:9.
[104] Rom 8:18 NRSV.
[105] Is 9:7 (9:6 LES2).
[106] Ps 72:7 (71:7 NETS).
[107] Is 13:10; Mt 24:29; Mk 13:24.
[108] Cf. Col 1:20.

related expenses as a result of their petty deliberation, and they appear also to be doing that which befits an organizer of the games. However, they do it in a trifling way, and these men are called "stingy," for they do not distinguish themselves, while they are found to be in no way inferior to those who were organizers of the games before them in "what is fitting."

This, then, is called *magnificence*: when there is greatness in that which is fittingly done. Magnificence exists especially at the time when one does what is fitting not because of some other person but because of oneself.

Take another example: if someone, being wealthy, [17] during small occasions and at small gatherings spends lots of money, this person is not magnificent. This is an excess of magnificence, as when we say that audacity is an excess of courage and superstition an excess of piety. For example, suppose someone serves his fellow dice players the very finest banquet and squanders more on it than another spends at a wedding feast. This happens for the sake of vainglory. And magnificence does not happen for the sake of vainglory.

Being led by the hand by perceptible examples, let us come to the things of which the word is speaking: the Savior accomplished what is fitting in great things. The righteous man also demonstrates what is fitting in great things. What is greater than saving the world, than making peace not with things that are on the earth alone, but also with things that are in heaven?[109] What is greater than to accomplish that for which the things in heaven, the things on earth, and the things under the earth bow the knee to the Savior to the glory of God the Father?[110] This glory is *magnificence*, and it has a kinship with majesty. It is said of God himself, therefore: "The Lord is king! He is clothed in majesty!"[111] This majesty and *magnificence* are the same thing. For whom was it fitting to save men other than one who had no sin?[112] He had no sin, knowing that it is good to avoid sin and to possess righteousness, that it is good not to repay insult to one who insults another,[113] not to avenge oneself on those who are disposed to evil. "When he suffered," it says, "he did not threaten."[114] Not only was he not doing things that are unworthy, but neither did he threaten to do them. A threat is an anticipation of fearful things. Indeed, when there is no longer an anticipation but something comes as a result, then there is no longer a threat.

Glory, then, *and magnificence you will confer on him*. And the statement *you will confer* is well said. This is conferred in addition to something else that is already established: for he did not begin to display this glory and magnificence among rational creatures for the first time when he appeared, but he did this at every moment and everywhere it was possible. The glory and *magnificence* that came by means of his appearance—through the cross, for example—have come as an addition.

[20:7] *Because you will give him blessing until the farthest age.*

Just as we have spoken about life—not that he himself should have it, for he has it already, but that those who draw near to him, who gather around his teachings, should have this.

And this blessing *until the farthest age* is distinct from the blessing that seems to exist among mortals, for this blessing is also spoken of on one occasion: "Because in his life his soul will be blessed; he will never again see light."[115] He will not see the light, even if he now seems to see clearly. He does not possess this glory on his own.

---

[109]Cf. Col 1:20.
[110]Cf. Phil 2:10-11.
[111]Ps 93:1 (92:1).
[112]Cf. 1 Pet 2:22.
[113]Cf. 1 Pet 2:23.
[114]1 Pet 2:23 NRSV.
[115]Ps 49:18-19 (cf. 48:19-20 NETS).

Therefore, the spiritual [18] blessings that are given in the heavenly places[116] are identical with this blessing that remains *until the farthest age*. For when someone supposes that he has received wealth as a blessing, he does not possess it *until the farthest age*, for it passes away together with the material life.

It is also possible to interpret this with grace and elegance in a moral sense: when one who has wealth so spends it that he finds a glory after these things are gone, of which glory it says, "As for the those who in the present age are rich, command them not to be haughty."[117] Then it says, "Storing up for themselves a foundation of good works."[118] The blessing of this person remains *until the farthest age*. And the things accomplished by this wealth remain indestructible. Likewise also in the case of other things: if in keeping with prudence—with what is truly prudence— a person should be glorified and blessed, he has the blessing remaining *until the farthest age*. If, however, someone presumes to be blessed by virtue in pretense, he has a blessing that is ended; for when the truth shines forth and deeds appear just as they are by nature, the blessing that accords with mere thinking is dissolved. At times it even presents a danger.

[20:7] *You will gladden him in joy with your face.*

The saying seems to be ambiguous, for by the phrase *you will gladden him in joy with your face*, on the one hand the following is meant: when you gladden your face, you will gladden him also.

Or perhaps both things gladden him: *you will gladden him in joy*, and *your face* will gladden him along with you.

This kind of saying appears also in Isaiah: "And the Lord, the Lord has sent me and his Spirit."[119] Some take it thus: "The Lord sent me; meanwhile his Spirit also sent me." And they say that the sending of the Savior in his appearance has taken place from the Father and the Holy Spirit. For it was said to her who conceived him or carried him in the womb, "The Spirit of the Lord will come upon you and the power of the Most High."[120] See! It seems here that he was sent from the Father and the Holy Spirit.

Others, however, read it thus, and this reading is better: "And the Lord, the Lord has sent me; and he has sent his Spirit also," the Father sending the Son and the Holy Spirit.

The former interpretation says this, that the Father and the Holy Spirit sent the Son. And each receives an interpretation of the reading that suits himself, as was already said.

Here too, then, is the *face* of the Lord who is spoken of here. And the Son is his image, "the exact imprint of his very being."[121] Therefore, about the *face* assumed by the Savior and every righteous *face* is it said, *You will gladden him in joy with your face*, for when the Son comes, then someone, having seen the exact impression, immediately sees the one whose impression he is also, for "whoever has seen me [19] has seen the Father."[122] The joy comes from God and his *face*.

One can also understand the words *You will gladden him in joy with your face* in the following way. He is now saying this about every righteous person, for your *face*—by which the righteous person has been created "in the image and likeness"[123]—will be shown to be his.

And I say: accidents, even though they are separable from essences, often occur as coexistent with them. Take color, for example, for the body is not first created and then colored; it is created colored. Nevertheless, we

---

[116]Cf. Eph 1:3.
[117]1 Tim 6:17 NRSV.
[118]1 Tim 6:19.
[119]Is 48:16.
[120]Lk 1:35.
[121]Cf. Heb 1:3 NRSV.
[122]Jn 14:9 NRSV.
[123]Gen 1:26.

say that color in some cases belongs among the accidents and can be absent. I added the words "in some cases," since in the realm of sensible things, color is neither added to nor lost from snow. Neither is humidity added to water, for it is essential to it.

Therefore, given that the rational being has been created good from the beginning, it is not good in the same way that God is, for man is not good in essence but in habit and disposition. Even if man, then, has been created "in the image and likeness of God,"[124] this is separable from man in the sense that it has an appearance that is able to be cast away and taken up again. But when God saves, every appearance will change. And this will be shown in the one that is saved.

[20:8] *For the king hopes in the Lord.*

This king hopes in the Lord. He hopes that there will be salvation for those on whose behalf he has come to suffer. He is not uncertain about the goal of what is pursued with zeal, but he hopes steadfastly, for "in the mercy of the Most High he is not shaken."[125] Therefore his hope does not fail.

And I give an example, though perhaps it is forced. No one hopes for things that are present. The one who is well does not hope to be made well; the wealthy does not hope to be rich. Hope, then, is concerned with future things. Hope and expectation are identical. Expectation is the genus to which hope belongs; specifically, hope is an expectation of good things from God.

Of things future, then, some have potential reality, so that they might happen and might not, since both outcomes transpire by chance, while other things will certainly transpire: as, for example, when I say knowledgeably that after so long a period of time there will be an eclipse of the sun. Only the wise person hopes for this, for the other is wholly ignorant of it, whether it happens or not.

It is good to remember this: that there are four questions to be resolved, two of them being simple and two being complex. The simple questions are that something is and what it is. Then the complex questions are how it is and why it is. Therefore, it is characteristic of the wise person to expect, according to knowledge, these things that will always come to pass.

For he understands both that there is such a thing as an eclipse and what an eclipse is: namely, a covering of the sun by the moon. And he understands how it happens: when the moon passes in a vertical line beneath the sun, an eclipse occurs. See! This is the "how" question. And the "why" question is as follows: when the sun travels around, it appears in different positions. Sometimes the circle of the moon is below the circle of the sun. It does not always pass directly below it. That is, there are two circles. When a body comes here and passes again into the position directly below the other, that which comes below conceals the one above it. In any case, they say that an eclipse is an interposition of the moon [20] before the sun.

It belongs to the wise person, therefore, to know this unerring expectation. And one can anticipate the things that happen by chance, for example, rain or a good harvest. But these predictions are often wrong.

Therefore he says, *You will gladden him in joy, for the king hopes in the Lord.* The one who hopes is a king. The hope and expectation of such a person is unerring. And he says,

[20:8] *In the mercy of the Most High he will never be shaken.*

Being pitied by the Most High, he is unshaken. For he is shaken at the time when his subjects are found to be unworthy of his rule. And he leaves them and abandons them.

---
[124] Gen 1:26.
[125] Ps 21:7 (20:8).

And, in their intent, we understand hoping in God to be the same as repenting.

It is characteristic of the Most High to bless rational creatures, just as the following also shows: "Glory to God in the highest, and on earth peace."[126]

[20:9] *May your hand be found against all your enemies, your right hand find out all who hate you.*

In the case of the body, one may contrast the right hand with the hand, for the right hand is a hand, but not every hand is a right hand. We have here a *hand* and a *right hand* that are named in relation to God. Of the true David who comes from David's seed this is also said in another psalm: "And he will set his hand upon the sea and his right hand on the rivers."[127] And note that it is simply the *hand* that is set on the sea, for the *right hand* is not on the sea but on his rivers. And again, "Your hand destroyed nations."[128] Observe: the military power of a king is often called *hand*, and executioners are called the *hands* of judges. The devil also knew that there is a *hand* that causes harm, for he did not say, "Stretch out your right hand," but rather, "your hand, and touch all that he has."[129]

May your hand be found against all your enemies.

Your hand that punishes your enemies will appear. So also do I understand the saying, "But the Lord's face is against evildoers, to destroy the remembrance of them from earth."[130] When they do evil things, they suppose that there is no providence, that there is no punishment for the sins that they commit. But when they receive an experience of a certain suffering, sometimes when they become aware of it they see the face of God. Now, "the face" I understand in this way: they know that there is a God. And just as "we contemplate the Creator by analogy from the greatness and beauty of creatures,"[131] so also from the greatness and harmony of the things that relate to his government the Judge is observed.

We have found, then, Pharaoh first behaving with contempt, and then, when he was stricken, laying hold of a conception of God. Once at least he says, "The Lord is just."[132] He who says earlier, "I do not know the Lord,"[133] now confesses that he both knows him and knows that he is just. "But I and my people are impious."[134] And when the face of God comes on Pharaoh, the worker of evil, the hand is found as well: for at some time evildoers need to know that there is a Judge, even if it does not happen in this life, but it must happen at some point. For this reason it is said, *May your hand be found.*

May your right hand find.

The hand is found by the enemies; the right hand, however, finds those who hate. Those who hate can be less wicked than enemies. Not everyone who hates is an enemy, but every enemy hates.

And as it was said that the hand of God is set on the sea, in order that by its sufferings he should bring an end to its agitation and saltiness, the right hand of the Savior **[21]** is on the rivers—and these are people who have life in the Spirit, "out of whose heart flow rivers of living water";[135] "the rivers lifted, O Lord; the rivers lifted up their voices"[136]—so the right hand of the Savior is found to be the one that saves, the one that exalts, according to the saying: "The right hand of the Lord exalted me, the right hand of the Lord did mightily. I shall not die, but I shall live."[137]

---

[126] Lk 2:14.
[127] Ps 89:25 (88:26).
[128] Ps 44:3 (43:3 NETS).
[129] Job 1:11 NETS.
[130] Ps 34:16 (33:17 NETS).
[131] Wis 13:5.
[132] Ex 9:27 NETS.
[133] Ex 5:2 NETS.
[134] Ex 9:27 NETS.
[135] Jn 7:38.
[136] Ps 93:3 (92:3 LES2).
[137] Ps 118:16-17 (117:16-17).

[20:10] *You have placed them as an oven of fire for the time of your face.*

This could be said about the enemies who are handed over to punishment.

If, however, it applies to both the enemies and those who hate, understand what is written in this way: see, those who are built on the foundation, Christ, if they are gold and silver, are only tested with fire, but they do not disappear. They are not consumed even when they are found by the fire. But if they are "wood, hay, or straw,"[138] they do disappear and they are set like an oven of fire—they are at last like smoke. Now, smoke is a byproduct of the useful activity of the fire. Therefore, when wood, hay, and straw are *for the time of God's face*, as it is set down—for there will be an appointed time when the Judge will be shown—those who are called "wood, hay, and straw" do not disappear so that they exist no longer—for it is impossible for them to disappear in this way—but they disappear insofar as they are hay. For this fire of punishment does not act on their essence but on their habits and qualities. This fire does not consume creatures but certain kinds of conditions, certain habits.

And teaching accomplishes the same end: it takes the unlearned and it makes him disappear, not insofar as he is a human but insofar as he is unlearned, for instruction brings his ignorance to an end. So also righteousness abolishes the unrighteous person, not so that he exists no longer but so that he is no longer unrighteous.

[20:10] *O Lord, confound them in your wrath, and a fire will consume them.*

Someone is confounded at the time when he begins to hesitate and repent. And *a fire will consume them* so that they are no longer such people.

[20:11] *You will destroy their fruit from the earth and their seed from the sons of men.*

The word *seed* is ambiguous. When it is defined in relation to fruit, it signifies the seed of a tree; when it is defined in relation to children, the seed of a man; for we often have the word *seed* in Scripture mentioned together with children.

It now falls to us to speak about the difference between the words. He is saying the following: While they were on the earth and had dealings with it, they were united to the earth. Instead of the works of the immaterial soul, they produced as their fruit the works of the flesh. This *fruit you will destroy from the earth*. The good and beautiful land, which receives the seed of Jesus, the seed he sows, brings forth fruit.[139] This is the same land, in its underlying substance, with that which produces thistles. And being a rational essence, the land is receptive of seeds. This land acquires its differentiation from our free will.

And their seed from the sons of men.

They sowed among the sons of men and not among the sons of God, for they are unreceptive to these seeds. Therefore, *you will destroy their seed from the sons of men*, where the [22] tendency toward bad fruit is present. If someone has virtue in his activity, the seed of vice is opposed so that it seems to be destroyed.

[20:12] *Because they inclined toward evil things against you.*

Against you who have made them straight. Their free will inclined toward evil. You know that in the case of perceptible works of art and representations bad work brings censure to the one who produced it, while what has been well done brings praise. For example, it was said in Sirach, "A work will be praised for the hand of

---

[138] 1 Cor 3:12.

[139] The "land" is frequently taken as an allegorical reference to the soul.

the craftsman."[140] . . . if someone bends from being "in the image."[141] Therefore, as far as it was up to them, they chose evil things against you.

[20:12] *They devised plots together, which they could not establish.*

And in order to be led by the hand from history to so-called history—I am not sure, however, whether it is a history—those who wished to build the tower that has its head in the uttermost height desired to do this but were unable to establish it.[142] And indeed they were scattered. God accomplishes his counsel at the time when a person desires rightly and according to his counsel. The one who pursues this "does all things with counsel."[143] To this counsel God adds the fulfillment.

[20:13] *For you will show them your back.*[144]

Often things that relate to God are said to belong to his body: "You are the body of Christ,"[145] and in this body are found eyes, ears, and hands.[146] Hence, "You will show your back to them." You will put them in their place behind this body of yours.

It is possible to understand this in the following way: the primary matters about God are called his "face," whereas these perceptible creatures are behind him, for they are after him. For example, to Moses, who is unable to see God's face, God passes by in his glory and shows him his back. Indeed, he recorded the book of Genesis immediately afterward.

To them, therefore, he will show his back, for toward the saints his face is set according to the prayer that they offer up: "Show us your face and we shall be saved!"[147]

[20:13] *Among your remnant you will prepare your face.*[148]

The others "who remain," besides those who "hate," are saints; they are the ones who remained in this condition.

And well did it say *you will prepare*, and not "you will give." He has his face ready, in order that everyone who desires to see it should be able to behold it.

[20:14] *Be lifted high, O Lord, in your power; we will sing and play psalms about your sovereign acts.*

For you do all things with power. At the beginning of the psalm the power of God is also praised in song: *O Lord, by your power the king will be made glad.*[149]

The power that gladdens the king, that accomplishes all that has been mentioned, is lifted high, not by being raised from a low place into a height; rather, it is lifted high when men no longer think mean things about it but think lofty things, as it truly is. And when we say, "I will exalt you, O Lord,"[150] we do not mean this: that we elevate you from lowliness into the heights. To exalt God is to confess his loftiness.

Finally, he sings in triumph—for in the case of a king alone is dominion mentioned, and there are dominions that belong to this king—he sings of what he is able to do as king. **[23]**

---

[140]Sir 9:17 LES2.
[141]Gen 1:26.
[142]Cf. Gen 11:4.
[143]Prov 31:4 LXX. There is no corresponding statement in the Hebrew.
[144]The NRSV has "you will put them to flight," where the Hebrew has "you will set them backward."
[145]1 Cor 12:27 NRSV.
[146]Cf. 1 Cor 12:15-17.
[147]Ps 80:3 (79:4).
[148]The LXX has "among your remnant" where the Hebrew has "with your bows."
[149]Ps 21:1 (20:2).
[150]Ps 30:1 (29:2 NETS).

PSALM 21 [22]

[**21:23**] *Toward the end. For the morning's help. A psalm of David.*

There is a spiritual day that comes by means of "the Sun of Righteousness,"[1] about which many things are set down in the Scriptures, and especially in the New Testament. "Let us live honorably," it says, "as in the day."[2] You know that even in the literal sense, those who do certain indecent things do them in the darkness, and especially when many good men are present. Certainly the one who is ignorant of good things is in darkness and practices many things characteristic of those who tolerate indecent behavior.

But whenever someone is illuminated by the true Light, "walking in the day," that is progressing—for walking signifies progress—he practices all things in a dignified way and thinks nothing of those who tolerate indecency. Describing this condition, the prophet Isaiah also says, "Out of the night my spirit arises toward you, O God."[3] This morning, therefore, is in need of help. For even when we have illumination and a beginning of the day, we need to abide in the light lest the day fail, lest it set.

Toward the end, then, *for the morning's help.* For when the day has begun with the favor of God's help, when the one who is being helped remains in the same determination toward the helper, he also remains in the help for the whole day. For if in the beginning, which has small brightness, one is helped, how much more when midday arrives!

You find, therefore, many things like this set down in the Scriptures. God appeared to Abraham at no other time than midday, for at that time the light has come into full strength. And finally at the zenith the sun has moved so that the air around us has no shadow. And it says these things allegorically, since even the literal sense guides us toward this.

The bride also says this to her bridegroom: "Tell me, you whom my soul loves, where you pasture your flock and where you cause them to rest at midday."[4] I have arrived at the beginning of the day in which you are the shepherd. The time of midday, when the light is in full strength, is what I seek.

"Where do you pasture? Where do you cause to rest?" in order that, by coming there as a companion with you I may be busy with your work, for I also desire to drive to pasture those sheep that you shepherd. The holy women who were shepherdesses, like Rebekah was, bear a symbol of such a condition.

For the morning's help, then. Who possesses the morning and the beginning of the day other than the one who is able to say, "The night is far gone, the day is near"?[5] For this reason also the women who sought Jesus, when he was crucified, did not see him at the time of midday, [**24**] but in the earliest time of the morning.

You know also that, in the event that took place in the time of the Savior, the word truly has universal significance for every virtuous

---

[1] Mal 4:2 (3:20).
[2] Rom 13:13 NRSV.
[3] Is 26:9.
[4] Song 1:7.
[5] Rom 13:12 NRSV.

person, whose works shine before men like a light.[6] We say that he arrives at the time of the morning when he receives the beginning of illumination, so that he says, "Early in the morning I will approach you and gaze upon you."[7] Similar also is what is said, "for you were darkness, but now you are in the light of the Lord."[8]

Toward the end, then, since he has received the anticipated goal, which the Savior's economy, as well as perfect virtue, accomplished.

Listen, then: this psalm is one that refers to a single person. The person who speaks is the same from beginning to end. Changes of persons are commonplace both in the Psalms and in the prophecies, as well as changes of speakers, of audience, and of topics: for everyone who speaks has the role of a narrator. And since he is not speaking as though to just anyone but speaks to specific persons, there is also a second person who hears the speaker and attends to the topic that he is narrating.

So the person who speaks here is one. Many words were quoted from this psalm in the New Testament, since the psalm has been spoken from the Savior's person. This very statement in its entirety, *O God, my God*—the Savior said this expression when he was on the cross.[9] The statement *they divided my garments for themselves* was an utterance from the Savior in the Gospels.[10] Also the statement *I will proclaim your name to my brothers*, Paul wrote that this was spoken from the Savior's person in the letter to the Hebrews.[11] Since, therefore, three testimonies are set down from the psalm that the person of the Savior is the speaker, one must assume that the whole psalm was narrated from his person.

And I say this out of necessity—and I adduced this as proof also in my statements about the inhumanation—since they[12] always quote to us the words of the Scripture that say that the Savior has had a body, for example, "a body you have prepared for me,"[13] and "since Christ suffered for us in the flesh."[14] We said: if only the word *alone* were added: "a body alone you have prepared for me."

One can sometimes wear multiple pieces of clothing. When someone says of himself, for example, "I have a mantle, I have a small cloak, a garment," but does not add that he has "only" this, he is not hindered from having the other garments also. Again, let someone possess, for example, a shield, a sword, a helmet, and a breastplate. If necessity requires him to say, "I have a shield," but he does not add that he has "only" this, the other arms are not removed from belonging to him.

So we have here something that is said by the person himself: *Deliver my soul from the sword!* If he also said in another place, "a body you have prepared for me," [25] and there is no mention of a soul, here on the other hand there is mention of a soul. And he has not said this only about his soul, just because he says, *Deliver my soul from the sword!*

[21:2] *O God, my God, attend to me. For what purpose did you abandon me?*

The word *abandonment*, when used in its proper sense, does not mean "to come into misfortunes." The martyrs, in any case, were not abandoned when they were cooked in the furnace, when they were handed over to the flame. But those who sacrificed, even when they suffered nothing, were abandoned.

---

[6] Cf. Mt 5:16.
[7] Ps 5:3 (5:4 LES2).
[8] Eph 5:8.
[9] Cf. Mk 15:34.
[10] Mt 27:35; Mk 15:24; Lk 23:34; Jn 19:24.
[11] Heb 2:12.

[12] The word *they* here refers to the Apollinarians, who argued that Jesus possessed no created spirit, the Word taking the place of the human spirit within him.
[13] Ps 40:6 (39:7); cf. Heb 10:5. The Hebrew has "Ears you have hollowed out for me," where the Greek text reads "A body you prepared for me." The NT follows the Greek text here.
[14] 1 Pet 4:1.

When someone, therefore, asks not to be abandoned, he is asking the following: not to fall away from his determined intention. Although someone who suffers nothing does not seem to fall into abandonment, yet at that very moment it befalls him because of his own vice, as I said of those who sacrificed.

Abandonment, therefore, is God's withdrawal from the one who is abandoned. Saul has suffered this: "you have not listened to me," he says, "not even in dreams,"[15] and he went away to the medium.

Sometimes when you observe, then, a rich Christian who has all things pleasantly but who takes refuge among astrologers, or séances, or takes pains for such things—these were abandoned. And when you see a poor man who fell from wealth but clings to God, such a person as Job was, this man was not abandoned.

Since, then, the Savior has come to a cross, and to men it seems to be an abandonment to fall under such a death, he says this phrase, *O God, my God, pay attention to me!* as though addressing this opinion of theirs.

And perhaps he is also speaking about the abandonment of his body, as it were, for the Hebrews were his body before this. That people, then, was abandoned. And he calls this his own abandonment, since he was their head.

O God, my God, pay attention to me. Why did you abandon me? He seeks the cause and the goal of the abandonment, for this is to say, "For what end did you abandon me?" The goal of the questioner is not that it should be known to him but that it should be known to his body, to his people.

[21:2] *Far away from my salvation are the words of my transgressions.*[16]

Lest we imagine him to be relating a myth here, we are compelled to grasp a deeper vision. The subject and the word about the subject are not the same thing. The majority perceive things that are perceptible, but they do not possess an account of them. It belongs to the great ones to possess an account of the subjects.

Indeed, in this way, even by speech do we separate one thing from another. I have already mentioned color and appearance.[17] While color is one thing and appearance is another, they are, however, inseparable from one another. And so we separate them by speech. Color admits intensification and diminishment. Appearance, however, does not admit intensification and diminishment, so that color is something different from appearance, even though it is never divided from it, even though it is never without it. Those who are concerned with the demonstration of this say these things by way of abstraction. By speech we abstract one thing from another, not in experience, not in reality. Therefore, although we say that the line is a "length without breadth," the perceived line is not [26] without breadth. It certainly has breadth. But we abstract breadth from the line by means of speech.

I am saying the following: those who have transgressions in experience and in reality do not see the account of them. For if they had known that they are harmful, that they end in destruction, they would not practice them.

And one can possess an account of transgression. For example, suppose it is a transgression committed against the law of God to murder a man in some way at any time. However, when a certain juridical authority, especially a minister of the true law, kills one who is worthy of death—as Agag was killed by Samuel[18]—Elijah and Samuel possessed the

---

[15] 1 Sam 28:15.
[16] The Hebrew poetry here, being somewhat terse, is variously rendered. Most English translations supply the word *you* and maintain the mood of a question. The LXX takes the half-verse as a new sentence, supplying the verb *are*.
[17] Cf. PsT 19.
[18] Cf. 1 Sam 15:33.

account of the transgression, not the transgression itself.[19]

The Savior speaks as Man. For the one who is driven toward despair is himself the speaker of these things: *Far away from my salvation are the words of my transgressions.* They are not *far away from* my *salvation*, for I did not know sin, I did not perform it. Yet I understand it in my thought; I know what sin is. Therefore also let the words of transgressions be far away from my salvation. Let my salvation not receive a kind of mixture so that it becomes diluted.

Sometimes, indeed, someone is saved, and because there is something good that exists within him; if evil existed instead, his salvation is diminished. That is to say, many have often asked the question: "If someone does many wicked things but does a few good things too, does he ruin those good things?"

To say that he ruins them signifies the removal of the hope of persons. To this I have often said that his punishment is lessened. Grant me to say this: let many perpetrate injustice, but let some of these not continue to do so; rather, let them become pitiful. His sentence is diminished, and these good things are not practiced by him in vain. Whenever someone sins primarily, he has the deeds "preceding him to judgment."[20] They run in front of him; they lead him by the hand to judgment. As for others, however, their sins follow them. When someone who practices good things also commits a few sins, these follow after him. "Likewise," it says, "are good deeds as well."[21] As I said about sins, so also will I say concerning good deeds. In any case, no one who practices the good remains useless.

He has his punishment reduced as a result of it.

He, however, who knew no sin and did not commit it[22] and has the words of transgressions far away from his own salvation; he has salvation that is pure. Neither sin nor transgression are mixed together with it, not even this: the word of a transgression.

[21:3] *O my God! By day I will have cried to you, and you will not listen to me, and by night, and it is not incomprehensible to me.*[23]

The condition of the life of men differs. Life has some advantageous circumstances, and it has some misfortunes. And in these human circumstances themselves there are pleasures, and these are called "day," and there are misfortunes, which are called "night." He is therefore saying the following: I cry to you both in the pleasant and luminous times, and you listen to me,[24] and by night I do this, and it does not become incomprehensible to me. For when you assent and the misfortunes are no longer obscure, then it has become evident to me.

He hears us shouting by day, and by night—that is, **[27]** when we are in the unfortunate circumstance—we have him as our helper and we received knowledge in actual fact because he helps us, for this is what the statement "and by night, and it is not incomprehensible to me" means. Even if it was incomprehensible to others that this one, since he was "the man from God,"[25] was abandoned, this was not incomprehensible to him, for he has come into this circumstance willingly: "I will go by myself to the mountain of myrrh."[26]

---

[19] There is some clarification of this cryptic remark in Didymus's comments on Ps 5:6 (5:7). He writes: "For we do not call murderers or men of blood those who, in accordance with the divine law, kill those who deserve to suffer this, since otherwise it would be fitting to call Samuel and Elijah these things, who killed many for the sake of religion." *Patrologia Graeca*, ed. Jacques-Paul Migne (Paris, 1857–1886), 39:1172A.
[20] 1 Tim 5:24.
[21] 1 Tim 5:25.
[22] Cf. 2 Cor 5:21; 1 Pet 2:22.
[23] LXX and the Hebrew differ here. The Hebrew has "but find no rest," where the LXX has "and it is not incomprehensible to me" or, by a different translation, "and there is nothing for my folly."
[24] This seems to be an obvious misinterpretation of the passage. The word *not* has been overlooked.
[25] Cf. Jn 9:16.
[26] Song 4:6 LES2.

Surely, his body is myrrh. He has gone to the mountain, because he endured death on behalf of all those who were embalmed for burial.

And that this is so, let us also learn from another psalm, namely that misfortunes are "ignorance" and "night." "By day," it says, "the Lord will command his mercy, and by night he will reveal it."[27] When we see men being shown mercy clearly and readily, God has commanded his mercy by day.

And "by night he will reveal it." For when you know that God also hands a person over to punishment in order that he should reveal his own mercy—for God does not hand men over to punishments with cruelty—in this night, this unfortunate circumstance, the mercy of God will be revealed.

And he commands his mercy "by day," when his compassion is evident. And "by night" can be said because of the unfortunate circumstance of those who are being punished. Despite the fact that they are beyond hope, yet he himself will show his mercy even in the night.

And it is not incomprehensible to me. I am not ignorant when I cry out by night. I am not unaware that you hear me.

[21:4] *But you, the praise of Israel, dwell among the saints.*[28]

Observe what he is saying. You, who dwell among the saints and are the praise of all who have a pure heart and see you[29]—for such people are Israel—did not abandon me. For when you dwell among the saints, and the saints suffer something, those are not abandoned. How in that case would you dwell in them, and not merely dwell, but as the praise of Israel?

One can also understand the words *But you dwell among the saints* in this way: even when some surrounded me with a miserable death and for this reason you seem to be cut off from me, yet you dwell among the saints, among those whom I teach, those with whom I am agreed. And if you are present in these, I have not been abandoned.

The saints can also be taken in a general sense in reference to the blessed, rational beings, to holy men, and to the "mysteries of the kingdom of heaven"[30] themselves. And God, because he is present in every place, is found in such ones, and all such ones are his temple: a multiform temple.

Therefore, you are *praise* in Israel, for the one who is truly clear-sighted and "has the mind of Christ,"[31] by which he sees God, is not crushed by affliction. You, however, are *the praise of Israel*; "in you we will be praised all the day long."[32]

[21:5] *Upon you our fathers hoped.*

Our fathers who hoped on you were answered, *and they were not put to shame.*[33] For by always receiving their prayers you were bringing them into your kindness, even if they died in the midst of afflictions: for your attentiveness to those who cry out to you is not the same thing as your making them to be without afflictions [28], but rather to render them free of the harm that is borne by the afflictions. So indeed was the petition interpreted: "Lead us not into temptation."[34] Therefore, even if the saints seem not to be heard when they pray, at that time they are especially heard, because they are shown to be athletes by remaining in their afflictions. Otherwise, what kind of accomplishment

---

[27]Ps 42:8 (41:9).
[28]The word translated "saints" can also be translated "the holy place." The NRSV, following the Hebrew text, has, "Yet you are holy, enthroned on the praises of Israel."
[29]Cf. Mt 5:8.

[30]Mt 13:11.
[31]1 Cor 2:16.
[32]Ps 44:8 (43:9).
[33]Ps 22:5 (21:6).
[34]Mt 6:13; Lk 11:4.

would it be if, when praying, one should remove oneself from the afflictions?

Question: The statement *our fathers*, is this spoken from the person of the Savior?

You know that in many things he accounts himself according to the Man.

[21:5-6] *They hoped and you delivered them; to you they cried aloud and they were saved . . .*

. . . not because no misfortune afflicted them, but because they prevailed in their afflictions.

To you they cried aloud.

When they shouted they were saved. The intensified shout we take to be prayer, for we do not cry in a loud voice. Indeed, thought is the speech of the soul; it is the voice of the inner man.

[21:6-7] *Upon you they hoped and were not put to shame. But I am a worm and not a man.*

The fathers, when they cried to you, were not put to shame, for they have obtained what they were expecting, what they were hoping to obtain.

Here he is teaching modesty: *I am a worm and not a man.* He is not denying that he himself is man, but only that he is a certain kind of man, since he is not calling himself a worm literally. Therefore, I am not that man about whom it is said, "For when there is rivalry and jealousy among you, are you not merely human?"[35] But I hold fast to the same disposition toward them; for their sake I patiently endure all things.

One can also understand this as follows: since the body has come to him not from the sowing of a man's seeds, but only from the substance that was taken from her who conceived him, in this sense he calls himself a worm, for the worm does not come from copulation but from the simple substance.

Here also from the simple substance that is present in the female he constructed for himself his body. Indeed, "he has been conceived in her"[36] and "has been born from her."[37] Now, other bodies are said to receive their formation "through women." Therefore, since she did not produce her offspring from a man's seed, he has not come through her but from her.

[21:7] *A reproach among men and an object of scorn among the people.*

I am not a reproach among men in general but among certain men.

[21:8] *All who saw me mocked me.*

Some people often want to falsify the generalization, for the generalization is sometimes broken, and a generalization turns out differently. When I say, "All men are mortal," I say this as a generalization. But when I say, "All grammarians are mortal," I am indicating certain men, and the generalization now stems from the grammarian and not from the man. "All the virtuous are righteous." I do not say the following, that "all men are righteous." So it is here: not all who saw him mocked him—in any case, the apostles who saw him did not mock him— but all those who saw me in this way, as an object of scorn among the people, as a reproach; for the others did not see him in this way.

[21:8] *They spoke with their lips; they shook their head.*

[29] If they had spoken from their heart, they would not have shaken their head. They spoke with many lips. And it is not strange if they have said these things about the one who has suffered and who appeared suspended on a

---

[35]Cf. 1 Cor 3:3-4.

[36]Mt 1:20.
[37]Mt 1:16.

cross. And God himself accuses them, saying, "This people honors me with their lips."[38] All these, therefore, who take joy in others' misfortunes, when they rejoice over the saints and righteous people, speak only with their lips. And those who were speaking arrogantly toward the Savior were certainly doing this: "Aha! You who would destroy the temple and rebuild it in three days!"[39]

Question: What does the shaking of the head mean?

Probably this also relates to the historical sense: they were doing this in scorn. In many passages the head signifies the mind. When someone, then, speaks in this way with his lips against the Savior, not beholding him as he must, he has the mind shaken, he has the intellect agitated.

And that *head* means "mind": "I gave their ways to their heads,"[40] and certainly this head did not possess anything. "And from there you will come away, and your hands will be on your head."[41] "You say, 'I have not sinned.' Behold! I am indeed going with you into judgment."[42] And when you depart from this life, you will have your deeds upon your head. And again, "The suffering he caused will return upon his head."[43]

But this word occurs in a praiseworthy sense as well: "The eyes of the wise person are in his head."[44] Now, the one who has become wise after being unwise does not have eyes that are displaced into a different place. Therefore he says this, that the wise man's power of discernment is in his head, in accordance with Christ, for this is what the sentence "Christ is his head"[45] means.

---

[38] Is 29:13.
[39] Mk 15:29.
[40] Ezek 22:31.
[41] Cf. Jer 2:37 NETS.
[42] Jer 2:35 (2:36).
[43] Ps 7:16 (7:17).
[44] Eccles 2:14 LES2.
[45] 1 Cor 11:3.

[21:9] *He hoped in the Lord. Let him deliver him! Let him save him, because he finds delight in him.*

They are speaking in mockery. I said earlier that people are accustomed to saying such things about the righteous when they are afflicted: "If he is pleasing to him, let him save him!" And he will deliver him, not because those people say this, for he is pleasing to him. He is fulfilling his economy. He has come to fulfill the Father's will, for "I have come down from heaven not to do my own will."[46] If, therefore, he is doing the Father's will, the Father finds delight in him.

[21:10] *For you are he who drew me out of the womb.*

Something credible may be said even in the case of the literal sense. Mary has conceived "when the Holy Spirit came upon her and the power of the Most High overshadowed her."[47] And just as God himself, who fashions bodies in the womb—just as he fashioned Jeremiah,[48] so he fashioned this body in Mary's womb. Since, then, the same virginity and purity was present in her body as in her soul, he himself drew him out of her womb. He has not done this as something exceptional, but just as after he had formed Adam, he caused him to become a man, so after forming him he led him out.

[21:10] *You are my hope from my mother's breasts.*

Even while I was nursing I made you known, that you are my hope, by summoning the magi—for he was still an infant when he despoiled magic[49]—while I was receiving milk,

---

[46] Jn 6:38.
[47] Lk 1:35.
[48] Jer 1:5.
[49] This is a play on words. As in English, in Greek the words *magi* and *magic* are closely related.

I was not nursing like other newborns, who are ignorant of God [30], but I had you as my hope.

[21:11] *Upon you was I cast from the womb.*

I, who committed no sin and had no deceit in my heart,[50] who "before knowing how to say 'father' and 'mother'" received "the might of Damascus and the spoils of Samaria,"[51] who chose "the good before I could choose evil"[52]—for this shows that he neither committed nor knew sin. All men, after the choice of evil things, choose the good. He, however, before choosing evil things, selected the good. And this means that he is without sin, that he has not known sin, because he did not sin in those things that relate to the age of childhood—the things that are not altogether evil—yet nevertheless exist before virtue.

This could also be said about every saint who came into life for this very reason. "There was a man sent from God, whose name was John."[53] "And he will be filled with the Holy Spirit, even from his mother's womb."[54] Each of these is able to say these words: *Upon you was I cast from the womb; from my mother's womb, you are my God.*

And when it is said about Samuel, "and this was before Samuel knew God,"[55] it seems to disagree with what has been said. Consequently, let us look at this more sensibly, as God the Word pleases. Job says, "And if I ate my morsel of bread alone and did not distribute food to an orphan, if I did not, like a father, teach them from my mother's womb."[56] How indeed was he able to provide for orphans from his mother's womb? Therefore, I understand this in the following way: he is describing a praiseworthy deed. And the deed receives its beginning at the time when the understanding is fulfilled. Therefore I can say as follows: he is saying, "I did not practice good things after evil things, but when my understanding was fulfilled it began with praiseworthy acts." So for the time being let us put aside those matters that pertain to his having received such a condition of being "pleasing to God"[57] from some other source.

Since, then, there is another birth besides the obvious kind, and that birth is, after a certain way of speaking, a "mother," someone is drawn out from a womb, from this particular womb, for no man is able to draw forth from this womb into the light except God alone.

And from the corresponding breasts, from which those who are just beginning to have reverence for God receive milk, from those breasts they have hope in God. Milk often signifies something else as well: "You who have been torn away from milk? Receive hope in your affliction."[58] The one who has just recently ceased from milk and is snatched away from his mother's breasts is unable to receive hope in his affliction. Often the infant is mentioned in addition to the mature man, while the intervening ages are passed over in silence: "when I was a child . . . when I became a man."[59] And he has become a man not by a first and single change but by a change of many things. [31] Therefore, he who bears the condition of an infant and has a weaker disposition is nourished with milk. But when someone is able to become mature, then he keeps away from milk and at that time prepares himself for the strength to compete, which pursues and attains

---

[50] Cf. 1 Pet 2:22; Is 53:9.
[51] Is 8:4.
[52] Cf. Is 7:15-16.
[53] Jn 1:6 NRSV.
[54] Lk 1:15 ESV.
[55] 1 Sam 3:7 LES2.
[56] Job 31:17-18.

[57] Phil 4:18; cf. Job 1:8; 2:3.
[58] Is 28:9-10.
[59] 1 Cor 13:11 ESV.

"affliction upon affliction, hope upon hope."[60] "For though by this time you ought to be teachers, you need someone to teach you again. You need milk, not solid food."[61] You see that he passed in silence over the middle stages, and he considered the highest ones. Often, therefore, such things are said, and the intervening stages are passed over in silence.

[21:11] *From my mother's womb, you are my God.*

Just as, according to the earlier interpretation, Job was instructing orphans "from my mother's womb," from the mother's womb, namely, from that time when I began to have knowledge, I did not worship another God, neither my stomach nor money.

If, however, there is another interpretation: "I came down in this way, because I have God as my God." However, we do not say this about everyone but about those of whom it has been declared in Scripture that they have probably never come into sin, men such as John and Jeremiah.

For you are he who drew me out of the womb. Of the phrase "to draw out," and according to an earlier, persuasive interpretation, I said as follows: since the part of Mary's body by which she gives birth had no breach passage, she has given birth with the cooperation of God.

You are my hope from my mother's breasts.

I did not begin to hope after my maturation, but I had you as my hope from my mother's breasts.

If this should be understood in relation to the saint, we say as follows: the heavenly Jerusalem is the mother of the saints. Those who hope in God receive hope from the breasts of this mother, from the things that she teaches them, for often the breast does not signify the part of the body but the milk itself.

Upon you was I cast from the womb; from my mother's womb you are my God.

Upon you was I cast. I was not cast on another, and then after that one on you.

This is interpreted in this way: when I began to know the fear of God, I revered you, I worshiped you.

And according to the deeper sense: I came in the same way that John did, after having you as my God. It says, "he will be filled even from the time,"[62] for the phrase "even from the time" is certainly not said of one who has not yet possessed the Spirit completely.

[21:12] *Do not depart from me, for affliction is near.*

He is speaking about the Passion. I am in need of your presence. And when these things are spoken from the person of the one who became man, they are not said to the Father individually nor to the Son, but we have said that they are spoken to God—the divinity of the Father and the Son is one. When we say, then, "Christ is head of every man, and the head of Christ is"—he did not say "the Father" but "God,"[63] for he now receives Christ as high priest and king. The divinity, therefore, is head, for if he had said, "the Father," he would be excluding the Son; if he had said, "the Son," he would be passing over the Father in silence. In fact he has said, "God," since the divinity of Father and Son is one, and God is one; God is truly one, [32] but the Father and the Son are not the same. Abraham and Isaac are both one man, but one is the father and the other is the son, for which reason they are not one in their personal relationship but one in their essence.

---

[60] Is 28:10 NETS.
[61] Cf. Heb 5:12 NRSV.
[62] Lk 1:15.
[63] 1 Cor 11:3.

[21:12] *For there is no one who helps me.*

No one else can help.

One can also understand the phrase *for there is no one* in this way: I did not cast my care on another helper.[64]

And one can also take the phrase *for there is no one who helps me* in this way: since all are against me, there is no longer one who helps me, as far as it comes into human reckoning. For this reason, do not depart from me!

And one can understand it thus: not even an angel is able to help such a one. He does not dare to help because you, who are greater than all, that is, the divinity, are present with him, and no one else is able to help in this circumstance.

[21:13] *Many young bulls encircled me, fat bulls surrounded me.*

Now he is speaking about the different orders of the Jews: the Pharisees, the Sadducees, and the others, the so-called scribes, for these ones are likened to these animals because they are proud, especially because these animals are also workers of the ground.

Now, it is also possible that the Jews are called "young bulls," while those who incite them are called "fat bulls." For example, "the peoples contemplated vain things"[65]—these are the "young bulls." "The kings of the earth stood side by side."[66]

We do not always take kings and rulers literally, for there was one king, and he was insignificant and no longer possessed a kingdom, for the rule of the Romans finally wrested it from him. Paul, however, explained who the rulers are: those who became responsible for the Lord's crucifixion, whose wisdoms, he says, are many.[67] And he says, "If they had understood, they would not have crucified the Lord of glory."[68] If they had known that they were doing this to their own destruction, they would not have dared to do it. As the prophetic word we were quoting a little earlier said, "He who touches you is as one who touches the pupil of his eye."[69] And they were compelled to put him to death because they thought that they would bring his governance to an end. However, it turned out to the contrary for them; they themselves were deposed.

[21:14] *They opened their mouth against me, like a lion that drags away its prey and roars.*

They were appointed to be young bulls. But they changed into savage brutality so that they opened their mouth against me like the roaring lion; for the lion greatly harms, especially when he roars. He indicates their wildness and malicious joy against the Savior insofar as he says, *Like a roaring lion they opened their mouth*, no longer keeping still, no longer pretending to be at peace. These people, then, who seem to be at peace while they meditated on the law of God were young bulls who work the soil. But when they desired to open their mouth against me and to say: "Away with him! Crucify him! We have no king but Caesar,"[70] they have done this like the lion that has eaten its fill. [33]

Question: The Passion had not yet taken place?

All of these words are spoken prophetically. The things that are possible before they exist, before they come into being by way of activity, have the possibility of both occurring and not occurring. And no one has assurance whether it will happen or not, for there is an equal probability for both outcomes. But

---

[64]Cf. Ps 55:22 (54:23).
[65]Cf. Ps 2:1 NETS.
[66]Ps 2:2 NETS.
[67]Cf. 1 Cor 1:18–2:6.
[68]Cf. 1 Cor 2:8 NRSV.
[69]Zech 2:8 NETS.
[70]Jn 19:15.

while someone who has foreknowledge, or God himself, might anticipate that this particular possibility will occur, when it comes to us, whenever it has already occurred, then we have assurance. For in the case of things that are and things that have already happened, we can say whether it be true or false, whether it has happened or has not happened. However, in the case of future things we do not have this ability, or we can only say that one of two things will occur, but not which one.

Since, therefore, a divine eye has also anticipated here the things that are to come, they are no longer as possibilities to him. For this reason he says, *They have pierced my hands and my feet.*[71] If another person were speaking he would not have said this, but: "They will either be pierced or they will not be pierced."

[21:15] *Like water I have been poured out, and all my bones have been scattered.*

He speaks here of the scattering of the body, of the disciples themselves, when all were caused to stumble and the word had its fulfillment: "you will all become deserters."[72] And an hour will come when you will all flee; you will all depart to your own homes and you will leave me alone.

Just as water that is poured out, then, always runs and does not remain, so also understand the words *they were poured out like water*. He did not say, "they *are* poured out," for they do not always remain so.

What he says about himself, he says about his own body, which is in the assembly of the faithful, the church.

My bones—the strong parts of my body, for the apostles were the stronger members of those who believe. And these men were scattered.

---
[71] Ps 22:16 (21:17).
[72] Mt 26:31 NRSV.

Question: His bones were scattered?
When the disciples were caused to fall away.

This poured-out water is always running unless there is an impediment somewhere. And the disciples, therefore, were scattered, they had been poured out like water. When they were around him, they had been like water that is gathered in a river, water that is a spring. But since they have come apart from him for an hour, they are like water that is poured out. And the water will one day stand still, for it is not always running. So also the confusion and the stumbling of the disciples will immediately be put to an end, which has also taken place.

[21:15] *My heart has become like wax, melting in the midst of my belly.*

The heart of this body, which is composed of the assembly of those who have believed, are the spiritual ones. And these, then, have become like melting wax, as many as are his heart. But even if the wax was melted, this has not happened outside his belly, for they are in his belly, in order that they should be born again. In any case, after the disturbance that took place, they were again shown to be the sons of the Savior.

Question: What kind of disturbance was this?
The forepassion was racked by suffering for a little while, but not so that remained so.

The melting of the wax does not always occur, but when it is melted, it changes into some vessel or something useful, and this heart is collected together again, when it comes not too far from the womb of him who generated it. [34]

Question: Why "belly"?
The belly is the very power of the Savior by which he forms and produces sons. If again it refers to the generative parts of the body, Paul, while he was in the body, begot, saying, "I

31

became your father through the gospel,"[73] and, "for whom I am in the pain of childbirth until Christ is formed in you."[74]

They do not come outside the belly; they are not orphans.

Question: *My heart has become like melting wax?*

I said that the things said about him as Man may also be said of every righteous person. When his heart is not light but has something material intermingled with it, it is melted. The melting, however, is for the good, for the wax, when melted, does not come outside the one who possesses it.

Then, *in the midst of my belly*. In the case of intelligible things, different names signify the same thing. I call a spiritual "sheep" one who is under the true Shepherd.[75] In another figure this "sheep" is also called "light."[76] For example, once when I was asked by a philosopher whether I could say from Scripture that the soul is incorporeal, I said as follows: each name that designates a body signifies only that about which it is said. For example, the sensible vine is nothing other than a vine, and that which is called stone in a corporeal sense is nothing other than a stone. However, when many things that are said about the same essence express dissimilarities, it is clear that that is an intelligible essence. So, for example, we say of God that he is incorporeal, since he is also called "light," "fire," "spirit," and "source." These things cannot be something that exists corporeally but intelligibly. Such conceptions apply to intelligible things. When, therefore, the man or the soul is called "light," and he is also called "sheep" and "tree"—for the soul is called both "tree" and "sheep"—all these things cannot be the case in a corporeal sense; therefore, the soul is an intelligible essence. So then, when you hear for "soul" the words *heart, intellect, belly, source*, do not take these as you do in the case of sense perception. The receptacle of the soul, then, by which the soul receives spiritual foods, is called "belly." Then, since it is also generative, I understand this "belly" again sometimes as receiving and taking in foods, and sometimes as procreative.

You know that wax is a byproduct of honey. The composition of the honey has happened earlier, and the wax exists for the sake of the honey, not the honey for the sake of the wax. In the case of the tree, just as the fruit does not exist for the sake of the tree but the tree for the sake of the fruit—for the tree protects its fruit—so also the wax is not something that takes precedence, but it is a byproduct. Therefore, when the soul possesses the primary virtues, it is honey. When, however, it possesses the things that follow closely behind them, something material has been mingled together with it. It is wax. This is why it says that sinners melt like wax "from before fire."[77] Surely honey is praiseworthy; it is a first-rate substance, it signifies sweetness. Just as it has the ability to make sweet, it also has the ability to heal. The principal goods of the soul, [35] its movements and activities, are like honey, while the secondary goods, those that have something of the sensible and the material intermingled with them, are wax.

Therefore, sometimes the man melts, sometimes what is material in the intellect and the heart falls off, so that the mind no longer possesses anything that is clinging to it but is in every way immaterial as it was in the beginning.

[21:16] *My strength is dried up like a potsherd.*

My strength has lost all its moisture and richness so that it may be likened to a potsherd.

---

[73] 1 Cor 4:15 NRSV.
[74] Cf. Gal 4:19 NRSV.
[75] Cf. Jn 10:11.
[76] Cf. Mt 5:14.

[77] Ps 68:2 (67:3 NETS).

One can say this in a different way: when what is muddy within us—and you know what this is—remains as mud, it disintegrates when moisture penetrates it. But when it assumes dryness and loses all the humidity that is foreign to its material, it becomes dry like the potsherd.

Each of the received analogies is understood in accordance with a particular point. And this has often been said: for if an analogy may be understood in conformity with all points, then it is not analogy but that very thing which we are wishing to demonstrate. Often the potsherd is censured because of a certain figural interpretation: the vessel that has been made out of pottery, when it is shattered, does not admit repair, it cannot be fixed. According to another figural interpretation, however, I say that what is constructed out of mud, when it is tempered by fire and a kiln, loses its plasticity, its fragility.

My strength, then, *is dried up like a potsherd*. And we take this in each of two ways: it has no more moisture, no muddy condition. And one can also take it in another sense: it has lost all of its bitterness, which came from the affliction that for a long time belonged to it.

[21:16] *And my tongue has been glued to my throat.*

It is customary in Scripture to call "silence" the gluing together of the tongue to the throat. When those who are my members, who surrounded me and were my disciples, are no longer there, lest I seem to convey my message in vain, I have become silent: *my tongue has been glued to my throat*. The tongue is not glued, however, when we are talking. By the movement of the tongue the word is produced. But when it is glued to the throat, there is silence. The silence, however, does not stem from him who is silent but from those who are no longer listeners. It says, for example, in one of the prophets, in Amos: "The fallen one shall be numerous in every place. I will inflict silence."[78] When they flee, I inflict silence, lest I should seem to offer them this instruction. And this is also one of his remedies. For example, in Isaiah he commands the clouds not to pour down rain whenever the vineyard bears thorns instead of grapes, whenever it practices lawlessness, even though he remains its waterer in order that it should practice righteousness.[79] The grape stands for righteousness; the thorn stands for lawlessness. And since, when watered, it has not yielded the appropriate fruit but anxieties and temporal pleasures,[80] he no longer speaks; for, for the most part, the bad in their way of life are only irritated by the words about virtue, and they learn to despise them. At certain times, indeed, he holds back the rain. And the rain and the [36] voice here signify the same thing, for they signify the divine teaching. Therefore, just as it no longer rains whenever good fruits are not produced, so he no longer speaks nor preaches whenever his listeners occupy themselves with other things.

And this divine teaching he tells to men. According to the conception, those who listen to the teacher are called "disciples," and when he is their shepherd, they are "sheep." Nevertheless, *they* are neither sheep nor humans any longer but have become "scorpions," according to what is said: "O son of man, you live in the midst of scorpions."[81]

"Numerous," then, "shall be the fallen one in every place; I will inflict silence."[82] However, this can be read differently, for the language is ambiguous. One can understand, "numerous shall be the fallen one in every place; I will inflict silence," in this sense: in every place of honor, for here *place* means "rank," as it does in other places. Of Judas, for

---
[78]Amos 8:3 NETS.
[79]Is 5:4-6.
[80]Cf. Lk 8:14.
[81]Cf. Ezek 2:6 NETS.
[82]Amos 8:3.

example, it is said that he deviated from the place of service with which he was entrusted. "Numerous," then, "shall be the fallen one in every place." In every order of those who ought to be prudent and temperate and to speak about things that belong to virtue, "numerous is the fallen one," but not all of them have fallen. "I will inflict silence."

One can also punctuate the passage thus: "Numerous is the fallen. In every place I will inflict silence." I am not silent regarding the mysteries but also regarding morals, for in every place where it was necessary to stand and to sit and to be prepared for listeners, a fall has happened, and I apply silence everywhere.

Therefore, the gluing together of the tongue to the throat signifies silence. "If I forget you, O Jerusalem, may my tongue be glued to my throat, if I do not remember you."[83] If I do not remember you, may I become dumb.

[21:16] *And you have led me down into the dust of death.*

The word is said either from the person of Jesus or from the person of holy men who have known themselves to have come into evils, being humiliated in the place of distress, for "you humbled us in the place of distress."[84] Those who say this are saints, however, as the context of the psalm shows.

That which we wear is called a "body of death,"[85] and it is also called *the dust of death*. However, it is not *the dust of death* in its very essence. But since those who are compelled to do so come from the life outside the body into this body, it is called a "body of death." *Into the dust*, then, *of death you have led me down*. If it were a body of life, it would instead be led upward, for to be led into life and blessedness and an immortal condition belongs to those who are led upward.

If the Savior says this, then this is meant: *You have led me*, as the Light, *into the dust of death*. I descended into a body that I should die for all, in order that "by the grace of God" I might taste "death for everyone."[86] Therefore, "dust of death" and "body of death" are spoken of in one sense about other men, and in another sense about the Savior. For if the body becomes "a body of death" whenever the one who is furnished with it sins, and Jesus did not sin, then he has come into the dust of death, which can assume death. For this reason, they are deluded who say that he is a man only seemingly, or that he has borne a heavenly body, and who attribute death to this body. **[37]** This is impossible. Without a body such as this, the divinity does not undergo death, for divinity is immortal. And just as God, while he is Light in truth and in essence—darkness is not dark to him—so neither is there death in life. It is impossible for life to undergo death. However, he assumed something that is able to undergo death and division, and this is known as the death of its essence. For many other things are said to belong to certain ones even though they are not essentially theirs, such as "my garment, my sandal." In the same way the body is not essential. If, then, Life says that it receives death, it says that it endures this according to what is external to it.

And I will speak of a paradox: as the body receives death, so Life makes the body alive. Even this common life, the intertwining of the soul with the body, bestows life-instilling motions on the body. Therefore, how much more so does Life make his body alive than the soul, which is given life by the primary and blessed Life?

And to say *you have brought me down into the dust of death* is good. He himself did not go

---

[83]Ps 137:5-6 (136:5-6 LES2).
[84]Ps 44:19 (43:20).
[85]Rom 7:24 NRSV.

[86]Heb 2:9.

down into the dust of death; his soul did not come into the dust of death. This, however, occurs with those who are embodied because of vice. Since he, however, received a body for the sake of the economy and the salvation of all, and God prepared a body for him, it says that he is carried down by God into the dust of death.

If, however, there were people, who say by way of confession, "our stomach clung to the ground"[87]—whenever someone is not nourished on the heavenly loaves, the heavenly food, but rather on the earthly, not the physical, earthly bread but that which is opposed to the true Bread[88]—this food unites the soul that is nourished by it to matter, and there follows a humiliation of the soul into the dust.

Here, however, the soul of Jesus was not humiliated into the dust, but he was led down by God. In a providential way he has come into this, for his soul has never committed sin even though it was capable of this. For if it were not capable of this, neither is it wholly to be praised. Acts of abstinence from sins, therefore, confer praises on the one who has abstained, when it would have been possible for him to commit them.

Question: Are dust and death the same thing?

No. For he has not said, "And you led me down into dust, into death." And if dust and death were the same thing, he would have said, "into dust, into death you have led me down." But he said, *into the dust of death*. The mortal body, capable of being dissolved from the essence that bears it, is *the dust of death*. And perhaps it is also the dust of death in a second sense as well, since it confers death on the soul that loves the body.

The body of the saints is dead, for "they always carry in the body the death of Jesus."[89]

The dead body, however, does not have passions, for how would this be possible? Is that which is subject to death alive? The body lives when it has been united to the soul. Then it has passions. When it has died, it does not have passions. By putting to death the members that are on the earth,[90] it has no more passions. [**38**]

Question: Then is the soul found to be a cause of sin?

The soul of the sinner is a cause of sin. For sin is nothing other than disobedience to a command, transgression of a law. The body is not subject to a command in order that it should also transgress it. The soul, when it goes off course, leads the body to offer service to sinful fantasies. The body is like an instrument. We do not say that the sword that kills is a murderer, do we, rather than the one who wields it? For how could this be possible? If, indeed, we do not attribute sin or righteousness to the irrational animal, which has a soul, do we attribute these things to the soulless body? By its own definition the body is without a soul.

[**21:17**] *Because many dogs have surrounded me, an assembly of evildoers has encircled me. They have pierced my hands and my feet.*

Punctuate the passage in this way: *because many dogs have surrounded me, an assembly of evildoers has encircled me,* therefore *they pierced my hands and my feet.* The word *because* is an etiological conjunction. It does not apply to the previous words, however: *you have led me down into the dust of death,* because *many dogs have surrounded me.* No. But since *many dogs have surrounded me, and an assembly of evildoers has encircled me,* because of this *they have pierced my hands and my feet.* If they were still human, they would not do this. He calls *dogs* here those people who have the manner of a

---

[87]Ps 44:25 (43:26 NETS).
[88]Cf. Jn 6:32.
[89]2 Cor 4:10.

[90]Cf. Col 3:5.

dog. Now, the dog's movements are reproachable in many respects. They are completely addicted to mating. They are accustomed, therefore, to calling those who are unbridled in their habits *dogs* and to calling such women "bitches." For instance, even the law, suggesting this thought, numbered the dog with the prostitute: "You shall not offer the fee of a dog and the wage of a prostitute."[91] It has not mentioned the fee of a donkey or a horse, for the wages for these were presented in the house of the Lord. And the dog is also shameless—"and the dogs are shameless in soul"[92]—and sycophantic. People, then, who have such motions are rightly called *dogs*. These, then, surrounded the Savior. When they were God's sheep, then they were distant from the condition of a dog. But when the people have become lost sheep, their destruction did not turn them into nonbeing, but into the condition of a dog, of a serpent, and of a scorpion. Finally, all these things were said about the Hebrews: "And they are all witless dogs, who know only how to bark."[93] Therefore, when the Israelites lost their senses against the Savior, then they became dogs. Their being *an assembly of evildoers* followed their becoming dogs, for when they were sheep, they were a divine flock. "So dogs have come around me and an assembly of evildoers. For this reason they subjected me to a cross," for the piercing of the Savior's hands and feet means nothing other than a cross.

Now, observe each thing individually: Is not an assembly of shameless souls, who are both unbridled and ready to bark with their howling insults, to hate and to wish to subject to death him who brought about the resurrection of the dead, restored the sight of the blind, and cleansed lepers, is not this assembly one that does evil? [39]

However, there is a praiseworthy assembly.

And some have said the following in the case of the literal interpretation: there have been many herders of irrational living creatures, and it was never recounted that a herd of cattle attacked its herdsman, nor a herd of goats its goatherd, nor the flock its shepherd, nor horses their keeper. Only humans attack their rulers, and history relates that many rulers, even those of good character and virtuous thought, were killed by their subjects. Therefore, if they were remaining sheep, they would not have killed him. Then, when they have become dogs—and this is the same thing as men who are dog-like in character, life, and condition—they were called *an assembly of evildoers*. And it is normal for evildoers to be roused up against their benefactor, to rebel against their "herdsman."

[21:18] *All my bones were counted.*

It has gone so far with them that they indicated my bones with a number, even though they are innumerable. Now he joins together the sense. This has indeed happened historically, that they divided his garments and cast lots for the tunic, woven in one piece.[94] In a certain sense, however, the passage stands in contrast with the passage that appears in the Gospel. For the soldiers have done these things. And the soldiers were not Hebrews, for a Jew was entirely forbidden from serving in the army: but since in a certain sense they have become the cause of his betrayal to the soldiers, they attribute the blame for this action to them.

[21:18] *They looked at me and watched me.*

Question: Did they *watch me* by contemplating me?

Turning their attention toward me, they saw the scattering of my bones. And the phrase

---

[91]Deut 23:18 (23:19).
[92]Is 56:11 LES2.
[93]Is 56:10. Didymus's text differs here from the LXX and the Hebrew, which say, "they cannot bark."

[94]Cf. Jn 19:23.

"to watch" is often said in the case of those who rejoice at misfortune.

And the powers of his teaching one can call "bones."

[21:19] *They divided my garments for themselves.*

With respect to this passage here, we no longer wish to remain at the literal sense, for it was already said that the soldiers also divided his garments, having made four parts of them, and that they cast lots for the seamless tunic, which was woven from the top from one piece of cloth.

I say: just as the body of Christ was called, according to a certain understanding, the assembly of the faithful, so the apostolic witnesses were showing, and we were saying, that the strong parts of this body are *bones*. So again we say that the divinely inspired Scripture is a body of the Savior, and the *bones* of this body are the strong notions, the contemplations of the other, superior thoughts. And the words are *garments*, for the understanding that accords with the thinking behind it is clothed by the words. Even if his *bones*, then, were numbered, yet they were not divided. They only saw them as they are not, for if they had beheld them as they are, they would have been strengthened by them and they would have appropriated them for themselves, so that they could say, "All my bones shall say, 'O Lord, who is like you?'"[95] Indeed, physical bones are not saying these words! Therefore, all who hold different opinions, who are deceived, divide the *garments* of the word. And they draw away the words into whatever they wish and they appropriate them, as for example: "The Lord created me as the beginning of his ways."[96] The word is a garment of the object of contemplation. The Arians drag it away [40] as they wish, and they think it is their own. The men of the church, in contrast, receive it as the Wisdom who says this wears it, while others receive other things. And in general one can almost always find the same words being treated by the heterodox in one way and then in another. They divided them, then, they stripped the words from the sense, and they dragged them away naked from their sense into their own desire.

[21:19] *And for my clothing they cast a lot.*

No one who owns something casts a lot for it, but when something can come to many people in common, then they cast a lot for those things. When someone leaves behind an only son and has him as his successor, all the belongings of the deceased belong to that one, and no lot is cast. But when many approach the one who is the legitimate heir, saying, "We too are children of that man," then a division of that person's garments takes place. Now, they do not divide the man himself, but only the words; for not with the same sense is the same word cited differently among the heretics. Each person drags the word away according to his own intention and desire. The virtuous, then, and the faithful man truly keeps the tunic of Jesus whole; he does not have it ripped up. For this reason he does not cast a lot; his is whole. Indeed, even if those ones cast a lot and have the words, the words do not become theirs; they do not become masters of them; for a man who is wise in Christ enters into the midst of them and shows that what the heretic supposes to be his are not his.

Question: *Garments* and *clothing*?

All the *garments* taken together are called *clothing*, but each one by itself is not called clothing. And just as many sheep, when they have been gathered, are called a "flock," but each one is not called a "flock," so men who have come together into the same place are

---
[95]Ps 35:10 (34:10 NETS).
[96]Prov 8:22 NETS.

called a "people," but each is not called a "people."

[21:20] *But as for you, O Lord, do not prolong your help of me.*

When those were devoting themselves to these things, when they also brought affliction against me, however, I called on you not to withdraw from me, *because affliction is near*.[97] And if affliction has come near from *the young bulls and the bulls that encompassed me*, from those who *scattered my bones*, from those who became causes to me so that *my tongue was glued to my throat*, yet as for you, *do not prolong your help of me*. The resurrection of the Savior, therefore, has immediately taken place; those who were caused to stumble were immediately converted to him. Therefore, help has not gone for a long time.

These things, however, the Man speaks, Jesus under the aspect of the Man: *Do not prolong your help of me*. The help that he seeks comes from none other than God. I said, however, that when God speaks, it does not always mean the Father, separating out the Son, nor the Son, separating out the Father, for the divinity is one. And that this is the case, we showed that the *help* is the resurrection from the dead. In one place it is said that he has handed himself over[98] and that he has raised himself,[99] while in another place the Father is said to have handed him over[100] and to have raised him up.[101] **[41]** From which it is shown that the one resurrection and the one work that takes place by the Father and the Son happens in accordance with only one divine activity. And when the Father acts, he accomplishes this by acting as God; and when the Son acts, he accomplishes this as God.

[21:20] *Attend to my complaint!*

For if you attend to my complaint, my help is not far off but acts as something that is near. Indeed, he says these things primarily about men, for he has not come primarily in order that he himself should die and rise again, but because of others. "By the grace of God he tasted death for everyone."[102] All died for themselves. This one tasted death by the grace of God for all. "The love of God urges us on, because we are convinced of this very thing: that if one has died for all, then all have died," in order that those who died might no longer be dead, "but might live for him who died and rose again for them."[103] A person can repay a human debt for another and can take on himself blame and disgrace for another. But no person can take death on himself for another. And see in any case: he only tasted it; he did not carry it; he did not devour it. Now, the one who is devoured by death is also the very one who devours it. "Death, having prevailed, swallowed."[104] This one swallows death: the one who is swallowed by it. And since Jesus "committed no sin,"[105] and death is swallowed through sin's conquest of a person and then devours the sinner—therefore he tasted death for everyone; but he only tasted it. And he has supplied the reason: "that through death he might destroy the one who has the power of death."[106] He overthrew death by death.

[21:21] *Deliver my soul from the sword!*

Jesus is also the one who speaks this verse, and he can say this about his own soul, over which he had authority to lay it down and to take it

---

[97] Ps 22:11 (21:12).
[98] Cf. Eph 5:2.
[99] Cf. Mt 28:6.
[100] Cf. Rom 8:32.
[101] Cf. Acts 2:32.
[102] Heb 2:9.
[103] 2 Cor 5:14-15.
[104] Is 25:8 NETS. The NRSV, following the Hebrew, has "he will swallow up death forever."
[105] 1 Pet 2:22.
[106] Heb 2:14 NRSV.

up again;[107] he can also say this about every soul that is reconciled to him. And as each of the saints is not simply called a "man" any longer but a "man of God," so also the soul that is determined to be pleasing to God is no longer simply called a *soul* but "God's soul." Therefore he says these things in each of two ways: of his own soul and of every soul that is reconciled to him.

The sword sometimes signifies chastisement, as when it is said, "All the sinners of my people shall die by the sword."[108] Indeed, it has never literally happened that all the people were killed by a sword. Some died because of it, but not all. He is now saying the following: all sinners will be tested by chastisement.

Sometimes it also signifies an evil power, even the devil himself; for when it is said to Mary, "And a sword will go across your own soul,"[109] it means the adversary. When he suggests or desires to suggest thoughts to someone, and that soul does not receive them, he goes across the soul. Like the arrow that is shot, [42] when it is not shot with aim, it passes across the target. He hurled a dart at Judas; he ventured against Judas. That one did not guard himself, he did not preserve the saying "Do not make room for the devil,"[110] and the devil has not passed across him, for he entered into him. He who says, "When the evil one kept turning away from me, I did not know him,"[111] did not have the sword crossing him. "Not knowing" here does not mean ignorance but not having been tested. Therefore, those who think little of something are accustomed to saying, "I do not know it," even when it is near, even when it is present.

Question: The word *deliver*?

The word *deliver* does not always signify this: "Deliver me, because I am overwhelmed and am under its power!" Deliver me lest I suffer something at its hand.

Question: Who is speaking?

There are those who wish to say this: "When one speaks about his own soul, who is the speaker? The body is the speaker." Those who say such things are deceived. In things that are composite, each of the parts in the composition is mentioned for the whole composition. "May your spirit and soul and body be kept sound."[112] Surely the spirit is something different from people, and the soul is something different from the body? So they themselves assume. We often say of a city that a wicked city has wicked rulers, a wicked populace, wicked laws that are not just. What is the city other than the wicked rulers, the members of the council, and the populace? And as we say of the human body, "the head of the body, the face of the body, the hand of the body, its foot," so the body is not something other than these things, though each part is something other than the body. Those who have successfully studied logic understand these things easily. Look, all things that have sensation and life are animals, and I say that the animal is not a human, nor a horse, nor an ox. And I am saying this because the man is not the whole genus, he is not the whole category "animal." I am saying that the individual species are different from the animal. And I am not saying that all of them together are different from it but that they are identical with it. So also in the case of the body I say that the hand is different from the body of a human, and the foot and the head. Now, all these are not different from the body, but each part is different from the whole body. This obtains also in the case of the man. When he says, "my soul and my body and my spirit," each thing is different from the compounded man. However, all of them together are nothing other than he is. When, therefore, it says, "My

---

[107] Cf. Jn 10:18.
[108] Amos 9:10 NETS.
[109] Lk 2:35.
[110] Eph 4:27 NRSV.
[111] Ps 101:4 (100:4).

[112] 1 Thess 5:23 NRSV.

soul"—indeed, not of Jesus alone is this set down. And each man says this: "Why are you deeply grieved, O my soul?"[113] "My flesh was changed because of oil."[114] And also "my spirit": "and my spirit searched."[115] Each part, then, is other than the composite. And I am saying that all of the parts, taken together, are not different from the composite, but they are separate—therefore, when he says, "my soul," the compounded man is the one who is speaking these words. See, he also said, "my bones and my soul," and see, he says, "and my spirit."

[21:21] *And my unique one from the hand of the dog.*

He said, *because many dogs surrounded me.* He is referring to these many dogs individually as one dog. He who was delivered from [43] each of the men who desire to lay traps for him was delivered from a man. And he calls his actions the *hand of the dog.* "And the word of the Lord came by the hand of Haggai."[116] In the case of the vicious, it has been said, "Thorns grow in the hand of the drunkard."[117] From the *hand,* then, from the action of the dogs who have surrounded me, being a single *dog* in their character, *deliver my soul!*

Some people are said to be solitary: "God causes the solitary to dwell in a house."[118] And it can truly be said that all these ones who take up residence have a single way of life and have been called "of a single way of life" for this reason, as the word says, "that you be united in the same mind and the same purpose."[119]

However, one can also say the following: he who has a purpose that does not change, a manner of life that does not become altered by another, is "of a single manner," for the wise is not altered like the fool,[120] but he shines forth like the sun.[121] And the sun has no alterations in its brightness.

This soul, then, is *unique* to him. I said that other souls become reconciled to him by means of virtue. However, they do not possess stability, certainty. Only this soul, because it neither committed sin nor knew it, is *unique.* He has many souls; however, he has this soul as *unique,* for it is unchangeable. I do not mean "unchangeable" in this sense: that it is not changeable, for in an absolute sense that which is called unchangeable signifies that it cannot be changed. Now, when I say that the righteous man is not changed toward unrighteousness, I say that the righteous is unchangeable inasmuch as he possesses righteousness, for on the one hand the unchangeable is not changed, while on the other hand that which is not changed is not always unchangeable.

This soul, then, is *unique* to him among the others because it alone is always joined to him. No thought, no argument, no disturbance separates it from him, for even when he is troubled, the disturbance is stopped at the point of a forepassion. Indeed, this was indicated by the word *now,*[122] because he is not intending a space of time in any breadth by the word *now,* but the punctiliar, that which is not time. All time has three dimensions. However, the word *now* does not have this: for it is an end of time.

"He began to be distressed and agitated."[123] He is able to receive a forepassion as far as its beginning, not equivalent to cowardice, for the forepassion is a test of nature, not a quality that makes a person vicious or

---

[113] Ps 42:5 (41:6 NETS).
[114] Ps 109:24 (108:24 NETS). The ESV text, closely following the idiomatic sense of the Hebrew, reads, "My body has become gaunt, *with no fat.*" The Greek does not translate the idiomatic sense of *min* but takes it literally: "My flesh was changed *because of* fat."
[115] Ps 77:6 (76:7 LES2).
[116] Cf. Hag 1:3 NETS.
[117] Prov 26:9 NETS.
[118] Ps 68:6 (67:7 LES2).
[119] 1 Cor 1:10 NRSV.

[120] Cf. Sir 27:11.
[121] Cf. Sir 50:7.
[122] Cf. Jn 12:27.
[123] Cf. Mk 14:33 NRSV.

virtuous, provided that he does not take in addition the things that follow after it, so that it no longer remains a forepassion. These things were often distinguished by us, that there are four stages. The forepassion alone is free from blame; it does not subject a person to blame. The passion, however, is subject to moderate blame; the disposition is, consequently, a vice; how much more the practice, once it is assumed!

[21:22] *Save me from the lion's mouth.*

Here one can call the devil a *lion*, for he makes an assault at the time of the Passion. For example, when on the fortieth day of the testing, it was said that "the devil departed from him," it adds in the Gospel: "until an opportune time."[124] Then he comes again when the Passion begins. And since I was saying that his traps are sometimes brought against the Savior's Man himself, and sometimes against those who belong to him, when Peter says—or rather when the Savior says to Peter, "See! Satan has demanded us for himself,"[125] **[44]** in a certain sense when he was rushing against the Savior he desired to devour his members. Truly he says, *Save me from the lion's mouth.*

One can also call that people a *lion*, for "my inheritance has become to me like a lion in a thicket."[126] May I not suffer these things that they desire to arrange for me. And he is saying these words because every rational essence, even when it is perfect, stands in need of the military help that comes from God.

Save me from the lion's mouth!

One can say that *lion* here refers to the multitude of the Jews, the people of Israel, for he said in Jeremiah: "I have forsaken my house; I have let go of my inheritance. My inheritance has become to me like a lion in a thicket."[127] As my people, I placed them in paradise, where there is abundant fertility. However, when they change into ferocity, then they crouch down, consequently, in fruitless woods—for the thicket is nothing other than a place of fruitless trees. Consequently, they lie in wait there. And my inheritance, which I used to possess in order that it should be a people and portion of the Lord, became wild against me to such a degree as to be compared to a *lion*—and not to a tame lion, for often lions are tamed when they come into regions where men live—but they are like a lion in a thicket, like a savage beast.

It is possible that this is said about the devil as well, for we also said this, that after the testing in the wilderness it was said, "He departed until an opportune time."[128]

[21:22] *And my lowliness from the horns of the unicorns!*[129]

By *unicorn* he means a strong animal. It does not submit to man; it is not tamed by man. *From the horns of the unicorns*, then, *save my lowliness*, referring to the cross and death as his lowliness. "He humbled himself and became obedient to the point of death—even death on a cross."[130] You defend my lowliness, therefore, from the horns of these ones—and these are certain evil enemies—at the time when I arise from the dead, for indeed "the kings of the earth stood side by side, and the rulers gathered together"[131] in order to surround him with death. Then God delivers him from his lowliness; he raises him from the dead.

Now, all these things have been spoken about the Man. In any case he added at once,

---

[124] Lk 4:13 NRSV.
[125] Cf. Lk 22:31.
[126] Jer 12:8 LES2.
[127] Jer 12:7-8 LES2.
[128] Cf. Lk 4:13 NRSV.
[129] The NRSV has "wild oxen" here instead of "unicorns."
[130] Phil 2:8 NRSV.
[131] Ps 2:2 NETS.

[21:23] *I will describe your name to my brothers.*

"'I will tell of your name to my brothers,' and again, 'See! I will put my trust in him,' 'Behold, I and the children God has given me.'"[132] Moreover, "Therefore he had to be made like his brothers in every respect,"[133] not only in respect of the body, but in every respect. In the divinity the only-begotten Son of God has no brother; for if he had a brother, he would not be only-begotten. Having brothers and being only-begotten are contradictory. The only-begotten does not have brothers. The one who has brothers is not only-begotten.

"Brothers," he calls the apostles and all who believed in him from the circumcision, for many of the Jews did believe. The Twelve and the Seventy[134] were among them. Those, then, [45] were his brothers according to the flesh. And those who receive "the Spirit of adoption"[135] become his brothers again according to the Spirit. For if "everyone who practices righteousness has been born of God,"[136] and "everyone who believes that Jesus is the Christ has been born of God,"[137] then there are many sons of God. Again, these, however, are not brothers of the only-begotten; they are not brothers in the divinity but in relation to the one who was made human. The apostles also, making use of this word, understood it in relation to the Man: "For this reason he is not ashamed to call them brothers,"[138] for he neglected having none of the things with which man is filled, since if he does not have all these things, he is not a man. I have often said that there are certain mixed things, such as honey water. If it is deprived of water, it is either only honey or, if it is mixed with another substance, it is not honey water. If, then, he had only a body, then he was not made like his brothers in every respect, for the appetitive soul is irrational. The soul without a mind is irrational, nor does it exist in the first place unless in connection with it, for appetitive souls perish together with the bodies whose souls they are. "In every respect," then, "he became like his brothers,"[139] not in one respect but not in another. The apostle says again, "in order that he might become the firstborn among many brothers, whom he foreknew and predestined to be conformed to himself."[140] You see that by way of acquisition he had his being the firstborn among many brothers when he became human, when he assumed the Man from the brothers. And when he says "firstborn" here, he is saying "more honored." And in this sense "the assembly of the firstborn"[141] is also named. It is impossible for everyone to be firstborn; however, it is possible for everyone to be honored. For this reason, Jacob also sought the right of primogeniture from Esau, the honor of the firstborn. Therefore, he is firstborn among many brothers, as he is also "the firstborn from the dead."[142] He is the first among all the dead, for since he rose again many others have become able to rise again.

Then it says that he announces the name of the Father, that is, he makes it manifest. When they come to know the Father and learn the name of the Father, then they also have knowledge of the Son included with it, for these two things include each other. I am claiming that the laws of relative things relate both to their existence and to their knowledge. It is impossible for one who knows one of two relative things not to know the one that remains.

And from the horns of the unicorns.

---

[132] Cf. Heb 2:12-13 ESV.
[133] Heb 2:17 ESV.
[134] Cf. Lk 10:17.
[135] Rom 8:15; cf. Gal 4:5-6.
[136] Cf. 1 Jn 2:29 ESV.
[137] 1 Jn 5:1 ESV.
[138] Cf. Heb 2:11 ESV.
[139] Heb 2:17.
[140] Cf. Rom 8:29.
[141] Heb 12:23 NRSV.
[142] Col 1:18 NRSV.

This is also called a "rhinoceros." And in the Twenty-Eighth Psalm this is also mentioned: "And the beloved will be as the offspring of the unicorn."[143] This animal is said to possess a size no smaller than the giant bull. And it is completely sinewy; it is dense; it has a horn above its nose; it is the strongest animal; when it becomes angry, its horn becomes so very strong [46] that it is harder than any elephant tusk. However, when it is not angry, its horn is tender like flesh. And sometimes, when it is hot, it unearths great rocks in order that it might lay itself in that place where it is cool. As I said, this animal has a horn that becomes very hard because of anger. But when it is calm, it is not so. Some, therefore, try to take its horn, for it is precious. So since they are desirous of it in such a state, they do not shoot it unexpectedly. It does not fall in the hunt; it is not captured with a trap or with anything else. However, they wound it with a bow. When it is angry, then they injure it with a dart.

Question: Of what person do we understand this? Of Christ?

If it is understood in a praiseworthy sense. It is understood in a praiseworthy sense in the Twenty-Eighth Psalm: "And the beloved will be as the offspring of the unicorn."[144] This signifies one who has a kingdom that is all his own. The kingdom of the Savior, then, has no defect, but it is absolute insofar as it belongs to God, who appeared in it. And in this sense he is referred to as a "unicorn." However, when it is understood in a blameworthy sense, it is understood in this way because of the wildness of the beast, not because of the horn.

Some, however, say that the phrase *from the horns of the unicorns* is understood praiseworthily in a hidden sense, because the tips of the cross had the appearance of horns.

[21:23] *In the midst of the assembly I will praise you in song.*

In the midst of the assembly he praises God in song, he who confidently and decently offers up songs. One who praises God in song must be righteous, for "praise befits the upright,"[145] and "praise is not beautiful in the mouth of a sinner."[146] And just as we say that the divine word is spoken with authority—when someone who is prudent teaches on prudence, he preserves his message with authority. When, however, a person is undisciplined and foul, he does not offer the message with completeness. His conscience fetters him—therefore, just as he has the word with authority who bears deeds that are consistent with what he is saying, and has the practical life, which is organically united to the contemplative life, so also *in the midst of the assembly* he who does not have any evasiveness praises God in song. For example, he teaches about prudence in order that he might be prudent. For at that time he praises God in song in the midst of the assembly, in order that when he teaches about compassion, he might be compassionate, in order that when he speaks about courage, he might be courageous. Therefore, whenever you see someone pontificating about courage, even though the person is cowardly, he does not do this *in the midst of the assembly.*

And that the word *midst* signifies confidence, one can also learn from another psalm: "The one who practices arrogance does not dwell in the midst of my house."[147] No arrogant person wished to appear before me. Drawing back, he was practicing this in a corner, [47] blushing.

In the midst of the congregation, the Savior praises the Father in song. But when I say the

---

[143] Ps 29:6 (28:6 LES2).
[144] Ps 29:6 (28:6 LES2).
[145] Ps 33:1 (32:1 NETS).
[146] Sir 15:9 LES2.
[147] Ps 101:7 (100:7).

Father, understand the Son also. He praises God, and the divinity of Father and Son is one.

[21:24] *You who fear the Lord, praise him!*

Not just anyone praises God in song, but one who has fear toward him. However, not every fear is fear of God; for there is a fear of punishment. This is not the fear of God. In any case "perfect love" toward God "casts out fear."[148] The one who has love toward God out of his whole heart, out of his whole mind, does not have passionate fear. So, for example, the disciples of Jesus were called away from passionate fear by the Savior, when he was saying, "Do not fear those who kill the body."[149] And those who say, "The Lord is a helper to me. I will not fear. What will a man do to me?"[150] have cast out passionate fear. For the fear of God is not passionate, and it is not a fear of punishment, but it is characterized by reverence. "Fear of the Lord surpasses everything,"[151] it is second to nothing, not even to love itself. And "those who fear him have no want."[152]

[21:24] *All you offspring of Jacob together, glorify him.*

Now, this can also be meant literally. Since that people that is from the patriarchs was called to praise God in song and to serve him, naturally this was commanded for all of them to do.

Nonetheless, since many of them have become sinners, we understand *all you offspring of Jacob* not as the evil kind—for it was said of this people "evil offspring"[153]—but when they come out of all wickedness, just as he did whose offspring they are. And here we mean Jacob the patriarch, and we say the following: since he has become a supplanter and from this virtuous act began to possess his name, all those who supplant vice by prevailing over hostile powers, which are evil antagonists, these ones are *Jacob*. Indeed, Hosea listed this among his manly deeds when he said, "In the womb he kicked his brother with the heel, and he prevailed with God and predominated."[154] To prevail with God and to predominate are a great manly deed. In this sense, he also enumerated his having kicked his brother in the womb.

And the Savior was also called "Jacob" in Isaiah: "Jacob is my child; I will help him."[155] And Matthew said that this saying has been fulfilled by Christ.[156]

[21:24] *Let all the offspring of Israel fear him!*

Passionate fear is not a glory, but the fear of God that attends those who have earnestly endeavored to possess him for a long time is. "My son, if, when you accept the saying of my commandment, you hide it with yourself, your ear will be attentive to wisdom, and you shall incline your heart to understanding."[157] And after a space, "And if you seek it like silver and search for it like treasures, then you will understand the fear of the Lord."[158] See? The fear comes after many virtuous acts and perfect virtues. **[48]** We speak as though this were somehow easy. However, when you see the manly deeds, the acts of courage, and the virtuous acts of Elisha, you will see in a certain way how the one who fears the Lord is not just anyone.

---

[148] 1 Jn 4:18 NRSV.
[149] Mt 10:28 NRSV.
[150] Ps 118:6 (117:6).
[151] Sir 25:11 NRSV.
[152] Ps 34:10 (33:10 NETS).
[153] Is 1:4 NETS.
[154] Cf. Hos 12:3-4 (12:4-5).
[155] Is 42:1 LES2.
[156] Cf. Mt 12:17.
[157] Prov 2:1-2 NETS.
[158] Prov 2:4-5 NETS.

[21:25] *Because he did not despise or scorn the petition of the poor.*

He calls "poor" here the Savior who descended, who became poor for our sake. And just as he has not simply become a curse but "in order that the blessing of Abraham might come to the Gentiles"[159]—and the curse that is productive of a blessing is not a curse in reality. The things that produce good things are good. Things that produce what is pleasing to God are themselves pleasing to God. The word *curse* indicates the cross, as the very apostle who wrote this word demonstrated. He said, "for it is written, 'Cursed is everyone who hangs on a tree'"[160]—and just as he has become a dead man, in order that he should cause the dead to become living and make them so, and he has come under death's control, in order that he should abolish death and set free those who are ruled by it, so also he has become poor, in order that they, for whose sake he has become poor, should become rich by his poverty.

And notice the difference: "You know the grace of our Lord Jesus Christ, that though he was rich, yet for your sake he became poor."[161] To become poor for our sake, not to be rich for our sake; for it was not said that he has become rich as he has become poor, but "though he was rich, yet for our sake he became poor." And just as he, because he has the form of God and is in the form of God, when he receives the form of a servant, does not leave the form of God,[162] so when he became poor for others he did not abandon his wealth. For we speak of his wealth not as we do in relation to the virtues of holy men, for he himself is the bestower of the virtues; he himself is the one in whom the virtues exist by participation. Therefore, while remaining rich he has become poor. And for the sake of others he has become poor, in order that those should become rich. And when we remain in the poverty that first seized us and do not strive to receive that wealth which his poverty grants us, as far as we are concerned he remains poor. For if he has become poor for the sake of others, in order that they should become rich, whenever they should become rich, he no longer remains poor. He becomes poor when he became flesh. When we beheld "his glory, glory as of the only Son from the Father, full of grace and truth,"[163] we have become rich instead of beggarly, and he himself was shown to be rich instead of poor. He has not become rich. That is to say, his glory has become evident, that he is "as the only-begotten from the Father, full of grace and truth."

He did not despise or scorn the petition of the poor, for it was sent up for the salvation of all. "But if anyone does sin, we have an advocate with the Father, Jesus Christ the righteous,"[164] **[49]** in order that he should forgive us our sins. Certainly, we have him as our advocate as long as we remain in sins. However, when we cease from having sins, he then no longer advocates completely for this. "Consequently he is able for all time to save those who approach God through him, since he always lives to make intercession for them."[165] If he intercedes for them that they should live, whenever they live he no longer offers up this prayer for them; rather, he then prays for the defense of their life, for them to persevere in it. This *petition,* then, *of the poor* man *he did not despise,* neither did he scorn him who offers it up.

Nor did he turn away his face.[166] Now, the face of someone who prays is turned away whenever God does not approve but even

---

[159] Cf. Gal 3:14 NRSV.
[160] Gal 3:13 NRSV.
[161] 2 Cor 8:9 ESV.
[162] Phil 2:6-7.
[163] Jn 1:14 ESV.
[164] 1 Jn 2:1 NRSV.
[165] Heb 7:25.
[166] Cf. Ps 22:24 (21:25).

Lectures on Psalm 21 [21:25]

opposes the prayer from being offered up. Once he forbade Jeremiah from praying on behalf of the people. Why? Because intercessors and advocates ought to offer up their advocacy on behalf of the repentant and those who are no longer sinners. Indeed, he says, "Do you not see what they themselves are doing? Their fathers,"[167] to the man, inclined toward idolatry and do not hold their ground. So also the face of Samuel was turned away when he heard, "How long are you going to mourn over Saul, even when I have rejected him?"[168] And the faces of those who go as ambassadors have confidence when those for whom they intercede agree with God's will.

[21:25] *Nor did he turn away his face from me.*

The poor man himself speaks about himself. A change of persons has taken place. The Spirit who writes Scripture says, *He did not despise or scorn the petition of the poor.* Next, that poor man himself, whose prayer was not an object of disgust, was not turned away, says, *He did not turn away his face from me, and when I cried to him he listened to me.*

[21:25] *And when I cried to him, he listened to me.*

It is a great thing to say this. Truly, this is not said as a mere expression, but whenever it is shown that the thing for which he prayed occurred. Therefore, this has happened.

[21:26] *From you comes my commendation in the great assembly.*

See! I have successfully completed the work of crying out; I have established it as a great assembly, "in splendor, without a spot or wrinkle or anything of the kind."[169] This, then, is my commendation: to establish this assembly. Just as it is no great thing to praise the one who is perfect, in whom wisdom is spoken,[170] because he drinks milk, so also this is no great thing, nor does this bring praise to one who possesses a superior life.

Not for such things, then, not for other acts is he praised, but for establishing a whole assembly, and not just any assembly, but a great one.

And this is also possible: my virtuous deed is a great source of praise for the assembly. [50]

[21:26] *My vows I will pay before those who fear him.*

Vows are paid for things about which one is thankful, things that have already taken place. The request that is offered up to God is called a "prayer." And when it is offered up with a promise, that "when such things happen for me, I will repay you with such things," this petition is called a "vow." For example, Jacob also was saying, "If God gives me bread to eat, of all that he gives me, I will tithe a tenth of them to him."[171] This is a vow. No one, after praying for something and not receiving it, will rightly say, "I will repay my vows."

Question: *Before those who fear him?*

He says this in order that they should derive profit from it, for they themselves will also learn to repay the vows that they make.

Before those who fear can also signify the following: not before those who offer sacrifices alone—for those who only offer sacrifices are unable to know what kind of thanksgiving is fulfilled, what kind of vow is repaid—but *before those who fear.*

---

[167] Cf. Jer 7:17-18.
[168] 1 Sam 16:1 LES2.
[169] Eph 5:27 NRSV.
[170] Cf. 1 Cor 2:6.
[171] Cf. Gen 28:20-22.

[21:27] *The needy shall eat and be satisfied.*

"Though he was rich,"[172] he has become poor because of our poverty. Therefore, he not only set free these poor ones, on whose account he undertook the things he has spoken of, but he also rendered them satisfied instead of hungry; for he is also the "Bread of Life,"[173] and his flesh is an immortal food, and his blood is a divine drink. Therefore, when those who became rich instead of poor because of the poverty of that one partake of these things, they will eat and be satisfied. The saying "Blessed are those who hunger and thirst for righteousness, for they will be filled"[174] is like this passage. They are not filled so that they cease from eating the Bread of Life, but when they chew on this Bread, they also possess him in a way that is tangible to them.

What is said in the Wisdom of Sirach will seem to contradict this "getting full," for Wisdom says there, "One who eats me will hunger for more, and one who drinks of me will thirst for more."[175] The passage here does not indicate a lack of satiety but rather the permanent love of the drink and the food. The one who eats Wisdom is never satiated but always is in a state of great desire. And the one who drinks Wisdom, like a divine stream or a wine that is harvested from the true Vine,[176] thirsts for more, that is, he is always in love with it. Therefore, to long for more and stretch out one's hands for this is the same thing as being satisfied.

The difference between a poor person and a needy one is often mentioned: the one who goes into poverty out of wealth, that one is called poor. And you also have this from Scripture: "The rich became poor and hungry."[177] A needy person is one who, because of his wretched circumstances, always provides for the necessities of life by enduring heavy labor. Therefore, according to their two conceptions they differ from each other; nevertheless, insofar as both exist because there is a lack of an abundance of things that they desire, they are alike.

As I was saying about Wisdom, that when it is drunk, it makes those who have drunk to be thirsty again, so also with divine **[51]** food—even the inhalation of air is a kind of food. And when we live, we inhale; even while we are not inhaling we are alive. So it is with both divine food and holy drink: they provide their advantage when they are offered and bestowed.

[21:27] *And those who seek him shall praise the Lord.*

I say the following: God is always in the process of being sought, even when someone finds him, for it was said, "he is found by those who seek him."[178] Therefore, in a certain sense he is always in the process of being sought. Now, a person can find him according to the knowledge that is partial and the prophecy that is partial,[179] and he is still being sought. And even the very seeking of God is beneficial. And Eunomius is out of his mind when he says that we understand God just as he understands himself. The one who understands God as God understands himself does not know in part, and those who say, "we know in part"[180] are lying. The one who knows God as he understands himself is not in the process of seeking him, for he begins to have him and has him already. Those who think in this way are

---

[172] 2 Cor 8:9.
[173] Jn 6:35.
[174] Mt 5:6 NRSV.
[175] Sir 24:21.
[176] Jn 15:1.
[177] Ps 34:10 (33:11 NETS). The Hebrew has "young lions" where the Greek text reads "the rich." Though not an exact rendering, the figural connection between the two is common throughout the Bible.
[178] Cf. Deut 4:29; Wis 1:1-2.
[179] Cf. 1 Cor 13:9.
[180] 1 Cor 13:9.

speaking falsehoods. Therefore, when we know him in the coming age or after all the ages when the last object of our desire has come, we know him as much as it is possible for us. "Beloved, we are God's children now; what we will be has not yet been revealed. What we do know is this: when he is revealed, we will be like him, for we will see him as he is,"[181] not as he himself is, but as it is possible for a perfect person to know him. After all, when, according to what is attainable by nature in the beginning, he offers himself for the finding, we have taken hold of what can be known about him: "For what can be known about God is plain in it,"[182] saying not simply God "himself," but "what can be known" about God. We know him, that he is creator, that he is provider, that he is unchangeable, immutable.

Now I wish to touch on a principle of logic. Proofs are forms of scientific knowledge. Indeed, there are two kinds of syllogisms—allow me not to mention for the present the disputative and the sophistical—the dialectical kind, which is called "*epichirematic*," is based on what is generally acknowledged. This proof is based on things that seem true to people, not from the nature of things. The demonstrative proof is based on the things themselves, not on the consensus of people but on the real existence of the subjects about which we are wanting to receive scientific knowledge. It is really impossible to provide an incontrovertible proof that is based on negations. There are proofs that are based on affirmations. Indeed, when I want to prove that mankind is rational, I do not say, "Mankind is not without a soul," [52] for indeed there are many other things that are not without a soul and yet are irrational. Therefore, I ought to prove it in this way: "Mankind is receptive of wise thoughts. Everything that is receptive of wise thoughts is rational. Therefore, mankind is rational."

So, when we have knowledge about God, even when this knowledge is perfect, we have it from negations, when we say that he is incorporeal. Incorporeality is the negation of a body. He is immortality, without a beginning, and immutable. Even at the end of things, then, when knowledge about God is perfect, it is not that knowledge which God himself has about himself. For he does not know himself to be unoriginate by the privation of origination, as the Eunomians themselves wish; nor indeed does he know himself to be immortal by the privation of death. We, by the privation of what we know, know what the word *immortal* means. However, we do not possess the ability to reach into that which is named in antithesis to death through scientific knowledge, and we speak of it by privation of death, by the negation of death. And so it is with all other things. For example, he is invisible. Not through a certain kind of affirmation do we learn that he is invisible; rather, since we know what the visible is, because we possess sensation and the faculty of sight, we understand the invisible through privation of this condition.

I say these words on account of the Eunomians, because it is impossible to have about God the same knowledge as God does. That is not the same knowledge that God himself has about himself. Additionally, our knowledge is a disposition of the soul. And dispositions receive growth and diminishment. The knowledge of God, however, which he possesses either about himself or about some other, is not a disposition; it is essential. And just as I call fire "warm," so I call warmed water "warm," and yet the water receives increase and diminishment. For this reason it can sometimes lose its warmth and regain it. The warmth in the fire, however, does not receive increase and diminishment, for it is essential to it. The knowledge of God is essential so that it is incomparable with the kind of knowledge that depends on a disposition. And things that are

---
[181] 1 Jn 3:2 NRSV.
[182] Rom 1:19.

incomparable to each other do not admit any likeness to each other.

However, they say these things idly, for since our doctrine proves that the Son is of one being with the Father and is of the same divinity because he is known by the Father and knows the Father, they wish to make his knowledge common with ours, saying: "As we know God, so also does he know God, because we know him perfectly, just as he knows himself. The Son, in the same way, possesses knowledge about him. For this reason he will not be different from us."

[21:27] *Their hearts shall live forever and ever.*

Often accidents are called by the same names as those substances of which they are accidents. We say that there is an essence that belongs to the soul. When God the Word says, "Do not fear those who kill the body [53] but cannot kill the soul,"[183] the word *soul* here signifies an essence. And when it says, "Bless the Lord, spirits and righteous souls,"[184] it is signifying an essence.

On the other hand, the word *soul* often signifies an accident of the soul, for when it is said in the Wisdom of Joshua, "An evil soul will destroy him who possesses it,"[185] it is calling the disposition and the understanding "soul," for the one who possesses this soul is the person. And again, "Having purified your souls by your obedience to the truth."[186] And that saying, "But you, O man, who are equal in soul with me"[187] has been derived from this: you who have the same desire that I do. And again, when it is said, "And you shall eat grapes, as much as fills your soul,"[188] here he calls the appetitive power "soul." So not all

words denote their underlying essences, but there are times when they also designate the things that are accidental to them. It is a contingent event for a human to know God. For this reason, the human is never called "knowledge" but a knower. Here the accident does not have the same meaning as the subject. The Savior is called both "wise" and "wisdom," both "knowledge" and "having knowledge," both "righteousness" and "having righteousness," and in this case I do not speak of accident and subject, but by analogy the same meaning is conveyed through two words. For when I say that the Savior is righteousness, I am neither saying that he is a habit, nor a disposition; and when I say that he is righteous—"but you rejected the righteous one"[189]—I am not speaking of the quality but of righteousness itself. We say the word *righteous* in this way in the case of God in general. I do not say that God is righteous by participating in righteousness but by bestowing righteousness.

Now, the soul in respect of its essence does not receive increase and diminishment. But that soul, in respect of which some are called "great-souled," does receive increase. The disposition, then, is called "soul" as a homonym.

Heart and "mind" mean the same thing. For when it says, "Where your treasure is, there also your heart will be also,"[190] there also is your mind. "Blessed are the pure in heart."[191] It is one and the same thing, then, to say "mind" and "heart." However, this is not so in relation to all things, but in relation to people. See! The soul of the person and the mind are immortal. It is to be asked whether the immortality is of one kind or another. Now, the sinner, because he has an immortal soul, never perishes, for one must not follow the

---

[183]Mt 10:28 NRSV.
[184]Dan 3:86 NETS. These verses are found only in the LXX.
[185]Sir 6:4 NETS.
[186]1 Pet 1:22.
[187]Ps 55:13 (54:14).
[188]Deut 23:24 (23:25 LES2).

[189]Acts 3:14.
[190]Mt 6:21 NRSV.
[191]Mt 5:8 NRSV.

opinion of those who say that the souls of the wicked come to an end in nonbeing, as the Stoics among the Greeks wish, and indeed as the Hieracites among the Christians do as well. Therefore, the soul is immortal and possesses the life by which it moves by nature. Now, it even belongs to the sinner to possess this life by which he is immortal. Not of the present, natural life does it say *their hearts will live*, but it says this in relation to that life that the believer and the one who knows God possess. If hearts live forever and ever in the blessed life, then it is obvious also that they always remain in essential life, which is [54] common to sinners and the virtuous.

Now, just as I say that all have the faculty of sight when living creatures have the faculty of sight, I also say that one who sees well has the faculty of sight optimally. And he would not see well, if he did not possess the ability to see; and again he would not see badly, if he did not possess the ability to see. Both the soul and the heart, therefore, possess eternal life, whether they are wicked or virtuous. Natural life acquires further life: for it would not be able to live like God or to live in faith, unless it were immortal, unless it were possessed of essential life.

Therefore, the hearts of these who eat and are filled, who fear God and praise him, they will live not for one age, but *forever and ever*. And a multitude of ages is signified, for he did not say "for the age." And just as "a Sabbath of Sabbaths"[192] and "a year of years" is mentioned, which has as many years as there are days in the year, so he will live "unto the age of ages."

[21:28] *All the ends of the earth shall remember and turn to the Lord.*

He prophesies about the salvation of all mankind, for that event must take place of which this saint speaks again in another psalm: "All the nations, as many as you made, shall come and worship before you,"[193] for God did not create the rational beings that they should sin, that they should erect demigods and serve them, but that they should honor God. And since this is the intention of the Creator, even though the intention of creatures became an obstacle to it, the intention of God must prevail.

When he remembers us, we in fact supply the reason for this remembrance, for he remembers those who remember him, just as he knows those who know him. When we ourselves remember, then he remembers us and calls us into salvation.

The phrase *they will turn* shows that no one is evil in essence, but in choice. And when the evil is strong enough to drive the free will here and there, the good will be strong enough to recall it to its former condition.

[21:28] *And all the families of the nations will worship before him.*

After turning, they worship. They do not first worship and then return. So he indicates their progress. It is a great thing to worship before God. That one worships before him who worships him as is right.

The cause follows: *because kingship is his*.[194] *Kingship* here does not mean "rule," but "those who are ruled," in accordance with which this is said, "when peoples gather together, and kingdoms, to be subject to the Lord."[195] When they were evil in condition, they belonged to another.

[21:29] *And it is he who is master over the nations.*

Since the kingdom is his and he himself has created the nations, he is also their master.

---

[192]Cf. Lev 16:31.
[193]Ps 86:9 (85:9).
[194]Ps 22:28 (21:29).
[195]Ps 102:22 (101:23).

Therefore, they return to their own master. They do not make God wealthy by returning, for they are already his.

[21:30] *All the fat ones of the earth* [55] *ate and worshiped.*

One must understand this in a different sense. Often the names of those who are mentioned come from who they were earlier, like when it says, "The prostitutes and the tax collectors are going into the kingdom of God ahead of you."[196] "Do not be deceived! Fornicators will not inherit the kingdom of God."[197] How then do they go into it? He designates them by their former name; those who were once fornicators and tax collectors, after they were transformed, preceded the wicked Jews into the kingdom. And again, "The sons of the kingdom will depart into outer darkness."[198] If they are sons of the kingdom, how do they come outside? They were once sons of the kingdom. So also here: they were once the *fat ones of the earth*. Those who think earthly thoughts, who honor the works of the flesh, and live according to the flesh and not according to the Spirit, those were the fat of the earth. But those who repent— for if all the ends of the earth repented, and these also are from the ends of the earth—by eating spiritual food, they turned away from being *the fat of the earth* and have become, if I may say so, the fat of the heavens, and they *worship* from then onward with a praiseworthy worship.

It is also possible, however, to take *the fat of the earth* in a different sense. Sometimes, people who have a superior portion of the fat of God are fat. "As though with tallow and fattiness let my soul be fully satisfied."[199] Those who are *the fat of the earth* in this sense, the sleek ones, who have a moisture that is full of life, worship by eating. The food prepares them to be worshippers, for if those who approach God "in Spirit and in Truth"[200] become worshippers, and both the Spirit and the Truth are a food, after they have it within themselves, they will be true worshippers.

[21:30] *Before him all those who go down into the earth will fall down.*

One can say that those who go down into the earth are the angels who are sent for service.

I can say this. It is saying, even if many are sent for the service of salvation, yet they are not themselves saviors. There is only one Savior who was sent. Let no one, then, suppose that everyone who is sent into the earth is of equal honor, for these worship. *Before him will worship all those who went down into the earth.*

Now, if someone, riddling darkly, should also say this statement about the rational soul of man, that these also descend into the earth, first he will say this: those that fell do not worship, but those that descend. For example, John and Jacob were those who descended into the earth. For when they were sent they descended; they did not fall by slipping, no one else pulled them down. Indeed, there are those who were pulled down by the tail of the dragon, as it is said in the Apocalypse: "with his tail the dragon swept away a third of the stars of heaven."[201] Indeed, it was said, he who in teaching and prophecy "teaches lawless things: this is the tail."[202] The true teacher is not the tail; he is a head. [56] However, the one who falls away from the true teaching and prophecy is a tail, for evil is something that comes after good.

---

[196] Mt 21:31.
[197] 1 Cor 6:9.
[198] Mt 8:12.
[199] Ps 63:5 (62:6 LES2).
[200] Jn 4:23.
[201] Rev 12:4.
[202] Is 9:15.

[21:30] *And my soul lives for him.*[203]

The Lord's Man says these things: my soul does not simply live, but lives for him. For I am his temple.

However, it is also possible that a change of persons has taken place, so that David, the singer of the psalm, says these things: "my soul lives for no other thing." There are those who live for sin, for wealth.

[21:31] *And my offspring will serve him.*

My offspring, my children, serve him; for if my soul lives for him, those who are my children according to virtue will serve him.

[21:31] *And a generation that is yet to come will proclaim to the Lord.*

The word *generation* means many things. However, by saying *that is yet to come* he indicates the calling from the Gentiles. For the adulterous and perverted generation was cast out, a twisted and evil generation. "A generation goes, and a generation comes."[204] The former one, the one of the circumcision, goes; the one called by the Savior through the gospel comes. When I say, however, that the one from the circumcision is cast out, this is not because it has circumcision, but as many as have the same practice and vice as they do, even if they are Greeks, are thrown out with them. And as many of the circumcision as accepted the Gospel, these are numbered with the church of the Gentiles. For just as in former times before the appearance, those who associated themselves with the law of God became proselytes of the Jews, so now when a Jew believes in the gospel and in God, he becomes a proselyte of the gospel of the Gentiles.

Question: It will be proclaimed to God?

Do not let the saying trouble you. It is also said in Jeremiah, "To you the nations will come and say, 'What lies!'"[205] See! Something is announced to the Lord. You hear that such things are announced to the Lord, not in order that he might learn—since then we idly send up prayers, as it seems to some heretics: "If he knows all our concerns better than we do, there is absolutely no need that we should pray"—but the purpose for this announcement is that which is made clear:

[21:32] *And they will announce his righteousness to a people that is yet to be born, that the Lord has done it.*

The fat who worship and go down on the earth, they will announce his righteousness to a people that is yet to be born, to the people from the Gentiles who will be born in virtue, who will be born "of water and the Spirit."[206] And the Lord has done this. We do not take the doing here to mean creation, for he made all things, but he made a people itself, calling the people that was not a people. Indeed, he chose those who were a people earlier, not because it was uppermost but because of his own beauty. Therefore, when those who were called from the Gentiles into the gospel receive the beauty that consists in virtue, then they become a people under God, as is set down about it: "And a people, which is being created, will praise the Lord."[207] [57]

---

[203]The Hebrew text reads *lō'* (not) where the Septuagint translates *lô* (for him) with the equivalent word in Greek. This results in the quite different readings of this last part of the verse. The ESV, following the Hebrew, reads "even the one who could not keep himself alive." Following the Greek, the NRSV has "and I shall live for him."
[204]Eccles 1:4 NETS.
[205]Jer 16:19.
[206]Jn 3:5.
[207]Ps 102:18 (101:19 NETS).

PSALM 22 [23]

[22:1-2][1] *The Lord shepherds me, and nothing will be lacking for me. In a place of tender grass, there he cause me to encamp.*

The soul of a person is signified by many names, for it is said to be a "sheep," a "human," a "plant," and many other things, such as a stone, as well. For when Peter writes, "you yourselves like living stones are being built up,"[2] he calls people "stones." The person is none of these things essentially, so it is fitting to understand all these things about him in an allegorical manner.

The soul itself grows and increases not in its essence, but in the practical and contemplative life. It possesses intellectual virtue; it can accomplish practical virtue. Therefore, the progress of the soul, as of the person, is spoken of: for indeed he is sometimes called "infant," sometimes "child," at times "youth," and at times "man." And we receive these descriptions not in relation to the characteristics or the development of the body, for the soul does not advance in years save only in virtue, in progress, in improvement.

Now, there are some infants who are able to improve by no other food but milk. So the apostle writes, "I fed you with milk, not solid food."[3] And Peter says, "Like newborn infants, long for the pure, spiritual milk."[4] "Spiritual milk," however, is not the kind you can taste; it is not corporeal, but it is the food that corresponds to the rational essence. The apostle also writes the following to the Hebrews: "For though by this time you ought to be teachers"—for they had been nourished by the Scriptures for a long time—"you need someone to teach you again the basic elements of the oracles of God."[5] Though you yourselves ought to be teachers, to advance the perfect teaching to others, you have become so small in the inner man as to become nursing infants. And he calls "milk" the elementary principles of the oracles of God, the introductory, elementary doctrines. And he says, "Everyone who lives on milk, being still an infant, is unskilled in the word of righteousness."[6] He does not possess the doctrine of righteousness. "Therefore let us go on toward perfection, leaving behind the basic teaching about Christ."[7] Leave the elementary teaching behind you! For it is only a beginning of the doctrine of Christ. Let us be led onward to perfection in order that, having become perfect in this way, we may be able to be perfect listeners to Christ, for "we speak wisdom among the mature."[8]

As I said already, the soul is sometimes called a sheep as well. When he is a sheep, he needs young grass, not meat, not the flesh of Jesus, not bread. On the contrary: he is not yet able either to have the appetite for these foods or to obtain them, even if they are brought to him. He needs grass, and spiritual grass at that!

---

[1] Didymus the Blind, *Psalmenkommentar (Tura-Papyrus)*, vol. 2, *Kommentar zu Psalm 22–26,10*, ed. M. Gronewald, PTA 4 (Bonn: Rudolf Habelt, 1968), begins here.
[2] 1 Pet 2:5.
[3] 1 Cor 3:2 NRSV.
[4] 1 Pet 2:2 NRSV.
[5] Heb 5:12 NRSV.
[6] Heb 5:13 NRSV.
[7] Heb 6:1 NRSV.
[8] 1 Cor 2:6.

Sometimes the soul is called a "plant" as well, and it needs rain, it needs the skill of the gardener, in order that, by increasing, it should produce perfect fruit and say, "But I am like a fruitful olive tree [**58**] in the house of God."[9]

And here, then, it signifies the condition of the soul as a sheep, which is, as it were, more irrational, with meekness and tranquility, by saying, *The Lord shepherds me, and nothing will be lacking for me*. I am wanting for nothing; however, I want for nothing as a sheep. As when an infant might say, "My nurse feeds me, and nothing will be lacking for me," he is clearly referring to the food of infants.

In order to explain, he says, *In a place of tender grass, there he causes me to encamp*. There is a green teaching that is well suited to sheep. And perhaps this is nothing other than the voice of Christ, for he says, "My sheep hear my voice."[10] The disciples of Christ who have become perfect in his instruction, being sheep no longer, do not simply hear a voice, but they are familiar with the teacher himself, for "you call me Teacher and Lord—and you are right, for that is what I am."[11]

In a place, then, *of tender grass, there he causes me to encamp*. He did not cause me to settle, but he caused me to encamp there. Now, the tent signifies progress. "I shall proceed to a place of a marvelous tent, as far as the house of God."[12] The one who makes progress has a portable house: virtue itself. However, whenever he arrives at the end itself, and the perfection of virtue, he no longer encamps, but he settles down. The saint who understands the magnificence and the progress was saying, "One thing I requested of the Lord, this will I seek, to live in the Lord's house"—not to live near it—"all the days of my life."[13] However, the novice has life, as well as the one who makes progress and the one who is perfected. For this reason, he who says, "Your mercy is better than lives,"[14] acknowledges a multitude of lives; for in whatever kind of life I should come, I am filled with your mercy and I am helped.

[22:2-3] *At a water of rest he nourished me, he restored my soul. He led me into paths of righteousness.*

Water is a drink that is suitable for sheep. Those who are given pasture as food and are nourished with water are not given wine to drink, for where bread is, there wine is also named: "Bread sustains a human heart"—and by bread the perfect food is indicated—"and wine gladdens a human heart."[15] Where there is grass, then, there too is water, and where there is bread, there wine is also found. The perfect banquet is replete with bread and wine; on the other hand, the condition of the soul as a sheep is helped by grass and water.

The *water of rest* can be called this because the one who draws it does not suffer toil, for "whoever drinks of the water that I will give" will have "a spring of water welling up to eternal life."[16] Being beneath the earth, the water is not drawn up, but because it gushes up, it comes to the one who drinks it. For this reason it is a *water of rest*.

In addition to nourishing, this water also cleanses. And since the soul, when it is cleansed, casts off sin—for this is cast aside with "a talent of lead"[17]—the water bestows rest. It does away with both of them together: the thirst and the filth.

Next, since he mentions pasture, grass, and water, he immediately transfers his discourse toward the inner man and says, *He restored my*

---

[9] Ps 52:8 (51:10 NETS).
[10] Jn 10:27 NRSV.
[11] Jn 13:13 NRSV.
[12] Ps 42:4 (41:5 NETS).
[13] Ps 27:4 (26:4).

[14] Ps 63:3 (62:4 NETS).
[15] Ps 104:15 (103:15 NETS).
[16] Jn 4:14 ESV.
[17] Cf. Zech 5:7.

soul. By restoration [**59**] change is signified. I no longer remain a sheep; I am no longer under a shepherd; I do not have an appetite for water.

He restored my soul. What, however, took place with my soul when it was restored? God led it *into paths of righteousness.* The *paths of righteousness* are the particular virtues or the practices of the virtues.

In many passages of the divine teachings, the word *righteousness* means virtue in general, for indeed there is a specific virtue that is also called "righteousness." When we say that there are four cardinal virtues, courage, righteousness, temperance, and prudence, one of the virtues is signified by the word *righteousness*.

And when it says, "And you, masters, act fairly and rightly,"[18] the right that accords with worth is here signified. And when it says, "a righteous scale and a righteous weight,"[19] it mentions what is productive of righteousness. Now, the right that distributes according to worth derives from it as well as the right that is, as they say, corrective. For righteousness is talked about in two ways: either as corrective or as distributing according to worth. And, in order that I may establish this from the Scriptures, the law commands, "tooth for tooth and eye for eye."[20] He who attacks someone violently and destroys his eye is delighted because he is punishing an enemy. The one whose eye or tooth is destroyed is grieved. The divine law grants the one who had first acted wickedly to suffer the same thing. And there comes a removal of his pleasure, and it is delivered over to the one who suffered because he experienced painful wounds, and there comes equality. This right, then, is called corrective. The distributive kind of right appears not in the equality of the nature of the subject, but in the proportionality of the distribution.

Paths of righteousness, therefore, are the paths that are worn out by it, the paths that are traveled by many.

However, *paths of righteousness* can also be the practical activities of righteousness, for then especially righteousness is traveled and worn out, when it is put into practice. And that practical virtue is signified by this word *righteousness* is confirmed by this: "One who walks spotlessly and practices righteousness, who speaks truth in his heart; he who did not beguile with his tongue, nor did evil to his fellow." And after a few words: "He who does these things shall never be shaken forever."[21] You see that by assembling all the particular virtues together into this one he called it "righteousness" in a generic sense.

"He led me," then, "upon paths of righteousness." There are also people who, before the written law, traversed this righteousness. Of Abraham it was said that "he kept all the decrees and ordinances"[22] of the Lord. Even though they were not yet given, yet he kept them, he lived according to them. Abel also is recognized for his righteousness.

The restoration of the soul, then, is the passage [**60**] that leads along the paths of righteousness, in order that a person may be a sheep no longer.

[22:3] *For his name's sake.*

Not so much because of my worthiness as because of his own name did he offer this to me. For even when someone rushes toward good things, even when he is desirous of them, unless God shows him mercy, he does not obtain the things that are desired. Even in the 118th Psalm it is said, for example: "I ran the way of your commandments, when you made my heart spacious."[23] Because you enlarged my

---

[18]Col 4:1.
[19]Lev 19:36.
[20]Ex 21:24.

[21]Ps 15:2-3, 5 (14:2-3, 5).
[22]Cf. Gen 26:5.
[23]Ps 119:32 (118:32 NETS).

heart and have given it breadth, I ran the way of your commandments. Therefore, one always obtains the things desired because of God.

For he created rational creatures, in order that they should partake of his name. By "name" I do not mean that which is composed of syllables, but that which demonstrates what is named by its quality. Indeed, the definition of *name* is rendered as follows: "Name is a summarizing designation that indicates the very quality of the thing named." And this is especially the case with a derived name. From wisdom someone is called "wise," and he does not have a mere designation, he does not possess merely a collection of syllables, but the quality that the name indicates, which wisdom bestowed on the soul. Therefore, *name* in a strict sense is a summarizing designation that designates the quality of the thing named. And when, therefore, you say the word *human*, this designates the quality of the human—and I am calling here the identity "quality"—for you mentioned the peculiar quality of the one named. Now, the peculiar quality of the human is humanity; for if you should speak of another quality, they share in it as well as others; it is not peculiar. Take, for example, a certain disciple of a physician, and let him understand nothing of the healer's art. Now, he is a reproach to the one who trained him the arts of healing, seeing that he knows nothing of them nor practices them.

[22:4] *For even if I walk in the midst of death's shadow, I will not fear evil, because* you are with me.

Since for his name's sake he restored my soul, he is with me. And since he is with me, warding off every evil, neither does the *shadow of death* draw near to me.

"Evils" are mentioned in two senses in Scripture, and perhaps also in ordinary language. The opposites of virtue, the types of vice, are called "evils," as when it says, "With laughter a fool practices evils"[24] and, "Turn away from evil and do good."[25]

And they also signify unpleasant misfortunes, since people say that pleasant circumstances are "goods." But the "goods" of men are not truly good. Because of this Abraham said to his neighbor, "you received your good things."[26] So, if he was talking about the virtues, he would not say, "your good things." **[61]** "The Lord will give good things to those who ask him."[27] He did not say, "their good things."

When, for example, Job says, "If we received the good things from the Lord, shall we not bear the evil?"[28] he is calling "evils" his ulceration, the lamentable death of his children, and the rest. And especially clear is what is spoken by Isaiah, when the prophet says the following about God: "And he, being wise, brought evils upon them."[29] It is not the part of a wise man to bring on another the forms of vice, which are evils; consequently, this is not the part of God either. And wicked men themselves, when they feign virtue, do not say, "We are bringing evil upon someone." But it is said of God that he brings evils on people as one who is wise. It is speaking of things that are painful. And observe the goal of the introduction of evils: "And his word will not be set to naught."[30] So that his word is not set to naught, he introduces painful things. For since they heard by his commanding word what they should do and what they should avoid doing, and they despised this word, and, inasmuch as it depended on their wicked condition, the word was set at naught, he brought evils on them lest his word be set at naught.

Now, both medical surgery and cauterization, when these bring health to the patient, are not evils.

---

[24]Prov 10:23.
[25]Ps 34:14 (33:15); cf. Ps 37:27 (36:27 NETS).
[26]Lk 16:25 NRSV.
[27]Mt 7:11.
[28]Job 2:10.
[29]Is 31:2 NETS.
[30]Cf. Is 31:2 NETS.

Now, he is not speaking here of that *shadow*, which we say that the law possesses—"since the law has only a shadow of the good things to come"[31]—but he calls here *shadow* that which exists before death. And sin preexists death. By *death*, however, I am not now speaking of the common kind. Look, painters make an outline before they paint images and forms. And that shadow is the beginning of the image. So then, *death* also possesses a *shadow*: sin. And this prefigures death and makes it known beforehand.

That is to say, when I come *in the midst of the shadow of death*, I do not fear it. Such was Joseph, insofar as he has come into the midst of death's shadow at the incitement that sought to drag him down into licentiousness, and he has *feared no evil*; that woman did not conquer him.

Question: Does the word *shadow* mean the common kind?

Since the discourse is not about common death, neither should one think about its *shadow* in this way. For just as that prefiguration of which you are speaking, being something sensible and subject to sight, conveys both what is sensible after the shadow and that which is visible, so also here the death only touches the soul since the *shadow* comes within the region of the soul. "When sin"—which was the shadow—"is fully grown,"[32] it becomes the mother of death, that is, it bears and produces death. *If, then, I walk in the midst of death's shadow*. [62]

Question: Has he come into afflictions?

Yes. If he had been afraid, he would have sinned.

Question: The phrase *in the midst* means that he is in sin?

I am not saying this. I am not saying that being afflicted is *the shadow of death*, but rather that giving way and cowardice from being afflicted is *death's shadow*, seeing that the martyrs have gone into *the midst of death's shadow*, but not into death. They were distressed, but what the affliction that was imposed on them promised, to this they did not consent. In a like sense the following was also said: "Lead us not into temptation,"[33] for they do not say this: "Do not allow us to be afflicted." If this were so, the apostles would never have declared the truth by saying, "We are afflicted in every way."[34] By "lead us not into temptation," we are saying this: "Let us not be conquered by the desire of the tempter."

I will not fear evil, because you are with me.

Since I have you with myself, I fear nothing from those who decide to harm me.

[22:4] *Your rod and your staff—they comforted me.*

You see that he was not inexperienced in the shadow of death. *Your staff*, becoming my support, and *your rod*, correcting me, *comforted me*. They have freed me from death, even when I have come into its *shadow*, even when I proceeded into *the midst of its shadow*.

The *rod* and the *staff* of God are understood also as correction and support: "He who produces wisdom from his lips strikes a heartless man with a rod."[35] It named the corrective and challenging word *rod*. And Paul writes to the Corinthians: "What would you prefer? Am I to come to you with a rod?"[36]

And *staff* is understood as support as well: "Your staves in your hands. And you shall eat it with haste—it is the Lord's pascha."[37]

---

[31] Heb 10:1 NRSV.
[32] Jas 1:15.
[33] Mt 6:13; Lk 11:4.
[34] 2 Cor 4:8 NRSV.
[35] Prov 10:13 NETS.
[36] 1 Cor 4:21.
[37] Ex 12:11 NETS.

[22:5] *You prepared a table before me over against those that afflict me.*

We connect the present words, then, with the introduction, for they are a consequence of the previous ones: when we were saying that after the drinking of milk "solid food"[38] is given, which is the wisdom of God spoken of among the mature.[39]

Now, the mode of living here follows after the bestial one. And when it has passed with tranquility and gentleness I remained without want, because I had been shepherded by you, for a *table* took the place of green grass. When I had the condition of a sheep, I was in need of instructions that are like grass and that have the quality of water. But when I made progress, my soul being restored by you on paths of righteousness, so that I was comforted by your rod and staff, then I became human. For this reason you no longer prepared grass but a *table*, and in my presence you revealed to me its nourishing and edible beauty. Your Wisdom [63] prepared this table for me. "Slaughtering her own sacrificial victims," she laid them on it. And "mixing her own wine,"[40] she set it on this table, and she calls everyone to eat and to drink from this table.

Now, in this place we are calling Wisdom's table the divine instruction. And offerings are laid on this table, for when we perform sacred offices and sacrifice the doctrines of piety in order to make them ready for nourishment, then the sacrifices are laid on the table. And none other offered them except Wisdom herself, who "prepared her own table."[41] For it did not simply say, "she prepared a table," but "her own table." And Wisdom's table has no other food laid on it except wise instructions.

Then she has also "mixed her own wine." She added water to it, in order that we, who are unable to take unmixed wine, should receive wine that has been mixed. There are certain inexpressible words, which are not. . . . Let these be wine. Whenever someone is capable of bringing these into spoken teaching, he has mixed the teaching, uniting clear water with these inexpressible words. These are the illustrations of Scripture, the sayings that are proclaimed in parables.

Again, since God the Word is Wisdom, and we were unable to receive the Word unmixed, he mixed the Word in the inhumanation, and we at last received the wine that has been mixed both from the doctrine of the inhumanation and of the majesty of the only-begotten. "And the Word became flesh and lived among us, and we have seen his glory."[42] Behold the mixture!

However, this mixture came from none other than from Wisdom herself. You know that the wine mixer sometimes completes the mixture in consideration of the drinker's condition. And Wisdom, therefore, mixed her own wine and did not give the same mixture to all, but only what each is capable of drinking. There are, then, puerile ones, among whom this mixture seems to be rather more watery. The portion of the inhumanation predominates. But when someone "sees his glory, the glory as of the only-begotten from the Father,"[43] the wine predominates.

This table, then, he did not prepare toward the back of his guest, not far away from him, but *before* him and *over against those who afflict* him. Exchanging this riddle for what is clearer, the apostle writes, "for a wide door for effective work has opened to me, and there are many adversaries."[44] Whenever someone holds a doctrine, and the door of a doctrine, strongly and effectively, he has many adversaries. Even the devil himself opposes him, wishing to

---

[38] Cf. Heb 5:12.
[39] Cf. 1 Cor 2:6.
[40] Prov 9:2.
[41] Prov 9:2 NETS.
[42] Jn 1:14 NRSV.
[43] Jn 1:14.
[44] 1 Cor 16:9 NRSV.

prevent the usefulness that comes from the performance of the doctrine. And sophistical and other wicked men oppose as well. They certainly oppose to such a degree that they plot against the one who receives the benefit of his teaching.

He prepared the table *over against those who afflict me*. I once spoke in relation to that passage about the infant Jesus: "for before the child knows how to call father or mother, it will receive the power of Damascus and the spoils of Samaria before the king of the Assyrians."[45] It would not be a great thing, if he received the spoils [64] possessed by the king while the king was absent. Rather, in front of him, while the king was present, he plundered what he took from him. Or did he not despoil the magi in front of the king of Assyria? For they were still working magic. They had not converted before they came to the child, but the demons were still active among them. The following thing, in any case, has been seen in the church: those who made it their custom to call on demons, when they did not have them obedient to them, knew that magic was overthrown by the child who was indicated by the star that appeared. These oppressive demons were present, and the works of kindness have appeared before their eyes.

One can also understand the phrase *over against* in this way: they were present, wishing to hinder, as much as they can, or wishing to harm him with an opposed intention.

[22:5] *You anointed my head with oil.*

You rendered me an "anointed one." In accordance with what is signified, this is said: "Do not touch my anointed ones."[46] And this saint was one of the anointed ones who was anointed by Christ "with the oil of rejoicing beyond your companions."[47] The man himself was anointed beyond the companions, beyond the other anointed ones, of whom it was said, "You came forth for the salvation of your people, to save your anointed ones."[48]

You anointed, then, *my head with oil*. In many cases the head signifies the intellect, as when it is said, "They eyes of the wise person are in his head."[49] At any rate, ordinary language says that the more stupid ones do not have a brain, that they have no head. The leader of a community is called the head of the community. And since the intellect also rules and governs our whole constitution as humans, it is named head. And many Scriptures teach this, which we have said many times.

He did not merely say, "it was anointed," but he added *with oil*. Indeed, there is also a contemptible oil, which the saint deprecates, saying, "But let not a sinner's oil anoint my head."[50]

[22:5] *And your cup was supremely intoxicating.*

Since not everyone can consume the whole bowl that Wisdom mixed, she distributes to each a cup, with which each, by receiving, can be gladdened.

Some of the Scriptures have "and my cup," the cup that you have offered me. However, the passage is said in both ways.

It is also *supremely intoxicating*. She offers the best wine to the drinker, a sober intoxication. The word *intoxicating*, however, stands for "gladdening." Therefore, we often call one who drinks a great deal intoxicated. However, mere touching and tasting is called intoxication.

---

[45]Is 8:4 NETS; cf. PsT 29-30.
[46]Ps 105:15 (104:15 NETS).
[47]Ps 45:7 (44:8).
[48]Cf. Hab 3:13 NETS.
[49]Cf. Eccles 2:14 LES2.
[50]Ps 141:5 (140:5 NETS). The Hebrew and the Septuagint differ here. Whereas the Hebrew relates that the rebuke of the righteous is oil to the psalmist's head, the Septuagint punctuates the verse differently. Translating *rāšāʿ* instead of *rōʾš*, the oil becomes the "oil of the sinner" and is therefore to be avoided.

And they give the etymology of the word *intoxication* in the following way: in antiquity there was not an abundance of wine. Immediately after it was discovered that the fruit of the vine makes wine, then they began to drink it at banquets and public festivals, after sacrificing. They did not drink it at any other time. And for this reason it is called intoxication.[51]

However, even to touch often signifies intoxication: "They will be intoxicated with the fatness of your house,"[52] that is, "they will be gladdened." Elsewhere, indeed, intoxication is mentioned with aversion: "those who are drunk get drunk at night."[53] Those are drunk with darkness and ignorance. However, those who are drunk [**65**] because they received a divine drink, that is, those who are gladdened, are soberly drunk. "Eat, drink, and be intoxicated, my brothers!"[54] says the bridegroom in the Song of Songs. By "be intoxicated" he does not mean this: "be controlled by wine," but rather "be gladdened."

[22:6] *And your mercy shall pursue me all the days of my life.*

Understand the phrase *your mercy* as you do the words *you anointed my head*. He does not anoint my head for a short time, but always, and so each of the anointed ones becomes an eternal christ.

All the days, therefore, *of my life* he pursues me. He does not permit me to be far away from him; indeed, this is permanent because he is present with me, and not for today or tomorrow, but for *all the days of my life*. Take *all the days of my life*, however, as the illuminations of the soul that take place by the Sun of Righteousness.[55]

---

[51]The same etymology is traced in Aristotle: *methuein = meta to thysai*. See Valentin Rose, *Aristotelis qui ferebantur librorum fragmenta* (Leipzig: Teubner, 1886), 99 (fragment 102).
[52]Ps 36:8 (35:9 NETS).
[53]1 Thess 5:7 NRSV.
[54]Song 5:1.
[55]Cf. Mal 4:2 (3:20). The final half verse, "and my dwelling will be in the house of the Lord for the length of days" (Ps 22:6 LES2), is either absent from Didymus's text or skipped.

PSALM 23 [24]

[23:1][1] *A psalm of David. On the first of the Sabbath.*

. . . has an appropriate heading, for it refers to the first day of the Sabbath. *The first of the Sabbath* is the eighth day, the one that follows it. This is also the first day of the Sabbath. And so, I suppose, since it is the beginning of a seven-day cycle, it is also called the eighth day, for the number seven is concluded at the seventh, at the seventh addition either of a day or another unit. The second day begins again from one. Sometimes this is called *the first of the Sabbath*, that is, the day after the Sabbath, and at other times it is called the eighth day, in order that the two weeks should be brought together.

While the saint gives a portion to those of the seven and those of the eight, the Jew has only the Sabbath. They have neither the first of the Sabbath nor the eighth day, because they do not entirely contemplate the meaning of the earlier week. Only the one who has the church's understanding, then, who according to another parable in the Gospel "brings out of his treasure what is new and what is old,"[2] only that one has the new day of the Sabbath. Having transcended the first week, he began the second week, which accords with the Gospel. And this eighth day is also called the *first of the Sabbath* since it relates to the first week.

The first verses of the psalm can be taken both literally and intelligibly.

By *fullness of the earth*[3] one must understand the earth's adornment, which Moses in any case spoke of, for when the trees and the animals came on it, it was said: "the adornment of the heaven and the earth was finished. And on the sixth day God finished his works."[4]

And in a literal sense we understand that the fruits and the animals are the *fullness of the earth*. And the apostle instructs, telling—indeed, advising—those who believe from the Gentiles and the Jews not to hold false beliefs about foods. He says, "Eat whatever is sold in the meat market without raising any question, for 'the earth and its fullness are the Lord's.'"[5] Now, meat [66] in particular is sold in the markets, but also the other goods that contribute to nourishment.

[23:1] *The earth and its fullness are the Lord's, the world and all those who live in it.*

Now, earlier I said that the earth was divided so that one part of it is arable, and one part of it is suitable for habitation. The part, then, that is ready for habitation is called *world*, and the part that is suitable for agriculture and the rest is called *earth*.

So God is the creator of both of them. For how would these be his, if he himself has not created them? *The Lord's*, therefore, *are the earth and its fullness*. Take the following in reference to them both:

---

[1] A good English translation of the commentary on this psalm can be found in Albert-Kees Geljon, "Didymus the Blind: Commentary on Psalm 24 (23 LXX): Introduction, Translation and Commentary," *Vigiliae Christianae* 65, no. 1 (2011): 50-73.
[2] Mt 13:52 NRSV.
[3] Ps 24:1 (23:1).
[4] Gen 2:1-2.
[5] Cf. 1 Cor 10:25-26 NRSV.

[23:2] *It is he who founded it on the sea, and prepared it on the rivers.*

It is either the earth or the world. The world, moreover, is the earth.

What is being said here is equal to what was said in this way: "him, who made firm the earth upon the waters,"[6] and to what was said by Job, "he, hanging the earth upon nothing."[7] For if it has been founded on the sea, it does not have a strong and rigid foundation but has its suspension on the waters. Now, every water has a floor that offers resistance to it. And since the sea has a floor that lies under it, clearly even that floor must have something that underlies it. However, nothing else besides liquid is found there. For this reason he says that the earth has been founded on the seas.

The earth maintains itself by gathering itself to itself in a mass. A resistant, hard floor does not allow it to be ordered in this way; rather, it rotates around itself. Indeed, the theories of the Greeks also say that straight lines sent out from the circle—straight lines that are not perceptible but are contemplated in thought—hold it firm in the exact center. And this is what its being suspended on nothing means.

And this is God's will, for "you founded the earth upon its own stability; it will not be moved forever and ever."[8] For how is it possible for the earth to be tilted, which has received its base in such a way by God's decree?

Since then the *earth* has been founded on the sea, and the world is a part of the earth, clearly the *world* also has its base on this liquid substance.

And he says that it was *prepared on the rivers*: not founded on the rivers, but prepared; for it is impossible to say that it has its foundation on the sea and on the rivers, but it has truly been *founded upon the sea* after being prepared with rivers, in order that by being in it as certain springs and flowing fountains they should benefit it. Unless such bodies have water intermingled with them, by which they are able to endure, they become dust.

Now, these comments related to the literal sense. And yet what follows can no longer be understood literally: *Who shall ascend into the mountain of the Lord? And who shall stand in his holy place?*[9] Though he is bound to speak [67] of the way of ascent and the place of cessation, he spoke of no such thing, but to the one who asked: "Who is he who ascends? And who is he who has stood?" the answer comes as follows: *One who is guiltless in hands and clean in heart.*[10] To be *guiltless in the hands* means to be pure in actions.

Next he speaks of a divine quality: *One who is guiltless in hands and clean in heart, he who did not occupy his soul with what is vain.* Now, this is understood in two ways. He occupies his own soul *with what is vain* who ponders vanities, and chooses them, and practices them; for in many passages these things that are not important: the sensible things, the temporal, are signified by the name "vanities," as when it says, "And you will realize where you were, when you placed your trust in vain things,"[11] in temporal things.

Sins themselves can also be indicated. He occupies the soul *with what is vain* who rises early and drinks wine and lingers until evening so as to be inflamed with wine, for "woe to those who rise early and pursue strong drink, who linger until evening, for wine will inflame them."[12] In another sense again they take pains to arise early in the morning and to hurry to the courts, where the doing of injustice follows. This person *occupied his soul with what is vain.*

---

[6] Ps 136:6 (135:6 NETS).
[7] Cf. Job 26:7 NETS.
[8] Ps 104:5 (103:5).
[9] Ps 24:3 (23:3).
[10] Ps 24:4 (23:4).
[11] Cf. Is 30:15 NETS.
[12] Is 5:11.

What is spoken to some by Isaiah also agrees with this: "The strength of your spirit is vain."[13] Here *spirit* means "intention." This is akin to what was said of the virgin, that just as she is pure in body, so also in spirit,[14] in intention and understanding.

"Vain," then, "is the strength of your spirit." When someone, then, is afflicted in his intellect and intention with "worries of life"[15] for vain things, the strength he possesses is vain. They squander the power of thinking on vanities. One can see, in any case, that such people are also more harmful. They squander altogether the whole strength of the intellect on such things.

There is a second interpretation of the phrase: *he who did not occupy his soul with what is vain.* God created mankind to be rational, not that he should merely have a thought and do nothing with it; for, for this reason he has created the rational creature: in order that he should receive virtue and practice it. *He occupied his soul with what is vain* not because God has taught it to do this, but because he has constrained his soul in this way. As when someone says, for example: "He has created mankind consisting of soul and body, and there are certain movements of the soul, and there are certain movements of the body. We have an activity of the limbs, like walking, making something with our hands, or seeing. Come now! If someone, therefore, never walks, even though he has feet, in a certain sense he has feet 'in vain.'"

And now for the anagogical meaning. The words that follow the earlier verses compel us to interpret them anagogically as well. That *earth is the Lord's*, "that honest and good heart"[16] that received the seed that Jesus sowed and bore fruit a hundredfold, or as much as a hundred, or sixty, or thirty.

I have often said that the same spiritual realities can be understood according to numerous conceptions, as when I said that the soul is called [68] both sheep and tree.

Here, then, the same soul is both *earth* and *world*. So when it brings forth the practical virtues, it is an *earth* that possesses *its fullness*. And when it possesses the divine gifts of the Spirit, it is a *world* that has inhabitants. It is not a wilderness, for he has not said, "Come! Let us forsake her,"[17] as was said in reference to the accused world. Now, this is the synagogue of the Jews. But this also extends to each soul that was previously inhabited and is now abandoned through its own fault.

With these thoughts the following is linked: *It is he who founded it upon the seas.* The place around the earth and the condition of those who dwell here are called "sea" and "seas." Having its existence, I mean its residence, among violent waves and brine, he founded the soul on these *seas*.

Now, this sea receives the dragnet of Jesus in order that good living creatures should be caught out of it: the virtuous ones.[18] When these ones, who are friends of virtue, are caught, in one sense they are said to be caught out of the sea, in order that they should come out of it, and in another sense they are said to be *founded upon the sea*, for they are founded here in order that they may appear to be "rooted and grounded in love."[19] And they are prepared *upon the rivers* that flow out of the belly of the one who has the Spirit[20] in order that they should receive these rivers that flow from the belly of each of the faithful. And the rivers are the different gifts of the Spirit.

To the one who asks because he wants to learn, *Who is he who ascends to the mountain of the Lord, and who stands in his holy place?* an answer is brought: "Are you seeking to know

---

[13]Is 33:11 LXX.
[14]Cf. 1 Cor 7:34.
[15]Cf. Lk 21:34.
[16]Cf. Lk 8:15 NRSV.

[17]Cf. Jer 51:9 (28:9 NETS).
[18]Cf. Mt 13:47-48.
[19]Eph 3:17 NRSV.
[20]Cf. Jn 7:38.

who is the one who ascends and stands? *One who is guiltless in hands and clean in heart, he who did not occupy his soul with what is vain.* This is he who ascends by means of progress. Progress, however, means ascent. Standing is the condition that relates to the perfect one, whenever someone becomes "perfect as the heavenly Father is perfect."[21] He stands in the holy place, except that he then transcends such a condition entirely and takes the beginning of another. For this reason it is also said in the Psalms, "I saw a limit to every perfection."[22] There are many limits, as obtains in the case of the learning of letters. Someone becomes perfect in the knowledge of the characters, and he begins with syllables, and when those reach their end again, another beginning occurs. It is not the property of a circle to receive either a beginning or an end. Therefore, when someone marks down the beginning of a circle with a symbol, then he will complete the whole circle. He comes again to the beginning, as obtains in the case of the sun. By such ends a person is always brought back to the same point.

The Jews, therefore, say probably that to *ascend to the mountain* means to ascend to the temple and to stand in it. The following context, however, excludes this understanding.

[23:3-4] *Who shall ascend onto the mountain of the Lord? And who shall stand in his holy place? One who is guiltless in hands and clean in heart;* [69] *he who did not occupy his soul with what is vain and did not swear deceitfully to his neighbor.*

It is set down in the Decalogue, "You shall not take the name of the Lord God in vain, for the Lord will not acquit the one who takes his name in vain."[23]

This must be understood both in an inner and perfect sense and in an introductory sense that is suitable to beginners. Strictly speaking, the new man who is ready to receive the laws of God "does not swear at all."[24] Therefore, he does not take the name of the Lord in vain. He uses it for no vain thing, contenting himself with "yes, yes," and "no, no."[25]

However, it is possible to say this to the novices: one must not swear falsely, for the one who names the name of the Lord falsely, insofar as this depends on him, took it in vain. For although he is able to give proof and assurance without an oath to the one who disputes with him, he is easily driven to the oath. They call this kind of assurance by means of an oath "unproven." Now, the secular authorities, when it was impossible for them to prove through documents or through witnesses—even then a person does not hurl himself into making an oath, but the judges, after wishing to find every kind of proof but not finding it, take refuge in this extremity.

He who did not occupy his soul with what is vain. And at once it added, *And he did not swear deceitfully.* For every perjurer swears *deceitfully*, for he knows well enough not to commit perjury.

This seldom happens in ignorance. Often, one pledges oneself falsely in forgetfulness, and again he receives a charge as in the case of involuntary sins. I mean the following: some people do not charge drunkards, even though they say what they should not say and do what they should not do, because they say that the intoxication by which these things happen with which they are charged, the things that take place after the intoxication, is involuntary. But drunkenness itself is voluntary; indeed, one should not get drunk.

---

[21] Mt 5:48.
[22] Ps 119:96 (118:96).
[23] Deut 5:11.

[24] Mt 5:34.
[25] Cf. Mt 5:37.

[23:5] *He it is that will receive blessing from the Lord.*

Having described who it is who *ascends onto the mountain* and who *stands in the holy place*, he also says that which follows on such a thing. This concerns the one who *ascends the mountain* of God and *stands in the holy place*. And after the ascent of the mountain, that the mountain peak is the holy place, the saint says, *he it is that will receive blessing from the Lord*, "every spiritual blessing in the heavenly places."[26] For it is said, "For even the lawgiver will give blessings."[27] The Lawgiver, however, does not give a blessing to those who transgress the law, but to those who translate it into action. And again, "Look, thus shall a person be blessed who fears the Lord."[28] The reverence is the cause of the blessing, the fear directed toward the Lord; for this reason it is said, "May the Lord bless you from Sion."[29] If God blesses such a person from Zion, he grants the blessing because of his superior virtue and right judgment. Behold, he says that the virtuous, the one *guiltless in hands* [70] and *clean in heart*, who *did not occupy his soul with what is vain* nor *swore deceitfully to his neighbor*, *will receive a blessing from the Lord*. He does not receive it from just anyone, for there are also men who bless one another and bless themselves, namely by saying praiseworthy things about themselves.

This one, then, *will receive from the Lord*. It is similarly said in Proverbs, "The blessing of the Lord is upon the head of the righteous."[30] The righteous person does not invoke the blessing on himself; men do not dispense it to him; rather, the blessing of the Lord is on his intellect, which is allegorically called "head."

[23:5] *And mercy from God his Savior.*

For even if someone has works that bring blessing, since the blessing is greater than the things that were done—and God gives beyond what we imagine and do—for this reason he needs mercy from him.

[23:6] *This is the generation of those who seek him.*

Since the inquiry comes in the singular, "*Who will ascend* and *who will stand?*" and the answer comes as though it is about one person, "*The one who is guiltless in hands and clean in heart*," though there is not only one who has arisen to accomplish virtue, he immediately adds, *This is the generation of those who seek him*, calling *generation* all those who have been born of the same achievements and virtues.

And by this contemplation a statement from the Gospel is unraveled for us. The Savior says, "All the righteous blood spilt upon the earth will be exacted from this generation," and he says, "from righteous Abel."[31] If he is indicating the Jews when he says "from this generation," then the exacting is unjust. Cain killed Abel, and others killed others before the calling of Abraham and the historical giving of the covenant. But he is saying: from such a generation, from those who are born from the devil by such works, as it says, "You are from your father the devil, and you choose to do your father's desires."[32] Now, desires make one a child of the devil. Again, those who have the same desires are one *generation*. The saying "a generation of upright ones will be blessed"[33] is also similar.

---

[26] Eph 1:3 NRSV.
[27] Ps 84:6 (83:7). The Hebrew text has "the early rain also covers it with pools." The Greek text reads "For even the lawgiver will give blessings." The words for "lawgiver" and "early rain" are homonyms in Hebrew (*môrēh*), and the words for "pools" and "blessings" differ by only a vowel (*bərēkâ* as opposed to *bərākâ*).
[28] Ps 128:4 (127:4 NETS).
[29] Ps 128:5 (127:5 NETS).
[30] Prov 10:6 NETS.
[31] Mt 23:35; Lk 11:51.
[32] Jn 8:44 NRSV.
[33] Ps 112:2 (111:2).

[23:6] *Who seek the face of the God of Jacob.*

Everyone who truly prays asks to receive the appearance of God, and this is *seeking the face of God*. Indeed, the saints send up prayer, saying, "Let your face appear and we will be saved."[34]

This is also possible to say. We received the heading of the psalm, *on the first of the Sabbaths*, and we were saying that the Savior's resurrection on the Lord's day is sometimes called the "eighth day" and is sometimes called *the first of the Sabbath*, according to different conceptions. *They seek the face* of the one who is going to visit them, when they hear that "by inclining heaven he will descend,"[35] that "the Savior comes."[36] For the heralds of the truth, who run before the one who visits them, hear: "Say to the daughter of Zion: behold! your Savior is coming to you!"[37] and: "Say to the cities of Judah: behold! your God is coming with strength."[38] They say this of him who supplants vice, in order that we should learn from him to trample on our enemies, on those who incite vice, "him who is at work in the sons of disobedience."[39]

When the economy achieves its goal—for "while you are still speaking, he will say, Here I am"[40]—the ascension of the Savior is immediately signified after the appearance, for the word that functions as a refrain says, *Raise the gates, O rulers of yours!* O rulers of yours, raise the gates. Or thus: raise your gates, O rulers: those that you supervise, that you guard.

And be raised up, O perpetual gates! The statement, demonstrating the greatness of the one who is about to go up and enter through the doors, says, *And be raised up*. As long as they remain here, they do not make room for his exaltation.

"Lifting" and "raising up" can also mean to remove them as obstacles, for so great a king has no need of an entryway.

And again: *And the king of glory shall enter.* The angels, who run before the Savior while he is being borne to heaven, say these words to the powers above, to the heavenly powers that raise the gates.

Next those inquire: *Who is this King of glory?* whom you announce beforehand that he will enter in, for whom it is necessary for us to raise and lift up the perpetual gates, not the temporal ones but the immortal ones?

Nearly similar to this is what is said in Isaiah as follows: "Who is this that comes from Edom, a redness of garments from Bosor? Why are your garments red?"[41] And against they ask. Even if this body, risen from the dead, and especially the former body of the Savior, does not have the characteristics of flesh because it has changed into a spiritual body, yet by the grace of him who ascends, traces are preserved in order to know from where the body that ascends has come. And for this reason, there is "a redness of garments from Bosor."

And just as, when he rose again from the dead and appeared to the disciples, desiring to assure them that the very body he used to possess has arisen, he showed them the marks of the nails, he showed them the wounds, not because that body has wounds, for it belongs to a hard and resistant body to bear wounds—but in order to convince them that he himself is the one who rose again. Next he entered in "after the doors were closed,"[42] lest from the sign of the proof of the resurrection they understand the resurrection poorly: that again after resurrection the risen body bears the characteristics of the corruptible body. In the same way also here, when he was being received into heaven, at the moment of his ascent he showed the characteristics of the flesh, not that they

---

[34]Ps 80:3, 7, 19 (79:4, 8, 20).
[35]Ps 18:9 (17:10).
[36]Is 62:11.
[37]Is 62:11.
[38]Is 40:9-10.
[39]Eph 2:2.
[40]Is 58:9 NETS.

[41]Cf. Is 63:1-2 NETS.
[42]Jn 20:19.

should remain. Nor did those things which he showed, such as eating and having the marks of the nails and other things, remain although he had them. [72] Not that we should eat did he eat after the resurrection, but in order that they should see that it was he himself, of whom he had spoken, who had risen again.

Luke says this same thing, indeed: "After his suffering he presented himself alive to them by many convincing proofs, appearing to them and eating together with them."[43] Observe that by eating together with them, he showed himself to be alive after his suffering.

[23:7-8] *Raise the gates, O rulers of yours! And be raised up, O perpetual gates, and the King of glory shall enter. Who is this King of glory?*

They inquire: "Of whom is this spoken that he will enter in, in order that we should open the doors for him and raise them up?" He says:

[23:8] *The Lord, strong and powerful, the Lord, powerful in battle.*

He composes the answer by naming his deeds. Just as in the beginning of the ascent on the mountain of the Lord, it was asked: "*Who will stand?*" and it was not answered, "This one," such as Abraham or John, but, "if there is someone *who is guiltless in hands and clean in heart,*" so also here he did not say "this one," but he showed the person of interest by his deed: *the Lord, strong and powerful, the Lord, powerful in battle.* He who puts to flight the kingdom on the earth, who overthrows the power of death, the devil, this one is also *strong and powerful, the Lord, powerful in battle.*

. . . comparing that prophecy that goes thus: "The Lord of powers will go forth and crush the war."[44] When he was coming down, these things were proclaimed beforehand. And when he rose again and was received into heaven, it is no longer said that "he will go forth," but after he came as *Lord, powerful in battle,* he overthrew the tyrants.

[23:9] *Raise the gates, O rulers of yours!*

Since they have said who it is for whom they have told them to raise the gates and open them, they say, since it is *the Lord, strong and powerful,* and *mighty in battle,* do not hesitate, do not delay.

And see: he says to those who are put in charge of the gates, "*Raise the gates!*" And since the gates, however, are rational, he also addresses himself to them, saying, "*And be raised up, O perpetual gates!*"

[23:9] *And be raised up, O perpetual gates! And the King of glory shall enter.*

Then he says, *The Lord of hosts, he is the King of glory.* Often armies are signified by the name "power." He is Lord of these powers, of the heavenly armies, for such powers also appeared to the shepherds to sing praise to God when Christ was born.[45] And he is the Lord of all these powers altogether, of the thousands and ten thousands who sing praise to him and serve him.

However, one can also understand powers in this way: each rational essence that pursues holiness is a power. Just as we say that a woman is musical or that a woman is educated, when she has these things, so also each essence that partakes of "Christ the power of God,"[46] is a power. He therefore is the Lord of these powers.

One must understand power, however, in two ways: either each rational [73] essence that participates in the power of the Savior himself is called "power," or the army of rational essences, which wage war in this way.

---

[43]Cf. Acts 1:3-4.
[44]Is 42:13.
[45]Cf. Lk 2:13.
[46]1 Cor 1:24 NRSV.

[23:10] *Who is this King of glory? The Lord of hosts, he is the King of glory.*

Do not seek who it is of whom we are speaking, for it is he, the Lord of powers. And you yourselves are powers, and each of you is a power according to the second sense. *Lord*, then. For this reason he said with authority: *he himself is the King of glory*. Paul also writes of this power and manifestation, "The mystery of godliness is great: He was revealed in the flesh, vindicated in spirit," and at the end, "He was taken up in glory."[47] The Lord who was taken up in glory is the Lord of glory; *he is the King of glory*.

It is not a bad time to include now a saying that is badly interpreted by some. By "the Lord of glory, who was crucified,"[48] they wish this one to be God the Word; for those who deny the perfect inhumanation say that "the Lord of glory, who was crucified," is God the Word himself. And there is in any case also the syllogism that those who stumble in this way repeat, and the thought comes from Apollinaris the heretic, who says that "the Word," by a change of essence, "became flesh,"[49] and he also has assembled such syllogisms as are found in his writings: "Christ was crucified. The crucified one is the King of glory. Therefore, Christ is the King of glory." Thus, however, they misapprehend the syllogism: "Christ is the King of glory. And Christ was crucified. Therefore, the King of glory was crucified."

And these people tell of monstrous things. The cross is plain: for it is the nailing up of a body. "They gouged my hands and feet."[50] He who says that God the Word, who is incorporeal, was crucified treats the cross as an allegory. However, if the cross is allegorized, so also will the resurrection be allegorized: all the things that took place are like dreams. These people also say this: for when they say, to deceive some people, "Is a body the same thing as a body?" and you say, "Yes," they reply, "Then truly this body is no different than God the Word." They are in fact two things. Therefore, we call them two things. For why is it absurd to call two things the temple and the one who dwells in the temple? For the body was called the temple of the Savior. And it is not said, "he was revealed as flesh," but "in flesh."[51] And again, "He was put to death in the flesh."[52] He has not said, "He was put to death as flesh." "Every spirit that confesses that he has come in the flesh."[53] This is why there are two: the flesh and the one who appeared in it, even if they do not wish it to be so.

Now, we are not speaking of the flesh without a soul, for this flesh without a soul, when it has been laid in the tomb [**74**], has become like leather, clearly. "My flesh will dwell in hope, because you will not abandon my soul to Hades."[54] So, if it were to remain in Hades, his flesh would not have the hope of resurrection.

Question: . . . ?

Earlier they asked: "Who is this King of glory?" and they heard an answer. Then, since the King of glory is not just anyone, they also ask a second time for a more perfect exactitude, and finally they received another answer: no longer the Lord, strong and *powerful, the Lord, powerful in battle*. For it was perhaps assumed that one of the powers under God gained the highest distinction. And therefore he says, *The Lord of hosts, he is the King of glory*. In this sense do I say that he is powerful, as Lord of the powers, and not as a power.

---

[47] 1 Tim 3:16.
[48] 1 Cor 2:8.
[49] Jn 1:14.
[50] Ps 22:16 (21:17 NETS).
[51] 1 Tim 3:16.
[52] 1 Pet 3:18 NRSV.
[53] Cf. 1 Jn 4:2 NRSV.
[54] Ps 16:9-10 (15:9-10).

PSALM 24 [25]

[24:1] *A psalm for David.*

The psalm is spoken of in relation to David; for one is said to be "of David" while another is *for David*. "Of David" is said when he himself was the one who had composed it or sung it. And it is called *for* him when it was produced for him, as when I also say, "This hymn of victory is for the athlete, for the boxer."

So it set down David as its model. However, the things that are said are not set down in relation to his person alone, but also if another may be found like him. And who is this David? He "who will carry out," it says, "all my wishes."[1] Let the psalm be said of all who carry out the wishes of God.

[24:1] *To you, O Lord, I lifted up my soul.*

It is not for everyone to say, *To you I lifted up my soul, O God.* Now, he alone lifts up his soul to God who is able to say, "My soul lives for him."[2]

God is on high. I do not mean this in a spatial sense—and these things have often been explained by us—but he is on high, with nothing being greater than he is.

Whenever someone, therefore, separates his own soul from things below, the devil and the causes of vice and vice itself, he raises it to God in order that it should live for him alone, in order that he should reconcile it to him, in order that it should become "united as one spirit" with him.[3]

To say this word is for someone great; it is the word of one who has an innocent soul. "If our hearts," it says, "do not condemn us, we have boldness before God."[4] When the heart is condemned because it is reproved by the conscience, it cannot say such things about itself.

However, such a person is rare, and perhaps because he is difficult to find he is regarded by some as though he does not exist. The author of Proverbs shows the scarcity further when he says: "Who will boast of keeping the heart clean, and who will be confident that he is clean from sin?"[5] He calls "clean in heart" the one who is rightly disposed toward piety and understands it. The one who has equipped himself according to the truth, that one has the heart pure. And the one who is free [75] from the practice of sin is confident that he is clean from sin. Now, that the truth and the things that are truly understood purify the soul and the heart, Peter the apostle writes, "having purified your souls by your obedience to the truth."[6] And James also writes, "Cleanse your hands, you sinners, and purify your hearts, you double-minded."[7] Those who make their own actions virtuous cleanse their hands, and those who cast away all double-mindedness purify their own soul, for he says, "And purify your hearts, you double-minded!" since for the most part those who think wickedly are double-minded. Sometimes they are at first stricken by an opinion and they are

---

[1] Acts 13:22 NRSV.
[2] Ps 22:29 (21:30 NETS).
[3] Cf. 1 Cor 6:17.
[4] 1 Jn 3:21 NRSV.
[5] Prov 20:9.
[6] 1 Pet 1:22 ESV.
[7] Jas 4:8 NRSV.

confined by it, and when they turn their attention to the facts and find that they are otherwise, they sometimes remain, somehow, in the false opinion that rules them.

The one who successfully completes the practical life, then, is shown to be clean from sin. The one who thinks truthful thoughts, who receives "the mysteries of the kingdom"[8] in his soul and is instructed according to them, has a pure heart.

This one, then, *lifts his soul to the Lord*. The one who lifts is not just anyone. Perhaps it is easy for anyone to say, but because of its own nature the thing is surpassingly difficult or nearly impossible to do. Moreover, this is so, since according to the apostle, "no one says, 'Jesus is Lord,' except by a holy spirit."[9] And these men themselves, when they say that God is their Lord, do not say it with the voice alone but with action and disposition. Whenever they are so disposed toward their Master that they practice whatever he desires and commands, they are his servants in reality, and since he repays the things that relate to the one who is really his servant, he is their Lord in reality.

[24:1-2] *O my God, I have put my trust in you; let me not be put to shame.*

He who has a precise understanding, having depended on it, speaks to all and is *not put to shame*. He who has trusted in virtue is not conquered by vice, for which reason he is *not put to shame*. To accept shame belongs to sinners, indeed. Some in fact "will arise to reproach and eternal shame."[10] Therefore, the word of the psalmist prays for there to be shame for those who are senseless: "Fill their faces," he says, "with dishonor"—he is speaking about wicked people—"and let them be ashamed and perish and know that your name is the Lord."[11] When those who are deep in evils sense this, they perish in that condition insofar as their qualities are evil. The unrighteous person, who has put his trust in unrighteous deeds, when he knows that he is unrighteous, is ashamed and perishes insofar as he is unrighteous, not insofar as he is a rational essence.

For this reason the apostles say, "We have renounced the shameful things that one hides."[12] We have renounced not only the obvious outrages that also create shame but also the hidden ones.

One can also understand this in this way: for some the effects of inebriation are secret. When they are exalted by wines, they were like those of whom Paul writes, "whose glory is in their shame";[13] in the things of which it is necessary to be ashamed, they themselves wish to be honored. For instance, it is possible to find men who wish to be honored for their drinking of much wine.

Question: How are these things secret?

I spoke of the "secret" in two senses: there are sins in the thoughts. Therefore, not only does the righteous person pray about the practices of sin, but also about the hidden sins, when he sends up his prayer: "Cleanse me from [76] my hidden faults!"[14]

Now, in another sense the unknown sins are called "secret." The saint, being confident about all the known transgressions, that they are far away from him, says: "Transgressions—who shall detect them?"[15] Rare is he who is aware of his transgressions. Therefore, since it is possible that I too am ignorant of them, "cleanse me from these!" "Spare your servant from strangers,"[16] for they are strangers to me, to my essence, both them and those who

---

[8] Mt 13:11.
[9] 1 Cor 12:3.
[10] Dan 12:2.
[11] Ps 83:16-18 (82:17-19).
[12] 2 Cor 4:2 NRSV.
[13] Phil 3:19.
[14] Ps 19:12 (18:13).
[15] Ps 19:12 (18:13 NETS).
[16] Ps 19:13 (18:14 LES2). The difference between the Hebrew and the Septuagint here hinges on how one takes the word *zēd*. Is it a reference to proud, insolent people or to internal dispositions?

activate them against me. And then he adds, "If they will not exercise dominion over me"—if the secret transgressions will not lord it over me—"then I shall be blameless." And he concludes, "and be cleansed from great sin."[17]

We began to say that these things are in the thoughts, and that they are so in such a way that they are undetected by the one who has them. How then is the one who is cleansed from these cleansed "from great sin"? You know that the word *great* is relative to something. To one who desires to be completely clean, even trivial sins seem to be great.

Now, I once took such an example: when a garment repeatedly gets dirty from elsewhere, even if someone should touch it or grab it, it does not seem to have received anything more. But immediately after it has been brought back from the fuller, even the touching of the fingers seems to be a defect, it seems to produce something unclean on it. The completely clean man, then, regards even the brief transgression in thought as a great sin.

One can also give the following explanation, which is able to help everyone: compared to the practice of sin, the sin in the thoughts is very small. When someone looks at a woman with desire[18] and checks his appetite at the point of the forepassion, he will not perform the practice of the sin. Therefore, when this forepassion is removed, someone is cleansed from great sin: he is cleansed from the practice of sin.

The one who says these things has arrived at such a state of cleanness that he says somewhere: "If I was contemplating injustice in my heart, let the Lord not listen."[19] He brings something damaging, as it were, and a penalty against himself, if he has injustice in his heart. He says, "Therefore God listened to me,"[20] where the implication of the phrase

"Therefore God listened to me" is that "I did not contemplate injustice in my heart." If I were contemplating injustice in my heart, let him not receive my prayer. "Therefore," then, "he listened to me."

I was saying the following: the one who has faith in God practices all the things that are worthy of being practiced, for I do not mean that he practices those things that God forbids.

I have already taken that passage: "And let them be put to shame and perish!"[21] And what follows after being put to shame and perishing other than knowing "that your name is the Lord"?[22] For example, God says to her who speaks presumptuously after doing and thinking evil things, "Be ashamed and receive your dishonor."[23] You were subjected to dishonor. You yourself have provided the cause, for you did those things that bring dishonor to you. Be ashamed, therefore, [77] of the things you did, and receive your dishonor, not by saying, "I did not sin." For she was saying to God, "I did not sin," so that God said, "Behold, I contend against you while you say, 'I have not sinned.'"[24] And I contend against you, not that I should condemn you, but that you should be ashamed and cease from dishonor.

[24:2] Nor let my enemies deride me.

My enemies deride me, then, when I say that I have put my trust in you but do things that produce shame.

They are my enemies; I am not their enemy. For this reason the Savior also says, "Love your enemies."[25] The qualifier "your" seems to be redundant, for it was only necessary to say, "Love enemies." However, since the servants of

---

[17] Ps 19:13 (18:14 NETS).
[18] Cf. Mt 5:28.
[19] Ps 66:18 (65:18 NETS).
[20] Ps 66:19 (65:19 NETS).
[21] Ps 83:17 (82:18).
[22] Ps 83:18 (82:19 NETS).
[23] Cf. Ezek 16:52 NETS.
[24] Jer 2:35.
[25] Lk 6:27.

Christ should not have enemies, but others wish to be their enemies, let them love them.

That passage in Aristotle seems in whatever way to be good for political behavior. Speaking about the primary and the secondary, he was saying, "We desire for our friends to be just in a primary sense, even when they are far away. We want our enemies to be just in an accidental way, in order that they should do no harm."[26] For their own sake, we also desire this. And the apostles of Christ pray for them, not in order that their enemies should not harm them but in order that those enemies should not be harmed.

[24:3] *Indeed, all those who wait for you will not be put to shame.*

The word *all* is often understood in Scripture as a universal negation; for we are not saying this, that some of those who wait are ashamed, while others are not, as the partial negation that says "Not all men are just" demonstrates. Here, then, it means "no one." None of those who wait for you is ashamed. And frequently in Scripture the universal negation is indicated by the universal affirmation taken in the opposite sense. You know that the affirmation in the opposite sense often follows the simple negation.

[24:3] *Let all who are lawless in vain be shamed.*

Understand the phrase *are lawless in vain* in this way: vice is exercised in vain, not to attract fame, not for reward. It is nonexistent; it has its being in something else. Therefore, when the one who has vice wishes to leave it, it no longer exists.

Some, however, either in ignorance or more like a sophist, say that virtue is also like this, because it also has its being in another. This, however, is a falsehood, for virtue exists essentially in God the Trinity. And by participation in the Trinity men possess the good, the righteous, and virtue. Therefore, even if they themselves are far removed from it, it exists. In God lies the virtue by which the virtuous are themselves virtuous.

But when vice is not exercised, it does not exist at all. For this reason many Scriptures teach that it does not exist. From this it is concluded that there are not two principles, opposite in essence, and that certain men are not wicked by design, as many of the heterodox wish: namely that no one is good or evil by his own free choice. Now, many absurd and impious conclusions follow these things. Look! If all who are good are such by design, [78] and the evil are essentially evil, all legislation is redundant, for the law cannot make the good good, nor the evil good. And if law is redundant, every kind of exhortation, incitement, counsel, and—in a word—the rational part of man itself is abolished, for one who does not possess choice and a will is not rational.

Moreover, even the appearance of the Savior is superfluous. Does he make the good person good? The good person is such out of himself. Or does he make the evil person to be good? By nature he cannot receive a participation in the good.

The sinner, therefore, sins *in vain*. Certainly in another psalm it is written of the great demon himself, the devil, the cause of all vice: "Crush the arm of the sinner and evildoer!"[27]

We have often said that the names that are given to the opposing power are names of a free will. So, for example, he is called "enemy," "devil," "Satan"—that is, adversary—and "sinner." And this, moreover, is the name of a free will. And every single time he is spoken of with an article: "See, I have given you authority to tread on snakes and scorpions, and over all the power"—not of an enemy but—"of the

---

[26] Aristotle, *Topics* 3.1 (116a).

[27] Ps 10:15 (9:36 NETS).

enemy."[28] And, "Deliver us"—not from an evil but—"from the evil one."[29] And here: "Crush the arm of the sinner and evildoer!"[30]

Then he adds, "His sin shall be sought out, and he shall no more be found on account of it."[31] Because of sin's nature, it is not found. Sometimes his sin is sought for and it is not found, because it is nowhere, not because it moved to another place, but it is not found because of itself, since it has no being in itself, but only by the one who enacts it.

And again, "And injustice lied to itself."[32] As we often say, "to lie" here we mean in this way: that the earth lies. Injustice, therefore, lies to itself, so that it no longer exists. It lies to itself because of its own nature.

So then, the lawless *act lawlessly in vain*, not so as to gain something but rather to be harmed. Those who had no knowledge of the law act lawlessly. I am speaking of that which is written, of the law that relates to teaching, for those who did not receive this are called *lawless*, as in the following passage: "Blessed are they whose lawless acts are forgiven!"[33]

Sin after the law, however, is not merely called lawlessness, but transgression: "Transgressions ensnare a man, and each one is bound by the ropes of his own sins."[34]

"Lawbreakers will not endure before your eyes."[35] The lawless person never comes before God at all. He does not come under the eyes of God except in another sense: according to the design of foreknowledge. However, they will not endure in the rank of the virtuous. They will not endure as the righteous do, of whom it is said, "The Lord's eyes are on the righteous."[36] By saying, then, "they will not endure," he shows that they once before have come, when they were keeping the law, but when they had become transgressors of it, they were cast out from the eyes of God. [79]

[24:4-5] *Make known to me your ways, O Lord, and teach me your paths. Guide me to your truth.*

God's *paths* are mentioned in two senses: either those that lead to him or those that he himself travels when he traverses the universe, it being necessary according to the design of foreknowledge or in order to benefit them that he also be in those who are receptive of him. Certainly he says, "I will live in them and walk among them."[37] And he who walks among them has paths that he himself travels.

Therefore we speak of God's *paths* in two senses: either as those that lead to him—and these are the virtues—or as those that he himself walks according to his own foreknowledge, judgment, administration, and grace. Therefore one must know the *paths* of God from him who makes them known.

And teach me your paths, either those that the ones who earnestly seek for you travel or those that you yourself travel when you traverse your deeds of grace.

And if it is permissible to expand on this: you know that before instruction some things must be familiar, for from what is known beforehand come scientific knowledge and proofs.

Therefore, *make known to me* both of *your ways*, for in this way will I learn *your paths*, by following those who wear them down by walking them, who travel ahead of me in good things, or because you went before "that we

---

[28] Lk 10:19 NRSV.
[29] Mt 6:13.
[30] Ps 10:15 (9:36 NETS).
[31] Ps 10:15 (9:36 NETS).
[32] Ps 27:12 (26:12 NETS). The Septuagint has "injustice lied within itself," and the Hebrew reads "and they are breathing out violence." The verbs for "lied" and "breathing out" are homonyms in Hebrew. The word *ḥāmās* is rendered both "violence" and "wrong."
[33] Ps 32:1 (31:1 LES2).
[34] Prov 5:22 NETS.
[35] Ps 5:5 (5:6 NETS).

[36] Ps 34:15 (33:16 NETS).
[37] 2 Cor 6:16.

should follow in your steps,"[38] having you as our model and rule of life.

Therefore before *teaching* comes *making known*. So they say that proofs and teachings come from what is familiar.

One can also understand it in this way, that common notions are known beforehand. And when we examine the teaching, we put it to the test by comparing it with common notions. For example, sometimes the teacher says something, and the common notion of the student anticipates it and he understands it, whether the teacher presented well or not. You will also find, therefore, in the case of these human, scientific examples, that knowledge is not advanced very well when the audience does not know beforehand what is necessary for them to know beforehand. For example, in many places this was said by us: that when someone is learning some things that are necessary to know beforehand in the process of learning, one must not speak with unclear words to that person, because they are not known to him.

Guide me to the truth.

After these practical virtues and those that relate to disposition comes the *guidance to the truth*; for "if you desire wisdom," he says, "keep the commandments, and the Lord will lavish her upon you."[39]

Wisdom and truth are the same thing, however. The Savior is truly said to be both: "Christ the power of God and the wisdom of God."[40] And he himself said, "I am the truth."[41]

[24:5] *And teach me, because you are God, my Savior.*

You are my God, because you created me; you are my savior, because you desired that I be made better. You, therefore, became my teacher! As he is creator, so also is he teacher.

[24:5] *And for you I waited all day long.*

I waited for you all the time of my life, in order to have you as my teacher and Savior; for *to you I lifted up my soul*, and to no other. I did not invoke another, to make known to me your ways **[80]** and to teach me your paths, but I asked you to become my teacher in these matters as well.

In many passages the whole time of our life is called *day*, according to the word: "For on account of you we are being killed the whole day,"[42] instead of which the apostle has written "all day."[43]

The whole time of the life of the saints can also be called *day*, because they are always in illumination: they are illumined by the true Light, the "Sun of Righteousness."[44] This day is not interrupted by night; it is unbroken.

So was it said in a psalm, "Our age is for the illumination of your face."[45] The life, however, which after extending to this moment passes through it, is called "age," for "he will be your servant for the age."[46] "I will not eat meat for the age,"[47] that is, "through my life." Since, then, the time of our life has served to illuminate your face—for we have come to proclaim your appearance beforehand—our age has completely served to the illumination of your face, to illuminate men and to manifest your visitation to them.

[24:6] *Remember your compassions, O Lord, and your mercies, for they are from the age.*

For if I called on you and lifted my soul to you, and requested other things to be given

---

[38] 1 Pet 2:21.
[39] Sir 1:26 NRSV.
[40] 1 Cor 1:24 NRSV.
[41] Jn 14:6.
[42] Ps 44:22 (43:23 LES2).
[43] Cf. Rom 8:36.
[44] Mal 4:2 (3:20).
[45] Ps 89:8 (90:8). The word translated as "eternity" in the Septuagint shares the same root ('lm) as the word translated as "secret sins" in English translations.
[46] Deut 15:17.
[47] 1 Cor 8:13.

me from you, yet I still do not ask these things worthily. Out of your compassions and mercies you bestow those things in agreement with the passage: "So it depends not on human will or exertion, but on God who shows mercy."[48] For even when we have done all things that are in our power, by the mercy of God do we do our utmost to reach their perfection. Since you are compassionate, hear me; since you are merciful, receive my prayers.

And your mercies, for they are from the age.

For you did not begin to be merciful yesterday or the day before that. You are eternal; you are eternally good.

[24:7] *Do not remember the sin of my youth and my ignorance.*

You see that he prays about prior ignorance and sin in accordance with the compassion and mercy of God, for it is no longer repentance that sends up a prayer for sins that are still being practiced. Repentances are for those who have gone beyond their sins. He says in any case, *Do not remember my sins and my ignorance* that I possess, but do not now possess, but belong to my youth.

The following is also possible, however: when the ignorant person is of such an age, he is young in the youth of opinion, in the untried strength of habit.

One can always find, then, those who confess and after words of repentance about sins that have passed, saying as follows: "We have sinned, we have acted lawlessly, we were impious."[49] How indeed could it be possible otherwise? The one who repents asks for virtue. How, then, is he who is still in sins able to possess or receive virtue? Indeed, "turn from evil and do good."[50]

[24:7] *In your mercy, remember me.*

Question: *Remember me?*

This is an idiom in Scripture that means "Know me."

[24:7] *According to your goodness, O Lord.*

Do not remember me on account of my virtue!

[24:8] *Kind and upright is the Lord.*

The one who is *kind* with *uprightness* is good, for often the word *kind* is understood as an accusation [81]: "Bad company ruins kind morals."[51] The *kind* morals are not understood here in a praiseworthy sense but instead as superficial morals.

And again the word *simple* is similar: "A simple person believes every word,"[52] that is, a naive person. And of the heterodox Paul writes, "By smooth talk and flattery they deceive the hearts of the simple-minded."[53]

[24:8] *For this reason he makes laws for sinners in the way.*

If he were harsh, if he were not kind, he would not *make laws in the way* of salvation *for sinners*, but he would repay them with chastisement. Therefore, he also *makes laws for sinners* themselves *in the way*, in order that by following this way they should attain salvation.

And see! He does not say, "for those who have sinned," but "for those who are sinners." By reproving those who are still sinners with exhortations, by establishing laws for them, he leads them into the way.

Question: *Is he speaking of the written law?*

This passage can be understood in all the senses of the word *law*.

---

[48]Rom 9:16 NRSV.
[49]Dan 9:5.
[50]Ps 34:14 (33:15); 37:27 (36:27 LES2).

[51]1 Cor 15:33.
[52]Prov 14:15.
[53]Rom 16:18 NRSV.

[24:9] *The meek he will guide in justice.*

He guides the meek judiciously, for again meekness also seems to the many to signify superficiality. However, when they are also guided with discernment, they possess a perfect virtue, which the Savior taught them to have, saying, "Learn from me; for I am gentle and humble in heart."[54]

The phrase *in justice* can also be understood in this way: because he judges these *meek* ones as able to receive help, *he guides* them.

However, the first interpretation in particular is appropriate to the passage because they come on the way with discernment when they have God as their guide. Or does he not guide them, he who says, "Learn from me; for I am gentle"?[55]

[24:10] *All the ways of the Lord are mercy and truth.*

In many places of the Scriptures *mercy* is joined together with *truth*. The *truth* is something great; if I may say so, it is beyond men. Observe, however, that all the rational and supernatural beings that remain above need the *truth*.

Here, however, we have a need of *mercy*, in order to be able to know the *truth*. Now, it was said in the verses before this: *By your ways, O Lord, and your paths, guide me to your truth*. So, a beginning of traveling these blessed ways comes from the *mercy* of God, and an end comes from his *truth*.

[24:10] *For those who seek his covenant and his testimonies.*

Not to those who merely *seek* but to those who seek intensely. There are those who search out the Scriptures, and those *seek* God's *covenant*. To search out and to seek are the same thing.

And his testimonies: his testimonies are the oracles of Scripture that have been attested by him. You know that what is testified cannot be gainsaid. Therefore, the undeniability of the divine instructions is often signified by the name *testimonies*.

Question: What did he himself attest?

That which he himself confirmed. Now, it is also possible for that which is irrefutable and suffers no annulment to be called *testimonies*, not because they were attested by someone but because their nature is of such a kind that they attest [82] to the truth. "And the witness in heaven," it says, "is faithful."[56]

With respect to God, when God is said to be attested, we are not claiming that the one who attests to him establishes him. John has come "to testify to the light."[57] Indeed, John, who testified to the light, did not provide the light with credibility and proof. The one who attests to knowledge shows himself to be knowledgeable, and the one who attests to virtue is shown to be virtuous. So indeed, those who are pleased with their pursuit and compete as they ought to are called witnesses. They showed themselves to be lovers of the truth; they showed themselves to be knowers of the truth. They did not establish the truth; but they established themselves. Therefore, things that are worthy of one who attests them are often called *testimonies*.

[24:11] *For the sake of your name, O Lord.*

Not for the sake of our zeal or our way of life, but *because of your name*. They also say this in another psalm: "Not to us, O Lord, not to us, rather to your name give glory."[58] For since we

---

[54] Mt 11:29 NRSV.
[55] Mt 11:29 NRSV.
[56] Ps 89:37 (88:38 NETS).
[57] Jn 1:7 NRSV.
[58] Ps 115:1 (113:9 NETS).

take our name from you and you are called our God, act because of your name.

[24:11] *And you will expiate my sin, for it is great.*

We clarify the phrase *it is great* in this way: when he desires such things, that the ways be made known to himself, that he be led to the truth, how does he have a great sin? Of the saying, "from my hidden transgressions, clear me,"[59] it was said before that even the small stain is a great sin for one who is wholly clean.

[24:12] *Who is the person who fears the Lord?*

Next he asks: *who, then, is the person who fears* God? Most of us think in this way; we often say as follows: "I merely wish to fear God." However, we do not understand what we are saying, for "fear of God surpasses everything,"[60] as the Scripture itself says. And again, "those who fear him have no want."[61] If the one who fears God has no want, he is completely satisfied.

The words *Who is the one?* can indicate scarcity and are an interrogative.

[24:12] *He will set a law for him in the way he chose.*

In the way God himself chooses.

It can also mean, however, *in the way* the man *chose*, for virtue, strictly speaking, is called "chosen."[62] Just as what is worthy of being loved is loveable, even when no one loves it, and what is worthy of being hated is detestable, even when no one hates it, so the "chosen" is to be chosen, even when no one chooses it; for even evils can be chosen, although they are not "choice." Rather, the faculty of choice about these things has been overthrown.

He will set a law for him in the way he chose refers either to the lawgiver himself or the one who is receiving the law. Both interpretations, however, are correct.

[24:13] *His soul will abide in prosperity.*

This man who fears the Lord has his soul abiding in prosperity.

[24:13] *And his offspring shall inherit the land.*

His offspring does not always indicate his bodily offspring—however, the sons of many holy men were proven to be wicked—but the offspring that is begotten [83] in teaching and the imitation of virtue.

[24:14] *The Lord is the strength of those who fear him.*

Next he speaks of the greatness of the one who fears God. Those who *fear* God have no other *strength* than he himself whom they fear. He is their strength, he is their king, he rules over them.

And his name has become the property *of those who fear him.*[63] It is not the possession of men, but of those who fear, for he has indeed given it to all, but it has become the possession of those who fear.

[24:14] *And his covenant is for showing to them.*

When covenants have been sealed, the written contents are no longer visible to the heirs. This *covenant*, then, does not always remain sealed, but at some point it will be unbound, in order

---

[59] Ps 19:12 (18:13).
[60] Sir 25:11 NRSV.
[61] Ps 34:10 (33:10 NETS).
[62] The word for "chosen" (*hairetē*) sounds like the word for "virtue" (*aretē*) in Greek.

[63] Ps 25:14 (24:14). This line of the Greek text corresponds to no Hebrew text.

that the inheritance should be rendered by what is written within.

So *he will show it to them*. And since in many passages it calls the divine word, both the old and the new, the word before his appearance and after it, a *covenant*, it is necessary for this covenant to be made clear; it is necessary for it to be unbounded. And it is a unbounded when the things declared beforehand are fulfilled by their consummation, according to the word: "so that what had been spoken was fulfilled."[64] For then it becomes firm, when the one who arranged it has died. For then comes the unbinding of the covenant. Even though it is not unbound because there is no objection to it, it has been effectively unbound; for when the things that are arranged are rendered, then the covenant has been unbound for those who have received them.

[24:15] *My eyes are ever toward the Lord, because it is he who will pull my feet out of a snare.*

Observe that unless we examine the words precisely, occasionally contradictions are found. The statement *"My sin is great!"*[65] no longer accords with the one who says, *"My eyes are ever toward the Lord,"* for one who always pays attention to the Lord with his eyes has no sin at all; he has a clean heart. In this way it is even possible to see God himself.[66]

So it is not that he sometimes sees and sometimes does not; when he keeps on having his eyes always toward the Lord, he says, "And I am continually with you."[67] And when I am with you, I do not sin. If someone does not part from God, he does not sin. "Those who distance themselves from you," then, "will perish."[68]

---

[64]Cf. Mt 2:23.
[65]Ps 25:11 (24:11).
[66]Cf. Mt 5:8.
[67]Ps 73:23 (72:23 NETS).
[68]Ps 73:27 (72:27 NETS).

Question: *And his covenant?*

The covenant of God is shown when someone is shown to be worthy of receiving what is promised in it. And the covenant of God has something more extraordinary than other covenants: human covenants are unbounded one single time. God, however, releases his daily. This one, then, shows his covenant to those who draw near to him and to those who are worthy.

Just as the things of God are superior in all other matters—for I was saying that this perceptible light, when it comes into our midst, illumines the one who has an eye; it does not provide assistance to the blind man. The light of God, however, when it appears, both bestows sight and illumines it all at the same time. Indeed, to those who are ignorant of him, to those who are blind, when he arises, he gives both the possession of the intellect's eye and the ability to apprehend the light—so his covenant is not unbound **[84]** only once, but when someone today makes himself worthy of being the son and heir of the one who arranged the covenant, then it is shown to him.

My eyes are ever toward the Lord.

Since "the Lord's eyes are on the righteous,"[69] it is necessary also for the righteous to have their *eyes* always *toward* him. They do not look at him at one time and then not look to him at another, but look rather at one of the forbidden things; for in the same way "no one can serve two masters,"[70] so no one can have eyes for God and for vice or the first doer of vice.

God is an intelligible essence, seen by the eyes of the mind. When the eyes of the mind become directed toward this one alone, they see nothing else. They are not inclined to see inferior things when they see God, just as the one who serves God is not inclined to serve Mammon.

---

[69]Ps 34:15 (33:16 NETS).
[70]Mt 6:24 NRSV.

The words "is not inclined" I mean in this sense, however: the unrighteous person is not inclined to practice righteousness. Indeed, I do not mean it in this sense, as when I say, "The human is not inclined to fly," but insofar as a righteous person is not inclined toward sin, and when he is a sinner, he is not inclined to virtue.

My eyes, then, *are ever toward the Lord.* I always see him. The one who sees God does not sin. "No one who sins has either seen him or known him."[71]

And observe the piety of the saints! When he by his free will was directing his eyes toward the Lord, that is, was not sinning, he attributes to God the achievement of sinlessness and says, "Since *my eyes are ever toward the Lord,* for this reason I am removed from the trap that sin prepares, for *it is he that will pull my feet out of a snare.*"

Some of the ancients made an investigation, which is useful to mention, because sometimes the eye of the inner man is named in the singular and at other times in the plural. So is it said in the Song of Songs, "You heartened us with one of your eyes."[72] "My eye brought down tears."[73] "My eye was troubled due to anger."[74] And sometimes it is in the plural: "I lifted up my eyes to the mountains,"[75] and in the present verse: *My eyes are ever toward the Lord.* And, "with the eyes of your heart enlightened."[76]

We possess a double way of knowing, for there is a knowledge of the truth when the mind receives into itself the form of each thing that is known. There are visible and invisible works of God.[77] And from the majesty and beauty of these things the one who created them is seen.[78] However, the eye that sees invisible things is our intellect, the pure heart, which also sees God.[79]

Now, we also possess the perceptive faculty of the eyes. And when it concerns itself with God's visible creatures in a manner that accords with how they were created and are by nature, then this faculty is sound. Come then! But when we, looking on the sun, suppose it to be a god, or looking on the heavenly order, believe them to be a horoscope, this eye does not see rightly; for it was necessary "that God's invisible attributes be clearly perceived from the creation of the world [**85**] in the things that have been made."[80] The invisible attributes of God are seen when we concern ourselves with God's visible creatures and in this way perceive the invisible attributes of God from the creation of this visible world.

We cannot see the technical skills and the thoughts in the mind of men since they belong to the invisible intellect. However, we receive the impression of the intellect from the works that are devised or from the scientific ideas, by which thought or skill the intellect has performed.

Observe with precision the skill of the inventor; he is the one who can receive into his own mind the reasons for the contrivances of inventors. It is similar with the others as well: we call that person a physician who knows the healing arts as he should, as the discipline dictates.

So when someone sees the invisible as he should—and I mean "as he should" in the sense of "as it is within his reach"—and he also sees the invisible creatures of God, among which is the soul of man, he has this *eye always looking toward* God and clean.

When he receives the perceptible creatures and the providence that relates to them rightly,

---

[71] 1 Jn 3:6 NRSV.
[72] Cf. Song 4:9 NETS.
[73] Cf. Jer 9:18; 13:17.
[74] Ps 6:7 (6:8 NETS).
[75] Ps 121:1 (120:1 NETS).
[76] Eph 1:18 NRSV.
[77] Cf. Col 1:16.

[78] Cf. Wis 13:5.
[79] Cf. Mt 5:8.
[80] Rom 1:20.

he also possesses the desire of the senses—I do not mean this desire of the body, but the understanding of the things that are perceptible, visible—rightly placed, and so he has *eyes that are ever toward the Lord*.

He speaks as a servant. And a servant is one who serves God, who confesses his lordship both in his disposition and his action, "who does the will of the Father in heaven."[81]

Because it is he that will pull my feet out of a snare.

Even if poachers and hunters lie in wait for me, because they wish to take me and to ensnare my foot as though in a trap, but I, having my *eyes always toward the Lord*, do not suffer this.

Indeed, in many passages of the divine instruction the deceits of evil people are called "traps." "In this trap, which they hid, their own foot was caught."[82] Often the enemies of the truth prepare traps, and in the traps they prepare for others, they themselves are caught. Certain stories like this are also in the history. Haman made ready a post to crucify the righteous Mordecai, and he himself was crucified on it.[83]

And of the great demon itself it is said, "A pit he dug and cleaned it out, and he shall fall into the hole he made."[84] Even if these things do not take place in this life, yet at least in the age to come he is trapped in the trap he prepared.

Many indeed pay attention to these sensible things and regard them as wrong, among which is the saying, "All who take the sword will perish by the sword."[85] This, however, is not incontrovertible. Rather, it is saying this: those who take a sword will fall under punishment. Now, in many places of the Scriptures the sword signifies punishment, as in the passage: "I will make my arrows drunk, and my sword will devour the blood of the wounded."[86] And, "My sword has become drunk in heaven,"[87] for he touched even those who had sinned there and as a form of punishment he dragged them here.

"Our soul was rescued like a sparrow from the snare of the fowlers."[88] And observe the difference: perhaps some of the ones hunted by these wicked fowlers are completely captured within traps, while others are taken only with the feet. Those, therefore, who say, "Our soul was rescued like a sparrow" were wholly ensnared; indeed, it says at once, "The snare was crushed, and we were rescued."[89]

Here, however, since the saint has *eyes that are always toward the Lord*, he says of the very littlest sins, "*My feet* have come into a *snare*." Therefore, draw them out from there, that becoming consequently unimpeded, they might run the way of your commandments and say, "Without lawlessness I ran and went straight on."[90]

[24:16] *Look upon me and have mercy on me.*

Whenever God *looks upon* them, *mercy* comes to those on whom he looks, for they are worthy of being seen; the sinner, indeed, is far away from the eyes of God and from his face. Adam, for example, when he sinned together with Eve, "hid from the face of the Lord God."[91] They do not endure being seen by the face of God, especially when they know for themselves that they have sinned.

The insolent Cain also removed himself from the face of God, for "Cain went away."[92]

---

[81]Mt 7:21; 12:50.
[82]Ps 9:15 (9:16 NETS).
[83]Cf. Esther 7:9-10.
[84]Ps 7:15 (7:16 NETS).
[85]Mt 26:52 NRSV.
[86]Cf. Deut 32:42.
[87]Is 34:5.
[88]Ps 124:7 (123:7 NETS).
[89]Ps 124:7 (123:7 NETS).
[90]Ps 59:4 (58:5).
[91]Gen 3:8.
[92]Gen 4:16 NETS.

He who goes away, however, does this voluntarily. Indeed, it was said of Adam and Eve that "the Lord sent them forth."[93] Although they desired to be inside, he sent them out, because it was no longer useful for them to remain inside. Nevertheless, they were smitten with the desire. The wicked are not so as the one who departs from the Lord's face. These are the ones of whom it is written, "Lawbreakers will not endure before your eyes."[94] Voluntarily, however, they come away from the eyes of God, for the eyes of God, when they look on them, illuminate those on whom they look.

[24:16] *Because I am only-begotten and poor.*

Aetius, the leader of the faction of Eunomius, was saying to some: "As though you were giving him great gifts, you say that Christ is the *only-begotten* of God. Many other creatures are also only-begotten. The sun, for example, is only-begotten."

I say to him: It is not the same thing for something to be *only-begotten* and for a child to be only-begotten or a son to be only-begotten, say I. These things, then, that are called "only-begotten" by some are not mentioned with the qualifying addition "son," "from the Father," or "child." The Savior, however, when he is named elsewhere, is mentioned with such a qualifying addition: "And we have seen his glory, glory as of the only-begotten Son from the Father."[95] Now, one who is the only-begotten from the Father is the Father's only Son. And again: "God so loved the world that he gave his only-begotten Son."[96] I say: when there is an only-begotten Son, it is therefore impossible for there to be another son of that one who has an only-begotten son.

However, none of the creatures is only-begotten. For even if the sun is only-begotten, it is not an only-begotten creature, not an only-begotten product, but an only-begotten sun. For example, we speak in this way about an only-begotten child of humans, not that the child is the one and only one, but that it is the one and only child **[87]** of that person. And there is the passage, "He who does not believe is condemned already, because he has not believed in the name of the only-begotten Son of God."[97]

Since, then, the one who says these words is not an only-begotten son, we will consider how this is said in a different sense; for even if you take the man David, he was not only-begotten. He had six other brothers.[98] In this way, then, it is necessary to understand the word "only-begotten" that was used here as the passage says, "And I alone am left, and they are seeking to take my life."[99] And in whatever sense they say that the sun is only-begotten because there is no other sun, when the saint is isolated and distinguished from other men by his way of life and his contemplative vision, he is only-begotten.

I am only-begotten, then, *and poor*. Nonetheless, the one who is *poor* in this way is rich, for "he is rich in speech and knowledge of every kind."[100] But in comparison with God, who looks on him and bestows him with gifts, he is poor. Indeed, as Abraham said, "Since I have begun to speak to the Lord, though I am earth and ashes"[101]—for he did not call himself "earth and ashes" in an absolute sense, but "since I have begun to speak to the Lord"—so also Moses, even though he had been trained in all the wisdom of the Egyptians and was capable with words, called himself "weak-voiced and slow-tongued since

---

[93] Gen 3:24.
[94] Ps 5:5 (5:6 NETS).
[95] Jn 1:14.
[96] Jn 3:16.
[97] Jn 3:18.
[98] Cf. 1 Sam 16:10.
[99] Rom 11:3; cf. 1 Kings 19:10.
[100] 1 Cor 1:5.
[101] Gen 18:27.

you began to speak to your attendant."[102] And this saint, then, even if he is rich—for nothing is richer than having one's *eyes ever toward the Lord*—yet, in comparison with the one who looks on him and has mercy, he saw himself as poor.

However, it is also possible to explain *only-begotten* as follows: I have only one soul. This soul, when it is ensnared, you will draw out of the trap, for it is unique to me.

[24:17] *The afflictions of my heart were broadened.*

I say: the *afflictions* of everyone are not *broadened* but of the one who bears them nobly. The apostle writes this, "We are afflicted in every way, but not crushed."[103]

Those who know the language of the Hebrews say that being crushed, when it is mentioned together with affliction, signifies the following: being afflicted in the faculty of the will, being crushed because one bears the things that afflict one nobly, as Job did: "although afflicted in every way, he was not crushed."[104] For how was he crushed, who says, "As it seemed good to the Lord, so it turned out; blessed be the name of the Lord"?[105] And the apostles who went forth "from the council, because they were considered worthy to suffer dishonor for the sake of the name,"[106] were not afflicted in their disposition, but they began to rejoice. Even in the case of perceptible things, however, the one who competes in expectation of a crown, seeing it lying there before his eyes, bears the blows nobly and rejoices because, although he is buffeted, he does not yield.

The word *affliction*, then, when it is joined together with *narrowness*, signifies the following: not being afflicted in the mind but bearing affliction nobly. When each of them occurs separately in Scripture, what *affliction* means, this *narrowness* means as well: "In affliction and narrowness: from these are a lion and a lion's whelp, and asps and the offspring of asps."[107] When *affliction* and [**88**] *narrowness* occur, that is, when the external things that afflict come, and the disposition is afflicted, and the faculty of choice of each person is afflicted, then moral characters become evident, the lion shows itself to be a lion—whether noble and strong or impetuous, for it shows both kinds of character. Whenever the righteous person, confident as a lion, endures afflictions nobly, then he appears as a lion in a praiseworthy sense. But when some impetuous person is crushed by affliction, he is shown to be fierce and the "whelp of a lion." In the case of lions, some are mature, while others are immature and like the whelps of lions and lions' cubs. You will also find it so with the wills of men; some are lions completely, while others took their birth just recently. The witnesses of the truth, when afflicted, were not crushed.

[24:17] *And bring me out of my necessities.*

He calls *afflictions* here *necessities*. And in other places it says, "And they cried to the Lord, and he rescued them from their necessities."[108]

One must certainly not follow the opinion of those who teach astrology, for those people say this: that necessity assigns certain things to men. However, when someone is godly and is wise in God, he is free from the things that are fated. Therefore, even the learned ones among the Egyptians, of whom is Hermes Tresmegistus, say that the wise person is no

---

[102]Cf. Ex 4:10 NETS.
[103]2 Cor 4:8 NRSV.
[104]Cf. 2 Cor 4:8.
[105]Job 1:21 NETS.
[106]Cf. Acts 5:41.

[107]Is 30:6.
[108]Cf. Ps 107:6 (106:6).

longer subject to necessity, that he is free from the world.[109] As the Savior says that it is possible for a person, while in the world, to be no longer of it,[110] whenever he has his thought above and his citizenship in heaven, so those learned Egyptians speak vaguely from what belongs to us, when they say that the wise person annuls necessity.

Certainly, some of those who concern themselves with astrology understand such words in this way: "Knots are the things to which I am subject. Free me from these; loose necessity!"

We do not understand the passage in this way; rather, he calls proofs "necessities." And this is also conveyed in Job: "Six times he will deliver you from necessities, and the seventh time no harm shall touch you."[111] What he is saying is as follows: the world was created in six days. The one who does not overcome it is under six necessities. This number, however, is perfect.[112] What he is saying is as follows: the one who loves the world and its parts and lives in this way is under a perfect necessity. But when he surpasses the world and rises above it, he takes a day of rest on the seventh day from the works of the world. And when he arrives on the seventh day, which is sanctified, pure, and reserved "for the people of God,"[113] he is untouchable.

However, this "touching" signifies drawing near to it and doing it harm. Therefore, when he says, "It is well for a man not to touch a woman,"[114] he does not mean this: that touching a woman's body by making contact with it is evil.

Bring me out of my necessities.

Now, since we have given our interpretation, observe what appears to me. I say: "*Bring me out of my necessities*, that by no longer being compelled by sin [89] I should become free for virtue. Then, in fact, do you bring me out of these, when you grant me forgiveness of sins."

However, one can also take this in this way: he calls *necessities* the future chastisements that are painful and oppressive.

The afflictions of my heart were broadened.

We do not often dispute about a variant reading. Now, however, it is necessary to know that it reads "they were broadened," and not "they were multiplied," for the one who is afflicted in the heart is no longer virtuous but even wicked. Now, the one who understands that the one saying these things is wicked, him who has his *eyes always toward the Lord*, does not have confidence in the words before this verse and those after it.

[24:18] *See my humiliation and my trouble, and forgive all my sins.*

He toils in this world, because he is still loaded down with "the body of humiliation."[115] It corresponds with this evil to be humiliated as well, for often affliction is called humiliation, according to the saying, "You humbled us in the place of affliction."[116] As we have come into the place of affliction, therefore we were humbled.

One can also say this: when he was having his eyes looking always toward the Lord, then he saw himself as humble, even though he is righteous, as I said about Abraham: he does not see himself as "earth and ashes" at any other time, save when "he began to speak to the Lord."[117]

---

[109] See A. J. Festugière, *La révélation d'Hermès Trismégiste* (Paris: Association Guillaume Budé, 1945), fragment 20.
[110] Cf. Jn 15:19; 17:14, 16.
[111] Job 5:19.
[112] A perfect number is one that is composed of the sum of all its factors, itself not being counted. The factors of 6 are 3, 2, and 1. And 6 = 3 + 2 + 1.
[113] Cf. Heb 4:9.
[114] 1 Cor 7:1 NRSV.

[115] Phil 3:21.
[116] Ps 44:19 (43:20).
[117] Gen 18:27.

[24:19] *See my enemies, that they multiplied, and with an unjust hatred they hated me.*

The one who is hated for no other reason than that he is virtuous is hated with an unjust hatred. So, for example, were the disciples of Jesus hated. Concerning these enemies, he teaches them to offer up prayer: "Pray for those who hate you; love your enemies!"[118]

We ourselves do not hate anyone, for it was said, "You shall not hate any man; you shall love every man." Those ones, however, do hate. And it is not our sin to be hated by some, but rather our misfortune, when we ourselves do not provide a pretext for the hatred.

He also says, "See my enemies, that they multiplied, and with an unjust hatred they hated me." They do not hate me with a just hatred. They were hating me as though I were unjust, as though I were arrogant. However, since they hate me while I am none of these things, they hate me unjustly.

Such people are also multiplied. For if the righteous person is hated because of virtue, he has all the virtues, according to what is often said by us about the concatenation of the virtues. The unrighteous hate the righteous, the intemperate the temperate, the vain the humble, and those who are involved in vice in general hate the righteous person.

The righteous person, therefore, is one, even if he possesses all the virtues, for vice divides those who possess it, for it is impossible for one person to have all the vices. The coward, therefore, cannot be rash, the superstitious cannot be impious, the impostor cannot be a fool. **[90]** In a certain sense, the Egyptian woman also hated Joseph when she made him experience chains and imprisonment like an evildoer.[119] This hatred was unjust. Jezebel was against Naboth and contrived his death.[120] This hatred was also unjust. And Herodias, the wife of Herod, brought about a most miserable death against John, as much as it was possible for her.[121]

The situations of those who are hated unjustly due to the decree and judgment of foreknowledge are partly clarified and partly not. The situation of John has become clear after his death, and the situation of others before their death: Susanna and Joseph.[122] Whether or not vengeance occurs here, no one can search out why it is here or not here, for these things occur due to God's judgment; indeed "his judgments are unsearchable."[123]

[24:20] *O guard my soul and rescue me; may I not be put to shame, because I hoped in you.*

When you *guard my soul* exempt from punishment and unharmed, I know that I will be delivered, for I am either rescued from evildoers or I receive a crown because I was afflicted.

[24:21] *The innocent and upright were joining me, because I waited for you, O Lord.*

I not only benefited myself, *because I waited* with the saving endurance—and endurance brings salvation, for "the one who endures to the end will be saved"[124]—I benefited many *because I waited for you*; I began to have many friends.

Now, he calls *innocent* here those who are free of vice, not those who are naive. In any case, the *upright* were joined closely with them. In relation to the approval of vice they are *innocent*, and in relation to the acquisition of

---

[118]Cf. Lk 6:27; Mt 5:44.
[119]Cf. Gen 39:17-20.
[120]Cf. 1 Kings 21:13 (20:13).
[121]Cf. Mk 6:19-28.
[122]Sus 60-62 and Gen 41:37-45.
[123]Rom 11:33.
[124]Mt 10:22 NRSV.

virtue they are *upright*. For example, the one who turns away from evil so that he no longer practices it has become *innocent*. And since, after turning away from evil, the doing of good takes its turn, the one who turns away from evil becomes *upright*. It is also possible to call the same people *innocent* and *upright* in this or another sense.

And one can also understand it in this way: those who are free of vice in practice are *innocent*, while those who think pious thoughts are *upright*.

[24:22] *Redeem Israel, O God, out of all his afflictions!*

Since he himself has succeeded in the request that concerns himself, he desires also for Israel, that is, for everyone who sees clearly and possesses understanding, to be provided with the same salvation, to be freed from affliction by God the redeemer.

However, it is not unreasonable to understand these things in relation to the Lord's Man also. Now, beginning from the psalm where we began,[125] we have said that the things spoken about the Man who is in the Savior are common to all the righteous, while those things are his alone that belong to him as God.

---

[125] This line suggests that the lecture series begins with Ps 20 as we have it. There Didymus discusses this theme at length.

PSALM 25 [26]

[25:1] *Vindicate me, O Lord, because I walked in my innocence.*

This is the voice of one who is exceedingly confident before God. Now, he whose heart does not condemn him, as the great disciple and Evangelist John writes in his epistle, has confidence before God: **[91]** "If our hearts do not condemn us, we have boldness before God."[1] The whole psalm, then, is offered up with great boldness.

And he speaks of some things as though they were already accomplished, and he relates other things as though they are present and being performed, and he declares other things as a kind of prayer of the speaker, for he says this, *Vindicate me, O Lord, because I walked in my innocence.* He did not say, "I will walk," but "*I walked.*"

And here he calls being devoid of malice *innocence*. The one who is converted according to the guidance of Jesus and becomes like children,[2] that one has come in innocence, and such a person is on the one hand an adult in his thinking, and on the other an infant in vice, as the apostle writes, "In your thinking," he says, "be adults, but be infants in evil."[3] One who is an infant in vice is not ignorant of it—for how would he be an infant in it, if he were ignorant of it?—rather, he does not enact it.

Indeed, he says this: *I walked in my innocence*. Here it is also different. In both ways he indicates being devoid of malice, as I said before, that one who is converted like children.

One who is converted, then, according to Jesus' teaching and becomes like children does not behave foolishly. He is not referring to the stupidity of infants but their inactivity toward evil things. I was also saying that the child, even when lying with a woman, receives no desire for her. Therefore, when someone becomes mature, he becomes free from the desire for intemperance in this way; he is an infant in vice and, being converted, has become like children.

For see that these children who are so in their period of life, when they are not converted, are so: silly and naive. One who is mature, however, after being converted has become such a one that he is free to be an infant in this way, to be innocent in this way. Now, in the case of newborns this does not appear; it is not free to be so, but its age does not permit it to have mature thinking.

The phrase *I walked* does not indicate interruption and cessation here but that I began this long ago or I began this from my mother's womb, for he says, "Upon you I leaned from my birth; from my mother's belly it was you who sheltered me."[4] And the saints also, of whom it was said, "Those whom he foreknew he also predestined to be conformed to the image of his Son,"[5] have this confidence.

[25:1] *And since I hope in God, I shall not grow weak.*

He no longer says, "I hoped," as he says, "*I walked.*" *Hope before God*, however, makes him

---

[1] Jn 3:21 NRSV.
[2] Cf. Mt 18:3.
[3] Cf. 1 Cor 14:20 NRSV.
[4] Ps 71:6 (70:6 NETS).
[5] Rom 8:29 NRSV.

strong and completely capable. "*Since, then, I hope in you, I do not grow weak.*" Of this weakness it is conveyed in many passages of the divine instruction: "He brought them out"—namely, the Hebrews—"with silver and gold, and there was no one among their tribes who was weak."[6] For when God brings someone out with gold—that is, with a pure intellect—and silver—with approved speech—he does not have any weakness. Those who are led upward in this way are not weak but are strong "through him who strengthens"[7] them. And just as the apostle says, "I can do all things"[8]—and he who can do all things is not weak—in the same sense also each of the wise, when made strong, is not weak. For how could the one who says to God, "I will love you, O Lord, [**92**] my strength"[9] be weak? One who hopes in riches will someday be weak.

If, however, the word *weakness* also means sickness—for it does mean this—he is saying as follows: when I hope in the Lord, I will not be sick in soul, I am always healthy; for "as for him who keeps the commandment, he is healthy."[10] This is not said of physical health, for many who keep the commandment grow sick, and many who transgress the commandments are healthy.

[25:2] *Prove me, O Lord, and try me.*

See his confidence! *Purge my kidneys* and see whether there is any unrighteousness in me. No one appeals to such a judge, who knows his secrets, who knows his innermost parts, to search him out, unless he has great confidence.

And indeed some, because of the superior purity of the one who is so bold, ascribe the psalm to the Savior's Man. Now, we have already said many times that the accomplishments of the Savior in the Man relate also to all perfect men.

Prove me, O Lord, and try me.

Lead me into the struggle! As when a certain competent athlete was saying to the prize giver, "*Prove me and try me*, if I am such a one as I profess to be!"

Now, God's proving of someone indicates this: that he is worthy of being proven by him. "But just as we have been approved by God to be entrusted with the gospel,"[11] "we determined to share with you not only the gospel but also our own souls."[12]

Someone shares his own soul with another when he trains him to be like in quality with the quality he possesses. "Not only, then," he says, "do we eagerly determine to share the gospel with you, but also our own souls." When someone becomes an imitator of the apostle and has his every disposition and practice, he has partaken of the apostle's soul.

However, one can also readily understand this as follows: we are even prepared to fight in front of you, for "because he laid down his life for us, we also ought to lay down our lives for one another."[13] When we, laying down our lives for the beloved, lay down not a certain spiritual and allegorically understood life but the life that we possess, this takes place in imitation of Jesus. And he himself truly laid down his human life, which is not understood allegorically.

[25:2-3] *Purge my kidneys and my heart. Because your mercy is before my eyes, and I was pleased with your truth.*

See that in all things he is confident in his own purity! Then, since these things seem to be beyond human ability, he says at once, *because your mercy is before me.* I know, however, that

---

[6]Ps 105:37 (104:37 NETS).
[7]Phil 4:13 NRSV.
[8]Phil 4:13 NRSV.
[9]Ps 18:1 (17:2).
[10]Cf. Prov 13:13 NETS.

[11]Cf. 1 Thess 2:4 NRSV.
[12]1 Thess 2:8.
[13]1 Jn 3:16.

even if I give proof of good things, even if I should hasten to run toward them, unless you have mercy on me, I am not perfected.

I was pleased, then, *with your truth*. Here, when the discussion is about the truth, there is no need to belittle oneself. Indeed, I am reminded of someone who says, "When you are asked, 'Are you a virgin?' say, 'Because of God I am a virgin until now, and until now I am also willing, and completely so, to put it to the proof.'" The one who is pleased with the truth of God has the mercy of God before the eyes. And having before his eyes the one who works together with him and perfects him, he will be confident because of what has already been accomplished by him.

For this reason, then, I say, *Purge my kidneys and my heart, because your mercy is before my eyes*. The kidneys are found joined together to the heart in many places of Scripture: "God is one who tests hearts and kidneys."[14] [93] "Moreover, until night my kidneys instructed me."[15]

And as when we hear the word *heart*, he does not mean the part of the body with which, by having it clean, he sees God.[16] And again, "Hear me, you who have ruined your heart,"[17] as no one destroys this bodily part, which is called by this name—unless of course he is dead!—when God removes a heart of stone and engrafts a heart of flesh instead,[18] so we understand the concept.

With this *heart*, therefore, the *kidneys* that are mentioned are not parts of the body. The generative seeds are said to be composed there first and from there easily to advance into the sexual organs. The kidneys, then, are reproductive and administer seeds. Since then there are also seeds, according to which the soul or the intellect generates, he names those *kidneys* together with the so-called *heart*. "You are near to their mouth," it says, "and far from their kidneys."[19] From these kidneys, O God, you are far away, not from their bodily members.

Therefore, examine my kidneys and my heart, put them to the test. I do not have seeds that can spread so that accursed children, children of destruction, are born, such as Judas had. For it was said, "Let them be born for destruction; let there be no one to support him,"[20] no defender for his children, not speaking about the children of his body. We probably do not even know whether he had children. It calls all the betrayers of the truth his children. Just as Paul begot through the gospel,[21] so that one through his betrayal begot those whom he preceded in betraying Jesus: "What are you willing to give me if I betray him to you?"[22] By this effort he has become a father of all the betrayers of the truth.

And I was pleased in your truth.

He who is pleased in God's truth is unashamed of his words, for Jesus said, "Whoever is ashamed of me and my words."[23] And if God himself is ashamed of the one who is ashamed of him, he himself also strengthens the one who has faith, remains in the truth, and prefers it to everything else, and he abides in him.

[25:4] *I did not sit with a council of vanity, and with transgressors I will not enter.*

Evils and goods cannot coexist. One who has good things cannot partake of evils. One who has equipped himself for vice, insofar as he is evil, is unreceptive of virtue.

And when there is a removal of the evils, whenever someone in agreement with nature desists from them by their free will, then the

---

[14]Ps 7:9 (7:10 NETS).
[15]Ps 16:7 (15:7 NETS).
[16]Cf. Mt 5:8.
[17]Is 46:12 NETS.
[18]Cf. Ezek 11:19.

[19]Jer 12:2.
[20]Cf. Ps 109:12-13 (108:12-13).
[21]Cf. 1 Cor 4:15.
[22]Mt 26:15.
[23]Lk 9:26; Mk 8:38 ESV.

children do not receive intemperance, but I am not saying that they themselves abstain from intemperance. The soulless and the irrational do not receive impiety, and I do not say that they abstain from impiety, for to abstain is a motion of the free will. In the First Psalm, indeed, it blesses the man who is perfect in the inner man: "Blessed is the man who did not walk by the counsel of the impious and did not stand in the way of sinners and did not sit down on the seat of the pestilential."[24]

The sophist and the trickster can say that neither the child, nor the irrational, nor the soulless "walked by the counsel of the impious [94], and did not stand in the way of sinners, and did not sit down on the seat of the pestilential." Denying that such things belong to the perfect man, he says: "How does one abstain from these things by having 'his will in the law of the Lord'?" Now, it does not belong to everyone to have "his will in the law of the Lord," for as many as seem to uphold the law by not sinning, when they do this because they are afraid of punishment, do not have "their will in the law of the Lord." If someone should convince them, for example, that there is no punishment, then they practice all that was forbidden. But the one who has "his will in the law of the Lord," even when there are numerous trials, even when many chastisements are threatening him, he does not rebel from the will of the law. So were the Maccabeans, so were the martyrs of the truth among ourselves.

Therefore, just as he does not say first that the perfect man has abstained from evils by having his own will in the law of the Lord, so here, after mentioning the goods that belong to him, he says next what he avoids and says: given that *I walked in my innocence* and, *hoping in you, I do not grow weak*, having *your mercy before my eyes*, since I am such a man, "I did not sit with a council of vanity."

Nothing else separated me from the council of vanity than being in such a way of life; indeed, let our way of life separate us from men, not space. Virtue separates the virtuous from ordinary men; knowledge separates the one who possesses it from the unlearned. So also here the one who walked in innocence and has God as his hope, and for this reason is strong and will not grow weak, "did not sit with a council of vanity."

And here someone might say, "The child, the irrational, and the soulless did not sit with a council of vanity." But those did not sit with a council of vanity because they could not by nature, not because they have walked in innocence and have hoped in God.

And with the transgressors I will not enter.

I never expressed approval with those who counsel vanities and who sit together because they practice such things, nor did I enter in with transgressors. Not only did I not sit but I did *not enter* in, for after entering comes sitting in their council.

Jeremiah, being of this choice and virtue, was saying, "I did not sit with a council of those who play, but I was reverent at the presence of your hand. I was seated by myself because I was filled with bitterness."[25] Indeed, he is saying these things to the Almighty. Playing is the same thing as counseling vanities, for here the game is not praiseworthy but is such a sport as those who built the calf were having, for it says, "They sat down to eat and drink, and they arose to play."[26] To play in this way is forbidden. Therefore, "I did not sit with a council of those who play."

And it has often been shown that the superficial things of life, which harm rather than help, which are easily shaken, are called "vain." The one who has his dealings with such men, even if he does not sit in the same place

---

[24] Ps 1:1.

[25] Jer 15:17.
[26] Cf. Ex 32:6 NETS.

with them, is sitting in the *council* [**95**] *of vanity.*

And with transgressors I will not enter.

Here he calls those who transgress the law "transgressors," not meaning those who have not had the law at all—those are "lawless" and are "without the law"—since he was far away from such people.

Question: *I will not enter?*

That is to say, I did not enter into their transgression. For to enter in with transgressors means to transgress, just as to enter into virtue means to act according to virtue.

[25:5] *I hated the assembly of evildoers, and with the impious I will not sit.*

Evildoers are either the same with those who sit together in vain or are not far from them. And perhaps those who sin in practical matters sit together for vanities, while those who think lies and hold heretical opinions are an *assembly of evildoers.*

And it is well to say *of evildoers.* No one who is evil by nature is said "to do evil," but one who has grown to do so and is able to withdraw from its activity.

[25:6] *I will wash my hands in innocence.*

The one who says, *I walked in my innocence,* and says, *Prove me and try me; purge my kidneys and my heart,* says, *I will wash my hands in innocence.* We say the following: the former deeds were related to the soul. They were indicating the disposition of one who is confident that he does not have unrighteousness in his *kidneys* and his *heart,* that he has walked *in innocence,* that he *hopes in God,* that he is bold and says, *Prove me and try me.* Since, then, I am such a person in inclination, I also have my actions clean. The disposition was washing my actions. *I will wash,* then, *my hands in innocence,* for I am not content merely with the disposition.

[25:6] *And I will go around your altar, O Lord.*

The priests, according to the law, being washed, used to go *around the altar.* And such an ordinance teaches that the priest must be clean in his deeds also. And indeed, a basin for washing "the hands and the feet"[27] was fashioned of no other material than out of mirrors. Moses received many golden and other vessels from the Hebrews to fashion many of the temple's vessels: the lampstand, the table. And some were made of silver, and others of gold, but he fashioned the basin out of the women's mirrors in order to teach that, by washing his own actions and the powers of the soul that can walk, a person ought to look at himself in the mirror.

And that such guidance is called a "mirror," James also writes. Of the one who "is a hearer who forgets" and not "a doer who acts,"[28] he says, "he looked at his face in a mirror and has gone away at once and forgotten what he was like."[29] He did not reprove looking at the face in a mirror but immediately turning away. Now, as the one who looks into a mirror [**96**], when he turns away from the mirror, no longer sees himself, so the one who supports the law without being a doer of the law transgresses, like the one who withdraws from the mirror and forgets in accordance with the < >.

"And all of us, with unveiled faces, seeing the glory of the Lord as though reflected in a mirror."[30] In the basin made of mirrors, then, the apostle also was washing his hands and was exhorting others to do so.

[25:7] *To hear a voice of your praise.*

You see that after the washing of the hands comes both the seeing of wonders and the hearing of the *voice of praise,* for virtue must not remain standing at the deed but also must

---
[27] Cf. Ex 38:8 (38:26-27).
[28] Jas 1:25.
[29] Jas 1:23-24.
[30] 2 Cor 3:18 NRSV.

reach vision and praise, as far as the knowledge of the good itself, the truth.

[25:7] *And to tell all your wondrous deeds.*

Hearing a voice of praise leads to proclaiming all the *wondrous deeds* of God. And he has no other discourse at all in his own speech than the discourse that relates to the *wondrous deeds* of God.

And so the priest who says these things is not the one who is a priest by succession according to the classes of priests who served daily in the law, but are like Samuel, who was always in the house. And also each of the saints, who can say, "And I am continually with you,"[31] is such. And here also it was said, "My eyes are ever toward the Lord."[32] The one who has his eyes always toward the Lord goes around the altar of God. Remaining ever with him, he always serves as priest.

[25:8] *O Lord, I loved the goodly appearance of your house and the place of the tent of your glory.*

In what way do a *tent* and a *house* differ? It was often said that the *tent*, on the one hand, indicates progress, for it is a *house* for travelers; it is a portable house. The *house*, however, is constructed in one place. Indeed, it signifies perfection.

I loved the place of the tent of your glory, when I was making progress. The glory of the tent, that is, of progress, consists in practical and contemplative virtue.

Magnificent is this one who can say, "All that we should do, we have done."[33] This person is magnificent. He possesses what is fitting, very properly, when he comes into virtue and piety. Of lovely appearance is the one who through celibacy accomplishes "how to please the Lord."[34] The one who is "holy in body and spirit"[35] has a lovely appearance. The goodly appearance of your house have I loved: perfection.

[25:9] *Do not destroy my soul together with the impious and my life with men of blood.*

He is not saying this: "Do not condemn me, being righteous, with the impious; do not drag me away to them!" At that time, however, you do not punish me together with the *impious*, when you prevent me from going into impiety. And I am prevented from going into impiety, when the accomplishments I confessed [97] to possess remain mine, when I remain walking *in innocence*, when *I hope in you so that I do not grow weak*. I am perfect. And being perfect, I am not *destroyed together with the impious*. No virtuous person is condemned together with the wicked.

Now, the form of the destruction is twofold: do not punish me with the impious, do not number me with those who are punished because of impiety.

And a second: preserve me in piety, in being well-pleased "in your truth," for "impiety will not deliver its friend."[36] Now, when it does not deliver, it destroys him.

And my life with men of blood.

May I not possess such a life as murderous men have.

In the anagogical meaning, those who boast what great men they are and cause the small ones in the church to stumble[37] are *men of blood*. May such things not be practiced by me so that I maintain a way of life with them. "This is life and length of days: loving the Lord your God with all your heart and all your soul."[38] The one who has this life does not have the life *with men of blood*; as far as the *men of*

---

[31] Ps 73:23 (72:23 NETS).
[32] Ps 25:15 (24:15 NETS).
[33] Cf. Lk 17:10.
[34] 1 Cor 7:32 NRSV.
[35] 1 Cor 7:34 NRSV.
[36] Eccles 8:8.
[37] Cf. Mt 18:6.
[38] Cf. Deut 30:20; 30:6.

blood are concerned, he is dead. And he is dead because he does not possess the way of life that they themselves possess.

[25:10] *In whose hands are acts of lawlessness.*

They still possess lawlessness in their actions. It is not that they had these in the past; rather, they have them now.

[25:10] *And their right hand was filled with gifts.*

One can even lead into error judges who accept bribes.

And even we who do not judge often accept gifts a little when we show partiality to someone. And when one acquires pleasures for himself, he accepts gifts; he receives gifts from himself.

[25:11] *But as for me, I walked in my innocence.*

None of those who accept bribes and have their right hand *filled with gifts*, none of the *lawless* and the *men of blood walked in innocence*. Such was Elymas the magician: an impious man, walking in lawless deeds, and having his right hand full of gifts, for he was seeming to be virtuous in order to deceive, and it was said to him, "You son of the devil, full of all deceit and villainy."[39] Now, he who has been filled with all villainy is unable to say, *I walked in my innocence*.

[25:11] *Redeem me, O God, and have mercy on me.*

He who *walks in innocence*, who is ready with the aforementioned accomplishments, says,

"*Redeem me!*" Even if I am among such achievements and all that belongs to virtue is granted to me by your cooperation, yet still you were burdening me with "the body of humiliation,"[40] still I am "in a place of ill-treatment."[41] For this reason, "*Redeem me!*"

[25:12] *For my foot stood in uprightness.*

The *standing of the foot* of the inner man in *uprightness* means the same thing as when he stands on the rock, according to the word: "You set my feet upon a rock,"[42] for *uprightness* is like a rock that cannot be shattered and is unbroken. My foot therefore is secure in my *uprightness*.

And *standing in uprightness* is the same thing as standing in [**98**] faith, for it says, "because you stand firm in the faith."[43] Such standing does not happen without Jesus. By him stand those who have this standing, so that he himself says, "There are some standing here,"[44] who are here beside me.

[25:12] *In assemblies I will bless you, O Lord.*

In church I will render you hymns of thanksgiving, not somewhere outside. He who professes to give thanks to God outside, in contrast with the church's considered judgment, does not *bless in assemblies*.

---

[39] Cf. Acts 13:10 NRSV.
[40] Phil 3:21.
[41] Ps 44:19 (43:20 NETS).
[42] Cf. Ps 40:2 (39:3).
[43] 2 Cor 1:24 NRSV.
[44] Mt 16:28.

PSALM 26 [27]

[26:1] *Of David. Before he was anointed.*

The psalms before this were "for David"; this psalm is titled *of David*. He himself produced it by the influence of the Holy Spirit.

He produced it *before he was anointed*. Now, David appears to be anointed three times. The first time was when he went to Samuel and was anointed, even the time when Samuel went to Jesse.[1] The second time was after Saul died. The rule was divided, for some had chosen David as king, while others Mephibosheth the son of Saul. When the son of Saul was betrayed by Abner because of the pretext of a woman, David was anointed over all the people in Hebron.[2] A third time also he was anointed.[3] On the first occasion again he is clearly a private person. On the second, it happened that he might rule a certain part of the people. At the death of Saul's son, next and again he has been anointed by all in order that he might rule over the remaining portion of the people.

We seek, then, which anointing he is speaking about here. One will say that he speaks about every anointing in general; he says that the psalm was spoken before he was anointed at all. And naturally if it preceded the first anointing, it is clear that it also preceded the second and the third. And if it preceded the second, however, it did not certainly precede the first. And if it preceded the third, it did not by necessity precede both the first and the second.

Now, the psalm certainly appears to have been spoken before the first anointing, that is, before every anointing. The psalm, therefore, comes *before he was anointed*.

[26:1] *The Lord is my illumination and my deliverer; whom shall I fear?*

If God illumines me and delivers me, whom do I fear? Neither a man nor an evil power nor the devil himself.

Now, the word *whom* here stands for the words "no one." Indeed, this use occurs frequently in the Scriptures: "What then are we to say about these things? If God is for us, who is against us?"[4] *who* here standing for "no one." "Who will bring any charge against God's elect?"[5] that is, "no one" will. And again, "Look, the Lord helps me; who will harm me?"[6] Therefore, though many things are signified by the word, as was said in other places, now the word *whom* stands for "no one."

The discourse is not about the perceptible life and a certain sensible illumination, then, for people are illuminated by the divine light in the intellect and the soul.

Now, life is always linked with salvation. Eternal life and eternal salvation are the same thing. For example, "Israel is being saved by the Lord with everlasting salvation."[7]

And that life is always linked with illumination, one can see from many examples: "The

---
[1] Cf. 1 Sam 16:13.
[2] Cf. 2 Sam 2:4.
[3] Cf. 2 Sam 5:3.
[4] Rom 8:31 NRSV.
[5] Rom 8:33 NRSV.
[6] Is 50:9 NETS.
[7] Is 45:17 NETS.

life was the light of all people,"[8] and again this saint prays, "Give light to my eyes, lest I sleep unto death."[9] He means that the one who lacks the true illumination sleeps unto death, not to the common death but to that which is opposed to the blessed life.

The Lord, then, *is my illumination and my deliverer*. He himself instructs me, he speaks to me in secret, [99] he illuminates me through what he tells me, and his word immediately prepares me to possess salvation.

Since I said that the illuminated person certainly has life—the Savior himself also says, for example: "I am the light of the world. Whoever follows me will never walk in darkness but will have the light of life."[10] The one who has the light of life fears no one, especially because the truth of God itself becomes a shield defending him, for "with a shield his truth will surround you."[11] For this reason he has immediately followed up with, *The Lord is my life's protector; of whom shall I be in dread?*

[26:1] *The Lord is my life's protector; of whom shall I be in dread?*

Who can produce fear in me? I am clothed with "the whole armor of God,"[12] I have "the shield of faith," which extinguishes "all the flaming arrows of the evil one."[13] If, however, the shield of faith extinguishes the arrows of the evil one, how much more those of the inferior archers, for there are also other wicked archers. For example, "Look, sinners bent a bow; they prepared arrows for the quiver, to shoot at the upright in heart."[14]

He fears no one. The whole armor of God is invulnerable and unable to be struck. His shield is truth. And no one can possibly come against the truth: "for we cannot do anything," he says, "against the truth, but only for the truth."[15] The whole armor is surrounding the one who has been armed like a hoplite, and it keeps him unscathed.

The Lord, then, *is my life's protector*. He is not saying this about the common life, for many of those who depend on God and were clothed with his whole armor have died the common death, not to say all. Besides this, many procured a violent death, among whom are Naboth and many apostles. Isaiah, for example, was sawed in two.[16]

[26:2] *When wicked people would approach me to devour my flesh.*

Those who intend to harm the soul eat the *flesh*. When anyone is found having *flesh*, he has enemies who are strong against him. His *flesh* is their food.

Now, it is *flesh* of which Paul says, "For the mind that is set on the flesh is hostile to God,"[17] and, "we are not in the flesh."[18] If he were speaking of the physical flesh, the statement would be false, for all the saints, who were in the flesh, were pleasing to God while they were wearing the flesh, and they cannot say, "We are not in the flesh." However, when someone mortifies the flesh and removes its works, he is not in the flesh. For this reason, it is said, "Those who belong to Jesus Christ have crucified the flesh with its desires,"[19] and they possess it as something that has been mortified, no longer active. The one who is crucified has hands that are prevented from acting and feet that are prevented from going where he wishes. Therefore, those who are crucified with Christ

---

[8] Jn 1:4 NRSV.
[9] Ps 13:3 (Ps 12:4 NETS).
[10] Jn 8:12 NRSV.
[11] Ps 91:4 (90:4 NETS).
[12] Eph 6:13.
[13] Eph 6:16.
[14] Cf. Ps 11:2 (10:2 NETS).

[15] 2 Cor 13:8 NRSV.
[16] Ascension of Isaiah 5:1.
[17] Rom 8:7.
[18] Rom 8:9.
[19] Cf. Gal 5:24.

crucified the flesh with its desires; they rendered it dead, so that from now on they might make known the death of Jesus in their own flesh: "We always carry the death of Jesus."[20]

The Lord is my life's protector; of whom shall I be in dread? When wicked people would approach me to devour my flesh, since they did not find the food for which they were longing, *they became weak and fell.* Observe, however, what has been connected to this! [100]

[26:2] *Those who afflict me and also my enemies—they became weak and fell.*

They have come to me to pull me down into weakness, to treat me wickedly; however, the suffering that they wished to make for me happened to them. For if they had found *flesh*, they would have eaten me and dragged me down into both weakness and sickness. However, since they did not find *flesh, they* themselves *became weak and fell,* subjected to hunger.

Those who afflict me and also my enemies— they became weak and fell.

The one who afflicts is not necessarily an enemy. Even the good man afflicts.

Indeed, many *enemies,* when they wish to entangle those against whom they are in enmity with afflictions and misfortune, are unable to do this unless God consents.

And many also *afflict* without being enemies. For example, parents afflict when they train their children, and masters afflict their servants, and they certainly do not do this as enemies.

One can certainly say that both groups, the group of *those who afflict* and the group of *enemies, became weak and fell.*

However, this is also possible: *those who afflict* are themselves *enemies* as well, for they do not afflict for the sake of correction and training. They are not of such a kind as those of whom it is said, "He who produces wisdom from his lips strikes a heartless man with a rod,"[21] and, "What would you prefer? Am I to come to you with a stick, or with love?"[22] These *who afflict* are not *enemies.* There is a time, however, when the enemy also afflicts; however, not out of necessity.

Question: What kind of death is this?

This is not to live according to wicked activities. The one who bears "the death of Jesus"[23] is not intemperate; he has been mortified toward intemperance; he has been mortified toward deifying his own belly; he has inactive the members that respond to fleshly passions; he does not allow any member to be autonomous, for he has blameworthy desires. Indeed, it is said, "Do not let your sin exercise dominion in your mortal body, to make you obey its passions!"[24]

[26:3] *Though a camp be arrayed against me, my heart shall not fear.*

Next, he explains how he is neither afraid nor fears, when he says, "*Whom shall I fear?*" and "*Of whom shall I be in dread?*" since the word *whom* seems to go too far. Even if a whole camp of evil men and forces will arrange itself for battle against me, my heart will not be afraid. Even if they kill the body, the heart remains unshaken; my thought is not overthrown. If a whole army should come against me with great generals, I have a heart that is fearless; my thought is not afraid.

And that the multitude of troops is called by this name: Jacob, when he was returning from Mesopotamia and was about to meet Esau, saw a *camp* of angels.[25] Indeed, how was there not going to be a *camp* around the one

---

[20] 2 Cor 4:10.
[21] Prov 10:13 NETS.
[22] 1 Cor 4:21 NRSV.
[23] 2 Cor 4:10.
[24] Rom 6:12.
[25] Cf. Gen 32:2.

who was about to come to an enemy that was superior and spiteful?

And Elisha was similar: a camp from Syria drew up for battle against Elisha. A divine camp has appeared around him, not in the literal sense but in the spiritual.[26]

The soul is led by the intellect; it is guided by it. And if someone wishes to understand "the will," this is possible. The word *heart* sometimes signifies [**101**] the will. Here, however, one should take it to refer to the intellect.

[26:3] *Though war rise up against me, in this I hope.*

Though more than a *camp* rises up *against me*, I have hope in my *heart*, which does *not fear*, which is empowered by divine fear: "The fear of the Lord surpasses everything,"[27] and, "those who fear him have no want."[28]

I have courage because this heart means everything to me. The virtues are the arms of piety. "Let us put on the armor of light; let us lay aside the works of the flesh."[29] The weapons of light are the virtues, godly thoughts, the mysteries and doctrines of the truth. Reinforced with these armaments, he is afraid of no one, he has his *hope* confident. *In this*, then, *do I hope*, not merely in my thinking, but in it so fortified.

[26:4] *One thing I requested of the Lord, this will I seek.*

God is a giver of many good things, for "he will give good things to those who ask him,"[30] and he satisfies the desire with his good gifts, for "he satisfies your desire with good."[31]

Someone can say very convincingly, then, that these good things are the particular virtues, the particular mysteries of the truth. When someone, therefore, possesses the whole group of virtues itself, if I can speak in this way, he possesses them all. Therefore he asks for one request: virtue in its totality.

When someone does not have the virtues as already genuine, he does not offer up one request. For when he makes progress and becomes greater in others, he needs again a request and he does not ask only one petition. The one who sends up a prayer for the whole of virtue and for the doctrines of piety sends up only one.

It is also possible to say this, however: there are many progressions. And these are indicated by the name "tent," as was often demonstrated. When someone, therefore, comes to a certain progression and asks to have God as a helper, to have him as a defender as well, he does not remain in this petition, for he changes from progress into progress. He is becoming superior to himself.

Now, many tents are mentioned, but only one *house*. The one who arrives at perfection, therefore, asks only one petition. *One thing*, therefore, *I requested of the Lord.*

However, this is also possible: their help, in order that they might be well-equipped against those who raise up war and encampments, does not ask only one request for itself. They seek many helps: a military defense, the security of walls, engines of war.

However, the one who has God himself as his helper and asks for this one makes only one request. He becomes "all in all,"[32] so that each of the perfected has him in his entirety: as bread, as light, as teacher, as shepherd.

One thing, then, *I asked, this I seek*. He who says "*I seek*" and "*I asked*" shows that the one who seeks and desires to find does not yet possess. However, no one yet has perfection

---

[26]Cf. 2 Kings 6:15-17.
[27]Sir 25:11 NETS.
[28]Ps 34:10 (33:10 NETS).
[29]Cf. Rom 13:12.
[30]Cf. Mt 7:11.
[31]Cf. Ps 103:5 (102:5 NETS).

[32]1 Cor 15:28.

unless he arrives at the very limit and goal of virtue and to union with God.

[26:4] *That I may dwell in the house of the Lord all the days of my life.*

I did not begin to ask just now, but when I began, I began because of the goal, for the one who begins a skilled profession begins **[102]** because of the goal of the profession.

Those who arrive at this *house* dwell there. "Blessed are all those who dwell in your house."[33] The one who possesses the blessed *life* is alive in *days* and does not come into nights. Even if he at one time came into a night, and then began to desire *life*, he comes outside the night.

[26:4] *To behold the pleasantness of the Lord and to visit his temple.*

As *I dwell in the house* of God *all the days*, so *in all the days I behold the pleasantness of the Lord and visit his temple*. Now, the *pleasantness of the Lord* is participation in him. And *his temple* is the condition in which God is found, in which God dwells. Perfect virtue is God's *house*.

"Christ, however, was over his house as Son, and we are his house,"[34] and, "Do you not know that you are God's temple?"[35] Aside from the fact that we called both virtue and perfect holiness a *house*, second, we can also call faithful men so. They become a *house* for this reason: because they possess virtue and holiness. Virtue is not called a "*house* of God" because of those who participate in it, but those who share in it are called so because of virtue.

The goal beyond all others, however, is particularly described. However, because this does not occur suddenly, we speak of the goals before the goal, for there are also goals before the goal: "I saw a limit to every perfection."[36] "When a person finishes, then he is beginning."[37] When he finishes, then, he sees the limit of a certain progression. Then, when he begins, he seeks to see another goal, and after all these he reaches the end beyond all others.

Take this example from me also in the case of the founding of a city. The one who, desirous of honor, wants to found a city that is rich and—what more do I need to say?—fit for a king begins with the act of building. He begins to quarry stones. He repeatedly completes the act of quarrying. When he prepares what he needs and as many things as he needs, then he begins to seek a place where he may raise the city.

"God" becomes "all in all,"[38] not all in each, but "in all." In one he becomes compassionate, when someone aspires to be like this; in another he becomes a good judge; in another righteous; in another generous; in another as a teacher in the presence of a disciple. And "in all" he becomes "all" to those who draw near to him, and not all in each, but one, two, or three charisms.

And that we should make it clear in the matter of the charisms, take those of the Spirit: one has a word of wisdom, another a word of knowledge, another a charism of healing.[39]

However, when someone becomes perfect and no longer merely possesses "the seal of the Spirit"[40] but the Spirit himself, then God becomes *all* in each.

I become a perfect protector and overseer of God's *temple*, when I do not have anything else before my eyes than this *temple* of God itself.

---

[33] Ps 84:4 (83:5 LES2).
[34] Heb 3:6.
[35] 1 Cor 3:16 NRSV.
[36] Ps 119:96 (118:96).
[37] Sir 18:7 NETS.
[38] 1 Cor 15:28.
[39] Cf. 1 Cor 12:8-9.
[40] 2 Cor 1:22.

[26:5] *Because he hid me in a tent in the day of my troubles.*

For this reason *I requested one thing and this will I seek, because he hid me in a tent on the day of my troubles.* Now, progress was being described. When many troubles were pressing in on me and wishing to do me harm, he concealed me.

However, sometimes the body is also called *tent*, for "the earthly tent weighs down a mind full of cares,"[41] **[103]** and "while we are still in this tent, we groan."[42] He repeatedly hides us, while we are in the tent, still wearing the body, lest we be harmed by it, whenever, as I said earlier, someone carries around "in the body the death of Jesus"[43] and mortifies it and subjects it to himself.[44]

[26:5] *He sheltered me in the secret spot of his tent.*

Indeed, *the secret spot of his tent* is not harmful but protective. However, the open spot of the aforementioned *tent* harms instead. I am so clothed with a body as though I am not in a body, when what is "mortal is swallowed up by life."[45]

"Being swallowed" and "swallowing" signify victory in Scripture: "When they rose up, then they would have swallowed us up alive,"[46] that is, "they would have conquered us," and, "Israel was swallowed up; now he has come to be among the nations as a useless vessel."[47] "All," it says, "who eat him will err."[48] Now, the one who eats swallows.

In the secret spot, then, *of his tent he hid me.* One who appears in a body, when he understands the cause and the mystery because of which he has come in it, can also have been hidden in its secret spot; for if he knows the mystery and the cause straightaway, he will torment himself, though he will not be consumed.

And this can also be said about the Savior or in reference to the Savior. If this is about him, *in the secret spot of his tent he hid me*, he began to possess a *tent*, he became man.

The descent of the Savior has a certain concealed mystery. After the Word-become-flesh has pitched his *tent* in him, he who is then able to say, "We have seen his glory, glory as of the only Son from the Father, full of grace and truth,"[49] was sheltered *in the secret spot of his tent*. Understanding the mystery of the Savior's visitation has become his shelter. The Jews, indeed, and as many as are like them did not comprehend and were not sheltered *in the secret spot of his tent*.[50]

However, it is also possible, according to the former interpretation for *the secret spot of the tent* to be the goal, for they make progress for the sake of this even when it is hidden from those who advance; for unless someone arrives at it, he is unable to see it as it is. When he arrives at the very limit of blessedness, then he will see God "as he is."[51]

Question: "Have we seen"[52] him already?

Yes, but we do not know him. "We know only in part."[53]

Question: Is the whole race of men the one who says these things?

The Lord's Man does not say these words, but the family of the righteous, the assembly of the saints, for the Son of God as Man does not say, "*The Lord is my illumination and my deliverer; whom shall I fear?*"

---

[41] Wis 9:15 NETS.
[42] 2 Cor 5:4 NRSV.
[43] 2 Cor 4:10 NRSV.
[44] Cf. 1 Cor 9:27.
[45] Cf. 2 Cor 5:4.
[46] Cf. Ps 124:2–3 (123:2–3).
[47] Hos 8:8.
[48] Jer 2:3 NETS.

[49] Jn 1:14 ESV.
[50] This paragraph refers to the Savior's spiritual indwelling in people such as Saint John the Theologian.
[51] 1 Jn 3:2.
[52] Jn 1:14.
[53] 1 Cor 13:9 NRSV.

I often said that what is said about righteous men is also said about the Lord's Man in common. However, they are not common in accordance with equality, for he is incomparably superior to all others in these things as well. I call them common in view of participation, as I call common the medical art of both the one who is perfected [104] and possesses it completely and of those who are still making progress. I do not call it common quantitatively, but qualitatively.

The fornicator is not *hidden* but comes outside the *tent*, for he does not abstain "from the desires of the flesh that wage war against the soul."[54] Now, the one who lives openly in all things according to the flesh, being intemperate, living in luxury, and entirely preferring pleasures to difficulties, even if they should be reprovable: that one has his own tent open, he has his body conspicuous. It is clear that he wears a body, for the one who says, "But you are not in the flesh,"[55] teaches that they are free from the passions of the flesh. And the one who is free from the passions of the flesh is hidden in the *tent*.

In another sense, the hidden part of the *tent* is that which is unfamiliar to all.

[26:5] *High on a rock you set me.*

Being set high on a physical rock is not so great a thing so that one sends up praise of thanksgiving. All the things that are accomplished by God, for which it is appropriate to give thanks, which one must commemorate in song, are not commonplace and cannot take place by the hand of anyone.

Therefore, the Word of God itself, which cannot be broken, is a rock, and anyone who comes around it is not struck. Indeed, it was said in other places, "Their judges were swallowed up close to a rock,"[56] or "their mighty ones." And the rulers, being indeed distant from the rock, suppose themselves to be strong and to rule over things that are unstable. But when they draw near the rock, they are immediately overcome.

Now, I also said yesterday that "swallowing" means victory: "When people rose up against us, then they would have swallowed us up alive,"[57] and, "those who devour Israel with open mouth."[58] The one who is overcome, therefore, is swallowed; the one who prevails swallows.

You have, indeed, a certain riddle that appears in the Exodus, when Aaron casts down his staff according to God's guidance, and it becomes a serpent. The Egyptian magicians also cast down theirs by their magical arts, and those became serpents. "And the rod of Aaron swallowed the rods of those people,"[59] for the scepter of truth, which the worshiper of God possesses, when it is thrown and stretched out, swallows the sophistries of the Egyptians, so that they confessed their defeat, saying, "The finger of God did this!"[60]

Therefore, as the staff of Aaron devoured the staff of the magicians, that is, it conquered them, and it concealed them and showed them to be nothing, so also with the rock on which the supplicant gives thanks, the mighty ones among his enemies, or their judges, were swallowed when they drew near to the rock.

Those who advocate the causes of the heterodox, though they seem to establish the heretical arguments as things strong and mighty, when the rock draws near to them, the truth, they are swallowed up and shown to be nothing.

And: "May they not say, 'We swallowed him up!'"[61] May they not boast that they have prevailed and have conquered me!

---

[54] 1 Pet 2:11 NRSV.
[55] Rom 8:9.
[56] Ps 141:6 (140:6 NETS).
[57] Ps 124:2-3 (123:2-3 NETS).
[58] Is 9:12 (9:11 NETS).
[59] Ex 7:12 NETS.
[60] Cf. Ex 8:19.
[61] Ps 35:25 (34:25).

High on a rock you set me.

He who has his feet stationed on this rock sends up praises of thanksgiving: "He put a new song in my mouth."[62] When **[105]** the feet of the one so helped stand on the rock, and his steps are made straight, then he will say, "He put a new song in my mouth," a song of victory. Therefore, the one set high on the rock offers songs of victory, after he has his own driving impulses secured.

[26:6] *And now, look, he set my head high above my enemies.*

The one who says *"And now"* shows that his head was frequently exalted above his enemies.

And he calls the intellect *head*, as has been frequently shown. For example, it is also said of it in Ecclesiastes, "As for the wise man, his eyes are in his head."[63] The wise man has a discerning mind.

And now, then, *he set my head on high.* And always wrestling with and prevailing over enemies—and the enemies who attack him are diverse—he says after each victory, *And now he set my head on high above my enemies.* Some people, being driven into intemperance, arose, as the elders did against Susanna, as the brothers and she who later imagined that she had become his mistress did against Joseph.

As soon as he speaks with thanksgiving, he shows that he did these feats not by his own power but with God as his helper.

[26:6] *I went around and sacrificed in his tent, a sacrifice with shouting.*

Shouting intimates victory, for it is an inarticulate cry against fallen enemies. Just as, for example, when they encircled Jericho and sounded a blast on their horns and raised the war cry, and the walls of Jericho collapsed at their cry.[64]

Now, Jericho is, according to an allegory, the place around the earth. It is translated as "moon," not in its waxing but in its waning, like the crazed man: for "the fool changes like the moon."[65]

Therefore, when he goes around his own tent, according to all its interpretations . . .

Progress was called a *tent.* The one who progresses and genuinely completes the progression goes around it.

And again the body was called a *tent.* When the inner man applies himself vigorously against the body, he goes around it and prevails over it.

When someone goes around the tent, the body of Jesus, through faith, he is shown to be a victor.

[26:6] *I will sing and make music to the Lord.*

In the earlier psalms, it was said by us that to *sing* indicates contemplation, to send up praises and songs without an instrument.

It was said that *to make music* is to make the melody of victory resound.

Both of these, then, have been undertaken by me: *I* will both *make music* and *sing. I will sing* when I contemplate the truth. The one who takes possession of the doctrines of piety, and holds the contemplation of them in knowledge and wisdom, *sings.* And the one who takes his body in hand like an instrument, as a kithara and a psaltery, and strikes all of its appetites and senses, which are its strings, when he is able to recite a psalm melodiously, that one *makes music.*

This saint, then, professes that he does both: singing and making music. The one who mortifies his body and subjects it to himself[66]

---

[62]Ps 40:3 (39:4).
[63]Eccles 2:14.
[64]Cf. Josh 6:20.
[65]Sir 27:11 NETS.
[66]Cf. 1 Cor 9:27.

[106] and practices the moral virtues, such as one who practices acts of charity, the one who completes gentleness, the one who is led by courage, this person *makes music*.

And the one who sees each mystery of the truth and is able to explain with skill each doctrine of piety, this one *sings*.

Question: In the Fiftieth Psalm, do we understand it as a certain confession for sin?

It is clearly found there: "When Nathan came," and reproached him about the wife of Uriah.[67] It was the right time for confession, and he offers up the psalm of confession then. After he had become king and had gone in to Uriah's wife, that psalm appeared. Here, however, it is sung *before he was anointed*, so that that psalm differs from this one both in time and situation.

Question: How then can he *make music*?

Because virtue is immutable. Judas did not *sing* and *make music* to the Lord. Those handed over "to Satan, so that they may learn not to blaspheme,"[68] had not possessed a certain *tent* and progress in faith and virtue.

In any case, observe, moreover, that different psalms are not spoken throughout about one and the same person, for we have said this, that they are about a kind of person who acts according to virtue or vice.

It is not the same thing to say, "The man is sinless," and to say, "The righteous man is sinless." The one who possesses righteousness is unable to be subjected to sin. How indeed could this be, if opposites are unable to coexist? He who possesses the evil cannot possess the good, unless he first turns away from the evil.

Observe the kind of person, not this person or that one! For when I say that the faithful one can do all things, I mean not this person or that one, but everyone who has faith. Even when, for example, someone who is faithful and has the ability to do and to achieve all things, but the things of faith change for the worse for him, I do not say that the faithful person does not succeed but that this person does not prosper.

Question: Is not the psalm after this one earlier in time?[69]

The psalms do not demand the kind of order that you yourself are seeking. That psalm is the one that accuses Doeg the Syrian. Saul was still king and was undoubtedly mighty, so that David had to flee, because he was slandered. And much later it takes place that he becomes the king of all after the final anointing—and this was the third. And after a long while the affair with the wife of Uriah takes place. He was, however, not yet king when Doeg put him in a bad light as the one who took the loaves and bread and the sword of Goliath.[70]

Therefore, the ordering of the psalms is not to be sought in this way, in the ordering of times, but in the achievements, but in the deeds.

The number fifty possesses something extraordinary, and because of its excellence the psalm of confession was given to it.

See this at least: according to the number fifty, the act of repentance is brought to perfection. For example, the Savior proposes the following, when the Pharisees murmur about the woman who was cleansed by him, who came to wash his feet with her own tears and to wipe them with her own hair: "A certain creditor had two debtors; one owed five hundred denarii, and the other fifty."[71] And observe that he formed the number of those who were repenting with the number five, for five hundred has an affinity with fifty, for when fifty is increased tenfold, it becomes five hundred. [107]

---

[67] Cf. Ps 50 surtitle.
[68] 1 Tim 1:20 NRSV.
[69] The student is referring to Ps 52 (51 LXX), which follows Ps 51 (50 LXX) in time but is about an earlier event.
[70] Cf. 1 Sam 22:10.
[71] Lk 7:41 NRSV.

Also, according to such a mystery that relates to the number, the psalm of confession is also ordered in this way, for the number is expressive of mercy. Certainly, those who are victorious in war are paid a fiftieth. And for those who do not fight but guard the baggage, those who fight and are victorious give a fiftieth.[72]

And the priest, beginning to serve as priest from twenty-five years old, remains until he is fifty. After the fifty years, he no longer officiates, but he guards the tent.[73]

Now, the order shows that it is necessary first to achieve virtue, to accomplish all things in a priestly manner, and to become a perfect priest, so that one arrives at the number fifty and then guards the things in the tent. And the order teaches that in the progressions of deeds there is a need for growth, but when someone is made perfect, he ought to guard what he achieved.

Just as the one who assumes health is in the condition of being made well, he is in the situation where medicines are given to him. But when he recovers his health tenaciously and has a secure tent, then he brings himself things that are preserving of health, not things that make him recover his health but things that preserve it.

For this reason God also places Adam "in paradise to work and to keep it."[74] "To work," that it should bear fruit, that it should produce perfect fruit, and then "to keep" the trees that bore the fruit.

Just as "working" and "keeping" signify two things—and "to work" means to put into action the things of virtue, the things of the knowledge of the truth, and "to keep" means to make these things perfect—so also the priest, as long as he is short of the number fifty, continues in priestly service. But when he fulfills this and is shown to be perfect, from that time onward he guards what is in the tent. He himself no longer works, but he receives the tribute of others who work: he receives the tithes.

Moreover, this number is the beginning of a second square. A square is a number that is factored by equal numbers: twice two, three times three. This, then, is seven times seven. And then the addition of one establishes the beginning of another square. [When one multiplies seven times seven with ten, one gets][75] seventy times seven. For this reason also, when the Savior was asked by Peter about repentance, "How many times can he sin? As many as seven times?" he says, "Not seven times only, but, I tell you, seventy times seven times."[76]

The number seven times seven is a square. And this has holy factors, for as we have frequently shown, the number seven is blessed from all sides: for "God blessed the seventh day and made it holy,"[77] and, "The eyes of the Lord that watch over the whole earth are seven."[78] Not that I am speaking of seven as three plus four, but it represents his most perfect contemplation and observation.

So also, indeed, on the Feast of Weeks, the Pentecost is observed, which accords with the old covenant and the new, for you have in the Acts of the Apostles, "When the day of Pentecost had come,"[79] the gift of the Holy Spirit was given, the different charisms of the Spirit were apportioned, for it was necessary that the number, seven times seven, be transcended and take the beginning of another such number, and so be perfected. [108] The number fifty, then, seizes on many great things.

---

[72]Cf. 1 Sam 30:24.
[73]Cf. Num 4:3.
[74]Gen 2:15.
[75]This is a conjectural addition by the editor, to make sense of the gap in the text.
[76]Mt 18:21.
[77]Gen 2:3.
[78]Zech 4:10.
[79]Acts 2:1 NRSV.

Again, the seventh month is perfect. The Feast of Tabernacles occurs in the seventh month according to the Hebrews.

Again, the land was sown for six years, but in the seventh year it went unsown.[80] That year used to remain reserved for the poor. And again, there is also the fact that if a certain festival is held every seven years, that year again is a multiple of seven.

Now, seven sevens is also observed as a Jubilee, according to what is said by the Hebrews. The Jubilee is the fiftieth year. Every fifty years certain public festivals were celebrated. And this year used to have more than the other years. We were saying that there are both seventh years and seventh months. In the fiftieth year, called Jubilee, a cancellation of debts used to take place.[81] Creditors, being compelled by the law to do this, used to pardon, they used to cancel their debts as they were able, and they used to collect no interest. And besides this, houses that had been sold and fields used to become redeemable during the fiftieth year. If the seller were able to restore its price, his own property, which he used to possess earlier, would be reinstated.

Now, the order intimates this, that even when someone should produce his own way of life—and frequently the way of life is called a "house," as the passage says, "When the one who hears the words of Jesus acts on them, he builds his own house,"[82] and again, "Because the midwives were fearing God, they made houses for themselves."[83] These things have been written primarily only of women who act as midwives, for they did not have a house earlier. Because of the fear of God they built these houses, the right ways of life, the ones accomplished with the fear of God. "House" has now been explained.

Moreover, someone recovers that field, which he used to possess earlier and neglected, relative to its care, so that he again sows good seed, sows toward righteousness, harvests in the fruit of life, and gathers the harvest of righteousness from it.

So never look at the superscriptions of the Psalms! This one is titled *before he was anointed*. When you investigate the superscription, this should surely not be the twenty-sixth. Furthermore, Absalom attacked his father after the affair with Uriah's wife; insofar as concerns the ordering of the numbers, it should come after the fiftieth, yet that psalm is titled the third. We observe the qualities of the numbers and in this way we understand the ordering of the thoughts, not simply the numbers.

Someone asked me about the word, "All wisdom is from the Lord,"[84] and I was answering that when he says, "every wisdom," he is speaking of every kind of wisdom in particular, but when he says "all wisdom," he is speaking of one as a whole. As also when we say "all the city," we mean one whole, and when we say "every city is governed according to law," we do not mean one, but all cities.

So even the numbers are laid out with the circumstances of the psalm, being put there by none other than God. And because he created all things in wisdom,[85] he also created numbers in wisdom. Therefore, tell me when you think that what was written in Isaiah was fulfilled. "And it shall be," he says, "that after seventy years Tyre will be restored to her ancient condition."[86] From when are the seventy years numbered? Not in this way, that we should understand it in the literal sense, but the seventy years are seventy periods of the "Sun [109] of Righteousness,"[87] for the Sun completes its revolution when it illuminates

---

[80]Cf. Ex 23:10-11.
[81]Cf. Lev 25:8-10.
[82]Cf. Mt 7:24.
[83]Ex 1:21.

[84]Sir 1:1 NETS.
[85]Cf. Ps 104:24 (103:24).
[86]Cf. Is 23:17 NETS.
[87]Mal 4:2 (3:20).

souls and reveals the doctrines of piety and emits its shining rays. When, therefore, someone is made perfect and ceases, because he has arrived at the goal of progress, then the seventy years come together for him.

As for the passage that is before us, the digression was not proper, but it was necessary considering the question.

[26:7] *Listen, O Lord, to my voice with which I cried aloud.*

When I prayed to you, I cried aloud with my voice for that which is best for me to be. And indeed in a surprising way: he sends up a prayer for a prayer, for the one who invokes someone for his earlier prayer to be heard offers a prayer for a prayer. When I prayed, I cried to you and again I return in order that you should listen to this voice with which I cried to you.

For not everyone who cries out in the inner man cried to God, but only the one who speaks things that are for God, the one who brings his request to him. The Sodomites also cry out, but not to God: "The outcry of Sodom and Gomorrah has been increased, and their sins are very great!"[88] And of the Ninevites it is said, "The cry of their wickedness has gone up,"[89] the abundance of their vice. And in Isaiah: "I waited for him to produce justice, but he produced an outcry!"[90] So the outcry of the Sodomites is an intensification of vice.

Now, the one who prays to God cries with an intensified voice, when he prays about great things, not about worthless and contemptible things, is the one who asks that good things be given to him. Now, the other Evangelist interpreted good things as the Holy Spirit, for writing about the occasion Matthew says, "He will give good things to those who ask him,"[91] while Luke says, "He will give the Holy Spirit."[92]

Now, the Spirit, although he is one, is a multitude of good things in accordance with his different charisms, for the one who has the Holy Spirit has the charisms of the Spirit, which are many good things. And he is one in essence on the one hand, and many good things in conceptions on the other.

Also, as God he is one in essence. However, he is called many things according to different conceptions: good, immutable, unchangeable, source, light. And again, the Savior likewise, being one in subject, is called life, truth.

"Ask," he says, "for the great things, and the small will be added to you."[93] So the one who asks for small things speaks to God, but not with an intensified voice. "Ask," he is saying, "for heavenly things, and the earthly things will be added to you."

He who offers up a prayer chiefly for sensible things does not cry out to God; he speaks softly to him. However, the one who asks for those things that are truly great, heavenly, and deifying cries out to God. And the cry is his thinking.

[26:7-8] *Have mercy on me and listen to me! To you my heart spoke.*

My intellect speaks to you; I ask for mercy from you. My heart awaits mercy from you, and it says to you, *"Listen to me!"*

These things correspond to each other: the one who is pitied by God is heard, and the one who is heard is pitied. One cannot say, then, that the one precedes the other. Now, hearing takes precedence over having mercy. But it is not at all earlier in time.

And as it is impossible to say that appearance comes before color, so neither can one say

---

[88] Gen 18:20.
[89] Jon 1:2.
[90] Cf. Is 5:7 NETS.
[91] Cf. Mt 7:11 NRSV.
[92] Lk 11:13.
[93] Cf. Mt 6:33; Lk 12:31.

that color comes before appearance. If there is color, there is also appearance. If there is appearance, it is also colored. The appearance is conceived of first. [110] There must be an appearance, in order that it may also have color. However, this "must" I do not understand temporally but conceptually.

To you my heart spoke.

He is indicating the persons. In every statement three persons are indicated: the speaker, the one to whom he speaks, and the one of whom he speaks. So the one who is presently speaking is also the person who is praying. And he speaks his prayer to none other than God.

[26:8] *I have sought out your face!*

My heart is what says, "Have mercy on me, and listen to me!"

I did not just before now seek your face; not only now did I pray, "Show your face, and we shall be saved!"[94] However, it signifies an intensive search, if *I have sought out.*

[26:8] *Your face, Lord, will I seek.*

My heart will seek your face, O Lord. Even if I "sought out" and had it illuminating me, yet I do not cease at this point. Again I seek it out.

[26:9] *Do not turn away your face from me.*

The eye that is healthy and preserves the ability to see, when light is present, has a desire for it, and it is never wearied by it, for the light does not bring about satiety for the eyes: "It is sweet to the eyes,"[95] as the Preacher says. And no one receives satiety from sweetness. There are sweet things that produce satiety, like the sweetness of honey. The sweetness of the light, however, does not produce satiety, especially when the eye has the ability that is proper to it.

And now from the sensible to the intelligible: the eye of the inner man, or the eyes, are never satiated, they do not receive satiety from the face of God, for when it appears it always illuminates and increases the desire as well. Indeed, "The light of your face was manifested upon us, O Lord."[96] It remains. The light of the sun, however, or of the sensible light in general, does not remain. When, for example, someone withdraws from looking at light or shuts one's eyes, he does not have it manifested. The intelligible light, however, remains manifest to the one who is illuminated; it is unable to be lost.

[26:9] *Do not turn away in wrath from your servant.*

Sometimes it seems that God *turns away*; however, he does not do so in anger. Some supposed that he turned away from Job when his possessions, his children, and his body were handed over to the one who demanded them, but this has not taken place in wrath.

May my actions never be so, out of our indifference, that your face *turns away in wrath* from me.

Both, then, are possible: may such things never be practiced by me so that, being provoked to anger, you turn away from me. Or it could be so: may I never be so provoked to anger that I am deprived of your presence.

[26:9] *Become my helper; do not damn me!*

Some copies have, "Do not abandon me." Now "to damn" is the same as to reject, to dismiss. For example, in Isaiah it is announced, "And he will damn him."[97]

---

[94] Ps 80:3 (79:4 NETS).
[95] Eccles 11:7.
[96] Ps 4:6 (4:7 LES2).
[97] Is 17:13 NETS.

LECTURES ON PSALM 26 [26:9]

And observe the precision of the word! The word *become* does not always indicate a beginning, but it shows that which the addition to the discourse intends. And here there is added *Become my helper*, for the One who becomes a helper to someone does not come into existence.

Now, I also said at another time that words that suggest a beginning, when they are spoken in an absolute sense, indicate an act of creation: "All things came into being through him,"[98] that is, "All things existed through him." "In the beginning God made the heaven and the earth."[99] It did not say, "He made into such a thing," but only this: "heaven [**111**] and earth."

However, when he says, *Become my helper! Do not abandon me!* he means this: "Become a helper to me." He indicates a relationship of helper to one who is helped. In this way we also say, "Become my teacher," and certainly this does not mean a coming into being, but "become a teacher for me."

Of this kind, too, are the words spoken about the Savior: "Consider that the apostle and high priest of our confession was faithful to the one who appointed him."[100] He made him an apostle; he did not simply make him, but he made him an apostle. And notice: the essence of the Son is eternal.

However, his becoming an apostle takes place at the time when some move away from him, for he is sent to those who are far away. And see that his becoming an apostle coexists with there being some who are far away from him, who have been separated from him.

Again he becomes a high priest, when they began to exist for whose sake he is consecrated priest. Not at that time, however, has the Savior's existence come into being, as those people think, but his office, his high priesthood.

So again it also says in the Acts of the Apostles: "Let the entire house of Israel know this with certainty: that God has made him both Lord and Christ."[101] He becomes Lord of those who flee toward him to serve him. And when, therefore, someone begins to serve him today, today he becomes Lord to him. And when someone submits himself to his rule and his priesthood, today he has become Christ to him, for "Christ" indicates nothing other than a king and a high priest. So, for example, Aaron was called "the Lord's christ," and kings were called "the Lord's christs," and of Saul himself it says, "The Lord is witness and his christ is witness."[102] And this is said, "Do not touch my christs."[103]

Become my helper, then, *do not damn me! Do not send me away from you*. It is said of some, "God will reject them, because they did not listen to him, and they shall become wanderers among the nations."[104] When they fall away, being also carried away there, they were damned here, no longer having a firm opinion. And he addresses us with the reason: "Because they did not listen." It is not desired by him to drive away some from him. But it is desired by him to send away those who do not listen, lest he seem to hate virtue. And since they did not listen, "in accordance with their many evil acts cast them out, because they embittered you, O Lord."[105] This is what it means to be damned.

They say, moreover, that the word *aposkorakizō* is derived from another, so that they say that the *kora* are the filings of iron. The filings are lightly sent away, like dust. Consequently, may I not become such a one so that I am damned. I wish to be a golden vessel or a vessel of bronze, surely not a filing! This, however, is sent away and cast out.

---

[98] Jn 1:3 NRSV.
[99] Cf. Gen 1:1 NETS.
[100] Heb 3:1-2 NRSV.
[101] Acts 2:36.
[102] 1 Sam 12:5.
[103] Ps 105:15 (104:15).
[104] Hos 9:17.
[105] Ps 5:10 (5:11).

[26:9] *And do not abandon me, O God, my deliverer.*

Since you are also my Lord—for I serve you—and my God—since I am a child of Abraham, and you are "the God of Abraham and Isaac"[106] and of their descendants, clearly—I am like a servant to the Lord, as one who is truly subject to God, serving him as one who is delivered serves his deliverers. Therefore, since you have done all these things for me, you do not abandon me. **[112]**

[26:10] *Because my father and my mother abandoned me.*

I wish to explain beforehand a saying from the Gospel, in order that this may be understood from that. Both the ancient Scripture and the Gospel and the very exhortations of the Savior teach a person to love father and mother. Listen! If someone hates his father, he does not hate him as his father, but as an impious man, and he does not hate him insofar as he is his father, but insofar as he is impious. And the one who loves his father, loves him for this reason, because he is truly . . . , when he raises him with fear and correction, when he raises him as a righteous man. And "a righteous father raises well."[107] So I said that nearly all the Scriptures order us about the honor due to parents and punish those who abandon their positions: "The one who insults his father or his mother will die by death sentence!"[108]

So hear now, "Whoever loves father or mother more than me is not worthy of me."[109] Nevertheless, "Honor your parents and love your father and your mother,"[110] but when one loves them more than God, he is discredited; for when one is determined to confess the truth when persecution threatens, and when he says, "Because of the old age of my father and my mother I do not wish to die," and he gives over in betrayal, he has loved his parents more than God; he has preferred the disposition toward his parents above piety toward God. And this is what is reproved.

So the Savior says in the Gospel, "Jesus turned," it says, "and said to the crowds, 'Whoever wishes to come after me, and does not hate his father and his mother, his wife, his brothers, and his children, cannot be my disciple.'"[111] If you established as law respect for parents and you promised me great rewards for the contest, when you were saying, "Honor your father and your mother, so that it may be well with you and so that you may be long-lived on the earth,"[112] how are you now saying, "Unless someone hates his father and his mother, he cannot follow me"? The hate here is meant in a different sense: not to prefer something to God. When one is determined to love God, especially in a time of danger, in a time of persecution, the love of God is to be preferred before all other things. "When a parent or the age of a parent pulls against this, prefer God, since otherwise you cannot follow me!"

So, hating one's father and mother does not indicate that hate according to which we abandon and feel disgust, but according to which we do not prefer them to God. The same goes for both wife and children; the same goes for brothers. "Yes, and he must even hate his own life,"[113] he says. The one who assumes death for the sake of witness hates his own soul, yet only because of the Savior; for notice what he says, he who hates his father "for my sake,"[114] not in an absolute sense. The Savior is to be preferred to all others. So then, someone even hates his mother for the sake of the Savior. This hate does not bear hostility. The one who hates his parents in this way, because of the Savior, is abandoned by them.

---

[106] Ex 3:6.
[107] Prov 23:24 NETS.
[108] Ex 21:17 (21:16).
[109] Mt 10:37 NRSV.
[110] Cf. Ex 20:12.

[111] Lk 14:25-26.
[112] Ex 20:12.
[113] Lk 14:26.
[114] Cf. Mk 10:29.

Therefore he says, *because my father and my mother abandoned me*. He mentions [113][115] abandonment again. I myself preferred the Savior to my parents; nevertheless I did not hate them, since I was offered to the Savior with great affection. So also do they abandon me, not because they hate me, not because they reject me with disgust, but just as I myself preferred the Savior over them, they themselves also preferred him over me. *My father*, therefore, *abandoned me*. And given that they did not abandon me as a wicked man but because they preferred God above me, for this reason *God took me for himself*.

[26:11] *Instruct me, O Lord, in your way.*

Not everyone who receives the law walks in the way of God, but the one who so receives the law of God as it has been given—and it is given as perfect. For "the law of the Lord is faultless, turning souls."[116] The one who has "his will in the law of the Lord,"[117] so that his will and the law's are one, that one has been instructed in God's way. And in a different sense those are concerned with the shadow of the law and live according to it—for example, those circumcised in the flesh, who keep the Sabbath, who pursue the works of the servile—those were not instructed in God's way, but only those who know that "the law is spiritual,"[118] those who recognize the truth of the law by means of its shadow, those who understand the spirit of the law revealed by the letter.

[26:11] *And guide me on a straight path on account of my enemies.*

The straight paths are the commandments of God, the virtues. To the one who turns away, he says, for example, "Will you not stop making crooked the straight paths of God?"[119]

Question: *On account of my enemies?*

Because, when they find me off the *straight path*, they harm me. This *straight path*, as long as I am on it, is near me, and none of my *enemies* is able to harm me. And of the doctrines of piety, therefore, you will say, "If he leads someone on the path of the doctrines of piety, none of the heretics is able to harm him." And the heterodox are the *enemies* of those who love the truth and of the orthodox.

[26:12] *Do not give me up to the souls of those who afflict me.*

Now, someone is given up *to the souls of those who afflict* when he is abandoned to their wills, to their souls. Joseph was not given over to the soul of the Egyptian woman who was seeking him and wishing to harm him,[120] nor was Susanna given over to the souls of the elders who were maddened against her, that is, she was not taken captive by the passions of their souls.[121]

[26:12] *Because unjust witnesses rose against me.*

Did not the elders arise against Susanna as *unjust witnesses*? Was not the Egyptian woman an *unjust witness* against Joseph? Therefore, just as unjust men rise up against the virtuous, so also all the evil powers and the devil himself rise up. For they really do testify, and all those who have false opinions are also *unjust witnesses* against the truth when they attest falsehoods. "For we cannot do anything against the truth, but only for the truth,"[122] say the wise.

---

[115]Lincoln Blumell, *Didymus the Blind's Commentary on Psalms 26:10–29:2 and 36:1-3*, Brigham Young University Papyri 1 (Turnhout: Brepols, 2019), begins here.
[116]Ps 19:7 (18:8 NETS).
[117]Ps 1:2.
[118]Rom 7:14 NRSV.

[119]Cf. Acts 13:10 NRSV.
[120]Cf. Gen 39:5-12.
[121]Cf. Sus 8-21.
[122]2 Cor 13:8 NRSV.

[26:12] *And injustice lied to itself.*[123]

He is saying the following: even if they have become unjust witnesses, yet the injustice, in accordance with which they bear false witness, tricks itself, fails, does not subsist, and is not among the things that endure. The word *lied* here does not mean "to oppose the truth," but as when we say that a field "has deceived," for this is also found: "Threshing floor and wine deceived them."[124]

[26:13] *I believe that I may see the good things of the Lord in the land of the living.*

By the *living* he does not mean those who have been compounded with flesh **[114]** and have the common life, which even the impious and the irrational animals possess, but according to that meaning with which the Savior said of the patriarchs, "He is God not of the dead, but of the living,"[125] even though the ones of whom he was saying these things had died in a physical sense. For "Abraham died and the prophets"[126] died, and Isaac and Jacob died, "and he was added to his people."[127] So he calls them *living* according to the soul, in which they partake of God, and their God is the one who gives life.

So this *land of the living* is not the ground under our feet, but that of which the Savior said that it was an inheritance for the meek, for "Blessed are the meek, for they will inherit the earth."[128] And this earth is other than the one that is visible, situated in the height, in heaven. For example, in the Thirty-Sixth Psalm it says, "Wait for the Lord and keep his way, and he will lift you up to inherit the land."[129] You see that the land that is inherited by the righteous is in the height. And again, "The righteous shall inherit the land and shall dwell on it forever and ever."[130] It is impossible to dwell on this earth forever and ever, inasmuch as it also is about to pass away with heaven—for "heaven and earth will pass away."[131] Again in Isaiah it says, "Then you shall trust in the Lord, and he shall bring you up upon the good things of the earth and feed you with the inheritance of your ancestor Jacob."[132] So they receive a reward of being brought up into a perceptible land, in order that they should eat the good things that grow out of it, especially since God feeds them. *I believe*, then, *that I may see the good things of the Lord*. One should understand *good things* in conformity with *the land of the living*. Those are the things of which it is said, "who satisfies your desire with good things."[133] *I believe, therefore, that I may see.* If he were speaking about this earth and its good things, and he were hoping to rule over it, he would not offer up a prayer about those things. For these things are seen, and "hope that is seen is not hope."[134] No one, then, hopes for what is present but for what is coming.

[26:14] *Wait for the Lord.*

He says to his own soul: truly, "May you see the good of Jerusalem."[135]

[26:14] *Take courage, and let your heart be strong, and wait for the Lord!*

Strong deep within, with respect to your heart, with respect to the delay of time, by waiting for the Lord you will indeed meet with the expected things for which you believed.

---

[123]The LXX differs here from the Hebrew, which has "and they are breathing out violence" (NRSV).
[124]Cf. Hos 9:2.
[125]Lk 20:38 NRSV.
[126]Jn 8:52.
[127]Cf. Gen 49:33 NETS.
[128]Mt 5:5.
[129]Ps 37:34 (36:34).
[130]Ps 37:29 (36:29).
[131]Mt 24:35; Mk 13:31; Lk 21:33 NRSV.
[132]Cf. Is 58:14 NETS.
[133]Ps 103:5 (102:5).
[134]Rom 8:24 NRSV.
[135]Ps 128:5 (127:5 NETS).

PSALM 27 [28]

[27:1] *To you, O Lord, I cried out; my God, do not pass me by in silence.*

The one who has hope in nothing other than God offers up prayers to him. For this is the thought of the prayer: to ask for good things from God. And when, at times, some people, for example, falling away from the true divinity, behave toward one of the things that exist as toward a god, those people shout. Of such a kind were the prophets of Baal. This cry, however, is not a harmonious noise formed by syllables but is intensified thinking; and thinking is the voice of the soul. So, the one who thinks in an intensified way toward God and asks those things that are indicated by his thinking, that one shouts to God.

[27:1] *My God, do pass me by in silence.*

The *silence* of God and *passing by in silence* differ. Frequently [115] God is silent because he is patiently waiting, not seeking to take revenge against those who ought to be punished. This is indeed frequently found in Scripture: "To the sinner," it says, "God said, 'Why do you recite my statutes and take up my words on your lips? You hated instruction and you cast my words behind you. If you were seeing a thief, you would run together with him.'"[1] And after a few words, "'These things you did, and I kept silent.'"[2] I did not seek to take revenge quickly, I did not bring on my wrath, "giving you an opportunity for repentance,"[3] for "I do not bring on my wrath every day."[4] For if he were bringing on his wrath every day, the universe would pass away, "but he is patient,"[5] and this is called his "silence." And in Isaiah, for example, he says to those who irritate him, with whom he is patient: "I have been silent. Shall I even always be silent and tolerate"[6] even you while you sin? I did not seek to take revenge, and this is my silence. But I will not always be silent, for at some time there will be an assault against those who have sinned. And in another psalm the saint shouts this very thing: "Do not keep silent nor be appeased, O God, because, look, my enemies made a tumult, and those who hate you raised their head. Against your people they laid villainous plans; they conspired against your saints."[7] Consequently, since they have done such things, *do not pass by in silence*. Then, bring against them the sentence that is deserved by them. Now, not to pass by in silence means this: when I send up my prayer, *do not pass by in silence*, do not put it off, but immediately bestow the gift of good things generously.

For if *you pass by in silence, I shall be like those who go down into a pit*.[8] Indeed, in many passages of the divine instructions, the *pit* means Hades: therefore, *do not pass me by*. In Scripture there are differences between wells and pits, and as for the most part wells are

---
[1] Ps 50:16-18 (49:16-18).
[2] Ps 50:21 (49:21 NETS).
[3] Wis 12:10.
[4] Ps 7:11 (7:12). The Hebrew text reads instead, "a God who has indignation every day."
[5] 2 Pet 3:9.
[6] Is 42:14.
[7] Cf. Ps 83:1-3 (82:2-4 NETS).
[8] Ps 28:1 (27:1); cf. Ps 143:7 (142:7).

understood with approval. Infrequently, however, they are also understood in a blameworthy sense: "But as for you, O God, you will bring them down into a well of corruption."[9] The well of corruption and the pit are synonyms. And appropriately, indeed, he sometimes calls vice and at other times Hades a *pit*, because, as the pit receives the waters that fall down from above, so souls that fall down from above come into vice and into Hades. And in the Twenty-Ninth Psalm he says, "O Lord, you brought up my soul from Hades; you saved me from those that go down into a pit"[10]—look, he mentioned Hades together with the pit. No one arrives there without a reason, but by falling out of the height, by flowing away from the kindred water that remains above. Even in the narrative itself, the *pit* is frequently put in a bad light; for example, those who were conspiring against Joseph cast him into a *pit*, and they put "Daniel into a pit."[11] The saints, however, dig wells and have their residence besides these: "from your wells of running water."[12] And these things are certainly not said of sensible waters.

Now, he *passes by in silence* whenever he does not quickly assent to a prayer when it is offered up. In this way he does not come out against those worthy of his wrath each and every day. And sometimes the quick finding of an answer produces contempt; what someone easily finds, [116] he frequently neglects.

[27:1-2] *Lest you pass me by in silence and I shall be like those who go down into a pit. Listen to the voice of my petition, as I petition you,*

"since I am petitioning you." Certainly, a *petition* is asking for those things of which someone is in need. For prayer comes in two forms: there is a time when it is offered up in order that what is lacking to us and the things of which we are in need should be, and sometimes in order that what we already possess should be preserved. This is not called a petition but a "prayer." It belongs to those who lack something and are in need either to ask for those things that do not belong to them—and this is strictly called a *petition*, even though it is a prayer—or to ask that the good things that already belong to the one who is asking should remain. Again, just as a certain servant *petitions* a master, so a creature calls on God and offers up a prayer. For the prayer is offered up with a word of praise, and therefore some *petition* men, but they never pray to men.

[27:2] *As I petition you, and as I lift up my hands toward your holy temple.*

"When I petition, *I petition you*. For this reason *I lift up my hands toward your holy temple*," and he appears to do this in a perceptible way. He speaks freely, saying, "If we had spread out our hands to a foreign god,"[13] but instead we *lift up* our *hands toward your holy temple*. Now, it is also possible to call deeds *hands lifted up toward* God's *temple*, for whenever our deeds accomplish certain things that are not human, the hands are lifted up toward the temple of God in order that they should be sanctified. For he who prays in God's temple has as his goal becoming a temple himself: "Do you not know that you are God's temple?"[14]

And as I lift up my hands toward your temple. If you are speaking about divinity, here God is found; he is a temple. Do we not frequently say that the subject which relates to these questions, if I may say so, the subject that relates to goods and evils, is also this subject which is called "dialectical argumentation" according to the dialectic philosophers?

---

[9] Ps 55:23 (54:24 NETS).
[10] Ps 30:3 (29:4 NETS).
[11] Dan 6:16 (6:17).
[12] Prov 5:15 LES2.

[13] Ps 44:20 (43:21 NETS).
[14] 1 Cor 3:16 NRSV.

And it is also possible to say then: that the assembly of the faithful is a *temple*, and they come to Jesus who loves them, and he makes them for himself as a home with the Father,[15] and therefore one must *lift up one's hands toward this temple*. One must imitate the saints, for "you, the praise of Israel, dwell among saints."[16] It is also possible that he has seen, like a prophet, the inhumanation and that *temple* of which he says, "Destroy this temple."[17] Becoming an imitator of Christ, he also *lifts up his hands toward* this *holy temple* and then leads the practical and contemplative life.

[27:3] *Do not drag me away together with sinners.*

God drags no one away together with sinners unless he sins. And the sin is voluntary; it is not coerced, it is not given by God. He is saying this, then: when you *listen to me* and *my hands are lifted up toward your holy temple*, then because I do not sin I am not *dragged away together with sinners*. For example, those who have not thought it right to have God in their knowledge, being built into a worthless *temple*, are filled with every kind of defect, with vice; these people are *dragged away together with sinners*. And this can also possess a more mystical sense. Frequently some appear, [117] in a certain sense, to be dragged away unwillingly in order to sin. However, it is not involuntary; it takes place from another who is willing it. Israel, when it was in Jerusalem, when it was governed according to the laws, was free from all sinners; however, while it was there in Jerusalem, it performed certain guilty acts that led it into Babylon, and there it did sins, but not those that it had done in Jerusalem, nor was it able to do them there. At that time, Israel did not begin to worship Bel, the idol of Nebuchadnezzar, but afterward its guilty acts dragged it away with the Babylonians who were sinners.

Question: How can this be said by a holy man?

The one who is holy in this life, always comparing himself with those who are better than he, sees himself as inferior, and he regards the inferiority as a sin—certainly this "sin" is not the transgression of the law. And it is also possible to see things this way: the saints often assume a role, for a teacher is effective at the time when he performs and practices what he teaches others. They must also simulate their words about repentance.

[27:3] *And do not destroy me together with workers of lawlessness.*

He prays this peacefully, since no one perishes in vain except a *worker of lawlessness*. Preserve me in keeping the law so that I do not act lawlessly. But if I should act lawlessly I would be *destroyed together with the workers of lawlessness*, unless I should run in your commandments, saying, "I ran the way of your commandments."[18] "I am *dragged away together*" means "I am numbered together with them."

[27:3] *Those who speak peace with their neighbors, but wrongs are in their hearts.*

He calls them *sinners* and *workers of lawlessness* because they seem to *speak peaceful* and friendly words, but do wicked things *in their heart* in order to harm those whom they flatter by their peaceful words. Surely this is also said in Jeremiah: "He speaks peaceably to his fellow but inwardly has enmity."[19] It is the same thing

---

[15] Cf. Jn 14:23.
[16] Ps 22:3 (21:4).
[17] Jn 2:19.

[18] Ps 119:32 (118:32 NETS).
[19] Jer 9:8 NETS.

"to speak peaceably with one's neighbor but inwardly to have enmity" and *to speak peace with neighbors while they work evils in their hearts.*

Question: What is *working evil?*
Things that are hostile to those whom they speak with the tongue. Sometimes the tongue follows the heart: "With the heart one believes for justification."[20] Whenever the word is in opposition to the will, then someone *speaks peace* with his *neighbor* while he speaks evil things *in his heart*: "As they were speaking peace to me, they were also devising treacheries."[21]

[27:4] *Give them according to their works!*

Question: *According to their works?*
If a certain physician, after going in to a patient, says that this one wants to be cauterized, then the physician wants him to be cut: so from those things that seem to be the same, the works are found to be different, for they take place from a different perspective. See what he says: *According to their works, the wickedness of their habits.*[22] The will is that which is concerned with such works, for which the one who says, "*Give them,* O Lord, *according to their works,*" believes that there comes a recompense.

[27:4] *Render them their due reward,*

Their due reward. For they themselves obtained it; therefore this is *theirs*. Come then! When someone does not punish one who should be punished, as judges frequently do either on account of corruption or aversion, they do not give what belongs to those people according to their works. But you, O God, *Give them according to the works of their hands,*[23] that is, for them.

Render them their due reward. Indeed, you are not irascible; certainly, you are not vindictive. It is their due reward; they sowed it for themselves. A physician often recommends a harsh remedy, when it can be of help; the one who cannot bear the severity arranges it differently [118] or excuses himself, but this is his carelessness. When, therefore, the physician says, "The remedy truly did not harm you," then this happened to you in accordance with your intemperance, since you took it negligently.

[27:5] *Because they took no notice of the works of the Lord.*

The works of the Lord are understood in many ways. Those things that he desires for us men to do are called *works of the Lord*. For when it says, "Cursed is the one who does the works of the Lord carelessly,"[24] truly these are not what God himself does but what he commands to be, and in this sense they are called "his *works*." So we frequently call "the works of a king" what he commands to take place, and these are called the works both of those who do them and of those because of whom they take place. Things that take place according to God's commands, then, are called *works*; the actions that are accomplished according to God's will are his deeds. Therefore, when someone perceives the *works of the Lord,* he practices them, he does not do them carelessly, but zealously and vigorously, with knowledge and understanding.

Sometimes creation is called "*the works* of God." When someone deifies the works of God—for example, he considers the sun to be God and the moon—he did not comprehend the *works of the Lord.* For if he were

---

[20]Rom 10:10. Didymus does not quote the full text, which continues, "and with the mouth one confesses for salvation." The fuller quotation supports his point.
[21]Ps 35:20 (34:20).
[22]Ps 28:4 (27:4).
[23]Ps 28:4 (27:4).
[24]Jer 48:10 (31:10 LES2).

comprehending it, he would not honor it with honors equal to God. However, to create belongs to God, not to become.

[27:5] *And of the works of his hands.*

He is the Creator of visible and invisible things: "In Christ all things were created, things visible and invisible."[25] Now, strictly speaking, the visible things are *the works of hands* since they are indeed material: "whose hands created all the host of heaven."[26] And the intelligible things are called simply "*the works of God.*" Therefore, when someone does not recognize either the visible or the invisible works of God, he will not know him either. For if "from the greatness and beauty of created things, their Creator is discerned analogically,"[27] then from what is visible and invisible one can have a perception of God. So these went wrong in two ways: they understood neither his *works* nor the *works of his hands*.

The one who understands the reasons according to which each of the things that took place has occurred understands the *works of the Lord*. Right now, we have an understanding of the work of God, which is man, when we know why he came into being, why he is composite, and what cause led him into this. For when we become aware that man is the principal work of God, we also understand of the other works that they have come into being for the sake of man's need, in order that some should bear his burdens, others provide shelter, and others food.

Question: Will he indeed understand these things also in the case of the teaching of the Savior in the Gospel?

It is necessary to understand what Jesus does: he broke five loaves of bread for five thousand people, he raised the dead, he restored the blind to sight.[28] One must therefore understand both these works and the works of Jesus' hands. For they have taken place for a reason: and even the fact that they took place in a perceptible way has occurred for the purpose of making him credible—and there is again a reason—and in order that those who are caught up in evildoing should renounce evildoing itself, and then that by them, as by symbols, we should perceive the healings of the soul. For there are also a recovery of sight, a resurrection from death, and a healing from paralysis that belong to the soul.

[27:5] *You will bring them down and build them up no more.*

Since, as I was frequently saying, evils and goods cannot coexist, one must destroy the evils in order that the goods might come to be in this way. Now, often divine Scripture calls such a mode of living a "building." It says thus: it is "God's building";[29] God builds it. And again Jeremiah says, "He sets up, he pulls down, **[119]** and he rebuilds";[30] he razes to the ground the wicked buildings in order that he should build God's temple, he uproots trees that do not bear good fruit[31] in order that those that bear edible and wholesome fruit should grow. They themselves built themselves in an evil way, but you yourself pull them down, not in order that they should remain in a state of demolition but in order that they should be well-built by you. And that God takes down those who built, in one of the Twelve Prophets, in the last one, it says, "'They will build, and I will tear down,' says the Lord."[32] Surely this is in

---

[25] Col 1:16.
[26] Hos 13:4 LXX. The Hebrew text reads differently.
[27] Wis 13:5.
[28] Cf. Mt 16:9; Mk 8:19; Mt 11:5.
[29] 1 Cor 3:9.
[30] Cf. Jer 1:10.
[31] Cf. Mt 3:10; Lk 3:9.
[32] Mal 1:4.

order that we should take our conviction from things that are indisputable. Those who moved from the East desired to build a city and a tower,[33] and God says, "Come, let us go down there and confuse their languages,"[34] and they will never do "all that they intend to do."[35] See! He overturned those who built badly in order that he should build them as God's temple.

[27:5] *You will never build them,*

in the way that they are, and perhaps this is also because such vice is theirs that they, after being demolished, are not now being built up. Now, that this will happen, it says in the psalms that follow, for example.

[27:6] *Blessed is the Lord, for he listened to the voice of my petition.*

He listened, for in the beginning he made a *petition* and he was heard. He turned his speech into a hymn of thanksgiving. And observe that God's delays become useful, in order that one who is helped should know who his helper was and should praise him in song and should receive in addition perfect virtue.

[27:7] *The Lord is my helper and my protector.*

For I have been afraid lest I be *dragged away together with sinners* and lest I *perish together with workers of lawlessness*. He listened to me, therefore, and did not allow me to suffer these things.

[27:7] *My heart hoped in him, and I was helped.*

As one who anticipated all things from God out of a genuine disposition, *my heart hoped in him*, not in word only, but it was so disposed that it had help or expectation from none other than from the Lord of the universe himself.

[27:7] *And my flesh revived.*

That *flesh* of mine revived, which becomes a tablet of God, a heart receiving the decrees and commands of God, when he writes on it by the living Spirit,[36] that it might show that they have become good by nature. The phrase "by nature," however, is not meant literally; rather, it means "in truth." *My flesh revived.* That which was corrupted revived. And this is also possible: if even now the *flesh* vexes, yet at the same time it *revives* when the corruptible becomes incorruptible, and the natural spiritual.[37]

[27:7] *And from my will I shall acknowledge him,*[38]

not in appearance, but willing this, as was also said about the psalm: "rather, his will was in the law of the Lord."[39] Not everyone who practices the law has his own will in the will of the law. For often one decides to perform it from fear of punishment, and there is a time when one also does it on account of vainglory, and the one who really meditates on the law of the Lord, not on account of another, has his own will in its will.

[27:8] *The Lord is empowerment for his people.*

Since he spoke about himself, however, lest he seem to be a lover of self, every such person has God as his *empowerment*, has him as king, has him as a support.

---

[33] Cf. Gen 11:2.
[34] Gen 11:7.
[35] Gen 11:6.
[36] Cf. 2 Cor 3:3.
[37] Cf. 1 Cor 15:44-46.
[38] The Hebrew reads instead, "and with my song I give thanks to him" (NRSV).
[39] Cf. Ps 1:2 NETS.

[27:8] *And he is a protector of the salvation of his Christ.*

Lest they be harmed, lest they be destroyed, he sets his shield before them, to preserve them unharmed. And if, on the one hand, he is speaking about himself, David is saying, *"the [120] salvation of my Christ,"* and if there is some other such person—for there are other christs as well. It is, on the other hand, also possible that the Savior is here called *"Christ."* And his *salvation* is not that by which he himself is saved but that by which he himself saves, and I call both "the remedies of patients" and "the remedy of the physician" not that by which he himself is healed but that which he himself prescribes for them.

[27:9] *Save your people and bless your inheritance.*

Then, after the things that concern him, he prays the words of his request for all the *people* and all the *inheritance* in general.

[27:9] *And shepherd them, and lift them up forever.*

"And the Lord shall stand and see and tend his flock in strength,"[40] and, "You who shepherd Israel, pay attention."[41] And again, "He himself will shepherd them forever."[42] However, whenever they transcend the ages, they are no longer shepherded but ruled; the king rules not over sheep but over men. So whenever they come into the rational condition, then at last they are ruled.

[27:9] *And lift them up.*

Make them exalted not for a first or a second day, but forever. And only the inhabitants of Pelusium,[43] desiring exaltation, say that "forever" means "through life," as in the statement: "I will not eat meat forever."[44] But the rest say that "forever" means that eternal age that befits you.

---

[40] Mic 5:4.
[41] Ps 80:1 (79:2 NETS).
[42] Ps 48:14 (47:15).
[43] This is a comment with some local color. Pelusium is located on the opposite side of the Nile's delta from Alexandria. Apparently, some of its inhabitants interpreted the words "for an age" or "forever" to refer to this life only.
[44] 1 Cor 8:13.

PSALM 28 [29]

[28:1] *A psalm for David at the departure of the tent.*

During this feast, the Feast of Tabernacles, when the whole festival was brought to a close—it was celebrated for seven days—the priests who were officiating within exited the tent on the eighth day. That day is called "the departure of the tent." The divine law commands them to participate solemnly in festivals on three appointed times of the year; these feasts are given at the public expense.[1] For the new moons, the Sabbaths, and the fast were not as important and not of such a kind. These are completely done at the public expense: Pascha, Pentecost—this is also called the Feast of Weeks—and the Feast of Tabernacles—and it took place in the seventh month of the year, for the Pascha took place in the first. Now, according to the axis of the year the seventh is opposite the first, and just as the first until the sixth completes half of the year, so from the seventh until the twelfth the other part of the year is completed. So they are opposed in relation to the axis. For the Pascha arrives when the sun is in Aries, and the Feast of Tabernacles is celebrated when the sun is in Libra. Beginning from the new moon, however, this is the Feast of Trumpets; however, it is not a feast done at the public expense. And they hold the fast on the tenth day, during which it is explained that they humbled their souls.[2]

So the month is the seventh, and for this reason the psalm that relates to the departure from the tent is appropriately the twenty-eighth. For this number is an equilateral triangle, having the number seven on all its sides. Count from one always amplifying by one.[3] So it was necessary that the feast that is observed during the seventh month of the year be arranged according to such a number, having the number seven on all sides. Now, the number seven is holy and incorruptible, "without a mother and without a father,"[4] as has been frequently shown. Therefore, those who transcend the tent and come outside it hasten to the house of God, perfection. Then "God becomes all in all."[5] For this reason the number seven is found there on every side.

Now the triangle, as a two-dimensional shape, having no depth but only length and width, bears a symbol of incorporeality and the intelligible essence; for this reason it is incorruptible **[120A]** on every side, "without a father, without a mother." No longer subject to a beginning, it is free from every beginning, for it is an incorruptible virgin. And they call it a virgin because it factors no single-digit number, nor is it factored by any.[6] Therefore, it is neither generated, "without a father, without a mother," nor does it generate, as an incorruptible virgin.

---

[1] Ex 23:14-17; Lev 23:4-44; Deut 16:1-17.
[2] Cf. Lev 16:29; 23:27.
[3] That is, if you start from 1 and add to it the numbers 2 through 7, you will get 28. See T. W. Mackay, "Didymus the Blind on Psalm 28 (LXX): Text from Unpublished Leaves of the Tura Commentary," *Studia Patristica* 20 (1989): 40-49. See also Lincoln Blumell, *Didymus the Blind's Commentary on Psalms 26:10–29:2 and 36:1-3*, Brigham Young University Papyri 1 (Turnhout: Brepols, 2019), 144.
[4] Cf. Heb 7:3.
[5] 1 Cor 15:28.
[6] In Greek, the single-digit numbers ranged from 1 through 10 and were expressed by the letters *alpha* through *iōta*.

The number two generates the number four, when it is doubled, and the number six when it is tripled, and the number eight when it is cubed—and the cube is an equal times an equal times an equal, 2 × (2 × 2 = 4)—but when it is multiplied by five it generates ten. Again three, when doubled, generates six; tripled, it generates nine, which is the most important square. Now, I was calling the square an equal times an equal—3 × 3 = 9 is a square—but when one cubes it, it becomes 27 (3 × (3 × 3 = 9)). The number seven, however, generates nothing; when it is doubled it falls outside the decade. Again, no number factors it, for no number, either doubled or tripled, makes the number seven. According to this, then, inasmuch as no number generates it, it is said to be "without a father, without a mother"; it is beyond every beginning. And insofar as it does not generate, it is an incorruptible virgin. And such is the end, which is no longer material nor impeded by vice, but is purity in every way; it is holiness. So, the heading also is correspondingly the departure from every tent, becoming free from every body. In general, in every liturgy that is performed in the tent, when it is finished and the priests finally depart, it is called "*the departure from the tent.*" And chiefly this is mentioned when the Feast of Tabernacles is fulfilled in the seventh month, as I said.

[**28:1**] *Bring to the Lord, O sons of God.*

Now he gives orders: "I do not simply summon priests in charge of the divine liturgy to offer up spiritual sacrifices of praise, but *sons of God.*" Now, the *sons of God* are sinless, for "everyone who practices righteousness has been born of God."[7] And "everyone who believes that Jesus is the Christ has been born of God";[8] "he who was born of God"[9] is his son. And no one who is a son of God sins, for "everyone born of God does not sin."[10] Therefore, when someone has been disciplined in the practical and contemplative life, he is sinless and, because of this, he is called "*a son of God.*"

Bring to the Lord, O sons of God. It is also possible that they are called "*sons of God*" in place of "free men," not living as slaves in a servile fashion, though they were slaves of ignorance and vice and the rest of sin. And what do these offer? *Sons of rams*—not merely sheep, but *sons of rams*. "Sons of rams" could be said periphrastically, just as when we say "sons of physicians" instead of "physicians," and here *sons of rams* means "rams," since they beget offspring in the flock, in which they become leaders of the flock. For some are able to lead others by their life and practice, even if they do not have a word of knowledge, even if they are not able to instruct as a teacher. So these are leaders of the flock of sheep, and when they possess something more than the rest, they are able to rule and lead them. You certainly find that even teachers in the church who do not have the spoken word, and at times do not have the internal word, partake of [**120B**] the truth even though they are equipped with a certain vulgar education. These, then, because they are rulers and leaders of the second rank, are called "*sons of rams.*"

[**28:1**] *Bring to the Lord the sons of rams,*[11] *bring to the Lord glory and honor.*

Next, on the one hand, he tells the *sons of God* this primarily: to *bring glory and honor;* on the other hand, it is perhaps possible that this is related to the rams in common. Now, those who live well *bring glory and honor,* just as indeed the one who sins and transgresses

---

[7] Cf. 1 Jn 2:29 ESV.
[8] 1 Jn 5:1 NRSV.
[9] 1 Jn 5:18 ESV.

[10] 1 Jn 3:9.
[11] This part of the verse is not attested in the Hebrew.

the law of God dishonors the one who gives it, just as the one who keeps it honors the Lawgiver. And in this way we truly honor Jesus, as we honor the Father. And by the kind of reasoning where we honor the Lawgiver by transforming the words of God into deeds and right thoughts, in the same way we also honor the Son with honor equal to God when we keep his words. We honor the Father when we understand the things he powerfully taught, especially that which relates to the teaching about divinity, such as: "One honors the Son just as he honors the Father."[12]

Just as we call him unchangeable, immutable in nature, holy, and him "who alone has immortality,"[13] we are being pious when we say the same things about the Son as well. For we say that he is "eternal one from eternal one, true God from true God, light from light, holy one from holy one," not light from what has been lit earlier on. For there are lights that have come into this condition in this way, from having been lit, "for you were darkness, but now in the Lord you are light,"[14] and are holy because they were sanctified. However, when such names are said about God they do not mean the same thing;[15] we are saying that the God who is able to make saints is holy. So the one who keeps the practical virtues, who transforms the words of Jesus into deeds, *brings glory and honor*.

And he also *brings glory* in the same way, for he says, "Let your light shine before men, so that men may see your works and glorify the Father who is in heaven."[16] And in the Apocalypse of John it is found, "Fear God and give him glory."[17] And furthermore Paul writes, "Glorify God in your body,"[18] and, "Whether you eat or drink, do everything for the glory of God."[19] Indeed, the one who has self-control and seeks to complete the things of the Lord because of celibacy in order to please the Lord: this person glorifies God in his own body. And just as statues are frequently glorified, whenever temples are gladdened and receive added adornments, so the temple of God is adorned whenever it possesses virtues, for "holy is your temple, admirable in righteousness."[20] *Doxa* here means "glory," not "opinion."

[**28:2**] *Bring to the Lord glory for his name.*

His people are entitled to be called "his priests." Indeed, in the tent they celebrate the rites of the holy service, serving none other than him. Since, then, the name of God has been conferred on you, *bring glory to his name* by serving him as is necessary, serving him as the laws prescribe, acting in this way so that he for whom you are named might be adorned. Likewise, in the opposite case, God is blasphemed whenever those who bear his name do prohibited things, so that it is said, "Because of you, my name is blasphemed."[21] And it says again in Ezekiel, "You profaned my name among the nations."[22] For whenever those who belong to God, even the faithful, practice [**120C**] the very things that are outside reverence for God, as much as is possible to then, they profane the Lord's name. Therefore, because of this the saints send forth their prayer, saying, "Not to us, O Lord, not to us, rather to your name give glory."[23] Insofar as it depends on our deeds, we are unable to obtain what we desire, that for which we pray; but

---

[12] Cf. Jn 5:23.
[13] 1 Tim 6:16.
[14] Eph 5:8.
[15] Both Jesus and his disciples are called "the light of the world" (see Jn 8:12; Mt 5:14), but the sense is understood differently.
[16] Mt 5:16.
[17] Rev 14:7 NRSV.

[18] 1 Cor 6:20 NRSV.
[19] Cf. 1 Cor 10:31 NRSV.
[20] Ps 65:4 (64:5).
[21] Cf. Is 52:5 NETS.
[22] Cf. Ezek 36:22 NETS.
[23] Ps 115:1 (113:9 NETS).

insofar as it is because of your name, we ought to obtain them in order that you might be glorified even by those things that we do for you.

And note this observation: the word commands *bringing glory and honor to the Lord* as though to servants—clearly as servants and worshippers. *"Bring to the Lord"* is uttered with absolute authority, to him who is truly Lord, who is truly God the unchangeable and immutable.

[28:2] *Worship the Lord in his holy court.*

Those who come outside the tent come into the *holy court*, and there it is necessary to *worship*. And that this differs from a tent just as it also does from a house we learn from one of the psalms—that is, the eighty-third: "How beloved are your tents, O Lord of hosts."[24] See, he admitted a longing for the tents. "My soul longs and faints for the courts of the Lord."[25] He has not yet arrived in the courts, but he has a longing to arrive in them, in order that he should worship there. After the courts is the house: "Blessed are all those who dwell in your house."[26] Those who pass beyond the courts, "planted in the house of the Lord, will flourish in the courts of the Lord,"[27] for perfection is not there.

Question: The one planted, is he planted in the perfect state?

Someone is introduced into the healing arts because of the end of the healing arts. There he has his planting, then he sprouts, and afterward he is said to be within the profession, after his progressions, for after the tents are the courts. So God alone is to be worshiped: "You shall worship the Lord your God, and serve only him."[28]

[28:3] *The voice of the Lord is over the waters; the God of glory thundered.*

Again, the God of glory thunders in a way that corresponds to what was said earlier about the number seven. Those things are also said about the voice, for the phrase "the voice of the Lord" is mentioned seven times: *the voice of the Lord is over the waters,*[29] *the voice of the Lord in strength,*[30] *the voice of the Lord in majesty,*[31] *the voice of the Lord as he shatters cedars,*[32] *the voice of the Lord as he divides flames of fire,*[33] *the voice of the Lord as he shakes the wilderness,*[34] *the voice of the Lord, which creates the deer.*[35] What is peculiar about each one will be discussed. Nevertheless, let us first look at *the voice of the Lord*. Certainly one must first understand the more preliminary sense. These things could be said about John, for he is *the voice* of the one who cries out. "'What answer,' they say, 'should we give to those who sent us? Who are you if you are neither the Christ nor the Prophet?'"[36] He says, "I am the voice of one crying out in the wilderness."[37] *The voice of the Lord* comes *over the water* because he is the Baptist and is appointed for baptism. This *voice* baptized even the Savior as Man and, after the heavens were opened, a *voice* was given: "This is my beloved Son, with whom I am well pleased."[38]

[28:3] *The God of glory thundered, the Lord, over many waters.*

Now *God* is said to *thunder* whenever certain sublime words are conveyed to men. For

---

[24]Ps 84:1 (83:2 LES2).
[25]Cf. Ps 84:2 (83:3 NETS).
[26]Ps 84:4 (83:5 LES2).
[27]Ps 92:13 (91:14 LES2).
[28]Mt 4:10; Lk 4:8.

[29]Ps 29:3 (28:3).
[30]Ps 29:4 (28:4).
[31]Ps 29:4 (28:4).
[32]Ps 29:5 (28:5).
[33]Ps 29:7 (28:7).
[34]Ps 29:8 (28:8).
[35]Ps 29:9 (28:9).
[36]Cf. Jn 1:20-22.
[37]Jn 1:23 NRSV.
[38]Mt 3:17 ESV.

example, it is said, "And the Lord thundered from heaven, and the Most High gave forth his voice."[39] The servants of this thunder are generated by it, and they are called "sons of thunder."[40] It is the bestower of its *glory*. For in the same way we call him both "God of righteousness" and "God of salvation" when he produces [**120D**] salvation and grants righteousness.

The Lord, over many waters.

Each of the baptized is baptized for his own sake and, in a certain way, receives something better than water: that is, the one who receives his own baptism was purified. Jesus alone, when he is baptized, is *over many waters*, for he was baptized on behalf of all, and each is baptized in order that he should be sanctified, but Jesus in order that he should sanctify. Therefore, since the many are sanctified when they are baptized, it is necessary that the Sanctifier be *over many waters*. Now, it is also possible to understand it as follows, given that his baptism is a sign. It is also said that there is "a serpent in the sea"[41] and that there is a "king over all that are in the waters."[42] However, Jesus has come and, according to a mystical sense, has reached as far as all the waters, for "Thus says the Lord, who rules over many waters: 'And so shall they be scattered,'"[43] the brothers who are zealous for virtue from the wicked ones. For those who are virtuous are cleansed and sanctified from unworthy things, since their purification remains.

In these examples, the symbolic was also appearing: in the beginning of the creation of the world as well an intermediate firmament was gained, so that water should be separated from water, and one should be above, while the other should be under it. So here as well the Lord has appeared *over many waters* in order that he should separate these, just as when he cleanses the threshing floor—"Indeed, he gathers the wheat into the barn, but the chaff he hands over to unquenchable fire":[44] a separation of the threshing floor appears. And when he hauls the dragnet, or others haul the dragnet, they toss the good ones into containers, but the rancid they throw away as well as the potsherds.[45] And all these things one must interpret anagogically: figurally and spiritually.

[**28:4**] *The voice of the Lord in strength.*

The voice of the Lord is the strongest, and this is what its being *in strength* means. And it is also possible that *in strength* means that "he makes others strong": "*the voice of the Lord* strengthens." Here I understand the word as a feminine noun in the dative case: *the voice of the Lord* is *in strength*.[46] However, whenever he strengthens those who draw near to him, this is the utterance that strengthens those who draw near and is shouted out by *the voice of the Lord*. So John, as a strong man, was saying, "You brood of vipers! Who warned you to flee from the wrath to come?"[47] He was speaking to so great a crowd; he clearly grew strong according to this strength. Paul also, when he was empowered, began to say, "I can do all things through him who strengthens me."[48] And each one of the prophets was strengthened. One says, "I will love you, O Lord, my strength,"[49] and another, "O Lord, my strength and my refuge and my help in the day of my troubles."[50] So one who powerfully and

---

[39] Ps 18:13 (17:14 NETS); cf. 2 Sam 22:14.
[40] Mk 3:17.
[41] Ezek 32:2.
[42] Job 41:34 (41:26 NETS).
[43] Nahum 1:12 LXX.
[44] Mt 3:12; Lk 3:17.
[45] Cf. Mt 13:47-48.
[46] The discussion of case is important here because a variant reading that he has just discussed, *enischyei*, takes the two words together as a verb.
[47] Mt 3:7; Lk 3:7 NRSV.
[48] Phil 4:13 NRSV.
[49] Ps 18:1 (17:2 NETS).
[50] Jer 16:19.

mightily brings good news has *the voice of the Lord in strength.*

John is understood in the place of all of Scripture; John is the expression of the Scriptures. For this reason he said, "I am the voice of one crying."[51] It is said indeed, "The Law and the Prophets were until John."[52] And the one crying out is the Word; therefore the expression of the Scriptures is *in strength*, when someone says it in the same way that it has been said. And the one who receives it according to its shadow alone and its letter does not receive *the voice of the Lord* that *strengthens*; rather, the one who is able to transform the letter into the spirit and the shadow [121] into the truth, that one was *strengthened* by *the voice of the Lord.*

[28:4] *The voice of the Lord in majesty.*

Since all that the voice of the Lord does is great and supernatural, producing what is befitting it, the *voice of the Lord* is *in majesty*. *Majesty* is nothing other than having what is befitting in great things.[53] So the voice of the Lord has the instruction not in small things, but it acts as guide and it causes one to advance into the letter and the truth. For this reason it is *in majesty.*

[28:5] *The voice of the Lord, as he shatters cedars.*

John again is the *voice of the Lord*, for again in the more introductory exposition *he shatters the cedars*, although he does not literally shatter them when he says, "Even now the axe is lying at the root of the trees; every tree that does not bear good fruit is cut down and thrown into the fire."[54] Therefore, the Pharisees were considered to be cedars, and the scribes along with them. And he said to these very people, "Do not presume to say to yourselves, 'We have Abraham as our father.' Even now the axe is at the root."[55] This *voice of the Lord* is against the *cedars* of Lebanon, and is truly against the wise of this world; these are the *cedars* of Lebanon.

Now, when the expression "the cedars of Lebanon" appears in Scripture, it is not always taken literally. "Open your doors, O Lebanon, and let fire devour your cedars."[56] Then he interprets who Lebanon is and who its cedars are: "Let the pine wail, for the cedar has fallen, because nobles have greatly suffered"[57]—behold! the cedars! "There is a sound of shepherds wailing because the pride of the Jordan has suffered misery,"[58] since the cedars of Lebanon are shattered. And there is the passage: *He will pulverize them, even Lebanon, as the calf.*[59] They prepare calves out of the arable land of Lebanon; always keeping them near the idols, they drive them to the altar. And material from the arable land of Lebanon is easily consumed by fire and broken down. Like the other cedars, men who always boast great things are broken and easily shattered, because they cannot endure. Similarly, the material of the arable land of Lebanon cannot endure before the flame of fire.

[28:6] *And he will pulverize them, even Lebanon, as the calf.*

Once the people made a calf, when as they were leaving Egypt they became negligent, after Moses delayed on the mountain. The delay, however, had come about not because of any responsibility of Moses', but because of the circumspection of him who was causing it. For he wanted him to remain simply lest he be

---

[51] Jn 1:23.
[52] Lk 16:16 ESV.
[53] The same definition for "magnificence" is found at PsT 16.
[54] Mt 3:10; Lk 3:9.
[55] Mt 3:9-10.
[56] Zech 11:1 NETS.
[57] Zech 11:2 NETS.
[58] Zech 11:3.
[59] Ps 29:6 (28:6).

despised—for what is easily found is most often despised. So after he went down he pulverized that calf until it was dust, he cast it into the stream that went down from the mountain, "and made the sons of Israel drink it."[60] This happened not in order that they should drink gold and gold dust but in order that he might teach that the things by which one sins are the very things by which one is punished. Who eats and drinks his own habits? Indeed, "they shall eat from their schemes,"[61] so they also drink of them. Those who have this experience say as follows: "He gave us water with gall to drink,"[62] and, "You will feed us with the bread of tears."[63] So he will pulverize that Lebanon like the calf: that is, he will shatter all idolatry like that calf. And one must not settle down with these words and their literal sense, because it is impossible for a calf that is made of gold [122] to be completely shattered like dust, even as this is not possible for bronze, or gold, or another molten substance. The passage mingles together certain things that are impossible with the literal sense not in order that we should withdraw from what is credible and of good quality in the literal sense itself, but that we should collide with it and then mount up by means of it.

[28:6] *And he that is beloved like a son of unicorns.*[64]

He that is beloved before all the priests, he that is beloved before all the *sons of God*—because these have their being sons from "the Spirit of adoption"[65]—this one, then, is the only-begotten and is Son in his essence. Those are *rams*, if they both lead the sheep and generate young, but none of them was sacrificed for the whole rational race. The only holy one, he was at that time led to the slaughter, and the wondrous Lamb was led to sacrifice. And probably the deeds are not characteristic of his magnificence but are characteristic of his being a Lamb; after condescending, he approaches like a lamb. *The beloved one*, therefore, is just as this beloved Lamb of his is. And he is loved in every way; there is nothing to find in this Lamb, this beloved one, which is worthy of hatred. Even if he punishes, he is beloved by the one who knows the reason for his punishing; and when he is sacrificed for the whole race, he is worthy of love. Strictly speaking, one who is truly beloved is not loved because of something else but because of himself. John called him "a Son of love";[66] "Love," then, is not merely being called "the beloved," but it was often called "the beloved of this unicorn."

Therefore, since the kingdom of the Savior is one—for it is not changed in order that he should at one time rule in one way, and then rule collectively, for even if we say that his kingdom is different, we call it so because of those who are governed—he indeed does not pass from a lesser to a greater kingdom, for he condescends from a greater to a lesser because of those who do not understand the greatness of his kingdom. "He reigns," then, "in Mount Zion from now until forever"[67] over a kingdom that is neither eternal nor limitless but advantageous to those ones. So whenever those are instructed, then he no longer rules over them in this way, "the Lord, ruling forever and ever and beyond."[68]

So the horn signifies a kingdom, and the Savior is called a *"unicorn."* Because he does

---

[60] Ex 32:20 NETS.
[61] Hos 11:6 NETS.
[62] Jer 8:14.
[63] Ps 80:5 (79:6).
[64] The NRSV reads, "He makes Lebanon skip like a calf, and Sirion like a young wild ox." The place name "Sirion" is rendered "he that is beloved." A different main verb is also used.
[65] Rom 8:15.

[66] This attribution to John appears to be mistaken. Cf. Col 1:13.
[67] Mic 4:7.
[68] Ex 15:18 NETS.

not abdicate the kingdom that is intrinsic to him, he is strong and has the kingdom unbending and steadfast so that he is also called a "rhinoceros." Again the passage makes a declaration about the Breath that the kingdom exhales. Who is so great that those who are breathed on by him are summoned in order to rule? As the Corinthians hear: "And would that you did reign, so that we might share the rule with you!"[69] The statement is not about the perceptible kingdom, as Abraham also heard: "You are a king from God among us."[70]

[28:7] *The voice of the Lord as he divides a flame of fire.*

A promise is given to the wise man that he will pass through water and through fire: "If you should pass through water, rivers shall not overwhelm you; if you should go through fire, the flame shall not consume you, because I am with you."[71] Moreover, those who have had the protection of these good actions in their experience say, "We went through fire and water, and you brought us out to revival."[72] So, as according to the passage, at one time a separation of the Red Sea has occurred by the staff of Moses, in order that the people should journey through and, treading on the sea floor, should proceed as on dry land,[73] so again *the voice of the Lord*, like the staff, separated and cut the sea in two. He will split the *flame* in two so that the one who passes through the *fire* [123] is not scorched by a *flame*, because he has *the voice of the Lord dividing the flame* in two. Now, as the sea, after it is divided in two, provides a walkable path, so also the flame of fire, after it is cloven by *the voice of the Lord*, becomes passable. We were saying that John is the one who accomplished what was spoken by such a voice, when he says, "I baptize with water; that one, however, with the Holy Spirit and fire."[74] He cleaves *the flame of fire* in two in order that we should be helped by it by passing through it, that we should be tested with fire by it.

Since many love the literal senses, when it is possible we will also speak in favor of this. A "moist breeze,"[75] as it were, going down into the furnace, began to *divide the flame*. For the following was not said, that they were not burned when the flame drew near with the fire, but that the "moist breeze" that went down began to divide the flame and they were free of the flame—even while walking around deep within the furnace, they were not drawing near to the flame. They were "in the midst of the sea, but the water made its stand as a wall on the right and a wall on the left."[76] They were not disturbed by the water.

Pleasure is also a *flame of fire*, and from one pleasure, learn about them all. For Paul said to some people, "Marry and do not burn."[77] *The voice of the Lord*, by introducing, keeping, and revealing self-control in action, *divides the flame of fire*; it renders the pleasure split in two, and it begins to obtain a passable way in its midst. One must also understand these things in relation to the other situations that set pleasure in motion.

[28:8] *The voice of the Lord, as he shakes a wilderness.*

The phrase "in *the wilderness*" was said for this reason: "the voice of one crying in the wilderness."[78] When the *wilderness* is *shaken* it no longer remains a *wilderness*; afterward a field is cultivated and a paradise appears. So

---

[69] 1 Cor 4:8 ESV.
[70] Gen 23:6.
[71] Is 43:2.
[72] Ps 66:12 (65:12 NETS).
[73] Ex 14:21-22.

[74] Mt 3:11; Lk 3:16.
[75] Dan 3:50 LXX.
[76] Ex 14:29.
[77] 1 Cor 7:9.
[78] Is 40:3; Mt 3:3; Mk 1:3; Lk 3:4; Jn 1:23.

the voice of the Lord *shakes the wilderness* in order that it should no longer be a *wilderness*. As when you say, "He shakes sinners," and when sinners are shaken in repentance, they are no longer such as they were before they were shaken.

[28:8] *And the Lord will shake the wilderness of Kadesh.*

A *shaken wilderness* could be the inheritance of the Gentiles, which formerly "was without hope and without God in the world";[79] however, after it was shaken, it no longer remained an idolater, it no longer remained without God. *The wilderness of Kadesh* could also be the "remnant, which remains according to the election of grace,"[80] for Kadesh is interpreted as "holy." So the Lord will shake even the wilderness of Kadesh, which was laid waste by the interpretations of the shadow, which was made desolate by the letter, about which Isaiah says, "If the Lord had not left us offspring, we would have become like Sodom and been made similar to Gomorrah."[81] Behold! This is Kadesh, because of its being converted from the shadow to the truth and from the letter to the spirit.

Question: How is this "holy"?

Because the *shaking* is certainly not always blameworthy; what is interpreted as "holy" *shakes the wilderness of Kadesh.* You recognize this, that "the remnant, which remains according to the election of grace,"[82] at that time possesses the spirit of the law and the truth. The saints did not know even the true law before the arrival of Christ, and not all do now, for in the same way a *wilderness* is in them: the many who take their stand only as far as the letter and the shadow. So for a good purpose he set these in motion in order that they might be called "Kadesh," and no longer "*the wilderness of Kadesh.*"

[28:9] *The voice of the Lord, as he creates the deer.*

The voice of the Lord creates those *deer* who destroy the poisonous kinds of serpents. [124]

Now, the deer has an odor and it attracts serpents, even if they are in the deepest dens, even if they are on a height, even if they are in a dwelling. And they strike them with a blow and kill them, or they even make use of them for food. Now, the following is also said about this animal: that when it grows old it searches for a serpent and, after eating it, it purifies itself; it sloughs off its old hide and its flesh is renewed. So the deer kills serpents. Those who can say, "We are ready to punish every disobedience,"[83] are *deer* who slay the serpents of vice. Again, those who received authority from Jesus "over snakes and scorpions, and over all the power of the enemy"[84] destroy these snakes. And the killing of the serpents also benefits them, because they lose the venomous impulse of the serpent.

When John calls them "a brood of vipers,"[85] he is a *voice* that *prepares the deer* in order that he may no longer call them venomous animals, and that they may no longer be serpents; rather, they are made ready to become *deer* who destroy the true serpents, the forms of vice.

[28:9] *And he will uncover forests.*

You have again the word of John: "Even now the ax is lying at the root of the trees."[86] Now, there is an uncovering of a forest whenever the uncultivated trees are felled and the bare earth

---

[79] Eph 2:12.
[80] Rom 11:5.
[81] Cf. Is 1:9 NETS.
[82] Rom 11:5.

[83] 2 Cor 10:6.
[84] Lk 10:19.
[85] Mt 3:7; Lk 3:7 NRSV.
[86] Mt 3:10; Lk 3:9 NRSV.

is exposed, able to be sown at last. I say then, even now "the axe is at the root of the trees that are wicked and wild." It is clear that he is *uncovering* the *forests*. For when the *forests* are exposed, venomous animals are no longer able to lie in wait there, but the deer trample on the venomous animals that were there before. They kill them and that place, which was once a *forest*, becomes a paradise.

[28:9] *And in his temple everyone says, "Glory!"*

when the *forests are uncovered*. For the vice of those who possess it is also a covering; whenever this is destroyed, the underlying nature is revealed and so one also becomes God's *temple*. And *everyone says, "Glory,"* not this one or that one, but everyone. And again there comes the full complement of good things, the end that is superior to all, the end of ends.

[28:10] *The Lord will settle the flood.*

Whenever the soul is submerged by purifying waters, then the flood is inhabited. Truly this flood, which is rare and leads into serenity, is praiseworthy. "I made my sin known and I did not conceal my lawlessness,"[87] and after a few words: "but during a flood of many waters they will not come near to him."[88] Let one contemplate the sequence of the whole passage. As a man, I made known my sinful practice and revealed it; "I said, 'I will declare to the Lord my lawlessness, against myself.'"[89] I decided to declare against myself, for the one who says, "I am a sinner and a worker of lawlessness,"[90] declares against himself. Moreover, you, because you are good, not only forgave the sin regarding that I confessed, but you even forgave "the impiety of my heart,"[91]

from which the practice of sin and lawlessness have stemmed. And here he calls the disposition "heart"; he is speaking of the inclination. **[125]** So someone could hold the great impiety responsible. You then, after I confessed regarding the small sin, forgave the greater, "the impiety of my heart," which extends even to the saints.

"Because of the impiety of the heart every holy person will confess to you at the appropriate time."[92] However, it is not an appropriate time to offer confession regarding this, when we were previously purified from the practices. For the one who can be freed from abominable deeds, even if he is involved in lesser sins, it is clear that he is also responsible for impiety. "Because of the impiety," then, "of the heart, every holy person will pray to you at an appropriate time." We, however, render appropriateness to the time whenever we despise the lesser sins and trample on them.

But when the shower of many purifying waters takes place, impiety no longer draws near to those to whom it used to draw near previously, for it disappears completely. Consequently, God inhabits this *flood*. Whenever the *flood* occurs and the things carried off by the *flood* are ruined, then the one who was submerged is inhabited: he receives divine gifts. Now, in the case of the flood that occurred during the time of Noah, this appears symbolically: after the earth was flooded and all the unrighteous deeds with which it was filled left, then at last it received a divine planting in conformity with its beginning. And in Nahum also such a statement is found: "Why do you calculate against the Lord? He himself will make an end of those who arise against him; darkness will pursue his enemies."[93] Then he says, "Nevertheless, by a flood, by a group of

---

[87]Ps 32:5 (31:5).
[88]Ps 32:6 (31:6).
[89]Cf. Ps 32:5 (31:5 NETS).
[90]Cf. Lk 5:8.
[91]Ps 32:5 (31:5).

[92]Cf. Ps 32:5-6 (31:5-6).
[93]Nahum 1:9, 8.

floods, he will make passages."[94] When the soul is deluged and is cleansed from the things that were previously disturbing it, a passage appears; it receives God, who walks around within it. So God *inhabits* such a *flood*, and whenever, after overwhelming by the divine flood what is worthy of perishing, he *dwells*, then *he will sit as king forever*.[95]

[28:10] *And the Lord will sit as king forever.*

Sitting signifies either teaching or a kingdom. It is said, for example: "for the throne of government is established by righteousness,"[96] or a seat; he has called the kingdom a "throne of government." And again, "They sat on Moses's seat"[97]—this seat has to do with instruction. Therefore, after all the instructions, and at the end there is no longer a need of instruction—and instruction is a guide toward the goal of virtue and knowledge. Then at last *the Lord will sit as king* when there are no longer hateful enemies. For, since he does not sit in relation to making war but rather is arrayed for battle, and sometimes he makes war: "The Lord of hosts will go forth and will shatter in war, and he will arouse his zeal and will shout with strength over his enemies."[98] When he comes out to us, he wages war—for there are enemies, there are those who are arrayed for battle—so that he then "might destroy the one who has the power of death."[99] And "every ruler and every authority is destroyed"[100] when God the Word rules together with the Father. *The Lord*, then, *will sit as king* **[126]** *forever*.

[28:11] *The Lord will give strength to his people!*

His voice, that one that he had *for his people*, the *people* then bless with hymns of thanksgiving, not one time only, nor while they are still being attacked and troubled, but when they are in peace at last. Or in another sense, peace comes when, just as every affliction, sorrow, and sighing flees away, so too does war. And these good things will commence at the end of the troubles.

[28:11] *The Lord will bless his people with peace!*

Not simply "the people," but *his people*. Indeed, when the aforementioned enemies are shattered and all are overthrown, then all have become one people of God, and it is blessed in that "peace which surpasses all understanding."[101]

Question: [. . .]?

I was saying that the number is a triangle where each side is equal: the number twenty-eight, that is. There are only four perfect numbers between one and ten thousand.[102] We say that a perfect number is the one that is composed and completed by the sum of its own factors: for example, the number six. This number is perfect. Six divided by two is three. These factors, when they are added together, complete it.[103] Now, not every number does this; there are some that are less than their sum, such as the number eight: eight halved is four, and the factors become seven.[104] Those who devote themselves to this activity call these numbers "subperfect," because they are less than perfect. And other are "superperfect,"

---

[94]Cf. Nahum 1:8.
[95]Ps 29:10 (28:10).
[96]Prov 16:12 NETS.
[97]Mt 23:2.
[98]Is 42:13.
[99]Heb 2:14 NRSV.
[100]1 Cor 15:24.

[101]Cf. Phil 4:7 NRSV.
[102]These numbers are 6, 28, 496, and 8,128 (Blumell, *Didymus the Blind's Commentary*, 155n8-9).
[103]In this example, and the ones that follow, 1 is assumed to be a factor as well. $1 + 2 + 3 = 6$.
[104]$1 + 2 + 4 = 7$.

which exceed their own factors when they are added together: the number twelve is such a number.[105] So there are only four numbers, the sum of which completes the number when it is divided into its own factors. The number six is such a number, and this is the first of the perfect numbers; the second is twenty-eight.[106] So it was necessary that the person who is here celebrated for his perfection be placed at the perfect number.

For if *in the temple of God, everyone says, "Glory!"* when he *sits as king forever*, when he sits and is not shaken, then his attendants have made their stand and are perfect. For God is, in a certain sense, *shaken* when those who are around him come into turmoil, into confusion. For example, when Adam was keeping God's command, he was his companion, and when he transgressed, "he heard the sound of the Lord God walking about."[107] He withdrew from him as soon as he himself began to flee "from the presence of the Lord God."[108] One may certainly also find this in Zechariah: "And he will come with a surge of his anger."[109] None of those who have genuinely taken their stand by him are under his anger. Therefore, this person who is mentioned and described here must be found nearby.

Sons of God are those who are ordered to draw near to what God said. I say: the genuine drawing near takes place from both: both from the one who draws near and from the one who is approached. Indeed, neither by violence nor compulsion does one induce another to yield to virtue. Indeed, if innumerable exhortations are made and he resists them, then he does not progress. "How often," he says, "I desired, and you were not willing!"[110] Virtue is not a matter of compulsion; it is a matter of the will. If you remove its voluntary character, it is no longer virtue. And the divine apostle, knowing this, writes to Philemon about Onesimus, "I was able to keep him near me, but without your consent I did not want to lest your good deed be something forced and not voluntary."[111] So, there must be an agreement between the one who exhorts and the one in whom the progress takes place, in order that the actions belonging to the exhortation be carried out. "'Return, O sons who are turned away, and I will turn to you,' says the Lord."[112] Since you yourselves turned away from me, I also thought to remove my presence from you. "They walked aslant with me, and I too will walk with them in skewed anger."[113]

There are Christians who have a robust way of life [**127**] but not speech. These are the *sons of rams*. And I said that they are called *"sons of rams"* periphrastically, instead of *"rams."* And I was also saying, according to a second interpretation, that those who have a word of wisdom and "have received the Spirit of adoption"[114] are sons who are commanded to do what God prescribes. And since many are chosen as leaders of churches and assemblies of the faithful who have a robust way of life but not an elevated insight or speech, these are the *sons of rams*. *Rams* also lead the flock in a certain manner, but not like a herdsman, not like a shepherd. Then I was saying that it is said either to the *sons of God* or to both ranks—to both the *sons of God* and the *sons of rams*—"*Bring to him glory and honor.*"[115] And I was saying that the one who keeps his law brings honor to God; the one who disobeys the divine law becomes established in the opposite: he dishonors the giver by his transgression. "Honor the Lord, and he will strengthen you."[116]

---

[105] $1 + 2 + 3 + 4 + 6 = 16$.
[106] $1 + 2 + 4 + 7 + 14 = 28$.
[107] Cf. Gen 3:8 NETS.
[108] Gen 3:8.
[109] Zech 9:14 LES2.
[110] Cf. Mt 23:37; Lk 13:34 NRSV.
[111] Philem 13-14.
[112] Cf. Jer 3:22; Zech 1:3; Mal 3:7.
[113] Lev 26:23-24.
[114] Cf. Rom 8:15.
[115] Ps 29:1 (28:1).
[116] Prov 7:1 LXX.

Question: To whom then does he say, *"Bring to him the sons of rams"*?

Again, when someone wishes to understand the *sons of God* as priests, in the way that is more foolish and according to the letter, he calls the offerings *"sons of rams"* in the case of the literal sense. But the whole psalm is clearly elevated. If you understand it literally, you receive both the *forest* and the *calf, Lebanon* and *the wilderness*.

Question: *The Lord will inhabit the flood?*[117]

Again, this is taken in both senses: it is called a *flood* whenever a multitude of cleansing water appears to wash the one in need of cleansing. And I presented such testimonies as these: "Because of this impiety of heart, every holy person will pray to you at the suitable time."[118] Now, you should not consider impiety here to be the intensified kind, but as someone says, "Cleanse me from hidden transgressions,"[119] "but at a flood of many waters."[120] When cleansing waters come and that impiety is washed away, the one who is completely cleansed departs not only from wicked deeds but also from evil thoughts. Take it in another sense also: when a great flood of oppressions comes, the holy one is also impeded from drawing near to God. For this reason he must not have such great sins as to be in need of a flood, but of a sprinkling. For it says somewhere, "I will sprinkle them and I will give them a new heart."[121] The sprinkling is not a flood; the saint, moreover, says, "You will sprinkle me with hyssop, and I shall be cleansed; you will wash me, and I shall be whiter than snow."[122]

---

[117] Ps 29:10 (28:10).
[118] Ps 32:5-6 (31:5-6).
[119] Ps 19:12 (18:13).
[120] Ps 32:6 (31:6 NETS).
[121] Cf. Ezek 36:25-26.
[122] Ps 51:7 (50:9 NETS).

PSALM 29 [30]

[**29:1**] *A psalm of an ode for David's dedication. I will exalt you, O Lord, because you upheld me.*

Many think that this psalm is about the building of the temple, but Solomon constructed the temple.[1] How, then, does David sing about the dedication of the house, unless one of the lovers of history, who never leaves the letter, might say that he spoke more like a prophet? Now, the majority of the half-verses of the psalm bear reference to the Savior, and one will be compelled, in order not to destroy the sequence of these verses, to interpret the other things that seem to come later as having reference to him. For the same psalm is also spoken from only one person; accordingly, the person of the speaker is maintained from beginning to end.

So the *ode* is for the *dedication* of the house.

So then, I say that it is first of all necessary to understand this in a general sense: the rational essence is a house of God. "Christ, however, was over his house as a son, and we are his house."[2] This house, which was prepared to [**128**] be God's house, underwent destruction and captivity, for it is rational. For when God says, "My Spirit shall not abide in these men, for they are flesh,"[3] the house was destroyed; it has suffered captivity. For on the one hand in the case of perceptible things, since the house is one thing and those who dwell in it are another, the house is not said to be taken captive but destroyed; and those who are in the house are taken captive when this house collapses and is razed to the ground. On the other hand, in the case of rational essences, it is possible for both terms to be used of the same person, according to two different conceptions. He is both house and inhabitant of the house. In accordance with the true thoughts and the upright intentions and the pious and true meditations, he is the house, and he is the one who dwells therein, if he is receptive of this.

Now, if it were in the case of perceptible plants, it is impossible for the plant to be that which is cultivated and that which cultivates: one cultivates the soil, and another is prepared when it is cultivated. Now, the soul frequently has the value both of the cultivator and the cultivated, so that it is a plant according to one conception and a farmer and gardener according to another one. So, for example, I said that someone also searches for himself, even though the seeker is not a different person from the one who is sought, when I cited the opinion of Heraclitus that says, "I sought for myself."[4] He is saying, "I sought myself." So the house and those in it, according to this way of seeing, differ according to two different conceptions. However, according to their primary subject and essence they do not differ; rather, the same subject is both house and the one dwelling in the house. Therefore, just as the house was destroyed, so those who have made it evil by their negligent residence there were thrust out of it.

When he was saying, "My Spirit shall not abide in these men forever,"[5] the one who

---

[1] Cf. 1 Kings 6; 2 Chron 3.
[2] Heb 3:6.
[3] Gen 6:3.

[4] Heraclitus, fragment 101.
[5] Gen 6:3.

corrects this damage is the Savior, "for he has come to seek out and to save the lost"[6] and "to build Jerusalem."[7] For when the Lord builds Jerusalem, he dedicates the house, restoring the soul into itself, making it zealous for virtue. Now, this was its primary movement, since it has come to be virtuous rapidly. When it endured captivity and was overturned as a house, its captivity is turned around, and the fallen house is rebuilt. After the rebuilding, next comes the dedication before God dwells there, for he says, "I will dwell in their midst."[8] And again the Savior says, "If anyone loves me, he will keep my word, and I and the Father will come to him and will make our abode with him."[9] It was built up, it was renewed, it has become new; then God also dwells there. And when God dwells within it, his spear-bearing angels also dwell in that soul, as well as the divine gifts of the Spirit and all the virtues. And in another psalm it is said, "When the house was rebuilt after the captivity: an ode for David,"[10] not before the captivity but after the captivity, for the soul must certainly come into the good. It is impossible for the fallen one to remain in misfortune, for this has not taken place in order that he might fall but in order that he might stand. For example, for the one who has fallen [**129**][11] there occurs a resurrection according to both things, both according to the soul and according to the body: "Sleeper, awake! Rise from the dead, and Christ will shine on you."[12] Here the one who sins is dead, for "the soul that sins, this one shall die,"[13] and "sin, when it is fully grown, gives birth to death."[14] This sinner, then, he raises into the life that was before the fall, for this was the life with virtue. So also is it said in Jeremiah, "He who falls, does he not rise up?"[15]

Furthermore, a resurrection of the body takes place, for its formation is not a fall, but the corruption took place after the formation. So for this reason it also is raised up.

And we say this in a universal sense: good things precede evil things. For example, debased art comes after artistry, and error after the truth, and disobedience after the law, for disobedience is nothing other than transgression of a command. And again, the prefix *para* is always objectionable: "misunderstand," "overlook," "transgress."[16]

So the virtue is first; for observe where the discourse is tending! The rational being has appeared, in order that it should possess virtue; truly it has not appeared in order that it should possess vice. So as far as concerns material life, nearly all begin with sin. And if this were granted, that the soul never lived before material life, then its personal situation would have begun with vice, and sin would not be sin, but rather virtue; for no one, when doing what is according to nature and what is proper, is said to sin.

Those who pursue the arts, therefore, and work according to them, when they do what is proper to the art, they are not said "to overlook," they are not said "to transgress."

So there takes place a building of the *house* that fell and a return from captivity. According to an earlier rule, we say that residing and a house are the same thing.

Moreover, one can also understand it in the following way, in order to take it more universal: the assembly of the faithful, the church, is the *house*, that "you may know how

---

[6] Lk 19:10.
[7] 1 Esdras 4:47.
[8] 2 Cor 6:16.
[9] Jn 14:23.
[10] Ps 95:1 LXX. The surtitle is missing in the Hebrew version.
[11] Didymus the Blind, *Psalmenkommentar (Tura-Papyrus)*, vol. 3, Kommentar zu Psalm 29–34, ed. M. Gronewald, PTA 8 (Bonn: Rudolf Habelt, 1969), begins here.
[12] Eph 5:14 NRSV.
[13] Ezek 18:4 NETS.

[14] Jas 1:15 NRSV.
[15] Jer 8:4.
[16] Each of these words is prefixed with *para-* in Greek: *paranoei, parablepei, parabainei.*

one ought to behave in the household of God,"[17] and, "I loved the goodly appearance of your house."[18] Now, these people who dwell in it are the faithful, who conduct themselves with virtue.

Now, if the soul is the *house*, then the inhabitants are virtuous thoughts, which are innate to it.

And both the building and the dedication occur together. And there is *renewal* whenever those who have previously come out of it take up residence within it once again.

A psalm of an ode.

We were saying, when we began with the Twentieth Psalm,[19] that there are *psalms* and there are *odes*, that there are psalm-odes and ode-psalms. And I was saying that the *psalm* signifies the action. And the one who plays the *psalm* strikes an instrument that is called a psalter.

It is also possible to sing even without a psalter, for the one who employs contemplation alone—to know God, to understand the truth and to partake of it, in order that you should understand it as it really is, since he has the practice being sung in every way—now, when someone reflects and throws himself with learning to understand what knowledge is, what "the mystery of the kingdom"[20] is, this one sings.

Again, as many as put things into practice and stop at this very thing alone, at being practical, these play a *psalm*, as we were also saying about the rams, that they have a robust way of life, even though they are elevated neither in respect of the way of life that they have nor in the individual deeds of their life. That person plays a *psalm*.

Now, when one who both plays a psalm and is practical and sings and is contemplative, when on the one hand he begins from practicing, there is *a psalm of an ode*; on the other hand, when he begins from contemplating, there is "an ode of a psalm." And we see these things taking place: frequently, certain people who desire to contemplate dedicate themselves to the virtues and to their corresponding actions, and taking the ability to accomplish them [130] from the very understanding of them, proceed to practice them. "An ode of a psalm" is created. The ode precedes: the contemplation.

"If you desire wisdom, keep the commandments."[21] The desirous one "sang"; he kept the commandments, "he played a psalm"; and again, by playing the psalm, he has it as his chorus. Therefore, it sometimes happens that one begins from the *ode* and then takes a turn with the *psalm*, and vice versa: the *psalm*, leading the way, in its turn bears to the soul an *ode*.

Therefore, when the beginning and the conception of the beginning of a profession start from a deed, there is a *psalm of an ode*; and when someone, beginning from the contemplation, receives a love of living according to virtue, there is an ode of a psalm.

So, in order to dedicate the house, it was necessary for the one introduced to dance in this way on behalf of the dedication of the house.[22]

This is called an "interdependence." Now, there is a "dependence," when one thing follows another and the sequence is not reversible. But when the sequence is reversible, so that the former thing that precedes becomes a follower and the follower becomes the thing that precedes, then there is an interdependence.

Certainly the expression *for David*, this one who successfully completed the dedication, to whom the victory and the hymn is ascribed,

---

[17] 1 Tim 3:15 NRSV.
[18] Ps 26:8 (25:8 LES2).
[19] Here again is an indication that the lecture series begins with Ps 20, as we have it.
[20] Cf. Mt 13:11.
[21] Sir 1:26 NRSV.
[22] Cf. 2 Sam 6:14-22.

[either the Spirit of Scripture says] or the psalmist himself. Even if the psalmist says it, he clearly speaks from the Holy Spirit. It is not the same thing to say, "a man says this," as it is to say, "a knowledgeable man says this." For when we say that a man is the one who announces something, the things that are announced are human, but when we say that one endowed with knowledge says them, they are related to knowledge. Knowledge inspires that one, and that one becomes, as it were, a servant of knowledge.

Therefore, the one who is "capable in the Lord" sings this psalm or this ode, the *psalm of the ode* or vice versa. And every practical person is "sufficient in the hand." And the Savior in particular has this quality, for the others also receive sufficiency from him. John, for instance, observing his greatness, was saying, "I am not worthy to untie the thong of his sandals."[23] When in turn sufficiency is granted by him, "our sufficiency is from God, who has made us sufficient to be ministers of a new covenant."[24] When those who are exhorted toward this and have received love of this thing become imitators of Christ, seeing him acting "sufficiently," they themselves also act "sufficiently" in accord with what is possible to them.

Now, when I began in the Psalms,[25] I was saying that the things said about the man whom the Savior assumed could be said about every imitator of his, certainly not what is said about him as only-begotten Son and as God the Word; I do not mean that those things could be said about men, but surely they could not be said about the celestial powers, about any created being whatsoever. So the things that are now said correspond to the Savior's Man; for this reason others are also able to do them.

[29:2] *I will exalt you, O Lord, because you upheld me.*

What I have often said, I will also say now: the things that are said about God are understood as about God, and the things that are said about men are understood as being about men. And sometimes the things that are said about men, if they are not said insofar as they are mortal and human but insofar as they are rational, could also be said about the angels and every intelligible essence in general, for according to the intelligible part man is of the same being with them, according to his capability of becoming perfect "as the heavenly Father is perfect."[26] For what greater thing is an angel able to enjoy, according to its own reach? Then the Savior [131] says to men, "I will come along with my Father 'and we will make our home with him.'"[27] What more does a good angel have to possess? And again, "Grant that, as I and you are one, these also may be one in us."[28] What greater thing does the heavenly essence have to obtain? We receive our differentiation from them in the more bodily things; the angel does not have flesh. And this is not to say that man has flesh in order to be rational, since in this case all things that have flesh would be rational.

So see! If someone among us says that he was exalted, lifted up from a humble place into a superior one above, then he must first have the ability to change location. It is impossible for a person who does not change location to be exalted or to be humbled: I mean in a spatial sense. Therefore, when the saint says, "*I will exalt you,*" he means this: "I will give thanks to you."

When someone understands Christ according to the flesh, he does not exalt him.[29] But when he no longer knows him according to the

---

[23]Lk 3:16 NRSV.
[24]2 Cor 3:5-6 ESV.
[25]That is, with Ps 21 (20 LXX).
[26]Mt 5:48.
[27]Jn 14:23.
[28]Cf. Jn 17:21; 10:30.
[29]Cf. 2 Cor 5:16.

flesh, but beholds "his glory, glory as of the only Son from the Father,"[30] and knows that he who has seen the Son sees the Father,[31] then this is the same thing as exalting him.

Next, that he says this with gratitude, the following sequence affirms: *because you upheld me*. By upholding me you exalted me. And when I myself was exalted, then I know your loftiness.

And it is possible to see this from the examples that are near at hand. Someone dedicates himself to knowledge, but he does not yet see its greatness, he does not yet see its beauty, he does not see its loftiness. However, when he begins to partake of it and, by adding little by little to what was already known, he improves, then, when he sees the greatness and loftiness of knowledge and skill, he exalts it, that is to say, he confesses its loftiness. Certainly when he understands its loftiness and greatness, then he sees himself to be greatly lacking.

"Your knowledge was made too wonderful for me; it became strong; I can never attain to it."[32] As much as I understand it, I also marvel at it; it becomes strong, and I can attain no further to it, inasmuch as I am in a body. Solomon also says this about Wisdom: "I said, 'I will become wise,' and it was far from me, far beyond what was, and a deep depth; who will find it?"[33] It was far from me, and when I desired to obtain it, it became far from me, farther than it was before. And at last he presents the reason: "It is a deep depth; who will find it?" The expression "Who will find?" can mean "No one will."

[29:2] *And you did not gladden my enemies over me.*

Many enemies were set against me, wishing to harm me. And I was saying that these things are said in common concerning both the Man of the Savior and those who imitate him. Both the saints and the Savior had *enemies*. However, absolutely no one is able to draw near to him in his divinity, in order to even attempt to harm him. And it is characteristic of enemies to approach for no other reason than to harm. And so from the person of Jesus as Man, and from everyone who imitates him and becomes his member, this is said, *because you upheld me*. For if you were not upholding me, my enemies would rejoice, after they had taken me under the power of their hand, and I would not exalt you.

One can also understand the saying from the person of the Savior, when we no longer make distinctions and say, "as God the Word" or "as man," as I was just now about the knowledgeable man. *I will exalt you, O Lord, because you upheld me*. You upheld me by giving me those for whose sake I came. "Here am I and the children whom God has given me."[34] [**132**] "I will give you nations as your heritage."[35] The Savior regards this as his own prize and as his own spoils of war. For this reason he says, "*You did not gladden my enemies*," for because the captives were reclaimed by me, I myself on the one hand will exalt you on my own behalf and on behalf of those who are victorious, and on the other hand those ones are *not gladdened*.

[29:3] *O Lord my God, I cried to you, and you healed me.*

This is the voice of one who was heard, for when he cried about healing, he was already obtaining what he was longing for. "I said, 'O Lord, have mercy on me; heal my soul, because I sinned against you.'"[36] He was not yet healed,

---

[30]Jn 1:14 ESV.
[31]Cf. Jn 14:9.
[32]Ps 139:6 (138:6).
[33]Eccles 7:23-24 NETS.

[34]Is 8:18 NETS.
[35]Ps 2:8 NETS.
[36]Ps 41:4 (40:5 NETS).

for the one who says this is confessing and repenting.

The person of the Savior, however, says this: "*I cried to you, and you healed me.*" I assumed a lash that is curative and healing "of every disease and sickness."[37] Why then did I have the lash? That it might become a remedy for those who were wounded. And my healing takes place whenever the lash heals others who are my body.

O Lord my God, then, *I cried to you, and you healed me.* When each of the righteous says this, he will be heard by the One to whom he was crying. "While you are still speaking, I will say, 'Here I am!'"[38] The phrase "I will say, 'Here I am!'" means: when you make known the matter for which you are making your request, I am fond of being present with you, for your prayer does not precede my granting of it, but it comes together with it. You have prayed; you have your object.

Let us take examples from the Scriptures: a leper approaches the Savior, saying, "If you choose, you can make me clean." He answers, "I do choose. Be made clean!" And the cleansing takes place so that one cannot separate the timing of it.[39] In conception alone the request happens earlier than the cleansing; it is not earlier in time. Again: "Do you want to be made well?" Immediately he adds, "Stand up, take your mat and walk!" And the doing of Jesus' command does not take place later.[40] You know that the mirror image imitates the appearance, and that it is not possible to say which of the two is first, but only in conception.

[29:4] *O Lord, you brought up my soul from Hades.*

After you healed me, you led my soul out of Hades. This could be said about Jesus: "Since I was having the lash and was wounded because of the sins of some men—and probably those who have sins are 'in Hades'—I descended there, in order that my lash, drawing near to them, might heal them."

The healing, however, consists *in my soul's* being *brought up* from there. "I have come there not that I should remain there, and not that I should merely depart and come, but that I should raise up those who are there." "He was put to death in the flesh, but made alive in the spirit, in which he also preached to the spirits in prison"[41] the proclamation; he raised them up. For their sake he descended there, and for their sake he says that he ascends, for he went forth in order to raise them up. He would not ascend if they would not ascend, for he did not descend for his own sake; neither does he ascend for his own sake.

And one can also say the following: our soul is rational in reality. Just as someone is said to be a "man of God," so also could his soul be called this. *You brought up my soul from Hades.*

[29:4] *You saved me from those who go down into the pit.*

Already today, those who go down into the pit were mentioned, that they are those who have fallen from above, for pits are not sources; they contain water that is supplied from somewhere else. And Hades is frequently called a *pit* in the Scriptures for this reason: the souls that end up there fall.

You saved me from those who **[133]** *go down into the pit.*

For even if I descended into Hades, yet I was not restrained in the *pit* like the waters that fall, but I was delivered; for this reason no harm has happened to me, such as happens to some of those who fall into Hades.

---

[37] Mt 4:23.
[38] Is 58:9.
[39] Cf. Mt 8:2-3.
[40] Cf. Jn 5:6-9.

[41] 1 Pet 3:18-19.

[29:5] *Play a psalm to the Lord, O you his holy ones!*

Next, *playing a psalm* and singing praise because he was upheld, he desires for those to accompany him in the hymn whom he brought up from Hades, who have at last been manifested as his *holy ones*, for both those during the time of Abraham and the other saints were there. In that place, moreover, there were other souls, but while the souls of the holy ones were manifested, the others were not, for we are not saying that the Savior has exalted all souls but those souls that eagerly awaited him there. So, I was talking about the saying, "Are you the one who is to come, or are we to wait for another?"[42] That man had known that he was about to die; for, being in prison, he sent this message, "Are you yourself going there or are you sending another?" not that he was in doubt, but he desired to serve him there by learning from him, by receiving orders from him.

He writes to the saints: the achievement is for us or for us and you in common. Therefore, just as I sing a *psalm of an ode*, so you also, sing *a psalm*! Strike your instruments in unison with our ode, which I offer up for you, saying, "I will exalt you, O Lord!"

[29:5] *And confess the memory of his holiness.*

The word *exomologēsis* here is not said in the sense of the declaration for sins, for this kind of confession is also mentioned, as when it says, "Confess your sins to one another."[43] Nevertheless, for the most part, thanksgiving is signified by the word *exomologēsis* in Scripture: "We will confess to you, O God. We will give thanks to you."[44]

The memory of doctrines is here aroused; he speaks of "his holiness." Learned recollections [make you aware of what you have heard,] not for the first time just now. When someone was made holy, he began to possess holiness after he participated in the holy one. And he has become so, in order that he might be holy, not in essence but by choice, after receiving the holy, the good in loan. So *recall to mind*, by *confessing* and playing a psalm, that *holiness* is appropriate to you. Welcome that for which you have been made! You were made to be saints, not to be profane! But you have entered into sordidness and profanity. *Recall* your *holiness to mind*, and desire to become so.

[29:6] *Because wrath is in his fury and life is in his will.*[45]

For this reason I exhort you, who have become holy, *to play* a song and *to confess the memory of his holiness, because* there is *wrath in his fury*: lest you encounter wrath and fury. For when I accomplish such great things, if you remain in the same things that were before my visitation, and in the very things because of which I have come, then *wrath* will take its turn, because after so much assistance and so much help and exhortation you remain in the same things.

Now, just as *wrath* comes *in fury*, so also there is *life in his will*. The one who follows his will and does it, praying to know it from him—for example, someone offers up a prayer and says, "Teach me, that I do your will!" By saying this [134] with a causal clause, "because you are my God,"[46] he shows that the will of God alone is life. And our will must also agree with his, lest he say, "How often have I desired, and you were not willing!"[47]

Life, then, *is in your will*. One can also call God the Word *"will"* here. And in him all things were created; all things have come into

---

[42]Mt 11:3 NRSV.
[43]Jas 5:16 NRSV.
[44]Ps 75:1 (74:2).
[45]The NRSV translates this verse: "For his anger is but for a moment; his favor is for a lifetime."
[46]Ps 143:10 (142:10 NETS).
[47]Cf. Mt 23:37 NRSV.

being through him.[48] Therefore, in the *will* of the one who brought us into being lies our *life*.

[29:6] *Weeping will find lodging in the evening, and rejoicing comes in the morning.*

The *evening* is an end of day and a beginning of night, as again the *morning* is a limit of night and a beginning of day. Opposites were frequently said to be unable to coexist: the good and the evil.

It is possible to understand *evening* as the end of the shadow, the end of the letter. And after the letter and the shadow have reached their end, whenever someone desires to live among them, he weeps instead because he no longer sees the cheerfulness of the letter, because he no longer observes the flowering of Scripture. However, after the life-giving Spirit appears and the new covenant comes to light, there is the beginning of a day, which brings *rejoicing*.

And now for the more popular interpretation: when the synagogue of circumcision reached its evening after the Sun of Righteousness[49] set for it—for "she who bore seven was abandoned; the sun set for her while it was still midday."[50] She was giving birth to seven; then she welcomed the Sabbath, in order that she might complete all things according to it spiritually and might become a mother of good thoughts and deeds, but she was abandoned; she did not receive the fullness of which John, after receiving, says, "From his fullness we have all received."[51] Because of this her soul succumbed to misfortune after the Sun of Righteousness set "while it was still midday," while this age was present, for the age itself is also frequently called "day." *And rejoicing*, therefore, *comes in the morning*.

[29:7] *But as for me, I said in my prosperity, "I shall never be shaken forever!"*

The reading is doubtful. It can be read in this way: "But as for me, I said in my prosperity, 'I shall never be shaken forever.'" When I was flourishing, I said this: "I shall never be shaken forever."

However, it can also be read thus: "I said, 'In my prosperity I shall not be shaken forever.'" Both ways of punctuating it make sense.

When I was flourishing, because I sowed to righteousness and harvested the produce of righteousness, I was so disposed that *I will no longer be shaken forever*. For if "the one who does the will of God remains forever"[52] and his "righteousness is immortal,"[53] after I brought forth the produce of righteousness and when I was flourishing, I spoke. Indeed, I spoke in this way by my disposition, as we said in relation to the saying, "No one says that Jesus is Lord,"[54] except by his disposition and his life.[55] When I was flourishing and bringing forth the produce of virtue, I confessed this, that *I remain unshaken forever* according to the saying, "The one who believes, and everyone who lives and believes will never die forever,"[56] and, "The righteousness of the Lord endures forever and ever."[57]

However, one can also interpret the words *I said in my prosperity* in this way: "When I was flourishing and considered resting a while, I said **[135]**, 'I will never be shaken forever.'" And if help had not arrived quickly, he would have been swept along, because he was confident in himself; he has great faith in his own fertility.

Therefore, certainly when the person of the Savior is the speaker of this, let the former interpretation prove the victor, and when it

---

[48]Cf. Jn 1:3-4; Col 1:16.
[49]Mal 4:2 (3:20).
[50]Jer 15:9.
[51]Jn 1:16 NRSV.

[52]1 Jn 2:17.
[53]Wis 1:15 NRSV.
[54]1 Cor 12:3.
[55]See the earlier discussion of this verse at PsT 75.
[56]Jn 11:26.
[57]Ps 112:9 (111:9); 2 Cor 9:9.

relates to the rest of us, let one also receive this interpretation.

[29:8] *O Lord, by your will you furnished my beauty with power.*[58]

He is speaking either in the form of a prayer or a thanksgiving.[59] Let us see what kind of beauty he is talking about. He is not speaking of bodily beauty but of the beauty of the soul and the inner man. Now, this beauty that is perceived by the senses, which assumes visible form in the face and in the form, has its constitution from the proportion of the members—when the human members are proportionate to themselves and are not [disposed] so that some are too large and others too small—for then the beauty would be distorted. The eye must be well-suited to the nose, and this to the mouth, for when the members are disproportionate, even if each on its own seems to be beautiful, yet they do not produce beauty in the face.

Indeed, he is saying this: by your will the individual virtues are interdependent, so that my thoughts are in proportion to my deeds. And in the Song of Songs the one who praises the bride says, "You are altogether beautiful, my companion, and there is no flaw in you."[60] For this reason "you are altogether beautiful," because there is no flaw and there is nothing in you that is beyond proportion and there is no ugliness in you.

[29:9] *To you, O Lord, will I cry, and to my God I will pray aloud.*

For us to expound this in a more popular way, it is possible to say, "*To you, O Lord,* as high-priest, as healer, *I will cry; and to my God will I pray aloud,*" not separating the Father from the Son.[61] And the one who prays aloud to God prays to the Trinity, for the Trinity is one God, not the identity of the number, if it is even necessary to speak of numbers there.

[29:10] *What profit is there in my blood, when I go down to corruption?*

I went *down into corruption; what* kind of *profit* has appeared? See, they persist in their own wicked deeds. However, he does not say this universally. And it is said, "you were bought with a price,"[62] by the blood of Christ, and, "not with perishable things like silver or gold were you ransomed from your futile way of life, but with the precious blood of Christ, like that of a lamb without defect or blemish."[63]

And the following is also possible: the entire assembly of those who are being saved is called Christ's body. Since, therefore, after the Savior appeared and assumed all the things that we have previously mentioned: the lashing, the cross, and the descent into Hades, not all repented, not all assumed virtue and faith, but some did and others did not. In accordance with this he says, "*He turned away my face*" from those ones who are my members, who are my body, "*and I became troubled.*"[64]

Therefore, when he defended, ransomed, and set us free by his own blood, how does he say, "What profit is there in my blood, when I go down to corruption?" It is of great benefit—but he was speaking to those who persisted in their wicked deeds. Therefore, inasmuch as it pertains to you, no benefit has come by my blood, when I went down to corruption. Consequently, he says this in order to awaken them to repentance. Because of this he has said,

---

[58] The NRSV has, "By your favor, O Lord, you had established me as a strong mountain; you hid your face; I was dismayed."
[59] Other versions of the LXX have the word *provide* here instead of "you furnished," which would turn the verse into a prayer.
[60] Song 4:7.
[61] "Lord" here would refer to the Son; "God" to the Father.
[62] 1 Cor 7:23 NRSV.
[63] Cf. 1 Pet 1:18-19 NRSV.
[64] Ps 30:7 (29:8).

[29:10] *Surely, dust will not acknowledge you or tell of your truth?*

Behold, there are some who are dust. And I have come to suffer, in order that I should transform them and make them heavenly [136] instead of earthly. Therefore, since they still persist in bearing the image of the earthly, they do not confess to you, and they will not proclaim the truth. I have come, however, in order that I should reveal the truth, after overthrowing falsehood and the lie, and to supply you with confession, in order that someone might cast away the image of the earthly and assume the image of the heavenly.[65] So he says, "*Dust will not acknowledge you*, will it?" If *dust does not acknowledge you*, insofar as it is possible to it, then there has been no benefit from my blood when I went down into corruption.

Then—since I said that he says this because of those who are involved in their former vices, and we confessed that he also ransomed many by his own blood—indicating those ones he says,

[29:11] *The Lord heard and had mercy on me.*

After indicating those ones, he calls their salvation the "*mercy of the Lord*," their being the objects of his mercy.

[29:11] *The Lord became my helper.*

"To *become*" signifies a relation, not an origination: "He has become to me a helper and defender, for my deliverance."[66]

[29:11] *The Lord heard and had mercy on me.*

I began to groan, because after I had descended into corruption, no benefit from my blood has come to some; however, by building my house with those who are shown mercy, I also show those who are still of such a kind that they will at some time be saved; he will at some time accomplish the remedy for them.

[29:12] *You turned my grief into joy for me.*

In his love for mankind, he struck himself for those who have died, in order that he might raise them; for at once someone was having the thought: if, though I have sinned, that one mourns and groans, how much more should I myself do this!

You turned, therefore, *my mourning into joy for me*. "Their gain is joy for me, and when they were sinning, mine was the lamentation and the mourning."

[29:12] *You tore my sackcloth and girded me with gladness.*

While I was in mourning, I was wearing *sackcloth*, an austere way of life, a coarse one, but it changed into *gladness*. We have also spoken in a similar vein about this word: "For if the deeds of power [done in you] had been done in Tyre and Sidon, they would have repented long ago in sackcloth and ashes."[67] We were saying that he indicates the austere and toilsome way of life, which applies to the one who laments, by the name *sackcloth*.

And with this *sackcloth*, someone receives ashes and sits, no longer acting in the moment, but he sits, he ceases from the impulse of vice. He was groaning for this: what tares, thistles, and thorny plants he produced; for he was unable to sit among the thistles and thorny plants, but after reducing them to ashes, showing them to be devoid of strength, and destroying that quality according to which they are noxious, he sat on them.

---

[65] Cf. 1 Cor 15:47-49.
[66] Ex 15:2.
[67] Mt 11:21 NRSV.

[29:13] *So that my glory should make music to you and I shall not be stunned.*

Some read a comma before: *I shall not be stunned.* When my glory makes music to you, then I am not stunned. This reading, however, is unsatisfactory to me. Many of those who are in the church read in this way, however.

Torpor often indicates a kind of repentance. For example, when Ahab repented: "Did you see how Ahab was stunned with remorse?"[68] and, "You made them drink a spirit of remorse,"[69] a spirit of repentance.

He is saying the following, then: my glory makes music to you, I do according to your will, and I do not experience remorse, *I am not stunned*. *I am not stunned* as though over an evil deed, so that I do it no longer. For this reason he continues and says, *O Lord my God, I will acknowledge you* [137] *forever.*

[29:13] *O Lord my God, I will acknowledge you forever.*

Since, therefore, *I acknowledge you forever*, by making music to your glory, *I am not stunned*, I do not experience remorse.

---

[68] 1 Kings 21:29 (20:29).
[69] Cf. Is 29:10.

PSALM 30 [31]

[30:1] *Toward the end. A psalm for David. In a state of ecstasy.*

The word *ecstasy* is ambiguous, because it means many things, one of which is "delirium" or "madness": the one who is demented "stands outside himself."[1] However, the word *ecstasy* also means "amazement," for the one who is amazed is said to be outside himself: "I considered your works and was beside myself,"[2] because I saw their greatness, the skill by which they have come into existence. And there are many passages that show that "amazement" is indicated by the word *ecstasy*. So, for example, Isaac "was amazed with very great amazement"[3] when he took the blessing from Esau.

And again *ecstasy* indicates someone's coming out of his former condition, as when it says, "And as for me, I said in my ecstasy, 'Every man is a liar.'"[4] When I came outside myself and was no longer a man, but became God, because I had received God the Word who had come to me, then I said, "Every man is a liar." For if we might understand this naively, it is a lie. If every man is a liar, and he is also one of the men, then he lies. However, if he lies that "every man is a liar," then they are not liars in every way.

The affairs of men are fickle and irregular. Of such a kind also is that of which the apostle speaks: "What no eye has seen, nor ear heard, nor the human heart conceived."[5] He himself, then, is not a man any longer, but he adds, "these things, however, God has revealed to us through the Spirit,"[6] to us who are no longer men, who can say with confidence: "We were beside ourselves for God; we behave sensibly at the same time for you."[7]

So the one who says these things in the psalm was outside himself, he has become other than himself, he has become God by partaking of God the Word; he has ceased being human. And observe with confidence that he does not speak about human things, but what is fitting for a deified man to proclaim and to sing.

[30:2] *In you, O Lord, I hoped; may I never be put to shame into the age.*

Indeed, I am not ashamed, whenever the things I request come to be, for the one who prays experiences *shame* when the things he anticipated do not happen.

Now, if we might understand the *age* in a more simple sense, he is saying this, "Let me not be ashamed for the whole duration of my life, by always obtaining what I ask to receive from you." For it was often said[8] that the time that compares to the life of man is called an *age*, as the statement shows: "I will never eat meat for the age."[9]

However, one can also say as follows: "Since you are eternal and your existence and Lordship extend into all the ages, and I also

---

[1] The word *ekstasis* can be broken down into the two words that compose it: *ek* (outside) and *stasis* (standing).
[2] Hab 3:2.
[3] Gen 27:33 LES2.
[4] Ps 116:11 (115:2).
[5] 1 Cor 2:9 NRSV.
[6] 1 Cor 2:10.
[7] 2 Cor 5:13.
[8] Cf. PsT 80.
[9] 1 Cor 8:13.

am immortal in soul, *may I never be put to shame into the age*, for I am always with you.[10] Now I know and prophesy in part, but the partial will be succeeded by the perfect,[11] so that my hope has become much greater, because it has the expectation of greater things in the future." So the one who *hopes in the Lord* is *unashamed*.

[30:2] *In your righteousness rescue me and deliver me.*

Indeed, he himself is the *righteousness* about which it is said, "Righteousness poured down,"[12] when he inclined heaven and came down. He has come [138] in order to bring unrighteousness to an end, for the world that was around the earth was full of unrighteousness. Indeed, "the earth was full of wrongdoing,"[13] as it was also before the flood, when "all turned away, and at the same time became useless; there is no one practicing kindness."[14]

So, just as the light, when it rises and comes where the darkness is, disperses the darkness—for at the appearance of the light the darkness disappears, and when virtue shines vice departs far away—so after righteousness appears and delivers those who call on it, every unrighteousness is deposed.

[30:3] *Incline your ear to me; be quick to deliver me.*

Even if I cry aloud to you, yet I am truly weak-voiced in comparison to your majesty. Therefore, unless you *incline your ear to me*, my shouting is not strong enough to reach you. Unless you condescend, you do not receive my voice.

And in another sense: since he does not mark all the lawless deeds of those who are judged and examined by him,[15] he must incline the ear, in order to hear them; for if he is of such great knowledge, and if he remains of such great power, the prayer does not reach him. Unless he consents, he does not receive the prayer. And he consents by condescending.

When you *incline your ear to me*, you receive me and you quickly remove me from those who prevail over me, from those who carry me away. And even if they are enemies, "be quick to deliver me."

Question: Was he saying these things *in a state of ecstasy*?

I did not say that "being outside himself" meant delirium here, but wonder. You do not understand this, that there is not only one perfection. He who is truly perfected says, "I saw the limit of every perfection;"[16] truly, because he does not yet possess the end beyond every other, our psalmist says these words here.

[30:3] *Become to me as God my protector and as a house of refuge to save me.*

Become for me an invincible fortress, an unassailable wall; become for me also a *protector* with your shield, with your armor. When you become my *protector*, none of my enemies can harm me. No wild animal can prevail over me, even the one that carries off its prey, about whom I was offering up my prayer: "Lest he snatch my soul like a lion."[17]

And as a house of refuge.

Become for me that which is called an asylum, where someone, when he flees, comes within walls; for it is a building that is a lookout for salvation.

---

[10] Cf. Ps 73:23 (72:23).
[11] Cf. 1 Cor 13:9-10.
[12] Ps 85:11 (84:12).
[13] Gen 6:11 NETS.
[14] Ps 14:3 (13:3).
[15] Cf. Ps 130:3 (129:3).
[16] Ps 119:96 (118:96).
[17] Ps 7:2 (7:3 LES2).

[20:4] *Because you are my empowerment and my refuge.*

You are all things to me: both *empowerment* and *refuge*. I flee to no one else, to no ruler, to no wealth. You are also my strength: from you I have my strength by partaking of you, insofar as I rule as king.

[20:4] *And for your name's sake you will guide me and nourish me.*

He is saying this: "Since your *name* has been invoked over me, *for the sake of* this *name of yours* that I bear, supply me with two things. Lead me, in order that I should finish the race without reproach and be able to say, 'Without lawlessness I ran and went straightforwardly,'[18] and, 'I ran the way of your commandments.'[19] And let me be nourished by you. Your Son is your Way and Bread." He is the Way, for he says, "I am the way."[20] He himself is therefore Bread as well.[21]

For the sake of your name, then, which you gave to me, that I might obtain salvation; for I prayed and said, "O God, in your name save me."[22]

[30:5] *You will bring me out of this snare, which they hid for me. Because you are my protector.*

Many enemies, certain rogues, prepared a trap for me in order to capture me. Therefore, not only do I call on you, in order that you might not allow me to depart there, but, even if I entered the trap, that you should lead me out of it. **[139]**

Now it is necessary to punctuate it in this way:

[30:5-6] *Because you are my protector, into your hands I will entrust my spirit.*

I do not entrust *my spirit* to another, but *only into your hands*. And given that the man who says these things is a saint, his spirit is that which is bound together to his soul, of which it is said, "your whole spirit and soul and body."[23] Some say that the spirit is no different from the soul; others say that the spirit is the soul's intellect; others say that it is the soul's will. According to all these interpretations together, however, God keeps the *spirit*.

If the *spirit* means the "soul," then he entrusts it *into the hands* of God, in order that, being sheltered, it should remain unharmed, not injured by enemies, not carried off. And that the soul is sometimes called *spirit*, Stephen teaches, for when he was about to die and requested that the sin of those who were bloodthirsty against him might not be weighed,[24] he said, "Lord Jesus, receive my spirit,"[25] instead of "my soul." And James, when he writes, "Just as the body without the spirit is dead,"[26] he calls the soul "spirit."

However, as I said earlier, there is a certain rational power that is bound together to the soul in such a way that it is inseparable from it, in order that it might be the soul's instructor, and it is called *spirit*. And since this exists together with the soul, when it is held by God, this says, "May such things never be practiced by me, so that my spirit come outside your hands; rather, may every virtue be accomplished by me, in order that my spirit might be in your hands."

It is also possible that he calls his own will *spirit*, so that he also desires for it to be protected in *the hands* of God.

Now, the interpretive senses will follow: the *hands* of God signify the two covenants. Into

---

[18] Ps 59:4 (58:5).
[19] Ps 119:32 (118:32 NETS).
[20] Jn 14:6 NRSV.
[21] Cf. Jn 6:35.
[22] Ps 54:1 (53:3 NETS).

[23] 1 Thess 5:23 ESV.
[24] Cf. Acts 7:60.
[25] Acts 7:59 NRSV.
[26] Jas 2:26 NRSV.

these, then, *I entrust my spirit*, desiring to understand the old, that is, the things that are commanded there, and the new. Let both of your hands embrace my spirit!

And it is also possible to say that there are not only two *hands* of God, for it was not said in the dual form but in the plural. Plural or dual do not differ in form. Nevertheless, if they are the two covenants, the hands are mentioned in the dual form. However, if all the power of God is called his *hand*—for we call the military might of a king his *hand*—into your military might, which is your guardian *hand*, *I entrust my spirit*.

God says to Jerusalem in the prophet Isaiah, "See, I have painted your walls on my hands, and you are continually before me."[27] Even within our imagination, we cannot say that there are physical walls written on God's hands, for he is incorporeal. Therefore, when he says, "your walls are written on my hands, you remain before me continually," with no one able to take you into exile—for the walls that are written on my hands are indestructible—no one is able to advance against them.

Therefore, just as the walls that are painted on God's hands are not perceptible, so also when he *entrusts* his own *spirit* into the *hands* of God, he shows that the spirit is not some trifling thing, but is either the rational essence that is bound to the soul or its divine intellect, which is unmingled both with matter and with vice. The intellect, when it preserves the quality of the intellect, is free from all matter; it is unmingled with bodily things, and in particular it is a nonparticipant in every kind of vice. For this reason it can be given into God's hands and be protected, for God does not protect the one who has vice. [140] In another way he protects it, however, by desiring to lead it away from vice.

Question: What are "the walls"?

"Walls" are named in Scripture in many senses. About Wisdom it is said, "She is proclaimed on the tops of the walls,"[28] and we certainly do not say that there are certain preachers who appear on the tops of perceptible walls, announcing things that relate to virtue. The virtues and the divine thoughts are walls that guard the intellect and the inner man. As long as someone is still beside the walls' foundations or has reached the middle of their ascent, he is not yet able to proclaim Wisdom; with difficulty he is able to understand it. However, when he arrives at the very heights of the walls, so to speak, when he transcends the world, when he becomes superior to the world, then he is able to preach Wisdom.

Again, it was said, "I have painted your walls on my hands."[29] The forms are analogous to the perceptible things. And the forms are the very thoughts of God; they are God's desires. And understand what is contemplated by means of an example: the one who wishes to construct a city represents its parts to his own mind and constructs the perceptible things according to those thoughts. Certainly, if he does not understand the plan rightly, for example, of the marketplace or the sanctuary or the other parts, he does not make the perceptible parts well.

The "walls," therefore, can be the forms, the desires that are written on God's hands. So these walls have their existence in the will of God. And I say, "In Christ," he says, "all things in heaven and on earth were created, things visible and invisible, whether rulers or powers—all things were created through him. And he himself is before all things and in him all things hold together."[30] In him things visible and invisible were created, as when the parts of

---

[27] Is 49:16 NETS.
[28] Prov 1:21.
[29] Is 49:16 NETS.
[30] Col 1:16-17.

the city were built in the mind of the architect, that is, in regard to those things that are governed by those ideas, for the ideas belong to those who govern.

In Christ, then, all things have held together. If in conception you wish to derive the idea from things that are, these things do not exist. They pass away together with the negation of the idea. So it is then with the "walls" as well. Every kind of certainty has been written on the hands of God.

If, however, you also say that the "walls" are the virtues, naturally the virtues also have ideas, the original habits. For example, I have righteousness, but not all of it, yet I have been created in accordance with it. Now, that which is thought without one who partakes of it is, as it were, an "idea," but not an idea such as you are accustomed to speaking about. So when you take away knowledge, the habits of the knowledgeable pass away with it, but when that knowledge is assumed, then the habits that are partial exist and partake of it. However, it is other than these, since it is truly more original and more secure. It certainly admits neither increase nor decrease; however, it admits this in those who partake of it. So "walls" also signify security.

[30:6] *You redeemed me, O God of truth.*

The one who becomes freed from every kind of disturbance is *redeemed* by God. The *God of truth*, therefore, redeems out of deception; insofar as he is the *God of truth*, he redeems from deception and from false belief. Whenever someone has thoughts that are mistaken and false, he is in need of God, in order that by his own truth he might bring him outside every deception. Again the God of righteousness redeems from unrighteous deeds. For example, it was said, "Hear me, O God of my righteousness!"[31] in order that you should bring me out of all unrighteousness, in order that you might subject to defeat those who work unrighteous deeds against me. [141]

And so it is in each case: Joseph was calling on the God of self-control, lest he fall into the snares of the woman who was persuading him into intemperance; and Susanna, lest she fall into adultery under the power of the elders. The God of self-control heard her, not that he is one thing and another.

[30:7] *You hated those who guard vanities uselessly.*

Since you are a God of truth, you also *hated those who guard vanities uselessly.* Vain things, however, are not true. And he called them "*uselessly,*" since in a certain sense they do not exist. Every lie is nonexistent. Of her who carried in her womb the temple of Jesus, when I say that "she has given birth to him," I tell the truth. However, if I say "she has given birth from a man," I am lying. It is not untrue that "she has given birth," but the lie occurs concerning the manner.

Every vice takes place uselessly; it has no purpose. He says, therefore, "You, O God, *hated those who guard vanities uselessly.*" When someone of those who guard such things receives a revelation, someone who hates such things will have ceased or may reproach himself.

[30:7] *But as for me, I hoped in the Lord.*

You therefore, O Lord, *hated those who guard vanities uselessly*, but as for me, *I hoped in* you as my *Lord*; for he was unable to say, "But as for me, I hoped upon you." But he says, "*I hope upon the Lord.*" He says these things as a servant. From the disposition of a servant and the work of a servant he says these things.

---

[31] Ps 4:1 (4:2).

[30:8] *I will rejoice and be glad in your mercy.*

In your mercy. For if I also confess you as Lord and hoped in you, yet not by my power does perfection occur but by your mercy.

[30:8] *Because you looked upon my humiliation.*

You looked upon my humiliation, which was about to take place. After you looked on it, you did not allow me to fall into it.

[30:8] *You saved my soul from necessities.*

In a more simple sense afflictions are called *"necessities"* in Scripture; for "six times he will deliver you from necessities,"[32] and, "They cried to the Lord, and he heard them and delivered them from their necessities."[33] He has brought me out of every affliction, after he assented, that is, to my invocation; for I sent up a prayer, in order that I might be delivered from the enemies, from the adversaries who pressed against me.

However, you can say in a certain sense that is finally more rational that *necessities* are vices. Out of "necessity" the wicked man does not receive righteousness. I am not saying that man is not receptive to righteousness, but that the unrighteous man is not.

[But being saved from tribulations means] not that one is free of afflictions, but that one is not defeated by them, for in this sense we also understood the word, "Deliver us from the evil one," and, "Lead us not into temptation!"[34] However, when the apostles of Christ and the other righteous ones were asking not to be tempted, they would never have been heard unless they were telling the truth when they said, "We are afflicted in every way, but not crushed."[35]

[30:9] *And you did not imprison me in the hands of an enemy.*

I am locked *in the hands* of those who conspire against me, when I was being defeated by necessities and afflictions. But when I was saved from them, I am not locked in their hands; I do not do what they desire to lead against me.

[30:9] *You set my feet in a spacious place.*

This can also be understood in two ways. The way of life that accords with the region around the earth and that accords with vice is said to be broad and *spacious*. And it is a great thing, when someone is in this broad and *spacious place*, not to be dragged down but to stand firm. The standing, however, comes from God. Therefore he says in gratitude, "*You set my feet in a spacious place.*"

My feet do not feel the affliction that surrounds them. For example, those who say: [142] "Who will separate us from the love of God? Will hardship or distress?"[36] will say, "*you set* our *feet in a spacious place.*" Even if the place in which we have come, and the Way on which we find ourselves, is narrow, yet we see it as *spacious* when you remove our affliction. By helping us, you make broader the way of affliction.

[30:10] *Have mercy on me, O Lord, because I am being afflicted.*

But you maintain that he certainly said, "*You set my feet in a spacious place.*" There the saint prays incessantly, for there is not one affliction, for there is not one difficult circumstance in life, for there is not one trial. When someone, therefore, after making his request, is delivered from a certain trial or from certain trials, again he sees others lying

---
[32] Job 5:19.
[33] Ps 107:13 (106:13).
[34] Mt 6:13.
[35] 2 Cor 4:8 NRSV.

[36] Rom 8:35.

in wait for him, and again he prays about those, for the things that are anticipated afflict him.

Question: Did he see them beforehand as a prophet?

Things like this, certainly even one who is not a prophet can see beforehand. I am in a place where there are many wicked people. And they hate one who is righteous there. Even if at one time, for example, they should assail and bring against him a certain trial or judgment and someone should emerge from it, because he knows that their next evil is sleepless, he expects such a thing again: "For they will not sleep," he says, "unless they have done wrong; their sleep has been taken away, and they do not fall asleep."[37] After he has been frequently delivered, he also prays about things that follow.

[30:10] *My eye was troubled by anger.*

My intellect was not *troubled by my anger*, but by the anger of enemies or by your anger; for you are angered against those who sin, and after I had sinned, I fell under *anger* and my intellect was troubled.

[30:10] *My soul and my belly.*

Not only my *eye*, he says, that is, my intellect, was troubled *by anger*. Moreover, the following is also possible: "In anger my eye was troubled." When I am angered, my intellect is troubled, for the passions perturb the intellect. And *my soul* also was troubled, the *eye* of which *was troubled by anger*.

And my belly. He calls "*belly*" here not the belly of the body but that one that conceives from the Bridegroom and bears children: "because of the fear of you we conceived in the belly and travailed,"[38] so that we no longer preserve the fruit that was conceived, but reject them as aborted babies.

Moreover, the following is also possible: since I was not nourished with the Bread of heaven,[39] which makes the belly calm, but received another kind of food that is harmful and noxious, therefore my *belly* has been troubled. So he does not despair of salvation.

Question: Is his soul being troubled?

Some wish to say that the soul has three powers, and in a rougher way, they say that it is divisible. Also they call its intellect the "rational part," for this is receptive of wisdom; this can obtain knowledge. The appetitive part does not receive knowledge; however, it is sometimes persuaded by the rational part; it is obedient, but it does not possess wisdom. And just as when the airy winds blow strongly, the ship becomes obedient to the pilot, even though the ship does not possess such motion, but is not opposed to the pilot when the winds are not opposed, so also the appetitive part again is obedient to the rational part, even though the former does not have thoughts.

So a person would not err by calling the rational part "intellect." The soul, however, is all the parts in conjunction. And take an example: one can consider a flower. The flower has such a color, but this is not the flower. It has such a fragrance, but the fragrance is not the flower. It also has such a shape. So all of these taken together are the flower. Therefore, when we say, "The flower is sweet-smelling," we only signify an aspect of it: **[143]** that it exudes a most pleasant odor. And again, when we say that it is bitter, we signify only its taste. However, the taste is not the flower, but all of these things together are the flower.

So, after he says about his own rational part or intellect that it has been *troubled* because of *anger*, he says this also about the whole soul. You know that when the charioteer is dragged down by evil the whole vehicle is harmed, and

---
[37]Prov 4:16 NETS.
[38]Is 26:17-18.

[39]Cf. Jn 6:31.

when the pilot is destroyed, the hull is also destroyed. So this *eye* that is mentioned is a certain power that is endowed with intellect, which governs the whole soul. Therefore, when this was troubled, the *soul* is troubled together with it.

Question: And what about the generative *belly*?

What I have often said, I will now say again: in the case of perceptible things, each particular thing is something and cannot be something else. The plant cannot be a golden nugget; the gold cannot be a human. In the case of intelligible things, however, it is possible for them to be so according to different relations and conceptions. For example, yesterday I was saying that the soul, when it seeks, also seeks to know itself; it has the character of both the seeker and the sought. And when it cultivates itself like a plant, the plant is not one thing and the farmer another, but a difference is formed in the conception alone.

So when he speaks of an *eye* and a *belly*, it is possible to use both of these words to speak of the same power; because it sees, the intellect is called an "*eye*," because it generates and brings thoughts to light, it can be a *belly*.

[30:11] *Because my life failed in pain and my years in sighing.*

Since *my life failed in pain*—for I always possessed a painful life—I do not sometimes groan, and sometimes not—I always groan because I long for virtue; I always suffer, I always sweat for the acquisition of the good. Therefore, since I suffer this through my life, in a certain sense, *my life failed in pain and my years in sighing.* Wherefore I call on you, in order that I be subject to such pain no more. For although I suffer pain in order to preserve the good, yet the pain of acquiring something is not the same as the pain of keeping what is possessed already.

Question: Why are the species generalized?

When you are asked for a definition of the human, you do not produce the definition of Socrates, you do not say, for example, "Dion!" "The human is a mortal, rational animal" is the definition of the species. And therefore, when I say that the righteous person is free from unrighteousness, I am not speaking of such and such a righteous person, but of the righteous person in general.

Therefore, since the beginning of the psalm has also run thus: *In you, O Lord, I hoped; may I never be put to shame forever,* understand all these words of everyone who hoped and who seeks an end without shame, with eagerness. For the one who speaks the praises of the rhetorician is not speaking of such and such a rhetorician.

[30:11] *And my strength grew weak in poverty, and my bones were troubled.*

Again, he is not calling the lack of property here "*poverty*." *Strength* is mentioned here in opposition to *poverty*. The *strength* in the soul, therefore, consists in its wealth, whereas the perceptible and bodily strength is by no means so. There are strong men who have owned nothing, and there are weak men who are masters of many possessions. It is as if someone might say about virtue or knowledge: "Since I became poor without virtue and knowledge, my strength, which I ought to have from the appearance of these qualities, has become weak."

My bones were troubled.

The *bones* are parts of the body that are suitable for supporting its other parts. When there are *bones* there can also be tendons, blood vessels, and the rest. So when the strong powers of the soul, called its "*bones*," are *weak*, the whole soul comes into weakness.

And that he is not calling the members of the body "bones": "All my bones shall say:

'O Lord, who is like you?'"[40] The bones of the body do not have any conception of God at all, that they should be able to say [144] whether someone is like him or not, for one must first know God and then speak like this. Therefore, when he says, "All my bones shall say," he is speaking of the strong powers of the soul, of those that are suitable for supporting its other powers: the perceptive powers, the imaginative powers, the powers of memory.

And again: "My bones were strewn near Hades,"[41] say those who confess and repent. Now, it is impossible for the bones of a body to be strewn near this place that is habitually called Hades. And even if it might be, as some think, a place behind the moon, the bones of the dead do not come there. But when the powers of the soul, called "bones" because of their strength, come under sin, "they were strewn near Hades"; they no longer preserve their own structure.

[30:12] *With all my enemies I became a reproach, and to all my neighbors exceedingly so.*

I was saying that this psalm, like those before it as well, is said from the person of the Savior in accordance with the Man. "In the sight of *my enemies I become a reproach.*" He intimates the cross, for in another psalm, which Paul understood to be from the person of the Savior, he says the following: "The insults of those who insult you have fallen on me."[42] I myself have taken them on myself. Certain people insult you, O Father, or O God, and these insults fell on me. And this is nothing extraordinary: often when a knowledgeable person sees those who mock knowledge, he absorbs into himself their insults.

His enemies are those who sin. And this is said, "For if while we were enemies, we were reconciled."[43] The sinner is an enemy of God; God is not an enemy of that one, for God is an enemy to none.

And to my neighbors exceedingly so.

His neighbors are those who profess to know his Scripture and call themselves his companions.

Exceedingly so, then. Come now, the Gentiles stood there as *enemies*, for they sin and are impious. I have become an insult in the presence of all of those when I endured the cross, when I went down into death. *And to my neighbors exceedingly so.* However, when those who should draw near to me and profess to have their dwellings near me do the same things as my enemies, the insult has come because of these especially.

[30:12] *And I became a fear to my acquaintances.*

Those who know me, after seeing me suffering these things, began to have a *fear* that is equal to reverence, or else they began to have a *fear* lest they suffer the same things.

[30:12] *Those who would see me outside fled from me.*

Those who would see me before this, after they saw the things that happened around me, have come *outside* me. Although they were not sent by me, yet they were fleeing outside. Everyone who flees from Jesus comes *outside* him, *outside* salvation.

[30:13] *I was forgotten from the heart like a dead man.*

The enemies, who insulted me, and my neighbors, who did this excessively, cast me out of their own *heart*.

---

[40] Ps 35:10 (34:10 NETS).
[41] Ps 141:7 (140:7).
[42] Rom 15:3 NRSV, quoting Ps 69:10 (68:10).

[43] Rom 5:10 NRSV.

Now, forgetfulness of the dead occurs quickly. Indeed, those who have experienced misfortunes in this way say, "From the time when the dead was buried," it says, "grief is taken away from the soul." In any case, men are eager to do this quickly.

"I was forgotten," then, "from the heart." They cast me out of their own heart, for they did not possess me purely. As the apostle says, "But it is Christ who lives in me."[44] "I was living in them no longer."

When someone who has the Word in himself no longer acts according to him, as much as is possible for him, he causes the Word to be ineffective and he passes into forgetfulness of him.

Understand the forgetfulness in this way, however, not that he did not know that he used to possess him, for many things like this are said both in ordinary language and in Scripture. For instance, we often say to friends, "You have forgotten me already!" instead of saying this: "You do not keep me wholly in your memory." And Scripture says, "An hour's misery engenders forgetfulness of luxury."[45] Now, the one who suffers affliction [145] for an hour forgets about luxury. And again, "And they will forget," it says, "their former affliction, and it will not arise in their heart."[46] You are to understand this in this way: that the one who comes out of affliction forgets about it.

Question: *With all my enemies I became a reproach?*[47]

He did not say, "with all men," but "*with my enemies.*" Now, enemies are wicked men; because they are unrighteous, they are enemies in their disposition. He is indeed an enemy of none, whereas many are enemies toward him. "Hear the word of the Lord, you who tremble at his word; speak, our brothers, to those who hate you."[48] Those ones hate and are enemies. But as for you, he is saying, call them "brothers," not as a word, not as an expression, but in your disposition: in other words, show them to be as brothers with your disposition of brotherly love. Hostility, however, is as follows: having a disposition that is opposed.

However, when the Savior also says this—we said that this can be said from the person of the Savior as Man—he means the Jews, who have become his enemies. Not all of them, however, have become his enemies, for even the apostles were Jews, they were Israelites. So he did not say, "with all the Hebrews, with all the Israelites," but rather, "for my enemies I became a reproach."

They reproach the righteous man according to the first interpretation. Moreover, the wicked reproach the Savior. So not every reproach conveys a cause for censure to the one who is being reproached. There are times when those who reproach are to blame, and those in turn are people who are reproached by sin. And indeed, in the scripture of Proverbs it is said to the wise man, "Do not acquire the censures of evil men."[49] By the added phrase "of evil men," he showed that there are reproaches of virtuous men as well. The disciples, for instance, are commanded to rejoice when they are reproached.[50] The above censures are not those with which the apostles are censured; they belong to evil men instead. Then, since it is in our power to do things that are worthy of reproach, he prescribes, "Do not acquire the censures of evil men, and do not strive after their ways."[51] For the one who strives after their deeds and their thoughts has become an evil man, having acquired for himself harmful reproaches.

---

[44] Gal 2:20 NRSV.
[45] Sir 11:27 NETS.
[46] Is 65:16 LES2.
[47] Ps 31:11 (30:12).
[48] Is 66:5.
[49] Prov 3:31.
[50] Cf. Mt 5:11-12.
[51] Prov 3:31.

About this reproach it is said that some arise "to reproach and eternal disgrace."[52] However, not all arise "to reproach and eternal disgrace," but only those who seem to be good here. When, even though they are considered to be virtuous and holy men, they rise again and the shameful things of their soul appear, these arise into reproach, for those who are manifestly evil arise again not into reproach but into punishment.

And if the Savior says this, then he is calling the cross a "reproach." For the apostle taught this: "The insults of those who insult you have fallen on me."[53] Again, "He who, for the sake of the joy that was set before him endured the cross, disregarding its shame."[54] Now, reproach and shame are the same thing. And see this at least, as far as it concerned him, joy was set before him because he had no sin. Therefore he disregarded the shame; he trampled over it.

He does not become a reproach for his friends and for those who have the same virtue, but for his enemies. See, for instance, the insults that they bring against the Lord's Man: "Were we not right in saying that you are a Samaritan and have a demon?"[55] No virtuous men brought this speech against him; no apostles and the others. Again, when they say, "He casts out demons by Beelzebul, the ruler of the demons,"[56] they are no friends, they are no men of virtue.

And to my neighbors exceedingly so.

The Jews were his neighbors, if the Savior is the speaker; and the neighbors of the virtuous man are the pretenders of virtue. They are my neighbors; they have their own dwellings close beside my house, for the true way of life is a house for the righteous man; for the one who has heard the words [146] of Jesus and transformed them into deeds builds his house on the rock, while the wicked man builds on the sand.[57] However, since both of them have becomes hearers of the words of Jesus, they seem to be neighbors, they seem to be akin.

"The homes of transgressors will require purification, but the houses of the righteous are acceptable."[58] Transgressors are not lawless people; rather, they possess the same law, but they transgress it. And when it is said, "Blessed are they whose lawless acts are forgiven,"[59] those do not have any experience of the law. "Transgressions hunt a man";[60] for the lawless, in a certain sense, do not wholly arise into judgment, in order to be even censured. Being censured is a lesser punishment. Indeed, the ones who received the law and transgressed it, these arise again "to reproach and disgrace." And that this is so, we will establish the prophecy of Daniel, for in it this is set down: "And many of those who sleep in the tomb of the earth"—he did not say "all"—"arise, some to life and others to reproach and disgrace."[61] However, in the First Psalm the resurrection is found in three ways: the impious arise again, not in order to be judged. The transgressors arise again into judgment, those who received the law and transgressed it, the sinners. The righteous are not raised in order to be judged, but in order to receive the promises.[62]

So here he says, "And many of those who sleep"; for he does not enumerate the impious in this way, as those who are not raised into judgment, but who arise "to reproach and everlasting shame." These, however, are the sinners. The righteous arise again "to eternal life." Concerning these two companies the Savior also says in the Gospel, "They will come out—those who have done good, to the

---

[52]Dan 12:2.
[53]Rom 15:3 NRSV, quoting Ps 69:10 (68:10).
[54]Cf. Heb 12:2 NRSV.
[55]Jn 8:48.
[56]Lk 11:15 NRSV.
[57]Cf. Mt 7:24, 26.
[58]Prov 14:9 LXX.
[59]Ps 32:1 (31:1 LES2).
[60]Prov 5:22 LES2.
[61]Dan 12:2.
[62]Cf. Ps 1:5-6.

resurrection of life, and those who have done evil, to the resurrection of condemnation."[63] He does not mention the impious here. Since therefore the company of the impious is excluded, he did not say that "all" rise again, but "many of those who sleep."

However, if someone should regard this interpretation as forced, although it is not so, and should say that the impious are grouped in with the sinners as well, then we understand the word *many* here as "all," for all are many, but not vice versa. In any case, let the *many* here be defined as "all." Furthermore, the apostle writes this: "For just as by the one man's obedience the many will be made righteous, so also by the one man's disobedience the many are made sinners."[64] Here too "all" are signified by *many*: all were those who were disobedient, all are those who were obedient. This is not reversible. If "some" are sometimes "all," however, by no means are the "many" always "all," for instance: "Many will say to my soul."[65]

And a fear to my acquaintances.

I have become a *fear to my acquaintances*, because I bear this condition, in which many insult me. Even the apostles, for instance, because they were afraid, were scandalized for a while. And here he is speaking of the passionate kind of fear that cowardice follows, even though it is not itself cowardice.

One can also understand a divine *fear*. Those who see me, who understand the mystery of my appearance and why I was crucified, they began to have a *fear* that is equal to reverence, about which it is said, "Fear of the Lord surpassed everything";[66] for see what he calls them: "my acquaintances." The virtuous are known by God, for the Lord knew those who are his,[67] and they know him.

Indeed, the apostle also says to the Galatians, "Formerly, you did not know him [**147**]; however, now that you know God, or rather are known by God."[68] When we know God, he knows us; for "if anyone does not recognize, he is not recognized,"[69] and clearly if someone knows, he is known.

Therefore, I became *a fear to my acquaintances*. Those who are worthy of being known and who know me began to have a *fear* that is the equivalent of reverence, of which it is said, "Then you will understand the fear of the Lord,"[70] after many virtuous actions.

Those who would see me outside fled from me.

Our Savior and Lord is at the same time God and man. However, he is seen and is observed insofar as he is man, for he is invisible because he is "the image of the invisible God."[71] And the image of the invisible must be invisible. But when it is said, "Whoever has seen me,"[72] understand the phrase "has seen" correspondingly with the following: "Whoever contemplates me with knowledge, who sees me divinely, who reaches out as though to one invisible, who also understands the mystery of my appearance and my Passion." Therefore, "those who see me outside" have become exterior, who know Christ only according to the flesh[73] are such people as those to whom Paul writes, "For I decided to know nothing among you except Jesus Christ, and him crucified."[74] They belong among those who are outsiders and they run outside me; they are like those who hear in parables: for the parable that is expressed obscurely has not made them outsiders, but their superficial understanding has led those who are outsiders to this end.

---

[63] Jn 5:29 NRSV.
[64] Cf. Rom 5:19.
[65] Ps 3:2 (3:3).
[66] Sir 25:11 NETS.
[67] Cf. Jn 10:14.
[68] Cf. Gal 4:8-9.
[69] 1 Cor 14:38.
[70] Prov 2:5 NETS.
[71] Col 1:15 NRSV.
[72] Jn 14:9 NRSV.
[73] Cf. 2 Cor 5:16.
[74] 1 Cor 2:2 NRSV.

I was forgotten from the heart like a dead man.

The one who understands that Jesus is Life—for he says, "I am the Life,"[75] and is the living Son of the living Father: for "I live because of the Father"[76]—they do not forget him at any time, for, being present in their mind, he always illuminates them, so that each says, "Christ lives in me."[77] Such a person is in Christ and has Christ living and acting within himself. However, wherever someone becomes aware that he is neither living in nor acting on him, he forgets him as though he were a dead man, for Christ does not live in all, but in those who act in accordance with him. And as many as consider themselves to be Christians and do not act in accordance with Christ do not have him living in them.

Behold! The wicked man lives according to vice; being "a lover of pleasure rather than a lover of God,"[78] he does everything as a hedonist. He regards the righteous man as a corpse, since that one is deprived of his wicked way of life and has no place for that life in his intellectual part.

[30:13] *I became like a broken vessel.*

I did not become a broken vessel, but I became *like* the *broken vessel*. Now, take the following example: men other than the Savior, when they are crucified, seem to have become useless vessels, vessels of destruction. This speaker of these things has become *like the broken vessel*, but he is not ruined. Just as he has become sin, even though he is not sin in the same sense as the others are, but in order that those might become the righteousness of God in him[79] he made himself similar to sin, so also he made himself like the broken vessel.

And it is not unknown that men are called vessels, and some are for honor, while others are for dishonor.[80] This vessel that accords with Jesus is not for destruction, for he knew no sin.[81] However, he has been made like the broken vessel. He has become a curse, in order to bring in a blessing.[82] Now, no curse brings blessing, but rather it corrupts the blessing, for no accursed person is blessed. This one, however, by becoming a curse has become the cause of blessing, not for one man only but for all who believe.

[30:14] *Because I heard the censure of many who were dwelling all around.*

I heard many censuring me who were not at all isolated from me. The Israelites were living near Jesus in his circle. They censured him: "He casts out demons by Beelzebul, the ruler of the demons."[83] "He is a sinner, for he does not observe the Sabbath."[84] They were all around him.

When those who were saying these things were Gentiles, they were not his circle. These have encircled him. Indeed, it says, "They surrounded me like bees a honeycomb."[85] They surrounded me [148] with hostile intent.

[30:14] *When they gathered together against me.*

He mentioned *enemies*, *neighbors* who *excessively* reproach him, he mentioned those who *forget him from their heart*, and he speaks of those who *dwell all around* and censure him. These were *gathered together* "to take his soul," particularly at the time when "the nations grew insolent and the people contemplated vain

---

[75]Jn 11:25; 14:6.
[76]Jn 6:57 NRSV.
[77]Gal 2:20.
[78]2 Tim 3:4.
[79]Cf. 2 Cor 5:21.

[80]Cf. Rom 9:21; 2 Tim 2:20.
[81]Cf. 2 Cor 5:21.
[82]Cf. Gal 3:13-14.
[83]Lk 11:15 NRSV.
[84]Jn 9:16.
[85]Ps 118:12 (117:12 NETS).

things,"[86] for here even the nations that grew insolent have not yet been wholly cut off from him and isolated. "Why did they grow insolent?"[87] They attacked the Hebrews more arrogantly. And the Hebrews contemplated the prophecies about me idly and vainly. All the groups that have been mentioned *were gathered together; they plotted to take my soul.*

The greatness of the one who is to be despoiled is shown, because *they were* all *gathered together to take* his *soul.* Not one, not two, not ten, not a thousand, but all of them together. The indestructibility and the difficulty—or rather the impossibility—of Jesus' soul being defeated is indicated. With difficulty they have been able to take my soul; rather, they have plotted to take it but have not taken it. "No one takes my soul from me; I lay it down of my own accord in order that I might take it up again."[88]

[30:14] *They plotted to take my soul.*

As far as their intention was concerned, they have come to kill him. However, if he himself had not given himself up, they would not have been able to do this. And indeed, at the moment when they came in order to arrest him, he was saying, "Whom do you seek?" And it says, "Jesus of Nazareth." When he said, "I am he," "they stepped back and fell to the ground." And again a second time: "Whom do you seek?" and he gave them the same answer, and they fell to the ground again. He said the third time, "I am he, therefore take me, but let these men go."[89]

For no one was able to be arrested with him. This was often said: that he did not allow this for the sake of not providing to the unstable a false preconception—that he himself was not the most courageous, but the one who suffered with him was. Therefore, even when Peter says, "I am ready to go with you even to prison"[90] and to lay down "my life for you,"[91] he replies, "Stop! Before the cock crows, you will deny me three times."[92] Now, if he had suffered together with him, it would be in doubt for whose sake he has done this.

And "he gave himself for our sins."[93] Moreover, the Father is said to have given him up, for he has done even this at the Father's good pleasure. And when Judas is also said to have handed him over, that one handed him over in a different sense: he has become his betrayer.

[30:15-16] *But as for me, I hoped in you, O Lord; I said, "You are my God." My inheritance is in your hands.*

Even if those have acted in this way and *were gathered together* in order to *plot* against me *to take my soul* and in order to do the other things, yet for my part I did not depart from hoping in you. *I said, "You are my God. My inheritance is in your hands."* The priestly interpretations say this, that the lots *in the hands* of God are, for example, the diaconate, the presbyterate, and the episcopate. And it is blessed to have the lots that someone has obtained by lot in the hands of God. Such a person is free from intrigues, for "no one snatches out of the Father's hand."[94]

"*My lots are in your hands,*" says the Savior. And to agree together with the interpretation that was given, we say, "Those whom I obtained by lot in order to minister to me, whom I appointed in the church as apostles, prophets, and teachers,[95] *are in your hands."*

---

[86]Ps 2:1.
[87]Cf. Ps 2:1 NETS.
[88]Cf. Jn 10:17-18.
[89]Jn 18:5-8. The three instances of "I am he" are rightly recorded by Didymus, but the text refers to the same "I am he" twice, which means the crowd only falls down once.
[90]Lk 22:33.
[91]Jn 13:37.
[92]Mt 26:34.
[93]Cf. Gal 1:4 NRSV.
[94]Jn 10:29.
[95]Cf. 1 Cor 12:28.

However, it is possible—Israel also, when it was called "my people," became his portion and *inheritance*—all the nations have been given as an *inheritance* to the Son. The nations are many lots. These lots are *in your hands*, kept safe by your active and protective powers, so that no one can possibly snatch them from your hand, for "no one can snatch them from the Father's [149] hand."[96] He did not mention: if someone does not take himself out of his hand, he cannot be snatched by another, since some will say: certainly even virtuous people were later dragged down into impiety. And lest I should speak out of appearances, Judas, for example, has himself taken himself out of his hand. For while it was night, when he was reflecting on the things that related to the betrayal, it says, "He went outside, for it was night."[97]

Therefore, *my lots*: each of those who believes in me is my lot. *In your hands* is what is fair for an *inheritance*, for the lot conforms to the *inheritance* when it is reckoned for many. We also say this more comprehensively: the hands of God are the two covenants. If someone is his lot, he is *in his hands*.

[30:16] *Rescue me from the hand of my enemies and from those who persecute me!*

Not all *enemies persecute*, but all persecutors are enemies. For evidence that "to persecute" here is not meant in reference to capturing but in reference to setting a trap, it says, "The enemy said, 'I will pursue and I will overtake.'"[98]

This pursuit does not happen for the purpose of imitation. On the contrary, those who pursue righteousness must love. Those who pursue righteousness for the sake of partaking of it and being made like it really pursue it. As when someone pursues knowledge, he acts in order that he might also see according to knowledge. So also must one understand the statement, "Seek peace, and pursue it."[99]

It can also be taken with a more ethical sense in this way: since the *hand of the enemies* and of *those who persecute me* is vice, forbidden practice, deliver me from their practice. May I not submit myself to their wicked deeds, to their practice!

[30:17] *Shine your face upon your servant; save me in your mercy.*

When you raise me up and make me free of my persecutors, then you have made your face visible. I, however, am your face, the "exact imprint of your very being,"[100] the "image of the invisible God."[101] Given that I assume "the form of a servant,"[102] *shine your face upon your servant*. Show that this servant has your form, that *your face* was resident within this *servant*. Therefore the phrase *"Rescue me"* is said in accordance with the conception of the *servant*, and the word *face* in accordance with the conception of the truth: the exact impression of the divine being.

In your mercy, then, *save me*. Raise me from the dead. And perhaps he also calls "his salvation" the salvation that is on behalf of those for whom he has come, in order that he should become for them "the source of eternal salvation."[103]

[30:18] *May I not be put to shame, because I called on you.*

Now, *I am not put to shame*, when the objects of my request are undertaken.

---

[96]Jn 10:29.
[97]Jn 13:30.
[98]Ex 15:9.
[99]Ps 34:14 (33:15 NETS).
[100]Cf. Heb 1:3 NRSV.
[101]Col 1:15 NRSV.
[102]Phil 2:7.
[103]Heb 5:9 NRSV.

Question: This word is not the Savior's, is it?

The changes of persons are abrupt, as it also happens in the Prophetic Books. Furthermore, concerning the mere man: each of us, for example, when we describe a man, sometimes we indicate him by means of his soul, and sometimes by means of his body. When I say, in order to quote from the Scripture, that a beautiful person is "ruddy with beauty of eyes,"[104] exceedingly great—then I say that the man is wise, he is a servant of God, he is submissive to the Lord, for the changes of expressions do not take place outside himself, in general. Whenever a composite being is talked about, the changes of persons move from one part to another.

Since, then, the one who says these things is not only a man, nor only God, but God-become-man, some things are said as from the Man, others as from God the Word or about God the Word. "And the Word became flesh and dwelt among us, and we have seen his glory, glory as of the only Son from the Father."[105]

You are to understand this in relation to the same person, for he does not say the following: "*Shine your face upon your servant*," on one who is other than me, but on me, your servant. **[150]**

[30:18] *May the impious be shamed and be brought down to Hades.*

The phrase *May they be brought down to Hades* has again a particular significance. He did not say, "Let them descend to Hades." To descend somewhere belongs to those who go down willingly. These, however, are not led willingly to Hades. And it is certainly said of Capernaum or to Capernaum, "And you, Capernaum, will you be exalted to heaven? No, you will be brought down to Hades."[106] It is led down by others. And they are put to shame when they know that they are impious. And they do not have any impulse of desire to descend into Hades. For this reason they are led down, in order that, by receiving a notion of where they are about to descend, they might be put to shame. They will reproach themselves all the more because they have become impious.

[30:19] *Let the deceitful lips become speechless, which speak lawlessness against the righteous.*

He is not cursing them; he is blessing them. For he did not say, "Let their lips become speechless." Whenever *the deceitful* lips are deprived of slanderous words, they have become *speechless*. He does not simply speak of their lips but of their "*deceitful lips.*" After these abandon speech, at last they speak with confidence and truth. So indeed it is said, "The Lord will destroy all deceitful lips and a boastful tongue."[107] When the boastful tongue, that is, the speech, is destroyed, that speech, from the time it is destroyed, speaks at last the Word of God.

[30:19] *With pride and contempt.*

Since the phrase "*against the righteous*" is indeterminant, it can be understood both of the righteous man and of the righteous deed, of which it is said, "You shall pursue righteousness righteously."[108] Now, the one who speaks against the righteous deed and against the one who has it and has been made like it speaks *with pride and contempt.* Indeed, the lips become different when they know in what kind

---

[104] 1 Sam 17:42 NETS.
[105] Jn 1:14 ESV.
[106] Mt 11:23; Lk 10:15 NRSV.
[107] Ps 12:3 (11:4).
[108] Cf. Deut 16:20 NETS.

of lowliness they are, when they know that the one whom they scorn is unworthy of their contempt.

[30:20] *O how great is the abundance of your kindness, O Lord, which you hid from those who fear you.*

Since he seemed to say some things in imprecation, we, however, observing the disposition of the speaker, say that they are not imprecations but rather intercessions. And he desires for good things to happen to them.

Since it would happen that those who were not ignorant of his kindness and the end of those who are saved would perish, he hid these things from the fearful. And he calls the "fearful" here those who have the fear of punishment, not the righteous, not those who have that fear in which there is no want,[109] not that fear that surpasses everything.[110]

He says the following: since your *kindness* is naturally connected with—is the same thing as—your goodness, and you do all things for the salvation of all, even the unhappy things and certain things that you allow to happen to unhappy people, yet since those being crushed were about to be harmed because of their superficiality, you *hid* your goodness *from those who fear you* but do not love you. For here we take fear as that which is opposed to love: "Perfect love casts out fear."[111] Now, love is perfect when we love something not for the sake of something else. Therefore, "perfect love casts out fear; for fear has to do with punishment."[112] It is not that, of which it is said, "There is nothing lacking to those who fear him."[113]

[30:20] *You accomplished it for those who hope in you, before the sons of men!*

You accomplished this concealment.

Many are *sons of men*, and they are not being reproached for this. Frequently, however, men and their sons, when it says, "You sons of men, how long will you be slow of heart?"[114] and when it says, "From heaven the Lord looked down; he saw all the sons of men"[115]— these *sons of men* are praiseworthy.

And I relate a paradox: when they are related to God, righteous men are also *sons of men*, but when they are related to the righteous, sinners are *sons of men*. It is of those men who are wicked **[151]** that Paul writes, "For as long as there is jealousy and quarreling among you, are you not merely human?"[116] And it says about them, "But now you die as humans,"[117] after they fell away from being gods and sons of the Most High. In comparison to holy men, who are called or named "gods," the wicked are called *"sons of men"*; however, in comparison to God the saints are called the virtuous, those over whom he turns his gaze. And again, "You will save men and beasts, O Lord. How you increased your mercy, O God. And the sons of men will hope in the shelter of your wings."[118] "A man is something great, and a compassionate man something precious."[119] Here the man who is "in the image and likeness of God"[120] is praised for his greatness. However, whenever someone falls away from being a son of the Most High and becomes a man, this man is wicked.

You accomplished for those who hope in you, before the sons of virtuous *men*—and those ones

---

[109] Cf. Ps 34:9 (33:10).
[110] Cf. Sir 25:11.
[111] 1 Jn 4:18 NRSV.
[112] 1 Jn 4:18 NRSV.
[113] Ps 34:9 (33:10).
[114] Ps 4:2 (4:3). The LXX has *barykardioi*, which translates a different pointing of the Hebrew text from that which we have in *Biblia Hebraica Stuttgartensia*.
[115] Ps 33:13 (32:13 NETS).
[116] Cf. 1 Cor 3:3-4.
[117] Ps 82:7 (81:7 LES2).
[118] Ps 36:6-7 (35:7-8).
[119] Prov 20:6 LXX.
[120] Cf. Gen 1:26.

know the completion, the concealment of the riches of your goodness.

[30:21] *You shall hide them in a secret place of your appearance.*

Them being the *sons of men* for whom you *accomplished* your mercy. Now, some are *hidden in the secret place* of God in this way: God has an appearance that appears through his own creatures, for it is said, "From the greatness and beauty of created things, their Creator is discerned analogically."[121] By analogy with creation he is discerned. For just as when someone sees a ship, he receives an image of the shipwright, even if he is not present, and the one who looks at a well-steered ship from afar immediately arrives at the conception that there is one who steers it, and the one who sees a chariot from a distance, when it is being handled in an orderly way, even when he does not see the charioteer, receives an estimation of him, in the same way, since the world is now governed in an orderly way and has a nature that is most beautiful, an image of the beauty and majesty of God becomes known. For if the things that come into being are great, how much more the Creator of them! Therefore, when someone received an image of God from the world and its arrangement, from the notion and laws of providence, he was not *hidden in the secret place of* his *appearance*. Such, however, are the philosophers among the Greeks, for they received a representation of God from the greatness and beauty of his creatures. The one who receives an image of God aside from creation, having seen the Son and through him the Father—for "whoever has seen me has seen the Father"[122]—this one has been *hidden in the secret place of* God's *appearance*.

Again, to speak in a more popular vein, Jesus had two appearances, one of man and one of God. As many as know him according to the flesh receive him in the manifestation of his *appearance*. However, as many as withdrew from knowing him according to the flesh and came to know him insofar as he is God the Word,[123] these were *hidden in the secret place of* God's appearance.

And again, since I was saying that the external representation of the world is an appearance, the doctrine in relation to which the things that came into being have appeared, are cared for, and are governed, there is also the hidden place of God's appearance, and the hidden place is that which relates to the doctrine of the Creator himself.

God often conceals his own goodness for the little ones who fear him. Yesterday, we have understood those who fear as those who abstain from vice out of a fear of punishment, if it is even fitting to call this an abstinence from vice. "Perfect love," it says, "casts out fear; for fear has to do with punishment."[124] The one who has knowledge of good and evil, both desiring the good and adhering to it, abstains from vice out of love toward the good; he removes himself from evil not out of fear of punishment, he turns away [152] from evil. When, for example, an argument persuades him that there is no punishment, then he practices the evil that he prefers.

God, therefore, often does not bring in vengeance immediately out of his goodness and benevolence. And he *conceals* the multitude of his rich goodness because of those who are afraid, because of the little ones, because of those who abstain from evil out of fear of punishment.

How great, then, *is the abundance of your kindness, O Lord!* He concealed it, for the knowledge of it was making them to perish in

---

[121]Wis 13:5.
[122]Jn 14:9 NRSV.
[123]Cf. 2 Cor 5:16.
[124]1 Jn 4:18 NRSV.

evil things. As when someone, in order to terrify a son, produces words of indignation and conceals his kindness, in which he does this as one who is about to punish; for if the son knew that the threat was in pretense, he would despise his kindness and would be spoiled and would become accountable to wrath.

In reality, great is his kindness; it is a great abundance. For the apostle also says to some: "Or do you despise the riches of his kindness and forbearance and patience? Do you not realize that God's kindness is meant to lead you to repentance?"[125] However, the one who does not understand this thinks that God is not displeased with his wicked deeds and for this reason does not seek to take revenge. Moreover, Peter, the supreme head of the apostles, when he writes his epistle, has also said such a word: "The Lord is not slow about his promise, as some think of slowness, but is patient, not wanting any to perish, but all to come to repentance."[126] Behold his kindness! It was not necessary for it to be known to the many, for they would still despise it instead. Therefore, you *concealed the abundance of your kindness* for the sake of those who fear you.

You accomplished it for those who hope in you, before the sons of men.

Those who hope are those who await the divine rewards and the promises that God was offering to give to those who live well. *You accomplished it*, then, *for those who hope in you.* You accomplished this concealment of the abundance of your kindness, lest those who hope in you also see this: that you do not bring in your anger because of some.

So he says, "*before men*." The abundance of your kindness is not always hidden, but insofar as they are men of whom it is said, "But now you die as humans,"[127] and, "For as long as there is jealousy and quarreling among you, are you not merely human?"[128] Therefore, *before these sons of men you accomplished this concealment of the abundance of your kindness*, for he also opens this for them.

The God of all is often called a man, not because he has become a man or is a man, but because in condescending toward men he so governs the things that concern them and becomes their judge in such a way that he becomes like a sympathetic man. "He bore with you as someone would bear with his own son."[129] He bore with your ways by nourishing you and governing you. The saying, "If you mark lawlessness, O Lord, O Lord, who shall stand?"[130] and, "His eyelids examine the sons of men"[131] are in unison with this. He sees the things that are practiced with his mere eyelids.

Therefore, just as the One who sent the Son, who was well pleased with his appearance, provides beneficial things, like a man governing men, so also this one is "the Son of Man." He is the Son of the Man that is understood in this sense.

And in another sense: in a certain way individual children belong to the whole race. And mankind as a whole has been made "in the image and likeness"[132] of God. Therefore the one who preserves the prototype, the universal, as it were: that one is the son of man. Now, since the soul of Jesus preserved being "in the image"—for he knew no sin and he committed no sin[133]—in this sense he is called the "son" of that man who has been created "in the image and likeness" of God.

It could also be said in a different sense: even if Jesus did not have a father as man, yet he had a mother. And the mother is human. And for the suppression [153] of docetism he has been

---

[125] Rom 2:4 NRSV.
[126] 2 Pet 3:9 NRSV.
[127] Ps 82:7 (81:7 LES2).
[128] Cf. 1 Cor 3:3-4.
[129] Deut 1:31.
[130] Cf. Ps 130:3 (129:3 NETS).
[131] Ps 11:4 (10:4 NETS).
[132] Gen 1:26.
[133] Cf. 2 Cor 5:21; 1 Pet 2:22.

called the Son of Man. Even if he does not receive his existence from a father, yet he is from his mother. Indeed, in this sense it has been said that he is "born of a woman,"[134] for the sowing of the seed comes from the man, but the formation and birth comes through the woman. Since, therefore, this one does not have his existence from a man and through a woman, he is rather "from" a woman—for he received his whole substance from the Woman, not like other men: "And Jacob begot Joseph the husband of Mary, from whom the Christ was born."[135] He did not say "through her"—and in this sense therefore he is called "Son of Man," for if he were merely called a "man," the docetists would assume that he appears to be a man, because he does not have his birth of beginning from a man. Therefore, to show that he is from Mary, he called himself "Son of Man."

Moreover, God the Word himself is sometimes called a "Son of Man," for when he says, "No one has ascended into heaven except the one who descended from heaven, the Son of Man,"[136] he is predicating this of God the Word. And he is called Son of Man in the same sense as when we often say that the soul comes from the parents. As when we say, "Jacob, God's holy one, is from Isaac," we are not saying this: that he is of such a kind and holy for this reason, but rather that this one, for whom it happened that he is holy, is from Isaac. And in this way, then, God the Word is the Son of Man. "Then what if you were to see the Son of Man ascending to where he was before?"[137] we do not understand as the body, lest we adhere to those who say that he has departed from heaven as a body. And nearly all the heretics say this, such as Marcion, Basilides, and Valentinus.

And we often say in this sense that "a man is wise, holy, and a friend of God," and he is the son of such a woman; indeed, he is not such as he is simply because he is her son. In composite things, we often predicate of the whole the things that belong to the part, as when we say, "an intelligent man, knowledgeable, healthy in body, handsome and tall," we speak sometimes of the body and sometimes of the soul. For some of the things that belong to the composite cannot belong to each one of the parts in the composite. Indeed, to be awake or to sleep is not said of the soul alone, nor of the body, for the soul does not do this without the body, nor does the body do this without the soul. Therefore, it is said of the composite.

You shall hide them in a secret place of your appearance.

God's creation is sometimes called "his *appearance*." "From the greatness of the beauty of creatures their Creator is discerned analogically."[138] They are not in his *secret appearance* but in his manifest one. When you see a physician at work, as one who executes his art skillfully, you see his *appearance*. For the works of medical science reveal the physician. And when we are able to see the analogy of the thought of the things that are skillfully made and the disposition of their maker, we no longer see his manifest *appearance* but his *hidden* one. So also in the case of God we say that when we perceive his creatures, from the creatures, and from the greatness of their beauty, we see the God who is an ocean of beauty and majesty, we have in our mind his manifest *appearance*. However, when we observe why, for instance, he has made heaven in this way or how and why it was created in such circumstances, then we have entered into the *secret place of* his *appearance*, into the understanding according to which he created.

"The Word became flesh."[139] See the external appearance. "And we have seen his glory, glory as of the only Son from the

---

[134] Gal 4:4 NRSV.
[135] Mt 1:16.
[136] Jn 3:13 NRSV.
[137] Jn 6:62 NRSV.

[138] Wis 13:5.
[139] Jn 1:14.

Father."[140] This is the secret understanding. In agreement with this, then, the apostle says, "Even though we once knew [**154**] Christ according to the flesh, we know him thus no longer."[141]

[**30:21**] *From human disturbance you will shelter them in a tent, from the contention of tongues.*

Those who are just now being rescued and ridding themselves from the *disturbance of men* are *sheltered* by progress, for the one who turns away from evil in order to do good, together with his refusal of evil, he does not have the good within himself perfectly.

He becomes a disciple of the solitary *tongue*: the *tongue* of God. Now, *tongues* designate words, and this has been shown frequently: "They bent their tongue like a bow,"[142] their speech. And, "Death and life are in the hand of the tongue."[143] The physical tongue does not have a hand in any way. But it has an activity: speech, which is called a "tongue."

[**30:22**] *Blessed be the Lord, because he showed his mercy wondrously in a city under siege.*

After turning his attention to what has been said and becoming aware of the words, he then sends up songs of thanksgiving in the form of a blessing, and says, "*He showed his mercy wondrously in a city under siege.*" I was saying that he concealed the abundance of his own kindness on account of mercy, in order to show mercy. Knowing the motive behind the concealment of the abundance of his kindness, he blesses the one who has done this and says that he has done this "*in the city under siege.*" We can say that the present life is *a city under siege*: the passage of time in this world, for in a certain way we are contained within a garrison.

Moreover, since in the book of Kings Zion is called a "city under siege,"[144] for "who will bring me to a city of fortification?"[145]—this fortification is praiseworthy, it is a garrison that is invincible, an unstrikeable shelter.

He showed, therefore, *his mercy wondrously in the city under siege*. If someone is outside this city, he does not know why God conceals the abundance of his kindness. We say, however, that these are the little ones who do not practice what is evil out of the fear of punishment.

Question: Is it not quoted, *His mercy for me*?

The greatness of God's mercy is carried off when you add the words "for me." It is universal. We sometimes help a certain person. When we do this because he is virtuous or because he is knowledgeable, we have done it not for that person only, but for every virtuous person, for every knowledgeable person. Therefore, it is unnecessary to have the words "for me." A certain lover-of-self added the phrase.

[**30:23**] *But as for me, I said in my ecstasy, "I have been cast away from the presence of your eyes."*

He is speaking about his former circumstance, in which he was searching and was agitated. Put outside myself with greatness of wonder and astonished at the economy of the concealment of God's kindness, I supposed that I was expelled from the *presence of God's eyes*. He is expelled from God's presence who practices things unworthy of his presence. Nevertheless, this one is not so wicked as the one who departs from the presence of God by his own free will. Truly Cain was such a one, for "Cain went away from the presence of the Lord God."[146]

---

[140]Jn 1:14 ESV.
[141]2 Cor 5:16.
[142]Jer 9:3.
[143]Prov 18:21.

[144]Cf. 2 Kings 25:2.
[145]Ps 60:9 (59:11 NETS); cf. Ps 108:10 (107:11).
[146]Gen 4:16.

He left spontaneously to evil, he embraced godlessness, he has become an originator of the notion that there is no providence. Of Adam, however, it is said that the Lord "drove him out."[147] Now, the one who desires to be inside is driven out. He was not as wicked as Cain.

And this one who says these things therefore said, "Since such things occupied my attention and I wondered, for example, about the prudence of concealing the abundance of your kindness from those who fear you, I supposed that I was expelled from the presence of your eyes."

And it is also possible to understand it thus: just as all who have drawn near with faith are "the body of Christ and individually members of it,"[148] so also the fullness of the divine powers, of the rational essences, are God's body. [155] And just as in the case of the members of Christ we say that those who see clearly are called "eyes," and those who are active are "hands," those who "do not lag in zeal"[149] are "feet"—for this reason "the eye cannot say to the hand, 'I have no need of you,'"[150] nor can the hand say, "Because I am not an eye, I do not belong to the body."[151] And notice this! The eye is greater than the hand, and this eye, which sees clearly because it observes God's designs, is unable to say, "I have no need of you," for you know that the hand has the practical ability that an eye, though of primary significance, cannot do. And . . . certainly this is also characteristic of presumption, when the greater can say to the lesser, "I have no need of you."

Men who see clearly are the *eyes* of God. And he says, "Since I occupied myself with deeds and did not understand them, I am not an eye. So I spoke as follows: 'Perhaps I have come outside of God's eyes, of those clear-sighted men who perceive with their mind.'"

[30:23] *Therefore you listened to the voice of my petition.*

Therefore you listened, because I knew: insofar as it depended on my ignorance, I was cast away from God's eyes.

[30:24] *Love the Lord, all you his devout ones!*

"Devout" are those who do what is right toward God, who observe that which the Savior said, "Give to God the things that are God's!"[152]

"Love the Lord!" Notice the purpose for which this is said! Those who were afraid were the ones from whom the mercy of God was hidden. And we considered the passage of John and clarified it in this way: "Perfect love casts out fear; for fear has to do with punishment, and whoever fears has not reached perfection."[153] So the perfect love is when someone, out of love for the good, flees what is evil. He does not remain free from evil because of the fear of punishment but because he has genuine love for the good. Opposites, however, cannot coexist.

[30:24] *Because the Lord seeks out truths.*[154]

The truth of God has a singular form, for the Savior says, "I am the Truth."[155] However, it becomes a kind of truth in those who partake of it. And just as it obtains in the case of knowledges and virtues—we do not say about each knower that he possesses the whole of knowledge, but a certain kind of knowledge, that is, a particular part of it. So as many knowers as there are, so many are the particular parts of knowledge, and as many partakers of the truth as there are, even so many—rather, even so many[156]—are the truths; they are as many as those who partake of it. However, I

---

[147]Gen 3:24.
[148]1 Cor 12:27 NRSV.
[149]Rom 12:11 NRSV.
[150]1 Cor 12:21 NRSV.
[151]1 Cor 12:16 NRSV.

[152]Mt 22:21.
[153]1 Jn 4:18 NRSV.
[154]The NRSV reads instead: "The LORD preserves the faithful."
[155]Jn 14:6.
[156]Here Didymus corrects a grammatical mistake, which is characteristic of oral style. He at first wrongly uses the masculine form

am saying those things before the perfect state. For there it is impossible to speak of many true ones or many truths, many knowers or many knowledges. For if hereafter there becomes of the faithful "one heart and one soul"[157] and they "are united in the same mind and the same purpose"[158]—if they are not united in everything, at least they are united in a certain respect—after all the goals, in the state that is the final object of our desire, it is impossible to differentiate one knower from another. As when, by way of hypothesis, if all physicians, according to all the parts of medical science, were to possess it to the highest degree, there would not be many physicians—there would still be many men, but not many physicians.

Since then the truth is one—for "grace and truth" came "through Jesus Christ"[159]—therefore the truth comes as one through itself, not each individual truth coming through itself. They come through the one truth, just as the individual virtues come through the universal and the individual knowledges through the universal.

The Lord, therefore, searches out these truths. For this reason strive how you may be able to receive a certain truth, for God searches these out. Even if you understand it in reference to the practical virtues, the truth of the practical virtues is determined from the disposition, if someone pursues it because of righteousness itself. Since "you shall pursue righteousness righteously,"[160] pursue righteousness itself righteously; pursue the practice of righteousness with the disposition [156] of righteousness.

Love the Lord, all you his devout.

He has provided a reason: since *the Lord seeks out truths, love the Lord*, the bestower of truths. In this way we also understand righteousnesses spoken of in the plural: "the Lord is righteous and he loved righteousnesses."[161] When in fact it speaks of righteousness in general, of its subsistence: "Righteousness peered down from heaven,"[162] it calls the Savior here righteousness. And just as he has become wisdom for us, so also righteousness.

[30:24] *And he repays those who act excessively with pride.*

After he demonstrated the littleness of those who fear, indeed he also speaks of men who trouble them, of certain sophists and tricksters; these men he called proud. And they act out their *pride excessively.*

However, the following is also possible: every vice becomes excessive, that is, in vain. And this is certainly said in Proverbs: "Do not quarrel with a man in vain,"[163] for although you act as an enemy, you can do nothing to him, when God does not grant it. Therefore, one does this in vain. And one shall not strive for vanities. And these proud people, then, act out their pride excessively, for not all against whom they exalt themselves will become subject to them, unless God grants this.

[30:25] *Take courage, and let your heart be strong, all you who hope in the Lord.*

Having spoken of all the contests, he incites us to perseverance, to courage. And he does not speak of those who fear but of those who *hope*. Now, we were saying that these people are those who do the good out of a longing for the promises. Those, then, are ready to become men, to grow *strong*, and to draw near to God. When each of these is united to him, he becomes one spirit with him.[164] And if each of those who is united to the Lord becomes one with him, when many are united to him, they all become one spirit by way of participation.

---

of the adjective and then switches to the feminine form. It is impossible to render this meaningfully in English translation.
[157] Acts 4:32.
[158] 1 Cor 1:10 NRSV.
[159] Jn 1:17 NRSV.
[160] Cf. Deut 16:20 NETS.

[161] Ps 11:7 (10:7).
[162] Ps 85:11 (84:12).
[163] Prov 3:30.
[164] Cf. 1 Cor 6:17.

PSALM 31 [32]

[31:1] *For David. Of understanding. Blessed are those whose lawless deeds were forgiven.*

The forgiveness of sins is a new birth, a birth upon birth. For this reason it is called regeneration. Just as the palinode means a song upon a song, so also regeneration is another birth that happens after a preceding birth. Therefore, it was necessary that the psalm about regeneration be placed with a number that has certain virtues. Now, it comes from the fourth square, five fives, and receives an addition of the first of the perfect numbers, six. For the first of the perfect numbers, added to the fourth of the squares, renders thirty-one. Five fives is a square. A square is a number multiplied by an equal number. So these numbers, after being added together, have produced that which corresponds to regeneration, for one must have one's constitution from the perfect number and from the square because of its solidity. The former birth has become subject to shaking. The serpent's deceit separated the first-created ones from perfect virtue and from keeping the divine command, which they had received from God. Therefore, it was necessary for the second birth to be more firm. It possesses its solidity from the square; it also has perfection from the number six, because the number that is composed and completed by its own parts does not lack anything.

Moreover, one must say this: although twenty-five is also a square, yet it has its result from the senses, for the senses are five: vision, hearing, taste, smell, and touch. Nevertheless, even in the things perceived by the senses there is perfection and stability, for the praiseworthy is given even in a manner perceptible to the senses, and it is perfected by the number six, by perfection.

And it is also necessary to recognize this: the psalm before this one—I mean the Thirtieth Psalm—delineates the human birth, for a man [157] who has been alive for thirty years is able to be a grandfather, and a woman who has completed thirty years is able to become a grandmother. And the students of physicians say these things: someone who has been alive for fourteen years is able to produce viable seed. Therefore, since this seed is sown as "the workshop of nature," a living creature is produced and generated in the fourteenth year. Afterward, this very same seed again is able to be fertile after it has lived for fourteen years and is considered a grandfather in its thirtieth year. And the third generation obtains perfection, especially in the periods during this earlier birth.

This birth, then, being more common among men, precedes the second birth, which according to the number that has been mentioned is found to have stability because of the number twenty-five and perfection because of the number six.

At last, let us see the beginning of the psalm itself, in order to know what mystery it contains. The psalm is titled *"of understanding,"* "of David's understanding," so that the sense that is contained within the verses is like when you say of the theories of medical science: "The things written come from the understanding of such and such a physician. According to Peter they belong to

Galen, according to others they belong to Menemachos."

So it is *of the understanding of David*. And the *understanding of David* is not more common among men, but it is divine; it also has the practice joined together to it, for it is said, "And understanding is good for all those who practice it."[1] Understanding is synonymous with wisdom, as when it is said, "A spirit of wisdom and understanding."[2] This understanding is contemplative; it has to do with the mysteries of piety and the doctrines of the truth. However, the practice is something different; it is that which is done, for "understanding is good for all those who practice it."[3] Furthermore, practical virtue possesses understanding and knowledge, for from where do we understand whether things are advantageous or ethical, unless we understand them? And Paul, for example, while writing practical advice, says, "May God give you understanding in all things."[4] He was speaking about what was useful to do, about the need for the teacher to be supported by his students. And since he seemed to be speaking about himself or seemed to be the teacher himself, having spoken cryptically that it is necessary for the teacher to be supported by the students, he says, "May God give you understanding in all things."[5]

Truly, "understanding" is versatile; the word is ambiguous, it has many meanings. And since he is speaking here about things that are hidden, it is set down in the sense of knowledge; it is analogous to wisdom, for the psalm contains mysteries.

And one must also say this: it is impossible to understand grammatical notions, unless someone has an understanding of letters, and it is impossible to understand philosophical arguments, unless someone has knowledge of their introductory principle. So also it is impossible to understand the things of God without divine understanding.

Why, however, is the *understanding* accredited to David alone or said to be from *David's understanding*? Observe that personal characteristics are sometimes from the giver and sometimes from the receiver when they discover them. For example, the Holy Spirit is sometimes called the Spirit "of Elijah" and sometimes the Spirit "of John" in Scripture.[6] Likewise, the gospel is sometimes called "God's," since God gives it and orders it, for it says, "set apart for the gospel of God."[7] And it is sometimes named from the one who serves it; for it says, "according to my gospel."[8] And sometimes it is called the gospel of those who are evangelized and have received the gospel. And sometimes it is mentioned in an absolute sense: "Repent and believe in the gospel!"[9] Such names, whether with or without an addition, signify the same thing, as I was saying: simply [158] the gospel and the gospel of God. Therefore, it means the same thing to say simply the gospel or the gospel of God. So then, the understanding is said to be on the one hand from God who gives it; and on the other hand it is said to be from the prophet and the psalmist who has received it.

[31:1] *Blessed are those whose lawless deeds were forgiven and whose sins were covered over.*

Sin is different from *lawlessness*. Lawlessness is the sinful practice of one who does not have a law, for the violator of the law is called a transgressor. "Transgressions ensnare a man,"[10] and "The transgressor, in order to sin, speaks

---

[1] Prov 1:7 NETS (LXX).
[2] Cf. Is 11:2 NETS.
[3] Prov 1:7 NETS (LXX).
[4] 2 Tim 2:7.
[5] 2 Tim 2:7.
[6] Cf. Lk 1:17.
[7] Rom 1:1.
[8] Rom 2:16; 16:25; 2 Tim 2:8.
[9] Mk 1:15.
[10] Prov 5:22 NETS.

within himself,"[11] although in another sense sin and lawlessness are identical, for John the Divine writes this in the letter according to him: "Everyone who commits sin is guilty of lawlessness; sin is lawlessness."[12] Consequently, when someone sinned, it is in a certain way lawlessness, yet he calls them two things. Indeed, by binding them together with a copulative conjunction, he showed that they are two. Then he adds, "And sin is lawlessness." Sin is nothing other than the genus to which lawlessness belongs, for I was saying that the species of lawlessness occurs whenever one who does not have the law practices it badly. And this is also called "*sin*" as well as the transgression of the law or disobedience, which I called "transgression." Just as when I say, "Everyone who owns a horse also owns an animal," animal is the genus. Not everyone who owns an animal owns a horse, but the one who owns a horse owns an animal. The one who has the species also has the genus. In this way, then, he also speaks here, when he says that lawlessness and sin are the same. Conceptually, however, there is a difference, because the one is general and the other particular; the one is a genus and the other a species. For I was saying that the word *sin* is set down in relation to transgression and *lawlessness*. So each of the two ways is sin: "for all who sinned apart from the law."[13] See! These are people without the law: they sin. "And all who have sinned under the law":[14] these are the ones who have wisdom, who have the transgression of the law. Both sinned.

However, a *forgiveness of lawless deeds* occurs whenever the divine law, the spiritual one that "converts souls,"[15] rules over the lawless. Then their lawless deeds are forgiven. So the forgiveness of sins does not take place all at once. Jesus forgives when he says, "The Son of Man has authority to forgive sins,"[16] and, "Son, your sins are being forgiven,"[17] for he does not say as follows: "Behold! Your sins were forgiven." He has given him a renewing power. And the activation of it, that comes in addition, brought vice to ruin.

Therefore, *blessed are those whose sins were forgiven*. At last they keep to the perfect law of God, which converts souls.[18] Therefore, a forgiveness of sins takes place whenever the divine law that accords with the gospel draws near, for this is the "spiritual law" by which souls are converted, as I said. And the sins that follow and grow during the transgression of the law have a concealing. The *sins are concealed*, but it is impossible for those who were once baptized to meet with the baptismal water again. However, their sins are concealed though deeds of repentance. But you might respond that sins, by having been concealed, survive because of the concealment. Does it not say that "love covers a multitude of sins"?[19] For it does not absolutely conceal the sins, but in another sense, for the one who loves carries out works of love; indeed, one who demonstrates love toward his neighbor in no way slanders him, insults him, or does him harm. And whenever someone does these things instead, this person does not have love toward him. All these things, when they are no longer being performed, are concealed, not that they are eradicated when they are concealed by it, but love, when it approached, concealed those things, [**159**] that is, it renounced them, it has put them outside.

Furthermore, if one must go into detail, love, after it draws near, causes sin in its activity to cease, even though the possibility still survives. When some possibility is concealed, so is the activity. For example, the repentant thief was having sin in its activity; he repented; the Savior gave him forgiveness.

---

[11] Ps 36:1 (35:2).
[12] 1 Jn 3:4 NRSV.
[13] Rom 2:12.
[14] Rom 2:12.
[15] Ps 19:7 (18:8).
[16] Mt 9:6.
[17] Mt 9:2.
[18] Cf. Ps 19:7 (18:8).
[19] 1 Pet 4:8 NRSV.

The activities, according to which he committed thievery, were thrown away. The possibilities remain, however, but they are concealed.

Indeed, one must not follow the opinion of those who say that vice is a deprivation. There are some—and the whole faction of the Donatists[20] says this, "It is impossible for one who has cast off virtue to receive it again." Just as it is impossible for one who has lost sensory perception to receive it again, and for this reason blindness and deafness are a deprivation, so also they think about virtue. And to us, as many as are more simple, or rather, who babble without learning, say that such a recovery is no longer possible, for they say that there is no repentance after these things, that it is impossible to receive virtue again, but that vice remains forever and ever and bears a punishment that is appropriate to it.

So, the sins are covered over in this manner of which I spoke. They proceed into the possibility of sin, for it is blessed to have the possibility of vice. Opposites cannot coexist. The one who has virtue in its activity has the possibility of vice, and this is indeed blessed. Therefore one must not have virtue in possibility but in activity. For this reason, from the beginning when God created mankind "in his own image and likeness"[21] and made him "upright,"[22] therefore just as the good was already in his account, immediately he has also given a law that prevents sin, in order that sin should always remain only in its possibility.

[31:2] *Blessed is the man whose sin the Lord will not reckon, and in his mouth there is no deceit.*

Paul understood this in relation to those of the circumcision and in relation to the Gentiles: "This blessing," he says, "is pronounced over the circumcision and over the uncircumcision."[23] In that section of the passage he referred to a law that was good, to the good law. Those from the Gentiles are lawless, for "even though they do not have the law, they are a law to themselves."[24] However, when they were called to judgment by the true law, not by that which conforms with common reasoning, they are no longer lawless.

And so the blessing can belong to both the lawless, the Gentiles, or to those who have their sins concealed, the Jews. And they had the law earlier, so that there is a separation between the circumcision and the uncircumcision. And this was before the gospel, when the race of men was divided into two kinds of men, into circumcised man and uncircumcised man. However, when our Lord was pleased to come, he united both groups together, creating the two into one new man.[25] The new man is not ethnic, the new man does not come from circumcision, but he is one new man just as he was also created as one man in the beginning. For at that time there was no difference between circumcision and uncircumcision. Just as, therefore, the man of circumcision and the Greek are created as one new man by repentance, by observing the former way of life—and the former way of life that precedes the law is evangelical. Even though, indeed, the Greeks sometimes mock, saying, "See when Christianity was first introduced; but we are earlier," we show that before Moses and before the statues were introduced and the production of idols, men's way of life was such as Christians now possess when they live according to practical and contemplative virtue.

Into that one man, then, he created and has made him new—new, not different—but new in distinction [160] from the old. Whenever a succession of the commands takes place, that command becomes old, as we have frequently said, because the newly arriving law renders

---

[20]PsT reads "Stoics" here, but the discussion is more appropriate to the Donatists.
[21]Cf. Gen 1:26.
[22]Eccles 7:29.
[23]Rom 4:9.
[24]Rom 2:14.
[25]Cf. Eph 2:15.

the former law ancient. So indeed the commandment of the Jews is the old one according to the shadow, since it was succeeded by the gospel. However, since the commandment of the gospel is without successor—even if the heaven and the earth, therefore, should pass away, the words of Jesus remain[26]—for this reason it is called the new covenant, since it is without any successor.

Therefore, even the life of the lawless and the life of sinners was removed, for their *lawless deeds were forgiven, and their sins were covered* over, and finally a man is created. He speaks of a lawless person or a sinner no longer, and he says, "*Blessed is the man whose sin the Lord will not reckon.*" Remember that I said: sin is the genus of lawlessness.

This can also be related to the "example"[27] for those who are being saved: I mean the Lord's Man. Blessed is this one, for sin is not reckoned to him, for he neither knew it nor performed it.[28]

And in his mouth there is no deceit.

The one who "speaks truth in his heart"—according to the psalm that says as follows: "Who walks spotlessly and practices righteousness, who speaks truth in his heart"[29]—the one who "speaks truth in his heart" has no deceit in his mouth; he has no deceitful word.

And it is also well said, "And there is no deceit in his mouth." Some do not have deceit in the mouth, but they have it in their heart, for to someone it is said, "Your heart is full of deceit."[30] And the apostle said to Elymas the magician, "O you, full of all deceit."[31] Therefore it is a great thing not to have *deceit* in one's *mouth* when one's heart does not have deceit, for it allows a certain prudent person to say all such things, since he is known not to have deceit.

And I say: he has no *deceit in his mouth* like the sophists do. I do not mean the teachers of rhetoricians but the sophists, who lie by their sophisms. A sophism is a lie, for even when it should come at one time from true premises, yet its conclusion is a lie.

[31:3] *Because I kept silence, my bones grew old from my crying all day long.*

This is expressed in hyperbaton:[32] "*because I kept silence from my crying all the day long, my bones grew old.*" And the clause "*my bones grew old*" is erroneously placed in this way: *because I kept silence* about these things, *my bones grew old from my crying all day long*. Not *from my crying all day long* have my bones become old, but *because I was silent from my crying all day long*. For before this I used to have the day that "the Sun of Righteousness"[33] makes. And I used to shout, first praying and then glorifying God, who gives me the day. *Since, then, I became silent from my crying all day long, my bones have grown old.*

And it was said by us before this that he calls "*bones*" the strong powers of the soul and the doctrines of piety. As, moreover, these bones support the whole body—for on them both the small veins and all the rest depend—therefore it is said, "All my bones will say, 'Lord, who is like you?'"[34] These physical bones do not have feeling or thought. Indeed, even when they are sawed in two they do not feel it.

My bones, therefore, *grow old.* They were removed. When they were united to God, then I used to cry aloud all the day long. But since silence succeeded the shouting, my bones have become old. Now I already said that things that are not succeeded . . .[35]

---

[26]Cf. Mt 24:35; Mk 13:31; Lk 21:33.
[27]1 Pet 2:21.
[28]Cf. 2 Cor 5:21; 1 Pet 2:22.
[29]Ps 15:2 (14:2).
[30]Sir 1:30.
[31]Acts 13:10.

[32]In hyperbaton, the word order is inverted.
[33]Mal 4:2 (3:20).
[34]Ps 35:10 (34:10 LES2).
[35]Here there is a large gap in the manuscript. Pages 161-76 of the codex (comprising Didymus's comments on Ps 31:3–32:13) are missing.

PSALM 32 [33]

[*He saw all the sons of men.*] [177]

... [he is like] the senseless beasts.[1] So he saw these [sons of men.]

[32:14] *From his prepared habitation.*

His *habitation*, as it were, his temple is the condition ... his throne. This throne is prepared and a habitation ... "Your throne is prepared from then on; you are from eternity."[2] The prepared ... concerning him as king. And we receive a notion of his throne ... He comes, and so when we hear about his temple we understand him to be ready with it ... it signifies, as it were, God's condition, God's majesty. A soul whose ... is not ... his habitation is prepared.

Furthermore, this is also possible: ready ... from the same participation he becomes ready in order to advance into the presence of God ... holiness in a brief space draws near to the one who possesses it, for that one begins with progress ... receive the participation. The *habitation* of God is ready, not ...

According to progress, from a little one he becomes a great one. When it is measured together with reality ... it is ready.

Now, sometimes the good itself is called "ready," as when it says, "My heart is ready, O God,"[3] for the one who has his heart prepared is a temple of God, is his prepared habitation. And again, "Has it been told to you, O man, what is good" and what is delightful "but to do judgment and to love mercy and to be ready to walk with the Lord, your God?"[4] And again, "Your ear inclined to the readiness of their heart."[5]

[32:14] *He looked down on all the inhabitants of the earth.*

There are others who *inhabit the earth* besides the sons of men, for men who did not preserve being in the image and were not ... inhabit ... the earth. And the sons of these men do not inhabit the earth, but they sojourn ... he provides beforehand, for just as "he makes the sun rise on the good," so he does "on the evil"[6] ... he watches all the sons of men, and the inhabitants ... irrational animals, for he was securing "nourishment for all flesh."[7] All those on the earth ... he falls into a trap, for we are not speaking indiscriminately of the sons of men and of those who *inhabit the earth*.

[32:15] *He who alone fashioned their hearts.*

In Scripture, making and fashioning are distinguished, for God made man "in his own image and likeness,"[8] but he fashioned man from "the dust of the earth."[9]

And Job, for instance, says both of these things, "Your hands fashioned me and made me."[10] If he is saying this expression in a strict

---

[1] Cf. Ps 49:12, 20 (48:13, 21).
[2] Ps 93:2 (92:2 LES2).
[3] Ps 108:1 (107:2 LES2).
[4] Mic 6:8 NETS.
[5] Ps 10:17 (9:38 LES2).
[6] Cf. Mt 5:45.
[7] Ps 136:25 (135:25).
[8] Gen 1:26.
[9] Gen 2:7.
[10] Job 10:8 NETS.

sense, then the inner man would be made, and the outer man would be fashioned. And as he has said . . . : "Remember that you fashioned me as clay."[11] The word *fashioning* . . . means . . . , for example . . . And the Creator can also, by the desire that the parents have, bring into being . . . in what was read earlier we were saying that "becoming" is different from "being created" . . . .[12] it is not fashioning in every sense. Indeed, hear what he is saying: he does not say that hearts have been fashioned by God individually, but "*alone.*" *Alone* the hearts were fashioned . . . heart to run together with heart. They are totally different and . . . [178] many should have, they have them according to a certain difference. It says the following in Proverbs, for instance: "As faces are not similar to faces, so neither are the hearts of people"[13] similar. Truly, it is difficult to find two similar faces. Even if the face of Polydeuces and that of Castor should be recounted, yet this is set down as a myth. They say that the hemispheres are meant by these two names. For this reason they say that they live day by day only in part, for the hemispheres are so: when the one hemisphere passes under the earth, the other passes over the earth . . . because the hemispheres are indistinguishable in appearance. That is to say, when you cut a sphere in the middle, the two hemispheres are indistinguishable. So let that be regarded as a fable. We grant, however, that such men as these have existed. . . . Therefore it is difficult for face to run together with face in appearance . . . they recognize. So "as faces are not similar to other faces, so neither are the hearts of people"[14] similar. Most certainly, "no one knows a person's thoughts except the spirit of that person, which is in him."[15] If no one knows the thoughts of a person except the spirit of that person, which is in him, then the spirits of men are each formed individually. And fashioning here he calls the "mixture," as it were, and . . . for I said that they are not classified among the more perceptible formation, such as the clay of a potter . . . hearts, he knows all their deeds, for since someone knows their deeds accurately, when from the . . . them. And on another occasion we were saying that the one who occupies his intellect with the inventions of machines . . . you can judge whether he makes the parts of the sundial well or badly. And in an image . . . so heart does not run together with heart. For this reason he alone is called "knower of the hearts of all,"[16] according to the prayer offered up by the apostles, when the disciples were choosing . . . no one else can discover the heart of man. And Job says, "You knower of the mind of men."[17] Even if another is inclined . . . this of God's.

He forms hearts by themselves. Each heart . . . the word *formation* does not signify the creation of the heart . . . for even the elders who approve of her valor that . . . have said, "What is shaped by your heart is good."[18] They are not calling the essence of her heart "good," but her inventiveness, according to which she schemed cunningly. In keeping with good, they say, it has happened . . .

And it is possible so say in a second sense that "what is shaped by the heart" is good at that time when it feels disgust at vice or ignorance, when it is preserved as it has been in the beginning. The man who was made "in the image and likeness"[19] of God is not said to have been formed but to have been created. And the man who was made of earth and

---

[11] Job 10:9 NETS.
[12] See *Patrologia Graeca*, ed. Jacques-Paul Migne (Paris, 1857–1886), 39:1325A. "The phrase: 'They became' signifies the being of those who are brought into existence; the phrase: 'They were created,' signifies the ordering that has taken place after their being."
[13] Cf. Prov 27:19 NETS (LXX).
[14] Prov 27:19 NETS (LXX).
[15] 1 Cor 2:11 ESV.
[16] Cf. Acts 1:24.
[17] Job 7:20.
[18] Judith 8:29 NETS.
[19] Gen 1:26.

matter is said to be something formed by God: "Remember that you formed me from clay."[20] And in reference to both of the active powers of God, it is said, "Your hands formed me and made me."[21] To shape the heart . . . is a formation of the heart, not to give it substance. And so that you should know, the first creation of our hearts did not have any variance; for this reason it was not said at that time that each heart was fashioned by itself. There was no variance with the others. Here this is said, after the descent. [179]

Question: What does the passage mean, "There was one heart and one soul"[22] of the disciples?

In this sense "of those who believe," in the sense that they were of the same opinion, for we do not understand that their hearts and souls were entirely one in every respect.

Question: So will the act of formation ever cease?

The formation of the individual soul will, since this also took its inception from us. It both took its inception from us and will be limited, when it comes to pass that all rational things become one, just as the Father and the Son are one. I wish to be in him "that as I and you are one, O Father, so we all may be one."[23]

Question: Is there a difference between something that is made and something that is created?

There is a difference. "To make" signifies an essence that comes out of nonexistence, but not its formation. The word *creation* indicates, however, a kind of ordering of what has come into being. The word *creation* is even applicable to lifeless things: "I make peace and create things that are evil."[24] And indeed, according to the common understanding, we say as follows: being the one who provides for all things, he both grants them peace and creates evil things. And in another sense, this passage was clarified by us in the following way: he creates evil things as the impure creation, in order that it should no longer be unclean; he creates in order that it should become clean; he creates the two into one new man in him.[25] He creates the evil things in order that they might no longer be evil; for instance, he creates evil men, in order that they should no longer be evil.

Question: So he creates the quality?

The quality, as it were, "for we are what he has made us, created in Christ Jesus for good works."[26] He has not said the phrase "for good works" of their composition but in reference to their existence. And they are created "for good works," in order that they should do good works.

Question: With the result that the formation stems from the quality?

Yes, in the sense that formation is a species of creation, for the substance of the heart was formed. Now, the heart is the intellect. The word *creation*, however, extends even to perceptible things: "And [your hand] created the world out of formless matter."[27]

Question: Does *formation* apply to the rational beings without any distinction?

Yes, to rational beings in general. It is found extending even to irrational souls.

[32:15] *He who observes all their deeds.*

He perceives deeds, since he knows the heart, and the beginnings of the deeds that takes place are taken from their perceptive faculty. Among us, many welcome men because of every possible reason, and those who become imitators of God do this for no other reason except that "it is better to give than to

---
[20]Job 10:9 LES2.
[21]Job 10:8 LES2.
[22]Acts 4:32.
[23]Cf. Jn 17:21.
[24]Is 45:7.

[25]Cf. Eph 2:15.
[26]Eph 2:10 NRSV.
[27]Wis 11:17 NETS.

receive."[28] Indeed, to give makes one like God, but to receive does not, for each of those who receives is receptive of something. God, however, is productive, and that is why it is said to be better "to give than to receive." Again, "Blessed are the merciful, for they will receive mercy."[29] There is a kind of small progression, for in order to be shown mercy, one is merciful.

Another, because of sympathy, shows mercy, because he fears lest he should encounter such things, being human. So, for example, Christians feed those who are in prison in accordance with sympathy. Sometimes others again, having seen someone stricken by a disease, have compassion because that one has deteriorated. And again others do this in pursuit of glory, in order that they might be glorified.

Each of these deeds, however, being imperfect, admits increase and diminishment, for the perfect alone is that which does not admit increase and diminishment, the fortunate and the unfortunate. And each of these acts has an infinite difference. Not only in intensity is there increase and decrease, but also it is understood in relation to the duration of time. So this infinity is only comprehended by God. He alone understands this. Because of this he knows the heart of each. And it is difficult, perhaps, to find one heart that is indistinguishable from another heart.

So we ourselves put into action these things of which we have spoken because of vainglory [180], because of sympathy. However, it is something different for saints to receive. Therefore, in the case of saints it is not called "compassion," for it says, "Contribute to the needs of the saints."[30] He who gives to a saint must receive real wealth rather than giving it.

[32:16] *A king is not saved because of much power.*

Even in the literal sense this is true. Many, despite having great power and a mighty hand of soldiers, fell into enemy hands, and the abundance of soldiers certainly does not save the king. Pharaoh went forth to pursue the Hebrews with a great force, and he was not saved because of his great power, for "the chariots of Pharaoh and his host he threw into the sea."[31] Moreover, we find in the other narratives of the Scriptures that a few frequently prevail over many. And in general it was said to the Hebrews by way of prophecy: "one" of you "will pursue thousands and two will remove ten thousands,"[32] "and because of the voice of five, many shall flee."[33] So even the historical interpretation is preserved.

However, the elevated sense has great coherence as well. Many, believing that they have a provision of arguments and a well-trained rhetorical power, suffer defeat; they are refuted by the truth itself, and in this sense we say: Even if someone should boast of a kingdom because of a peculiar degree of preparation, because of a peculiar degree of sagacity, by means of such excellent things he is by no means saved by this great might.

And it is also possible to understand it in this way: since certain people are kings in an allegorical sense, as the Corinthians were, of whom Paul says that they were kings[34]—and Abraham was also "a king from God"[35]—the one who allows himself, out of his own strength, to be a king in this way and does not wait for God who has mercy is not saved by his own power. In a similar way, the city that is guarded without the collaboration of God does not remain in safety, nor does the house that is

---

[28] Acts 20:35.
[29] Mt 5:7 NRSV.
[30] Rom 12:13 NRSV.

[31] Ex 15:4 NETS.
[32] Deut 32:30.
[33] Is 30:17 NETS.
[34] Cf. 1 Cor 4:8.
[35] Gen 23:6.

[32:16] *And a giant will not be saved by the greatness of his own strength.*

This also has an historical sense. Goliath was a huge giant and possessed an abundance of strength, and he trusted in nothing other than in his complete armament, his own strength, and his size. However, he was also arrogant, for which reason he did not survive, for the one armed with "the name of the Lord"[37] conquered him and destroyed him. And we certainly find in the Scriptures that many great ones are overpowered, since they were placing on themselves too great a value. Amalek was prepared for war, and he supposed that he was stronger than Israel, for Israel was not at all prepared for the business of warfare; nevertheless, when Moses lifted up his hands Amalek was defeated and humiliated, and the lifting of the hands overpowered him, and he was not saved because of his own strength.[38]

We say again: when anyone who is an enemy of God, having "proud obstacles raised up against the knowledge of God,"[39] casts himself on the strength that he possesses and in which he prizes himself, he is by no means saved. Sometimes, the man who is wise in the things of God reproves him and overthrows him from the arrogance that he possesses.

[32:17] *A horse is unreliable for deliverance.*

Many again think very highly of a horse, but God the Word shows that even the arrogant snorting of horses is easily destroyed, for "some glory in chariots and others in horses, but we will boast in the name of the Lord, our God."[40]

See? "A horse is unreliable for salvation." With many horses Pharaoh was professing that he would take the Hebrews by storm. And those did not have even one horse; however, their salvation has proven [181] unreliable, it failed, it did not succeed.

Furthermore, it occurs in Proverbs: "A horse is prepared for the day of battle, but salvation is from the Lord."[41] You see that it is unreliable for salvation, unless this is undertaken by the Lord.

Let this suffice for the literal sense. As for the deeper sense, the body is often called the soul's "*horse,*" and the soul is a cavalryman or a horseman. It says, "I will strike every horse with alarm and its rider with madness."[42] Therefore, when someone is carried along on a body of those who are devoted to pleasure, he obtains madness because he fulfills his desires. Afterward salvation comes. The horse is stricken with alarm: it comes outside itself. For at last, when it is tormented and brought into subjection, it no longer advances according to its own desires, but it avoids these.

Bardaisan was alive in previous days, in the days of Antoninus, the emperor of the Romans. And in the beginning, he was of the school of Valentinus, but he defected to the church; he has become a presbyter.[43]

[32:17] *And by the greatness of its power it will not be saved,*

either the one who makes use of horses or the army of many horses, for the statement "*A horse is unreliable for salvation*" is true in each of the two ways, even if there are many, for it is not only said of one horse. Often the whole troop of cavalry is called a horse. Therefore, either the abundance of the power of the

---

[36] Cf. Ps 127:1 (126:1).
[37] 1 Sam 17:45.
[38] Cf. Ex 17:11-13.
[39] 2 Cor 10:5.
[40] Ps 20:7 (19:8).

[41] Prov 21:31.
[42] Zech 12:4.
[43] This anecdote about Bardaisan appears out of place, although perhaps he is being upheld as an example of a "horse" that was stricken with alarm and thus converted.

horseman who makes use of horses or the abundance and power of the horses does not deliver him.

[32:18] *Look, the eyes of the Lord are upon those who fear him.*

This is the equivalent of saying, "The eyes of the Lord are on the righteous."[44] And it says this again in the Twelfth Psalm, "Regard and listen to me, O Lord my God!"[45] So *the eyes of the Lord are upon those who* not only "fear," but *fear him*, for there is also a passionate fear, which perfect love drives out from those who have the fear of God.[46] There is fearing, and there is fearing God, for fear toward God is not passionate, but it signifies rising above all things. So indeed it says, "Fear of the Lord surpassed everything,"[47] and, "There is no lack for those who fear him."[48]

Because they are righteous, they are worthy of being observed by God.

[32:18] *Those who hope in his mercy.*

Observe: those who fear God *hope in his mercy*, for although they do all things that are at hand to do, they await mercy from him, as was said a little earlier: "It depends not on the one who wills nor on the one who exerts himself, but on God who has mercy."[49] And no one is able to keep his own city from being destroyed, either the citadel of his body or that of his soul, unless God watches over it together with him.

Those who hope in his mercy: he has mercy on those who fear him.

[32:19] *To rescue their souls from death.*

For this reason his *eyes are on those who fear him* and on *those who hope in his mercy*, in order that he might deliver *their souls from death*. We understand death here not as the common one that the pious and the impious, the righteous and the unrighteous, die, but there is a death of the soul that drags the soul away from the blessed life. Away from this death we turn to flee far away; of this it is said: "The soul that sins shall die."[50] And again, "Sin, when it is fully grown, gives birth to death."[51] And since this death follows sins, God, who grants forgiveness of sins, will deliver those who have been seized beforehand from the death that follows afterward.

[32:19] *And to keep them alive in famine.* **[182]**

Them: those who *fear him* and *hope in his mercy*. Just as he delivers *souls from death*, so he also *keeps them alive in famine*. Certainly such a thing has often taken place in history. He truly sustained the people of the Hebrews during a very long journey in the wilderness by giving them manna, offering it to them daily.[52] Even in the case of individuals you will find this: for example, Elijah was nourished by the widow and by the angel who appeared to him with the bread and the cup of water.[53] And again, when Jezebel was pursuing Elijah and all the prophets of the Lord, Obadiah, the supreme commander of King Ahab, nourished more than fifty men in two caves, after God made him ready to do this.[54] In any case he said this to Elijah when he met him: "And your servant is one who fears the Lord."[55] Now, the

---

[44] Ps 34:15 (33:16 LES2).
[45] Ps 13:3 (12:4).
[46] Cf. 1 Jn 4:18.
[47] Sir 25:11 NRSV.
[48] Ps 34:10 (33:11).
[49] Rom 9:16.

[50] Ezek 18:20 NETS.
[51] Jas 1:15 NRSV.
[52] Cf. Ex 16:35.
[53] Cf. 1 Kings 17:10-11; 19:5-6.
[54] Cf. 1 Kings 18:4.
[55] 1 Kings 18:12.

one who fears the Lord nourished those men because of the Lord.

Since it has, then, anagogical meanings—these other comments have been produced according to the history—again those who fear his fear and hope in his mercy he nourishes, offering them the Bread of life[56] who came down from heaven,[57] whose flesh is "true food."[58] Because he is the Savior of all, he supports them. Not only in one sense does he do this, but according to their situations: he delivers in battles by restoring people from their enemies and not allowing them to fall into captivity, he saves those who are ill, he saves also as a helmsman, when we are in upheaval within the ocean of life's sea.

Question: Does he grant each person to have a spring?

In the one whom he is "a spring for eternal life,"[59] this is sustained when he comes into a dry place. And, "Open your eyes, and be filled with bread."[60] The one who opened the eyes of the soul and was filled with divine words, which are chewed in the manner of bread, does not die of hunger, for "the Lord will not let a righteous soul starve."[61] Whoever craves bread without opening his eyes to the bread within himself lives in famine; for the soul possesses many foods within itself from God.

[32:20] *Our soul waits for the Lord.*

He means the following: since we know these things, that the eyes of the Lord observe those who fear him—even if at some time they have been in death, he delivered them, and even if at some time they have been in famine, he nourished them, and even if at some time we were in a certain kind of necessity, we endure, because we know that we will ever profit from these things. And our soul, even if it should come into death, will be delivered.

[32:20] *Because he is our helper and protector.*

You see that he began to transition then into a plural number: "From heaven the Lord looked down; he saw all the sons of men."[62] When at times certain discordant and contradictory things are said, see whether they are said about one person, for then a contradiction appears. But when these things are said of a church, or a city, or a house, there are no contradictions: for some things are said of some people, and other things are said of others.

And you should also know this, that the saints do not offer up prayers and thanksgivings for themselves alone, but for those whom they lead. It is not the same thing, for something that needs to be applied to one person to be said, and for it to be said to a multitude: for example, a whole people, or a nation, or a city. It is impossible for the same person to be good and evil at the same time, both temperate and undisciplined. And the apostle writes to the Corinthians, as to those who have become rich "in speech and knowledge of every kind."[63] Does he not say again, "It is reported that there is sexual immorality [**183**] among you"?[64] If he were saying these things to one person, they would be discordant. However, since the whole church is addressed with these things, and in the congregations there are people of one kind and people of another—in order for each to receive assistance for himself. So, for instance, he reproves those who are deluded about the resurrection, and those who wait open-mouthed, conserving the gifts, and about food sacrificed to idols. How then have these become rich "in speech and knowledge of every

---

[56]Jn 6:35, 48.
[57]Cf. Jn 6:33, 41.
[58]Jn 6:55.
[59]Jn 4:14.
[60]Prov 20:13 NETS.
[61]Prov 10:3.

[62]Ps 33:13 (32:13 NETS).
[63]1 Cor 1:5 NRSV.
[64]1 Cor 5:1.

kind"?[65] These are different people than those of whom he was speaking.

So also the saint is not speaking about himself alone—for he was a teacher—but about all those who were inferior to him, and have death, and encounter famine, because they did not come for their own land. He is not saying all these things about all of them, but all these things about certain ones; he applies particular things to each.

Since he is *our helper and protector*, for this reason *our soul waits* for him. We know, however, that even when we undertake something good, even when we desire to run to good things and wish to carry them to their perfection, unless he works together with us and has mercy, we are unable to accomplish these things. He is a *helper*, offering to us the things of which we are in need; he is our *protector*, setting his own shield before us in order that the opponents should not be able to wound us.

[32:21] *Because in him our heart will be glad.*

Some are gladdened in strength, about rule, dignity, and praises; our ground for joy, however, is the *helper* and *protector* himself.

[32:21] *And in his holy name we hoped.*

We ourselves hoped in the name that was named over us. And since this seems to be said in relation to another group—I do not mean that those who fear the Lord are also in death—observe: *we hoped* in one who is present. However, no one hopes in things that are present, but in things that are future and anticipated, for "hope that is seen is not hope."[66]

And when they sometimes say in the form of a petition: "Hallowed be your name,"[67] they are not saying this: "Let that which is not holy become so," but let this manifested, let this appear. And it appears as holy, whenever it both gives us aid and protects us. And when we were commenting on the Gospel, we mentioned many interpretations in relation to this, in relation to the saying, "Hallowed be your name," and this was understood: since we bear it, work together with us lest we blaspheme it; sanctify it, preserve it as holy in us, for it is spoken in the imperative mood. He says in the optative mood: "May your name be hallowed."

And another interpretation: when knowledge of your majesty comes to men, so that they do not deify another, when you become "all in all,"[68] your name is hallowed, removed from demons.

[32:22] *May your mercy, O Lord, be upon us, even as we hoped in you.*

May your mercy be upon us. The petition is not offered up by those who already have your mercy. For he did not say, "May your mercy be preserved," but *"may it be, even as we hoped in you."* For this reason we hoped in you. Observe that "in proportion to faith"[69] he gives the gifts, and all are not given to all in the same measure, but with the measure of the faith that preceded. And so it is here as well: *as we hoped*. There are some who hoped quite perfectly, and there are others who are not so, but according to a kind of advancement, **[184]** and others who hoped in an elementary way. "In proportion to" our "faith," indeed, *may your mercy be upon us, O Lord, for so have we hoped*.

---

[65] 1 Cor 1:5 NRSV.
[66] Rom 8:24 NRSV.
[67] Mt 6:9; Lk 11:2 NRSV.

[68] 1 Cor 15:28.
[69] Rom 12:6 NRSV.

PSALM 33 [34]

[33:1] *For David. When he changed his appearance before Abimelech, and he let him go, and he went away.*

To those who have read the Histories of the Kings, the narrative that is cited here is well known. When David was pursued by Saul and was about to be captured, he went away to Gath, to King Achish.[1] Here, however, he is named Abimelech. The word is a double name, for also in Scripture double names are related, as in the case of Moses's father-in-law: he is called both Jethro and Reuel. And Thomas is also called Didymus. And there are certainly many such double names: it seems that Matthew is called Levi in the Gospel according to Luke.[2] However, he is not the same, but the Matthias who was appointed in place of Judas and Levi are one person with two names. This comes to light in the Gospel according to the Hebrews.[3]

So it is possible that the king of Gath is called both Achish and Abimelech. However, it is also possible to reach a different conclusion. Many kings are named by a common name and by their own proper name, as all the rulers of Egypt are called thus: "Pharaoh." However, their names are found to be Sumachi or Neco, so that Pharaoh is the name of his rank, as the name "Caesar" is among the Romans.[4] Therefore it is also possible that this Achish, on the one hand, is the name of his rank, and that Abimelech is his actual name.

But whatever the case may be, the sense does not contradict either. Therefore, as you will: the one is a name of his rank, and the other his proper name. The grammaticists distinguish this from an appellative, for even the proper name is used in two ways: it is distinguished from an appellative and from a name used analogically. "Man," and the names that indicate a common essence of the species and genera, they call "appellatives," and the names that indicate this one or that one, they call "proper" names. However, the proper name is also said to differ in meaning from the name used analogically. I often say, "That which is equal corresponds." A quantity is said to be equal to a quantity. I say, however, that it "agrees and corresponds." This is an analogical use, for agreement and correspondence are only spoken of in reference to tones. And again we say that those who are of the same opinion and are of one mind "correspond." A proper expression, in the case of those who think the same things and have the same notions, is "to have the same opinion," "to think the same thing"; to agree, however, is an analogical use.

So it is possible that Abimelech is a proper name, which is not distinguished from an analogical name but from an appellative, whereas Achish is the name of a rank. So the narrative is clear: he saw that King Saul was pressing with his military strength against one man, David himself, and that the heavily

---

[1] Cf. 1 Sam 21:10.
[2] Cf. Lk 5:27, 29.
[3] The text referred to here is not extant. A fragmentary outline of the text has been reconstructed through citations from the church fathers. For a helpful discussion and reconstruction, see J. K. Elliott, *The Apocryphal New Testament: A Collection of Apocryphal Christian Literature in an English Translation* (Oxford: Clarendon, 1993), 3-10.

[4] The reading is uncertain here.

armed ones were against the unarmed one. He fled there. Then, since it was unsafe to go into a foreign city or country—for at that time in particular there began to be a suspicion of spies because the neighboring cities were always at war among themselves—he changed his appearance to a madman, even letting his saliva flow, and he began to go around, beating the doors at the gate, in order to seem to be possessed by demons.[5] In any case, the people of Achish counseled against him. He responds, "Do I lack mad men that you bring him to have a fit in front of me?"[6] And he sent him away, and he departed.

Such a condition, then, is called a "change of appearance," and indeed the alteration indicates a qualitative change. Truly, the qualitative changes has taken place willingly and not unwillingly; for changing unwillingly [**185**] takes place as when someone, because they are afraid, turns pale or, after being mistreated or because someone disturbs him, he seems to turn red. So, this alteration of the appearance has taken place willingly. And since "David" is often interpreted anagogically, as it was said in the earlier passages, as the Savior, you will say that the alteration of the Savior's appearance is his assumption of "the servant's form."[7] Moreover, here no change has taken place from one form into another, but there is a concealment of one form by another form that is clearly visible, for it is impossible for there to be an alteration of the unchangeable appearance. And indeed, of the Savior himself it is said in one of the psalms, "This change was of the right hand of the Most High."[8] The Savior is frequently called "the right hand of the Father," and especially in the thought of the psalmist. And he was changed when he became flesh, when he became a curse.[9] He endured becoming sin, in order that sinners should become the righteousness of God in him.[10] So the alteration is here an assuming of something, not a change, for may no one seek a change in the one who is unchangeable! "And if he is not unchangeable," as someone was saying, "he is something odious."

"This change," then, "was of the right hand of the Most High."[11] The right hand of the Most High is unchangeable. However, he has become sin, not as if by chance, but in order that he might accomplish righteousness.[12] Now, sin that accomplishes righteousness is not a change from a state of being without sin into being sin, for sin makes people wicked; it produces unrighteousness. This "sin," however, makes those who possess it into righteousness.

So when the Word becomes flesh and takes the "form of a servant,"[13] he was changed according to his appearance, not by way of a transformation, as I have already said frequently, but by way of an assumption. And the words, "We have seen him, a glory as of the only Son from the Father,"[14] indicate the glory that is his by nature. Therefore, in addition he began to possess a glory that is appropriate to the compounded flesh which he became.

"This change was of the right hand of the Most High." Not that we are speaking here of a change, which he himself accepted when we said that he was changed by the assumption of the servant's form; rather, this was a change that he himself caused to change. For he abolishes wrath; he does it to accomplish his mercies. After refraining from boasting and exalting for a little while, he says, "because I will remember your wonders from of old. And I said, 'Now I have begun.'"[15] I spoke of all the gloomy things, because I did not speak after I

---

[5] Cf. 1 Sam 21:13.
[6] 1 Sam 21:15 LES2.
[7] Phil 2:7.
[8] Ps 77:10 (76:11 NETS).
[9] Cf. Gal 3:13.
[10] Cf. 2 Cor 5:21.
[11] Ps 77:10 (76:11 NETS).
[12] Cf. Mt 3:15.
[13] Phil 2:7.
[14] Cf. Jn 1:14.
[15] Cf. Ps 77:11, 10 (76:12, 11 NETS).

had been troubled, because guards have surrounded me, but at last: "Now I have begun." But now I will relate what came after those things, the things that succeeded the gloomy things. "This change was of the right hand of the Most High."[16] Next he says, "What god is great like our God?"[17] "You made known your power among the peoples."[18] Behold! This is the change. Therefore, at that time he changed his appearance.

You can understand the king of Gath in a more allegorical vein as the king of this world, the devil. So the country of the foreigners is the place near us. And just as when the place on earth is called Egypt, then the one who rules over it and tyrannizes it is called Pharaoh; and as when Babylon is mentioned, so is Nebuchadnezzar; and when Assyria is mentioned, so is an Assyrian king; so when Gath is mentioned for the region around earth, one must again understand this person, its king, as a certain evil power. "He changed," therefore, "his appearance" "when he took the form of a servant";[19] for the devil thought that he had power over him to the extent that he even plotted death against him. "He tasted death by the grace of God for everyone."[20]

And the sign of this change: *he let him go*. He has proven unable to constrain him. And I am speaking of what is a paradox: If he has proven unable to hold back his diminution, what might he do about his divinity? Where are you who say that the Word was crucified, the Lord of glory?[21]

He let him go, then, *and he went away*. He departed from him, for he has not gone there because of the one who delayed him there, but in order that after completing the economy he should return and draw away many from there. Therefore, he has come even into Hades and raised up from there [**186**] many souls of the righteous. However, when you hear about "bodies,"[22] by no means contemplate the tents, for many suppose this. It is not absurd to say that this miraculous thing has happened in addition to the other divine miracles, but watch out lest it contradicts the whole sequence of the economy. Know this: that if people had recognized their own kin, it would have been difficult if they had remained in unbelief.

And furthermore, Peter in the Acts of the Apostles says of David, "And his tomb is with us to this day."[23] One must observe this: if anyone were to be raised at all, David would be raised. Therefore, the souls that were transferred from the earth we call "the bodies of the saints."[24] And we speak in this way, when we say that the whole church is the body of Christ. And in the resurrection it is said, "each in his own order."[25] Now, the proper orders of those raised from the dead are determined by nothing else than the progress of souls. Those who have the same virtue, faith, and piety are ordered together into one order. "Christ," then, "the firstfruits, then those who belong to Christ, each in his own order."[26] Those who belong to Christ are those who have different orders. And in order to receive from a different passage: as on the earth that received the seed, which bears fruit a hundredfold, sixtyfold, and thirtyfold, different orders appear, for it is not only one, or one heart, that bears a hundredfold, sixtyfold, and thirtyfold—indeed, our interpreters say this: those who pursue virginity obtain the hundredfold, those who pursue divine marriage the thirtyfold.[27]

---

[16] Ps 77:10 (76:11 NETS).
[17] Ps 77:13 (76:14 NETS).
[18] Ps 77:14 (76:15 NETS).
[19] Phil 2:7.
[20] Heb 2:9.
[21] That is, the Apollinarians.

[22] Mt 27:52.
[23] Acts 2:29.
[24] Mt 27:52.
[25] 1 Cor 15:23.
[26] Cf. 1 Cor 15:23.
[27] Cf. Mt 13:1-23.

They perceived the diminishment and inequality of the numbers, not the nature of the numbers. Certain perfect ones bear fruit. These, however, are signified by the number one hundred. And indeed it says in promise, "The youth will be a hundred years old!"[28] And Abraham, when he was a hundred years old, was called a "father" by means of promise.[29] And the number is most excellent in every way, for the number ten, when it is multiplied by ten, yields one hundred. And we were saying that the number ten contains everything; it contains all the numbers.

Again, the number sixty seems to have an affinity with the world, for the world was created in six days. So as many as become citizens of the world, and transcend this, and inherit the world that is signified by this world—and the number six was called perfect—these are another order.

And perhaps those prophetic people who, in addition to the two divine persons they have, also have the Holy Spirit abounding in them, these are the thirty. And the thirty has a kinship with the worshiped Trinity. Or perhaps because the Savior, after he become thirty years old, began the noblest way of life and the speaking of his gospel, those who have now drawn near to him bear fruit thirtyfold.

Listen! The virtues are interdependent, so that one who has one of them has all of them. We understand this in the case of the one who is very mature. However, when someone is in the process of advancing, he sometimes has one virtue that is superior, that one from which he began or for which he struggled, as it is also in the case of professions. You often see a grammaticist, a musician, and a physician, and he has one area that is superior, in which he possesses his whole propensity. We also learn this from the Beatitudes. For does not the poor in spirit possess the other virtues?[30] The poor in spirit is also sympathetic, and because of this he suffers, for if he were not sympathetic, he would not be poor in spirit. He has gentleness, for if he were inclined to anger, he would not be able to be blessed. He has righteousness. So those who are called by a different name are admired for their dominant and superior habit.

Question: It says that they saw many of them in the Holy City.[31]

However, the Jerusalem "that kills the prophets"[32] was not "holy," which the Savior abandoned when he said, "See, your house is left to you, desolate."[33] They appeared in the Holy City, the city of the living God, to those who live on earth and have their citizenship in heaven.[34]

Question: What does "they appeared"[35] mean?

These grosser senses apprehend gross things. The number thirty-three is divisible by three, eleven, and thirty-three. The sum of their quotients is fifteen.[36] And frequently the number fifteen was said to refer to the Two Testaments, for they "give a portion to [187] seven and to eight."[37] Indeed, it was said by us in previous discussions that it is also a triangle, and when this is granted it has five as the length of its sides. This has an affinity with the senses.[38] How indeed would this not happen after the change of appearance had taken place?

Question: When we say that he remained there?[39]

Not in the first instance. In another visitation that took place there. Roughly in the

---

[28] Is 65:20.
[29] Cf. Gen 17:5; 18:9-14; 21:1-7.
[30] Cf. Mt 5:3.
[31] Cf. Mt 27:52-53.
[32] Mt 23:37.
[33] Cf. Mt 23:38; Lk 13:35.
[34] Cf. Phil 3:20.
[35] Mt 27:53.
[36] $33 \div 3 = 11, 33 \div 11 = 3,$ and $33 \div 33 = 1. \; 11 + 3 + 1 = 15$.
[37] Cf. Eccles 11:2.
[38] Cf. PsT 156.
[39] See Emanuela Prinzivalli, *Didimo il Cieco: Lezioni Sui Salmi: Il Commento ai Salmi scoperto a Tura*, Letture cristiane del primo

beginning of the books of Kings this took place, but that event happened near the end, when at last they accomplished it in the war with Saul.[40]

Question: Was he not first released and then he went away?

By no means compare the anagogical meanings with the literal meaning! Therefore, I also enumerate for you the passage about Abraham: "He had two sons, one by a slave woman and the other by a free woman."[41] And he did not have them while he was Abraham. Abram had Ishmael with Hagar; however, Abraham had Isaac.[42] And then comes the statement, "She corresponds to the present Jerusalem."[43] He is not speaking precisely, in order that you should understand correspondence here as symbolic. *Correspondence*, however, is used in many ways. For example, in grammar the aspirated consonants are said to be corresponding to the smooth ones, and the long to the short. And in logic things that are opposed are called "corresponding." You divide the category "animal" into the rational and the irrational, into the mortal and the immortal, into those that have feet and those that do not. The rational does not correspond to the mortal but to the irrational.

Now, "to correspond" here is meant by the apostle principally as symbolism. To speak more coarsely: there is a literal sacrifice and a literal circumcision, and both have spiritual forms. One must not understand the circumcision in the flesh as corresponding to the spiritual sacrifice, and the more bodily sacrifice does not correspond to the spiritual circumcision but to the spiritual sacrifice.

Question: What do the passages, "By the word of the Lord the heavens were made firm,"[44] and again, "because the word of the Lord is upright" mean?[45]

The same things seem to be one thing and another in conception, when they are not perceptible by the senses. The Holy Spirit is one, and we speak of his various gifts. When you consider the gifts, it seems that there is a multitude of Holy Spirits. You have, for instance, "and the Spirit of prophets is subject to prophets."[46] And he is called both the Spirit of Elijah and the Spirit of Elisha. These are not different Spirits in essence, but in conception and in relation to those who partake of him he is called "Spirits" in the plural.

And so the Word of God, when he was still with God—for "the Word was also with God"[47]—has no relationship to another but to God alone, and later on to those who partake of himself, for "he called them 'gods' to whom the Word of God came."[48] The Word of God was indeed with him. Therefore, his Word is with God absolutely, but he came to those who partake of him relatively.

Sometimes those who partake of him partake of one aspect, as I said about the Spirit, for one has the Word of wisdom, another the Word of knowledge, for this Word is not one thing and another in his hypostasis. There are some who have the

---

millennio 37 (Milan: Paoline, 2005), 449-50n35. The student's question is based on the apparent inappropriateness of making David into a type of Christ in the episode at Gath. For David "remained" in Gath (1 Sam 27:3) after this brief appearance there (1 Sam 21:10-15). Christ, however, did not return to hell after harrowing it.

[40]Didymus responds to the student that the two episodes are different, the one coming earlier in the book (1 Sam 21) and the other later (1 Sam 27). For him, the type (David = Christ) can be connected episodically, and one need not maintain the correspondence in the same way throughout the entire narrative.

[41]Gal 4:22 NRSV.
[42]Cf. Gen 17:5.
[43]Cf. Gal 4:25 NRSV.

[44]Ps 33:6 (32:6).
[45]Ps 33:4 (32:5). Undoubtedly Didymus's recent exposition of this text—which is lost to us—would illuminate the student's question further. The student appears to be examining Didymus's claim about the lack of a full correspondence between symbol and reality. Two different things, "to create" and "to be upright," are predicated of the same spiritual reality. How is this to be understood?
[46]1 Cor 14:32.
[47]Jn 1:1.
[48]Jn 10:35 ESV.

knowledge of spiritual things, the knowledge of the truth, of the doctrines of piety; however, they are not able to explain something about them in detail. And we ourselves have known men who understand altogether intelligently and are unable to tell anyone about it. These possess the Word of knowledge. And whenever, in addition to having this knowledge, someone also has the ability to explain it in detail, to teach it, and to convey to others the thoughts that are within himself, there is the Word of wisdom. Indeed Wisdom herself says, "I prolonged words,"[49] that is, in the manner of instruction.

Therefore, the same Word of God comes to the prophets and is both with God and with those who became "gods" because of their closeness with him. And we do not seek the same relationship, for in the case of the Father it is unsurpassable. His closeness with God is not in accordance with condescension, but his closeness with those who [188] become "gods" takes place in accordance with their worthiness, ability, and the proportion of the progress they have attained. And to the prophets it happens as follows: "The Word that came to Jeremiah."[50] He did not say "that is" with Jeremiah but "that came" to him. And when he comes, he comes according to the measure of that person.

Here too, then, we have variously explained the "upright" Word of God, whose works are received in faith. We have said that it can be understood as the instructive Word.

Question: What kind of "spirit" should we understand there?[51]

According to a certain conception, you will understand the "spirit" of God's mouth in place of this: when, by means of the Word, he brings the Spirit to the knowledge of those he judges worthy of receiving him. "Remove from yourself a crooked mouth!"[52] "And his bold mouth invites death."[53]

When the Spirit is with God and with the Son, he is not called "the Spirit of the mouth," but when he renders service to those who are able to receive him by way of the Word.

Question: So you do not call someone a partaker of righteousness who is only a practitioner of it?

Right, I call one so who has righteousness with knowledge and is able to clarify it to another, just as he himself possesses it.

Question: You do not say that he does this by means of the word?

I do not say that he does this by means of the spoken word.

[33:2] *I will bless the Lord at every opportunity; continually shall his praise be in my mouth.*

He *blesses* God *at every opportunity* who gives thanks to him in every adversity. Moreover, the apostle writes, "Give thanks in every circumstance!"[54] He who gives thanks to God does not do this only for pleasant things but also for unpleasant things. Job certainly not only blesses God for prosperity, the well-being of his children, and for the rest of his wealth that surrounds him, but also when he is deprived of all these things all at once. For example, after he was deprived of all his children, of all his possessions, he blesses God and it says, "Job did not sin at all before the Lord, and he did not charge God with folly."[55] The one who says the following about providence, "God ought to do thus or thus," attributes folly to God, and as far as he is concerned, God did not know what he ought to have done. Truly, when someone says, "The

---

[49] Prov 1:24 LXX.
[50] Jer 11:1.
[51] Ps 33:6 (32:6). In the same verse the student has been asking about, it reads: "By the word of the Lord the heavens were made firm, and by the spirit of his mouth all their powers." The word for "spirit" here can also be translated "Spirit" or "breath."

[52] Prov 4:24 NETS.
[53] Prov 18:6 LXX.
[54] 1 Thess 5:18; Eph 5:20.
[55] Job 1:22 NETS.

elderly should die before the young, parents before their children, and the healthy should not die, but the sick," he attributes folly to the One who governs and provides beforehand. "He did not charge," therefore, "God with folly." "Blessed be the Lord."[56]

So, since there are also different opportunities, and it is appropriate to give thanks in every one of them, he says reasonably, "*I will bless the Lord at every opportunity.*" There is not a time when I do not bless the Lord. Even if impending events are unpleasant, I accept them as a good. And another word says, "Accept as a good thing from the Lord everything that happens to you!"[57] Would you not say, when you see a sick person being attended by the best physician, that he blesses the physician because he longs for health? Indeed, when he . . . him and cuts him with a surgical knife in order that he should be restored to health, he welcomes it, not only when he offers him pleasant remedies. And he looks not at whether the things administered to him are gratifying or unpleasant but to their usefulness and advantage.

So *every opportunity* is meant for the blessing of God. *Opportunity*, however, we understand in each of two ways: both the suitable occasion and the condition of the one who is being helped. So we say that in the case of the healthy, the time for luncheon is midday and the time for dinner is the evening, but in the case of one who suffers, we do not understand the suitable time in this way: by watching the time, but we understand it by observing how his body is faring. In each of the two ways the saint blesses God *at every opportunity*, for he knows that he is subject to providence and that the one who provides knows better than he does what things are advantageous to him.

"Rejoice always, pray without ceasing, give thanks in every circumstance."[58] If the saint always rejoices, he is never plunged down or dispirited at the misfortunes that come near him, for he even rejoices over these things; he rejoices as over contests. He perceives the victory that succeeds the struggles, and because he anticipates the crowns and the rewards, he rejoices, even when the circumstances are unpleasant.

Therefore, *I will bless.* **[189]** And lest someone suppose that the blessing happens only with the expression of words, for example, that someone says this only in promise, it adds, *Continually shall his praise be in my mouth.* When I celebrate him in song, I bless him.

Continually shall his praise be in my mouth. Now, we are not saying this, lest something impossible should follow, that he continually praises with the expressed word. Now, this is impossible, for when he sleeps he does not do this, when he eats from time to time he does not do this. Rather, one must praise in this way: "All that I do, whether I eat or drink or sleep, I undertake these things while giving thanks to God." Without a doubt one must also understand the command "Rejoice always" in this way. If you receive gratitude as an action, the one who is sleeping does not do this. He has gratitude in his potential. "Pray without ceasing." If you understand praying demonstratively, one cannot complete this without interruption. Certainly, if it was prescribed in a literal sense, it is said that he prays "three times a day,"[59] then we should allow that prayer takes place at noon, around the ninth hour, and at evening. Such then is praying without ceasing; prayer is nothing other than the requesting of good things from God. So whenever someone, through everything that he does, asks for good things from God, he prays. Even if one should not use the particular form of prayer, when he has a desire of obtaining things that are beneficial, he prays. The desire is itself a prayer, for he has

---

[56]Cf. Job 1:21.
[57]Sir 2:4.
[58]1 Thess 5:16-18.

[59]Cf. Dan 6:10.

the desire. Whatever he always does, even if he is prevented from making the particular form of prayer, yet he is praying to God.

So indeed also in the Wisdom of Sirach it is said, "The narrative of a pious person is always wisdom."[60] How is he always able to describe wisdom in detail? When we understand it in this way—and these things are frequently understood in ordinary language in this way—that we generally often seek someone and desire to get to know him, where it is possible to encounter him. They say, "He is always resident in this place of healing and he is there without interruption," although he does not pass the whole day long in this way, but when he is in session, it is so: he is quite assuredly in session there.

He did not simply say, "Continually shall there be praise," but "his praise." For the one who seems to praise without upright thoughts, without those that are truly theological, does not offer up praise for his own benefit; he does not praise God.

[33:3] *In the Lord shall my soul be praised.*

My soul is not commended for any other reason primarily than for partaking of God, for as another desires to be commended for his artistry, or for knowledge, or for rank or honor, so the saint desires for his own soul to be commended by the Lord. He does not recognize any other praise for his soul than this. For even if, as I said, someone is commended for knowledge, yet this praise, when it is compared to another that comes for the sake of God, is no praise at all. So we often say, "Nothing is sweet besides honey." However, there are also other sweet things, but when they are compared to honey they are not sweet.

And in another psalm it says, "From you is my praise in the great assembly."[61] The praise, which you give to me, comes into being in relation to no other than to you.

In the Lord shall my soul be praised. "In you," it says, "shall we be commended all day long,"[62] all the time of our life being called "day." And it is possible to understand the phrase "in you" either as "in consequence of you" or "by you." And both interpretations coincide in the saint. He is both praised because of God and he has praise from God himself.

[33:3] *Let the meek hear and be glad.*

Just as the wicked person desires to hide what he says and does, whenever it has not been renounced, so the virtuous and the one who is dedicated to God desires what he says and what he does to be well-known by all. He wants his light to shine before men, in order that those, when they see it, should glorify God.[63] He wants his words to enter others, for it is said, "Converse while walking."[64] Now, the one who converses with others does not converse primarily for his own benefit.

Since therefore I determined *to bless the Lord at every opportunity* and to have his *praise continually in my mouth*, so that my soul is praised in him, "Hear, O meek, and be glad!" Imitate me, and become so yourselves!

Now, if he is speaking to those who are more meek than he, he says, "Hear, O meek," because I who am instructed by you and stand below you am becoming so! For what belongs to the lesser also belongs to the greater. When disciples are praiseworthy **[190]** and praise the Lord—how much more are their teachers who also surpass them. So understand this in each of the two ways: either hear and be glad, you are greater in meekness than I am, because you have produced such a disciple or companion.

---

[60]Sir 27:11 NETS.
[61]Ps 22:25 (21:26 LES2).
[62]Cf. Ps 44:8 (43:9 NETS).
[63]Cf. Mt 5:16.
[64]Prov 23:31 LXX.

[33:4] O magnify the Lord with me.

After speaking to them about the meek, he then turns his speech around: "And before me *magnify the Lord with me.*" Now, someone magnifies God by not imputing to him a weightiness of little significance, but when he is able to understand his majesty. Truly the sun, when it rises, does not immediately appear in all its magnitude. However, in the course of a brief period it appears greater, for it certainly does not acquire any growth, but the one who sees it improves; he sees it better. "Magnify God"—think great things of God—"with me!" For the words "magnify God" mean to think great things about him.

[33:4] And we will exalt his name together.

The designation "God" has been named over the virtuous, for they are called by his name. Whenever, then, we possess actions and thoughts appropriate to his name, then his name is exalted not in a scattered way, but *together*, when we are established "in the same mind and the same purpose."[65]

Furthermore, it is possible to say that the name of God is exalted together in another sense: some drag down the name of God into lifeless matter, when they call images "gods." In a certain sense, they mistreat the name of God. And others bear the name because of their own belly, because they deify it in their teaching, because they are gluttons and all-devouring. Therefore, if we do not regard any of those things that is not God to be God, but only the Creator of all things, then we have *exalted his name together.* All of us are commanded by the prayer in the Gospel to say, "Hallowed be your name."[66] However, even if this word appears in imperative form, in any case we say it in prayer; it is therefore a prayer.

So according to all the senses of the exaltation of his name and its being sanctified do we understand this. Practice nothing that is profane, nothing wretched and mean, in order that the name of God should be exalted, in order that it should be sanctified. Keep the name of God separate from every fallen thing, from every earthly deed, for then the name of God is hallowed. And this will take place especially when "God becomes all in all,"[67] when eternal joy overtakes sorrow, pain, and groaning as they flee away.

[33:5] I sought out the Lord, and he hearkened to me.

He did not simply say, "I sought," but I have done this intensely. *And he hearkened to me.* This shows that the presently mentioned seeking happens through prayer, for this has been added: *and he hearkened to me.* Moreover, if one who desires to know God seeks for him, as much as is possible, yet the seeking has no end. Being heard means perhaps to find, to become perfect. *I sought out the Lord, and* he was found by me. So indeed is it written in Wisdom, "He is found by those who do not doubt him; he reveals himself to those who seek him."[68] And again, "Seek the Lord, especially when he should draw near to you."[69] Here, then, the phrase *"he hearkened"* signifies the following: that the seeking out has taken place through prayers. Praying without ceasing,[70] he seeks God out and had him listening, when he found the one who was being sought.

[33:5] And he delivered me from all my afflictions.

We have often spoken about these things, that God's deliverance from affliction does not

---

[65] 1 Cor 1:10 NRSV.
[66] Mt 6:9; Lk 11:2 NRSV.

[67] 1 Cor 15:28.
[68] Wis 1:2.
[69] Is 55:6.
[70] 1 Thess 5:17.

mean coming out of the reach of affliction, for if the apostles tell the truth when they say, "We are afflicted in every way,"[71] and again, "It is through many persecutions that we must enter the kingdom of God,"[72] a person must never be free from affliction. However, when someone does not understand deliverance in this way, then [193] the saints were never heard. Always being afflicted, in difficult circumstances, they brought their life to an end at their final breath.

[33:6] *Come to him and be enlightened, and your faces shall never be put to shame.*

Having spoken of the disposition that he has toward God, and having spoken of the things that are from God, which are useful to those who seek him out and to those who are heard, he exhorts either all or many and says, "*Come to him and be enlightened.*" Not to those who have already been enlightened and are able to say, "The light of your face was shown to us, O Lord,"[73] does he say, "Come!" For those who already come to him are light. For instance, the apostles, after they had come to him, heard, "You are the light of the world."[74] And they enlighten others.

Come, then, you who are far away, *to him and be enlightened!* And from your enlightenment comes your being without shame. And *your faces shall never be put to shame.* For after they have been enlightened, they become, as those who in thanksgiving . . . have said, "The light of your face was shown to us."[75] When the word is fulfilled: "The Lord will be a perpetual light,"[76] all shame will disappear.

When it was before sin, there was no shame: "Adam and Eve were naked and they were unashamed."[77] They were naked from every vice; they did not have a garment covering their rational part; their reason was not covered over by irrational passions. However, when sin comes, and then both the thinking and the way of life are moved by passion, the shame also comes into being. When, therefore, we approach the light, which we abandoned when we were sinning, our faces are not ashamed; we have great boldness, for it says, "If our heart does not condemn us, we have boldness before God."[78] When someone sees himself as innocent through his heart and conscience, he has boldness before God in every way, so that he says, "As the Lord lives, before whom I stand."[79] And it is the voice of one who is bold that says, "Early in the day I will approach you and gaze upon you."[80] I have seen many things, but I will observe still more; I will contemplate esoteric things.

And your faces shall never be put to shame.

We were saying that, when there is sin, the face of the soul is covered by shame, so that its beauty and the proportional arrangement of its parts is no longer seen. However, when illumination takes place, then "one reflects the glory of the Lord with an unveiled face."[81] No one, having his face covered, reflects the glory of God, but only if someone casts off the coverings that come afterward. Indeed, those who received the impression of how far beyond themselves they have progressed in wickedness say, "Disgrace has covered our face."[82] Disgrace has become a covering for us: the shame of our face.

---

[71]2 Cor 4:8 NRSV.
[72]Acts 14:22 NRSV.
[73]Ps 4:6 (4:7).
[74]Mt 5:14 NRSV.
[75]Ps 4:6 (4:7).
[76]Is 60:19.
[77]Gen 2:25.
[78]1 Jn 3:21.
[79]1 Kings 17:1.
[80]Ps 5:3 (5:4 LES2).
[81]Cf. 2 Cor 3:18.
[82]Jer 51:51 (28:51 LES2).

[33:7] *This poor man cried aloud, and the Lord heard him.*

It indicates someone who is poor in sin, who is impoverished in every vice. When someone, having become free of vice, having forsaken the riches of ignorance and vice, cries to God, he has him listening to him.

And perhaps, as I explained during this hour in an accustomed sense, that what belongs to the lesser also belongs to the greater, exhorting those who are already enlightened and who bless *the Lord at every opportunity*, being rich, he says: even the *poor man*, if he draws near and *cries aloud*, will be *heard*.

Furthermore, it is possible that this was said about the people from the Gentiles: the people who, "being without hope and without God in the world,"[83] drew near to him, cried aloud, and had him listening to them. Indeed, after other verses, it says in the same psalm, "Rich men became poor and grew hungry,"[84] speaking of those from the circumcision who became poor because they have forsaken the Law and the Prophets. For this reason he also says demonstratively, *"This poor man"*—he has become worthy of being indicated by holy men and by the Holy Spirit himself.

Moreover, it is possible that this is spoken about all people in general: that in comparison to God the giver of riches, who bestows great things, [194] we are all poor.

Question: Did not Jesus "become poor for our sake"?[85]

Certainly, and observe the apostle's exactitude: "that though he was rich, he became poor for our sake."[86] He was not made rich. "Although he was rich he became poor for our sake." Why did he become so? "So that by his poverty we might become rich,"[87] for poverty that is productive of wealth is not really poverty. And as he became "a curse for us,"[88] so that we might receive a blessing, and a curse that produces a blessing is not literally a curse but is this very thing: a curse that produces blessing, so also is he a poor man. "He, being in the form of God, did not regard equality with God as something to be exploited, but emptied himself, taking the form of a slave."[89] Behold! the poverty with which he became poor! Being truly always rich, being always in the form of God, and being "the exact imprint of God's very being,"[90] "after taking the form of a servant,"[91] he endured all that belongs to the poverty. He has become "sin for our sake, so that we might become the righteousness of God";[92] a curse, so that we might inherit a blessing; he endured death and has been put to death, so that we might take back eternal life.

"We became very poor."[93] We descended, reaching as far as your condition, in this way, that we might raise you up after the compassions of God went before us.[94] As some have spoken of such an example about the saints: while sailing in the ship of this life they saw many who had fallen out of the ship, and because they did not know how to swim they had been driven down into the depth. Then they leapt into the depth and appeared to suffer the same thing with those who were submerged, but they have done this for the sake of helping them, so that they might raise up those who are incapable of rising up by themselves.

---

[83] Eph 2:12.
[84] Ps 34:10 (33:11).
[85] 2 Cor 8:9.
[86] 2 Cor 8:9.
[87] 2 Cor 8:9.
[88] Gal 3:13.
[89] Phil 2:6-7.
[90] Heb 1:3.
[91] Phil 2:7.
[92] 2 Cor 5:21.
[93] Ps 79:8 (78:8 NETS).
[94] Cf. Ps 79:8 (Ps 78:8).

[33:7] *And from all his afflictions he delivered him.*

To *deliver from all afflictions* has already often been explained by us: that one is not overcome, not that one becomes free of things that oppress.

[33:8] *The angel of the Lord will encamp around those who fear him and will rescue them.*

An *angel*, encamping around those who fear God, *delivers* them from every enemy, from every affliction, from every defeat. Someone, then, will say the following: "Is one angel sufficient to save all those who fear God from the adversary?" Observe: because God willed it, one angel killed 185,000 with one sword.[95] Yet perhaps he was not a pure angel, since otherwise he would not have performed the service of punishment. How much more is the perfect man, who preserves holiness, who is "an eyewitness and servant"[96] of God, able to deliver many who fear God.

And if the explanation seems forced to someone, then one can understand it in this way instead: as it says, that "God made man"[97] so that he might rule over the irrational animals. And we do not mean the specific man individually, we do not mean so-and-so, but the whole species. "I made the earth and man upon it."[98] He named the whole species in this way. The angel, therefore, can also indicate here the whole race in general, because those who fear the Lord have the angels encamped around and encircling them, delivering them from every affliction.

Indeed, you also have the following in the Gospel: "Take care lest you cause one of these little ones who believes in me to stumble, for their angels continually see the face of our Father in heaven."[99] They are those who stand beside God, they see his face, they see what is invisible in an invisible way. So see, many angels of the many little ones were spoken of, whereas one angel of those who fear the Lord is mentioned. He is mentioned in the singular, even though he is not one.

Furthermore, one can say as follows: the little ones do not fear God, but they possess the fear that is pathological, for "perfect love casts out fear," and "fear has to do with punishment."[100] "Do not fear those who kill the body but cannot kill the soul."[101] However, those fear God who possess the surpassing fear of God, of which it is said in Sirach, "Fear of the Lord surpasses everything,"[102] [195] which comes to the one who seeks it after much progress.

So these ones who fear the Lord can have one angel encamping around them and delivering them, even the Savior himself, of whom it is said, "and his name is called 'Angel of Great Counsel,'"[103] for in many Scriptures an angel appears to be mentioned, which does not refer to a particular created being. Jacob also says of him, "The Angel who delivers me from all evils."[104] However, no one can deliver from all evils except the Savior, who has authority to forgive every sin.[105] And when the sin is forgiven, then the penalty that follows it, the painful things that follow it, pass away together with the vice.

As soon as a kind of encampment and wall comes around them, it preserves them from being harmed. And indeed, in Zechariah, the eleventh of the Twelve Prophets, it says, "Jerusalem shall be abundantly settled,"[106] and

---

[95]Cf. Is 37:36.
[96]Lk 1:2.
[97]Gen 1:27.
[98]Is 45:12.
[99]Cf. Mt 18:6-10.
[100]1 Jn 4:18 NRSV.
[101]Mt 10:28 NRSV.
[102]Sir 25:11 NRSV.
[103]Is 9:6.
[104]Gen 48:16.
[105]Cf. Mt 9:6.
[106]Zech 2:4 NETS.

it says, "And I will be around them like a pillar of fire and a wall that encircles them."[107] And he is a pillar of fire in order that those who draw near to harm might be harmed instead, for immediately in this very passage of the prophet it says, "For he who touches you is as one who touches the pupil of his eye."[108] "Touching" here means "harming," as the following word demonstrates: "Do not touch my anointed ones!"[109]

[33:9] *O taste and see that the Lord is kind!*

Often it was said by us that the perceptible and bodily things are as follows: each of them is merely that which it is. For example, the pomegranate is nothing other than a pomegranate; so is bread. However, the food that nourishes the inner man is mentioned according to different conceptions. Indeed, it is called Light, it is also called Source, it is called both Bread and Flesh, and True Food. So he says, "*Taste*" with the invisible palate of the inner man, "*and see that the Lord is kind*," that he is good. Merely *taste*, know that he is nourishing; see the Source of goodness, the Source of kindness.

[33:9] *Blessed is the man who hopes in him.*

The one who hopes in the kind Lord himself—for he *tastes* of him—will also get to know his sweetness, and from this nourishment he will possess all things and will grow strong, because he is fed like an athlete, so that he no longer struggles "against blood and flesh, but against rulers and authorities."[110]

Taste and see that he is kind. If someone is weary and sick in soul, let him taste him as something nourishing, as something that procures health, as something that wards off harm. This food not only satiates, but it also wards off and repels things that are harmful.

Blessed, then, is not simply "the human," but *the man*, who overcame "childish ways,"[111] who did not walk "by the counsel of the impious" nor stood "in the way of sinners" nor sat "on the seat of the pestilential" but has "his will in the law of the Lord."[112] This man has his own will in the law of the Lord, for many observe the law lest they be punished or in order to seem to be praiseworthy. The saint, however, the perfect man, has his own will in the law of the Lord, so that his will is no different from the will of the law. And this is the will of the law: to prohibit vice and to command virtue. Therefore, whenever someone becomes his own law—for "these, though not having the law, are a law to themselves"[113]—so that his own law has been interwoven with the law of the Lord . . .

[33:10] *O fear the Lord, all you his saints, because those who fear him have no want.*

I exhort all the saints to fear the Lord himself. And it is said in Isaiah, "He himself will be your fear."[114] Let him himself become your fear! And just as he becomes Food to some and to others a Wisdom that renders them wise, and to others Righteousness, and those for whom he has become Righteousness become righteous, so also they partake of holiness, for he himself is also **[196]** Holiness, "who became for us wisdom from God, and righteousness and sanctification and redemption."[115]

Fear God, then, *all you his saints*. They are *his* saints, for they are not merely called "saints" without being "his." As many as feign holiness on the one hand seem to be saints, but they are not God's.

---

[107]Cf. Zech 2:5.
[108]Zech 2:8 NETS.
[109]Ps 105:15 (104:15 NETS).
[110]Eph 6:12.
[111]1 Cor 13:11 NRSV.
[112]Cf. Ps 1:1-2 NETS.
[113]Rom 2:14.
[114]Is 8:13 NETS.
[115]1 Cor 1:30 NRSV.

And he provides the reason why he says "all": because *those who fear him* truly *have no want*. The fear of God makes them want for nothing and complete.

Fear the Lord, all you his saints.

Given that *those who fear him have no want*, in order that you should become complete, fear God himself. And the fear of God is certainly not pathological, as I said, but is the equivalent of reverence, the equivalent of piety. Whenever we receive an impression of God, fear at once increases, piety is present; for we are not afraid in the sense that we are terrified of him, not as though he were a kind of bogey, but as of one who is surpassingly worthy of veneration.

And since the church is holy, when it stands at the Savior's right hand in glory, all those who fill it are saints. So the following can also be said concerning the calling of the Gentiles: "*Fear the Lord, all you his saints!*"

[33:11] *The rich became poor and hungry, but those who seek the Lord shall not suffer decrease in any good thing.*

The former people, who together filled the synagogue before the appearance, although they were rich, fell into poverty. When the kingdom of God was taken from them,[116] when the understanding of the divine Scriptures departed, when they turned away from the ancient Scripture and it withdrew from them, instead of being rich they have become poor. For since this wealth benefits its possessor in every way—for it becomes both his food, and it also becomes his protective clothing—he says that these wealthy ones became poor and suffered hunger. They cast away the spiritual food; they turned away from the "Bread of Life."[117]

Therefore they became poor, but when they themselves also became poor, those who seek out the Lord do not suffer any decrease in good things, but they become full of them, they will partake of them completely. For just as the kingdom of heaven has been taken away from them, this the mother of Jesus also says, "He has filled the hungry with good things, and sent the rich away empty."[118] Those who were rich long ago were sent away empty, for even if they have the books of Moses and of the Prophets, yet they are bereft of their divine fulfillment. Indeed, the fullness of the divine Scriptures is not its shadow, but the truth and the Spirit.

Those who seek out, then, *the Lord*—to *seek out* indicates intensity—are filled with all good things. Concerning this the psalmist also says somewhere, while conversing with his own soul, "Bless the Lord, O my soul, who satisfies your desire with good."[119] And, "Delight in the Lord, and he will give to you the requests of your heart."[120] Those who convert from the shadow of the law and from the partial knowledge and prophecy[121] find all good things. Now, strictly speaking the things that are good, which want for nothing and are most complete, are the spiritual goods of the law, for these also lead us by the hand even face to face with the truth, which brings perfection, in which no one will be imperfect.[122]

[33:12] *Come, O children; hear me.*

After having spoken about the necessity of taking up fear toward God, and that some, by falling away from it, have become wretched and poor, and that those who seek out the Lord, whom they fear, are filled with all good things, at length he prolongs his instruction for all those who have become his children, saying, "*Come, O children; hear me!*" They are

---

[116]Cf. Mt 21:43.
[117]Jn 6:35, 48.
[118]Lk 1:53 NRSV.
[119]Ps 103:1, 5 (102:1, 5 NETS).
[120]Ps 37:4 (36:4 LES2).
[121]Cf. 1 Cor 13:9.
[122]Cf. 1 Cor 13:12, 10.

not children according to the flesh. However, those who pursue wisdom are children of the sage; those who desire to be sanctified are children of the saint; those who complete righteousness are the children of the first Righteous One himself, for it has been said by us at the beginning of the psalm that the psalm can be spoken from the person of the Savior as man. And those who are concerned with virtue are the children of the Savior, those who strive [197] to take up the knowledge of the truth.

Therefore, he summons them, while they are still far away, not in order that they might come by being moved, by shifting from one place to another, but from one disposition to another, from an inferior condition to the greater and more perfect condition.

[33:12] *I will teach you the fear of the Lord.*

And the children to whom he is addressing his speech could be "infants in Christ,"[123] who do not have the perfect fear, not the fear that makes them want for nothing, but the fear that produces abstention from the practice of vice, the fear of punishment, for such people are children because they are immature. For while the one who fears the Lord does not lack anything, these are imperfect because they do not have the perfect love that casts out the aforementioned fear,[124] which is nothing other than participation in God. And "God is love."[125] And as the one who partakes of righteousness is righteous, so the one who draws near to this love and becomes one with it is a child of wisdom, a son of love.

[33:13] *What man is he who wants life?*

When they were in the inferior fear that brings punishment and terrifies with punishment lest anyone sin, they were a multitude. But when at last they strive to draw near to the one who summons them that they might be taught the fear of God, consequently as though to one person are the things that are narrated said, for being established "in the same mind and the same purpose,"[126] and each being united to the Lord and becoming one spirit with him,[127] they forsake their multiplicity. For the multitude, especially the multitude in the soul and the inner man, results either from opposition or from a difference according to excess and deficiency. When all those who are called have virtue but do not have it equally, then there is a multitude. However, this is not the multitude that accords with opposition. However, whenever they have opposite perceptions, they are many because of the vice that is present, for vice is not unifying but rather divisive. For example, we speak of the interdependence of the virtues, but not of the interdependence of the vices. It is impossible for the vices to be interdependent on each other, for they are excesses and deficiencies. And excesses and deficiencies are opposites. So all who perfectly assume virtue are one and become one by the work of God. For example, all who believe according to the right faith have one heart and one soul,[128] while the wicked do not possess this. Therefore, he also calls some of them "double-minded."[129]

So he addresses the word to only one man. *Man* is singular in essence, however, for even if there are different and numerous men, they have multiplicity from the qualities that correspond to them. Certainly, according to the first substrate that is receptive of the qualities, they are one, for all are consubstantial. So it is characteristic of man to desire life, of man who preserves the creation in the

---

[123]1 Cor 3:1 NRSV.
[124]Cf. 1 Jn 4:18.
[125]1 Jn 4:8.

[126]1 Cor 1:10 NRSV.
[127]Cf. 1 Cor 6:17.
[128]Cf. Acts 4:32.
[129]Jas 4:8 NRSV.

image. A mare-crazed horse does not desire life.

Question: What does, *Who is the man?* mean?

Who does not signify scarcity or impossibility. It indicates the peculiar quality that we call the individual, so that the following should result: if a certain man is of such a kind, let him come and learn the fear of God.

[33:13-14] *And loves to see good days? Stop your tongue from evil and your lips from speaking deceit.*

The coming among *good days* immediately follows the desire for life and the learning of the divine fear. Surely we are not as stupid as some are, so as to suppose that the pleasure of the body and surrounding wealth make for *good days*. Indeed, you have many such things in Scripture: "Honor your father and mother so that it may be well with you and so that you may be long-lived on the good land that the Lord God is giving you."[130] If you understand this in relation to this earth and these parents in the common sense, then he is deceived. Of this present land it is not said "that he is giving you."

Stop your tongue from evil.

I invite you to learn the fear of the Lord, in order that you might become holy by learning it, in want of nothing, lacking no virtue. **[198]** So come now, that you might *stop your tongue from evil*. Let the *tongue* of the inner man no longer possess evil. And it becomes free *from every evil*, when it possesses the good and proclaims it. And that the *lips* no longer *speak deceit* follows on the *tongue's* ceasing from *evil*, as well as that they interpret something peacefully, for one acts deceitfully in order to do evil. "Their tongue is a wounding arrow; the words of their mouth are deceitful."[131]

These are the ones who are from the heresies, who are champions of godlessness.

Indeed, someone can also say the following regarding this passage: since at that time especially, when he was saying this, all people were rushing headlong to evil, so that at last laments were being sung over them, to such people as these he was saying this. For he did not say "each of my brothers," or "each of our brothers," that is, of the saints, but of those who wanted to have one father, of those who have been born of the devil, because they desire to do his desires: for "you are from your father the devil, and you choose to do the devil's desires."[132] Of such brothers, then, who have been born in the name of their father and of evil, he says, "Every brother will strike with his heel,"[133] for their father is also of such a kind as this. He led everyone who was under himself to deceit and subjects those who follow him to malice. "And every friend" of such a kind "will mock."[134] He is not speaking of those who really are friends. Jesus says to the disciples, "You are friends."[135] And he has produced the reason: "because I have made known to you everything that belongs to the Father."[136] None of these friends will mock. For this reason they are free.

Therefore, to those who are really of such a kind is the word addressed: "They will never speak the truth."[137] About those who do not speak the truth comes the word, "He did not remain in the truth."[138] The one who did not remain in the truth has at one time been in it. However, we do not say of someone that he does not remain in a profession when he did not practice a profession or many professions and changes from some to others. If he had not

---

[130] Cf. Ex 20:12 NETS.
[131] Jer 9:8 NETS.

[132] Jn 8:44.
[133] Jer 9:4 LES2.
[134] Cf. Jer 9:5 LXX.
[135] Jn 15:14.
[136] Jn 15:15.
[137] Jer 9:5.
[138] Jn 8:44.

been in the truth, it would bring no reproach against him that he did not remain in it.

And observe the dogma: how "he wants all men to be saved and to come to the knowledge of the truth."[139] If no one can oppose his will, how, when he wants all to be saved and to come to the knowledge of the truth, do some fail in this, not to say most? Since he is willing, when we desire it and an agreement between the two wills takes place, salvation occurs; for no one is good without willing it, no one is saved without willing it, no one is able to know the truth without striving to draw near to God and without keeping his law. For this reason the Savior also says in the Gospel, "If anyone wants to come after me, let him deny himself and let him take up his cross and follow me."[140] "If anyone wants": as far as it depends on the Savior, he desires for him to do this, but he does not compel by force, he provokes his free decision, he awakens his will. "If anyone," then, "wants to come after me," "if anyone wants to follow me"—for "to come after me" signifies following—"let him take up his own cross," let him be crucified to the world, let him put to death "his members which are earthly,"[141] let him become inactive in relation to the world. The one who is crucified has his feet prevented from walking where he wishes, his hands prevented from doing what he wants.[142] Therefore, whenever someone is crucified to the world, he neither walks according to it anymore nor does the things that belong to it; moreover, the world is crucified to this person who was crucified to it, in order that even the world becomes inactive against him, neither marching against him nor doing things that harm him.

"If anyone," therefore, "wants to come after me," not intermittently, for the virtue that is defined as without interruption is a virtue and is a perfection, not like the other actions. So, for instance, writes the apostle, "Rejoice always, pray without ceasing, give thanks in every circumstance."[143] The one who always rejoices always possesses the virtue, for he rejoices for no other reason than in order to be honored by pleasing God.

And loves to see good days.

To see here means to experience, and to experience *good days* means to receive their benefit.

Stop your tongue from evil.

Pay attention to your speech, put it to the test, desire to possess speech that cannot be condemned, as the apostle writes to Titus to have "sound speech that cannot be censured."[144] The one who has innocent speech also fulfills many other commands of Jesus. [**199**] It is impossible for someone who does not have innocent speech to observe the command, "Let your 'Yes' be 'Yes' and your 'No' be 'No,'"[145] for one who is untrustworthy sometimes takes back his oath. However, when he never has a word that is reproachable, when someone never is in doubt whether he speaks the truth, or whether he also does as he says, whenever he will be required to keep his oath, and his yes is yes and his no is no, then such speech is innocent.

And again, the one who expounds the doctrines of the truth and presents them knowledgeably also has innocent speech regarding them. No one can reproach him as a liar, as one who thinks wickedly, as one who is outside the truth.

[33:15] *Turn away from evil and do good.*

He is saying the following: if you happen to be involved in evil, if you had put it into action and are active in it, since I am summoning you

---

[139] 1 Tim 2:4.
[140] Mt 16:24; Mk 8:34.
[141] Col 3:5.
[142] Cf. Jn 21:18-19.
[143] 1 Thess 5:17-18.
[144] Titus 2:8 NRSV.
[145] Cf. Mt 5:37.

to the doing of the good, *turn away from evil*. It is impossible to be free of both. However, let infants be excluded for the moment. The one who is not involved in good is involved in evil; the one who is free from evil partakes of the good.

Turn away, then, *from evil*. The turning away, however, is voluntary, for he is commanding and advising. And no one commands or advises one who does not possess free will. I summon you to do the good. In no other way, however, can you do it and act according to it, if you do not *turn away from evil*. So indeed is it said in Isaiah, "Cease from your evil deeds; learn to do good,"[146] for insofar as someone is active in his own evil deeds, that is, in vices, this person can in no way learn to do good. And again, the divinely inspired apostle writes, "Test everything; hold fast to what is good; abstain from every form of evil."[147]

So then, *turn away from evil and do good*. It is not enough to *turn away from evil*, unless someone also *does the good*; for it is possible for one who is prohibited from evil to *turn away* from it from fear of punishment that leads to this, but this person does not *do the good* voluntarily, for when you remove what is voluntary from the good, it is no longer wholly good.

[33:15] *Seek peace, and pursue it.*

The evil is confounding and effects disturbance in the soul, for the genus of vice has an abundance of discord. Some of the vices occur by deficiency, others by excess, such as cowardice and rashness, such as superstition and impiety.

Pursue peace itself. For to pursue in this way does not signify this: "chase it away." And you also have in the Proverbs: "he loves," it says, "those who pursue righteousness."[148] God, that is, loves those who pursue him. And the righteousness that is pursued is virtue in its entirety. [. . .] So says Wisdom, "Evil people will seek me but will not find me."[149] The evil seek wisdom, insofar as they are able, desiring to conceal it and suppress it. But those who desire to become wise do not seek wisdom in this way, but they pursue it.

And I say, since you are fond of explications: Herod was seeking Jesus in order to kill him. The Jews often sought him in order to kill him. The disciples, however, were seeking him in order that they might receive help, in order to partake of him. For instance, someone said to him, "The crowds seek you, because they desire to see you."[150] For they were desiring to believe, to see marvelous works, to hear words, and to obtain healings. So to pursue is ambiguous.

[33:16] *For the eyes of the Lord are on the righteous.*

Again there is a great exhortation, a great instruction. He says the following: *the eyes of* God are ready to see and to save, and he has ears ready to listen. *Turn away*, therefore, *from evil, and do good; seek peace, and pursue it.* For immediately you will have God as your overseer. Desire only to be righteous, pursue righteousness, and you have *the eyes of* God placed on you and his ears ready to receive your prayers that you make to him.

[33:16] *And his ears are toward their petition.*

It was often said that the things that are said about God anthropomorphically one must not understand literally, as the anthropomorphites suppose, for they want there to be a human

---

[146] Is 1:16-17 NETS.
[147] 1 Thess 5:21-22.
[148] Prov 15:9 NETS.
[149] Prov 1:28 NETS.
[150] Cf. Lk 4:42; Mk 1:37; Jn 6:24.

face for God, and they say that the man "in the image and likeness" of God[151] has come into being [**200**] according to the structure of his body. Such a notion, however, was overturned by wise men, for they say, "If man is 'in the image of God' in this way, because he imitates God in a bodily way and his body bears a likeness to God, how is God said to have wings: 'In the shelter of your wings you will shelter me?'[152] Certainly, mankind is a wingless animal, so that he is not 'in the image and likeness' of God according to the body."

However, when you understand what the wings of God are, you will observe that man also has such spiritual wings that lift him up. Again the eyes: since they understand everything according to the literal sense, man, having two eyes, is not "in the image and likeness" of the one who has seven eyes.[153] And so one removes those things that are elevated from the sense, and the things that are removed from the senses, in man's case, preserve the likeness to God.

[33:17] *But the face of the Lord is upon evildoers.*

He is saying the following: *evildoers* are not righteous. And being unrighteous, they are not overseen by God, nor are they heard. Nevertheless, they do not remain devoid of the imagination of him. And whenever they meet with certain misfortunes and come into the awareness that they have come into these because of the evil things that are practiced and thought by them, they receive a representation of him. So, for example, Moses also, when Pharaoh and all his army pursued him, heard God: "I will be glorified in Pharaoh and in all his army, and the Egyptians shall know that I am the Lord."[154] How indeed did they know? Perhaps when they had become submerged and were no longer able to flee they received a vision of God. Moreover, in the Psalms it is found, "Let them be put to shame and dismayed, let them perish and know that it is your name, O Lord."[155] After they perish, after they are put to shame, they know God, and this is what his being made visible means, and his having his *face upon evildoers*.

Question: How does he say elsewhere, "But you turned away your face, and I became troubled"?[156]

There it is said in a different sense: it is the voice of the Savior. So listen: he is not saying that he turns away his *face* from *evildoers*, but from those who have it manifest. And after being troubled for a little while, they supposed they were outside his face; therefore, they were also troubled. They received an impression that something was displeasing to them. However, the turning away of the face here has taken place in order to awaken those who formerly saw it and do not have it turned away, in order to regain it. As far as those who do evil are concerned, however, this is not the cause, but in order that they might perceive that they are condemned by the administration of God, that by the providence of God they are in misfortunes. And this also comes to pass for a useful end:

[33:17] *To destroy the remembrance of them from the earth.*

Not *the remembrance of them* in an absolute sense, but *from the earth*, so that they no longer regard the earth, no longer meditate on earthly things. As we say, "He drove such a man out of the land, where there are many prostitutes." Indeed, it is not a curse that he took him out from there, having placed him in the opposite circumstances.

---

[151] Gen 1:26.
[152] Ps 17:8 (16:8).
[153] Cf. Zech 4:10.
[154] Ex 14:4 NETS.

[155] Ps 83:17-18 (82:18-19).
[156] Ps 30:7 (29:8 NETS).

Lectures on Psalm 33 [33:18]

[33:18] *The righteous cried, and the Lord listened to them.*

And most naturally, since he has *ears upon them*, when *they cry* out they find him *listening*. Notice that it was said in a twofold way, praiseworthy and blameworthy. And it is praiseworthy for the eyes of the Lord and the ears of the Lord to be on the righteous, and it belongs to correction for the face of the Lord *to destroy their remembrance from the earth*. For even if there is a better end, yet it comes through pain, like health through cauterizing, surgery, and very harsh potions that are necessary to drink.

To the other group, the former one, he says therefore: since the ears of God are open to the petition of the righteous and his eyes oversee them, when they cry aloud they do not fail to obtain their petition, for *he listened to them*.

And to the other group, to whom it was said, "*The face of the Lord is upon evildoers*," in what follows he says, *the death of sinners is evil*.[157] Not every death is evil, but the death of sinners is. Not of the common death is the present word, for that is the death of a living creature, not of a quality, not of a sinner, not of a righteous person. So even if you understand the common death, when he dies while a sinner, he has death [201] as an evil—for punishment will receive him—and if you understand the other death that is truly appropriate to the sinner, "sin," it says, "when it is fully grown, gives birth to death."[158] Sin, however, is not fully grown without those who practice it, but in people who practice it.

The death that follows them, therefore, is evil. Now, in the case of the former definition, we say that death is evil that produces evil, which is harmful. Here, however, according to the second interpretation, we call it evil because it is outside goodness. The grammarians recognize as evil, then, "something bad that harms." "And all the evil diseases of Egypt, I am not inflicting upon you,"[159] the troubling plagues that the Egyptians endured according to the history. And when it says, "Abstain from every form of evil,"[160] we are not speaking of this troublesome evil, for neither does it belong to us to abstain from these. They are sent by God; even when we are unwilling, these things assail us because of preceding vice.

To the words, "*But the face of the Lord is upon evildoers*," is later added, "*The death of sinners is evil*," either evil in one sense or evil in another. It is evil in both ways, for they obtain punishment and the wicked condition—which is equal to vice—that drags them away from the blessed life. "Remove the evil deeds from your souls before my eyes."[161] Observe the exact significance carefully: since he named the evils of souls, and these are seen by none other than God, he says: do not feign a removal of the evil deeds from your souls before my eyes since I see, even when not face to face. This is equivalent to what is said by the Savior that it is necessary to practice almsgiving in secret, in order that "the Father who sees in secret will reward you."[162]

[33:18] *And from all their afflictions he rescued them.*

And it was said in other verses of the psalm that to be delivered from all afflictions does not mean to be free from being afflicted, since otherwise the saints were never heard, so that Paul can say, "We are afflicted in every way."[163]

---

[157] Ps 34:21 (33:22).
[158] Jas 1:15 NRSV.
[159] Deut 7:15.
[160] 1 Thess 5:22.
[161] Is 1:16 NETS.
[162] Mt 6:4.
[163] 2 Cor 4:8 NRSV.

[33:19] *The Lord is near to the brokenhearted, and the humble in spirit he will save.*

As the dialecticians and the logicians say, that it is necessary to establish and to demonstrate what is not evident from things that are evident, this is indeed true. It is impossible for things that are unknown to become known from things that are similarly unknown, and all the more from things that are even more unknown. Therefore, from things that are evident, things that are not evident are made known, and from the things that are known the things that are unknown. Now let us understand another Scripture more clearly. It is also said in Proverbs, "Before affliction a man's heart is exalted, but before honor it is humbled."[164] He is saying as follows: the proud is humbled, because he is not broken. But when he is broken by efforts for modesty, he is exalted.

"Before affliction a man's heart is exalted." The arrogant man hears words against pride, and sometimes he receives the experience of afflictions, because he has become haughty. If he humbles himself before this affliction, which is more favorably applied to him by means of labors for humility, his heart is not exalted. Before the rebuke, so to speak, and before the scourges, he has his heart exalted. Truly, when he humbles himself before afflictions, he knows that he was exposed to things that do not accord with his desire because of his own arrogance.

One must also understand the following word in this way: "Capernaum, will you be exalted to heaven? No, you will be brought down to Hades."[165] Now, to be brought down to Hades signifies affliction. Before this affliction it behaved haughtily.

"Before honor it is humbled." It is necessary first to be humbled willingly, in order to obtain honor, for glory comes next, after modesty. For this reason the Savior also used to say, "He who humbles himself will be exalted."[166] And observe carefully: "Everyone who exalts himself will be humbled."[167] Here, "he will be broken." Before this affliction he has his heart exalted, playing the braggart, behaving haughtily. Again, it brings glory to the one who humbles himself that he is modest. Before this glory it is necessary to be humble; it is necessary to labor in order to receive a reward. So he receives the honor of modesty from God. So indeed Peter also counsels, saying, "Humble yourselves under the mighty [202] hand of God, so that you may be exalted in due time."[168] And indeed, Job says, God is he "who sets on high those that are lowly."[169]

And here he is not calling those who are weakened in heart "brokenhearted." The word *brokenness* sometimes means such a thing as not having wholesome thoughts, not having straight understandings. This brokenness of the heart requires a physician, and a physician who heals the hidden part, for it was said, "When the Lord builds Jerusalem he will also gather the scattered people of Israel, he who heals the broken in heart."[170] These were broken, that is to say, they were wounded.

So also, for example, is the one who went down from Jerusalem to Jericho,[171] that is, into the region around the earth and into its citizenship, called "Jericho" because of the translation of the name—for *Jericho* is translated as "moon." And it is said that "the fool changes like the

---

[164] Prov 18:12.
[165] Mt 11:23; Lk 10:15 NRSV.
[166] Lk 14:11; 18:14.
[167] Lk 14:11; 18:14.
[168] 1 Pet 5:6.
[169] Job 5:11 NETS.
[170] Ps 147:2-3 (146:2-3).
[171] Lk 10:30.

moon,"[172] like the moon, the light of which does not grow but diminishes. The bride, however, who is praised in Song of Songs, is "peeping forth like a beautiful dawn," "fair as the moon."[173] This alteration occurs for the better, in order to be made perfect, for the moon is changed in each of two ways. Changing from being crescent-shaped, it becomes a full moon. And there are four phases of progression in its growth: crescent-shaped, half-shaped, convex, and full. And again from the full moon it passes to the convex, and from the convex to the half-shaped, and from the half-shaped to the crescent-shaped. So indeed the bride of the Word peeps forth like the dawn, the perfect soul, the church, which is led in procession to him. And it is changed so that it becomes beautiful, as fair as a full moon.

And after this it says, "as outstanding as the sun."[174] And from the light of the moon it comes to that of the sun, when that prophecy is fulfilled, which says, "The moon will be like the sun."[175]

Therefore, someone will be broken in heart, when he is filled with broken thoughts, with thoughts that are alien to the truth that enjoys good health. Of these broken ones the Savior becomes a physician, for it is "he who heals the broken in heart and binds up their fractures,"[176] binding up their wounds.

And as an example I take this: a certain person is often broken because of an adversary when he contends in a struggle, and he obtains a crown. These fractures do not bring him any reproach. However, when he is broken by wild beasts or robbers, we reprove him—I am not speaking literally, for it is possible for someone to suffer this in ignorance—"Why do you go where there are wild beasts, or why did you have dealings with the spiritual robbers of evil?"

And the humble in spirit he will save.

Here he calls "*spirit*" the intention. This means the same thing as what was spoken in the beatitudes of the Gospel: "Blessed are the poor in spirit,"[177] those who are poor in their intention. And these are those who practice modesty because of a right reasoning, who have heard what is said by the Savior, who says, "Learn from me; for I am gentle and humble in heart."[178] And intention and heart are the same thing. Therefore, just as the Savior is humble in heart, so also those who learn this from him become humble in their intention. And these are the poor in spirit who do not desire to be rich in pride.

[33:20] *Many are the afflictions of the righteous, and from all of their afflictions he will rescue them.*

It was already frequently said by us that he delivers from all of them. *Many are the afflictions of the righteous*. I said that they continue throughout life even until the last breath.

[33:21] *The Lord guards all their bones.*

If they are delivered from all afflictions so that they do not fall under their power and become broken, then all their strong powers, called "*bones*," are preserved by God. Moreover, it was said before this that the powers of the soul are called its bones, for they are suitable for upholding the whole soul, like the perceptible bones do for the whole body. It would be impossible for the flesh and the other parts to stand otherwise; the parts suitable for upholding the body are the bones.

---

[172]Sir 27:11 NRSV.
[173]Song 6:10.
[174]Cf. Song 6:10 NETS.
[175]Is 30:26.
[176]Ps 147:3 (146:3 NETS).

[177]Mt 5:3 NRSV.
[178]Mt 11:29 NRSV.

And the strong powers of the soul, for example, the power of memory, or [203] the contemplative, or the aesthetic, when they are rigid and are preserved in perfection, they have this from God, not by their own power. Therefore, they start desiring this from their free will, but they achieve perfection in this after God works together with them.

[33:21] *Not one of them will be crushed.*

If they are righteous and they cried out to God and were delivered from all afflictions, *not one of their bones will be crushed*, that is, "not one power" of theirs.

And, in order to begin from the more perceptible powers: there is a certain power of sight. Whenever it does not look in order to desire the beauty of women nor to be overcome by the desire for beauty, this bone is not crushed by the Lord, but is preserved unharmed by him. Whenever one, looking to heaven, sees the sun and the moon and does not worship and serve them, but understands from the visible creation the one who created all things, even perceiving him analogously from the greatness of his creatures and their beauty,[179] then this bone that accords with sight was strengthened. To understand it more perceptibly, whenever someone does not "accept a groundless report"[180] but discerns by what kind of words he should be persuaded and by which he should not, and with what he should agree and what he should refuse—"Incline your ear to the words of the wise,"[181] and, "Do not accept a groundless report"[182]—this one has also the bone, the hearing, the sense of the ears, unbroken, healthy.

[33:22] *The death of sinners is evil, and those who hate the righteous shall go wrong.*

The *bones* of the righteous are preserved by the Lord, and *not one of them is crushed*, while *the death of sinners is evil*.

And it was already said by us that "evil" is said in two ways. If, however, the death that drags away from the blessed life follows sin, according to the passage: "Sin, when it is fully grown, gives birth to death,"[183] then this death is evil.

Again, since they are handed over to punishment after they depart from life, they have died again in order to be punished. So it is said, "Precious before the Lord is the death of his holy ones";[184] for how was it possible for this one to be evil or his death to be evil when he is planted together with the death of Christ? "For if," it says, "we have been united with him in a death like his, we will certainly be united also in resurrection,"[185] and, "If we have died with him, we will also live with him."[186]

And those who hate the righteous shall go wrong.

When the sinner receives an intensification of sin, he hates the righteous person. And by hating the righteous person he hates virtue. Indeed, sinners hate the righteous one not insofar as he is human—certainly they do not hate sinners—but insofar as he is righteous. And the one who hates a physician insofar as he is a physician hates the medical art. Because of this they will go wrong, they will be punished.

---

[179] Wis 13:5.
[180] Ex 23:1 NETS.
[181] Prov 22:17 NETS.
[182] Cf. Ex 23:1 NETS.

[183] Jas 1:15 NRSV.
[184] Ps 116:15 (115:6).
[185] Rom 6:5.
[186] 2 Tim 2:11 NRSV.

[33:23] *The Lord will redeem the souls of his servants.*

Now he says: even if an evil death attaches itself to sinners, and transgression will befall those who hate the righteous, yet he redeems the good *souls of his servants*. He redeems their souls from the preceding afflictions that seized them. Again, you can receive this in each of two ways: he both redeems from punishment and he redeems from sin, for if he redeems from sin, it follows that one is redeemed from punishment.

[33:23] *And all those who hope in him shall never go wrong.*

All those who hope in God *shall not go wrong* as those who hate the righteous go wrong. For if, in the case of those who hate the righteous, the transgression indicates a sentence and a punishment, in the case of those who hope in the Lord, not going wrong means not being punished, not being sentenced, not falling into the hands of those things that cause torment.

PSALM 34 [35]

[34:1] *For David. Render judgment, O Lord, on those who do me wrong; fight against those who fight against me!*

No one demands that God become his judge, if he has thoughts like those of an unrighteous person. This is not the voice of an unrighteous person but of one who is wronged, of one who prefers rather to be wronged than to wrong.[1] And a person does not simply prefer to suffer wrong, but when both doing wrong and suffering wrong lie before him, if both things cannot coexist—for both are not possible—he chooses rather **[204]** to be wronged than to wrong. For indeed the one who does wrong suffers punishment, and the unrighteous are unable to inherit the kingdom of God.[2]

As for the one who suffers wrong, on the other hand, there is no need for him to experience these things, for he suffers wrong willingly. And supposing that he is unable to help himself, yet he does not wear himself out because he cannot take revenge, not even by reflecting on the fact that the one who is wronged is pitied and has many who feel sympathy for him. And the unrighteous one, even when no one punishes him, is to be punished. Even this very fact that he covers the unrighteousness at all and desires to defend himself as though he is not unrighteous is his punishment. His conscience condemns him.

And there is great boldness in the one who speaks the psalm: *Render judgment, O Lord, on those who wrong me; fight against those who fight against me. I myself do not fight against them. And "among those who hate peace I am for peace."*[3] I have faith in the Holy Spirit, who says, "Hear the word of the Lord, you who tremble at his word; say 'Our brothers!' to those who hate you, so that the name of the Lord might be glorified, but they shall be put to shame."[4] "Hear the word of the Lord, you who tremble at his word; say 'Our brothers! to those who hate you," in order that we should speak with actions rather than with the voice, for those who say, "Jesus is Lord," with their voice alone hear, "Why do you call me 'Lord, Lord,' and do not do what I tell you?"[5] However, the one who calls Jesus "Lord" "in the Holy Spirit,"[6] in participation with the Holy Spirit, by those things which he practices and thinks, according to the Spirit cries that Jesus is "Lord."

"Say," therefore, "'Our brothers!' to those who hate you." Let those ones hate, but as for you, call them brothers by your actions, not as a mere expression, but do to them what is fitting to be done to brothers, for in this way the name of the Lord is glorified. For it is acknowledged that someone does these things because of God. For insofar as it concerns his being hated, he would not have called those who hate him "brothers."

"But they shall be put to shame." Indeed, after they are put to shame they do not perish.

Therefore, the saint fights against no one. However, when he is attacked he does not

---

[1] Cf. 1 Cor 6:7.
[2] Cf. 1 Cor 6:9.
[3] Ps 120:6-7 (119:7).
[4] Is 66:5.
[5] Lk 6:46 NRSV.
[6] 1 Cor 12:3.

strive to avenge but to suffer no harm and, so to speak—though drastic and yet for clarity's sake—he makes use only of a shield, he does not make use even of a defensive sword, of a defensive weapon that is able to wound in turn and to strike back.

Fight against those who fight against me.

While they were still wronging him and fighting against him. Therefore, in order that they should no longer wrong him and fight against him, he asks God to be his ally, not in order to wrong them, not in order to fight against them, but in order that he should remain unharmed, when wronged and attacked. And the nature of the rational being, if it does not suffer corruption, has this property. *Fight against*, then, hinder them from surrounding me for destruction.

[34:2] *Take hold of arms and shield, and rise up to help me!*

The shield of God extinguishes the fiery darts of the enemy, the evil one.[7] Take hold of this shield; place it around me! I do not say the following: "Surround yourself with the shield." Take hold of it in this way in order to be gracious to me, in order to protect me.

Arms and *shield* can mean the same thing. Moreover, they perhaps signify types of arms.[8]

It is possible that he is praying for the inhumanation to take place, for when he takes hold of the man who is able to protect us and to fight on our behalf, then he *took hold of arms and a shield and arose to help* us. He arose from the bosom of the Father,[9] in order to bend heaven and come down,[10] in order that he might appear as our defender; for he himself has come not to make war against us but to fight for us, and he has come not simply to suffer but to suffer for our sake.

And see carefully: he has come "by the grace of God to taste death for everyone."[11] We were all subject to death, our whole race as mortal. Now, what is mortal is subject to death. He said of the one who suffered such things, then, that "he tasted death." And that he did not endure the whole whirlpool of death—for this seems to be **[205]** fitting—the word in Isaiah: "by his bruise we all were healed"[12] was clarified in this sense by me. And he calls the cross his "bruise." As far as the nature of the cross and the magnitude of its affliction are concerned, it is not a bruise. However, for him it is a bruise; since it is a bruise to him, it does not harm the one who has it; rather, he helps those for whose sake he was receiving the bruise.

So also "by the grace of God he tastes death." Without doubt when he came into death he destroyed death. And the Savior's Passion again is the destroying of the passions, for by coming into the passions he destroyed them; he was not overpowered by them.

And just as, by becoming a curse, he dissolves the curse so that he might bestow a blessing in its place,[13] so we also say that he has come under an imprecation not in order that he should suffer something but in order that he should dissolve the imprecation and extend a blessing in its place.

Did he not "make him who knew no sin to be sin for our sake, so that in him we might become the righteousness of God?"[14] He becomes the sin that makes those who have righteousness—righteousness itself. He is not simply called "sin," but sin for the purpose of making those who were formerly mastered by sin into righteousness, and not just any

---

[7] Eph 6:16.
[8] The *hoplon* is a general word for arms but can refer to a hoplite's round shield. The *thyreos* was a shield that was shaped like a large door and was thus longer than it was wide. It could be rectangular or oviform.
[9] Jn 1:18.
[10] Ps 18:9 (17:10).

[11] Heb 2:9.
[12] Is 53:5.
[13] Cf. Gal 3:13-14.
[14] 2 Cor 5:21.

righteousness, but the righteousness of God. And this indicates the intensity of the participation in the quality: for those who have participated to be called by the same name as the quality they possess. They have as a quality the righteousness of God! He won the victory to such an extent and prevailed so that they might be called not "righteous" but "righteousness" itself.

And in many places within Scripture you will find such things. It says, "God is love."[15] See the greatness of love! "God is love." By the two names the same essence is made known: God and love.

Then it says that the one who draws near to God and loves him with his whole heart, and with his whole soul and strength,[16] becomes love; for the things that are said about love one after the other: "Love is not arrogant, or boastful or rude; it does not resent misfortune; it bears all things, believes all things, endures all things,"[17] are these things not strange when they are said about the virtue? For I do not say that the virtue endures or bears or believes. The one who possesses love, he called by the same name as "love."

So also those who possessed righteousness, because of the "sin" that came into being for our sake, become the "righteousness of God," no longer merely being God's righteous people but the righteousness of God. And this indicates the intensity of the perfection, of the progress.

Question: In Scripture are there many optatives presented in the imperative form?

And probably also in other books; and not to digress too far away: "Hallowed be your name," that is, "May your name be hallowed." "Let your kingdom come, let your will be done": "may your will be done."[18] "Let the deceitful lips become speechless"—that is, "may they become" so—"which speak lawlessness against the righteous."[19]

Question: He is praying to him?

Yes, to him. I say: when I wish to receive something from another, and I mean from another besides God—then he would not pray to him but to God in order that he might grant us such help, in order that he might lead such a commander into our midst. However, whenever someone prays to God himself, because he desires to receive something from him, he addresses the request to him as well and has the expectation of receiving from him. As when I say to God, "Approve of my request!" I offer up a prayer about a prayer. "Hear me, O Lord, because I cried out to you!"[20] and I am offering up a prayer about a prayer; for since there is need of God's cooperation even for a prayer to be heard, I call on him again as a co-laborer through prayer, in order that he should fulfill my prayer and listen to it.

This is the very thing I ask: that you arise to help me not as one unarmed, but as one who grasps a shield. Take my body and my soul, for through these you can help me. Often a physician who has great importance cannot heal insignificant animals or unimportant men. Sometimes, therefore, he prepares one of his students, who are inferior and far beneath him, in order to be able to go to such a person and heal him.

So to *take up arms and a shield* is to assume what is human, to receive the form of a servant.[21] And many things like this habitually happen in this way. So he is saying as follows: if you prefer to help me as God, the help is too high for me. [206] Help me by becoming a man.

And indeed he says to him, "Gird your sword on your thigh, O powerful one, in your bloom and beauty."[22] You have bloom and

---

[15] Jn 4:8.
[16] Deut 6:5.
[17] 1 Cor 13:4-7.
[18] Mt 6:9-10.
[19] Ps 31:18 (30:19).
[20] Ps 141:1 (140:1).
[21] Phil 2:7.
[22] Ps 45:3 (44:4 NETS).

beauty, for you committed no sin, neither did you know it. Therefore, "gird your sword on your thigh." Frequently the word *thigh* means the generative organs, as when it says, "Every thigh will be defiled by moisture,"[23] it indicates euphemistically and in a dignified way the organs that serve generation by the "thigh." For this reason also Abraham, sending away his own servant for the requesting of Rebekah in marriage, says, "Put your hand under my thigh, and I will make you swear,"[24] for since he was about to assume the care of a virgin and to lead her from a faraway place to a faraway place, necessarily he guaranteed his self-control.

However, this is also possible: since the one who comes for the salvation of all is going to come forth from my loins, "put your hand" there, "and I will make you swear!"

And indeed, the Scripture names many such things in a way that is noble. Concerning the dragon, that is, the devil, it says, "Look now, its strength is in its loins, and its power in its belly's navel."[25] In the case of the man it named the loins, and in the case of the woman it called that organ "the belly's navel" in a noble way. From the parts that are close by it indicated that one: the use of which it prohibited.

[34:3] *Pour out your sword and close up those who pursue me out of opposition!*[26]

Multiply the sword; give me a sword that is against the foes! And the living Word of God is the sword.[27] And again the Word belongs to the Spirit: "and the sword of the Spirit, which is the Word of God."[28]

To pour out, however, always indicates abundance; as when it says, "I will pour out of my Spirit upon all flesh,"[29] it indicates the abundant giving and rich supply through this word. "The love of God has been poured into our hearts."[30] And again, "Your name is perfume poured out."[31] Perfume that is poured out comes outside of the vessel that contains it and emits its fragrance to the farthest place. For example, when the Savior was in Israel and alone—for "in Israel his name is great"[32]—his name was in a vessel. But when the words "how admirable is his name in all the earth"[33] come to pass, and that passage is fulfilled: "Like your name, O God, so also your praise is to the ends of the earth,"[34] he has become perfume that is poured out.

This word, then, indicates an abundant supply. Therefore, he is saying the following: arm each of us with a sword, pour out the sword: for then you block those who pursue us out of hostility. For then we become heavily armed soldiers, we approach them armed with swords, not in order that I should kill them but I in order that I should suffer nothing.

Question: What does the phrase "*close up*" mean?

Close up means many things, and especially the gathering together, as it were, of the conclusion, which prevents the attack of the one who wants to speak craftily: this has become a "closing up." Indeed, dialecticians are accustomed to saying, "I closed him up."

However, it also means something else, as it is found in the philosophy of Paul: "God closed up all in disobedience so that he may be merciful to all."[35] And observe with care the sequence of the statement: those of the Greeks who have believed surpassed those of the Jews who believed in the Savior. And earlier again

---

[23] Ezek 7:17 LXX.
[24] Gen 24:2-3 NETS.
[25] Job 40:16 NETS.
[26] The NRSV has instead, "Draw the spear and javelin against my pursuers."
[27] Heb 4:12.
[28] Eph 6:17.
[29] Joel 2:28.
[30] Rom 5:5.
[31] Song 1:3 NETS.
[32] Ps 76:1 (75:2 NETS).
[33] Ps 8:1, 9 (8:2, 10).
[34] Ps 48:10 (47:11).
[35] Rom 11:32.

the Jews were opposing the Gentiles from being called into salvation, for they were saying, "Are you receiving into salvation those who are from accursed ancestors, those who are from idolaters, from polytheists?" So he has made a closing up; he reproved them both.

And it is possible to furnish such an example: suppose someone has a son who remains close to him and another who was rejected because of past vice. If, after the rejected son repents, and the father wishes to receive him back, and the son who remained close opposes this, saying, "Does this one become a joint heir with me? He has done such and such," then the Father accuses that one for other sins: "This one was not excluded from the inheritance for this reason. You also should be cast out: you have done such and such," then finally he no longer opposes it. For he too was "closed up," that is, he was hemmed in by accusations, even as that other one was.

He has done this "so that he may be merciful to all." For he has brought accusations, not in order to show them to be of such a kind, but in order to prevent each of them from the one who remained; for the Greek no longer surpasses the Jews because of the cross that was given to the Savior by them, nor did the Jews surpass the Greeks, for all were found to be subject to sin.

So, he says the following: "For just as you were once disobedient to God," you Greeks [207]—even if you now welcome the gospel and intend to be pious, yet at one time you also hurled stones—"but have now been set free by their disobedience"—if Israel had not become disobedient, you would not obtain salvation, for they were opposing and preventing this—"so," he says, "they too," the Jews, "they have been disobedient, in order that, by the mercy shown to you, they too should be set free."[36] At last, as a conclusion, he added, "For God has closed up all in disobedience so that he may be merciful to all."[37] This is the depth of his justice: "O the depth of the riches and wisdom and knowledge of God! How unsearchable are his judgments and how inscrutable his ways! 'For who has known the mind of the Lord? Or who has been his counselor?'"[38] of him who enclosed all in disobedience?

In the case of enemies, the phrase "close up" is understood thus: when every way is taken away from them in order to attack them and to harm them dreadfully, for someone is closed up in this way. As if with a syllogism he debated with the Jew: "Do not find fault with the calling of the Gentiles, for you also have done the same things." Again to the Greeks who overcame the Jews and say, "You murderers of the Lord, and you so-and-so's," he says, "'Once you were disobedient,'[39] you were idolaters."

[34:3] *Say to my soul, "I am your salvation."*

Say, O God, through your actions *to my soul*, *"I am your salvation."* And at what time are you saying, *"I am your salvation"* other than when you save or when you give all things to my soul, acting as its guide for salvation?

[34:4] *Let them be ashamed and embarrassed who seek my soul.*

These are those who do wrong, these are the ones who make war, about whom he said, *"Render judgment on those who do me wrong, fight against those who fight against me!"*

"Let them be ashamed," he says, "and embarrassed." There can be no rage against them, but shame on the things they do, for thus they will cease. Certainly those who knew this, that they have come into shame, say, "We slept in our shame, and our dishonor covered us!"[40]

---

[36] Rom 11:30-31.
[37] Rom 11:32.
[38] Rom 11:33-34 NRSV.
[39] Rom 11:30.
[40] Jer 3:25.

This belongs to those who knew that they have come into shame and that they were concealed because of dishonor.

And this shame and dishonor had come from sin. Such a thing he also says in Ezekiel to a certain one who was overly confident and was behaving impudently: "Be ashamed and receive your dishonor!"[41] As when someone, for instance, may be condemned to serve in public works, such as in the bathhouse or in the mines, and he thinks highly of himself for this, we say to him: "Be ashamed! Know that you are in dishonor!"

Question: The shame of Adam was also thus?

Yes, for not all shame is of the same kind. Indeed, the Scripture itself says, "There is a shame that brings on sin, and there is a shame that is a glory and a joy."[42] And observe carefully: many pride themselves in things for which it is necessary to be downcast, to forget, and to believe to be dishonorable. So says the apostle: "Their god is the belly; and their glory is in their shame; their minds are set on earthly things."[43] In the things of which it is necessary to be ashamed, about these things they speak openly, and we see that such things are also done by people naturally. The one who eagerly awaits the Savior, God the Word, knowing that they are transformed by him into becoming more glorious and conformed to the body which he himself has,[44] no longer think highly of the works of shame.

[34:4] *Let them be turned backwards and let them be put to shame who devise evils against me.*

The word *backwards* is used differently in various passages of Scripture. "To be turned backwards" conveys reproach. For example, Lot's wife, while withdrawing from that region of destruction, heard, "Do not look around backwards,"[45] do not give your consent to what you have abandoned.

Again in other places it is said, "May my enemies be turned backwards!"[46] May they be turned toward what is behind them, in order that they should no longer travel the same course as that of enemies.

"No one who puts a hand to the plow and turns toward what is behind . . ."[47] "Behind something" was not said, but only "toward what is behind." For whenever the plowman turns, he tramples on the straight furrow. And the trampling of the straight furrow impedes the work. Sometimes praiseworthily and sometimes blameworthily, however, a person is said to turn toward what is behind him. When he strives to traverse the divine way and is turned away, this turning is blameworthy, to come into the things behind him. When, however, someone hurries toward vice and then withdraws with words of repentance and turns away, this turning that comes from repentance is praiseworthy. [208]

So he is saying: since they proceed toward vice and their desire is to do me harm, let them be turned backwards from this objective.

In each of two ways, then, they *devise evils against me*. When they desire to enfold me with sin, they devise evils against me; when they desire to plot, willing to bring against me something harmful, again they devise evil against me.

The two elders who raged against Susanna have done both of these things: they devised evil by wishing to drag her into adultery. Falling short of this, they devised the other kind of evils: to condemn her to death, for her to be stoned. Think the same things of both Joseph and the Egyptian woman. She also

---

[41] Cf. Ezek 16:52 NETS.
[42] Sir 4:21.
[43] Phil 3:19 NRSV.
[44] Phil 3:20-21.
[45] Gen 19:17 NETS.
[46] Ps 6:10 (6:11).
[47] Lk 9:62.

devised the evil of fornication, into which she desired to drag him down. However, failing in this she put her hand to the other manner of evil, spreading a false accusation against him, through which the one who was considered to be his master was moved against him, as though against one who must be punished.

[34:5] *Let them become like chaff in the face of the wind.*

Let them become worthless. This is also said in the First Psalm: "Not so are the ungodly, not so! Rather, they are like the chaff that the wind sends away from the face of the earth."[48] He reveals their worthlessness not so much as a worthlessness of essence but as a worthlessness of intention; for "their mind is set on earthly things,"[49] and all who are of the flesh and its members are chaff, because they have no path, no firm place to sit.[50]

Therefore, a slight *wind* moves them. And this *wind* can be either an affliction or a deceptive argument. So, for example, some are carried off "by every" deceptive "wind of doctrine, by the trickery"[51] of those who act as ambassadors for that doctrine, which is perverse to those who practice it.

[34:5] *And an angel of the Lord afflicting them.*

They have *an angel of the Lord afflicting them.* In the previous psalm "an angel of the Lord, encamping around those who fear him, delivered them."[52] Here, however, an angel of the Lord afflicts them, because he is a kind of punisher and is sent down to take vengeance on them.

However, it is also possible to understand the angel who "encamps around those who fear

him" in a good sense, for he who makes use of shame *afflicts* the sinner, who persuades him to turn away from the pleasures that he practices.

[34:6] *Let their way become darkness and a fall,*

their way, not the way of God, not that of virtue, not that of the commandments of God, as it is said: "I ran the way of your commandments,"[53] but *their way,* in which they boast, in which they suppose that they run in the light. Let them know what kind of way their way is, let them fall, for this *fall* is fortunate. Just as the one who turns away from running the straight path falls into a great evil, so the one who strives to run to evil, when he slips and falls, receives a beginning of repentance.

[34:6] *And an angel of the Lord pursuing them,*

as I said, in both senses: either reproaching and striking or punishing them.

[34:7] *For without cause did they hide for me the destruction of their snare.*

Vice is frequently called a *destruction,* for it corrupts the truth, it makes the inner man evil instead of good, unrighteous instead of righteous, ungodly instead of pious.

And that vice is called corruption: "Bad relationships corrupt good morals,"[54] it says. This corruption—for it is not a bodily corruption of the members—corrupts the morals. And the corruption of the morals is ethical vice.

"Bad relationships" are deceptive relationships. And, to make use of an image that is introduced in Proverbs, the whore—whether false opinion or intemperance—the adulterous woman, corrupted the good morals of that

---

[48]Ps 1:4.
[49]Phil 3:19.
[50]Cf. Ps 1:1.
[51]Cf. Eph 4:14 NRSV.
[52]Ps 34:7 (33:8).

[53]Ps 119:32 (118:32 NETS).
[54]1 Cor 15:33.

youth, for she made advances against him with certain sophistical words: "I have a peace offering; today I am paying my vows"⁵⁵—punctuate the word *today* wherever you wish. "Therefore I came out to meet you."⁵⁶ But she is lying. She did not go forth in order to pay her vows, but as one "gripped with amorous desire."⁵⁷ [209]

For without cause did they hide for me the destruction of their snare.

Many trips and false thoughts rise up for those who are not able to define words of equivocal meaning. The word *destruction* and *ruin* indicate many things in Scripture: "If anyone destroys God's temple," it says, "God will destroy that person."⁵⁸ In this same passage two meanings of *destruction* are found: "If anyone destroys God's temple," through sin—he is speaking of the body, for "your bodies are a temple of the Holy Spirit within you, whom you have from God."⁵⁹

The whole of vice is also *destruction*. And, in a more strict sense, *corruption* is called a species of vice: the dissolution of virginity. Indeed, we say that the virgin has been corrupted and that the child who has just now tasted sexual pleasures has been corrupted. Nevertheless, even if the whole genus of vice is called corruption, even if it is a species of vice, they are included in one signifier, for such corruption destroys and drags down both the soul and the body.

It is said in the prophet, "Due to uncleanness. You were corrupted with corruption."⁶⁰ Now, uncleanness is a vice of the soul. Indeed, it was said in Proverbs of a certain wicked person, "He is ruined by impurity of soul."⁶¹

And in the Lamentations of Jeremiah it is said, "Her uncleanness was from her feet,"⁶² that is, her way of proceeding is uncleanness, for she travels on the forbidden way of death itself, the evil path.

"Due to uncleanness," then, "you were corrupted with corruption." Uncleanness, however, is the vice of the soul, as was said, according to the twofold sense of the aforementioned "corruption," both according to the genus and according to the species of vice, that is, both according to intemperance and according to the other types of vice.

"Due to uncleanness you were corrupted with corruption," one can also understand as the other meaning of *corruption*: "If anyone destroys God's temple, God will destroy that person."⁶³ God, however, "destroys" by testing. And just as the word *destruction* is said in two senses, when understood in relation to the soul, for we say that the one who sins is called destruction and that the one who is punished is also destruction: "Fear," then, "him who can destroy both soul and body in Gehenna!"⁶⁴ Destruction here is punishment, which is also called corruption.

"Due to uncleanness you were corrupted with corruption" can also mean: for this reason you have fallen into punishment, because you loved to be unclean, because you were eager to have uncleanness of the soul.

And this uncleanness is the opposite of cleanness, which, when it comes to the heart, brings the presence of God and the vision of him, for "blessed are the pure in heart, for they will see God."⁶⁵ Concerning this it is said, "Cleanse your hands, you sinners"—and you become clear then, when you pursue "justice justly"⁶⁶—but also "purify your hearts,"⁶⁷ and

---

⁵⁵Prov 7:14 NETS.
⁵⁶Prov 7:15 NETS.
⁵⁷Prov 7:15.
⁵⁸1 Cor 3:17 NRSV.
⁵⁹1 Cor 6:19.
⁶⁰Mic 2:10 NETS.
⁶¹Prov 6:16 NETS (LXX).

⁶²Lam 1:9 NETS.
⁶³1 Cor 3:17 NRSV.
⁶⁴Mt 10:28.
⁶⁵Mt 5:8 NRSV.
⁶⁶Deut 16:20.
⁶⁷Jas 4:8 NRSV.

also the right thought by means of the contemplations of the truth.

Without cause, then, *they hid for me*, desiring to corrupt me, to bring me down into vice, or even to plot against me and lead me into affliction. And they do both of these things in vain—for here *without cause* means "vainly"—either because I have afforded them no cause—so the one who has prepared to suffer wrong and to undergo humiliation rather than being involved in hostilities will say, "Those who surround me with corruption do this in vain, because God is my helper," or, "They do this without reason because I have afforded them no cause."

For example, when Susanna was condemned to death by the elders because she was being slandered, she could say, "They deliberated against me without reason, even though I gave them no cause." Joseph could also say these things as well as the disciples of Christ when they were being persecuted, condemned to death, reproached on account of the name of Christ.[68] For when someone conspires against Christians for no other reason than that he is a Christian, those who conspire plot against him without reason; for sometimes some come against Christians, and because they want to harm them, they invent a reason of their own accord.

[34:7] *Without cause they cast reproach on my soul.*

For I did not do anything worthy of reproach. Moreover the words "without cause" were clarified in another sense, though I have afforded no cause, I suffer for the name of Christ and for no other reason. And again, "Do not acquire the disgrace of evil men."[69] [210] "Do not acquire," when it is within our power to acquire it. However, when some surround us with reproaches even though we did not acquire them, *without cause they cast reproach on* our *soul*. Will you not say that Jezebel and her accomplices have reproached Naboth without cause, that without reason they hid for him the destruction of their snare?

Question: *Their snare?*

He calls their snares not those in which they are trapped but those in which they wish to trap others. The dramatic composition that was rehearsed against Susanna by the elders was *their snare*, not one in which they themselves are trapped, but one in which they were wishing to trap that woman, and to subject her to punishment and shame.

[34:8] *Let the snare of which they are unaware come upon them!*

He is saying the following: those who are capable of composing plots against some and who plot against them without cause never undertake this before their eyes, because they are able to take them by surprise with the things that they have prepared. For example, "He who digs a hole" for his neighbor "will fall into it."[70] They certainly do not consider something: that they themselves fall down into the hole, since otherwise they would not dig it.

So they did not know that the trap was coming on them, which they were preparing for another, in order that they should encircle him and catch him.

Which they did not know, then, which they did not have before their eyes, since otherwise they would not have made it ready.

[34:8] *And let the hunt, which they concealed, let it catch them.*

In order that they should escape the notice of others and hunt them down unnoticed, they

---

[68]Cf. 1 Pet 4:14.
[69]Prov 3:31 NETS (LXX).

[70]Sir 27:26 NETS.

concealed. Let it catch them. "They dug a hole in front of me, and they fell into it."[71]

[34:8] *And in the snare—they shall fall in it.*

In this *snare* that they made ready for others, *they will fall.* After the fall of others, they themselves fell into such contraptions that some invent and that then turn against themselves. This occurs by a kind of interweaving of providence. The doctrine of providence has a vast interweaving, although it is unknown by many, not to say, by all.

[34:9] *But my soul shall rejoice in the Lord.*

Moses says, "You shall do to him just as he connived to do to his neighbor!"[72] After these things have taken place, my soul will rejoice, knowing that it has suffered no harm.

Question: Is he rejoicing over them?

No, but he is in awe at providence and rejoices that he was not ensnared. For instance, the soul of Susanna rejoiced, not because the elders were condemned but because she was set free from their accusation. And that has happened as an accident.

And, for example, the saints, praying when they are in affliction, pray only this very thing: "Do not let us be overwhelmed by the affliction," not in truth praying against those who surrounded them with the affliction. For they receive it as a contest, not as a punishment. And the one who receives it as a contest is not so: as though he is against the adversaries so that they might no longer exist. "Lead us not into temptation";[73] indeed, he has not said, "Strike those who tempt us!"

I was once asked how the sexual union of the saints happened without pleasure—does it not say, "Let marriage be held in honor, and let the marriage bed be kept undefiled"?[74]—and I answered that the saints only have relations with their legitimate wives when it is the right time for conception. After conception they do not have sexual relations. Then I said that their intention was not a pleasure that they desired to pursue, but was to procure the begetting of children. Necessarily, however, pleasure is also involved, but they do not come together for the sake of it.

And in the case of food the same thing transpires: there is a person who feeds himself for no other reason than to satisfy the appetite, for the sake of being filled. However, when it happens as a consequence that the things eaten are also pleasurable, they are not taken for this reason, because they are pleasurable. And especially in the case of healing medicines this happens: frequently the remedy is pleasant, but one has not administered them because of the pleasure. Certainly, even if it is unpleasant, he employs it as a remedy, since he uses it for the sake of health and its benefit.

Therefore, sometimes even when those who make an assault against the righteous suffer the same things, he rejoices because he has not fallen into their hands. Then let the question follow as to whether and what they have suffered. However, I should be surprised if this is in accordance with a saint who is perfect. To rejoice because those who were trying to treat him boldly have suffered something is appropriate to one who is making progress, but not to one who is perfect.

Question: What is the difference between the phrase "in [*epi*] the Lord" and the phrase "in [*en*] the Lord"?

The one who understands the prepositions without refinement will say that there is no difference.

However, it can be understood in this way: for example, someone rejoices over (*epi*) his own child when it is healthy. He rejoices in

---

[71] Ps 57:6 (56:7 NETS).
[72] Cf. Deut 19:19 NETS.
[73] Mt 6:13; Lk 11:4.

[74] Cf. Heb 13:4 NRSV.

(*en*) the drinking of wine. It has this situation, and then that.

From another passage let us understand the demonstration: "Everyone who confesses in [*en*] me before men"—he did not say "over [*epi*] me"—"I also will confess him."[75] However, if the preposition [**211**] had been put down without a reason, the word "in [*en*]" would be set down in the case of denial also: "And everyone who denies in [*en*] me, I also will deny in [*en*] him." However, it would be impossible for the one who denies him to deny that he is in Christ or for Christ to deny the one who is in him. Therefore, the one who denies has been separated from him whom he denies. The one who denies God has been separated from God, and God has been sundered from him. However, the one who confesses him is in (*en*) him, in order that you should not understand the confession in voice alone, for those who honor him with their lips on the one hand confess, but on the other hand they are not in him.

Therefore, since our relationship with God is different, sometimes we are said to rejoice over (*ep'*) him as over a deliverer, as over a benefactor, as over a general who secures victory for us, and sometimes we are said to rejoice in (*en*) him as in wisdom, as in sanctification, as in righteousness.

So he who confesses Christ is in him. And take from another example: the one who confesses knowledge is unable to confess it in any other way unless he might understand it.

Question: Is a person in Christ as he is in an essence or as in a quality?

Let those considerations be set aside for the moment, for right now the inquiry is about the difference between the prepositions. Whether someone participates in an essence or in a quality, let this be for another occasion.

And yet it is one and the same: for God is not one thing when he becomes the Father of the righteous, another when he is their Creator, another when he is their King, but only in conception. From what we know, we understand the conceptions, since it was impossible to separate conception from conception there. God is light.[76] He is also sanctification and righteousness and wisdom,[77] and it is impossible to separate substance from substance.

However, we separate relation from relation. Let there be a man who is a father, and a master, and a teacher, and a ruler: certainly he is not distinct from himself. However, when you hear that he is a ruler in relation to those who are ruled, and a king in relation to his subjects, and a father to the one who was begotten by him, and a master to his servant, and a physician to one who is cured by him, and a teacher to his student, he is not distinct from himself, but the relation that is referred to some and to others creates the difference. So, just as it happens that he is a father, and a teacher, and the rest, it also happens that the student is the same person as the one who is ruled and as the.... And again, since he is not always related as one to one—for one may find a son of one person, and this same person is the student of another, and the friend of another . . .

[34:9] *It will delight in his saving act.*

Saving act he calls salvation here, for in many passages that which saves means salvation.

There are times when that which effects salvation is called thus, as when it says, "The ends of the earth have seen the saving act of our God,"[78] that is, the Savior.

My soul, then, "will delight in his saving act." He does not seek salvation from any other besides God himself, from him who saves with

---

[75] Lk 12:8; Mt 10:32.
[76] 1 Jn 1:5.
[77] 1 Cor 1:30.
[78] Ps 98:3 (97:3).

[34:10] *All my bones shall say, "O Lord, O Lord, who is like you?"*

It is the first theology to know what the holiness of God is and who can be likened to him or who cannot. Therefore, he attributes this theology and knowledge of God to his own bones because of which he stands, because he is not speaking about his own bones—these bones that hold firm the other members of the body, the flesh, and the sinews—but of the strong powers, of which we have often said that they are the bones of the inner man himself.[80]

All my bones, then, *shall say*: the strong doctrines, my vigorous movements, according to which I know and understand, they confess God, that none of the created things is like him.

Question: How then is the word *"who"* meant?

In the sense of impossibility, as the word, "O God, who shall be likened to you?"[81] We do not understand this in the case of the Son, for he does not obtain the likeness in the future, but as the "exact imprint of God's very being,"[82] he is eternally like him.

Therefore, it can be understood in each of two ways: if it is about the essential likeness, no one is like him. However, if it is taken in relation to the likeness that accords with virtue and holiness, the one who is like him is scarce.

[34:10] *Rescuing the poor from the hand of those too hard for him.*

If in this case, the likeness is understood, it indicates scarcity. God delivers the *poor* man and the needy man *from the hand of those too hard for him*. And this applies also to men, rulers for instance, the rich, those who are powerful in another way [212] in the city, and especially to evil powers and the devil himself. Therefore, God alone delivers from these.

And when, as I said, he delivers from the affairs of men, even the one who is able to do this is rare, for it is no great thing to deliver from lesser men. Those who raged against Susanna seemed to be too hard for her, for they were rulers and judges, and that woman lived at home and was an ordinary citizen. And God delivered her *from those too hard for her.*

And this also must be recognized: everyone who is weaker than someone is *poor* in this respect: he is unable to help himself, he cannot aid himself and bring himself out of the difficult circumstance that hems him in.

[34:10] *Both poor and needy from those who despoil him.*

Now, it certainly happens that the same person in subject is *both poor and needy*. If one is devoid of wealth, one is *poor*, whereas if one has enough for oneself through hard labor, he is *needy*; for "the rich became poor."[83]

If then, you interpret these things anagogically, you understand the man of the Jews who believed as the *poor* man, and the *needy* one as the one who has no hope but is still godless.[84]

[34:11] *When unjust witnesses rose up, they kept asking me about things I did not know.*

The *unjust witnesses* ask him, whom they wish to testify against, what he *does not know*.

And here *what I did not know* means "what I did not know experientially." The phrase "not knowing" sometimes signifies ignorance:

---

[79] Is 45:17 NETS.
[80] See PsT 33.
[81] Ps 82:2 NETS. The Hebrew text does not have the phrase "Who will be likened to you?"
[82] Heb 1:3 NRSV.
[83] Ps 34:10 (33:11 NETS).
[84] Eph 2:12.

"Formerly, when you did not know God,"[85] indicates ignorance. And it also means "not having experienced," as when I say, "him who knew no sin,"[86] having not experienced sin. In one respect, therefore, he does know it; he understands its nature. However, he does not know it, because he did not make use of it. So indeed, both in the case of married women and women in general, it is said, "he did not know her," "he knew her." Here knowing means experience. "Now Adam knew his wife Eve." This was said at the time when he has been united to her, for it added, "and after she conceived she bore a child."[87]

Therefore, unjust witnesses are those who speak against someone what does not pertain to that person. Such also is the word, "When the evil one turned away from me, I did not know him."[88]

[34:12] *They repay me bad things for good, and childlessness for my soul.*

It was necessary for them to know that for their own good I did not experience nor know what they are asking me about, for they were going to be punished, and because of this they will not be punished on my account, insofar as it depends on me.

In this way we also interpreted the passage from the Gospel: "Be favorable with your accuser while you are on the way with him!"[89] And since the definition of favor is as follows: "Favor is intending good things for your neighbor for his own sake"—for often I desire good things to be given to him, that I might gain something from him.

So, they desire to punish me, who have harmed them in no way but have even offered them the possibility of salvation.

Of such a kind also is what is said by Jacob to Laban: "Discover if there is anything of yours with me, and take it."[90] I desire nothing of yours; I am benevolent to you; I restore to you what is yours.

For the good things that I did for them . . . And I have done good things to them lest they be appointed to be punished on my account, when I did not yield to them. Would not Susanna also say of the elders: "They wanted to drag me down into adultery; I did not let myself be persuaded by them. I have done something good to them: insofar as it depended on me, they have not come into sin to render me childless"? The phrase "*They repay me*" is said in respect to both: just as they repay me with evil for good, so also they repay my soul with *childlessness*.

Question: What are the offspring of the soul?

Right thoughts, the noblest actions. "Because of the fear of you we conceived and travailed and gave birth."[91]

[34:13] *But as for me, when they troubled me, I would put on sackcloth.*

Observe: he called their evil deeds and the purpose of their desiring to render him *childless* "troubling," like one who has spoken the troubles of a sophist. They *trouble* me rather than harm me. Nevertheless, I dressed myself in *sackcloth*, both lest I fall into their hands, as one abandoned, and for their sake: that they might cease from their arrogance against me. I clothed myself in a certain austere way of life. I bore a sign of repentance partly lest I suffer harm from their troubling and partly lest those ones perish. And how much more is it for their good, if they should also cease!

---

[85] Gal 4:8 NRSV.
[86] 2 Cor 5:21.
[87] Gen 4:1.
[88] Ps 101:4 (100:4).
[89] Mt 5:25.

[90] Gen 31:32.
[91] Cf. Is 26:17-18 NETS.

[34:13] *And would humble my soul with fasting.* [213]

I not only dressed myself in sackcloth, that is, in austerity of life, but I also *would humble my soul with fasting*, both in the literal sense and in the principal sense, no longer consuming anything of those things that are distressing.

And also the fasting in the literal sense often comes to our assistance, for we have seen many things accomplished because of fasting: the city of the Ninevites not falling to its ruin, the race of the Jews being saved from Haman.[92]

[34:13] *And my prayer shall return into my bosom.*[93]

In many Scriptures the dominant part of the soul and the intellect are signified by the name *bosom*, as when it says, "For the unrighteous, everything will turn around into their bosom."[94] This is equal to the saying, "I have given their ways into their heads,"[95] for again the heads indicate the dominant part of the soul: "His toil shall return upon his head."[96]

The saint prays for good things to happen. And prayer is nothing other than "asking for good things from God." When someone obtains the good things for which he was praying, his *prayer* was *returned into* his *bosom*. He was not left in the lurch and he did not remain outside; his voice was sent up and dispersed into the air, but he obtained what he asked for. And this means that his prayer was not sent up in vain but that "he who satisfies your desire with good things"[97] conveyed what he asked for into the heart of the one who prayed. He who desires them is satisfied with them.

"This will be the contempt in their bosom in the land of Egypt."[98] And, "The wife who is in your bosom,"[99] whom you love dearly, who is unanimous with you, who is like-minded with you. [217]

And my prayer shall return into my bosom.

The one who asks for good things from God prays. Whenever he obtains what he asks, his *prayer* is *returned into* his *bosom*, into his dominant part. And I illustrated from several passages that the dominant part of the soul is frequently indicated by the name "bosom." "This will be their contempt in their bosom in the land of Egypt."[100] And again, "All things come upon the unrighteous into their bosom."[101] Now, the bosom here means kinship. So indeed one was resting in Abraham's bosom,[102] because he had the same courage and steadfast endurance as he; and at last: "the wife in your bosom,"[103] your own wife, who lives together with you.

[34:14] *Like a friend, like a brother of ours, so was I pleasing them.*

He says the following: no one has a pretext for being angry with me, no one receives from me any motive for being hostile toward me; for to each one just as I was like a friend, like a brother, so also I was pleasing because of mutual love, devotion to my companions, and brotherly love.

[34:14] *As one grieving and sullen, so I used to humble myself.*

So I used to humble myself, because of them. Those whom I held to be neighborly and brothers were brought together against me,

---

[92]Jon 3:5-10; Esther 4:16.
[93]The NRSV reads, "I prayed with head bowed on my bosom."
[94]Prov 16:33 LXX.
[95]Ezek 11:21.
[96]Cf. Ps 7:16 (7:17 NETS).
[97]Ps 103:5 (102:5).
[98]Hos 7:16 LXX.
[99]Deut 13:6.
[100]Hos 7:16 LXX.
[101]Prov 16:33 LXX.
[102]Lk 16:22-23.
[103]Deut 13:6 NETS.

they were making war with me, as it says in the beginning of the psalm: "*Render judgment, O Lord, on those who do me wrong; fight against those who fight against me!*"[104] Afterward he says, "*Indeed, they were speaking peaceful words to me and they were devising treacheries in wrath.*"[105] For this reason, like one grieving for them and like one sullen about them, so I used to humble myself, for if indeed they were supplying me with things that gladden, I would be uplifted, I would rejoice, I would be made happy from cheerfulness.

Question: What does "So I used to humble myself" mean?

When someone has a beloved and longed-for son, and sees him stricken with fever, he *humbles himself*, since he sees him whom he desired not continuing in this way, being afflicted in this way. Therefore, since I was bestowing opportunities for virtue, relating to them as though to a neighbor and brothers, and they were showing themselves to be hateful and hostile, *I used to humble myself* over them, although I should rejoice over them. What do you suppose Paul did about Hymenaeus and Alexander? Did he not humble himself when he saw them making shipwreck of the faith?[106] Was he not formerly like this toward them: Did he not love them, did he not provide them with opportunities for blessedness?

Now, when what is said is from the person of the Savior, he can say these things about Judah and the whole people of the Hebrews.

[34:15] *And against me they were glad and gathered together.*

And do you wish to know that it is a humiliation to be downcast over sinners? Paul writes to the Corinthians. Stimulating them into repentance, he says, "Lest somehow when I come, I may find you thus and God should humble me."[107] The saint is exalted when he sees those who received help from him improving. And a father is exalted, when he rejoices and is gladdened over children.

If they were preserving toward me the love that I was preserving toward them, I would not be humbled, but I would be exalted because I have them of equal condition with me, because I have them as companions.

And against me they were glad and gathered together.

I, however, was so disposed toward them out of tenderness, as one most personally attached. They, however, gathered together out of opposition against me. They were glad or, being glad, they gathered together against me, in order to buy something more evil and troublesome against me.

[34:15] *Scourges gathered together against me, and I did not know.*[108]

I said in the previous readings from one of the psalms that the same afflictions are for some scourges, and for others they are contests, when the text was cited: "Many are the scourges of the sinner."[109] "Scourges" here can also enumerate evil powers.

They were *gathered together, and I did not know*, and this passage is analogous to the following: "When the evil one was turning away from me, I did not know."[110] The evil one drew near; I did not afford him any room, because I was persuaded by the apostolic judgment that says, "Do not make room for the devil."[111] I have not known him by experience.

---

[104] Ps 35:1 (34:1).
[105] Ps 35:20 (34:20).
[106] 1 Tim 1:19-20.
[107] 2 Cor 12:20-21.
[108] The NRSV has instead, "Ruffians whom I did not know tore at me without ceasing."
[109] Ps 32:10 (31:10). Because pages 161-76 of the manuscript are missing, these remarks are not extant.
[110] Ps 101:4 (100:4).
[111] Eph 4:27 NRSV.

It is said that one of the ancient philosophers used to be whipped, in order that he should denounce his own city, in order that he should accuse [218] his fellow citizens. Taking care lest he should blurt something out against his own will, he bit through his own tongue and severed it and hurled it at the one who was doing him violence. That one could not say, "I did not know," for necessarily he knew a little, otherwise he would not have provided security for himself from another source.

Not so the saint. Isaiah was sawed in two with a wooden saw. And note carefully the malice of Manasseh the apostate, who worshiped idols. And since the idol, which he himself erected, fell down after Isaiah had looked on it and certain others, he put forward accusers, and they have brought against him two accusations: first, that when Moses says, "No one can see my face and live,"[112] he himself says that "he saw the Lord of Sabaoth sitting on a throne."[113] However, if they had paid attention carefully, they would have recognized his slander. He did not at all say that he did, nor did he, see his face. He saw it veiled, so that we should demonstrate that they are slanderers as to the literal sense.

This accusation, then, they have brought against him, as well as a second: "The rulers of the clear-seeing race, the holy priesthood, the kingly people[114] he called 'rulers of Sodom,'[115] and the people whom God loved, whom God honored, he called 'people of Gomorrah.'"[116] Because of these two accusations they slandered him, even though they knew that they were not called so by him before.[117] But when the idol fell down, lest they appear as though they were avenging that which clearly was not God, however, they imputed a certain accusation against him.

Isaiah may also say, "Scourges gathered together against me, and I did not know." And observe the malice of Manasseh: in order that for a long hour he should remain subjected to torture, he sawed him in two with a wooden saw, in order that the flesh, being scraped by those teeth, should endure a greater pain and for a longer time.[118]

Question: Because they bring punishments as though against an evildoer, they are also called "*scourges*" in accordance with this?

Yes. Yet I myself did not know that they were scourges, for I competed and I was crowned by means of them. Then I would experience them as such, if I were such a person as they seemed to punish.

As an example: in a certain sense, those who pursued a false accusation against Susanna also scourged her a little, for she had fallen into such dread as to say, "There are narrow places on every side for me."[119] If, as though against an adulteress, they were deriving their frauds, they were scourges. She, however, did not know them; for she was not intemperate.

Let virtue, therefore, be as fish glue for the saints. Let fire be brought to it, for example, the blazing desires of shameful passion. She did not know that a blazing desire was what was present to her; that is, she did not experience it. But the fish glue, because it corporeal, is consumed by the fire, and only then the fire attacks that which was smeared and was not harmed earlier. However, because virtue is fireproof, the fish glue, as it were, always remains, and the fire never prevails against the one who possesses virtue.

Question: "He made the Most High his refuge and no scourge drew near his tent?"[120]

We have found many people who were scourged and who have died while being scourged. Therefore, when we say that

---

[112]Ex 33:20.
[113]Is 6:1.
[114]Ex 19:6; 1 Pet 2:5, 9.
[115]Is 1:10.
[116]Is 1:10.
[117]Martyrdom and Ascension of Isaiah 3:7-10.

[118]Martyrdom and Ascension of Isaiah 5:1-14.
[119]Sus 22.
[120]Ps 91:9-10 (90:9-10).

someone who is scourged with perceptible whips does not feel the pain from them, this is not a contest. This is no great thing, and everyone would be able to endure this. They simply did not recognize them, even though the scourges forced them to experience them and to do something against their will.

Look, the examples of Susanna have become clear; let that of Joseph also be taken. Scourges were brought against him as against an intemperate person, and he did not know anything either. Naboth was plotted against and was whipped because he "blessed" God, as the accuser said, that is, he "blasphemed," and he did not know it, for he did not renounce piety.[121]

Question: Is it not said in an improper sense, "He will hide you from the scourges of the tongue"?[122] What is "the scourge of the tongue"?

You cannot understand it in a perceptible sense. It is a lying word, a slander.

So also the evil powers, since they assail the dominant part of the one who is unguarded against them more than scourges do, are called "scourges." And because these scourges are of such a kind, *they gathered together*. And to gather together against someone is characteristic of a rational being.

[34:15] *They were separated and they were not repentant.*

Unanimity toward evil things is a great evil; it is harmful. Once, indeed, those who came [219] from the East and came into the plain of Shinar,[123] where Nebuchadnezzar erected his image,[124] were in agreement. And see that this is wicked. And it is translated "a grinding of the teeth."

Now, often "teeth" are understood in place of "words." Indeed, "he shattered the teeth of sinners,"[125] and we certainly do not say that these are perceptible teeth, for this was never recounted. And, "The molars of lions the Lord shattered."[126] He says these things not about the perceptible teeth of four-legged wild beasts but of men like these.

Unanimity toward evils is a very wicked thing. And the scattering of these and their separation is something good. If those should perceive that they were scattered because of their own vice that came from agreeing together and by the mercy of God—as the Sadducees and Pharisees were once of one mind against Paul, when they led him even into the barracks, and the commander of the garrison has given him to them in order thereby to understand more about him. They, however, had the goal of taking him to put him to death. And they had thought it fitting to bring him forth and to station him on the flight of stairs.[127] "When Paul noticed that the one part was of Sadducees and the other of Pharisees,"[128] he said something that put an end to and broke apart their unanimity, for he said, "I am on trial today concerning the resurrection of the dead,"[129] and they were divided, for some said, "He says nothing reprehensible," while others pressed against him.

If they had been repentant because of this division, they would no longer have plotted against Paul. At that time they were not repentant; they did not understand the cause of the division.

And David certainly prays somewhere and says, "And divide their tongues,"[130] for their tongues are divided when they begin to say

---

[121]Cf. 1 Kings 21:10 (20:10).
[122]Job 5:21.
[123]Cf. Gen 11:2.
[124]Cf. Dan 3:1.

[125]Ps 3:7 (3:8).
[126]Ps 58:6 (57:7 NETS).
[127]Acts 21:34-35.
[128]Acts 23:6.
[129]Cf. Acts 23:6 NRSV.
[130]Ps 55:9 (54:10 LES2).

things that disagree. Indeed, this has also taken place with the elders against Susanna: their tongues were divided; the first said some things and the second said others.[131] If they had been repentant, they would have ceased their accusation and they would not have continued what they undertook.

They were separated, then, *and they were not repentant*. The one who divided them in order for them to repent and change their behavior has done this. They themselves, however, did not know the cause of their separation and division.

Question: What does *they were not repentant* mean?

They did not change their minds. To repent is to repudiate one's own former thinking and first disposition.

For example, when Ahab has become aware of the things that happened earlier, God says to Elijah, "Have you seen how Ahab is smitten with remorse?"[132] For he repented with weeping. And this transformation of his he has called his repentance. And when the saint says, "So that my glory may make music to you and I shall not be stunned with remorse,"[133] he is saying, "I shall not experience regret." And in the case of the others, who do not proceed rightly, it happens that they repent.

[34:16] *They tried me; they mocked me with mocking.*

It is necessary for them, being repentant, to cast away their anger against me, but they even inflicted, attacked, tried me, and mocked me. But even when they tried me, they did not find me as they wished; I did not enter into temptation, I was not caught in the trap of their temptation, for in this way too is interpreted the word "Lead us not into temptation."[134]

---
[131]Sus 52-59.
[132]1 Kings 21:29 (20:29 NETS).
[133]Cf. Ps 30:12 (29:13 NETS).
[134]Mt 6:13; Lk 11:4.

They mocked me, they despised me. And again I, boldly withstanding their mockery, showed it to be nothing.

[34:16] *They gnashed their teeth at me.*

Someone gnashes the teeth sometimes against another, sometimes against himself, whenever he experiences regret, meeting with pains from what he practiced: "Where there will be weeping and gnashing of teeth,"[135] for since they are being punished because of their own impieties and sins, when they become repentant they weep and gnash their teeth.

However, another gnashes; for this reason it is said of the devil, "He has gnashed his teeth at me,"[136] and of the wicked it says here, "*They gnashed their teeth at me.*" Failing to obtain what was desired, they gnashed because they did evil in vain, or because they stumbled on the knowledge of what they desired to do, suffering what they desired another to do.

Question: Must one understand the *teeth* as words?

When it signifies repentance and the wrath of those who did not accomplish what they intended to do, we understand this, that *they gnashed their teeth*, so that the gnashing of their teeth signifies their repentance, either their repentance or the torment that comes on them because they have not succeeded.

However, if you want to understand *teeth* in a different way, it is not from this passage: because often it is possible [220] to comprehend a true object of contemplation, but not from this passage. And because it is true, those who are unable to make the thoughts level with the words welcome it. The masticating powers of the soul are often called its *teeth*. And by these masticating powers that break down foods, if one may use them opportunely, one

---
[135]Mt 8:12; 13:42, 50; 22:13; 24:51; 25:30.
[136]Job 16:9 NETS.

eats "the Bread of life,"[137] the fruit of the "Tree of life,"[138] the flesh of Jesus.

However, if someone may use them badly, he eats the flesh of the dragon. And the flesh of the dragon is godless doctrines, great sins; for as the body of Jesus reaches maturity because of doctrines, as it says, "puffed up without cause" in his intention, "a mind of flesh, not holding fast to the head, from whom the whole body, joined together, will grow with a growth that is from God."[139] He is saying the following: the one who has a fleshly mind, that is, one who is disposed to what is fleshly and perceptible, has his mind puffed up without reason, because it is fleshly, and he does not grasp the head of the doctrines. He does not hold firmly to the Savior himself, who is the head of the doctrines. Moreover, the great theological doctrines are the head of such a body, "from whom the body, being joined together by its every ligament and by its sinews, will grow with a growth that is from God."[140] So indeed we also, when a greater number of words and many topics arrive at a single resolution, say that the argument has been made into one body.

When we understand that there are masticating powers of the soul, we say something that is true, but not in relation to the passage that is set forth. And if, however, you should take it this way, that some make use of these masticating powers treacherously, according to the passage, "If, however, you bite and devour one another,"[141] and, "those who devour Israel with open mouth,"[142] and these assume a punishment, then it is possible for the passage, "They gnashed their teeth at me," to be understood in this way. They gnashed these teeth, and for this reason they will endure their affliction, for "you broke the teeth of sinners."[143]

[34:17] *O Lord, when will you take notice?*

When will you observe so as to hinder them and to set me free from harm? Indeed, we have frequently said that "take notice" and "look" . . . signify that the passing over of something indicates patience.

O Lord, when may you take notice? For when you may take notice, you will do me good, looking favorably on me, having mercy on me, and you will make them be apart from the desire that was for the evil, so that I am not harmed by them, nor do they remain any longer in the savage vice they currently practice.

[34:17] *Restore my soul from their ravages!*

He spoke of many enemies besetting him and who did many things to him in an evil way. And from the beginning of the psalm this is established: *Render judgment, O Lord, on those who do me wrong; fight against those who fight against me!* and what follows: *And when are you taking notice, O Lord? . . . They gnashed their teeth at me. . . . Scourges gathered together against me and I did not know.*

Therefore, he says, "Make my soul free of them!" for he used to be free of them. Indeed the word *restoration* recalls this to mind. No one who arrives at a place where he has never come before is said to return, but he is one who comes from one fatherland to another fatherland or from one place to another.

Therefore he is saying as follows: "They desired to trap my soul, because it is holy, to subject it to corruption." Then he is restored from the malice of the evil ones, when he suffers nothing from them, when he is not endowed with a quality like them.

---

[137] Jn 6:35, 48.
[138] Gen 2:9; 3:22, 24; Rev 22:2.
[139] Cf. Col 2:18-19; Eph 4:16.
[140] Cf. Col 2:19; Eph 4:16.
[141] Gal 5:15 NRSV.
[142] Is 9:12 NETS.

[143] Ps 3:7 (3:8 LES2).

Susanna was raised in keeping with self-control, and she was very prudent, being instructed in accordance with the law of Moses. As far as the elders who attacked her were concerned, she was caught red-handed in adultery. And she called out, saying, "Restore my soul!" Lead it away from the perversity of these men into the same self-control. Everyone who is schemed against will say these things. And the souls of martyrs is restored when these are not corrupted by temptation.

And that "to restore" has this meaning, it says in one of the psalms: "You are the one who restores to me my inheritance."[144] According to this meaning we say that man has been restored into paradise, [221] because an entrance for him there has come into being when the repentant one heard, "Today you will be with me in Paradise."[145]

"Restore," therefore, "my soul." They have done evil to such a degree that they have become like wild beasts against me.

[34:17] *My only-begotten one from lions!*

"Restore *my only-begotten one from lions.*" He calls his own soul *only-begotten*. He possessed it as his *only-begotten* one; he had it "alone." It is not possible for me to be tempted in multiple souls, since it is certainly *only-begotten* for me.

And in another interpretation: "God has made man upright";[146] "in his own image and likeness"[147] he created him. Whenever he remains in this condition in which he was created, he does not come outside himself; he does not become free of himself.

Since, then, it is the person of the Savior who says this, the soul that Jesus possessed has belonged to no other. Our souls, however, become the possession of those who dominate us, for by whom someone is defeated, to this one also is he enslaved. And it is possible to transfer from the one who is truly Lord to other masters and from some to others, when sins become discordant: for the one who repents is restored from the wickedness of those who dragged his soul into vice.

Since, then, the soul of Jesus "has in every respect been tested as we are, yet without sin,"[148] it has never belonged to any other except the one who assumed it. Because of this he calls his own soul "*only-begotten.*"

Furthermore, *my only-begotten one* should also be clarified in this way: all souls belong to the Savior, "receiving the outcome of faith, the salvation of souls. Concerning this salvation, therefore, there was both careful search and inquiry by the prophet."[149] Those, then, who "receive the outcome of faith" belong to the Savior. They are indeed his members, who are all together his body.

This soul, however, is his in another sense than those are, for this one he chose to possess as an instrument and a temple, in order that by it he might produce actions, by it he might produce salvation. In this way indeed, even when it came into Hades, it was not held there, for his soul was unique.

Now, often the word *only-begotten* means "only." Aetius the Arian, then, the father of Eunomius, who cast him into a pit, used to say, "How great a thing," he said, "are they conferring on Christ: that he is God's only-begotten." He says, "There are also other only-begotten things: the world is only-begotten, the sun, the earth." I respond to him: it is not the same thing to be called "only-begotten" and an only-begotten offspring and an only-begotten child. Therefore, Jesus alone has been called an "only-begotten Son," for it has been said, "we have seen his glory, glory as of the only-begotten Son from the Father."[150]

---

[144]Ps 16:5 (15:5 NETS).
[145]Lk 23:43 NRSV.
[146]Eccles 7:29.
[147]Gen 1:26.
[148]Cf. Heb 4:15 NRSV.
[149]Cf. 1 Pet 1:9-10.
[150]Jn 1:14.

And the "only-begotten from the Father" is an only child. And it is always so: "for God so loved the world that he gave his only Son."[151] He never simply called him "only-begotten" but "only-begotten Son." And again, "because he has not believed in the name of the only-begotten Son of God."[152] Therefore, if something is a unique creature, as you say, then it is only-begotten; but there is no only-begotten work—for there are other works of God—there is not an only-begotten creature.

When also the saint says, "Look upon me and have mercy on me, because I am only-begotten and poor,"[153] he is saying the following: "I am alone." And when Elijah says, "I alone am left, and they are seeking my life,"[154] he could be called "only-begotten," but not as a son or a child.

And here then he says, "*My only-begotten one from the lions*," the fierce ones who have become feral against me. Rescue and redeem my soul, because it is unique to me, for it alone did not know sin,[155] it alone "has been tested in every respect, yet without sin."[156]

Question: How was it restored?

He has not come into sins, but insofar as he was amid the cruelty of adversaries he took care lest he suffer this. Now we speak from the person of the saint. And the examples of both Susanna and Joseph are evident.

Even the devil himself has plots, thoughts befitting a sophist, which each and every virtuous person is able to discern. Paul says, for instance, "We are not ignorant of his designs,"[157] of his designs, his deceptions, the very acts of falsification, his sophistical thoughts by which he wishes to deceive us.

Therefore, "restore" us! For to be afraid at all was itself a forepassion. And he desires to become free of the forepassions as well, for he did not say "from my wicked act."

Question: Into the state of impunity?

Even though he has been frightened, he did not now say, "Restore me into impunity," into no longer having even a forepassion. [**222**] I have a sense that I have been troubled. "Restore," then, "my soul." "Why are you deeply grieved, O my soul, and why are you throwing me into confusion? Hope in God, because I shall acknowledge him."[158] For he did not speak to another; he was conversing with his own mind. "Why are you deeply grieved, and why are you throwing me into confusion?" You have near you the one who brings confusion to an end. As when someone would say to one who has a fever and has neglected it: "Why are you moaning so? A physician is present who can liberate you from your fever!" "Hope," then, "in God, because I shall acknowledge him." When he persuaded himself to hope in God, he was restored from fear and confusion, which fear and which confusion have come from the malice of evil powers and the devil himself.

My only-begotten one from lions.

He named these evildoers themselves, who wished to attack him, "*lions*," who make an assault and like scourges come against him.

[**Question:** The soul of the Savior?]

Since it "has been tested in every respect as we are, yet without sin,"[159] we grant to it the forepassion. Now the forepassion is not a sin. For if you do not grant this, you introduce another essence for his soul. And it has no renown, nor is it worthy of praises and crowns, if it was not disturbed. For example, you have in the Gospel, "He began to be bewildered and agitated."[160] For to begin is nothing other than

---

[151] Jn 3:16.
[152] Jn 3:18.
[153] Ps 25:16 (24:16).
[154] Rom 11:3 NRSV; cf. 1 Kings 19:10, 14.
[155] Cf. 2 Cor 5:21.
[156] Cf. Heb 4:15 NRSV.
[157] 2 Cor 2:11 NRSV.

[158] Ps 42:5 (41:6 NETS).
[159] Cf. Heb 4:15 NRSV.
[160] Cf. Mt 26:37; Mk 14:33.

a forepassion. This beginning is this very thing: it is only a beginning, it has nothing after it. This soul alone, before the choice of evil things, chose the good.

[**Question:** What do you call a forepassion?]

This was frequently discussed. The essence of the rational soul is receptive of that which it is natural to receive. It is receptive of anger, concupiscence, grief, confusion, fear. Whenever the thing that provokes it to fear is present, the rational essence is disturbed in every way. And sometimes it immediately checks the disturbance so that nothing comes after it. They call this a forepassion.

Question: Are you saying that a human and a quality are the same?

When I say that a man has died, I am not speaking of the quality: for example, of the righteous man. The death of the righteous is certainly not the dissolution of the soul from the body, but his ceasing from being righteous. This is the destruction of the righteous man.

Often, because we are ignorant of the false opinions of the impious we stumble on them. And by stumbling on those we destroy orthodoxy.

Question: How are you claiming that I have not understood? I do not concede that he is righteous.

But when another understands as was said and grants him to be righteous, the same person is both righteous and unrighteous. Now, hear why the followers of Protagoras took a different view—now Protagoras was a sophist.... He says that for things that exist, being is in appearance. He says: "I appear to you who are present to be sitting, while to one absent I do not appear to be sitting. It is unclear whether I am sitting or not sitting." And they claim that all that exists is in appearance: for instance, I see the moon, while another does not see it. It is unclear whether it is or is not. To me, who am well, comes the perception of honey, that it is sweet, while to another comes the perception that it is bitter, if he is feverish. It is unclear, then, whether it is bitter or sweet. And so they desire to express the doctrine of indeterminacy.

Therefore, when we also say, "Since it does not appear plain to me with what purpose he has spoken, I regard him as unrighteous and impious," but when it seems plain to another with what intention he has spoken, he appears to that one to be righteous and pious. And again, another does not understand what has been said by him. To him he is neither pious nor impious. And we fall into the opinion of Protagoras.

Let us observe, then: one must first understand the facts and in this way either explain or not explain them. The one who has said that he did not speak rightly and was not wholesome, what kind of understanding does he give the words?

Question: How then does Job speak?

When I say, "May the day perish in which I was born!"[161] I am saying, "Let my beginning perish, for I have come from better things into worse," for it is beneficial that the evil perish. As when Jeremiah says of the people of the Hebrews—and each of the Hebrews who was taken captive will say—"May the day of the captivity perish," he does not say the following: "Let the captivity be no longer." "Let that day," he says, "not be, let it depart," for did the day still endure? He was 148 years old when he was saying these things. How did that day, on which he was born, remain? For it departs and it is impossible to cause it to return. And he says, "Let it not be longed for!"[162] for who prays that [225][163] that day that passed by so many years ago return again? Therefore he curses the beginning of the flesh, the beginning of mortal life.

---

[161] Job 3:3 NETS.
[162] Jer 20:14 NETS.
[163] Because of a mistake in the modern reckoning of the manuscript, there are no pages 223-24.

Question: Does he not sin, then?

The one who insults Satan does not sin. Does not the impious person, "when he curses" the impious "Satan, curse his own soul?"[164] He curses Satan, not insofar as he is God's creature but insofar as he is evil and impious. However, he himself is also impious. Therefore he curses himself, and this curse is not blameworthy.

When someone curses himself because he is impious, he hates the cause of his being invented as Satan was.[165] Impiety, however, is the cause. And probably he will have ceased or, not ceasing, he will have been punished.

When the captives curse the day of their own captivity, they are not saying this, that they may no longer be subject to the captivity—far less do they ever have the captivity as a kind of cause—and they curse it.

Question: Does he himself also curse "that day"?[166]

And why did he add also the word *that*? For one day is no different from another. Then he says, "May he who is about to subdue the great sea-monster curse it."[167] Why did he not say, "he who created the sun, he who founded the world," but "he who is about to subdue the great sea-monster"? For the Savior, after having come, also "subdued the great sea-monster" and abolished the beginning of men, so that he might give them another beginning "of water and the Spirit,"[168] which is strictly called "regeneration." Now, a regeneration is one birth on another, just as a palinode is one ode on another.

And he called the resurrection of the dead "regeneration," for he says to the disciples, "In the regeneration you yourselves will also sit upon twelve thrones,"[169] that is, "in the resurrection, in the age to come."

When I say, "May I not see this day," being in affliction or in sickness, I do not say of the time, "May I not see," since it passed away, for time does not turn back.

Question: Has he said that that cause of his birth is a sin?

Again, I am not saying this, but that the one who curses a day or blessed a day blesses or curses not by observing the time but by looking to the things that have taken place in the time.

I say this: does he not say, "It is far better to depart and to be with Christ"?[170] He is not saying that departing from this life is better.

Question: Will he say that being involved in it is better or worse?

Neither worse nor better.

Question: But indifferent?

If something is indifferent, then what is contrary to it is also indifferent.

Question: It is not as an evil, but is evil in view of what is better?

Opposites are unable to coexist. If one of these things is good, then the other is evil, and if one of the two is evil, then the other should be considered good, as obtains in the case of virtue and vice, in the case of unrighteousness and righteousness, in the case of piety and impiety. When the one is wicked, then the one that remains is good. And whenever one of the opposites is not wicked, neither is the other one. White and black are opposites, and since the color white is indifferent, being neither good nor evil, so also is the color black.

Question: You yourself do not say that to come outside the body is good, according to the one who says, "It is better to depart"?

Contemplate this according to its goal: the one who departed comes to be with Christ.

Question: Is this word *better* a comparative?

Pay attention to what you are saying. Things that are spoken of by way of

---

[164] Sir 21:27.
[165] The text here is corrupt.
[166] Job 3:8 LXX.
[167] Cf. Job 3:8 NETS (LXX).
[168] Jn 3:5.
[169] Mt 19:28.

[170] Cf. Phil 1:23 NRSV.

comparison are spoken of in this way because they are of the same kind, not because they are opposites. As when I say, "Sodom was justified more than you"[171]—Sodom has not been justified—"more than your sins, O Jerusalem,"[172] because it killed prophets and has become a traitor to the Savior. That Sodom besieged one man: Lot. "That city was justified more than you." It was not simply justified—for it has not been justified—but "more than you." And when it says again, "He loved evil more than goodness and deceitful lips more than speaking justice,"[173] these things are said comparatively, not antithetically; for this is being said, that when one is denied immediately the other is established.

"To depart," then, "and to be with Christ"—if you say that it is indifferent "to remain in the flesh,"[174] then this too is indifferent. In fact, it has been demonstrated by us that things that are compared and set in contrast with one another are so: when one of the two is wicked, the remaining one is virtuous. If it is good to be "departed with Christ,"[175] to withdraw from the world, to be free of the flesh, then to be in the flesh is also good, even if [226] according to you it is inferior.

Paul desires for the inferior to perish in order that he might come into possession of the greater. And the loss, however, I speak of in this way: as its impediment, as its cessation.

Now John was desiring to remain thus, as he was on the day of his birth.[176]

Question: Does he not deny what is greater, then?

In no way desiring a better thing, he believes this to be neither better nor good. He does not pray for such a condition to pass him by. And to pass by is "to perish," to exist no longer. He is disturbed by the words destruction and *trouble*. But a person should not be troubled.[177]

Paul therefore was not troubled at such things. "We know only in part," he says, "and we prophesy only in part; but when the complete comes, the partial will come to an end."[178] Now, to come to an end conveys a better impression than to perish. In this way we ourselves have often said that for the partial to come to an end is not absolute, but to come to an end of being partial. And we understood an analogy like this in relation to the expression "down payment."[179]

Question: How do we conclude whether he is righteous or a sinner?

You do not wish to learn only this, for many things are involved in it. If you would remember what you heard, you would not always be troubled about these things. I said: let there be a king who rules over the earth, of whom all are convinced that he is righteous and that whatever he does, he does as one who is righteous.

"Bless the Lord, O my soul."[180] If I should preserve it in this way, doing that for which it was established by the Creator, it is "one of a kind." However, if at another time it acts differently, and I serve others, the soul is not unique to the one who possesses it, but sometimes it belongs to him, and sometimes it becomes independent of him.

And, to take in addition a word from the Gospel: the younger son, who traveled abroad from his father's house, had become free of himself: his soul was no longer his own. Indeed, when he repented, it says, "But when he came to himself."[181] Consequently he has become his own; his soul at last has become his. This is like the phrase "Know

---

[171]Cf. Ezek 16:44-58.
[172]Cf. Mt 23:37; Lk 13:34.
[173]Ps 52:3 (51:5).
[174]Phil 1:24.
[175]Cf. Phil 1:23.
[176]He is speaking about John the Baptist here.

[177]This paragraph continues to refer to John the Baptist.
[178]1 Cor 13:9-10 NRSV.
[179]Cf. 2 Cor 1:22; 5:5.
[180]Ps 103:1, 2, 22; 104:1 (102:1, 2, 22; 103:1).
[181]Lk 15:17.

yourself!" The one who knows himself is in himself.

[34:18] *I will acknowledge you in great assembly, among a weighty people I will praise you.*

The assembly is called *great* and numerous when it is filled with those who are individually great, for this assembly is not called great and numerous when it is composed of insignificant, ordinary men. The apostle "speaks wisdom among the mature."[182] These, coming to the same point and being "united in the same mind and the same purpose,"[183] are a numerous and great assembly.

And just as I call an assembly wise, when those who fill it up are wise individually, and I call a city tranquil and wise, when the citizens are peaceable and wise individually, so I call an assembly numerous and *great*, when those who fill it up have greatness, and a greatness that is of the soul, which is of the mind, not of the body.

Again, he calls that which is of value *a weighty people*, for things that are of value and most worthy of honor they are accustomed to calling weighty. Scripture also attests this, for when the queen of Sheba came to Solomon, it says that she came "with a weighty force."[184] And it calls the "weighty force" her very possessions that she had brought. She has offered many precious stones, many spices, gold, silver, and other things that complete her wealth. And that force of wealth was called "weighty," that is "precious," "highly valued."

He says, therefore, that when each of those who fill up the *people*, as I said regarding the assembly, is most worthy of honor, is precious—for "there is glory, honor, and peace to everyone who does good,"[185] when the good that is done has glory and honor—then a people is full of value.

So was it said about it that it was "a royal priesthood, a holy nation."[186] The "holy nation" is filled up by those who are holy individually; the "royal priesthood" is composed of many worshippers of God.

Among a weighty people, then, *I will praise you*. He is preparing himself also so that he is able to offer up a song of praise. And he can do this at that time when he becomes upright in [227] soul and mind, for "praise befits the upright."[187]

[34:19] *May those who are my enemies unjustly not rejoice over me.*

Great is the confidence of the one saying these things. They are hostile toward me unjustly. Though I give neither motive nor cause for them to press against myself in enmity, they do this. Since, then, they rejoice as enemies, whenever I encounter misfortunes, may I not encounter misfortunes so that those rejoice over me, so that they occupy themselves with me, for the one who desires to lead another into intemperance rejoices over him at that time. Being wicked, he rejoices whenever he falls down into the things with which he was eager to enfold him. So let this not be for me, so that those who hate me unjustly rejoice over me.

[34:19] *Those who hate me without cause and wink with the eyes.*

Unjustly and *without cause* mean the same thing as "without any grounds."

And wink against me *with the eyes*: they not only speak against me with words but even *wink with the eyes*. And frequently, since whenever the heterodox agree in evil in favor of

---
[182]1 Cor 2:6.
[183]1 Cor 1:10 NRSV.
[184]Cf. 1 Kings 10:2 NETS.
[185]Rom 2:10.

[186]Ex 19:6; 1 Pet 2:9.
[187]Ps 33:1 (32:1 NETS).

those who harm us—to whom they wink with their eyes, with their thoughts—they agree in impiety.

[34:20] *Because as they were speaking peace to me, they were also devising treachery in wrath.*

This is one form of impiety: although they were speaking peaceful words, they were not doing peaceful actions. And this is to be unjust. He speaks peaceful words among friends, among companions, as one who displays mutual affection, and he devises treachery in wrath. And I say: wrath is an appetite for vengeance. And the one who approaches another treacherously certainly wants to harm that one, so that the deceitful man is also inclined to anger. And in appearance he does not appear inclined to anger often, because he speaks peaceful words. Indeed, this is also said in Jeremiah of someone: "He speaks peaceably to his fellow but inwardly has enmity."[188]

To me, he says then, *they were speaking peace*. *They were* not simply *speaking peace*, but *to me*. Desiring to deceive me, *they were speaking peace*, for the man who is truly peaceable does not speak peace to another while having another mind against him.

So indeed the Savior, in addition to other things, says that "the peacemakers are blessed, for they are sons of God."[189] To be peacemakers is characteristic of sons of God. And he called "peacemakers" those who make peace. Whenever they lead those who are divided in opinion into agreement and friendship, they are peacemakers.

And in themselves they are also peacemakers. And after first making peace within themselves, so that they do not have thoughts or actions that make war against themselves, they then made peace within themselves. And they also transfer this peace to others, for as they themselves are, they desire those who are instructed by them to be. They instruct the soul to live in peace with the body and the body to be at peace with the soul, for whenever the soul "punishes the body and enslaves it,"[190] and the soul rules while the body is ruled, there is peace between body and soul.

Therefore, just as they established peace within themselves, so also they do this among the others who desire and love one another, or even among those who contend with one another. For this reason, it is also said in the Didache, the book of catechesis: "You shall make peace among those who fight."[191] And the one who brings others who fight into peace and agreement first makes peace within himself; he has no combat within himself, he does not have thoughts that conflict with him.

[34:21] *And they widened their mouth against me.*

They widened their speech *against me* by speaking peace. Their mind, however, was constrained by deceit, gathering together into the same purpose not praiseworthily, but so that they do not have the proper virtues.

This is also possible: *They widened* (their mouth) *against me*—as those who speak peace and devise treachery in wrath, they decided to deceive me. Then, consequently, they began to laugh out loud with a wide mouth and to unfold their speech against me.

In the Histories you have such examples: Delilah, who is introduced in the book of Judges as a whore, was deliberating for deceits to be brought against Samson, in order that she might give him to the [**228**] foreigners who wanted to kill him. And she was saying, "By what means will your strength become weak or how will you become weak like one among

---

[188] Jer 9:8 NETS.
[189] Mt 5:9.

[190] 1 Cor 9:27.
[191] Didache 4.3.

men?"[192] He did not tell her the truth. Then she, supposing that he was telling the truth, bound him and did the other things, and as if she were joking, said, "Foreigners are upon you, Samson!"[193] See, she was widening her mouth against him. For a long time she was begging him and nagging at him. And when she supposed that she had captured him within her nets, she said, as though she were joking, "Foreigners are upon you, Samson!" And see that she, who spoke peace for a long time and devised treachery in wrath, when she supposed that she had become his master, widened her mouth, speaking arrogantly at last.

[34:21] *They said, "Good, good, our eyes saw!"*

Those who believe that they have someone whom they were desiring within their power are accustomed to speak in this way: "Good, good, what we were desiring, our eyes saw! We no longer see you so, as you supposed yourself to be, but as we ourselves were wishing. We have found you easy to catch."

[34:22] *You saw, O Lord; do not pass by in silence!*

Do not pass by in silence means "Do not be patient any longer," for we demonstrated this from many passages: "I was silent for an age; and I shall not always be silent, shall I?"[194] I was patient; I did not proceed against the wicked deeds that were done. But this will not always be so. Again, the goodness of one who threatens one who must immediately be punished is recognized, in order that by his threat he might awaken him and lead him to repentance.

And in another psalm it says, "But to the sinner God said, 'Why do you recite my statutes and take up my words with your lips? You hated instruction.'"[195] Then at the end, "These things you did, and I kept silent"—I did not proceed against you—"You assumed lawlessness—that I would be like you!"[196] But my patience does not always remain, for "I will reprove you and show in your face"[197] your sins. And the threats of God, therefore, come according to his great goodness. The name *judge* is implied in the name "righteous."

[34:22] *O Lord, do not be far from me!*

May such things not be done by me, so that you withdraw from me, you who are my helper, my defender. Now, God withdraws from the wicked, even as he draws near to those who draw near to him. The great apostle James also writes, "Draw near to God, and he will draw near to you."[198] As when you would say to a wicked man, "Draw near to virtue, and it draws near to you." So we understand God's presence not spatially but relationally and in reference to a disposition.

[34:23] *Wake up, O Lord, and pay attention to my trial!*

This is the voice of one who has confidence. No one who is charged for adultery or murder or anything else says to God, "*Wake up and pay attention to my trial.*" For you know that vigilance at the trial will condemn him.

Therefore, the voice of one who is confident in his purity and irreproachability says, "*Pay attention to my trial*. Investigate what concerns me and what concerns those, because they speak to you in vain about me, because they hate me without cause."

Often the word *awaken* indicates alertness. For example, we frequently say, "Awaken this

---

[192]Cf. Judg 16:6.
[193]Cf. Judg 16:9 NETS.
[194]Is 42:14.
[195]Ps 50:16-17 (49:16-17).
[196]Ps 50:21 (49:21 NETS).
[197]Ps 50:21 (49:21).
[198]Jas 4:8 NRSV.

person to pay attention to himself," and it certainly does not indicate a bodily posture.

However, even when you want to understand this as awakening from sleep, it is said, "Wake up! Why do you sleep, O Lord?"[199] God sleeps when he does not wish to chastise on the spur of the moment. Therefore, he says this not as one despairing, but desiring to learn the reason, since your wisdom does nothing as though by chance. Even when you are patient, even when you defer punishment, even when you throw down those who attack me unjustly, tell me the reason. For in this way someone wise who knows the reason may become even more patient, even more enduring.

[34:23] *My God and my Lord, to my case!*

You are both *my God and my Lord*; awaken to my trial, decide my case!

He is not praying for his own enemies to suffer bad things, for to the saint who loves his enemies his prayer is that they no longer be his enemies, that they no longer be such people. However, this seems somehow to indicate punishment. However, it is a punishment [229] for the lover of pleasure to become free of pleasures, for the intemperate to go far away from intemperance. He desires that they perish insofar as they are such people.

This, furthermore, is not for everyone to say, "*My God*," then, "*and my Lord.*" For that person truly calls the Savior "Lord" who does what the Savior tells him to do, for he says, "Why do you call me 'Lord, Lord,' and do not do what I tell you?"[200] And again, "They profess to know God, but they deny him by their actions."[201] The saints call God "God" not merely in word but by becoming oriented toward him and by serving him as priests, as worshippers.

But they also serve him by doing his will, for "not everyone who says to me, 'Lord, Lord,' will enter the kingdom of heaven, but only the one who does the will of my Father in heaven."[202]

He is called "God" insofar as he is Creator, for "in the beginning God made the heaven and the earth."[203] So he is also called "God of the spirits and of all flesh,"[204] in relation to his creative activity.

And he is called "God of the saints" in another sense, in relation to the service rendered to him. In this sense indeed he is called the God of the patriarchs themselves. And in relation to creation, which meaning I was indicating, he was the God of all, of all that he has made.

And again he is *Lord* of all, because he himself bestows being on them and governs them under his own care.

And in another sense he is *Lord* of those who do his will, of those who practice what he commanded, even as a master to his servants.

[34:24] *Vindicate me, O Lord, according to your righteousness.*

According to your righteousness, vindicate me.

Again, what is said seems proud and of a different opinion from other passages. The difference stems not from content but from expression. It says, "Not any living will be counted righteous before you,"[205] that is, "no one living." And he calls "living" the one who lives according to the soul, therefore righteous in the highest degree; however, not before you, and in comparison with you they are nothing.

Just as when you may say also about lamps, that they do not illuminate before the sun—and this does not mean that they do not illuminate, but only in comparison with the

---

[199]Ps 44:23 (43:24 NETS).
[200]Lk 6:46 NRSV.
[201]Titus 1:16 NRSV.
[202]Mt 7:21 NRSV.
[203]Gen 1:1 NETS.
[204]Num 16:22; 27:16 NETS.
[205]Ps 143:2 (142:2).

sun. Thus is meant what is said in Job: "And the stars are not pure before him."[206]

Therefore, he does not say this expression, *according to your righteousness*, in an absolute sense: not according to your insuperable righteousness, but according to your righteousness by which you judge the affairs of men. Do not judge me according to their enmity but according to your righteousness, for your righteousness detests the unrighteous.

[34:25] *May they not say in their hearts, "Good, good for our soul!"*

Even if they should not say it verbally, may they not even say in their hearts to their soul, *may they not say, "Good, good!"*

[34:25] *Nor may they say, 'We swallowed him up.'*

May they not say, "We have prevailed over him and conquered him!" For this was frequently explained as well: that in Scripture swallowing indicates victory.

[34:26] *May those who rejoice over my evils be both shamed and embarrassed.*

Bring salvation to those who are *shamed* and *embarrassed* over what they do wickedly, for since they wish to encompass me with calamities and desire to be made glad after they have seen what they are eager to see fulfilled, let them be ashamed. For, when they are *shamed*, they will no longer press against me; when they are *embarrassed* they will no longer do these things that bring censure and reproach.

Question: Is he referring to painful circumstances, not to vices, as "evils"?

Truly, in no way did he have vices who says, "Vindicate me, O Lord, according to your righteousness," who says, "Those who rejoice over me unjustly."

[34:26] *Let those who brag against me be clothed with shame and embarrassment.*

May those who speak great things against me arrogantly and rejoice over me be put to shame and embarrassed; let them recognize themselves! And this happens to them for the good, and I also no longer have them as oppressors. He chiefly prays for them, and secondarily he prays for himself.

Question: *Be clothed?*

As we say that someone is clothed in virtue, that someone is clothed in vice, that someone is clothed with "a garment of salvation": "Let my soul be glad in the Lord, for he has clothed me with a garment of salvation and with a tunic of joy."[207] The quality becomes, as it were, a garment of the person who is of such a kind.

[34:27] *May those who want my vindication rejoice and be glad!* [230]

When "those who brag" are mentioned, "they will be clothed in embarrassment and shame," while *those who want my vindication* and peace *rejoice and are glad*. When the enemies are shamed and disgraced, the friends *rejoice and are glad*. And these are the ones who desire my salvation, my virtue, my righteousness.

[34:27] *And let them say always, "Let the Lord be exalted!"*

They exalt the Lord always, then, when I myself always remain in righteousness, remain in the midst of evils while I do not fall subject to them.

---

[206] Job 25:5 NETS.

[207] Is 61:10 NETS.

[34:27] *Those who want the peace of his servant.*

Of me, his servant. Let them say always, "May the Lord be exalted!" when they see me living in peace, when they see me not falling under the power of disturbance, or confusion, or strife, or combat.

We were often saying that sometimes by the individuals the whole is shown, and we made use of the following witness, saying: "Who will ascend unto the hill of the Lord, and who will stand in his holy place? He who is innocent in hands."[208] Next he says, "He will receive a blessing from the Lord."[209] He does not speak of a specific person, but if someone is like this, if someone ascended unto the hill and stood on the hill of the Lord, and is innocent in hands, everyone, if there is anyone like this, "will receive a blessing from the Lord."

Likewise, in the Eighteenth Psalm it is said, "The law of the Lord is blameless, converting souls. The testimony of the Lord is reliable."[210] And after saying many things, he says, "for your servant also keeps them."[211] He does not speak of himself alone, but if there is any such servant of God.

Therefore, being inclined to diminish himself, whenever he speaks of achievements, he attributes them "to the servants of God," but whenever he speaks of transgressions, he attributes them to himself.

Some of those who draw near to God are called sons of God, while the servants stand beneath these. For out of being servants they become friends and sons.

The greater, therefore, are "those who desire," the sons, as it were, who are "perfect as their heavenly Father is perfect."[212] They desire for there to be peace even for those who are inferior to them. Or it is thus, that all desire the peace of each servant.

[34:28] *And my tongue will meditate upon your righteousness, your commendation all the day long.*

He will meditate by giving thanks. Whenever what I asked for takes place, my tongue meditates on your righteousness. I always describe this in detail, I proclaim it in hymns, I express it in descriptive words.

"Day" here he calls all the time of human life, as it says in other places: "For your sake we are being put to death all day long,"[213] that is, through life.

He is not speaking about the *commendation* of God, however, in a strict sense, for it is called a hymn and a praise (*ainos*) in the case of God, and a commendation (*epainos*) in the case of men. That which is accurately called the praise (*ainos*) of God could also be called his commendation (*epainos*). And possibly the commendation of God can be interpreted as the commendation that he himself gives, for he praises those who are worthy of this. It says, "Then each one will receive commendation from God."[214]

---

[208]Ps 24:3-4 (23:3-4).
[209]Ps 24:5 (23:5).
[210]Ps 19:7 (18:8).
[211]Ps 19:11 (18:12).

[212]Mt 5:48.
[213]Ps 44:22 (43:23 NETS).
[214]1 Cor 4:5 NRSV.

PSALM 35 [36]

[35:1-2][1] *Toward the end. To the servant of the Lord, David. The transgressor of the law speaks in order to sin within himself.*

Concerning the *end*, it was often said that that is the goal for the sake of which all the others exist, but it exists for the sake of nothing else. It is called the last object of desire. We desire some things for the sake of another. None of those is the *end*, but they are productive of the *end*. The *end*, however, is that which exists for the sake of nothing else, but all the others exist for it. A person wants to learn grammar: he learns it well, he studies, he listens to a teacher, and none of these is his end. However, the very acquisition of perfect knowledge is the end.

So there is a last goal, perfect virtue, after which it is impossible to seek something else that is fit for accomplishing. We make use of laws for the sake of virtue; the giving of laws is not the goal. We are persuaded by counsel, by the teachings of one who presents moral instruction; however, all these things exist for the sake of another. And perfect virtue itself, the insuperable virtue that is established after all progress, is the goal.

Every servant of God pursues this end. Because of this it says, "*To the servant of the Lord, David.*" When it says, "*To the servant,*" this goal does not belong to this David, the son of Jesse, alone, but to everyone who became a servant to God. When, for example, we praise someone for grammatical knowledge and say that he is competent both to write as is right, and to read as is appropriate, and to interpret as maintains harmony, we are not speaking about that person alone but about everyone who masters grammar.

However, let us consider his service, [231] in order that we should also see the other fellow servants in this way. "I have found David," it says, "son of Jesse, to be a man after my heart, who will carry out all my wishes."[2] The wishes of God are the particular virtues. And virtue in general is referred to as a single will, for it says, "Not everyone who says to me, 'Lord, Lord,' will enter, but only the one who does the will of my Father."[3] Here he called virtue in general "will" in a singular way. And someone does the particular virtues by acting according to all the wishes of God, when a person is a doer of God's wishes, when a person changes his commands into actions, when a person forsakes mere opinions when the truth of God has been revealed. This is a servant of God.

And observe carefully: the man who says these things was a king, and he set the service of God before the kingdom! For it is a great nobility to be God's servant. It has often been said, certainly, that the saints position themselves by titles in this way: "James, a servant of the Lord God, Jesus Christ,"[4] and, "Paul, a servant of Christ,"[5] and when Jonah is asked, "From what country are you and of

---

[1] Didymus the Blind, *Psalmenkommentar (Tura-Papyrus)*, vol. 4, *Kommentar zu Psalm 35–39*, ed. M. Gronewald, PTA 6 (Bonn: Rudolf Habelt, 1969), begins here.

[2] Acts 13:22 NRSV.
[3] Cf. Mt 7:21 NRSV.
[4] Cf. Jas 1:1.
[5] Rom 1:1.

what people?"[6] he then answers, "I am a servant of God."[7] And just as those who, because of the dignity of their own class, are arranged first in worth and dignity, so these saints confess the service of God to be the greatest nobility, the surpassing glory, and the great dignity.

The servant of God, knowing the will of God, knows also the things that are contrary to God's will. Impiety, transgression, and every form of vice oppose the will of God. Therefore, the servant of the Lord, knowing the end, the virtue that is after all, also knew transgression, for the knowledge of opposing things is the same. The one who possesses medical skill knows not only the things that produce health by way of medicines but also the things that harm, so that he makes use of some things, while he turns away from others. Therefore, the servant of the Lord, who rehearses the song *toward the end*, says:

The transgressor speaks within himself in order to sin.

The passage is ambivalent. It has one meaning, thus: "The transgressor speaks within himself in order to sin." "Within himself he speaks in order to sin." First he consents to the transgression and sin, and in this way he comes to practice it. It is impossible for one who is not predisposed to sin to sin. "The transgressor," therefore, "speaks within himself in order to sin." "He speaks within himself." In fact, it should be read in this way, that "the transgressor speaks within himself in order to sin."

However, it is also possible to understand the other half of the ambiguity in this way: "The transgressor *only* speaks within himself in order to sin," for he knows that he lacks the audacity to sin. Every sinner, when he continues to sin, conceals the evil deed; no one indeed shows himself who he is. Even if there is a whore and she wishes to be sexually involved with certain ones, she does not wish for the one who unites with her to call her a whore. Therefore, they are all the more condemned, because they wish to conceal what they do. No one, however, who does the good wishes for it to be unknown—even if he does this at times for the sake of modesty—but he strives to have such deeds made known before men, in order that the heavenly Father might be glorified. For "let your light shine before others, so that they may see your good works and give glory to your Father in heaven."[8]

[35:2] *There is no fear of God before his eyes.*

No one who has the divine fear before his eyes sins, for the divine fear is destructive of sin. It belongs to those who despise it, who came outside the divine fear, to sin. So, for example, the divine scripture of Proverbs introduces Wisdom, saying, "The fear of the Lord hates injustice, also pride and arrogance and the ways of the wicked."[9] If the fear of God hates these things, then no one who possesses it acts unjustly, for "the fear of the Lord hates injustice." He is not overbearing, he is not offensive, he is not arrogant. The word *insolence* sometimes means "insult," and sometimes "showing off" and "boasting." "And the fear of God hates the ways of the wicked." And "the ways of the wicked" are the impious intentions, the acts of transgression.

Therefore, since he does not have the fear of the Lord *before his eyes*, for this reason *he speaks within himself in order to sin*. "But by the fear of the Lord everyone turns away from evil."[10]

---

[6]Jon 1:8 NETS.
[7]Cf. Jon 1:9.

[8]Mt 5:16 NRSV.
[9]Prov 8:13 NETS.
[10]Prov 15:27 NETS (LXX).

[35:3] *Because he practiced deceit before him that he might find lawlessness in him and hate him.*[11]

He practiced deceit before himself. He hides the evil by deceit, knowing that if he does not conceal the transgression by means of deceit, when it is found out it produces aversion in the one who has found it and recognized it. Therefore, lest he be hated because of the transgression, he conceals it by means of deceit, for the one who finds it hates it.

You know that they also [232] often overshadow their evil deeds with plausible arguments, in order that they should remain hidden. For example, the false prophets, though they are "ravenous wolves"[12] in their intention, carry with themselves a sheepskin, in order that they may be regarded as sheep. And for what reason they desire to be known as sheep is clear, because they hate the disposition of the wolf but they conceal it, because when it is found out, it produces aversion. However, no one is so foolish as to say, "I love lawlessness and I hate piety"—for one who clings to piety and is delighted to do it does not wish to hate it—for when this is shown, it is shown that he also bears chastisement.

[35:4] *The words of his mouth are lawlessness and deceit.*

The words that he brings forth are lawless and deceitful. And when he sins morally by being intemperate, wrathful, and unrighteous, he has his words as lawlessness. And when he has erroneous opinions, he has them as deceit, for he acts deceptively lest the impiety of his words become clear, and they become trampled, and someone rejects them with disgust.

Question: Did he not say "transgression" instead of "lawlessness"?

Transgression is also *lawlessness*; lawlessness, however, is not always transgression in every way. When the one who does this is beside the law, is outside it, this is lawlessness. However, when, after receiving the law, he transgresses it, he acts beside the law, this is transgression. Transgression, therefore, is also lawlessness, but lawlessness is by no means always transgression.

From his habit, the one who acts beside the law and does things that make war against the law, as far as it depends on his actions, is judged. When, however, we look at the disposition of the one who acts, and the one who has received the law does not act according to it, he transgresses. And again, when <someone has no> knowledge of the law—I mean of the written law—he is merely lawless. "All who have sinned," it says, "under the law."[13] Those who sin under the law are transgressors. Those who have not had the law sin "apart from the law."[14] Nevertheless, that which is practiced is one and the same. From the choice and disposition of the one who acts I understand the difference so that sometimes it is called lawlessness, sometimes transgression.

[35:4] *He did not want to understand to do good.*

Lest anyone suppose that nature is what divides a servant of God from a transgressor and the virtuous from the wicked, he attributed both to the will and says that one is either wicked or virtuous as a consequence of his own will: *He did not want.*[15] Another, however, wants to understand to do good. The virtuous wants this very thing: to practice good things. Again, the one who is not in these things by

---

[11] The NRSV reads instead, "For they flatter themselves in their own eyes that their iniquity cannot be found out and hated."
[12] Mt 7:15 NRSV.
[13] Rom 2:12 NRSV.
[14] Rom 2:12 NRSV.
[15] This is a veiled reference to the Manichaeans.

his own desire has come outside these. Therefore, the word establishes the autonomy and freedom of the will, that no one is a transgressor because of his constitution, that no one is good merely in accordance with his essence, for all men are of one essence. And because of our choice or our neglect we are either wicked or virtuous.

[35:5] *He plotted lawlessness on his bed.*

He is saying the following: that he not only performs lawless deeds when he goes out and acts, but even after he has lain on his bed he plots lawlessness. It is necessary to imitate that man who is blessed, who meditates on the law of the Lord by day and by night: "Rather, his will is in the law of the Lord, and on his law he will meditate day and night."[16] The one who meditates day and night on the law of the Lord does not plot lawlessness on his bed but the law. It was said by Moses, the master of sacred truth, from the person of God, "And all these words that I command you today shall be in your heart and in your soul."[17] Then, "while going on the road and lying down and rising up."[18] If he speaks the words of God even while lying down, he does not plot lawlessness on his bed.

It is also possible to call the body the soul's "bed." Even when the soul is in a body, yet it already meditates on becoming free from it, by mortifying the body and subjecting it.[19] So, for example, it is said of those who have such an intention, "You are not in the flesh."[20] They certainly had flesh, but they were not under the control of the flesh's intention. "The mind that is set on the flesh is hostile to God."[21]

And again, "Those who are in the flesh cannot please God."[22] If he is speaking about this flesh, then all the saints who were in it did not please God. But to think according to the flesh in intention, to depend wholly on the flesh, is therefore to become fleshly. And who is the one who becomes fleshly besides the one who sells himself to sin? "But I am of the flesh, sold into slavery under sin."[23]

He plotted lawlessness on his bed. According to the elevated sense: *he plotted lawlessness* by means of *his bed*, the body. However, it was necessary, while remaining on this bed, for him to lament over himself and to weep because transgression is in his thought, [233] so that he says aloud, "With my tears I will drench my couch."[24] This is the voice of one who is repentant, and one who is repentant does not plot lawlessness. And of others it was said in Micah the Prophet, "He came devising troubles on his bed, and as soon as it was day he would execute them."[25] In the nights they often think about transgressions, and as soon as it is day they accomplish them. However, it is necessary to be repentant since at one time transgression has taken place on the bed, for the word commands the following: "Be angry and do not sin; what you say in your hearts, be repentant about it on your bed."[26] For when you are repentant, the devil finds no room.[27]

[35:5] *He was set on every way that was not good, and he was not indignant with vice.*

He avoided every good way. And "ways" are the virtues. And certainly the apostle says to Elymas the magician: "Will you not stop making crooked the straight paths of the

---

[16]Ps 1:2 NETS.
[17]Cf. Deut 6:6 NETS.
[18]Cf. Deut 6:7 NETS.
[19]Cf. 1 Cor 9:27.
[20]Rom 8:9 NRSV.
[21]Rom 8:7 NRSV.

[22]Rom 8:8 NRSV.
[23]Rom 7:14 NRSV.
[24]Ps 6:6 (6:7 NETS).
[25]Mic 2:1.
[26]Ps 4:4 (4:5).
[27]Cf. Eph 4:27.

Lord?"[28] They are straight and good. And the virtues are called "straight" because they are means, for there is no deviation in something straight. "God knows the ways on the right, but those on the left are twisted."[29]

And it is also well said that the way was *not good*, for he did not say "evil." What is *not good* is not definitely evil. It is impossible for someone to present himself to *every* evil path, because there are oppositions even in respect to vice. The cowardly person cannot also be rash, nor can the impious person be superstitious. These, then, are *not good*. They are the same things by way of negation, but not the same things by way of affirmation. *He was not indignant with vice.*

[35:6] *O Lord, your mercy is in heaven, and your truth as far as the clouds.*

Of those who inhabit the earth, we say of their way of thinking, "Their minds are set on earthly things."[30] These God the Word accuses in the prophet Jeremiah and says, "You made your dwelling deep in the earth."[31] If it is possible, you even desire to be below the earth, thinking of nothing elevated, not having "citizenship in heaven,"[32] not having your heart there with those who say, "Let us lift up our heart to the High One in heaven."[33] Therefore, the following is also said of some: "But they sought my soul in vain; they will enter into the lowest parts of the earth."[34] And Moses also, in the song of victory against Pharaoh and those with him, was saying, "You extended your right hand; the earth swallowed them."[35] Nevertheless, according to the narrative, the earth had not swallowed them but the water. Indeed, it is said, "They sank at once like lead in violent water."[36] And indeed, when God extends his right hand against the wicked, they are swallowed by the earth: they become wholly earthly, they are handed over "to degrading passions,"[37] they are given over "in the lusts of their hearts to impurity"[38] to serve "the creature rather than the Creator."[39]

In heaven, then, is *his mercy*, for "you do mercy to thousands, for those who love you."[40] As by a kind of ladder of mercy one ascends into heaven, for the nature of God's mercy belongs not to things below but to things above. Therefore, even if the goodness of God sometimes comes on the earth, that is among men—for it was said, "the earth is full of the Lord's mercy"[41]—those who are the objects of his mercy are raised by his mercy into heaven.

"*And as far as the clouds*," he says, "is *your truth*." One should not follow the opinion of those who take away divine providence from the earth and say that it is confined to the borders of the moon because it says, "Your truth is as far as the clouds." "Clouds" are the prophets, who administer to us spiritual rain, the spiritual rain by which the paradise of God is watered, the seed that fell into the good ground, which Jesus sowed so that it might become a hundred times as much, a hundredfold, sixtyfold, and thirtyfold.[42] Therefore, as far as these clouds that administer the spiritual rain, of whom it has been said, "Let the clouds shower down righteousness,"[43] is the truth of God. If someone is a cloud, because he is capable of pouring out spiritual rain and righteousness, that one has the truth of God.

---

[28]Acts 13:10 NRSV.
[29]Prov 4:27 NETS (LXX).
[30]Phil 3:19 NRSV.
[31]Cf. Jer 49:8 (29:9).
[32]Phil 3:20.
[33]Lam 3:41.
[34]Ps 63:9 (62:10 LES2).
[35]Ex 15:12 NETS.
[36]Cf. Ex 15:10 NETS.
[37]Rom 1:26 NRSV.
[38]Rom 1:24 NRSV.
[39]Rom 1:25 NRSV.
[40]Cf. Deut 5:10.
[41]Ps 119:64 (118:64).
[42]Cf. Mt 13:8, 23; Mk 4:8, 20; Lk 8:8.
[43]Is 45:8 NETS.

[35:7] *Your righteousness is like the mountains of God.*

The *mountains of God* are interpreted in many ways in Scripture. When it says, "You yourself wondrously give light from everlasting mountains,"[44] he calls the saints "everlasting mountains," who look no longer at things that are seen, which are temporal, but at things that are unseen, which are eternal.

"Draw near to the everlasting mountains!"[45] These perceptible mountains are not eternal. And if earth and heaven disappear, the excretions and the parts of the earth, the mountains, pass away with it, they disappear with it, so that those mountains are not eternal. However, as many as look to the eternal things, the invisible things [234], the higher things, the things that are most high, those having an elevation of their way of life are mountains, having the sublimity of a pious way of thought. "Draw near," then, "to the everlasting mountains," draw near in disposition, assume the same lofty way of thinking with those ones.

However, it is possible to say that the mountains of God, according to another interpretation, are all the higher places on which the ninety-nine sheep remain when Jesus came to save the one that went astray from the mountains, the sheep that fell down from there and appeared in wandering, persecution, and death.[46]

Your righteousness, therefore, *is like the mountains of God*. Righteousness among men, whenever it will exalt those who possess it, makes them like the mountains of God.

According to another explanation, it is possible to say that those whom he saved are the *righteousness* of the Savior who appeared. For "for our sake he made him to be sin who knew no sin, so that in him we might become the righteousness of God."[47] Those who became the righteousness of God in the one who became sin for our sake are like the mountains of God, like the angels, like the archangels, for they were united to the creation on high.

O Lord, your mercy is in heaven, and your truth as far as the clouds.

God has mercy in one way, and men have mercy in another. Indeed, the mercy that is produced by men and the useful service to the neighbor is human, for they understand how to help, to feed, and to do the rest only in a human way, and this mercy, in any case, draws near to the earth, that is, to things human. However, when God has mercy he raises those who are lifted up so that he leads them up into heaven. *In heaven*, indeed, *is your mercy*.

And it is also possible to say this: when you are merciful, you are not merciful in a human way. For even if you "give nourishment to all flesh,"[48] even if you bestow health on the sick, yet this righteousness does not touch heaven. And in order to speak more plainly: that which touches on the grace of God concerns not only the righteous but also the wicked, both the rational and the irrational; it is not heavenly. And those things alone belong to heaven and escort outsiders into heaven, which are truly good . . .[49] And in another psalm you have, "The earth is full of the Lord's mercy."[50] He has mercy on the earth by sending down that mercy, which is suited to those on earth. And the mercy that "he does to thousands, for those who love him,"[51] is heavenly and raises into heaven.

And it is possible here to say that heaven is the rational essence, the existence endowed with intelligence, for some have understood

---

[44]Ps 76:4 (75:5).
[45]Mic 2:9 LXX.
[46]Cf. Mt 18:12-13.
[47]2 Cor 5:21 NRSV.
[48]Ps 136:25 (135:25).
[49]The text is corrupt here.
[50]Ps 119:64 (118:64).
[51]Deut 5:10.

the word, "in the beginning God made the heaven and the earth"[52] in this way, where "the earth" signifies the more bodily existence and essence, and "the heaven" signifies the rational one. So is it said in other places as well: "The heaven of the heavens is the Lord's."[53] And "heaven" cannot be this one that appears, which is in our view only, but all of it. And the "heaven of heaven," being divided sevenfold, is the divine condition, for God is said to be in heaven not because he is in a place. Indeed, it is said in the Gospel, "No one has ascended into heaven except the one who descended from heaven, the Son of Man."[54] Only Jesus descended from that which is truly heaven, that is, from the condition that is appropriate to God, from the contemplation, as it were, of God.

For example, the devil happened to be in heaven, for he fell down from there with those who blasphemed and were incited by him. Indeed, it is said to him, "You said, 'I will ascend to heaven.'"[55] Being in heaven, how does he ascend to heaven? He was in heaven, in that place where the other divine and blessed essences are. Deciding to become "like the Most High,"[56] he called likeness to the Most High "heaven." Correspondingly, only God is in that which is called "heaven," not because it is a place, or a kind of body, or a creature, but a condition, as it were, God's condition, God's contemplation.

Therefore, the one who receives a desire of being God proposes vanity, that it is possible "to ascend above the clouds and to set his throne above the stars and to become like the Most High."[57] Especially because he said, "I will be like the Most High," it was necessary for him to understand that likeness to the Most Hight is not possible in the future. And he bears the same existence without any limit: the same one is from infinity past and into infinity future, without beginning and without end. And the one who says, "I will be like him," indicated that he was not like him earlier. And the one who is like him not will never be just as God is. Therefore, the deed rose up in him as far as his desire, and he fell away even from the heaven that was at hand to him, for he was in heaven in a different sense. And after he said, "I will ascend [235] into heaven," he fell down from the heaven that he did possess. For "how did the Day Star, which rises early in the morning, fall from heaven?"[58] By saying, "How did he fall?" he showed that he was in heaven, and by saying, "I will ascend into heaven, and I will be," he showed that he desired to come into another heaven.

It is good to understand the *clouds* in conformity with "heaven." We were saying yesterday that the word *clouds* often signifies divine natures, for when God speaks about Israel as though it is a vineyard, and because it produced thorns instead of grapes—instead of the appropriate fruit they produced shameful desires, and these the Savior called "thorns"—he says, "I will command the clouds not to wet it with rain."[59] This rain, however, is not perceptible, for which reason neither are the clouds that flow into it. Indeed, it was said, "Let the clouds shower down righteousness!"[60] Righteousness, however, rains and descends from clouds that are not perceptible.

And I will say something extraordinary: there is a kind of truth that does not primarily reside with God. Paul says, "the truth of Jesus is in me,"[61] as though there is another truth that is not strictly called "the truth of Jesus"; for all things are his, he is the Creator of them

---

[52] Gen 1:1 NETS.
[53] Ps 115:16 (113:24 LES2).
[54] Jn 3:13 NRSV.
[55] Cf. Is 14:13 NETS.
[56] Is 14:14 NETS.
[57] Cf. Is 14:13-14.

[58] Is 14:12.
[59] Is 5:6.
[60] Is 45:8 NETS.
[61] Cf. 2 Cor 11:10.

all. His creatures, however, because they are knowable, have an innate knowledge and truth that someone can understand from what is knowable. So there is a truth, for example, in grammar, and in geometry, and in the other sciences. He is not, then, calling that truth the "truth of Jesus," not that it is also not his: for the knowable things, by which come knowledge and truth, are his creatures.

And I say: let a certain inventor devise a clock. There is, no doubt, a knowledge in the thing that was devised according to which it has come into existence, for by having the knowledge of the inventor, he devised it. And there is a truth in the device, when it maintains its proportions in the very manner by which it is a perfect clock. Therefore, if someone should receive that knowledge from that visible clock, he would have the knowledge of the one who invented it. And the clock is indeed an intermediate between these two characters: both of the one who has made it and of the one who became knowledgeable about it from observing it.

Let us consider by way of example: those who are knowledgeable know what they know, not insofar as they are simply knowledgeable but insofar as they strive to be so, and they know things as they are when they ascend to the very limit and end of knowledge. Therefore that progression toward all things could be called the knowledge and truth of the knowledgeable person, not that it does not belong to God and is only elementary, for this is gained for the sake of the truth of God. The prototype and the whole form of the truth is the Savior, and it is possible to partake of this truth. The one who partook received a condition called "truth," of which the saint said, "The truth is in me,"[62] and, "I did not conceal your truth in my heart."[63] This other truth has appeared, because the seal that is made in wax or some other material comes from the truth of the original signet ring.

Certainly, a certain difference is still found with respect to another quality that is, so to speak, more human. The quality itself does not receive amplitude and diminishment in itself. However, it receives these things in the one who has the quality. And that which receives and that which does not receive are not identical. They are somehow different and yet not different. And if someone has become a certain quality by habit and disposition, he receives amplitude and diminishment. And this can be seen by itself: for the one who desires to see a quality with precision does not understand this very quality from the one who has the quality, but from the quality itself he knows the one who has it to have been made so.

[35:7] *Your judgments are a great abyss.*

Among men a great contrast is found both in their external circumstances and in the states that come from their disposition. One can find a contrast because of external things. Some are rich while others are poor; some are rulers while others are subjects; some are healthy while others are sick. Correspondingly, these things also apply to their habits: some are, as it were, sharp in soul, and others lazy in nature, and some are conspicuous for virtue, and others for vice.

And great is the difference between these! For no one among men is in perfect virtue, even if someone strives toward this, even if he progresses in it. And where there is amplitude and diminishment, there is a great infinitude. So too vice. And it is good to say: virtue, even though it receives increase and diminishment, will at some time come to the end, when there is not a more virtuous than the virtuous, a wiser than the wise. Vice, however, is always within an infinitude. It does not have an end at all: For how is it possible for there to be one

---

[62]Cf. 2 Cor 11:10.
[63]Ps 40:10 (39:11).

end when vice itself is discordant and diverse? There is an infinitude in excess and insufficiency, but in the golden mean a certain fixed end is received.

Since, then, we humans do not have the ability to say, even if some do—for they do not seem to have knowledge—why a certain man is poor and another wealthy [236]—for it is as when you say, "It is more or less incomprehensible." We often say that God, considering that such a person, if he finds wealth or honor, becomes proud and tramples on all, does not give it to them, and then we find such people walking erect and having wealth in every way. Likewise also in the case of health and in the case of the motions of the soul, we say that the difference between these comes by the decision of God. And that it comes by God's decision, let us understand the passage from the Gospel and let us clarify it, if it is possible for someone to be led by the hand to this narrative. The Savior says in the Gospel: "Woe to you, Chorazin! Woe to you, Bethsaida! For if the miracles done in you had been done in Tyre and Sidon, they would have repented long ago, sitting in sackcloth and ashes."[64] If the extraordinary miracles had been done among the Sidonians and the Tyrians, they would have been provoked to repentance. The cities that were mentioned, Bethsaida and Tyre, experienced these things—why have the extraordinary miracles appeared there, where they did not repent? The statement is like an abyss. The apostle called the judgments of God "incomprehensible."[65] No one examines them; no one can comprehend their depth. Examining with difficulty the things that are done and the things that are decided, as it were, we receive a vision that God is the one who judges and orders each thing. And we cannot say in each case why such a person, for example, is strong and another is weak. We do not have the ability to speak about them individually.

And as I once said that healing is circular, and if someone takes each remedy by itself, he appears to take it while he is being deluded sometimes, and he accuses the physician. And he would understand it well, if he should understand why certain other remedies appeared before it, and certain others will be after it, and until when it is so that his health might return. However, one who is not a physician cannot comprehend this.

Therefore we receive a vision about them so that we always understand also that these judgments come by God's decision.

Your judgments, then, are not simply *an abyss*, but a *great* one. Now, what is simply *an abyss* undoubtedly has depth, it even has its depth as indefinite, but how much more one that is *great*. And he indicates an emphasis by the word *great*, as he also indicates the "incomprehensibility" of the judgments. In other psalms it was spoken about this. Speaking about God, the psalmist was saying, "The deep like a garment is his clothing."[66] And in another, "And he made darkness his concealment."[67] It speaks about obscurity and incomprehensibility. Being hidden, this darkness of obscurity, of incomprehensibility, is also a garment that is like an abyss.

[35:7] *Men and animals you will save, O Lord.*

He saves *men and animals*. And if we understand *animals* in the usual sense, we also understand those who are perceptibly *men*. And he governs them all, both the rational and the irrational animals, the rational in accordance with themselves, and the irrational since they existed because of the rational, for the irrational fulfill the needs of the rational. They carry loads for them, they draw the plow,

---

[64]Lk 10:13; Mt 11:21.
[65]Cf. Rom 11:33.
[66]Ps 104:6 (103:6 NETS).
[67]Ps 18:11 (17:12).

they provide service in another way. Then, since even these can succumb to harm and death, he saves them as well. He also saves men. *Men, then, and animals you will save, O Lord.* The same incomprehensibility of judgment is also found in these things again, because on the one hand he saves all men, but he does so differently: some after great suffering, others with a kind of rest and joy.

However, if he is saying that men are saved with what is truly salvation and prays about that which has been said, that the Savior "became the source of eternal salvation for all who obey him"[68]—the saint, contemplating this meaning, was saying, "Our God is a God who saves"[69]—then the animals here one must understand allegorically. For of those who have drawn near to piety and to the very instruction of the gospel, some are called "disciples" and others "sheep": "My sheep hear my voice."[70] They hear only a voice. And the voice is the obvious explanation of the Scriptures, which approaches and strikes the soul and its hearing, but not its intellect. Therefore, his sheep hear the voice of Jesus like a perfect and true Shepherd.

And when he says to some, "You call me Teacher and Lord—and you are right, for that is what I am,"[71] I am truly a teacher. And I am your Lord, for you serve me by keeping my laws—these are not sheep [237] but disciples, disciples of wisdom, disciples of truth. And the sheep are sheep of the Shepherd. And there is another respectful conception of the Savior's being himself a shepherd. Since he desires to save and to improve all people, and the salvation and improvement is accomplished when it happens according to the habit of the one who is capable of being helped, according to what he is capable of, he calls some listeners only to his voice, and other listeners to his word, his teaching. Therefore he saves those who are called men in this way and animals. And he also saves sheep in order that they might be sheep no longer but should become men instead of sheep. Indeed, the Twenty-Second Psalm hints at this in riddles. "The Lord," it says, "shepherds me, and nothing will be lacking for me. In a place of grass, there he made me encamp; by water of rest he reared me."[72] He speaks as a sheep. He reports with thanksgiving the things that took place from the Shepherd. Then he says, "He restored my soul. He led me."[73] And after a brief space he adds, "You prepared a table before me."[74] There is no longer a place of grass, no longer a pasture, no longer is he led to pasture, but there is a table on which is set "the Bread of life,"[75] "the Bread that came down from heaven,"[76] the flesh of Jesus, the true food.[77] And after the progression of the table he also partakes of a cup,[78] which Wisdom, "who mixed her own wine,"[79] first drank. It is your cup, since you drink it before me, and it is my cup, since you have measured out for me what I am capable of drinking.

[35:8] *How you increased your mercy, O God!*

Men are also saved by God's *mercy*. And the mercy of God is *increased* and his liberality appears at that time when he saves animals as well. As when you talk about a perfect teacher, because his goodness is made known when he instructs wise and perfect listeners, and his goodness is increased when he even condescends to the foolish, when he attempts to lead them to a better condition. So, for example,

---

[68]Heb 5:9 NRSV.
[69]Ps 68:20 (67:21 LES2).
[70]Jn 10:27 NRSV.
[71]Jn 13:13 NRSV.
[72]Ps 23:1-2 (22:1-2).
[73]Ps 23:3 (22:3).
[74]Ps 23:5 (22:5 NETS).
[75]Jn 6:35, 48.
[76]Jn 6:41.
[77]Jn 6:55.
[78]Cf. Ps 23:5 (22:5).
[79]Prov 9:2.

the teacher of Christianity is "a debtor both to Greeks and to barbarians."[80] He is a debtor not only to the wise but also to the foolish. And to the wise "he speaks wisdom among the mature,"[81] and to the foolish he does not speak wisdom, but he extends those instructions that detach them from their foolishness, in order that, by no longer being foolish, they might receive wisdom at last. Again to the Greeks, to those who have a Greek mind, which is exacting and able to comprehend, he speaks as to Greeks. And to those who are barbarians in soul he says those things that detach them from their barbaric tribe, from such thought that is more uncultivated.

[35:8] *But the sons of men will hope in the shelter of your wings.*

The *sons of* these *men*. So, if according to the former interpretation "the mortal, rational animals," men, and the animals that serve them are mentioned, then the sons of these men have hope *in the shelter of* God's *wings.*

These *wings* are intelligible, elevating the intellect. So indeed the saint says, "Who will give me wings like a dove?"[82] We do not speak in this manner: that he prays for the wings of a perceptible creature to be given to him, for this is impossible. And one cannot desire impossible things nor pray for them. "As an eagle yearned for his young."[83] At that time they were given wings, they were able to be received "on God's back."[84] And what is there for us to do to be so furnished with wings? Hear what the prophet Isaiah says: "Those who wait for God shall change their strength; they shall grow wings like eagles; they shall run and not be weary."[85] And another prays,

saying, "Your youth will be renewed like an eagle's."[86] Indeed, whenever the saint says that he has become winged, it is necessary to understand the wings of this one as virtue, understanding, and wisdom, for these things raise the man heavenward.

They are sheltered under God's wings. Their shelter comes from God's wings. And they are sheltered then, in order that they should put on wings, in order that they should be made to hatch, since they became eggs under God's wings. Now, eggs are unformed souls that did not yet receive the formation of Christ. So whenever they have appeared under his wings, then they are formed and they become living creatures, in an allegorical sense, in the inner man.

He does not say the following: "sons of the mortal animals," but of those who truly preserve the man who is "in the image and likeness"[87] of God. Furthermore, it is possible that the phrase "sons of men" is spoken periphrastically instead of "men."

[35:9] *They will be intoxicated with the fatness of your house.* [238]

Not every intoxication is reproachable. "Do not get drunk with wine," it says, "in which is debauchery."[88] And in the usual sense it is possible that excessive drinking has been called the wine of debauchery, for it damages the good senses and sometimes makes the person fall into sin. Therefore, this intoxication is reproachable.

And of those who are of false opinions and introduce impious doctrines, offering them like food and wine, it is said, "These people eat the bread of impiety."[89] And because those ones eat and seek out the bread of impiety, they are the ones of whom it has been said,

---

[80]Rom 1:14 NRSV.
[81]1 Cor 2:6.
[82]Ps 55:6 (54:7 NETS).
[83]Deut 32:11.
[84]Cf. Deut 32:11 LXX.
[85]Is 40:31 NETS.

[86]Ps 103:5 (102:5 NETS).
[87]Gen 1:26.
[88]Eph 5:18.
[89]Prov 4:17 NETS.

"You gave him as food to the Ethiopian peoples."[90] For as those who accept the doctrines of piety are fed by the body of Christ, so those who feed on impious doctrines and drink the wine appropriate to this food, the wine of debauchery, eat the flesh of the dragon, of the devil himself. "Do not get drunk with wine," then, "in which is debauchery."[91] And it is characteristic of the impious to drink such wine, "for they will get drunk with illicit wine."[92]

However, there is also a praiseworthy intoxication, in order that I should say as others have said, a "sober" intoxication, making those who have drunk to be sober-minded. For example, in the Song of Songs Jesus began to address his companions, "Eat, drink, and become drunk, brothers!"[93] God the Word says these things to his own brothers, for after he became man he began to have brothers who conducted themselves as he did, who received his teachings and were adopted as sons. "Eat," then, "drink, and become drunk!" Eat the spiritual food which Wisdom prepared for you, for "she prepared her own table."[94] And drink that wine which leads to an intoxication that is sober.

And here, then, he did not speak in an absolute sense, but he said, *"They will be intoxicated with the fatness of your house."* According to one interpretation the church is called "the house of God," for it is said to Timothy by Paul, "If I delay, I wrote to you how you ought to behave in the house of God, which is the church of the living God."[95] The fatness of this house is the perfect instruction, the wisdom spoken among the mature,[96] "the solid food," of which they partake, "whose faculties," belonging to the inner man, "have been trained by practice to distinguish good from evil."[97] And these drink the wine that is harvested from "the true Vine."[98] These, then, are intoxicated with the fatness of God's house. The fatness of this house of God is the perfect teaching, the complete knowledge of the truth.

However, if you also call the Savior's Man a house, since he says, "Destroy this temple,"[99] "and he was saying this about the temple of his body,"[100] not that he had only a body as his temple, but that this part of the temple was able to be destroyed by man.... Certainly, he received the destruction of the temple only in relation to the body. And when he says, "I lay down my soul, in order to take it up again,"[101] he does not say, "Destroy my soul."

Therefore I was calling such a thing a paradox once, when he lays down his soul in order to take it up again, "and no one takes it from him, but he himself has the power to lay it down and to take it up."[102] Observe why: life was not taken away from him by a common death. And indeed, those who were crucified together with him were cut off in their legs in order that they should die. Then, even though the Savior did not suffer this, he was found to have died. Then "he bowed his head and gave up his spirit."[103] However, if no one took his soul, but he himself laid it down of his own accord in order to take it up again, this happened in this manner, as it says in one of the psalms, "I became as a helpless person, free among the dead."[104]

And indeed, according to the usual sense, we will say that those who depart with sins

---

[90] Ps 74:14 (73:14 NETS). The Greek takes 'am laṣiyyim to mean the people of the steppes or the wilderness, i.e., the Ethiopians (see Ps 71:9). The Hebrew does not designate a nation.
[91] Eph 5:18.
[92] Prov 4:17.
[93] Song 5:1 LES2.
[94] Prov 9:2 NETS.
[95] Cf. 1 Tim 3:14-15.
[96] Cf. 1 Cor 2:6.
[97] Heb 5:14 NRSV.
[98] Jn 15:1.
[99] Jn 2:19.
[100] Jn 2:21.
[101] Jn 10:17.
[102] Cf. Jn 10:18.
[103] Jn 19:30 NRSV.
[104] Ps 88:4-5 (87:5-6 LES2).

and "are constrained by the cords of their own sins"[105] are not free dead people. Therefore, since Jesus committed no sin nor knew it,[106] he was free among the dead. Only this soul appeared there as free. And indeed, the guardians of the gate of Hades shrank before it in fear.

In a second sense, he became "free among the dead" in this way: all who depart life and leave the body, when they are virtuous, are led by the hand by the illuminating angels, while others are taken away by certain punishers. So is it said, "The poor man died and was carried away by the angels to Abraham's bosom."[107] The soul has not gone there by itself, but angels have carried it off. And to another, who loves life, it is said, "You fool! This very night they demand your soul from you!"[108] When his soul is demanded and it is carried off by certain punishers into Hades, only the soul of Jesus went forth free: neither did it need angels to guide it, nor was it dragged away, since it has no reasons for being dragged off. This, then, is to lay down and take up the soul, and "No one takes it from me," he says. "I have power to lay it down in order to take it up again."[109]

The divine instruction [**239**] from the Savior, after he became man, is the fatness of the house. And here is the paradox: things that are said from the side of the spiritual, the intelligible, are not paradoxical. Things that exist in a perceptible way are not something else as perceptible things. However, that which is intelligible can also be understood in a perceptible way. Therefore, in perception, it is impossible to receive the same person as a high priest and a lamb. Jesus, however, is both lamb and high priest. It is impossible, in a perceptible sense, to understand the same one as a door and a house. Jesus, however, is both, both a door leading into the house and that house into which the door enters. And all intelligible things in general are like this. And indeed, we say of the soul of man that it cultivates itself, that it is on the other hand the tree, that it is a land that receives seeds and bears fruit, and that it becomes a bride of God the Word and bears children of salvation. And it also becomes a sheep. And we receive profit because of the different conceptions and names. When the soul is called "land," the potent instructions are in a certain way seeds, and when it is called a "bride," the seeds are what is sown in her, and the adornments around her are the practical and moral virtues, as well as the contemplative and perfect ones. Again when she is called a "sheep," the teachings are called a "pasture," the instructions are called "grass." So everything is able to be one thing and something else at the same time.

This, however, must also be understood: the so-called house is also the vine that produces wine, and again it is the flesh that nourishes, and it is the gardener who cares for the trees, in order that they will bear fruit. And see that he is both gardener and vine, both shepherd and sheep. When these things are understood according to different conceptions, they show that it is an intelligible essence of which these things are said. Once, indeed, when a Greek was asking, "From what place are you able to show from your Scripture that, for example, the soul is intelligible? For all that is reported about it also indicates the properties of bodies," I said this very thing in response: "Inasmuch as each of the bodies has one form, it is that according to which it is. But when something is said to be everything by participation, it is nothing perceptible. God is spoken of, the spirit is spoke of, light is spoken of, as though it were fashioned as a man and had members. A spirit certainly does not have members. God does not have sitting and arising, feet and the rest. From this it is

---

[105] Prov 5:22.
[106] Cf. 1 Pet 2:22; 2 Cor 5:21.
[107] Lk 16:22.
[108] Lk 12:20.
[109] Jn 10:18.

established that the essences about which these things are said are certain intelligible ones."

[35:9] *And you will give them drink from the torrent of your delight.*

The gushing fatness of the house, in addition to the drinking, can also lead to a sober intoxication. By *torrent of delight* he speaks in the sense that it is said, that "a river of delight goes out of Eden and waters paradise."[110] The abundance of teaching, of the participation in instruction, is called a *torrent of delight*. *You will give them to drink*. And it is well said, *you will give them to drink*, since after this torrent they also arrive at the source itself. Like infants, they are given drink, and to quote from the apostolic passage, Paul writes to those who are novices, "I gave you milk to drink."[111] And those who cannot drink by themselves are given drink; those who are being instructed are given drink. When they are watered from this river of delight, at last they come to life itself, from which this river flows: *because with you is the source of life*,[112] since the source of life is with you. He did not say, "the source of life will be," but "the source of life is with you." He is the *source of life* perpetually. Indeed when those who are given to drink abound, then he flows, and this stream comes from the source, being called a *torrent of delight*.

[35:10] *Because with you is the source of life; in your light we will see light.*

Observe here the source again. He has spoken in two ways. The light has also been called "source." In the literal sense, however, and in corporeal opinion, these things cannot be. And when what is good flows from him and he does not receive them from somewhere, like a reservoir, then he is the head, he is the fountain of life. And what am I saying? He himself used to say, "I am the life."[113] Now, to say "life" and "source of life" is the same thing. Life indeed, since it makes alive and leads into immortality, is also a source, since it receives that which makes alive not from somewhere else, but it has them within itself.

In your light we will see light.

Now, if this expression may be directed [240] to the Father, it says the following: since the one who has seen your Son, who is the true light, sees you who are light, by your light we will see you who are light, for "whoever has seen the Son has seen the Father."[114] And he is "the image of the invisible God,"[115] showing the one whose image he is, and he is "the exact imprint of God's very being,"[116] manifesting God's being. *In your light*, then, *we will see light*. And if this may be directed to the Son, by your shining instruction and teaching we will see you, being light.

Where he says, *Prolong, O God, your mercy to those who know you*,[117] he speaks of that knowledge about which it is said: "And this is eternal life, that they know you, the only true God."[118] These ones who have knowledge are loved by God. And God "does mercy to thousands, for those who love him."[119] We understand the phrase "to thousands," in this way: this number has a kinship with the One. Therefore, those who draw near to God, to the One, even becoming "one spirit with him,"[120] consequently become thousands and ten thousands. But this is said like this: "The chariotry of God is ten thousand strong,

---

[110] Cf. Gen 2:10.
[111] 1 Cor 3:2.
[112] Ps 36:9 (35:10).
[113] Jn 11:25; 14:6.
[114] Cf. Jn 14:9.
[115] Col 1:15 NRSV.
[116] Heb 1:3 NRSV.
[117] Ps 36:10 (35:11).
[118] Jn 17:3.
[119] Deut 5:10.
[120] 1 Cor 6:17 NRSV.

thousands of those flourishing."[121] For we do not understand the "thousand" in this way, as ten hundreds, but because of the kinship that it has with the One. And mercy comes to them. Therefore, if the compassion of God extends to the thousands, as it is said, "for his mercy endures forever,"[122] clearly he is saying here, "Prolong your mercy to those who know you." In another way he has mercy on those who approach him in the manner of repentance, on those who seek the forgiveness of sins. He has mercy on those who know him so that they may be strengthened and may rise up to the end that is beyond all the others.

[35:11] *And your righteousness to the upright in heart.*

Now, the upright in heart and the pure in heart are the same. Therefore, it is an excellence that belongs to the pure in heart to see God, for "Blessed are the pure in heart, for they will see God."[123]

[35:12] *Let the foot of arrogance not come to me, and let not the hand of sinners shake me.*

Let not the *foot of arrogance* enter into my mind, that is, let not a path of arrogance come into me, for often limbs are said in place of the best and the worst ways of life. For example, in Proverbs it is said, "for the feet of folly bring down those who deal with her, to Hades with death."[124] As many as proceed according to folly by dealing with the feet of folly are brought down into Hades. Therefore, as are the feet of folly, so also is the foot of arrogance. *Let the foot of arrogance*, therefore, *not come to me*: let not a path of arrogance come into my soul and my mind.

And let not the hand of sinners shake me. Now, the deed is often called a "hand," as when it says, "Thorns grow in the hand of the drunkard,"[125] shameful desires, intemperate pleasures.

[35:13] *There those who practice lawlessness fell.*

Where the *foot of arrogance* and the *hand of the sinner* are, *there those who practice lawlessness fell*. Nature did not lead them into the fall, but the activity and the practice of lawlessness.

[35:13] *They were thrust out and will surely never be able to stand.*

For since they themselves brought themselves down to the foot of arrogance, and they are handed over to the hand of the sinner, which they preferred to have, this handing over is also called their expulsion. And God, who does what is beneficial, expels them, lest they become able to remain in evil. Therefore, even though nature or a kind of compulsion does not overthrow him, yet his practice does, because it is lawlessness and vice. Therefore God expels him, lest he remain, lest he have his condition immovably in vice.

And indeed, it is necessary to clarify the Scriptures on a higher level. And the one who is truly wise in God does this. Nevertheless, if they might not be clarified in this way but in an inferior way, neither is their grandeur displayed, nor the greatness of the one who has given them. The Jews, indeed, receiving them in the common and human way, are said "not to understand either what they are saying or the things about which they make assertions."[126] **[241]**[127]

---

[121] Ps 68:17 (67:18).
[122] Ps 106:1 (105:1).
[123] Mt 5:8 NRSV.
[124] Prov 5:5 NETS.
[125] Prov 26:9 NETS.
[126] Cf. 1 Tim 1:7 NRSV.
[127] Lincoln Blumell, *Didymus the Blind's Commentary on Psalms 26:10–29:2 and 36:1-3*, Brigham Young University Papyri 1 (Turnhout: Brepols, 2019), resumes here.

PSALM 36 [37]

[36:1] *A psalm of David. Do not be provoked to jealousy with those acting wickedly.*

The one who enters into a struggle, when he runs toward victory and has a goal of overcoming this and obtaining it, endures every kind of pain for the sake of overcoming. Indeed, for this very reason the judges of the contest set out crowns beforehand, in order that the contestants, when they see them, should endure every pain. And since the knowledge of opposites is one and the same, the one who understands what this knowledge is and receives a desire for it knows what shame the vanquished incurs. And he does two things: he chooses victory, and he avoids the things that flee from victory, shame and the things that produce it. He is truly perfect who knows what is necessary to avoid. Therefore, the one who is prepared in this way must be strong so as to say, "I have fought the good fight; I have finished the race; I have kept the faith. At last the crown of victory is laid up for me,"[1] the voice of one who competed and completed the race, as therefore the one who strives for such success, for the perfection of the word, must do. Because of this it is necessary for such a disposition, which is detached from things that are harmful and produce what is inferior, which also strives for victory and the things that produce it—and the things that are productive of victory are the things of virtue—to be found in such a number.

For the number thirty-six is a perfect number, for it is six times six. Indeed, the numbers that are rolled up on themselves are perfect. It has been said that the number six is perfect, for a perfect number is the one composed by its own parts. This number six, after it is multiplied by itself, makes the number thirty-six. Therefore, it was necessary for the perfect person who was brought to such a state and such a disposition also to have arrived at such a degree. This squared number, which has six on each side, after it is multiplied in accordance with an amplification of one, becomes fifty-five, and the number fifty-five is a right triangle. And this figure indicates an incorporeal essence: therefore, the amount indicates that the one who is made perfect transcends bodies, gives no thought to temporal things, and has a longing for things that are unseen, because they are eternal. The number 36 is as follows: it can be halved, divided by 3, 4, 6, 9, 12, 18, and 36, and this renders the number 55.[2] From the parts of thirty-six, then, is this number composed. And observe how the sum arises: beginning from one, we always count by an increase of one from one until ten. See that the amplification climbs until ten. And the number one has the same relationship with ten as the ten has with one hundred, and as the one hundred has with one thousand. It was therefore necessary that the one who here authors the righteous psalm be found in relation to this number.

Do not be provoked to jealousy with those acting wickedly. When you see those who act wickedly having success, becoming rich, enjoying good health, *do not be provoked to*

---

[1] 2 Tim 4:7-8.

[2] That is, 18+12+9+6+4+3+2+1=55.

jealousy. The word "to become jealous" has this force. At times some provoked others to be jealous: whenever, therefore, they provoke to jealousy those whom they wish to imitate, those become jealous. For example, often some servant lives together with a married woman from the city, and the servant, wishing to corrupt her marriage, provokes the latter woman to jealousy. And she provokes her to jealousy at the time when she pretends to be with her husband. To be envious is one thing, and to be jealous is another. When a woman is an adulteress, the woman from the city, being prudent, does not imitate her; she is not provoked to jealousy so that she thinks about the same things and pretends. Therefore he is saying as follows: when at times you see people who act wickedly and commit lawlessness, do not become jealous so that you wish to imitate them. Those people, however, provoke you in order that you might imitate them. You, then, do not become jealous, do not become provoked.

Without a doubt, God also in a certain fashion provokes the synagogue of the Hebrews to jealousy. For when his separation took place and he dissolved the lawful nuptial bonds, he pronounces a calling of the Gentiles in order to provoke them to jealousy. Indeed, as many of those as were provoked to jealousy remained by a good jealousy "a remnant, chosen by grace."[3] And that this notion is strong, the reading also suggests: "They made me jealous with what are not gods, they provoked me with their idols. So I will make them jealous with what is not a nation, I will irritate them with a nation of impious ones."[4] "They made me jealous with what are not gods": they were established in order that I might be their God—and I am their God when they [242] are my people[5]—and since they began to hold onto idols so that God says, "They provoked me with foreign things; by their abominations they embittered me. They sacrificed to demons and not to God,"[6] they provoked God to jealousy. And he himself "makes them jealous with what is not a nation,"[7] that is, with what is not one nation, save that they were not a nation before their calling. Therefore, "I will make them jealous over what is not a nation," but for all who are called, all the Gentiles, he opened the doors of salvation.

Since, then, according to the preceding argument, they did not wish to dwell with God, but "as a woman is faithless toward her companion, so the house of Israel was faithless toward him,"[8] in order to provoke them to a good jealousy, he calls the church of the Gentiles. For by no means has the calling of the Gentiles taken place for the destruction of Israel, but for their arousal, since God imprisoned all in disobedience in order to have mercy on all: "for just as you were once disobedient to God"—and he is speaking these things now to the same people—"but have now been set free because of their disobedience, so they have now been disobedient in order that they too may be set free. For God imprisoned all in disobedience so that he may be merciful to all."[9]

And we have said at another time that we are accustomed to saying that those who are joined together in speaking have been imprisoned together, when it leads one to the opposite conclusion from what he desires. For he did not, as the heretics suppose, imprison them in order to disobey, but because they were disobedient he showed them to be so, and so a way has appeared for all to be saved. For no longer can someone contradict the words, "Do not be provoked to jealousy by those who do evil," by also mentioning the punishment of right imitation and jealousy. He immediately

---

[3] Rom 11:5 NRSV.
[4] Deut 32:21.
[5] Cf. 2 Cor 6:16.
[6] Deut 32:16-17 NETS.
[7] Deut 32:21.
[8] Jer 3:20.
[9] Rom 11:30-32.

established how it must be. *Hope in the Lord, and practice kindness.*[10] Do not become jealous when you are deprived of what you desire. Insofar as you believe them to be good, *hope in the Lord and practice kindness.* Here to be envious is to imitate, for when you are provoked to jealousy by those who do evil, you immediately envy *those who practice lawlessness.*

The one who practices lawlessness was harmed in his disposition; he has come outside goodness and for this reason he is called an "evildoer." Not everyone who desires evils also does them, nor does everyone who practices evil do it because he contrived it beforehand. For people do many things without premeditation, and the oracles call these "involuntary sins."[11] Therefore one must offer a sacrifice for these also.[12]

[36:2] *Because like grass they will quickly wither and like herbs of grass they will quickly dry up.*

It is possible that is was said of those who practice lawlessness, *like herbs of grass they will quickly fall,* and of those who do evils that *like grass they quickly wither.* Both expressions apply to both together, so that the evildoer dries up quickly like grass and like herbs quickly falls—and after they fall they certainly wither.

Often the thing that produces the punishment and the punishment have the same meaning. "If anyone destroys God's temple, God will destroy that person."[13] The one who destroys God's temple sins, and the destruction of God's temple is nothing other than to become subject to sin. And God will destroy this person who destroyed God's temple: God will punish him. And by the name "destruction" is the same punishment and the deed that bears the punishment; destruction has been shown in both ways. And it has been said again in the Gospel, "Fear him who can destroy soul and body in Gehenna."[14] Here destruction indicates punishment.

It is not the same thing for a man to die and for an evildoer to die. The man who dies has his soul sundered from his body; the evildoer, when he dies, does not die insofar as he is human, but insofar as he is an evildoer he casts off the life in wickedness, and it will be well with him. For since the soul, being mutable, changes little by little in adverse circumstances, some in one way and some in another, whenever it repels the adverse circumstance that is blameworthy, it receives its opposite, which is praiseworthy: "Turn away from evil and do good."[15] And I said the following: even if "heaven and earth shall pass away,"[16] "the word of the Lord remains forever."[17] The word according to which the flesh has become errant is that which passes away, but the word according to which it has come into being remains forever. Therefore, there will be a resurrection.

[36:3] *Hope in the Lord and practice kindness, and dwell in the land.*

You provoke to jealousy, and you are jealous, because you see sinners wealthy, glorified, and honored. Do not look only at things that are present. Hope, therefore, concerning things that are not present, that they exist, and practice kindness according to virtue, with confidence.

[245][18] [36:9] [*Because the evildoers shall be destroyed.*]

. . . so as to be brought to an end. But they are destroyed insofar as they are evil, in order that

---

[10]Ps 37:3 (36:3).
[11]Cf. Lev 5:17.
[12]Cf. Lev 5:17-19.
[13]1 Cor 3:17 NRSV.
[14]Mt 10:28.
[15]Ps 34:14 (33:15); 37:27 (36:27).
[16]Mt 24:35; Mk 13:31; Lk 21:33.
[17]1 Pet 1:25.
[18]Didymus the Blind, *Psalmenkommentar (Tura-Papyrus)*, vol. 4, *Kommentar zu Psalm 35–39*, ed. M. Gronewald, PTA 6 (Bonn: Rudolf Habelt, 1969), resumes here.

they should no longer be so. And it also indicates chastisement. And again the chastisement is a hindrance to vice.

[36:9] *But those who wait for the Lord—they shall inherit the land.*

Those who wait for the Lord inherit the already interpreted "land," which is in the height, which is in heaven. And this, David was saying: "I believe, in order that I may see the good things of the Lord in the land of the living."[19] He was a king. And it is customary for a king to possess the good things of his own land and to rule over it. No one, however, believes in order to receive what he already possesses, but he believes that he has received it. However, this one says, "I believe in order that I may see," not "that I have received" those "good things," which God gives "to those who ask him"[20] when they pray about them genuinely.

Those who wait for the Lord, then, *will inherit the land*. Perseverance is the greatest reward for virtue. "Suffering produces perseverance."[21] You see that perseverance comes after suffering. Therefore, that one waits for the Lord—as is necessary for one who has perseverance—for none other than him. And as wisdom comes to some, and righteousness, and sanctification, so also perseverance. So says this David himself in another psalm: "And now, what is my endurance? Is it not the Lord?"[22] Those who compete for virtue and piety always strive to have this perseverance. The singer himself again says somewhere, "Waiting, I waited for the Lord."[23] I did not simply "wait," but I did so "waiting," just as, "You shall pursue justice justly."[24]

The servants of God have an inheritance. And understand the paradox: it is characteristic for children to inherit, not servants. The surpassing goodness of the one who is being succeeded in the inheritance, just as it is fitting to their condition and nature, leads those who are servants into an inheritance. And I once used this saying as an example: "By grace you have been saved through faith, not of works."[25] And I was saying that it is not completely impossible to have faith without works, for "faith without works is dead."[26] He says then, "through faith, not of works." And I was giving such an example: whenever there is a person who loves humanity, in return for what some work for and what service they provide, he gives them a wage that exceeds the value of their compensation. I also took such an example: let there be a certain landowner and let him have entrusted his farm to someone, and let him say to him, "If you should care for it as is necessary and work it as is appropriate, I would give it to you as a gift. Take it as an inheritance." We say that that person did not receive the inheritance because of works but because of the grace of the one who bestowed it. "There is an inheritance for those who serve the Lord."[27]

[36:10] *Yet a little while, and the sinner will be no more.*

He is saying the following: *Do not be provoked to jealousy with evildoers, nor envy those who do lawlessness.*[28] God created you as a living creature who loves the good. And it is characteristic of those who love good not to desire what is temporal and present, for things temporal and present are also the possessions of sinners. Therefore, do not become jealous of him, when he is rich, when he is healthy, for he

---

[19] Ps 27:13 (26:13 NETS).
[20] Mt 7:11 NRSV.
[21] Rom 5:3.
[22] Ps 39:7 (38:8 NETS).
[23] Ps 40:1 (39:2 NETS).
[24] Deut 16:20.

[25] Eph 2:8.
[26] Jas 2:17.
[27] Is 54:17.
[28] Ps 37:1 (36:1).

does not always remain so. And when [I say this], I do not mean his essence, but his quality.

Question: What does *temporal* mean?

If you wish to understand it readily: because he no longer sins, the sinner seems to be no more. And then he does not accomplish the works of sin. And "sin has a fleeting pleasure,"[29] as Paul writes. The pleasure of sin no longer exists. For the many, therefore, we say that because he no longer sins it seems that the sinner no longer exists. And as for the truthful account: sin neither was from the beginning nor will it be forever, for of its supreme form, idolatry, this was said: "They did not exist from the beginning, nor will they last forever."[30] Now, if the very pinnacle of the vices had no beginning, in the same way it is clear that it will neither be endless eternally.

Yet a little while, and the sinner will be no more. You have, then, in the Ninth Psalm as well, "Crush the arm of the sinner and evildoer."[31] He did not say "of a sinner," but "of *the* sinner." And if the arm of "the sinner" is crushed, how much more the arms of those inferior to him!

[36:10] *And you will seek his place and will never find it.*

Again in the common sense, for it is needful to provide the more popular interpretations as well. The place of the sinner seems to be the region around the earth, for here lawlessness occurs, here sins are accomplished. Therefore the earth will pass away with the heaven.[32] *You will seek his place,* therefore, *and you will never find it.*

The position of each person is strictly called his "*place.*" For example, it is also said about Judas that he absconded from his place of service: "from which Judas turned aside."[33] The position in service is a kind of "place" of service, for when Paul says, "The apostles are appointed first, second prophets, third,"[34] ranks are being indicated through the placement. And indeed, even among the military ranks they say: he has the place of a beneficiary, of an adjutant, and in the churches it is similar. The position of the sinner will not be found when he is no longer a sinner. And *his place* was sin.

[36:11] *But the meek shall inherit the land.*

While the sinner, after a little while, will no longer be, nor his place be found even when it is sought, the place of the meek [246] remains forever, for it is eternal . . . , it is immortal. And of the virtuous it is said, "His righteousness endures forever and ever."[35]

The meek, then, that is those who have meekness, those who practice tranquility, will inherit the land, for the tranquil person is meek. Indeed, it is unnecessary to address certain others who say that that person is meek, even when he becomes angry at things at which one must be angry.[36] This meekness, however, is more political and is rhetorical. Why? For the virtuous person is free from anger; and indeed in the previously quoted verses it was said, "Cease from anger, and forsake wrath!"[37]

[36:11] *And they will take delight in an abundance of peace.*

At what time does the *abundance of peace* come? Whenever the prayer of those who say,

---

[29] Heb 11:25.
[30] Wis 14:13 NRSV.
[31] Ps 10:15 (9:36 NETS).
[32] Cf. Mt 24:35.
[33] Acts 1:25 NRSV.
[34] 1 Cor 12:28.
[35] Ps 112:3, 9 (111:3, 9 NETS).
[36] See Aristotle's discussion of anger in *Nicomachean Ethics* 1125b-1126b.
[37] Ps 37:8 (36:8).

"May grace and peace be yours in abundance,"[38] is answered. He who is able to say, "Among those who hate peace I was for peace,"[39] has an abundance of peace; he takes delight in the abundance of this peace. It is also possible to say that after they were transferred from this region where enemies and disturbances are, they come into the land of the meek, where peace lives freely.

I also said earlier that such a topic is assigned among the topics of dialectics: "What kind of virtue requires what other kind?" And it says: when all are just, there is no need of courage. And it calls courage the more political virtue, which joins combat with enemies. When all are just, there is no need of courage. However, when courage is present, there is a need for justice.

And here, then, they take delight in an abundance of peace, when they are meek. Now, the meek, as was said by us, is untroubled in the presence of anger. And observe the greatness of the virtue from the one who taught us and prepared us to imitate himself: "Learn from me," he says, "for I am gentle and humble in heart."[40] He did not simply say "humble" but "humble in heart." I am gentle in disposition, in heart. The one who possesses modesty is "humble in heart."

And since the word from the Gospel appeared, it is necessary to refute those who say that Jesus did not possess an intellect but only an irrational soul.[41] In all the Scriptures, both new and old, the heart is mentioned instead of the intellect, for when it says, "Hear me, you who have ruined your heart,"[42] you who have ruined your understanding. And a "heart of stone"[43] is the foolish understanding. If then he has a heart, then this has virtue—for he is gentle in the heart and humble—he has assumed a perfect man.

[36:12] *The sinner will watch the righteous closely and gnash his teeth at him.*

He is saying as follows: the sinner always wants to be an enemy of the righteous, and not only an enemy, but he even wishes to be murderous against him.

And observe carefully how *he will watch him closely* is used. *To watch closely* strictly indicates this: to watch closely how someone might harm another. Someone has been armed: he who wishes to strike him with darts watches him closely to see what member of his is exposed, and there he shoots the dart. Since, therefore, the righteous man has been fortified, he is not exposed but is clothed with "the full armor of God,"[44] and "has taken the shield of faith,"[45] and is wholly guarded.

And in the event that the word "watches closely" (*paratērēsetai*) is used instead of "watches" (*tērēsei*), for frequently words that are said with the preposition have the same meaning as words without them—for example, "going" (*bainōn*) and "descending" (*katabainōn*): the one who descends *goes* downward. If therefore "watches" can be understood, it means two things: either "to watch closely" was meant or "to guard." When indeed the Savior says in the Gospel, "Holy Father, watch them,"[46] he means "guard them." "While I was with them, I was watching them,"[47] instead of, "I was guarding them." And those who say, "You will watch us from this generation,"[48] are saying "you will protect us."

And "to watch," as I said, means "to watch closely." So it is said, "He will watch your head,

---

[38] 1 Pet 1:2 NRSV.
[39] Ps 120:6-7 (119:7 NETS).
[40] Mt 11:29 NRSV.
[41] This is the position of Apollinaris on Jesus's soul.
[42] Is 46:12 NETS.
[43] Ezek 11:19.
[44] Eph 6:11.
[45] Eph 6:16.
[46] Jn 17:11.
[47] Jn 17:12.
[48] Ps 12:7 (11:8).

and you will watch his heel."[49] The saint watches for the head of the serpent, in order that by killing the head of vice, he might have the whole of the serpent put to death. And the serpent cannot observe the head of the man, but the heel; he observes his extremities, the powers that draw near to the earth. A fatal wound does not happen, nor any damage, to the heel. So it has been said in other places as well: "The lawlessness at my heel will surround me: then I was afraid on the evil day."[50] If the lawlessness was observing my head, it would have touched my head like the head of that one of whom it is written, "His toil shall return upon his own head,"[51] and again, "I gave their ways against their heads,"[52] instead of "against their intellect."

And it was also good to call him *the righteous*, not merely "a righteous," but the perfect righteous person, the irreproachable. For it is often said regarding those who are progressing, with the word that is predicated of the perfect, for example: "The wise do not turn away from the mouth of the Lord."[53] None of the wise comes away from the word of the Lord, doing all things with reason. And it is said, "Rebuke a wise man, and he will love you."[54] See! A wise man [247][55] is subject to reproaches. This one is progressing and beginning. The perfect, however, is untroubled; he is not subject to reproaches; he does not "turn away from the mouth," that is, from the word, of God.

"Inform a righteous person, and he will continue to receive,"[56] and, "A righteous person is his own accuser in his introduction."[57] He abstains in every way from that with which he will accuse himself. And the one who is truly, perfectly righteous does not sin, for "everyone who does righteousness has been born of God,"[58] and "everyone who has been born of God does not commit sin."[59] He who does not sin is perfectly righteous, about whom the Savior in the Gospel has also said, "Many prophets and righteous people longed to see what you see, but did not see it."[60]

However, it belongs to one who accuses himself to *gnash the teeth*, for after he observed him he did not seize him, he did not strike him, he did not wound him, and so on account of his lack of success he gnashes the teeth. And frequently the gnashing of the teeth signifies repentance, as also in the Gospel concerning the one who was bound feet and hands and cast into the "outer darkness"[61] "which is prepared for the devil and his angels."[62] "Then there will be weeping and gnashing of teeth."[63] And the word *there* here again signifies such a condition.

[36:13] *But the Lord will laugh at him, because he foresees that his day will come.*

This is about the sinner, who gnashes his teeth against the righteous, for *he foresees that his day will come*. Because the Lord *foresees that his day will* come in which he will be condemned, he *will laugh* at the sinner.

However, let not such words spoken about God be understood in a human way. We understand their sense, however, in a manner befitting God. Indeed, it was said, "He who resides in the heavens will laugh at them, and

---

[49]Cf. Gen 3:15 NETS.
[50]Ps 49:5 (48:6).
[51]Ps 7:16 (7:17 NETS).
[52]Ezek 9:10; 22:31.
[53]Prov 24:7 NETS (LXX).
[54]Prov 9:8.
[55]Didymus the Blind, *Psalmenkommentar (Tura-Papyrus)*, vol. 5, *Kommentar zu Psalm 40–44,4*, ed. M. Gronewald, PTA 12 (Bonn: Rudolf Habelt, 1970), recovers this page of the manuscript.
[56]Prov 9:9.
[57]Prov 18:17 LES2 (LXX).
[58]Cf. 1 Jn 2:29.
[59]Cf. 1 Jn 3:9.
[60]Mt 13:17 NRSV.
[61]Cf. Mt 22:13.
[62]Mt 25:41.
[63]Mt 22:13.

the Lord will mock them."[64] This does not portray God as a man; we do not understand it in a human way in the case of God.

And again in Exodus it says, "how I have mocked the Egyptians."[65] Here the mockery has such a sense: he did not bring lions to them, not dragons, not the other great wild animals, but the gnat, the dog-fly, [after] the frog and the caterpillar.

Question: What does the phrase "he threw them into the sea" mean?

But there it does not say, "I have mocked them."

[36:14] *The sinners drew a sword and they bent their bow to bring down the poor and needy.*

They prepared a sword, in order *to bring down the poor and needy*. It is turned back and proceeds into their heart, according to what is said: "He who digs a hole for his neighbor will fall into it."[66] And again, "And let the trap which he concealed capture him."[67] And in the Preacher it says, "A serpent shall bite him who demolishes a wall."[68] A serpent shall bite him who demolishes the wall of another, who demolishes the safety of another.

They drew a sword. From the scabbard they drew it into the open.

The sword can also be the word spoken with deceit, for they draw it in order that they might strike them by means of it. You have what is said in Proverbs: "There are some who speak who wound with a sword, but the tongues of the wise heal."[69] There are some who by speaking wound with a sword. And let this word "sword" be read in the dative case. There are some who by speaking wound with a sword. Those who corrupt good morals with wicked conversations[70] wound with the sword when they speak. "And their tongue is a sharp sword."[71] Their word, like a sword, harms and wounds.

By speaking, then, there are some who wound with a sword, but the tongues of the wise, the words of the wise, heal. These swords belong to healing; they do not wound, they do not strike, they do not traumatize, but they heal the wounds that have come by other words.

The dominant part of the soul is a bent bow, which was so prepared so that arrows are loosened from it. These, however, are evil thoughts, harmful words. "Look, sinners bent a bow; they prepared arrows for the quiver."[72]

[36:14] *To slay the upright in heart.*

Here we understand *the upright in heart* as the wise man who is reproached and as the righteous person who accuses himself.

In the Gospel stands a word from the person of the Lord: "All who take the sword will perish by the sword."[73] And many think that he says this, that the one who slays a man will certainly be slain. But this does not seem to be undeniable. Many murderers have met with a natural death. But he is saying the following: "Everyone who brings punishment against someone will be exposed to punishment; everyone who desires to harm someone with a sword, with his sharpened mind, or with his tongue and word, will be subject to the same things."

Question: *To bring down the poor and the needy?*

They are not able to bring down the rich, they are not able to bring down the one who is rich "in knowledge and speech of every kind,"[74]

---

[64] Ps 2:4 NETS.
[65] Ex 10:2.
[66] Prov 26:27 NETS.
[67] Ps 35:8 (34:8).
[68] Eccles 10:8.
[69] Prov 12:18.
[70] Cf. 1 Cor 15:33.
[71] Ps 57:4 (56:5 LES2).
[72] Ps 11:2 (10:2 NETS).
[73] Mt 26:52 NRSV.
[74] 1 Cor 1:5.

Lectures on Psalm 36 [36:15]

but the poor and needy, even if he seems to be upright in heart, as I said before, like the wise man who is reproached and the righteous man who accuses himself, but then the sword, being turned against those who sharpened it, strikes and kills them. Likewise also the bow is shattered in pieces.

[248][75] [36:15] *May their sword enter into their own heart, and their bows be crushed.*

[And it is good that it is said, *May their sword enter into their own heart.* This harmful sword, the sword of enemies, is not naturally connected to the heart. It enters it from outside.

In fact, such a thing] is written in Isaiah: "Your affliction will come from far away."[76] Affliction is alien; it arrives from outside. However, "the kingdom of God is within"[77] the heart of those who possess it.

[36:16] *Better is a little that the righteous has than the great wealth of sinners.*

Earlier, in reference to the passages, "Do not be provoked to jealousy with those acting wickedly and do not be envious of those who commit lawlessness,"[78] and, "Do not be provoked to jealousy so as to do evil,"[79] we were saying: when you see someone who possesses bodily and external goods, "do not be provoked to jealousy" so as to imitate that person, because you know that these things do not endure. For the one who leaves the body does not possess bodily goods—now, health and strength are the bodily goods—the one who comes outside this life no longer possesses the external goods: wealth, status, rule, and small renown. Only the goods of the soul endure. Unless the one who possesses them casts them away, no one takes them from him.

Therefore, he is saying the following: even when the sinner possesses many things, and the righteous *a little*, what is sufficient for his stewardship, this is *better*.

And this is also possible: even when someone possesses a certain virtue, being only in its elementary stage, this is better than the wealth that sinners have.

Again, it could also mean as follows: there are some who follow the church's mind neither richly nor with delight, but are only in its elementary stage. Therefore, even when the heterodox are rich and seem to be forceful in speech and powerful enough in dialectical arguments both to speak craftily and to prepare disputatious arguments, yet their wealth quickly fails; it has promise only in the present life. For the *little that the righteous has* remains to him, it goes with him, it never comes outside him, but rather he will receive this as an addition. But since "treasures shall not profit the lawless, but righteousness shall deliver from death,"[80] even when the one who is eager for righteousness has *a little*, he possesses much: for if it is *more than the wealth of sinners* it is not a trifling amount—only in comparison with the perfection of that which is eagerly sought after by the righteous is it *little*—and it surpasses the wealth of sinners.

[36:17] *For the arms of sinners will be crushed, but the Lord upholds the righteous.*

So even if they possess great wealth, their *arms will be crushed*: their deeds and their active powers. And that the passage is not about perceptible arms, we do not observe sinners absolutely everywhere encountering a crushing

---

[75]Michael Gronewald, "Didymos der Blinde, Psalmenkommentar (Nachtrag der Seiten 248/49 des Tura-Papyrus)," *Zeitschrift für Papyrologie und Epigraphik* 46 (1982): 97-111, restores pages 248-49.
[76]Is 10:3.
[77]Lk 17:21.
[78]Ps 37:1 (36:1).
[79]Ps 37:8 (36:8).
[80]Prov 10:2 NETS.

of the arms, nor do the virtuous remain free of this.

He *upholds* them therefore so that they do not suffer crushing, nor anything else that damages them. And the saint also says, "And the Lord became my support."[81] And again in the Song of Songs the Bride is seen "coming up, clad in white, leaning on her beloved."[82] "To be upheld" and "to lean on" mean the same thing.

[36:18] *The Lord knows the ways of the blameless.*

God knows the good, and he does not know the evil. Here "to know" and "not to know" do not mean "to understand" and "not to understand," for God understands not only the ways of the blameless but the ways of all the rest as well. Indeed, he says, "I have given their ways to their heads."[83] If he were ignorant of their ways, he would not give them to their heads, that is, he would not punish them for them. Therefore, "to know" here means "to be tempted," as it also says in the Preacher, "Whoever keeps the command will not know an evil word."[84] And who must know the evil word better than the one who knows the command? Is not the Word of God good? Therefore he is saying as follows: the one who keeps the command will not be tempted by an evil word. So too must this be understood: "The Lord knows those who are his."[85] "Formerly, when you did not know God, you were enslaved to beings that by nature are not gods. Now, however, that you have come to know God, or rather to be known by God."[86] God, then, knows the one who knows him.

Truly, the one who is completely sinless is *blameless*. And vice is a flaw. For example, God the Word says to his own bride who is "without a spot or wrinkle"[87]: "You are altogether beautiful, my companion, and there is no flaw in you."[88]

[36:18] *And their inheritance will last forever.*

The inheritance of the blameless, clearly, for they do not desire temporal things. For if they are righteous and blameless, they have become free from fleeting pleasure of sin,[89] "looking no longer at what can be seen, which is temporal, but at what cannot be seen, which is eternal."[90]

Their inheritance, then, *will last forever*. Now, it was said above that "the meek shall inherit the earth."[91] For "those who wait for the Lord—they shall inherit the earth."[92] This is the *inheritance* that *will last forever*. For if someone does not cast it away by himself, no one is able to take it from him. [249]

Some want to establish from this that virtue is really immutable. And when Arius, because of his arrogance, was about to begin this schism, while he was still within the church he was teaching such things and was saying that virtue is immutable. And he was making use of those words, "'Love never fails';[93] love is immutable." And he was teaching this, since he was about to say that the Son is changeable. And he was saying, "For this reason the Son does not undergo a change, since he is guarded by the hand of God. He himself is not immutable, but his protection does not fail." And as many perfect men as he introduced, he always used to say, "He was not perfect," for instance, "David was not perfect; the devil was not

---

[81] Ps 18:18 (17:19 LES2).
[82] Song 8:5.
[83] Ezek 9:10; 22:31.
[84] Eccles 8:5.
[85] 2 Tim 2:19 NRSV.
[86] Gal 4:8-9 NRSV.
[87] Eph 5:27 NRSV.
[88] Song 4:7.
[89] Cf. Heb 11:25.
[90] Cf. 2 Cor 4:18.
[91] Ps 37:11 (36:11).
[92] Ps 37:9 (36:9).
[93] 1 Cor 13:8.

perfect." And their argument resolved to call no one perfect.

... "And no one snatches out of the Father's hand."[94] And it is impossible for the one who is protected by God to be snatched out by someone, but he will suffer this if he comes outside his hand. For example, Judas, when he departed from Jesus, has come outside his hand and in this way was snatched.

And by way of another analogy this was said: "The birds of lofty flight cannot be hunted. When because of a certain greediness for the things below them they descend, however, then they can easily be caught." So the one who is under the shelter of God's hand cannot be snatched away, but the one who comes outside of it is snatched away. "They," it says, "were thrust away from your hand."[95] When did this take place? When they became disobedient to God, for "God will reject them, because they did not obey him."[96]

[36:19] *They shall not be put to shame in an evil time, and in days of famine they shall be fed.*

Those who are blameless in their way, whose ways God knows, *shall not be put to shame in an evil time*, that is, in a time of oppression, for often in times of oppression many incur shame, as when some sacrifice to the gods as testimony. The *time is evil* when it produces suffering, for here the opposite of good is not being indicated by the word *evil*, but that which brings suffering, that which brings harm.

In an evil time, then, *they shall not be put to shame*—those who are blameless in their ways. If someone was put to shame when he was subjected, ignobly, to an affliction that took hold of him, then he was *put to shame in an evil time*. An *evil time* has come against Susanna, for there was a conspiracy that was bringing her to death, and she was *not put to shame*, for her virtue was made known, her temperance has appeared. However, the *time* becomes *evil* because of the things that are practiced, for the divine Paul writes the following, saying, "Distressing times will come. For people will be lovers of themselves."[97]

And in the days of famine they shall be fed. Even in the case of the literal sense, this often transpired: a famine overtook the whole race of the Hebrews in the wilderness, and God rained down heavenly bread and meat on them, "bread in the early morning, and meat in the evening."[98] Nevertheless, in the literal sense these things have also not taken place: for the manna was that which was flowing both morning and evening, yet the manna itself was a food that was transformed according to the desire of the one who ate it.[99] Now, often it calls "bread" every kind of food, as when it is said about Moses that for a whole "forty days he did not eat bread and did not drink water."[100] He is not saying the following: that he did not eat the bread that habitually nourished him but ate some other things—for he did not eat anything else—but he means every kind of dry food by "bread" and every kind of moist nourishment by "water." So too the Savior in the wilderness neither ate nor drank for forty days and forty nights.[101] When a famine arrived, Elijah was fed by ravens, when God sent to him bread early in the morning and meat in the evening.[102]

And in general the righteous man always has God nourishing him: "The God who sustains me from my youth."[103]

And this must be said in relation to the elevated sense: it often happens that there is a

---

[94] Jn 10:29.
[95] Ps 88:5 (87:6 NETS).
[96] Hos 9:17.
[97] 2 Tim 3:1-2 NRSV.
[98] Cf. Ex 16:8.
[99] Cf. Wis 16:21.
[100] Ex 34:28.
[101] Cf. Mt 4:2; Mk 1:13; Lk 4:2.
[102] 1 Kings 17:6.
[103] Gen 48:15 NETS.

scarcity of the word that brings salvation or that the bread that nourishes the soul is not available. By way of a threat God promises to bring on a famine, "neither a famine of bread nor a thirst for water, but a famine of hearing the word of the Lord."[104] When a famine was brought in because there was no bread and no water, the wise man has bread within himself, for he has a command to "open his eyes and be filled with bread."[105] The one who opens these perceptible eyes is by no means filled with bread, but rather the one who opens the eyes of his soul. When someone "enlightens himself with the light of knowledge,"[106] he has his eyes opened, for "the Lord will not let the soul of the righteous starve."[107] And both of these words are said proverbially, for which reason he is not saying these things about perceptible bread but about the bread that concerns spirit and soul. Therefore the righteous man, having in himself "the Bread of Life"[108] and "a spring of water gushing up to eternal life,"[109] does not starve. For just as someone receives "a spring" to have "in himself water gushing up to eternal life," so when he opens his eyes he is filled with the bread [250][110] that feeds the soul, that gives it water to drink. Indeed, in the same prophet where it is written, "I will send a famine on the land, neither a famine of bread nor a thirst for water, but a famine of hearing the word of the Lord,"[111] it is added, "The fallen one shall be numerous in every place; I will apply silence."[112] The famine is for those who have fallen. And a silence of the divine word is added to these. *In the days, therefore, of famine they shall be fed.*

[36:20] *because the sinners will perish.*

In two ways again we understand the destruction of sinners: either they are destroyed insofar as they are sinners, or they receive an experience of sufferings. The righteous "are not put to shame in an evil time,"[113] but sinners are put to shame. When they are ashamed because they know how deep they are in evils, and they blush because of their sin, sometimes they despise their sin and become free of it, and they are destroyed so that they are sinners no longer.

[36:20] *And the enemies of the Lord, as soon as they are glorified and exalted, disappearing like smoke, they vanished.*

Sinners can be *the enemies of the Lord*. And it is also possible to call those who go astray according to their morals *sinners*, and to call those who transgress the divine laws and think impious thoughts *enemies of the Lord*, those who are outside piety, who think what is false.

These *enemies of the Lord*, then, *as soon as they are glorified and exalted*, immediately *vanished like smoke*. And see, he always likens sinners to smoke. And in another psalm, for example, it is said, "As smoke vanishes, let them vanish; as wax melts from before fire, so sinners will be destroyed from before God."[114]

This word teaches that sinners are not of a different nature. Smoke is a byproduct of fire, and wax is a byproduct of honey. And the honey receives its origin beforehand. And since it is composed in no other way than in wax, the wax is constituted as an accident. The honey does not exist because of the wax, but the wax because of the honey, and the fire does not exist because of the smoke, but the smoke because of the fire.

The *sinners*, therefore, *vanish like smoke*, which is a byproduct, for to sin and to be at

---

[104]Amos 8:11.
[105]Cf. Prov 20:13.
[106]Hos 10:12 LXX.
[107]Cf. Prov 10:3.
[108]Jn 6:35, 48.
[109]Jn 4:14.
[110]Didymus the Blind, *Kommentar zu Psalm 40–44,4*, restores this page.
[111]Amos 8:11.
[112]Amos 8:3.

[113]Ps 37:19 (36:19).
[114]Ps 68:2 (67:3).

enmity with the Lord is a byproduct. And the rational creature has come into being in order that it might be receptive of virtue. But that which is receptive of something is not such a thing in essence. Men indeed are not good in essence, for they were created because of this: in order that they might become good by participation in the One who is truly good. And that which is receptive of vice follows after that which is receptive of virtue. And in the same way evils are always after goods, evil art after skill, disobedience after obedience.

Therefore, sin is a sequel of virtue; it would not be constituted if the erring creature were not receptive of vice. Likewise also the wax is a byproduct. This disappears, indeed, and does not come to an end in nonbeing but transforms into something better.

And sinners, then, become smoke because of vice itself, for vice is in this way like lawlessness: "As the unripe grape is harmful to the teeth and smoke is harmful to the eyes, so transgression is to those who practice it."[115] You see that transgression becomes smoke to the eyes that meet with it.

However, there is no need of great violence for the smoke to be destroyed, for it is destroyed quickly. For this reason sinners are *like wax that melts from before fire*, and *as smoke disappears, let them vanish*. Smoke is a byproduct, as I said, of fire, for it arises either when there is fire or when fire has passed.

The enemies of the Lord, then, even if they are astoundingly arrogant, even if they are exalted as those who are fairly powerful, as those who are illustrious, are extinguished like smoke at the same time that they are exalted. It is ours to see their vanishing, since even if they remain glorified for a certain time and are exalted, thinking great thoughts, yet to the one who is able to look at that in which they think great things, immediately they are found to disappear.

[36:21] *The sinner borrows and will not pay back.*

What God gives for the benefit of men and the soul, those who receive do not take as something that is due them. For no one receives something in this age according to his due, but he borrows it with thanksgiving, he gives the good as a debt, in order that after he completes it, profit might be derived from it and he might give interest.

I understand the word concerning *righteousness*. If I, after repaying, also give the interest, I bring the works of righteousness to God. However, if after receiving the word about righteousness I will do nothing in righteousness, after borrowing from God I have not repaid. For God gives, in order that we might work; God bestows, in order that we might change words into actions. And he lends his divine silver, of which it is said, "Silver refined by fire, tested in the earth."[116] The one who borrows, therefore, repays interest and that which he received.

[36:21] *But the righteous is compassionate and gives.* [251][117]

Not only does he repay what he borrowed, but he even becomes the benefactor of others. By being merciful, he derives profit. And "he who has compassion on the poor lends to God."[118] The one who borrows from God is righteous, storing up an abundance of good deeds and rational silver, and he is the benefactor of another, for the wicked harm those who associate with them, whereas the righteous benefit them. And that the wicked man is harmful is obvious. So it is said in Proverbs, that the wise man benefits and improves: "Rebuke a wise man and he will love you."[119]

---

[115] Prov 10:26.

[116] Ps 12:6 (11:7).
[117] Didymus the Blind, *Psalmenkommentar (Tura-Papyrus)*, vol. 4, *Kommentar zu Psalm 35–39*, ed. M. Gronewald, PTA 6 (Bonn: Rudolf Habelt, 1969), resumes here.
[118] Prov 19:17 NETS.
[119] Prov 9:8.

When he is rebuked, he receives the rebukes well, so that he loves the one who rebuked him. And because he loves the one who rebuked him, he no longer practices the things for which the rebuke has taken place. The one who practices evil is like "a brother of the one who injures himself."[120] Therefore, the wicked man harms himself above all.

The righteous, then, *is compassionate and gives*, and he is generous, and in general he shares his goods with his neighbor. Those who say, "when a brother or sister is naked and lacks daily food, 'Go in peace. Eat your fill,'"[121] and does not give to them their necessities, benefits them not at all, since he is not *compassionate and gives*.

However, one can also understand it in this way: the sinner, even though he borrows from God the common notions that are given to him and the commandments, "will not pay back" either what he has or what he has received: either the capital or the interest. But *the righteous* God *is compassionate and gives* all the more. That man, though he receives, does not repay, but God himself *is compassionate and gives* all the more. And I say: compassion and doing what is honorable appear when the receiver is ungrateful. "He is kind to the ungrateful and the wicked,"[122] he gives. The receivers are ungrateful—for because they do not repay what they must repay, they are found to be ungrateful and wicked—but God is still kind, even to these ones.

For this reason the righteous is all the more compassionate and gives. The imitator of God, then, "who shows mercy to the poor and lends to God," even when the one who borrows from him does not yield what he owes, is still compassionate: he still gives.

And take for example the parable of the Gospel about the talents. "To each according to his own ability"[123] he has given his rational possessions, not to each according to his nature but according to his ability, which he established for himself by his free choice. "To one he gave five talents, to another two, to another one."[124] "The one who had received the five talents traded with them"[125] and doubled them. After he had borrowed he paid back. The one with the two talents did likewise. The one who received the one and buried it in the ground neither traded with it nor returned interest; he buried it in the ground. Whenever you see a man who has the ability to be a benefactor or to behave cordially and does not do so, what he received he buried in the ground, he buried it in his material way of thinking. And when he is asked about it, when at last the appointed time of the gathering together of those who have received the rational treasures arrives, he says, "Here you have what is yours."[126] And he even accused God, desiring to attribute his own sluggishness to another: "I knew you," he says, "I knew that you were a harsh man, gathering what you did not plant, reaping where you did not sow; so I was afraid, and I hid your money in the ground,"[127] and I gave it to no one. From what he has said, he had his reproach and his condemnation: "O you wicked servant! You knew, did you, that I gather what I did not plant,"[128] when I gather the good things that are not mine, take back what is mine with interest from those who have received from me, when "I reap where I did not sow"?[129] In every respect, I would have received what is mine, if you had given it to a bank, in order that it should be increased. So he was deprived even of this.[130]

---

[120]Prov 18:9 LXX.
[121]Jas 2:15-16.
[122]Lk 6:35 NRSV.
[123]Mt 25:15.
[124]Mt 25:15 NRSV.
[125]Cf. Mt 25:16 NRSV.
[126]Mt 25:25 NRSV.
[127]Mt 25:24-25.
[128]Cf. Mt 25:26.
[129]Mt 25:26 NRSV.
[130]Cf. Mt 25:27-28.

Therefore the sinner also, when he often borrows, when he does not repay what he ought to repay, he will sometimes be deprived of those good actions. He himself will no longer receive, even though the righteous is all the more compassionate and gives.

[36:22] *Because those who bless him shall inherit the land.*

Those who bless the righteous. It should be received according to both interpretations: either the righteous man or God. He who does those things that he requires of him blesses God, so that he says, "I will bless the Lord at every opportunity."[131]

Moreover, the righteous man is blessed, for "the blessing of the Lord is upon the head of the righteous"[132] and, "This one will receive a blessing from the Lord."[133]

It mentions that "land" of which it is said, "And he will lift you up to inherit the land."[134]

[36:22] *But those who curse him shall be destroyed.*

He truly curses the righteous, who says about him ungodly things, about whom or to whom God says, "Woe to them, for they have run away from me! Wretched are they, because they have acted impiously against me. I redeemed them, but they spoke lies against me."[135] "I," he says, "redeemed them," I led them to the bath of regeneration,[136] bestowing perfect forgiveness of sins, abolishing their lawless deeds. They, however, spoke lies against me, not doing those things for which they were called. And I had forgiveness on their sins, for I did not redeem them for this purpose, that they should sin, but that they should become free from sin. When, therefore, after the ransom and the reward money, someone does what is reprehensible, he slanders it, to say in a certain sense, "He did nothing beneficial for me." He is speaking lies against him.

[36:23] *The steps of a man are directed by the Lord, and his way by his will.*

The man voluntarily travels from the worse things to the better, from things temporal to things eternal. And it belongs to him [252] to will the good, since "it depends not on human exertion or will, but on God who shows mercy"[137] to accomplish the journey blamelessly.

The steps of a man are directed by the Lord.

The steps are not given, for it belongs to us to desire to pass from things that are wicked to things that are good. For example, in the Catholic Epistle by him John writes, "We know that we have passed from death to life."[138] "We have passed," not "we were dragged." Force does not set us down into this, when God directs our steps, when he grants the goal to those steps that become straight in this way. And you have many such examples in Scripture: "I ran the way of your commandments, when you made my heart spacious."[139] When God enlarges the heart, after he has given breadth to the intelligence, someone traverses the way of the commandments. His heart was not enlarged because he ran but because God enlarged it, causing every kind of narrowness that stems from wicked thoughts and afflictions to leave; because of this he ran the way of God.

And again, you should not regard as a contradiction when it is said in Jeremiah, "I know that man's way is not his own nor shall a man journey and direct his journey."[140] You are the one who [directs it.] And the word of the

---

[131]Ps 34:1 (33:2 NETS).
[132]Prov 10:6 NETS.
[133]Ps 24:5 (23:5 LES2).
[134]Ps 37:34 (36:34).
[135]Cf. Hos 7:13 NETS.
[136]Cf. Titus 3:5.

[137]Rom 9:16 NRSV.
[138]1 Jn 3:14 NRSV.
[139]Ps 119:32 (118:32 NETS).
[140]Jer 10:23.

prophet can have a sense in two ways: Nebuchadnezzar threatens the demolition of Jerusalem and the deportation of the whole Hebrew race. The prophet was saying: since he was threatening and we bestowed the causes of our suffering this ourselves, "I knew that the man's way is not his own." You are able to prevent his way against us, for even if a man regards himself as being someone great, yet his expedition is not accomplished if you prevent it.

It is also possible to understand it thus, according to the previously explained interpretation of the passage: "So it depends not on human will or exertion, but on God who shows mercy."[141] Determine to run the way of salvation. It is not ours to bring the way to its conclusion, but to desire to come to the end of the journey, so as to say aloud, "I have finished the race."[142] However, to direct the course is from him; to act as guide is from him. "Guide me to your truth."[143] The one who is guided by God does not keep straight by himself. However, he desires to keep straight and he has given himself to the one who is able to lead him into perfection. Such things, which are according to God, I say, and look to him, are richly completed, and one cannot separate one from another. Someone desired the good, he is eager to become an imitator of God, to prepare to assume virtue; after determining, he does not stop himself at his determination, but he is active, he practices, he is zealous, he habituates himself to do good things. "Has it been told you, O man, what the Lord seeks from you but to love mercy and to do justice and to be ready to walk with the Lord your God?"[144] The one who prepares himself to walk always with the Lord God is unimpeded in every way. Let him only prepare himself for this, saying, "My heart is ready, O God; my heart is ready."[145] However, no one of those who is impeded by shameful thoughts or a certain state of anxiety can say, "My heart is ready, O God; my heart is ready," for he has fetters, he is "bound by the ropes of his own sins."[146]

God wills the way of the one who is being guided in his steps. And a man walks it according to God's will, he runs the way of life, of him who has said, "I am the way."[147] He walks and he runs on him.

And his way by his will.

Furthermore, it is possible to say the following: he whose steps are directed by God desires the way of God into which God leads him, on which he instructs him and guides him. Even if at times, then, he happens to fall, he is not broken to pieces.

[36:24] *Whenever he falls, he will not be knocked down.*

Take the following example: let there be a certain excellent runner, who both possesses swiftness of feet by nature and is perfectly trained in the runner's profession. When this one, who can run so swiftly and has the legs of the inner man trained, sometimes stumbles while running, in a certain sense he receives only a brief impression of stumbling, for he is neither vanquished nor does he, as it were, bending after he is struck, cease from the race. Even if, therefore, he at times happens to meet with a kind of slip, he is not broken to pieces. Judas slipped from the way of truth and fell down, for it is said, "falling headlong, he burst open in the middle."[148] However, he would not have fallen headlong if he had not been knocked down.

And well said is the saying, *Whenever he falls, he will not be knocked down.* Even if a kind of stumbling takes place, he gives "no room to the devil,"[149] so that he overturns him in every way and repulses him.

---

[141] Rom 9:16 NRSV.
[142] 2 Tim 4:7 NRSV.
[143] Ps 25:5 (24:5 NETS).
[144] Mic 6:8.
[145] Ps 57:7 (56:8); 108:1 (107:2).

[146] Prov 5:22 NETS.
[147] Jn 14:6.
[148] Acts 1:18 NRSV.
[149] Eph 4:27.

Someone saw a woman with desire as far as the forepassion. He seemed to fall, but he was not knocked down. For when he yields to following the thought and the desire of her beauty overcomes him, then he is knocked down, then he fell. So are the elders who became crazed against Susanna.

[36:24] *Because the Lord steadies his hand.*

The practice is often called *hand*, the active power. By steadying his active power, he does not allow him to fall down completely. He finds a place where he may press his hand. And the Lord becomes his support, according to what was said before this, "And the Lord became my support."[150] He masters his active power so as to say aloud, "You seized my right hand, and with your counsel you guided me."[151] Behold! the mastery . . .[152]

[36:28] [*And the seed of the impious shall be destroyed.*] **[255]**

. . . is impiety. And it proceeds against God. *Seed* stands for "the offspring of the impious." And the seed can also be, as it were, the disposition of the impious. And it is profitably destroyed. The seed is destroyed, lest it produce something that still lingers.

[36:29] *The righteous shall inherit the land and dwell on it forever and ever.*

On the aforementioned land.

[36:30-31] *The mouth of the righteous shall declaim wisdom, and his tongue speaks justice. The law of his God is in his heart, and his steps shall not be tripped up.*

The mouth of the righteous speaks wisdom. When the wise man has been illumined, he produces luminous words, for it is said, "The wisdom of a man will illuminate his face."[153] He who speaks this wisdom has the face of his intellect illumined, for "the conversation of the godly is always wisdom."[154] And again the one who pays attention to him who says, "Open your mouth with a divine word,"[155] saying, "I opened my mouth and drew breath,"[156] speaks wisdom. *The mouth, then, of the righteous shall declaim wisdom.* He always recites wise things, not only the contemplations of piety but also the things of practical wisdom.

His tongue speaks justice. He speaks all things judiciously. He does not pronounce an "idle word."[157] For he knows that "by his own words a person is justified, and by his own words he is condemned."[158] Because of this he speaks judiciously. And as the thoughts of the righteous are judgments—for "the thoughts of the just are judgments"[159]—they do not simply possess thoughts that are thrown away but thoughts that are examined, tested, and regulated. From such judgments a speech that has been subjected to judgment is produced. And because of this the *tongue* of the righteous *speaks justice.* For if he speaks these things that he considers, and he considers thoughts that are examined and tested, then his speech is of the same kind.

And at length he supplies the cause: "his law" is not in his ears alone but "in his heart." For "God puts his laws in their hearts and writes them on their minds."[160] The one whose heart, then, has been filled with the law of God, for this reason both *declaims wisdom* and *speaks justice.* And after this takes place and is accomplished, *his steps are not tripped up.* He travels in a straight line, he does not collide, so to speak, he has feet that are winged. And one

---

[150] Ps 18:18 (17:19 LES2).
[151] Cf. Ps 73:23-24 (72:23-24 NETS).
[152] Pages 253-54 of the codex are missing here.
[153] Eccles 8:1.
[154] Sir 27:11 LES2.
[155] Prov 31:8 NETS (LXX).
[156] Ps 119:131 (118:131 NETS).
[157] Mt 12:36.
[158] Mt 12:37.
[159] Prov 12:5 NETS.
[160] Cf. Heb 10:16, quoting Jer 31:33.

who has winged feet does not slip, does not fall. Indeed, the wise man has put on "the readiness of the gospel of peace."[161] "The readiness of the gospel" becomes sandals on the feet of the righteous, for these sandals are winged, bearing him aloft. So also God says to the soul, "I shod you with shoes of hyacinth."[162] He did not rely on another to supply this footwear, but he himself put them on. And hyacinth loves to imitate the color of the ether. Therefore, "I dressed you with ethereal sandals."

[36:32] *The sinner watches for the righteous and seeks to put him to death.*

He does not watch in order to imitate him. Paul writes to men who are in Christ, "Considering them in order to provoke love and good deeds"[163] and the rest. They consider them in order to imitate them. Indeed, "obey your leaders,"[164] "who spoke the Word of God to you; consider the outcome of their way of life, and imitate their faith."[165] Here the consideration is praiseworthy.

The sinner, however, considers *the righteous*, not in order to imitate, not in order to receive him favorably, but in order *to put him to death*. And the sinner puts the righteous to death in two ways: when he turns him away from righteousness, he puts him to death, or he puts him to death when he insidiously brings death against him, as the elders proposed to do against Susanna.

[36:33] *But he will never abandon him to his hands, nor have him condemned, when he is brought to trial by him.*

Even if the sinner should apply himself to this, God will not abandon the righteous into his hands. And we were mentioning a variety in the word *abandonment*.[166] Even when Naboth was killed by those who took counsel against him, he was not abandoned into their hands, for he would have been abandoned then, if he had done what they desired.[167] The martyrs were slain by some people, but they were not abandoned into their hands. And they would have been abandoned then, if they had sacrificed.

When the sinner is subject to judgment with the righteous, the righteous is not condemned. The elders stood in judgment with Susanna, and she was not condemned when they were subjected to judgment, for they were shown to be lying slanderers. [256]

[36:34] *Wait for the Lord and keep his way, and he will exalt you to inherit the land.*

Then he exhorts: even if there are many things that disturb, even if there are many enemies who wish both to harm you and to kill you, yet *wait for the Lord and keep his way*, so that you may cry aloud, "I have finished the race."[168] For then he will exalt you and you will inherit the earth. He showed the reward for steadfast endurance: he will make you exalted, he will take you aloft, he will lead you into heaven itself.

[36:34] *When he destroys sinners, you will look on.*

He says the following: you will see sinners being destroyed, and you will know that you yourself inherited the land. Because you waited for the Lord and kept his way, you did not succumb to them.

---

[161] Eph 6:15.
[162] Ezek 16:10.
[163] Heb 10:24.
[164] Heb 13:17 NRSV.
[165] Heb 13:7 NRSV.

[166] See PsT 25.3-5.
[167] Cf. 1 Kings 21:13 (20:13).
[168] 2 Tim 4:7.

[36:35-36] *I saw the impious being highly lifted up and being raised up like the cedars of Lebanon. And I passed by, and behold, he was no more, and I sought him, but his place was not found.*

Frequently the *impious* consider themselves to be great, and they raise themselves to a great height *like the cedar* that is in *Lebanon*. Furthermore, it is possible, since it is said with an article, to understand even the devil himself: I saw him raised up against all the others, saying, "I will take the whole world with my hand, I will seize it like eggs that have been forsaken,"[169] I will snatch it like a nest. You know that the one who encounters a nest easily takes the eggs. Even if at this moment they have become young birds, again he has encountered them while they are unable to have strong and rising flight. As a result of a great boasting, of arrogance, he was considering that he was possessing the whole world, that is, all men, thus: before him they were like lifeless eggs, made like the young chicks who are unable to be lifted up but still linger in the nest.

I saw, then, this *impious one*, saying, "By my strength I will do it, and by the understanding of wisdom, I will remove the boundaries of nations and I will plunder their strength,"[170] I saw him being highly lifted up. I mounted up in thought into the life that is after these things, into the doctrine of providence, and I saw him no longer, nor was his place found, even after it was sought. Impiety has come to an end; there is no longer any impiety. It is not among the immortal things, as it says about righteousness: "Righteousness is immortal."[171]

Question: "Like the cedars of Lebanon"?

Often Scripture indicates the proud by this tree: "And the Lord will crush the cedars of Lebanon."[172] There are also praiseworthy cedars. Scripture indicates those who are great in this life by this name: "Open your doors, O Lebanon, and fire will devour your cedars."[173] Then he explains, "Because the nobles suffered greatly."[174] He called the nobles "cedars." There are then praiseworthy cedars, but the present discourse is not about them.

And I passed by, and behold, he was no more.

I passed by in my mind and I saw him being *no more*. I saw him becoming insolent because of wealth, because of human rule. *I passed by* in thought and saw that the impious is not among those who remain. He still exalts himself like Lebanon and its cedars; indeed, I sought for his place among the things that are, and I did not find it.

God has made all things "exceedingly good."[175] "Out of the mouth of the Lord good and evil will not come."[176] He is not saying this, that neither good nor evil come, but while the good will come from the mouth of the Lord, the evil, on the contrary, will not. The goods therefore are in the plural. For this reason, there is no place among the things that are for the evils, for God has made all things "exceedingly good." And "he does not delight in the destruction of the living. The generative forces of the world are wholesome, and there is no destructive poison in them, and the dominion of Hades is not on earth."[177]

[36:37] *Mark innocence, and behold uprightness, because there is a remnant for the man of peace.*

Now, he is saying these things: "Turn from evil, and do good, and dwell forever and ever."[178] He says, *Mark innocence, behold uprightness*, by becoming free of every kind of vice. And that

---

[169] Cf. Is 10:14 NETS.
[170] Cf. Is 10:13 NETS.
[171] Wis 1:15 NRSV.
[172] Ps 29:5 (28:5 NETS).
[173] Zech 11:1.
[174] Zech 11:2 LXX.
[175] Gen 1:31 NETS.
[176] Lam 3:38. The sense is opposite if read as a question, as in LES2 and the NRSV.
[177] Wis 1:13-14 NETS.
[178] Ps 37:27 (36:27).

one is "innocent" according to the present meaning.[179] The one who possesses virtue also sees uprightness.

Because there is a remnant for the man of peace.

He is saying the following: it is impossible for the peaceable man to disappear utterly. Even if he is left alone, yet he possesses a *remnant*.

[36:38] *But the transgressors shall be destroyed together.*

The transgressors are destroyed contemporaneously, for this means that they encounter destruction "together."

[36:38] *The remnant of the impious shall be destroyed.*

However, there is a *remnant* for the peaceable person. The remnants of the impious will meet with destruction.

[36:39] *But the salvation of the righteous is from the Lord.*

He says the following: even if *the righteous*, when they are schemed against, seem not to have obtained *salvation* from men, for example Abel and as many other righteous people as were conspired against, yet their salvation is *from the Lord*: the eternal, not the temporal, salvation.

[36:39] *And he is their protector in a time of affliction.*

Even if a *time of affliction* overtakes them, he is their *protector*. He sets in front of them his own shield, so that they remain unharmed: by no means in body, but in soul.

[36:40] *And the Lord will help them and rescue them.*

By helping them, he rescues them. Even if it is not here, yet [257] at the same time they will be rescued; for when they are schemed against thanks to their reverence and seem to die, yet [they do not suffer this as by a kind of] punishment. And this is truly to be helped by God, to be rescued by God. And [since his salvation has both forms], by helping he rescues. He rescues them from the grievous circumstances that have surrounded them [and helps them in their actions.]

[36:40] *And he will deliver them from sinners and save them, because they hoped in him.*

Since they hoped [in no other thing that produces] salvation other than him, he will deliver them from the sinners and will set them free from every [damage that they are eager to bring against him.] And here the one who harms the righteous, as he supposes, actually harms himself. This indeed God [hints at in riddles in the prophet]: "He who touches you is as one who touches the pupil of his eye."[180] For the one who schemes [against someone] does not harm his own [sensible pupil.] And he took the example in order to show that the [one who schemes against someone] is harmful to himself . . . [for it is not necessary to punish that one when he acts against] himself.

Question: How do we understand the word *bow*?[181]

The dominant part of the soul, having been stretched taut, [is often called a "bow."]

---

[179]Elsewhere, Didymus understands the word *innocence* negatively. See PsT 90.14-15.

[180]Zech 2:8 NETS.
[181]Ps 37:14 (36:14).

PSALM 37 [38]

[37:1-2] *A psalm of David. In remembrance of the Sabbath. O Lord, do not rebuke me in your anger.*

There is a difference between remembrance and reminding, for someone is reminded when one person [says to another what he did not think about on his own. However, when someone on] his own reexamines in his mind the earlier things, he remembers. So indeed, some have called these the "remembrances of those who desire to learn." Those who desire to be saved come "to the recognition of the truth."[1] It is the same thing to come into the recognition and into the remembrance. For someone remembers what he knows. No one is said to remember what [he does not know. For it is necessary to have learned it] earlier. [The brothers] of Joseph recognized him, and he himself refreshed their memory, for they knew him [and he knew them. Therefore when] he takes *remembrance of the Sabbath*, he has the beginning of something good. "Sabbath" indicates rest . . . he keeps the Sabbath. One does not keep the Sabbath in the six days, but whenever one surpasses these things and [then should arrive on the seventh. This world] in which we sojourn, things visible and temporal, has come into being in six days. [The one who is in it does not find Sabbath rest.] However, whenever he transcends these things and then passes above the world and above the heavens . . . , in heaven, at that moment he has the Sabbath rest. This, strictly speaking, is the Sabbath observance. Even [while dwelling on earth a person is able to observe the] Sabbath, for the one who walks on earth and has citizenship in heaven,[2] this . . . to the world has his mind keeping the Sabbath rest in heaven. And at some time there will begin [a resting for us who are burdened,] when we possess our heart and already observe the Sabbath, "the delightful one, the Sabbath holy to God,"[3] [when we desire to follow] the one who says, "Come to me, all you that are weary [and carrying heavy burdens," "and learn from me; for I am gentle] and humble in heart, and you will find rest for your souls."[4] [For when we trust him, not in a kind of] figurative way do we observe the Sabbath, but in truth [we keep the Sabbath. And that the Sabbath observances that the Jews keep] are not original is evident, for it says, "Let no one condemn you in matters of observing festivals or new moons, (or Sabbaths), which are only a shadow of what is] to come."[5] Now, if the festivals and new moons are like the shadow of the things to come, and] the Sabbaths [are associated with them, these Sabbaths are foreshadowing. [And it is possible by the true Sabbath-keeping that remains] "for the people of God"[6] to have a rest that exists.

In remembrance of the Sabbath. O Lord, do not rebuke me in your anger.

Therefore, the Sabbath was remembered, on which no servitude [imprisoned, for he was once in it, but he fell away from it after he

---

[1] 1 Tim 2:4.

[2] Cf. Phil 3:20.
[3] Is 58:13.
[4] Mt 11:28-29 NRSV.
[5] Cf. Col 2:16.
[6] Heb 4:9.

sinned. Therefore, when] he is led there, he remembers the most beautiful [rest there, for the person who recites] the psalm [is the person of one who repents.] The one who truly repents [desires to be reproved and to be instructed about his lawless deeds], for thus the repentance will be demonstrated to be genuine. [For if, though he produces words of repentance, he does not desire to be reproved,] he seems to do this in a feigned way. Therefore, it is necessary to show the true repentance . . . , in order that it might appear how great and how beautiful it is.

[37:2] *O Lord, do not rebuke me in your anger, nor discipline me in your wrath.*

[258] [After receiving an awareness of it], he then brings to God [a question] about sin. This, then, is what he says: "I will ponder about my sin."[7] Teach me why I am a sinner! Because he took remembrance of his own sin he says these things. [And this is the paradox:] on the one hand he knows the sin, on the other hand he does not understand it, for since he has the experience of it, he knows [it but does not understand it. However, if] he had understood that it is harmful and destructive and produces the greatest destruction, [he would have recognized it. Therefore,] the one who receives an experience of it [can] know it and in another sense not understand it. By mere [faith, again, someone understands] without having the experience. The Man who is in relation to Jesus is said not to have known sin [nor to have committed it.[8] In] another sense of "knowing," no one knew it better than he did, for how has he come [to take sin away, unless] he knew it?

O Lord, do not rebuke me in your anger, nor discipline me in your wrath.

The passage can have such a sense: often when a kind of anger and beating arrive, they show such a person to be a sinner. [So indeed Israel, when it] was seduced into great impiety, was handed over to the Assyrians, subject to the Babylonians. . . . And because the handing over of Israel has taken place, not by chance, but by means of previous sin: "Jerusalem sinned a sin,"[9] it took place for her disgrace. She sinned a great sin, and she did not merely "sin," but she sinned a "sin." "Jerusalem sinned a sin." Whenever someone, then, because of previous sin, falls into painful circumstances that [rebuke him, he receives an experience of God's anger.]

Therefore, he did not say, "Do not rebuke me at all," nor, "do not discipline me at all," [but *not in anger, nor in wrath.*] "Everything that is reproved by the light becomes visible."[10] The reproof that is by the light is through instruction. The saint does not excuse himself from such reproof. Again, someone is disciplined in anger [whenever, through painful circumstances, he receives an impression of what] he practiced in ignorance and thought wickedly. He desires to be reproved in the same way that it is said [of the wise man who is reproved.][11] And this reproof is not in anger, but is said by way of revelation. After the sin becomes manifest and . . . Anger is weaker than wrath, however, just as the rebuke is weaker than the painful discipline.

And perhaps he is speaking entirely from the person of those who are overwhelmed by vice: "May the Lord discipline us before [we fall into painful circumstances. For this reason, show] us the judgment, show us the punishment that succeeds the [transgressions] . . . threaten us—do not bring the things threatened into effect—and [reprove us about

---

[7] Ps 38:18 (37:19).
[8] Cf. 2 Cor 5:21; 1 Pet 2:22.
[9] Lam 1:8 LES2.
[10] Eph 5:13.
[11] Cf. Prov 9:8.

our sins as if] in judgment, show us what we must do with discretion."

... ["Or have you not read in the law that on the sabbath] the priests in the temple break the sabbath and yet [are guiltless?"[12] Either he is saying the following: if] the Sabbath is broken [by works of every kind], then the priests can be said also to profane it because of [their service. By sacrificing and] performing [the rest of their] sacred ceremony, they seem to profane [the Sabbath no differently than the disciples] profane it. Or perhaps, according to the opinion of the [Pharisees, who were scandalized by his disciples] and said: by plucking ears of grain on the Sabbath "your disciples are doing what is not lawful to do on the Sabbath,"[13] he said this response in order to show that there is [a difference between the works. So indeed the priests perform] the priestly [works] and they are not guilty of transgressing [the Sabbath. According to those who] think [in this way, they in every way profane the Sabbath], yet they are without blame. For not as [works of servitude are the priestly deeds that are performed for God,] so that the one who does them does not transgress the Sabbath . . . in the world, in action, and in desire . . . he may find rest: for "come to me, all you that are weary and carrying heavy burdens, and I will give you rest."[14] . . . a more elevated anagogical sense, which the divine ones call . . . and the Sabbath observance that will be mentioned. Just as someone, while walking on earth [259] has citizenship in heaven, so someone, while he is in the world, arrives on high by his deeds and keeps the Sabbath. The Sabbath does not simply prohibit work but the work of servitude. The priestly elevation of office, however, being superior to the world, makes people free. Not like works of servitude are the works of God—the works of God being here not what God does but what he commands those who trust in him to do.

And man will receive not another body instead of the corruptible one, but the corruptible one itself changing into incorruptibility and the animate becoming spiritual. See indeed what he is saying! That which is different from the body is incorporeal. Therefore, if someone may say that what we should receive is different from a body, he does not know what he is saying, for he used the word *body* in both cases. "It is sown a perishable body, it is raised an imperishable body. It is sown a weak and dishonored body, it is raised a strong and glorious body. It is sown a natural body, it is raised a spiritual body."[15] In a certain sense, then, the body that is raised is both different and the same as the one that has fallen. When, however, he says that if there is a natural body, there is also a spiritual body, he is speaking of the difference conceptually and he is saying, "But it is not the spiritual that is first, but the natural, and next the spiritual."[16] The "first" and the "next" seem to be two things, but I speak in this way, as when I say that man is first an infant and next a child, and not first the child but the infant. And I am certainly not speaking of two *hypostaseis*; I am not speaking of two men but of one and of two periods of life. Therefore, in whatever way the periods of life do not make the one who changes ages of a different being, but in character or in intention a change occurs or an alteration, in the same way, too, a man comes from the child and the man is not a different person from the child but the same person.

Someone therefore comes truly and corporeally in heaven and observes the Sabbath at that time, no longer walking on earth and having his citizenship in heaven,[17] but already

---

[12] Mt 12:5 NRSV.
[13] Cf. Mt 12:2.
[14] Mt 11:28 NRSV.
[15] Cf. 1 Cor 15:42-44.
[16] 1 Cor 15:46.
[17] Cf. Phil 3:20.

being seated in the heavenly places,[18] already living under "the great high priest who has passed through the heavens."[19]

And because the things that concern men did not begin from vice but from virtue, he speaks *in remembrance of the Sabbath*. When someone comes into virtue, he remembers that he was once in it. Now, I wish to intimate a deep subject. If the beginning of men and of the soul was in this life, then vice comes before virtue, and virtue is something confiscated later on. We have a life that is with a body; we have a life that is also without this. And that after leaving the body we come into an incorporeal life is probably evident to everyone. However, let it be sought out whether this was also before the body. This is not clear, however: but let it be sought out and examined. If, then, the life of the rational being comes from the material life, then vice is before virtue, for we see that the reason begins after it has been filled up by vice. But if, as maintains the truth, virtue was before vice—for "God has made man upright, but they themselves searched out evil reasonings."[20] And see that the seeking of evil reasonings comes after the uprightness. And virtue prepares uprightness. "And a man, although he is in honor, does not understand. He was comparable to the senseless beasts."[21] He has not arrived at the human from a beastly way of life but has come to the beastly from the human. And in general, at least, the good things always precede the reproachable things. Art must precede debased art, knowing something erroneously comes after knowing rightly, for how are we able to say at all that this is erroneous, unless we may have known what is straight?

For this reason, then, he says, "*in remembrance of the Sabbath*." And since to observe the Sabbath is to pass the time virtuously and to live in a way that is pleasing to God and to serve, doing what God desires, the life of men began from virtue. In the more bodily life, however, this is not clear, for the virtue of those who are with the body is confiscated, it is taught. For this reason, the one who enters into the good remembers it.

Question: What does the number thirty-seven mean?

You cannot throw yourself at every number. Now then, someone might say this, that the number thirty-seven is composed of two holy numbers, for the three is also praised in Scripture. For example, one produces the triple-ten by bearing only one of the fruits of the Holy Land: for "one bore a hundredfold, one sixty, and one thirty."[22] And lest we always say the same things, one should be once and for all content to say that the number three is holy, whether it is encountered in ones, in tens, or in hundreds.[23] [260] Furthermore, the number seven is holy, for it was often said of this that it is incorruptible; it is a virgin; it is without a father, without a mother.

O Lord, do not rebuke me in your anger, nor discipline me in your wrath.

He does not simply try to avoid being rebuked or disciplined but shuns these things in anger or wrath. However, a person can be disciplined rationally and knowledgeably, in accordance with which sense the saint prays, saying—rather, he praises and blesses— "Blessed is the man whom you discipline, O Lord, and teach him out of your law."[24] He showed that this discipline comes in accordance with teaching. Now, both rebuke and discipline often come through anger and wrath, through painful things, through harsh things. Furthermore, a rebuke frequently comes when that in which one is in guilty error is demonstrated by a word, for it says the

---

[18]Cf. Eph 2:6.
[19]Heb 4:14 NRSV.
[20]Eccles 7:29.
[21]Ps 49:12 (48:13).

[22]Mt 13:8; Mk 4:8.
[23]That is 3, 30, and 300.
[24]Ps 94:12 (93:12).

following: "Rebuke a wise man, and he will love you."[25] The wise man rebukes the less wise and him who is as a beginner. . . . And again, "Everything that is reproved by the light becomes visible."[26]

And many say of a rebuke such things: that a rebuke is like a contradictory syllogism.[27] Say, for example, someone is in vice. By bearing the argument that separates the vice from the virtue syllogistically, and by knowing the good, he receives an estimation of the evil. And this rebuke does not come with anger but with instruction, for since the knowledge of opposites is the same, when we know the good, we possess knowledge of the evil.

And from the Scriptures one can take examples: the Ninevites have come into great vice, so that "the outcry of their wickedness came up"[28] to God, calling for the punishment and recompense. But God sent a proclamation of repentance. They welcomed the proclamation. They were disciplined; they were not rebuked in anger or wrath. The Sodomites, for example, were rebuked and disciplined in anger and wrath. So while he would not shun being rebuked in a knowledgeable way, he does not desire to be rebuked by these things.

[37:3] *Because your arrows were stuck in me.*

For this reason, I seek to avoid the rebuke that is in anger and the discipline in wrath, since *your arrows were stuck in me.* I received an understanding of the punishments that are brought against the undisciplined, against those who do not accept rebuke. And in many places of the divine instruction "arrows" signify punishments. As when Job, when he comes into many grievous afflictions, says, "The arrows of the Lord are in my body."[29] That dreadful ulceration he called "the arrows of the Lord" in his body. And this is a paradox: he even introduces providence through this saying. These painful experiences, the kinds of arrows that wound me, have not begun for me without God's decision, "for they are the arrows of the Lord; their wrath drinks my blood; when I begin to speak, they pierce me."[30] And observe carefully that that painful and torturous wound he called the "arrows of the Lord." And again in the great song of Deuteronomy, God says, "I will make my arrows drunk with blood, and my sword will devour the blood of the wounded."[31] In many places the sword means punishment. "For if you are not willing, nor listen to me, the sword will devour you."[32] Such is what is spoken in Isaiah: "My sword has become drunk in heaven,"[33] that is, the punishment even touched some of the heavenly ones. And since God subjected "the angels who did not keep their own position to eternal chains,"[34] the sword of God has become drunk, the power of punishment, that is, even in heaven. And here also understand the same things: when someone, thinking that he has his citizenship in heaven,[35] being himself a heaven so that "he declares the glory of God,"[36] when he falls unexpectedly into punishment, then the sword has become drunk in heaven, among those who are declared to have a heavenly citizenship. Such is the saying, "The sons of the kingdom will be thrown into the outer darkness,"[37] because they are not truly sons.

However, it can also be understood in a praiseworthy way: "Your arrows are sharp, O powerful one—peoples shall fall under you."[38]

---

[25]Prov 9:8.
[26]Eph 5:13.
[27]Aristotle, *Prior Analytics* 66b11; *Sophistical Refutations* 165a2.
[28]Jon 1:2.
[29]Job 6:4.
[30]Cf. Job 6:4 NETS.
[31]Deut 32:42.
[32]Is 1:20.
[33]Is 34:5.
[34]Cf. Jude 6 NRSV.
[35]Cf. Phil 3:20.
[36]Ps 19:1 (18:2).
[37]Mt 8:12 ESV.
[38]Ps 45:5 (44:6 NETS).

Your arrows, which wound for desire and love, have been sharpened, for you are powerful and you powerfully send your words, and you wound those who are struck for love. Indeed, the soul that suffers this, or the church, says, "I am wounded with love."[39] There are, then, praiseworthy arrows; there are, then, blameworthy ones. But since these were mentioned together with wrath and anger, they do not wound for desire and love, but they give on the impression of precisely how far someone is in evils.

[37:3] *And you clamped your hand on me.*

In many places, again, the punishing power is indicated [261] by the name "God's hand," as when he says to Pharaoh, "Now when I stretch out my hand I will strike you."[40] And, "See, the hand of the Lord will be on your animals in the plains,"[41] for in this way those animals were subjected to destruction. And again it is said, "Your hand destroyed nations."[42] When the active, creative, and protective hand of God is mentioned, it is called "the right hand." This hand truly leads to salvation. He who has received the experience of being led by it says indeed, "You seized my right hand,"[43] the active power for good things.

[37:4] *And there is no healing in my flesh from before your wrath.*

The word *flesh*, being an ambiguous word, signifies different things in Scripture. At times *flesh* is used to signify our perceptive mode of thought, for when it is said, "I will draw forth from them their heart of stone and I will give them a heart of flesh,"[44] he calls a "heart of stone" the foolish thinking that is detached from every sensation. Instead of this a fleshly heart is given, perceptive and yielding to the laws of God. That which is yielding and perceptive, then, is often called "flesh."

And *flesh* is used when it is being contrasted with *spirit*. And it calls "spirit" the reason, while it calls "flesh" that which is contrasted with reason. Therefore, whenever someone meditates on the things of the flesh, and practices them, and lives in accordance with them, he is far away from the spirit. However, when he follows the spirit, the true reason, and especially the reason that partakes of the Holy Spirit, then he leaves the flesh inactive. Concerning such flesh and the spirit that is distinguished from it, he says, "But you are not in the flesh but in the spirit."[45] However, they were in the flesh, they were still burdened with the body. In their disposition, they had come outside it. And just as some, while living on earth, can have citizenship in heaven, so someone, while still in the flesh, comes outside it when he follows the spirit. And this is what is called a "blessed exodus." Some, however, who are ignorant of how the wise have spoken of a blessed exodus, often say when they have been asked, "They have expelled themselves from life either by reasonings or passions." This, however, is not a blessed exodus, but whenever a certain one, being holy in body, becomes free of it in his preoccupation and disposition, so as to say, "We are not in the flesh but in the spirit,"[46] and again, "The mind that is set on the flesh is hostile to God."[47] "And those who are in the flesh cannot please God."[48] And it comes to mind that he is not speaking about this flesh, for all the saints, while they were in the flesh, pleased God. There is, therefore, a

---

[39]Song 2:5 NETS.
[40]Ex 9:15.
[41]Ex 9:3.
[42]Ps 44:2 (43:3 NETS).
[43]Ps 73:23 (72:23 NETS).
[44]Cf. Ezek 11:19 NETS.

[45]Rom 8:9.
[46]Rom 8:9.
[47]Rom 8:7 NRSV.
[48]Rom 8:8 NRSV.

"flesh," which the one who becomes free of, is pleasing to God: the material, pleasure-loving inclination.

And perhaps when someone becomes a spiritual person he abandons the flesh, nor is he troubled when wrath presses on him. However, he who still strives to live in this way is troubled whenever something painful is expected and approaches.

Often, the composite is indicated by one of the parts in the composite. When the saint says, "Why are you deeply grieved, O my soul, and why are you throwing me into confusion?"[49] Then he produces the indication in respect to that which is more precious. Again when it says, "I punish my body and enslave it,"[50] indeed, he is not speaking about that which is distinct from the body, but since the body is subordinate, and the soul ruling, when the body is subjected to the soul, being ruled by it, being also ruled with reason and with God's law, it is punished and enslaved.

Since, then, I see wrath pressing on me, for this reason my flesh also is troubled. For this reason the saints do not fear a kind of rapid death. He has become forgetful that he bears flesh. And whenever he looks to this very thing, that he is entangled in flesh, and has received flesh, which can be separated from the soul, on the contrary he is shaken by death.

"All flesh is grass, and the glory of man is like the flower of grass."[51] Again it says, "To you all flesh shall come,"[52] that is, every man. "All flesh shall see the salvation of God."[53] All the ambiguous things are separated by certain qualifications from those things that have the same name. When it is said in Scripture, "he who gives nourishment to all flesh,"[54] we understand every living creature that exists.

And when I say, "I will pour out of my Spirit on all flesh,"[55] I am speaking of that flesh that is naturally inclined to receive the gift of the Spirit.

[37:4] *There is no peace for my bones from the appearance of my sins.*

Since I see my sins present. Not everyone receives a knowledge of their appearance except the one who repents and desires to flee from them. The one who sins, and ignoring [262] this very thing, that he sins, does not see the *appearance of* his own *sins*, does not see their shame. However, the one who understands what he does and sees that he accomplishes them by transgressing the divine law has the appearance of his sins revealed.

And by *bones* he certainly does not mean those of the body, except according to the lower sense, as was also said of *flesh*. And this passage was quoted in the earlier lectures: "All my bones shall say, 'O Lord, who is like you?'"[56] If the bones say, "O Lord, who is like you?" then they received an impression of the Lord and, if I may speak in this way, of his form, so as to know that no one is like him. However, the likeness and the unlikeness to God make manifest the knowledge of God and the teaching about God, so that he is not speaking about the bones of the body but about the strong and robust doctrines of the soul and its powers. For then the physical bodies are supported by the bones, for they would be unable to have tendons and blood vessels and the rest, unless they had bones.

Question: *There is no peace for my bones?*
Whenever the powers of the soul are interdependent, they have peace. Whenever the irascible part is not at odds with the rational part, and the appetitive part with the intellect, then there is peace. Again, when

---

[49] Ps 42:5 (41:6 NETS).
[50] 1 Cor 9:27 NRSV.
[51] Cf. Is 40:6 NETS.
[52] Ps 65:2 (64:3 NETS).
[53] Is 40:5 NETS.
[54] Ps 136:25 (135:25 NETS).

[55] Joel 2:28 NETS.
[56] Ps 35:10 (34:10 NETS).

someone possesses discordant doctrines—and the many possess such doctrines; they carry a certain doctrine with themselves and then they bring in another, which overturns the one they have held first. And the wise man, especially the man who is wise in God, must have concordance in the powers of the inner man and in the things he must think, for in this way there is peace in his bones.

[37:5] *Because my acts of lawlessness went over my head.*

He is saying the following: *my lawless acts,* which ought to be under my feet and trampled over, have come over me, they rule my intellect. And in many places the head signifies the intellect, as in this one: "The eyes of the wise are in his head,"[57] that is, they are in his intellect. In any case, the one who has said this very thing, "The eyes of the wise," clarifies it in other passages when he says, "The wisdom of a man will illuminate his face,"[58] no doubt calling the inner man, the intellect, "face."

My deeds have become a heavy burden, they drag me downward. I must bear that burden that Jesus gives me to carry and the yoke that he puts on me, for this is a wicked burden, as this very passage says: "My lawless deeds, a heavy burden, weighed on me."[59] "Come" then, he says, "to me, for I will give you rest,"[60] I take the burden from you and the things that oppressed you were taken away: "for my yoke is easy, and my burden is light."[61] This burden exalts the one who bears it, it bears him above; this burden is furnished with wings. The burden of vice is downwardly heavy; it throws down. So it says of the wicked, "You will sink like lead in the mighty water."[62]

[37:5] *Like a heavy burden they weighed on me.*

And this is not for everyone to know that vice is a heavy burden, other than the one who received an impression of its irksomeness. Then indeed, someone grows weary of the things that convey this burden, when he receives an impression of the weight of vice. And then he comes to Jesus. However, the one who rejoices in the burden of vice instead strays from Jesus. For this reason it is also said in Isaiah, "Egypt worked hard, the commerce of the Ethiopians. And the lofty men of Saba shall come over to you, and they shall be your slaves. And they shall prostrate themselves before you because God strengthens you, and there is no God besides you."[63] "Egypt worked hard," then, when he received an impression of how deep he is in wickedness, when he worships idols and occupies himself in superstitious folly, with those who foretell the future, with necromancy and the very demons who oppress them. And when he does not have an awareness of them, he does not "work hard." "The commerce of the Ethiopians," then, or "the merchandise of the Ethiopians," works hard at that time. And he calls "Ethiopians" those who have become black in the inner man. So indeed the devil in the Epistle of Barnabas and in the Shepherd is called "the black one," not in body but darkened in understanding, because he came outside **[263]** the brightness of the saints. Therefore these Ethiopians have commerce or merchandise, where their commerce is. And then they work hard, whenever they receive an impression of how deep they are in evil, for as long as someone takes pleasure in sinning, he does not work hard.

[37:6] *My wounds stank and festered from the appearance of my foolishness.*

I had wounds from the darts of punishment or even from the darts of the evil one that

---

[57] Eccles 2:14.
[58] Eccles 8:1.
[59] Ps 38:4 (37:5).
[60] Mt 11:28.
[61] Mt 11:30 NRSV.
[62] Ex 15:10.

[63] Is 45:14.

have been tempered with fire,[64] for he also is said to possess flaming arrows. Therefore, whenever someone receives lacerations, that is, the thoughts and ideas of evil things and impieties, he is among wounds. And whenever these grow, and have an exhalation and emit an odor, finally they create decay. *My wounds stank and festered.* From where did I have the wounds; from where has their decay come? *From the appearance of my foolishness.* I must disdain foolishness to withdraw from it. And someone creates foolishness whenever he does not acquire wisdom. The pricks of thoughts and desires: these produce wounds. It is necessary to heal these quickly. Someone saw a woman with desire. He had a wound. Let him heal! Let him arrest the impulse at the forepassion, for in this way the desire may neither emit a bad smell nor produce decay. However, when the intention persists, it produces these things: decay and an odor, and that an unpleasant one.

Whenever one does not have this prudence so as to know what should be done, what should not, and the so-called indifferent things, which are mixed, he is in foolishness. And foolishness nourishes and strengthens sins that seem to be petty, so that they are made comparable to wounds, and they become filth and decay. However, understand the odor and the decay appropriately to the being about whom the discussion runs, for nothing corporeal is shown, for many foolish people are healthy and have strong bodies.

[37:7] *I was wretched and bowed down completely.*

Often things that are unpleasant and painful produce fatigue. And indeed, the body itself makes the one who has been loaded with it wretched. The apostolic saying, which runs thus: "Wretched man that I am! Who will rescue me from this body of death?"[65] suggests this sense. For since I am in the body of death, I am wretched, and not just anyone will make me free from such wretchedness other than the Savior, for he immediately added, "I give thanks through Jesus Christ,"[66] who set me free from the body. We say, then, that wretchedness arises for the soul from the body of death. We do not understand the body to belong to death absolutely, but only such a body. Whenever someone uses this body so that he commits sin to death, then he is afflicted with a body of death. And it is possible for one to make it not a body of death, for whenever I remove from it the things that make it a body of death, then it is a body of death no longer.

And just as this perceptible body has both a material existence and the form of a body, it is also possible to separate this body from the gross body. When the body has only three dimensions without matter, then this body is not an essence. In these common things, then, when it is said, for example, that "in a body there is color," hence also in a certain body, by saying that there is "color in a body," he showed that he means this visible body, which we touch. But when he says that the body is one form of the quantity, he does not mean this body, for how can an essence be the form of an essence? So "body" is ambiguous, for the one is understood in three dimensions without matter. And this is the quantitative body, for the body with matter we do not understand as only three dimensions without the underlying essence but with it. This body is something else.

The body, then, is a body of death at that time when its actions and movements take place sinfully. **[264]** It is therefore possible to separate this from the body. When I receive an eye that does not see in a harmful way, that does not look adulterously, I remove the eye of

---

[64] Cf. Eph 6:16.

[65] Rom 7:24 NRSV.
[66] Rom 7:25.

death from its substance. And when this takes place for each part and for each sense, the body of death is chased away. We do not throw away the body but the body of death. And when we see the wicked man changing into a virtuous man, we say that the wicked man was brought to ruin, but not the man.

And I was bowed down.

Vice is heavy; it bows down the one who has it. For always, when great burdens are placed on someone, they pull down and bend the one who carries them. For example, it says of that woman who had "a spirit of infirmity" for eighteen years that "she was bent over and was quite unable to stand up straight."[67] She would never raise herself up. The sinner, therefore, bends forward and looks downward. Indeed, it says, "They set their eyes to incline at the ground."[68] And again in Jeremiah it is said, "Let those who have turned away be recorded on the earth."[69] Those who have forsaken the divine source are recorded, they are registered as citizens on earth, as those who have their citizenship below and bear "the image of the earthly man."[70] Now, "the names" of the disciples "are written in heaven."[71] He does not mean these names that are composed of syllables but their own qualities, which indicate their soul and their intellect. For the definition of *name* is given as follows: "'Name' is a summary appellation that indicates the quality of the thing named." And this is an appellative name: "man," "heaven." Therefore, their names are inscribed, that is, they are recorded.

[37:7] *All day long I would go around sullen.*

Even if "I was bowed down completely" from the fatigue that assaulted me, yet I am not insensitive to this. Indeed, sullen, I go around with "godly grief, that produces a repentance that leads to salvation and brings no regret."[72] And, sullen in this way, I go around all day long. And well did he say, "I go around." He does not remain downcast but he goes around. He did not "hollow out a place to sit in the earth,"[73] he did not lay his back on the earth, but he goes around. *Sullen*, then, *I would go around.* I would do those things that would transport me out of the fatigue. And I am guided out of the fatigue when I put away from myself the causes of the fatigue.

[37:8] *Because my soul was filled with mockeries.*

My soul was filled with sins. Now, *mockeries* are sins. The one who deceives mocks the one who is deceived, and in this way his soul is filled with mockeries.

Now, in some variants it reads "my loins." The sperm are said to be constituted around these. Whenever someone therefore sinks down into intemperance and pursues being a lover of pleasure rather than a lover of God, he has his loins filled with mockeries.

[37:8] *And there is no healing in my flesh.*

For as long as I have been filled with these mockeries, not only is my flesh not sound, but it is sick, so disposed that it does not receive healing. Just as it is impossible for the one who is perceptibly sick, while he is still in the sickness, to welcome health, so the one who is filled with mockeries is unable to make his flesh at peace, that is, temperate, or not at odds with itself.

---

[67] Lk 13:11 NRSV.
[68] Cf. Ps 17:11 (16:11 NETS).
[69] Jer 17:13 NETS.
[70] Cf. 1 Cor 15:49.
[71] Lk 10:20 NRSV.

[72] Cf. 2 Cor 7:10 NRSV.
[73] Jer 49:8 (29:9).

[37:9] *I was mistreated and I was utterly humiliated.*

It is possible to speak here of a willing mistreatment and humiliation. Since I have become aware of the height of vice, its harmfulness, and its vanity, I reduced myself freely into humiliation, in order that I might be exalted, for "whoever humbles himself will be exalted."[74]

One must understand the mistreatment and humiliation similarly. And this takes place willingly at the time when, as I said, that which is exalted humbles itself in order that it may be exalted by God.

And it is also possible to understand it in this way: because of the painful and heavy burdens that have beset me *I was humbled; I was utterly mistreated*. I had the mistreatment intensified.

[37:9] *I would weep because of my heart's groaning.*

I would not lament in a feigned way the evils that have surrounded me, but *because of my heart's groaning*. Knowing what one must groan about, I would groan.

[37:10] *And before you* [265] *is all my desire.*

The righteous person always has a love and desire for the virtues and things that are done in a praiseworthy manner. Indeed, it is said of the righteous person, "The desire of the righteous is completely good."[75] And all that is good has the boldness to be in front of God. *Before you*, then, that is, in front of you, *is all my desire*. "My desire" must be understood here as praiseworthy, of the same kind as that desire of which this psalmist himself says, "Bless the Lord, O my soul, who fulfills your desire with good things."[76] All such desires of the righteous person, therefore, being able to be spoken of with confidence, are before God.

However, it is also possible to understand the saying with the different meaning of *desire*. Because of this I was humiliated and exceedingly bent down, because of this I groan and my groaning comes from my soul and my heart, since I knew that every desire which I had, which was wicked, is obvious to you; no desire is outside of your presence. However, the word *before* is more noble.

[37:10] *And my groaning was not hidden from you.*

Having a good desire and desiring to be in good things and in virtue, insofar as I see myself lacking these things, I groan. And this groaning comes from a desire of beauty, from the expectation of what is better. Even if I often remain unobserved when I groan, lest I seem to exalt myself and thence repent only in appearance, yet my groaning is before you; it was not hidden from you.

The Egyptians certainly used to crush the Hebrews. When "the sons of Israel" took pleasure in the works of the Egyptians, their groaning had been hidden from the face of God. However, when they began to groan over their works, when they received an awareness of the works of Pharaoh, that they drag down, are earthly, and proceed free from God, then they groaned, and their groaning was not hidden from God, for he immediately set them free. However, when they took pleasure in them, they were found there, they did not obtain freedom.

This groaning corresponds to "the grief that produces repentance leading to salvation."[77] And this grief is different from the grief of the world, which produces death. Indeed, when

---

[74] Lk 14:11.
[75] Prov 11:23 LES2.
[76] Ps 103:1, 5 (102:1, 5).
[77] Cf. 2 Cor 7:10.

you see a man groaning because he does not obtain what he desires, even when these things are evil, this groaning is destructive.

[37:11] *My heart was troubled, my strength failed me.*

When the heart is troubled, that is, the intellect, then the strength becomes far removed. And this is the strength that is appropriate to peace and to the tranquility of the heart. The one who learned from Jesus, "for he is gentle and humble in heart,"[78] does not have a troubled heart, for he imitates Jesus. And the one who imitates Jesus is free from all trouble. And as long as he does not have this trouble, his strength remains to him, so that he says, "I can do all things through him who strengthens me,"[79] and, "I will love you, O Lord, my strength."[80]

[37:12] *And as for the light of my eyes—it too is not with me.*

The light of my eyes has become far from me. And the light of the true eyes, which perceive penetratingly, is the knowledge of the truth, for it is said, "Enlighten yourselves with the light of knowledge."[81] That the discourse is not about these eyes, nor the light that is perceived by the senses, hear the one who says, "The commandment of the Lord is radiant, enlightening the eyes."[82] The keeping of the radiant commandment no doubt illuminates the eyes of the inner man, for there are many who are keen-sighted and are also transgressors of the commandment of the Lord, and on the other hand there are people who are weak-sighted who keep it and embrace it. By no means, then, of the physical eyes is it said, *And the light of my eyes is not with me.* It forsook me, however, because I turned away from it, because I myself did not keep it constantly with me. **[266]**

"My heart was troubled, my strength failed me."

Whenever the intellectual faculty suffers disorder, the strength becomes far distant, for when the mind is in good health and the intellect is perfect, strength belongs to the one so disposed, so as to say, "I can do all things through him who strengthens me."[83] "I will love you, O Lord, my strength."[84] And someone is abandoned by this strength when he suffers disorder in the heart, when he has confused thoughts. For this reason, it is necessary to keep watch not to give "room to the devil,"[85] who arouses disturbances, in order that our strength should remain and we be able to say, "The Lord is my strength and my song of praise, and he became my salvation."[86]

And the light of my eyes is not with me.

Whenever the heart is troubled, and the corresponding strength leaves the heart, then even the light itself is not with the one who suffered these things, for it is necessary to "sow unto righteousness and reap unto the fruit of life," in order to "enlighten yourselves with the light of knowledge."[87] When therefore the heart is troubled and the strength that empowers the inner man becomes remote, then the very light of the eyes that illumines the inner man leaves this one who has betrayed himself to darkness and ignorance.

[37:12] *My friends and my neighbors drew near opposite me and stood.*

Such things happen to occur in critical times. And Job certainly was saying such things when he had come into a critical situation: "And my

---

[78] Mt 11:29.
[79] Phil 4:13 NRSV.
[80] Ps 18:1 (17:2 NETS).
[81] Hos 10:12 NETS (LXX).
[82] Ps 19:8 (18:9 NETS).

[83] Phil 4:13 NRSV.
[84] Ps 18:1 (17:2 NETS).
[85] Eph 4:27.
[86] Ps 118:14 (117:14).
[87] Cf. Hos 10:12 (LXX).

friends became merciless; they recognized strangers rather than me."[88] And in the Books of Wisdom it is written that the friends are only present and give proof of and seek the things of friendship then, when the one whom they "truly love" is in abundance. But whenever his affairs, his external circumstances, come into a kind of confusion, then those become far away.[89]

Indeed, there are three kinds of friendship. There is friendship in itself, when a person is pursued for no other purpose than for beauty of life and virtue. But if there is a purpose, it is wealth. When those prerequisites are missing, then the friendship will have come to an end. But this friendship is said to be of a second kind. It comes into existence for the sake of profit. And a third kind of friendship is for the sake of pleasure. Many are pleased to be friends of monks, not in order to be monks, but in order to say, "The monastics love me." And others are their friends for the sake of wealth, although they expect nothing from them but sometimes even give to them bountifully.

One can call the *neighbor a friend*, without distinction, or the friend a neighbor. And in the same way those who are neighbors in close familiarity are my brothers in kinship.

Question: Is it necessary to take this in relation to bodily things?

If you might mean it in a spiritual sense—and there are both friends and kin in spirit— observe: whenever a person diminishes himself and is no longer such as he was, those whom he formerly held for friends become estranged from him, because he is lesser than himself, so to speak, because he has become wicked. Surely the words that follow are recited no longer as though they are about a wicked person or by a wicked person. Although he is completely troubled in heart, he is not an outcast, for the one who destroys this heart is different. It was said indeed in Isaiah, "You who have ruined your heart."[90] Now, the heart is ruined whenever the understanding becomes free of its appropriate condition. And it is troubled when it receives a kind of confusion. And it happens that I am troubled because I receive thoughts and ideas that are not fitting.

They drew near opposite me and stood.

Not as companions, not as friends, not in order to be united with me, but *opposite me*, in order that they might oppose me by coming near. I had such an observation both in Zechariah and in the 108th Psalm. About Judas it is said, "Let the devil stand at his right."[91] And about Joshua the high priest, the son of Jehozadak, "the devil stood at his right to oppose him."[92] And see that both of Judas and of Joshua the high priest, most pure and holy, the devil stood on the right. But it is said in the case of Joshua, "to oppose him." He stood in order that he might be an adversary to the things on the right hand, in order to make war against it, because by the right hand one accomplishes the things that one must practice and has such a disposition. However, this is not so in the case of Judas. He has already secured dominion over the right hand **[267]** things of Judas. He has given to the devil himself a place in these things.[93]

And here *they stood opposite*. For this reason they *drew near*, in order to besiege and trouble.

[37:12] *And those nearest me stood far off.*

There are two kinds of friends: there are two dispositions of those who are neighbors. Whenever those who were formerly enemies become friends in pretense and obscurely, they do this in order to oppose. And, to take from the catechetical instruction of the Shepherd, I say: there are two angels with man, and the

---

[88]Job 19:13.
[89]Cf. Sir 6:10-12.
[90]Is 46:12 NETS (LXX).
[91]Ps 109:6 (108:6).
[92]Zech 3:1.
[93]Cf. Eph 4:27.

one suggests evils, and the other goods, and one is an angel of righteousness, while the other is an angel of injustice. Therefore, when the angel of injustice draws near, the one who suggests evils, the good angel is far away, as again after that good angel approaches, the evil one opposes. For as opposites are incompatible, the good and the evil; indeed, one does the evil whenever the good is far away.

And if it is the person of the Savior who says these things, he can say, "Those who were once my friends have become far away, my sons, those whom I begot and reared. After they repudiated me they have become distant. And those who believed from the Gentiles, after becoming friends, are at last near and 'opposite me,' that is, 'opposite my face.'" For we no longer understand the *opposite* to mean "adverse" but "in front of the face," "before."

[37:13] *And those who seek my soul did violence, and those who seek evil things for me spoke vanities.*

None of those who love my soul do it *violence*, but he draws near or becomes one with it. However, the rest do it violence, and by speaking evil things against that one to whom they do violence, they speak *vanity*, nothing useful, nothing that contributes to the knowledge of the truth, but about vain things, for all vain things are evils, wicked, and even temporal, which are seen, most lightly put away, and destroyed.

It is necessary to seek the soul for its benefit. By adding *evil things* to *those who seek my soul* and *do violence* it is clear that they are wicked. The one who received the sinning soul into repentance, and leads the soul that slipped away from the truth into this, seeks the soul in a praiseworthy and beneficial way. The Savior, for example, "came to seek out and to save the lost."[94] When he seeks the soul, he seeks in order to lead it to salvation, in order to return it according to its former condition. Therefore, as the Savior does this through instruction and perfection in the good, so also the disciples of the Savior, both angels and men, do this. And none of these *speaks vanity* when seeking the soul; none of these *seeks evil things* for it but things good and beneficial.

[37:13] *And they contemplated treacheries all day long.*

They used to contemplate iniquities all their life long, for how would they not intend this? They had "perverse thoughts which separate from God,"[95] and their heart had become perverse and crooked, which the saint denied having, saying, "A crooked heart did not cling to me!"[96] Therefore, the one who has crooked thoughts *contemplates* perversions all day long, deeds and thoughts that accord with his perverse ideas. These perverse thoughts are surely placed in the soul by the devil, for it is said, "The serpent, the crooked dragon."[97] He twists things. For example, it is said in other places, "All the crooked ways shall become straight."[98] The crooked ways receive straightening whenever they lay aside crookedness. And the one who contemplates this all day long has crooked deeds, a crooked faculty of choice, and a contorted disposition as well.

[37:14] *But as for me, I, like the deaf, would not hear, and like the mute, not opening his mouth.*

He reports his own praise. The one who repents, when the devil suggests evil or crooked thoughts, like a kind of deaf person, let him not hear, let him not occupy himself with them, let him not present to them the hearing of the inner man, but let him be just as

---

[94] Lk 19:10 NRSV.
[95] Wis 1:3.
[96] Ps 101:4 (100:4 NETS).
[97] Cf. Is 27:1.
[98] Is 40:4 NETS.

a mute, as a deaf person who does not open his mouth. And here he does not call the one who lost his hearing "deaf," but he calls deaf the one who does not speak, for often, especially in Scripture, this meaning for the speaker is present: "When the demon had been cast out, the deaf person spoke."[99] He did not say, "the deaf person heard." However, I do not mean this, that this passage does not also signify the one who is deprived of hearing. It indicates both things.

Again, to Moses who said, "I am weak-voiced and slow of tongue,"[100] God said, "Who gave man a mouth to speak, [**268**] and who made him hard of hearing or deaf, seeing and blind?"[101] Here it is possible that the word *deaf* applies both to the speaker and to the one deprived of the sense of hearing. And the passage, "when the demon had gone out, the deaf person spoke,"[102] signifies a deaf person who has not the faculty of speech, who does not have an active tongue.

[37:15] *And I became like a man who does not hear and has no retort in his mouth.*

He means the following: I have not become a man who does not hear but *like a man who does not hear*. I did not receive the words and the reports of those who act deceptively, even though I am able to respond to them. Knowing that reproaches are not conveyed to such a person at the right time, like one who is unable to rebuke him, I was silent. The discourse shows that both reproaches and refutations ought to be done at the right time. We understand what is the right time from our opponent and the interlocutor. Just as food, when it is given at the right time, benefits and fulfills, so when it is offered at the wrong time, it harms instead. "Do not rebuke evil people, lest they should hate you!"[103] The discourse does not teach one to avoid being hated by the wicked, but it means the following: you are to rebuke in order to bring benefit. When someone is led to rebuke at the wrong time—for "there is a rebuke that is untimely"[104]—it does not benefit that one who is rebuked, but rather it makes him even more wicked, so that he also hates the rebuker. Indeed, "rebuke a wise man, and he will love you."[105] If the wise man, when he is rebuked, loves the one who brings the rebukes, clearly the one who hates the rebuke is wicked. It is said indeed in other places also, "An undisciplined person will not love those who rebuke him, and neither will he associate with the wise."[106] The undisciplined person utterly dislikes those who rebuke him, but the wise person desires this. None of what the wise man says reaches the wicked man, who hates those who rebuke him.

Question: *And has no retort in his mouth?*

"To retort" is used in two ways: often a person is unable to retort. He lacks such confidence and does not have such a power of speech so as to retort, and he simulates one who does not hear. For example, a certain heretic is present. He speaks impious doctrines, heretical opinions. Unless we are able to rebuke the things said by that one, we are called *like men who do not hear*. For to listen to such conversations troubles rather than benefits. Indeed, it is said, "Bad company ruins kind morals."[107] If someone who has a kind morality knows this very thing, that he is unable to advance against bad company, he should not bestow his hearing but should become like a deaf man.

And another, though he has the ability to rebuke the most disgraceful conversations, does not do this when he knows that it is not

---

[99] Lk 11:14.
[100] Ex 4:10 LES2.
[101] Ex 4:11.
[102] Lk 11:14.

[103] Prov 9:8 NETS.
[104] Sir 20:1 NETS.
[105] Prov 9:8.
[106] Prov 15:12.
[107] 1 Cor 15:33.

at that moment useful to that person to be rebuked. For I was saying that just as foods for healing are offered at the right time, so also are the medicines for the soul. And in what way such things are medicine for the soul, for example, it says, "Reproach, rebuke, and encourage!"[108] When you make something manifest by rebuking the sinner, reproach! When again you reproach, after making the reproach sufficiently, encourage! Let one remedy of the soul succeed another! And it is not for just anyone to know these things but for the one who knows the cure of the soul.

[37:16] *Because in you, O Lord, I hoped; it is you, O Lord my God, who will listen.*

Since *I hoped in you*, you yourself listened to me! I am confident that all the things that can be done by that one on my behalf will be done. For this reason, because I am confident in you who are greater and know how and in what way one should rebuke, I was silent. "I have become like a deaf man, having no retort in my mouth."

And it should be punctuated thus: since I hoped in you, you yourself listen to me! For, having become to that one both mute and not having rebukes in my mouth, I cry out to you in my mind.

So appears what happened in the exodus in the case of Moses, at the moment when Pharaoh pursued him with all his strength and his host, and in a certain sense the Hebrews were shut in so that they were unable to travel any further. The host of Pharaoh and the tyrant himself pursued, while the Hebrews, the "sons of Israel," were pursued. And the former were heavily armed and brought with them every kind of armament and military power: both cavalry and infantry. The latter, at this very moment, were carrying only the staffs in their hands. They were hemmed in and they were no longer able to advance any further, for they were unable to hurry forward because the sea prevented them, nor were they able to turn to the right or to the left. It remained only to fall into the power of their enemies once more. Therefore, being caught in a kind of trap and within nets, **[269]** the Hebrews were agitated and contended with and blamed Moses: "Was this not the matter that we told you in Egypt, saying, 'Leave us alone, in order that we might be subject to the Egyptians?'[109] And behold! we perish in this wilderness." Moses the commander himself was speaking words of encouragement: "Take courage! Stand and see the deliverance from the Lord that he will perform for you today. For as you have seen the Egyptians, you shall never again see them, time without end."[110] It was necessary for the commander to say such things to the people without fainting, for he was not able to send up prayer openly. Those people were supposing that he himself also despaired of deliverance. But he was speaking things to reassure them, while to God he was crying out the things that are with the mind. And in order that God should show that it does not come accidentally when help comes, he says, "Why are you crying out to me?"[111] He was crying out to God in secret, but he was speaking words of encouragement. It is, however, a great evil, when a certain terror arrives and the commander thrashes about, as it were. He leads into desperation.

[37:17] *Because I said, "Never let my enemies rejoice over me."*

I said this: for this reason I was silent and have become like a deaf person and like one who has no retort, lest perchance after I dare to do these things, they, becoming superior to me,

---

[108] 2 Tim 4:2.

[109] Ex 14:12 NETS.
[110] Cf. Ex 14:13 NETS.
[111] Ex 14:15 NETS.

should rejoice over me, they will jest against me. For this reason the apostle also says: do not do such a thing, "lest Satan rejoice over you because of your innocence."[112] Certainly that one rejoices over the one who is harmed. "I will exalt you, O Lord, because you upheld me and did not gladden my enemies over me."[113] For if you were not upholding me, because I neither exalted you rightly, nor in the way that I ought to do, they would rejoice over me. And in other places it says, "Do not rejoice over me, my adversary, for I have fallen, yet I shall rise again."[114] You rejoice over my fall, but know that I shall rise again. Therefore, when I stand up, your joy changes into grief, and your songs of jest are transformed into lamentations.

[37:17] *And when my feet were shaken, they boasted against me.*

Even when a trembling of *my feet* takes place, *they boast against me.*

And it is possible to say the following: since "my heart was troubled within me, my strength failed me, and the light of my eyes is not with me," my feet were agitated; however, they did not fall. And that such things happen to those who repent in particular, it is also possible to learn from another psalm: "How good God is to Israel, to the upright in heart! But as for me, my feet were almost shaken; my steps nearly slipped, because I was envious of the lawless."[115] This is the person of one who repents. The repentant person does not report what he says out of the disposition of one who feigns repentance; I knew that "as the God of Israel is good," he does what he does "to those who are upright in heart." Right now, however, I am insecure—he then introduces the repentant one—I almost stumbled and fell.

And I quote the apostolic word that harmonizes with this: "We know that the law is spiritual"—we the perfect, the disciples of the Spirit, who received the divine and spiritual law—"but I am of the flesh, sold into slavery under sin."[116] Not the one who knows that the law is spiritual is of the flesh, sold into slavery under sin, for he was distinguishing himself from those. "We know that the law is spiritual," he says of the saints in general. "But I am of the flesh, sold into slavery under sin." And this very brief phrase, "I am of the flesh," suggests many doctrines indeed. Not by nature, not because of my creation am I so, but "because I was sold into slavery under sin." And the one sold under a certain master is so because he becomes so; he is not fleshly by nature, for because of his sale such a condition has come on him.

And here: "How good God is to Israel, to the upright in heart. But as for me, my feet were almost shaken," the feet of the soul, that is. And the word *almost* means this: that he has not been totally agitated, for the one who says, "I was almost killed," shows that he was not killed. "My steps were nearly dispersed." I was running well, I was walking as I ought to do, I was traveling with upright steps. These were almost dispersed, however. And they are dispersed whenever the runner stops and veers toward the things that were behind him. And from this very word observe carefully: take, for example, someone who goes up to a lofty place on a gritty [path] < ... >.

Therefore, after they have seen the trembling of my feet and not a fall at all, they boasted against me, they have spoken arrogant words. [270] One might say with a different expression, "Do not rejoice over me, my adversary, because I have fallen. I will rise again."[117] However, he who now speaks did not fall entirely, but his feet were only confused,

---

[112]Cf. 1 Cor 7:5.
[113]Ps 30:1 (29:2 NETS).
[114]Mic 7:8.
[115]Ps 73:1-3 (72:1-3 NETS).

[116]Rom 7:14 NRSV.
[117]Mic 7:8.

for if the one who fell arises again and leaves in his wake the rejoicing of the enemy, how much more the one who did not fall! It is easier to stand and to hold up the feet when a person is agitated than for someone, after having fallen, to rise again. Therefore, if the difficult thing happens, how much more quickly is the easy thing accomplished.

[37:18] *Because I am ready for scourges.*

Even if I have become in motion, my strength abandoned me, the light of my eyes was not with me, and my feet were confused, *I am ready for scourges*, for I do not try to avoid being scourged by you, since you discipline a beloved son.[118] "Do not despise the Lord's discipline, for whom the Lord loves, he disciplines, and he punishes every son whom he accepts."[119] Since therefore I am a son, even though I have brought on myself the reasons for my scourgings, I pray not to be boasted over by them, as though those were destroying me. But *I am ready* to be scourged by you.

[37:18] *And my pain is always before me.*

I suffer *pain* because I have arrived completely among those who bring punishment, among those who bear scourges.

The one who is grieved with "a godly grief, which produces a repentance that leads to salvation,"[120] has the pain always before himself. Just as the one who has a dead friend and groans over him and weeps as long as he sees him, so the one who comes among those who bring him pain, as long as he sees them, he groans and weeps and always has the pain before himself. Suppose, for example, someone has come into an incurable disease: from the pain of this disease he has pain before him.

When a certain physician or the help of God brings the disease that causes pain to an end, he at once casts off the pain and says, "You turned my grief into joy for me."[121] And he says, "The Lord heard and had mercy on me."[122] And to speak more plainly, Lazarus, the brother of those who were related to Mary and Martha, has died, and as long as he was dead, these grieved and indeed groaned to such an extent that those who came in order to comfort them were weeping with them. And when he said, "Lazarus, come out!"[123] and their grief was cast away, they were no longer suffering. Indeed, a feast of thanksgiving was even celebrated, and "Lazarus was one of those at the table."[124]

As long as I have the causes of pain, I have it always before me. Therefore, when you yourself listened to me and applied the scourges profitably like a painful remedy, I no longer suffer because I was healed.

[37:19] *Because I will report my lawlessness.*

He means the following: when I report my lawlessness I do not conceal the pain, for by always commemorating and expounding the pain, I maintain that I have arrived in it. And I do not so much report it as I desire to find the one who heals it. "I will be anxious," then, "over my sin."[125] Not every sinner shows anxiety over his sin. Cain sinned and heard, "Have you sinned? Be still."[126] If he had been still, he would have been anxious over his sin, how to cast it away and no longer carry it out, by no longer being made like it.

---

[118]Cf. Prov 3:12.
[119]Prov 3:11-12.
[120]2 Cor 7:10.
[121]Ps 30:11 (29:12).
[122]Ps 30:10 (29:11 NETS).
[123]Jn 11:43.
[124]Jn 12:2 NRSV.
[125]Ps 38:18 (37:19).
[126]Gen 4:7.

[37:19] *And I will be anxious over my sin.*

Here lawlessness and sin can be understood without any contrast. Of this John also writes in his epistle, saying, "Everyone who commits sin also commits lawlessness; sin is lawlessness."[127] *I will be anxious*, then, about my lawlessness, which is *sin*. Indeed, I will report it, I will not conceal it, I do not await something to rebuke me from outside, I do not await so that another should say to me, "You are in sin and lawlessness." It was quoted by us, "The righteous is his own accuser in his introduction, so that when the adversary attacks, he is refuted."[128] And we understood that statement thus: he is saying, "You yourself, tell of your sins first, in order that you may be justified." Do not await the accuser. In one's introduction one must reproach oneself, for when this takes place, then that one is put to shame, since you yourself were anxious about [271] your sin, how you shall no longer carry it out.

[37:20] *But my enemies are alive and are stronger than I.*

For this reason I call on you as my helper, for this reason I have made myself ready to be scourged by you. Since then, because I sin and have lawlessness, *they are alive and are stronger than I*—for they are nourished on my vice—for this reason do for me what I ask, for "I am anxious over my sin." Therefore scourge me, apply your painful remedy that I might be healed, for then at last those become weaker than I, they are trampled under my feet, for Jesus alone can trample Satan under the feet of the saints. And again, "The God of peace will shortly crush Satan under your feet."[129] So long as he is not yet trampled, then, neither he nor those who are beside him, they live.

[37:20] *And those who hate me unjustly were multiplied.*

However, it is a great praise that he was hated unjustly. When, for example, someone might hate another as arrogant even though he is not arrogant but is even completely devoid of pride, he hates him unjustly. The elders who proceeded against Susanna hated her because they did not conquer her. This hatred is unjust. The Egyptian woman hated Joseph. This hatred is unjust.

[37:21] *They were slandering me, since I was pursuing righteousness.*

I did not harm them, for no one who "pursues justice justly"[130] and pursues righteousness—here the word *pursue* is not to pursue with hatred, but it means "to aspire," as when it says, "Seek peace, and pursue it."[131]

[37:21] *And they cast me off, the loveable one, like a horrid corpse.*[132]

I myself did good things for them, and it was necessary for me to receive from them good things for good things. But they gave me evil things for good, insensitive to how deep they are in evil, and I am of such a disposition toward them that I am not such as rejoice at their misfortunes, but loving them, I also desire for them to come outside of evils. They shunned me, the loveable one, whom it was necessary to love, like a horrid corpse; like the putrid corpse, they fled from me.
  And well also is he called "the loveable one," not the "loved one." For he was hated.

---

[127] 1 Jn 3:4.
[128] Prov 18:17 LXX.
[129] Rom 16:20 NRSV.
[130] Cf. Deut 16:20.
[131] Ps 34:14 (33:15 NETS).
[132] Most texts of the LXX do not contain this part of Ps 37:21.

[37:22] *Do not forsake me, O Lord; O my God, do not stand far from me.*

Even if they themselves forsook me because "I was pursuing righteousness," but as for you, *do not forsake me, do not be far from me.* Now, God forsakes someone when he is worthy of suffering painful things. And I do not mean this, that he receives an experience of painful things in this way. He has not been forsaken, but he is abandoned when, experiencing the painful things, he is outdone and overcome. You do not forsake me then, when you do not stand far from me.

I was united to you; I have become one spirit with you. When I remain so, I have you present with me. When someone is united to the Lord, the Lord is united to him. "My soul clung to you."[133]

[37:23] *Attend to my help, O Lord of my salvation!*

You turn from me when I sin, not when I am unjustly hated, nor when some boast over me.

And you are the Lord and the God of my salvation. Now, salvation does not pertain to the flesh; it is not found in relation to the external things but in relation to the soul itself. This is what is called "eternal salvation," for "he became for all who obey him"—Christ, that is—"an eternal salvation."[134] An "eternal salvation" does not belong to the flesh, which salvation physicians produce, which deliverance a pilot provides for those who embark with him, for after a space these will again have died. But the salvation of God is eternal; he himself is their salvation.

---

[133] Ps 63:8 (62:9 NETS).

[134] Heb 5:9.

PSALM 38 [39]

[**38:1-2**] *Toward the goal. By Jeduthun. I said, I will guard my ways lest I sin with my tongue.*

He is one of the priestly singers. In the book of Esdras[1] and in the Paraleipomenon[2] a record of each name of those who wrote them down is made. And this man is one of them, and he himself either composed the psalm for David or, after receiving it when it had been made by David, he recited it. And it is a work of the priestly singers to recite the psalms, both those that they themselves have composed and those that others arranged.

This is also a song of victory. Often he has the sinner molesting him, [**272**] but after he overcomes and tramples on him and takes him under his power, he sends up the song, for no one sings a song of victory when he is at war and being attacked, but when he has proven victorious. For example, both Moses and the whole Jewish multitude, not when they had to do with Pharaoh did they recite the victory song, but when they saw him after he was submerged under the water: "Let us sing to the Lord, for he has been glorified gloriously; horse and rider he threw into the sea."[3] When the horse and its rider were thrown into the sea, and God cast the chariots of Pharaoh and his army into the Red Sea, then the song of victory was sent up at the right time. And David in the Seventeenth Psalm says, "On the day when he delivered him from the hand of all his enemies and from the hand of Saul, then he said, 'I will love you, O Lord, my strength,'"[4] and the rest of what the song contains. Prayer comes before the war and in the war, but a hymn and song of victory comes after the demolition of war, after the enemies are conquered.

I said, "I will guard my ways lest I sin with my tongue."

Perhaps the beginning of every practical sin comes from a word. To the young man who was overcome, the adulteress in the book of Proverbs, representing either a real woman or false belief or a kind of betrayal, after beginning with words has been able to conquer him. So it is said, "With much conversation," or charm, "she seduced him." "And with the snares of her lips she compelled him."[5] And see only that the beginning of the sin has taken place as a word. The elders also, who raged against Susanna, moved a word against her.

Therefore, whenever someone does not sin with the tongue, he traverses his ways well, for I said that the beginning of these ways is speech. And, conversely, the beginning of all good works again is speech. But in the meantime he is not speaking about these ways. And he added, *lest I sin with my tongue.* It is not the same thing to sin with the tongue and to say, "My tongue will meditate on your righteousness."[6] "The beginning of your words is truth."[7] The cause of my saying your words is your truth. I will make this known when I know it. In the case of the virtues and the ways that are good, truth is the beginning, the

---

[1] Cf. 2 Esdras 21:22-23.
[2] Cf. 1 Chron 25:1; 2 Chron 5:12.
[3] Ex 15:1.
[4] Ps 18 surtitle and Ps 18:1 (17:1-2).
[5] Prov 7:21.
[6] Ps 35:28 (34:28 LES2).
[7] Ps 119:160 (118:160 NETS).

cause. However, in the case of the ways that are forbidden, from which one must keep away, from which it is fitting to draw back, speech is the beginning, as was already said.

[38:2] *I set a watch for my mouth.*

Remember how he said, "lest I sin with my tongue." *I set a watch for my mouth*, for since "by one's own words a person is justified, and by one's own words one is condemned,"[8] one must place a guard around the mouth, in order that in this way I should speak some things and not others, that we should say what is beneficial and pass over what is harmful in silence. For a person cannot produce words that justify and condemn at the same time.

Such a thing is said in the Proverbs with an enigma: "Death and life are in the hand of the tongue."[9] Now, the "hand of the tongue" is speech, the operation of the tongue. The one who speaks what is beneficial and leads into the kingdom has life in the tongue. However, the one who speaks things contrary and forbidden has death in his speech, called his "tongue." And in another scripture it says, "Make a balance and a scale for your words."[10] One must speak in a way that is measured, one must have a balance and place words on each side of the scale. And when the right words tip the scale, it is fitting to choose those and declare them, and to turn away from the wicked ones. Again it is said, "The lips of the wise are devoted to perception."[11] Whenever someone speaks with understanding, his lips are bound; he does not open them for every word but only for the word that is of help. "O Lord, I will open my lips, and my mouth will declare your praise."[12] The one who has lips that are bound for perception, after perceiving that what he is about to say is beneficial, he opened them. And whenever that which [273] is produced brings harm, he bars and binds his lips with perception, he binds his speech.

[38:2-3] *When the sinner marshaled against me, I became dumb, I was humbled, and I was silent from good things.*[13]

Often, when *the sinner* appears, he provokes and calls out to what is dear to him. Sometimes, then, when he marshals, and it happens that he marshals with our consent, for if we do not give him room,[14] he is not able to marshal. And to marshal in this way means to make war at close quarters. It is necessary to be silent, for he often provokes. Indeed, for this reason the serpent, marshaling in front of Eve, provoked her speech and harmed her. However, it was necessary to be silent, and receiving an impression of one's own weakness or of the previous sin, not to say anything to him, but to be *silent from good things*. And the statement *to be silent from good things* does not mean this, "not to say good things," but to possess a silence that has meditated on good things. For example, when I assume the virtue of a prudent man, I know it is necessary to answer from the good, that is, from prudence. I was silent before the woman who appeared close beside me and provokes me to sin. If, then, that young man were answering nothing to the adulteress, out of right understanding, she would not "seduce him with much conversation," nor would he "be caught in the traps of his own lips."[15] I became silent, therefore, when the good things that persuade me not to answer that one came to aid me.

He does not mean, "I become silent, lest I speak good things," but "lest I speak things that provoke." And this silence has come on me

---

[8] Cf. Mt 12:37.
[9] Prov 18:21 LES2.
[10] Sir 28:25 LES2.
[11] Prov 15:7 NETS.
[12] Ps 51:15 (50:17).

[13] The NRSV reads, "'As long as the wicked are in my presence.' I was silent and still; I held my peace to no avail."
[14] Cf. Eph 4:27.
[15] Cf. Prov 7:21.

out of an understanding of the good things that prevent such conversation. "There is one who keeps silence and is found to be wise."[16] The one who is silent in this way is found to be wise. And it is wise to know to whom one must speak and to whom one must not, and when to offer words and when not to. Therefore, "there is one who keeps silence and is found to be wise, and there is one who keeps silence, for he has nothing to answer."[17] Even this person has a kind of judgment, a little, for because he knows that he has no answer, he is at peace. "And there is one who keeps silent, because he knows the opportune moment."[18] This person is perfect.

[38:3] *And my suffering was renewed.*

The suffering is renewed then, when the sinner stands near. He has recalled to his mind what he practiced, for which it is necessary to feel pain. And the pain has received a renewal, as it were. Now, an inauguration (*enkainismos*) means dwelling in a house for the first time. Therefore, a renewal (*anakainismos*) means to lead what is already fading away and remains motionless to blossom forth. *My suffering*, therefore, *was renewed*. After saying, "I guarded my ways lest I sin with my tongue," I knew that I sinned. Therefore, *my suffering was renewed*. And it is a blessed thing for the one who has sinned to come into a renewal of the suffering and not of the pleasure, for the one who rejoices in what he practiced also renews them by bringing them into being again. However, the one who suffers, after sensing that he must keep watch on his ways and must not sin with his tongue, renews his suffering by weeping and grieving "with a godly grief that produces repentance."[19] While he changes his mind completely, he suffers because he has come into such things completely.

[38:4] *My heart became hot within me.*

He can mean the following: my heart acquired heat, as it were, even from the renewal of the suffering.

Furthermore, he can mean this as well: since I fervently rebuked myself, groan, and lament my suffering, *my heart became hot*, it has become red hot. "With" this, indeed, "my meditation, a fire burned,"[20] which consumes me and . . . for there was grass, wood, and the rest.[21] I have the fire that destroys the grassy elements not only when I am being perfected but also when I meditate on my suffering.

And well did he also say *within me*. The heart within is warmed so that it even causes its warmth to pervade things outside it. For example, those who marry and burn[22] do not have their heart warmed within but have the heart spreading the warmth into their external parts. [274] As when it is said, "I was troubled and did not speak."[23] The one who had a certain trouble in his mind or in his thoughts and did nothing according to the trouble of his thoughts nor spoke anything, experiences having been troubled and not having spoken—such a person has his heart warmed within.

[38:4] *And in my meditation a fire will be kindled*

within me. And so in each of us, two men come together, one of whom is the outer, and the other the inner man. When, therefore, trouble comes to the soul and does not stir up trouble for the outer man, but keeps it within so that the soul despises it and weeps over it, it

---

[16]Sir 20:5.
[17]Sir 20:5-6 LES2.
[18]Sir 20:6 LES2.
[19]Cf. 2 Cor 7:10.
[20]Ps 39:3 (38:4).
[21]Cf. 1 Cor 3:12.
[22]Cf. 1 Cor 7:9.
[23]Ps 77:4 (76:5 NETS).

has the heart warmed within, not in order to practice it but in order not to practice it.

In my meditation fire is kindled. With the voice of others, their practice, and their understanding, a fire is kindled, which touches them, burning them. "Their heart was fired up like a fiery kiln."[24] Here the meditation, like fire, was kindled, having combustible material underlying it. And the meditation and the burning warmth of the saint are what comes by means of the ardent Spirit. Therefore the fire kindled in order that he might accomplish something, not in order to harm and kill. "Were not our hearts burning within us on the road, while he was opening the Scriptures to us?"[25] This burning is praiseworthy. And observe in the case of the craftsman: some things are heated in order to be reshaped and to pass into a vessel: gold and silver, for example. However, when timber is heated or something else, the heat is harmful.

[38:4] *I spoke with my tongue.*

Even if I did not allow it to come outside but remaining within me, it provided me with burning because of my meditation; I then spoke at last with my tongue, "Make known to me, O Lord, my end."[26] I spoke this with my tongue, for this is the tongue that by nature belongs to its possessor: for example, when the prudent person, speaking the things of prudence, speaks with his own tongue, he speaks with the tongue of the prudent man, not with the tongue of man. And the one who pursues learning his own end and addresses his question to God: with my tongue, not with the tongue of a deceptive man, but with my tongue I spoke because I desire to know my end. This word of mine is not feigned. Whenever a certain hypocrite speaks about prudence even though he is not prudent, he does not speak with his own tongue. The prudent man, however, when he relates words about prudence, speaks with the tongue of the prudent. No hypocrite, then, speaks with the tongue that is by nature but with the feigned tongue. The wolf, when he wears sheepskin and approaches the flock of Christ,[27] does not speak with his own tongue but imitates the voice of the sheep in order that, as when like encounters like, he might harm them.

[38:5] *Make known to me, O Lord, my end and the number of my days—what it is.*

Observe that it is a penitential person who says these things. He prepared me to keep watch over my ways, to set a guard over my mouth. When the sinner stood near before me and provoked me, I received good things in my mind, which persuaded me not to speak to him. I am saying the following, then: since I perceived myself failing on many occasions—for I barely began my progress—"make known to me, O Lord, my end," that I might know how much time of life remains to me, whether it is sufficient for my perfection and fulfillment. So indeed another was saying, "Tell me the scarcity of my days. Do not take me away in the middle of my days!"[28] In a certain sense I am in the middle of the days that come from the Holy Light. Therefore, do not take me away in this way. Therefore fulfill my days. And God fulfills the days of some, not by granting them increase, for when he says, "With length of days I will satisfy him,"[29] about the righteous we do not mean this: that he makes him live for many years. There are also impious people who have lived for many years.

And the number of my days.

---

[24] Hos 7:6.
[25] Lk 24:32.
[26] Ps 38:5.

[27] Cf. Mt 7:15.
[28] Ps 102:23-24 (101:24-25).
[29] Ps 91:16 (90:16 NETS).

With "the number of my days" it is also possible to say the following: you illumined me many times, I have been in the "days," for each illumination is a day. Show me, then, the number of my illuminations, in order that I should know what is lacking to me. [275] As when someone, having assumed a desire for skill or knowledge, was saying—and he has not yet acquired perfect knowledge of his discipline—he says, "Make manifest to me what the clear points of the skill are, so that I might know what kinds of things I possess and what kinds of things I lack."

It is blessed to have deeds, works, and thoughts numbered, which are worthy of being enumerated. For example, of the adulteress it is said, "Innumerable are those whom you have slain."[30] By no means does he mean this, that they are infinite in number, but that they are not worthy of being recounted. They are left with no word or number.

[38:5] *That I may know what I lack.*

When I learn the number of my days and my end, up to when it occurs, I know in what things I am lacking, what those things are that I did not yet learn. Therefore, those who awaken a desire of knowledge tell their audience in a more general outline at the beginning the theories that were already grasped by them, in order that they might also know how much they lack and might receive the desire to succeed and to assume them.

[38:6] *See! You made my days palms.*

The first reading, which is more common, is this: "You made my days old." I am not young or newly formed, I did not begin to live just now, but "you made my days old."

Moreover, this must be said: that which comes later always makes that which came earlier old. So, for example, laws are rendered ancient. So he is saying the following: the old days that I had, when I was living according to the old man, have grown old, they have gone: I have put on the new.[31]

See! You made my days palms. Since the word *palm* is ambiguous—it both signifies the one who competes in wrestling and also indicates a certain measurement—it is possible to understand it in both senses. He is saying, "You made my days in wrestling and in struggling," for we always have those who assault us. And sometimes a human temptation seizes us, and human desires make war on us and wrestle us, and sometimes evil forces do so: for "our struggle is not against blood and flesh"—not ours, but surely that of others—"but against the rulers, against the authorities."[32] In order that this may be so, "you made my days into contests."

Moreover, this could be said about a measurement: as the days that I live are forever and ever, they have the significance of a palm. And just as it calls all the nations, though they are many, "a drop from a jar"—since all the nations are like a jar of rational drops—and a "weight in a balance"[33]—their weight lowers the scales until it tips, not so that the plate of the scale lowers completely, so in comparison with the magnitude of the ages and the blessedness of the days, with which the one who is able to live well is furnished, are my days: "The one who loves father and mother will be long-lived,"[34] it says. And this is already found not to be so in the literal sense.

[38:6] *And my substance is as nothing before you.*

The word *substance* signifies many things. For the present, however, there is need of two

---

[30]Cf. Prov 7:26 NETS.
[31]Cf. Col 3:9-10; Eph 4:22-24.
[32]Eph 6:12.
[33]Is 40:15.
[34]Cf. Ex 20:12.

meanings. Sometimes essence is called "substance," as when the Son is called "the exact imprint of God's substance,"[35] of God's essence and existence. And sometimes the perfect endurance, by which someone endures things that are painful, is called "substance." Therefore he speaks in both senses: "The essence of my soul *is as nothing before you*," compared to you, a certain great essence. And although it ought to be perfect in likeness to you, the Father, I degraded it. And that this is so, he says of some, "The sons of Zion who have been raised up as precious as gold and silver, how did they become as earthen vessels?"[36] See! Their essence was debased. One must understand this sensibly: they have become earthen vessels. Gold, when it is defiled, is debased, and much of its value is abandoned. The one who does not preserve the worth that belongs to him from God "becomes like the mindless beasts,"[37] and because of his meanness his essence was considered as nothing.

And since it also means endurance, he says: even if I waited steadfastly, wishing to see my end, and I call on you to make this known to me, yet even then this endurance of mine, which is thus, is something little before you.

[38:6] *But all is vanity, every living man.*

One must understand this in two ways: all things that are because of man are vanity, as the Preacher fittingly explained.[38] In comparison with that which is highly exalted, perfect, and truly eternal, substance is vain, except "every living man." So then it is possible to say: even if all the other [276] creatures besides man are vanity, mortal animals, for example, which are temporal and may be without a soul, yet man alone is alive, alive with that life that they live like Abraham, for "he is not the God of the dead, but of the living."[39]

And the man who lives according to the human flesh is himself also vain. One must therefore make the following distinction: all these things are vanity; for if they are mortal, after they have died they are no more. Man, however, is living. And even when he dies, he still lives. Or one must think thus: a living man who does not become free of the merely human life is himself vanity, so that it should therefore read thus: "But all is vanity, even every living man." Or thus: "But all is vanity; man, however, is alive."

Question: The essence is *as nothing*?

Even when man lives differently from how he would live as a mortal, in comparison to the superiority and greatness of the divine life and God himself, the source of life, he is nothing. The small things and the things that are called smaller than nothing are so called in relation to the things relative to them. The small, however, has no delimited quantity, for it is called this in reference to what is great. We sometimes say that the palm's breadth is greater than the breadth of a finger. In the *Categories*, for instance, you have a small mountain and a great grain of millet.[40]

[38:7] *In fact, a man passes through as an image.*

I said that he says the following: "All is vanity," about all the others besides man. Man alone is alive. And he possesses something more than the others. He has an immortal soul. Nevertheless, even if he is alive, yet he does not always possess this motion, for it says, *In fact, a man passes through as an image.* He did not say whether he passes through as a praiseworthy or blameworthy image, but of whatever kind when someone passes through, of

---

[35]Heb 1:3.
[36]Lam 4:2.
[37]Ps 49:12 (48:13).
[38]Cf. Eccles 1:2.

[39]Mt 22:32.
[40]Aristotle, *Categories* 5b, 21-22.

whatever kind when he acts, he is as a kind of image. And to one who understands it more generally, it ought to be said that it relates either to the image of the heavenly man or the image of the earthly man.[41] And from such a passage it is established that man is free of will, for if he were good because of his constitution, he would always walk in the image of the heavenly man; if he were essentially evil, he would walk in the image of the earthly man.

And it is possible to separate these general images into specific ones. And I say that one passes through in the image of a fox, another in the image of a lion, and a certain one comes bearing another image: a stallion crazy for the mare, and another comes in the image of a dove, but *every man passes through as an image.*

[38:7] *Surely, they are troubled in vain.*

But the wicked *are troubled in vain. Surely, they are troubled in vain.* And he now speaks about vain trouble, because this effort has to do with human things. Indeed, *he lays up treasures and does not know for whom he gathers them.*

[38:7] *He lays up treasures and does not know for whom he gathers them.*

It was clearly said by the Preacher, "He does not know whether he will be wise or foolish,"[42] the heir of his possessions. And often what a person stored up, the heir abandons. And sometimes, even within the passing of a year, he transfers those things to others. Therefore, one should not strive in order to treasure up in this way, for "treasures shall not profit the lawless, but righteousness delivers from death."[43] Therefore let one store up the righteousness that delivers from death and from every other evil. And this wealth is treasured up in heaven. "Do not store up for yourselves treasures on earth, but store up treasures in heaven."[44] For since, where the treasure is, there also is the intellect, called "heart,"[45] let one store up in heaven in order that we should have our intellect there, and one must avoid treasuring up on earth, lest we have our understanding there. It is said of some, "Those who store up injustice and wretchedness in their lands."[46]

Therefore, the man who *passes through as an image* does not know, when he treasures up, for whom he gathers them, for it is unclear to him what will come along afterward. For this reason the virtuous understands to store up treasure in heaven. He has the wealth that consists in good works. Exactly this Paul also writes to Timothy: "As for those who are rich in the present age, command them not to be haughty about wealth, but to set their minds on God, who provides all things."[47]

One must also speak about the blameworthy wealth, for example, the heretical opinions of impious doctrines. And the one who treasures up these things does not know for whom he gathers them. And he bequeaths it to another, for "what is falsely called knowledge"[48] has promise only as far as the present life, for after the truth shines on it, it is dispersed and [277] disappears.

Question: *In fact, as an image?*

Even if every man is alive, yet he is not infallible in living in a praiseworthy way. For if he were remaining in the true image, the first one in which he was created, he would not be troubled, he would not store up treasure in vain. In fact, he passes through as an image even when he has become alive, and by no means as the first image, but simply as an image, for the rational creature can never

---

[41]Cf. 1 Cor 15:49.
[42]Eccles 2:19.
[43]Prov 10:2 NETS.
[44]Cf. Mt 6:19-20 NRSV.
[45]Cf. Mt 6:21.
[46]Amos 3:10.
[47]Cf. 1 Tim 6:17.
[48]1 Tim 6:20.

become free from acting according to reason. And in every way that he acts, he acts either praiseworthily or blameworthily, and when he thinks certain things, he also practices the same things.

Question: *Surely they are troubled in vain?*

It was often said by us already that the changes that happen in this way have a kind of difference. Then, when they do not preserve this image in which they have come into being, those who are troubled in vain are a multitude. And when it indicates the life of man, that "every man is alive" and "in fact, man passes through as an image"—it does not indicate the same image, but since the images are different, and especially those that are blameworthy and fallen, the troubled are many.

[38:8] *And now who is my endurance? Is it not the Lord?*

What has been spoken was said of others. But I say about myself, "*Who is my endurance? Is it not the Lord?*" I do not wait for another. And just as "wisdom, righteousness, and sanctification come"[49] to those who partake of them, so also endurance, the Lord himself, comes to the one who awaits him.

[38:8] *And my substance is from you.*

Of the Lord he says that he is his endurance. And to him, the Lord who is his endurance, he says, "*And my substance is from you.*" Substance here can mean the strength by which someone is able to endure, because when you cooperate with me and are my endurance, I endure all things. And *the substance from you* is praiseworthy for me.

One can also understand "essence" here for *substance*. Even the essence of my rational soul, of the rational being, is from you, for you have given me a soul. I have the soul from you, not

beginning from seeds, not according to the explanation proposed in the Stratiotical heresy,[50] but *my substance is from you.*

[38:9] *From all my acts of lawlessness rescue me!*

Not from some, but *from all,* that I might become free of every blameworthy image.

[38:9] *You gave me as a reproach to the foolish.*

From the outset, we said that the whole psalm presents a person who is repentant and progressing. A wicked deed is to be reproached by a righteous person but is praised by a foolish one. The fool indeed reproaches for good works and for zeal. Because of this it is said in Proverbs, as though there were a difference between kinds of reproaches, "Do not earn the reproaches of evil men,"[51] for he did not say in general, "Do not earn reproaches," but those "of evil men." Do not be reproached for wickedness, for there are those who are reproached for good things. So says Jesus to the disciples, "Rejoice and be glad when others reproach you!"[52] One should not avoid this reproach, for it is good and it leads to the kingdom of heaven. One should flee, however, from the reproaches of evil men.

[38:10] *I became dumb and I did not open my mouth.*

Who is the fool who reproaches besides that sinner who stands near before him, as long as "he became dumb and did not open his mouth"? And here again he means the same thing: *I was dumb and I did not open my mouth.* I did not respond to him, to what he reproaches. And I often said this, that in another sense the apostle teaches this, saying: "After a

---

[49] Cf. 1 Cor 1:30.

[50] This heresy proposes a "world-soul."
[51] Prov 3:31 LXX.
[52] Mt 5:11-12.

Lectures on Psalm 38 [38:10-11]

first admonition have nothing to do with a heretical man!"[53] In other words, do not open your mouth to him. Nevertheless, when you have an apologetic word and can say a word in your defense about yourself, "I have done what is in my power," rebuke him. When after rebuke he is not restrained, or "after a second one also"—for some of the variants have "and after a second"—be turned away from him, "knowing that he is sinful."[54] It is unnecessary to rebuke the one who is "self-condemned."[55]

[38:10-11] *Because you are the one who made me, remove from me your scourges.*

Do not scourge me, for I am your creature. "And he punishes every son he accepts,"[56] naturally, when the son has reasons for being scourged. Therefore, forgive me those things, grant me forgiveness, for in this way I will be no longer scourged. But as for the present, I am still liable to scourges. [278] And indeed, the one who made the Most High his refuge does not have evils approaching him, nor a scourge drawing near his dwelling.[57] Make me, then, such a person so that I am no longer liable to scourges, remove from me the way that is necessary to punish. Since then I say, "From all my lawless deeds deliver me!" when he delivers me I am no longer liable to punishment.

In a certain sense, therefore, he was whipping him also by means of the fool, and he says that the reproaches of the fool are scourges. If God does not hand him over to the fool, he is not stronger than him, nor does he oppose the one who is not yet handed over.

[38:11] *I departed due to the strength of your hand.*

The strength of your hand lies on me, which disciplines, which strikes, which subjects to punishments. Since, then, it has become strong on me, I departed. I left my former life; I left behind my former condition, for I did not depart so that I was no more, so that I became devoid of strength, but so that I left behind the condition that made me necessary to punish.

I departed.

I who say these things, who confess, who say, "You made me a reproach to the foolish," I departed, being set free from my former condition. And this is a praiseworthy departing: it is not a blameworthy one. "And Esau came in from the field, departing,"[58] when he desired to eat stew. Here the word *departing* is used instead of "fainting" and "desiring nourishment." It is frequently said in a praiseworthy sense as well. "They departed and went away"[59] or "turned away"—for it is also related in this way. This desertion is blameworthy. "Faith has come to an end from their mouth."[60] This is also blameworthy. When, however, someone leaves unbelief and vice behind, this departure is not blameworthy. So is it said, "My soul longs and departs for the courts of my God."[61] Whenever he receives a desire for the courts of the Lord, which are "in the Father's house,"[62] he departs insofar as he is a soul, he casts away being merely natural, he becomes spiritual.

[38:12] *With reproofs for lawlessness you disciplined a man.*

You do not reprove when I do not commit lawlessness. Reproving for lawlessness, you

---

[53] Titus 3:10.
[54] Titus 3:11.
[55] Titus 3:11.
[56] Prov 3:12 NETS.
[57] Cf. Ps 91:9-10 (90:9-10).
[58] Gen 25:29.
[59] Jer 5:23.
[60] Jer 7:28.
[61] Ps 84:2 (83:3).
[62] Jn 14:2.

discipline a man. You make him know that he is a man, that he is rational, that he is in the image of God. And in this way he is instructed after he is reproved. It is blessed to be disciplined, not with anger[63] but with reproofs, for we were saying, "All that is reproved by the light becomes visible."[64] And this reproof is a demonstration and a revelation. "Reproof" never occurs in Scripture in a praiseworthy sense, or only seldom. Behold that it is said, "All that is reproved by the light becomes visible."[65] And those outside call the demonstration a "reproof": "He reproves the opposition." Indeed, they say that a reproof is a contradictory syllogism.[66] Again, suppose someone says, "To do injustice is beneficial," for there are those who have such an opinion, that injustice is beneficial and righteousness is without a doubt harmful. "The righteous man," they say, "does not increase his wealth, but the unrighteous multiplies riches." Therefore, we make such a contradictory assertion: "Injustice must be renounced. Everything that must be renounced is harmful. Injustice, therefore, is harmful. What is harmful is not beneficial. Therefore, injustice is not beneficial." The contradictory syllogism has come, and this contradictory syllogism is called a "reproof."

Those who practiced dialectics formerly were not doing this as they practice it today. Therefore, they are sophists rather than dialecticians. They have a goal of wrangling, and they present quarrelsome proposals, which prevail and persist among them. The one who is truly a dialectician, however, since he tries to argue according to both sides—and there is one that is true, and the other is false—knows from his dialectical argumentation according to each of them, of what kind is the true one and of what kind is the false one. And the true one itself becomes visible because the false one is shown, for the knowledge of opposites is the same.

[38:12] *You cause his life to melt like a cobweb.*

Like a spider's web, [**279**] you cause his soul to melt, his soul, according to which he is merely natural. Concerning a certain wicked man or wicked woman it is said, "She was windborne by the cravings of her soul."[67] Whenever someone, by means of her soul, for example, invents prophecies for herself or, as it were, "pious doctrines," "she becomes windborne by the cravings of her soul." She is not being inspired by the Holy Spirit.

Indeed, in another book I explained the difference: that man is fleshly who wages war according to the flesh,[68] who in his passions is an image of the flesh, who is sold into slavery under the flesh, who became fleshly and has been sold under sin.[69] However, a spiritual man is one who transcends the condition of the merely natural, when he is inspired by God and does and practices all things by the Holy Spirit. And the natural man is one who is neither fleshly nor spiritual. And perhaps the wise men of the world are all of this kind. They consider themselves to be austere in the motions and thoughts of their own soul. And for this reason they do not receive the things of the Spirit, for since they prefer their own affairs and consider their own thought to be great, they do not receive the things of the Spirit, regarding them as foolishness.[70] Indeed, there are even some people, and their heresies are wholly constituted both by Greeks and by Christians, who say that allegories are foolish, that they are fantasies. And they claim that their contemplations of intelligible things are false, since they suppose that all things are

---

[63] Cf. Ps 38:1 (37:2).
[64] Eph 5:13.
[65] Eph 5:13.
[66] Cf. PsT 260.8-9.

[67] Jer 2:24 NETS.
[68] Cf. 2 Cor 10:3.
[69] Cf. Rom 7:14.
[70] Cf. 1 Cor 2:14.

bodies and subject to sensory perception. Therefore, these "natural" men cannot receive the things of the Spirit, because they suppose that they are themselves austere and are able to see all things by their own power.

His soul in such a state, therefore, not his essence, but his condition in which he is only a soul, *you caused to melt like the cobweb.* The cobweb, however, is altogether so weak, so that it is said, "They weave the loom of a spider. Their weaving shall not become a garment."[71] It is saying that the melting of the soul is as the easily broken construction of the animal that is called a spider. When the soul is consumed, this melting happens for its benefit, for that which is cobweb-like in it is weak, and finally it is rendered free of vice. Therefore, you melted the soul of this man, who is reproved with reproofs for lawlessness, like a cobweb.

[38:12] *Surely, every man is in turmoil for nothing.*

All men who are outside God's discipline are troubled with rebukes in vain. This man, however, when he was troubled by being rebuked, when his soul was melted like the cobweb, did not suffer this in vain, for he received a change for the better. However, when someone like this, a mere man, should not be under discipline, not being subject to reproofs, he is troubled in vain according to the passage previously quoted: "In fact, a man passes through as an image; surely, he is troubled in vain."[72] The one who does not wish to be troubled but to have tranquility of spirit becomes God because he receives the Word of God, for "he called them 'gods' to whom the Word of God came."[73] And these are not troubled in vain, but even when it happens that there is a slip or a forepassion arrives, they say, "I was troubled and did not speak."[74] Their disturbance is arrested as far as the forepassion.

Question: Are they troubled by themselves?

Sometimes they are troubled by themselves and sometimes by certain ones who oppose them.

[38:13] *Listen to my prayer, O Lord, and to my petition!*

There seems to be a difference between *petition* and *prayer*. That one sends up a petition, who knows himself to be in need and lacking, in order that he may be filled.

The one who prays, while he has this appearance, sometimes asks also for the presence of goods that are above. The one who asks to receive something from God either asks to receive what he does not have or asks that what he has might remain with him. This, strictly speaking, is *prayer*: it is a request sent up while the one who prays considers to be divine the one to whom he sends up the prayer. When it says, "A prayer of the prophet Habakkuk: O Lord, I have heard of your reputation and I marveled. You will be known in the midst of the living creatures; when the years draw near you will not be recognized."[75] Behold! This is a prayer. However, when a person, being in need, asks only for certain things that he lacks, the *petition* is that which is offered up as a prayer, as it were.

Moreover, one can understand it in this way: there are those who ask for the more bodily things, such as health, wealth, and the rest. Since they are in need of these things, they often consider it worthy **[280]** to receive them. However, the one who wishes to possess the fullness says, "O Lord, our God,

---

[71] Is 59:5-6.
[72] Ps 39:6 (38:7).
[73] Jn 10:35.

[74] Ps 77:4 (76:5 NETS).
[75] Cf. Hab 3:1-2.

give us peace, for you have granted us all things."[76]

Since also, as one inadequate, I pray that certain things be given to me—for right now I am still under instruction—hear my petition. And since I am about to obtain those things I am lacking, having become filled, I ask greater things, I ask for heavenly things and I say, "Our Father who is in heaven, hallowed be your name"—he does not ask for this as one who lacks it—"Your kingdom come."[77] Make it to come! And it comes at that time when our God reigns in actuality.

[38:13] *Give ear to my tears!*

When I see myself lacking, I weep, carrying out and establishing that "godly grief, producing a repentance that leads to salvation,"[78] in accordance with which I say, "Every night I will bathe my bed; with my tears I will drench my bedding."[79] And since he is also one who lacks the perfect and highest virtue—again he moans, saying, "we who are in this tent groan,"[80] and again, "You set my tears before you, as even by your promise."[81] You see: "As by your promise you set my tears." Now, what kinds of tears are these, or what are the characteristics of those who weep in order that they should laugh? For "blessed are those who weep, for they will laugh."[82] These set their tears as by the promise that they should laugh, that they should be filled with "indescribable and glorious joy."[83]

[38:13] *Do not pass by in silence, because I am a sojourner on the earth.*

Do not pass by me *in silence*, when I pray, petition, weep, and produce such tears, which "those who sow will reap with rejoicing."[84] "Do not pass by in silence, therefore, but approve and grant what I have requested," for passing by in silence sometimes indicates deferment and sometimes also patience, when it takes place toward sins: "These things you did, and I kept silent,"[85] that is, "I did not punish you."

When I was an "inhabitant" I neither dared to make a request nor to pray. Now, "inhabitants" are those who are guilty of vice and impiety. So it is said in Jeremiah, "From the face of the north evils shall be kindled for those who inhabit the earth."[86] Not "for those who sojourn." And in the Apocalypse of John three times in succession is it said, "Woe, woe, woe to the inhabitants of the earth!"[87] Therefore, if I were an inhabitant, I would not say, *"Do not pass by in silence."*

[38:13] *And a visiting stranger, like all my fathers.*

The "sojourner" and "stranger" are the same. So Paul, in the epistle according to the Hebrews, when he made a catalogue of all who were well-pleasing by faith, called them "sojourners" and "strangers."[88] None of those is an "inhabitant," none is "indigenous," but a "stranger." He has come into this place from elsewhere; he has not been born here.

Our fathers in virtue were therefore all strangers on earth as well, as were the patriarchs and the others who begot children in accordance with divine instruction, such as prophets, teachers, and law givers.

---

[76] Is 26:12 NETS.
[77] Mt 6:9-10; Lk 11:2.
[78] Cf. 2 Cor 7:10.
[79] Ps 6:6 (6:7).
[80] 2 Cor 5:2.
[81] Ps 56:8 (55:9 LES2).
[82] Lk 6:21.
[83] 1 Pet 1:8 NRSV.

[84] Cf. Ps 126:5 (125:5).
[85] Ps 50:21 (49:21 NETS).
[86] Jer 1:14.
[87] Rev 8:13 NRSV.
[88] Cf. Heb 11:9, 13.

[38:14] *Let me be, that I may revive before I depart and am no more.*

Here he uses *revival* in a praiseworthy sense, which has the same force as "Take delight in the Lord."[89] "I have found relief for myself,"[90] says Ephraim. That relief, however, is blameworthy. Therefore, someone revives in a praiseworthy manner, when he obtains virtue, when he "takes delight in the Lord," when he receives an impression and conception of "the paradise of delight." Since, therefore, many things are lacking to me—for I send up my petition for this reason, in order that I may be filled with what is lacking, for he said this in the beginning of the psalm, "Make known to me, Lord, my end, and the number of my days—what it is—that I may know what I lack."[91] When he knows what he lacks and acquires these things, he has these things cultivated, then he revives.

He then says the following: leave me to remain in this life, in order that I should revive after being instructed, before I depart from this life and am no more. He is not saying this, "I will no longer exist," **[281]** but I will be such a man as I wish to be. For the soul does not depart into nonexistence, but understand: one must understand the words in conjunction with those who say them. When the righteous and the one who is wise in God says, "I devote myself to everything in order that I should become rich," do not understand what is said in connection with perceptible wealth. And when there is another person, whether a merchant or a physician < . . . >. This saint, then, is also a wise man. He says indeed that he has "no other as his endurance than the Lord" and that "his existence is from him."[92] Therefore, this wise man, when he says, "Leave me to live, having hope in this life only, in order that I should revive by eating and drinking, according to the passage: 'Let us eat and drink, for tomorrow we die!'"[93] yet in conjunction with the person it is also necessary to understand the revival and the phrases "Leave me" and "I will be no more." The one who says these things is immortal. Therefore, when he says, "I will be no more," he is not saying the following: "I depart into total corruption, I come to an end in nonexistence," but, "I am no longer just as I pray to be. 'Before I depart,' then, from being so, before I depart from life 'and exist no more' as I prayed that I would be." When a sinner says, "Correct me, discipline me in order that I should no longer be," he surely does not mean that he departs into total corruption.

---

[89] Ps 37:4 (36:4 NETS).
[90] Hos 12:8 NETS.
[91] Cf. Ps 39:4 (38:5 NETS).
[92] Cf. Ps 39:7 (38:8).
[93] Is 22:13; 1 Cor 15:32.

PSALM 39 [40]

[39:1-2] *Toward the goal. A psalm for David. Waiting, I waited for the Lord, and he paid attention to me.*

The psalm being now set forth could be spoken both by every saint who resolutely and magnanimously passed the time of life and by the Lord's Man, for the apostle in the letter to the Hebrews, quoting passages from it, has understood them to have been spoken about Christ. This passage above all: "Sacrifice and offering you did not desire,"[1] until "in the scroll of the book it is written of me."[2] The psalm, moreover, is from a single person. The same person who begins recites and sings until the end of the psalm.

With thanksgiving, then, he says to God, "*Waiting, I waited for the Lord, and he listened to my petition.*" The phrase *waiting, I waited* has such a sense as when someone might say, "I healed medically, I wrote grammatically." There are those who wait impatiently, but rather by means of great insensitivity or sometimes because of their love of glory. So says the apostle, "I do not lay down my body in order to boast."[3] By casting my body and soul for the sake of praise, one does not *wait, while waiting*, for he waits always knowledgeably, and as it is necessary to wait, not in order to receive what one hunts for from men, whether glory or praises. Therefore, he is one who waits in this way, as is necessary, as when I say, "According to wisdom I acted wisely."

God was said in the previous psalm to be the endurance of the righteous person: "And now who is my endurance? Is it not the Lord?"[4] The one who with this endurance bears the painful things that befall him patiently will say, "*Waiting, I waited for the Lord.*" With a longsuffering disposition I endured the painful misfortunes, for many, as I said, endure painful things for a reason. God, then, is the endurance of the saint. So it is also said in Jeremiah, "O exalted throne of glory, our sanctity! O endurance of Israel! O Lord of Israel!"[5] The one who has been fashioned in accordance with this endurance and who derives his name from it will say, "*Waiting, I waited for the Lord.*" He speaks as a servant. He who serves God confesses him to be Lord by his very deeds, thoughts, and words. He says that "Jesus is Lord" "in the Holy Spirit,"[6] for not everyone who names Jesus as Lord does this in the Spirit. Indeed, even hypocrites do this. "On that day many will say to me: 'Lord, Lord.'"[7] And what does he answer them? "I never knew you."[8] I never knew you as those who served me. And again, "Why do you call me, 'Lord, Lord,' and do not do what I tell you?"[9] Therefore, the one who calls Jesus "Lord" in this way, by doing the will of his heavenly Father,[10] that one calls him "Lord" "in the Holy Spirit." This, then, is the voice of a servant.

---

[1] Ps 40:6 (39:7); Heb 10:5.
[2] Ps 40:7 (39:8); Heb 10:7.
[3] Cf. 1 Cor 13:3.
[4] Ps 39:7 (38:8).
[5] Cf. Jer 17:12-13 NETS.
[6] Cf. 1 Cor 12:3.
[7] Mt 7:22 NRSV.
[8] Mt 7:23 NRSV.
[9] Lk 6:46 NRSV.
[10] Cf. Mt 7:21.

[**39:2**] *And he listened to my petition.*

Being in need, I asked for certain things, and God, being attentive to my petition, has fulfilled these things. Since I indeed "waited while waiting" . . . the command of which the Savior [**282**] said, "The one who endures to the end will be saved."[11] And the statement "I waited" belongs to one who is at peace.

Question: And as what kind of person did the Lord say this?

Truly, we have not said this out of necessity. If, then, you understand the statement from the person of the Savior—for it has come as far as a forepassion, for he has not come among the passions. So Jesus "began to be grieved and agitated."[12] As far as a beginning such things have come to him, for we do not claim that any other is immutable besides the Trinity. Since, then, the soul that Jesus assumed is something other than the Trinity, it was able to receive a forepassion and a beginning of being "grieved and agitated." And I quote an apostolic saying: "For the sake of the joy that was set before him he endured the cross, disregarding its shame."[13] If it has not happened that he flees while in the forepassion, then there was no manly action and no struggle.

Question: *He paid attention to me?*
That is, "he approved."

[**39:3**] *And he brought me up out of a pit of wretchedness and from miry mud.*

When each of the saints says this, "a pit of wretchedness," he speaks of the region around the earth, for a pit is where the waters that fall from above collect. Often, therefore, in the divine Scriptures both the region around the earth and Hades are indicated by this name, for when it is said in the Twenty-Ninth Psalm from the person of the Savior as man, "You saved me from those that go down into a pit,"[14] for I myself do not go down into a pit. I have come there for the sake of others. No other forced me to go down. Moreover, this seems all the more evident from the passage, "I was counted among those who go down into a pit; I became like a helpless man, free among the dead."[15] I am not among those led down into the pit, but "I was counted" among them. I counted myself among those ones. "I became," therefore, "like a helpless man." Although he is not helpless, he has become like a helpless person, for when the Jews came to arrest him, if he had not given himself up, they would not have been able to arrest him. If he is "free among the dead," then he is not among those who by nature go into Hades because of their free will and their action, but he accounted himself in this way.

He brought me up, then, *out of a pit of wretchedness*. The one who mortified his own body and made it his servant,[16] and lives on earth while he has acquired citizenship in heaven,[17] that one was brought up from a pit of wretchedness and from the miry mud. And now indeed he was powerfully brought up from the world, and from mud, and mire, of which the body of clay is fashioned. "And God formed the man with the dust of the earth."[18] And again Job says, "Remember that you fashioned me as clay!"[19]

And Jesus will also say these things as man: "I have come into the pit of wretchedness, I was accounted so, in order that I should set them free of wretchedness and from the miry mud, for because of them I have come into the miry mud." When, therefore, this mortal body changes into an incorruptible one, the one who

---

[11] Mt 10:22; 24:13; Mk 13:13 NRSV.
[12] Mt 26:37 NRSV.
[13] Heb 12:2 NRSV.
[14] Ps 30:3 (29:4 NETS).
[15] Ps 88:4-5 (87:5-6).
[16] Cf. 1 Cor 9:27.
[17] Phil 3:20.
[18] Gen 2:7.
[19] Job 10:9 NETS.

wears it is no longer restrained by mire and wretchedness but was delivered from these.

[39:3] *And he set my feet upon a rock.*

And let this be said also of the righteous in general. And "rock" should be understood in these passages as the unbreakable and indivisible Word of God, whom no tempest or violent wave moves. Often, then, in the holy words, mention of a rock occurs, though it cannot be understood in a physical sense, for when the saint says in thanksgiving to God, "High on a rock he set me,"[20] he does not mean the following: "Lifting me up, he set me on a physical rock," but on his unbreakable and indivisible Word. Paul interpreted this stone and said who he is, namely, Christ: "For they drank from the spiritual rock that followed them, and the rock was Christ."[21] And again the same psalmist says after other things, "Their strong ones were devoured like rocks."[22] Those of the Egyptians who drew near to the rock seemed to be nothing. And in this way "the rod of Aaron swallowed the rods"[23] of the magicians among the Egyptians, that is, it overcame them. When, therefore, it says, "Death is swallowed up,"[24] "Israel is devoured,"[25] when, therefore, those who seem to be strong draw near to the rock: sophists, certain debaters, or even evil spirits, they are swallowed up, they are proven to be nothing. Therefore, on this rock, Christ, whereas the strong ones of the Egyptians who **[283]** draw near, after they approach him, are devoured, the feet of the one who is benefited are established from being disturbed, from being resisted by enormous waves, and from having enemies. When he is in the pit of wretchedness, when he is in the miry mud, endurance comes into being. However, he does not always suffer them. And when, after endurance receives its goal, he becomes free of these things, the feet of the one who is benefited are at last established on the aforementioned rock.

[39:3] *And he directed my steps.*

And observe carefully that the discourse leads us far away from the literal sense. No one who stands is walking; no one who is walking stands. When someone therefore has been established in Christ so that he shouts, "Who will separate us from the love of God?"[26] he has his passages directed, for he strives always for the higher things, for the heavenly things, while God directs the steps of the one who runs, for "it depends not on human will or exertion, but on God who shows mercy."[27]

[39:4] *And he put a new song into my mouth.*

Into the mouth of the inner man, that is, into my faculty of reasoning. *A new song*: how this word is used, the significance of the word *new* has often been said by us. That which is without a successor is new, while that which is replaced is old. And this has often been demonstrated by many examples.

[39:4] *A hymn to our God.*

The one who is truly brought up from the aforementioned circumstances, both from the pit of wretchedness and from the miry mud, had a perpetual victory. The song of victory for a perpetual [victory] is always new. And what this new song is, he explains, "It is a *hymn to our God.*" When we celebrate God in a hymn, when we receive an opinion about him,

---

[20] Ps 27:5 (26:5 NETS).
[21] 1 Cor 10:4 NRSV.
[22] Ps 141:6 (140:6). In Hebrew the verse reads, "Their judges are cast down at a cliff."
[23] Ex 7:12 NETS.
[24] 1 Cor 15:54.
[25] Hos 8:8.
[26] Cf. Rom 8:35.
[27] Rom 9:16 NRSV.

that he is within our reach, when we come to the goal, we sing a new song, for that which is without successor comes at the end. Therefore, the hymn that is sent up by him in thanksgiving to God is a new song.

[39:4] *Many will see and fear and put their hope in the Lord.*

Many will see me brought up from the pit of wretchedness and from the miry mud, and having received a standing for my feet on the rock, and my steps guided, and me singing a song and a hymn, and *they will fear* so that they also come into such a way of life, *and they will hope* so that they too may obtain these things that belong to me already.

[39:5] *Blessed is the man whose hope is in the name of the Lord.*

David once had a single combat with Goliath, and he did not hope in a shield.[28] You see that the name of the Lord has become his hope. And it is used in a sense that is close to what is strictly called "hope"—now, hope is nothing other than the anticipation of good things—some people frequently call the things they already possess their "little hopes." For example, the rich call "my little hope" not that which is anticipated but that which is already present. And therefore those who already possess it regard the name of the Lord, which is already present, as their hope.

[39:5] *And he did not look toward vanities and lying madnesses.*[29]

The one who looked toward the Lord does not look toward vanities and lying madnesses. He does not look toward a full armament, nor toward the size of a body, nor toward military action, nor toward some other thing that can fall short.

Now, divinations are called "mad lies." Now, there are *madnesses* that are not false: for example, those who are inspired by God, those who are inspired by Christ, are possessed by divinity, but these madnesses are not false but true; that is, they are inspiration. For if there were not also true madnesses, he would not say, "He who does not hope in false madnesses."

The Kataphrygians, being ignorant of how these things are said, understanding both madness and ecstasy according to one meaning, say that Spirit-bearing men have spoken in ecstasy, that they have prophesied. And indeed they are right that they did so in ecstasy, not indeed as a dementia, not as delirium. For example, when Paul says, "If we are beside ourselves, it is for God,"[30] he is not speaking of madness but of standing apart from what is merely human and . . . having given. And this word [284] is used also for astonishment: "And after these things, the sons of Israel shall return and seek the Lord their God and David their king, and they shall stand in awe at the Lord and his good things."[31] Here *ecstasy* means "amazement."

[39:6] *You have done many things, O Lord my God; many are your wonders.*

After gaining an experience of the kindnesses mentioned, since he enjoyed not only these good things but, so to speak, was reared into these things from his mother's womb—and this anointing of his, while he was a child, has taken place contrary to expectation,[32] then, he also says, "*You have done many things, O Lord my God; many are your wonders.*" They are

---

[28]Cf. 1 Sam 17.45.
[29]The NRSV reads, "who do not turn to the proud, to those who go astray after false gods."
[30]2 Cor 5:13 NRSV.
[31]Hos 3:5 NETS.
[32]Cf. 1 Sam 16:13.

many and great, "and in your deliberations," according to which you do wonders, "none will be likened to you."[33] No one will be able to do such wonders, no one will be able to bring someone out of a pit of wretchedness, out of miry mud, to establish his feet on a rock, to guide his steps, and all the rest.

If the phrase "There is no one who will be likened to you" is said in reference to the Father, he is not speaking about the Son, for none of the things that are created will be likened to him. However, the Son will not be likened, for he is eternal, he is the "image"[34] and "exact imprint of God's very being."[35] He is not one who possesses likeness in things that are coming in the future, for he is like already.

Question: *In your deliberations?*

The thoughts about individual things are strictly called "deliberations." Just as deliberation is the speech of the soul and at the same time to say many things in expression does not take place, so also the thoughts about individual things are called deliberations.

A topic in syllogistic reasoning was assigned, asking whether knowing and thinking are the same, and it was said that they are not the same, for while many things are suddenly known, not many things are thought, so that to know is not the same as to think. One can receive an idea of a whole genus and of a whole species. However, it is impossible to know each of them individually, to think of each thing in turn all at once.

Question: To think in the literal sense?

No, but only in the case of the individual objects of thought. As it is impossible to say many things at the same time but to know many things is possible, whereas thinking is a kind of speech of the soul, it is not possible to think many things at the same time. God therefore has such deliberations so that he knows all things at the same time, and in any case differently than we do as men. For it is said in Isaiah, "As heaven is far from the earth, so are your thoughts from my thought."[36] He wished to demonstrate the supremacy of his own thought by way of a perceptible example, for his thought is not spatially removed from the thought of men, but it is removed by the grandeur of its supremacy.

[39:6] *And in your deliberations no one will be likened to you.*

None is compared to the deliberations of God. As when you would say, "No one will be compared to God in respect of creation." For even if there are "creators" among men, yet they do not provide the underlying material of the things that are produced. For example, the builder, when he makes a couch or a chair, does not also create the wood by his art. He merely confers an end on the preexisting material. God, however, confers a form on it, not by discovering a material, but he brings it into existence together with its form.

[39:6] *I proclaimed them and I told of them: they multiplied beyond number.*

You know that when we do not understand something as is necessary and we desire to report it to another, how we then speak in this way and in that, while we know that we did not encompass what we wanted to say. And this one also says, "I proclaimed and I told." Since no one is like you in your deliberations, "I *proclaimed and I told.*"

However, one can also understand it in this way: *I proclaimed* in my disposition, in my thought, and *I told* it perceptibly in my expression, for it is first necessary to think and then to speak in this way.

---

[33] Ps 40:5 (39:6).
[34] Cf. 2 Cor 4:4; Col 1:15.
[35] Heb 1:3 NRSV.

[36] Is 55:9.

Question: *They multiplied beyond number?*
The deliberations, to which none compares.

[39:7] *Sacrifice and offering you did not desire.*

He then says, "You brought me up from a pit of wretchedness and from the miry mud, you set my feet upon a rock, you directed my steps." Inasmuch as it is possible with these thankful words and with deeds that are even greater, it was necessary to sacrifice and to burn an offering to God. But you did not desire perceptible [285] whole burnt offerings, the bodily sacrifices that come from the slaughter of animals and the rest, which were the foreshadowing things.

[39:7] *You fashioned a body for me*

instead of these things. The apostle therefore explained that this body is the rational and unbloodied sacrifice.[37] Therefore, when a certain greater sacrifice is found, then he no longer desires the former sacrifices; they are not desired by him.

Do not let the teaching of the Dimoirites trouble you, for they say, "Do you see that [he fashioned] a body?"

Indeed, the one who says, "*You fashioned a body for me,*" does not say this: "only [a body]." For the one who possesses a complete Man has a body, but not only a body. Now, I said that the psalm has one person speaking from the beginning, for from the beginning until the end the person who speaks is presented as one and the same. Therefore, just as he said here, "A body, however, you fashioned for me," so also in the lines that follow he will say, "Those who seek my soul to remove it."[38] See! He has both a soul and a body. Pay attention! And since the discourse is about perceptible sacrifices that are replaced by the Spirit, he mentioned a sacrifice that succeeds them. However, the soul has not become a sacrifice in this sense, but the body.

And it is good that he did not say "you created" a body, but you yourself "fashioned" it "when the Holy Spirit came upon" Mary "and the power of the Most High overshadowed her."[39]

For this reason you did not desire those sacrifices and offerings any longer, since "you have fashioned a body for me," which was about to be sacrificed for all. And the following can be said: for this reason you did not desire sacrifice and offering, since you fashioned a body for us, which we can offer and sacrifice to you: "I appeal to you by the mercies [of God], to present your bodies as a rational sacrifice."[40]

In other versions there lie the words, "Ears, however, you fashioned for me." Therefore, the one who interprets this reading says: since you did not desire sacrifice and offering, "you fashioned ears for me," by which I hear about those things that are indicated by the perceptible sacrifices: for instance, of the intelligible sacrifice of praise, "Offer to God a sacrifice of praise."[41] You summon me at last into listening, you are no longer seeking perceptible sacrifices, so that what is said is something like this: "The instruction of the Lord opens my ears."[42] The unmusical man does not have an ear to listen to words about music.

And another of the translators also said, "Ears, however, you dug for me," since you eliminated their obtuseness, you eliminated that which hinders the hearing of them.

Question: How do we understand this in relation to Jesus?

I said that allegories are not explained like the literal senses. And I have frequently employed the example of Abraham and the two

---

[37]Cf. Rom 12:1.
[38]Cf. Ps 40:14 (39:15 NETS).
[39]Cf. Lk 1:35.
[40]Cf. Rom 12:1.
[41]Cf. Ps 50:14 (49:14 NETS).
[42]Is 50:5 NETS.

women.⁴³ I said to you that the soul of Jesus is not an immutable essence. It is of one substance with other souls, and all the good that it possesses it has from God the Word. Since, then, it also possesses the art of listening well, it has it from the Savior. It belongs to the one who uses it as a temple.

[39:7] *Whole burnt offerings and sacrifices for sin you did not require.*

The things of the shadow you neither required nor approved of. "What to me is the multitude of your sacrifices? I am full. I do not want whole burnt offerings of rams and the fat of lambs."⁴⁴

[39:8] *Then I said, "Look, I have come."*

Then I, for whom you fashioned a body, said, "*Look, I have come,*" that is, since this is the goal of his appearance, to bring the shadow to an end, for sacrifices and whole burnt offerings to be offered no longer, I myself have come in order to fulfill the sacrifice, when I will come as a whole burnt offering.

[39:8] *In the scroll of the book it is written of me.*

The head of the book refers to "all the Scripture that is inspired by God."⁴⁵ For the chief point of Scripture is the way of life that relates to Christ. In a secondary sense, let it also be said to relate to other things, for if the appearance was not going to take place, the ancient Scriptures would not have announced the gospel beforehand.

Question: This was written regarding the Pentateuch?

He calls all of Scripture a book, the "scroll" of which is the goal for which the Scriptures have been given: salvation, the visitation.

Question: Was the origin of the world then narrated first because of this?

It was narrated first to show the origin of the world before men, and after this the origin of men, [286] in order that the appearance should have an occasion. He is "the Lamb of God who takes away the sin of the world."⁴⁶ When it is said that Adam transgressed "by disobedience"⁴⁷ and the Savior has been shown to be righteous "by obedience,"⁴⁸ does it not make reference to the Savior, who is a type of the one to come, since Adam himself is a "type of the one to come"?⁴⁹ "This is a great mystery, and I am applying it to Christ and the church."⁵⁰

And, when a book is mentioned, that it is by no means necessary to understand it in the literal sense, Ezekiel hears from God, "Open wide your mouth."⁵¹ And he sees a book in God's hand, and he says, "Take it and eat, and your belly shall be filled."⁵² And it says, "This book was inscribed on the front and back."⁵³ It is inscribed within according to its spiritual and intelligible senses, and without in its perceptible and manifest senses. However, the wise one consumes both, and he finds a harmony between both the symbols and the originals. And in Isaiah again it says, "And these sayings shall be like the words of the book that is sealed. If they give it to a man who knows his letters, saying, 'Take, read,' he answers: 'I cannot, for it is sealed.'"⁵⁴ And the unlettered man says, "I do not understand letters."⁵⁵ [For it makes no difference] whether it is sealed or unsealed. And we understand again the divinely inspired Scripture, and the

---

⁴³Cf. Gal 4:22-24.
⁴⁴Is 1:11.
⁴⁵Cf. 2 Tim 3:16.
⁴⁶Jn 1:29 NRSV.
⁴⁷Rom 5:19.
⁴⁸Rom 5:19.
⁴⁹Cf. Rom 5:14 NRSV.
⁵⁰Eph 5:32 NRSV.
⁵¹Ezek 2:8 NETS.
⁵²Ezek 3:3.
⁵³Cf. Ezek 2:10.
⁵⁴Is 29:11.
⁵⁵Is 29:12 LES2.

one who understands letters, yet cannot read because of the seals set on the book, as the people of the circumcision, and the one who does not understand letters as the people from the nations.

[39:9] *I desired to do your will, O God.*

For this reason "I said, 'Look, I have come!'" because I desired to do your will after you did not delight in sacrifice and offering.

Those who believe wrongly about Christ say that there are different wills, for he also says here, "I have come. I desire to do your will," and in the Gospel [he says], "I have come down from heaven, not to do my human will, but the will of him who sent me."[56] Because of those who say, then, that there are two wills, we will answer: variances in wills take place either in excess or deficiency or opposition. The one who is progressing in virtue desires righteousness as well as the one who is perfected, yet the will of the perfect is not one and the same as that of the one who progresses or of the beginner. And either a multitude or a duality of wills takes place either in excess or in deficiency, and it also occurs in accordance with opposition when one prefers good things while another chooses evil things, when one desires to be saved while another wills to sin. To attribute such a will to the Son, therefore, a will that even has opposition, is the uttermost impiety!

And now I address myself to the Manichaeans. To these the following must be said: the will of the Savior is found to be good, for he says that he has come down from heaven "to do the will of God."[57] And to do the will of God is good. And again, "He has come to seek out and to save the lost."[58] And again, "If you choose, you can make me clean."[59] If this is the will of the Son, then he desires all things that are beneficial. . . . If, however, the will of the Father is opposed to him, I leave it to you to observe what follows. If excess and deficiency are found in their wills, in their disposition, then even the Father as well as the Son, having a disposition, that is, a quality, even the Father will no longer be incorporeal: he is no longer a simple essence, he is no longer uncompounded. Neither in excess, nor in deficiency, nor in opposition should his will be spoken of, for the will of the Son demonstrates that it is good. Nevertheless, he says that this will of his is to complete the will of the Father. But it is not appropriate to attribute this to his divinity: neither is it contrary, nor does it differ in excess or deficiency. Therefore, one must understand these things of him as man.

[39:9] *And to do your law in my innermost belly.*

There is a spiritual food that spreads into the belly of the inner man. And that the law, however, is a spiritual food is probably evident to everyone, for it is not a perceptible **[287]** food.

Now, this belly is often praised, and it is in the following: "Because of the fear of you we conceived in the womb."[60] And as this belly conceives in the womb from the divine Spirit—and this is the fear of God—so also it receives divine food into itself. Because you no longer want sacrifice, offering, or whole burnt offerings, I began to have the spiritual law as my food.

[39:10] *I told the glad news of righteousness in a great assembly.*

A great assembly is that which is composed of those who are individually great, of whom Paul said, "We speak wisdom among the mature,"[61]

---

[56] Jn 6:38.
[57] Cf. Jn 6:38.
[58] Lk 19:10.
[59] Mt 8:2 NRSV.

[60] Cf. Is 26:17-18.
[61] 1 Cor 2:6.

so that the gathering of these ones, then, is *a great assembly*.

With *righteousness* is not meant the kind according to the law, of which the apostle says, "As to righteousness under the law, I was blameless."[62] This righteousness, then, I proclaimed in the great assembly, for if he were to proclaim the letter and the shadow, he would not declare good news to great ones but to infants.

Question: What kind of righteousness?

The kind of which the Savior was saying, "Unless your righteousness exceeds that of the scribes and Pharisees,"[63] is this not the righteousness according to the shadow? Therefore, of ours—of the disciples' righteousness—the Savior says, "Let your righteousness abound more than that of theirs." And he says that theirs was done in ignorance.[64] For this reason let us not be ignorant of God's righteousness, but let us proclaim it!

[39:10] *Behold! I will not restrain my lips.*

He refers to speech here as "lips." Often when speech summons us to say something in front of mean and uninitiated men, we restrain our own lips, we do not have them unbound, but we condescend, we conceal, we speak in proverbs, and our lips are restrained. However, when he speaks to perfect men and to the great congregation, he does not restrain his lips, since nothing impedes him from speaking to them.

Moreover, it is possible to say the following: as the word says, "And on his law he will meditate day and night."[65] He never restrains his own lips, always declaring the words of God. And understand the word *always* in this sense: as is necessary and as it is befitting for him to do this, for even when he is silent, he speaks in his mind, and when he sleeps, when he sleeps as a righteous man, he does this with reason. He meditates on something good even during silence.

[39:10-11] *O Lord, you knew my righteousness.*

After he bore on many occasions what is so-called self-testimony—for "to tell the glad news of righteousness in a great assembly" is something great and, so to speak, superhuman—he says to God, "*You knew my righteousness.*" This righteousness, which I announce, I possess and I have been fashioned in accordance with it.

And since the psalm may be spoken about the Man of the Savior: because he knew no sin, but the sin that has occurred is productive of righteousness.[66] Now, reproach and shame are the same thing. And see this at least: as far as it concerned him, joy was set before him because he had no sin. Therefore he disregarded the shame;[67] he trampled over it.

And the following is also possible: even if some speak blasphemy about me in ignorance, yet you know my righteousness. As Susanna also said, "You know that they give false evidence against me."[68]

[39:11] *I did not conceal your truth in my heart.*

The one who knows the righteousness of God does not conceal the truth that is yoked to it in his heart. Truth is said to be yoked to righteousness, when it says, "Truth sprouted from the earth, and righteousness peered down from heaven."[69] It calls the Savior the righteousness that has peered down from heaven, for it says, "He bent heaven and came down."[70] And "he sprouted from the earth" when it received the fulfillment of his visitation.

---

[62] Phil 3:6.
[63] Mt 5:20 NRSV.
[64] Cf. Rom 10:3.
[65] Ps 1:2 NETS.
[66] Cf. 2 Cor 5:21.
[67] Cf. Heb 12:2.
[68] Sus 43.
[69] Ps 85:11 (84:12).
[70] Ps 18:9 (17:10).

And it is also possible to understand it in this way: when truth sprouts from the "earth," it sprouts out of that good and beautiful soul that hears the word [**288**] and bears fruit.

Righteousness therefore peers down from heaven. And in another psalm it says, "Mercy and truth met; righteousness and peace kissed."[71] Those who are well acquainted with the Histories find that wars and troubles begin because of injustices. Truth, however, has the mercy of God; for if God does not show mercy, one cannot know the truth: how great it is and of what kind it is. For this reason, then, "mercy and truth met."

And mercy can also be as follows: for example, the one who loves his neighbor as himself[72] is merciful toward his neighbor, and he himself requires an equal mercy from him, for the truth is also made manifest. Therefore, just as righteousness goes before peace, so also mercy goes before truth. However, both are one and the same.

Therefore, when someone is ashamed of Jesus and his words,[73] he is ashamed of his truth.

[39:11] *And I spoke of my means of salvation.*

The confession of the truth is *my means of salvation.*

And if he also calls Christ the truth, he again calls him the *means of salvation,* and I spoke of my means of salvation and made your truth manifest. I speak of *my means of salvation,* which is Christ, whom I make manifest.

[39:11] *I did not conceal your mercy and your truth from a large gathering.*

We said that mercy is yoked together to truth.

And a *large gathering* he calls that gathering of the nations that believed, and was composed of all the nations. Both the wise person and Jesus, as Man, say this.

[39:12] *But as for you, O Lord, do not keep your compassions away from me.*

By your compassions I have come to speak blamelessly and as is necessary. Do not keep them from me, then, so that I remain such as I am. "Let your compassions quickly overtake us, O Lord, because we became very poor."[74] When your compassions are far away, then poverty comes. That one, from whom they were not removed, is kept wealthy. And he is wealthy when he has received truth and mercy.

[39:12] *Your mercy and your truth supported me always.*

When you were compassionate toward me, *your mercy and your truth supported me.* "Do not," therefore, "keep your compassions away from me," so that your truth and the mercy that is yoked to it might remain, assisting me in this way.

[39:13] *Because evils encompassed me, of which there is no number.*

For this reason, "do not keep your compassions away from me," because many *evils encompassed me,* which cannot be put down by a number either because of their multitude—if distresses are meant, they do not have a number because of their multitude. If, however, the other "evils" are meant, the moral evils of which it is said, "With laughter a fool practices evils,"[75] they do not exist in a certain measurement or number, for they not belong among the things that are; they are the conceptions of men, they are the transgressions of the divine laws. Understand, then, the double meaning of the "evils."

---

[71] Ps 85:10 (84:11 NETS).
[72] Cf. Lev 19:18.
[73] Cf. Mk 8:38; Lk 9:26.

[74] Ps 79:8 (78:8 LES2).
[75] Prov 10:23.

[39:13] *My acts of lawlessness overtook me, and I was unable to see.*

One can also understand this in this way: "because evils encompassed me," which are not subject to number—as it was said just now, in two ways—for this reason indeed "my lawless deeds overtook me." However, from another beginning point this must be read with the phrase joined together to it: "because evils encompassed me." *But as for you, O Lord, do not keep your compassions away from me because evils encompassed me, of which there is no number.* Therefore, let the words *Your mercy and your truth supported me always* precede both. Therefore, here he is saying the following: he calls "lawless acts" here the active powers of habits and the lawless deeds that are subject to them. *My acts of lawlessness, therefore, overtook me, and I was unable to see,* for they are harmful to the eyes of the mind, they cause blindness to the eye of the inner man. Therefore, since they overtook me, I am unable to see.

It is also possible, however, to understand them as habits. Now, the former interpretation understood them as the active powers. And these overtook me, and when they pursued me they took me as their subject, [289] and for this reason *I am unable to see,* for lawless acts are harmful to the eyes of the inner man.

[39:13] *They multiplied beyond the hairs of my head, and my heart failed me.*

If you want to understand the sins themselves, they overtake someone when he falls into their power and sins; for when it suffers this, the intellectual part of the soul is harmed.

If, however, you understand the active powers themselves, they are often called ambiguously by the name "habit."

And my heart failed me.

Since the lawless acts that overtook me and removed my sight from me *multiplied more than the hairs of my head, my heart failed me.* I no longer have the heart of a wise man, for the heart of the one who says these things is carnal. When, therefore, the carnal heart fails someone, it becomes hard.

[39:14] *Be pleased, O Lord, to rescue me.*

Since lawless acts overtook me, and I am unable to see, and they multiplied more than the hairs of my head, *be pleased to rescue me,* lest my heart remain alone.

If, however, the discourse is about the hairs of this head, he has spoken hyperbolically. When lawless acts take place, they cannot exceed the multitude of the hairs of the head. Therefore, it was spoken hyperbolically. But if not, he is saying this: indeed, the hairs of my head, that is, the insensitive movements that are not fitting to what is truly the intellect, are "hairs," for the hairs are those things that are attached to those things that are insensitive in us. Therefore, he is saying the following: when my lawless acts overtake me and I am no longer able to see, the hairs of my head multiplied, the things pondered insensitively, the things that are thought foolishly. For this reason my heart, the intellect itself, abandoned me. It is no longer my intellect, because it is seduced into sin.

[39:14] *O Lord, attend to helping me!*

Indeed, I ask you to be pleased to rescue me for no other purpose than that you attend to helping me. And you help me when you set me free from the enemies that dominate me.

[39:15] *May those who seek my soul, to take it away, be put to shame and embarrassment at the same time.*

I was saying that the psalm is spoken by the same person. And when a man is the speaker, he sends up his petition about the body and the soul. When, therefore, the Son of Man, the temple that has come forth from Mary, says these things, we will say to those who claim that he has assumed only a body because it is said, "you fashioned for me a body"—behold, he also says this, and the same person is the one who is now declaiming. Those who receive knowledge of the truth are put to shame and embarrassment.

[39:15] *May those who desire evil things for me be turned backward and embarrassed.*

It is a great advantage for vice to be turned backward, for to press forward is harmful. Therefore, *may they be turned backward*, so that they do not extend their way, so that they do not press forward into what is worse.

[39:16] *Let those who say to me, "Good, good!" be immediately clothed in shame.*

He is praying about those whom he says "*immediately*," lest they persist in evil, lest they say incessantly: "*Good, good, good!*" It is characteristic of those who rejoice in the misfortunes of others to say: "*Good, good*," at those who suffer something unpleasant.

[39:17] *May all who seek you rejoice and may they be delighted in you, O Lord.*

Speaking about his adversaries, that they be both put to shame and embarrassed and turned back, when they say spitefully, "Good, good!" he says, "*May those who seek you rejoice and be delighted in you, O Lord.*" We rejoice and are delighted, when we find you after seeking you, for the one who seeks something is made glad and cheered when he finds it. Therefore, even when painful misfortunes come on us, even when other things harm us, we seek to find you as our helper. And then, appearing, you help us and you say, "*While you are still speaking, look, here I am.*"[76] **[290]**

[39:17] *And let them say continually, "Let the Lord be magnified!"*

Since after finding you, they give thanks, *let them say continually, "Let the Lord be magnified!"* May they possess those things because of which they ought to sing and be glad.

And this is also possible: may ingratitude never be theirs!

[39:17] *Those who love your salvation.*

The salvation of the righteous, or the one who becomes the agent of their future salvation. *Let them say continually, "Let the Lord be magnified!"* Because they love your salvation, they also continually magnify God for it.

[39:18] *But as for me, I am poor and needy; the Lord will take thought for me.*

For this reason I ask that your help be given to me and that you be well pleased to rescue me, because *I am poor and needy.* I am unable to come to my own aid; I cannot set myself free from the things that threaten me, if you yourself do not help me.

I am poor, then, *and needy.* Now, the difference between these words has been spoken of elsewhere.[77]

[39:18] *You are my helper and my protector; O my God, do not delay!*

Since I called on you as my helper and protector, setting your shield in my defense—and this shield is the truth, for "with a shield his truth will surround you"[78]—*do not delay*, lest the struggle pass beyond my power. When you know that it is timely to assent, to help, and to rescue, let this happen, for as far as it depends on my strength and my nature, I am too weak to help myself, to set myself free from the evils that threaten me.

---

[76] Is 58:9.
[77] PsT 50.23-28.
[78] Ps 91:4 (90:4 NETS).

PSALM 40 [41]

[40:1-2][1] *Toward the goal. A psalm for David. Blessed is he who considers the poor and the needy.*

Many understand this psalm, too, as coming from the person of the Savior, because the words set down here are understood in the Gospel as having been spoken by the Savior, and the deeds and thoughts as being about the Savior.

Blessed, it says, *is he who considers the poor and the needy.* Now, in view of the ethical sense, many have given the following interpretations: the *needy* and the *poor* are different, and anyone who shares with these must give his charity proportionally, for then he acts intelligently. One need not feed every poor person with food. There is such a thing as one who is in need of food because he has previously lived wastefully—he lingered in drunkenness, he squandered all that he used to possess indecently and wickedly—whereas another is in need either because of long sickness or a large number of children. Therefore, one should give to each with understanding. Therefore, if someone does not have enough to give to all, to those to whom he ought to give, he ought to do this with understanding, and if he can he becomes compassionate like the Father in heaven,[2] who causes the sun to rise not only on the good but also on the evil.[3] However, when it is not possible for him to give to all, he ought to do this with understanding.

It is also possible for this to be understood about the Savior, for "he became poor for our sake"[4] and not for some other reason. "For our sake he became poor," in order that he might set us free from poverty, in order that he might remove us from wretchedness. It says, "For our sake he made him to be sin who knew no sin"—this is his poverty—"so that in him we might become the righteousness of God."[5] He was delivered [from death, he was not] overpowered by it.[6] Even if he has become sin, yet he did this not in order to remain sin but in order to set free those who . . . "You know the grace of our Lord Jesus Christ, that though he was rich, yet for your sake he became poor."[7] And this is the paradox: "though rich" he is poor, and this poverty makes us rich or is productive of riches. He is not poor in an absolute sense but in view of his wealth.

[40:2] *In an evil day the Lord will rescue him.*

He rescued Jesus "in an evil day," when they surrounded him and said, "Crucify, crucify him! We have no king but Caesar!"[8] And he was also delivered from the evil day, because by becoming sin he has become creative of righteousness.

The word *understanding* is meant in the sense of doing well to brothers who are in

---

[1]Didymus the Blind, *Psalmenkommentar (Tura-Papyrus)*, vol. 5, Kommentar zu Psalm 40–44,4, ed. M. Gronewald, PTA 12 (Bonn: Rudolf Habelt, 1970), resumes here until the end of the commentary.
[2]Cf. Lk 6:36.
[3]Cf. Mt 5:45.
[4]2 Cor 8:9.
[5]2 Cor 5:21 NRSV.
[6]Cf. Acts 2:24.
[7]2 Cor 8:9 ESV.
[8]Cf. Jn 19:15 ESV.

need, for the apostle also says about the offering: "Think over what I say, for may God grant you understanding in all things."[9]

Now, understanding is the knowledge of what is comparable [**291**] and what is incomparable. Comparable things are ones that are similar, ones that are equal, when we bring together one with another and find it to have the identity either in similarity or in equality. The one who has understanding therefore knows what is linked to what and what is not.

[40:3] *May the Lord preserve him, and quicken him, and bless him in the land.*

Concerning both it can be said: the Lord will preserve the poor and needy. For this reason he also led the one who understands into the same thing with him. Somewhere it was said once that when you see, for example, one who is sick and a physician who has suddenly come there because of another motive, observe that the divine decision of providence has led the physician, a compassionate physician, in order that by having sympathy for the sick man he should help him as a physician.

And he either *blesses* the poor and the needy and makes *him live in the land*, or the one who understands and received understanding in relation to the poor and the needy. When you say this about the Savior, he preserves him and bestows life on him, for even if "he was crucified in weakness, yet he lives by the power of God."[10] Understand the phrase "in the land" in common with both.

[40:3] *And may he not hand him over to the hands of his enemies.*

He does not hand over such a person into *the hands of his enemies*. Such a person has many enemies, he has many who lie in wait for him, for since he is a blessed man and has understanding in relation to the poor and the needy according to all the interpretations that were given, he also has many who lie in wait for him, for God will deliver him from their hands. The one who hands himself over to them, however, is not delivered from the hand of his pursuers.

[40:4] *The Lord will help him on his bed of pain.*

Here he is speaking about the poor man. Even when he comes on a bed of sicknesses and when such a condition is painful to him, God helps him. Consider what is said about the paralytics in the Gospels: the one who was placed bedridden for thirty-eight years used to remain on a bed of pain so that he was unable to be stirred up, nor to be roused. And other such paralytics were described in the Gospels. However, not everyone one who has pain on his bed and infirmity is rescued. Ahaziah, in fact, fell from the bed in his upper chamber and died.[11]

When, however, it is interpreted anagogically, the body is frequently called the bed of the soul. And there are many scriptures that advocate for such a view. When someone, therefore, is in the corruptible body and in the earthly tent, which "burdens the mind full of cares,"[12] then he is "upon a bed of pain." But when God helps him, he causes him to mortify the body and to make it subject to him,[13] and he is no longer cast down on the body, but he at last takes up his bed and walks.[14]

The body, therefore, is a bed. The lover of pleasure, the one who gives himself up to his passions, the one who welcomes the works of the body and practices them, suffers pain on a body, but God helps him and makes him well,

---

[9] 2 Tim 2:7.
[10] 2 Cor 13:4.
[11] Cf. 2 Kings 1:2.
[12] Wis 9:15.
[13] Cf. 1 Cor 9:27.
[14] Cf. Mk 2:9; Jn 5:8, 11.

in order that, after becoming well, he himself is no longer cast on the bed, but he himself lifts it, even as they say that it happens when the soul rules the body.

Question: Of what kind are the "sixty mighty ones," who are mentioned with praise, who are around the bed?[15]

From Abraham until [Solomon there are] nineteen generations, and from [Solomon until Christ there are forty-one]. These, then, are the sixty mighty ones who are around the body of the Savior, performing to him the service of his birth.

However, one must also say as follows: in six days the world has come into being, and this is a perfect number, as has often been explained, for counting by tens the number sixty is six. Therefore, the one who surpasses the world and passes above is mighty, being "a man instructed in warfare," having a sword "upon his thigh."[16] Therefore, these sixty mighty ones are around the bed of Solomon, around the Lord's body, encircling it, observing for what reason the Savior was made embodied. "Sixty," then, "mighty ones are around it, all holding a sword."[17] They are armed with swords. And there are swords that the wise hold: "Holy ones will boast in glory, and they will rejoice in their throat," "and a two-edged sword is in their hands."[18] They have two-edged swords in their hands. And they also have them "on their thigh."[19] And since the dramatic action is a wedding hymn about the nuptials of the bride and the groom, he wishes to show the temperate ones around the groom [292] and he says that they have a sword on their thigh, cutting away the shameful appetites.

[40:4] *You turned his whole bed in his infirmity.*

He is saying the following: no brief healing has he given the one who suffered great things, but he turned "his whole bed" from infirmity, in order that he might be no longer unwell but healthy, as I said about the paralytic.[20] Moreover, you will say about Lazarus, who has a body that is covered with sores, that when he was transferred from there by the angels,[21] his whole bed was turned, his whole infirmity. He had no longer been cast down sick. Indeed, he at last passed into Abraham's bosom.

[40:5] *I said, "O Lord, have mercy on me."*

Now he says the following: that which is within our power works together in order to be saved from the bed of infirmity and to be helped from the bed of pain, for this I did: *I said, "O Lord, have mercy on me. Heal my soul, because I sinned against you."* You see that when he sinned, then he began to be ill, and then he had been cast on a bed and a couch. Therefore, when someone knows the one who can deliver, then he will achieve that which is desired, similarly to this: "I am willing. Be cleansed!"[22] "Stand up, take up your mat, and walk!"[23]

I therefore *said* this, "*O Lord, have mercy on me!*" By saying, "*O Lord, have mercy on me,*" I showed that by myself I was not able to be shown mercy.

[40:5] *Heal my soul, because I sinned against you.*

I sinned against you. In this way, probably nearly all of us sin against God because we are ignorant of many things about him, overlooking many of the things in his laws that it is

---

[15] Cf. Song 3:7.
[16] Cf. Song 3:8.
[17] Song 3:7-8.
[18] Ps 149:5-6.
[19] Cf. Song 3:8.

[20] Cf. Ps'l' 291.15.
[21] Cf. Lk 16:22.
[22] Mt 8:3; Mk 1:41; Lk 5:13.
[23] Mk 2:9.

necessary to do. *I sinned*, therefore, *against you*, but when I said, "*O Lord, have mercy on me*," I had the object of my request.

[40:6] *My enemies spoke evils against me: "When will he die and his name perish?"*

I was saying that this psalm was spoken from the person of the Savior as Man. And since the Jews, his enemies, have become, as it were, the betrayers of the truth, who did not understand the one who appeared, and Judas has become so as well, though he is one of the disciples,[24] he speaks about the enemies who have come against him, once in the singular, relating the accusation of betrayal to the chief, and once in the plural, because of those who follow him and put Jesus to death.

And this does not occur here only, but also in the 108th Psalm it is said, "They spoke against me with a deceitful tongue. And they surrounded me with words of hatred. In return for my love they would slander me, but I, I would pray. And they rewarded me evil for good and hatred for my love. 'Appoint a sinner against him, and let a slanderer stand on his right'"—it says this in the singular about Judas—"'When he is tried, may he come out as condemned, and may another seize his position.'"[25] Once it speaks therefore about Judas, and once it speaks about those who were in agreement with him, and for this reason in the same verses sometimes it speaks in the singular and sometimes in the plural.

Also here it says then, *My enemies spoke*. They have said the following: the evils, which they regard as evil, they spoke against me: "*When will he die and his name perish?*" For they supposed that when Jesus died his teaching was extinguished and the reputation around him, and they were saying, "*When will he die?*" But it turned out opposite to what they supposed. When he was alive and was in life, his name did not gleam in the same way as it did when he was crucified and raised up to heaven.

In the anagogical sense this must be understood about the heterodox: for as many as do not think rightly but say deceptions and impious words about the Savior, those said evils against him. And since there is a certain leader of heresies, the liar or his prompter, the devil, for this reason it also speaks in the singular about such a one.

Question: Did the soul of the Savior sin then?[26]

His soul is utterly virtuous; there is not a time when he sins. **[293]** As we speak of a "man of God," so also we speak of a "soul of Jesus." Sometimes we call the "soul of Jesus" that one that he assumed, and sometimes we call a "soul of Jesus" that which is so oriented to him, in accordance with which sense it is said, "All souls are mine."[27] And if all souls belong to the Savior, then each soul does as well.

Question: Does the soul of the saints sin?

The soul of the saints is said to sin in this way, when it comes into the forepassion. And we often used that example: when a garment that has been dirtied receives a certain contamination from touch, it does not appear at all. But when you bring me a garment that is completely clean, freshly coming from the fuller's shop, even if you touch it, it is said to have been stained.

Question: Does the body not come into sin?

My soul comes into a forepassion. In fact, "he began to be grieved and agitated."[28] From here those who attach the appetitive power, called irrational, to Jesus are rejected. The irrational creature is indeed able to begin to be grieved, but certainly not to be agitated. From being agitated and being grieved the

---

[24] Cf. Mt 26:14.
[25] Cf. Ps 109:2-8 (108:2-8 NETS).
[26] Cf. Ps 41:4 (40:5).
[27] Ezek 18:4.
[28] Mt 26:37; Mk 14:33.

Evangelists attributed the beginning to him. However, a beginning is not that which comes after the forepassion; for instance, the passion is not a beginning, but the forepassion itself is a beginning. And in another psalm, for example, it is said, "He is my supporter; I shall not be shaken too greatly."[29]

Question: What does it mean to be agitated?

It is a grief of the rational nature, when mulling over the causes of grief in the mind.

[40:7] *And were he to enter in order to see, he would speak falsely.*

Now, he speaks about Judas: if at some time *he were to enter in order to see, he would speak falsely*, as I was saying just now that the one who has something more with respect to other teachings has something more than other men, so also Judas had something more than the other betrayers, for he derived advantage for a long time and had a residue and an ember of the earlier instruction.

Therefore he would frequently approach Jesus, so that he was even found in the paschal meal, but "he would speak falsely" when he was saying "Rabbi" and when he kissed him.[30] Jesus says, "Do quickly what you are going to do."[31] He was showing words of honor to Jesus. However, he was speaking them falsely, for he has spoken them in order to show him to those who have come for his arrest, not truly in order to show the respect due to the teacher, as he did it earlier. Therefore all that does not come in speech truly is uttered falsely.

[40:7] *His heart gathered lawlessness to himself.*

Even if his heart gathered lawlessness, yet it did this for none other than himself. "What will you give me if I betray him to you?"[32] His heart resolved to commit lawlessness when he gave his heart to the devil, "and after the mouthful the devil entered into him."[33] Judas therefore has committed lawlessness. It was lawless to betray Jesus, for him to be found as the enemy of the teacher who had benefited him so much.

Therefore, this lawlessness, which he gathered when he considered that he would surround his teacher with death, he has gathered against himself, for it did not cling to that one. Therefore, he arose from the dead, and all their [efforts] were shown to be [for nothing other than] his greatness.

[40:7] *He would go outside and talk.*

This took place [when he was about to betray Jesus], and with a kind of honor he would approach him, then "he would go outside"—his heart resolved about [this—"and he would say" to those] who came for Jesus' arrest, "This is the one. Arrest him!"[34] *He would go outside [and talk. Therefore he would go in]* and go out. Some indeed are accustomed to say that he is neither outside nor inside.

The end [of the betrayal taking place, he realized] that he had betrayed Jesus. And it says, "when he saw that he was condemned, he went and hanged himself."[35] [It is ambiguous. This is possible:] "When he saw that" Jesus "was condemned" by Pilate, he experienced regret exceedingly, "and went and hanged himself." [However, the following is also possible:] "When he saw that he" himself "was condemned" after such a great teacher was betrayed, [he experienced regret exceedingly because he himself] **[294]** had betrayed [him], and going away he brought an end to his life by hanging.

---

[29] Ps 62:2 (61:3).
[30] Cf. Mt 26:49; Mk 14:45.
[31] Jn 13:27 NRSV.
[32] Mt 26:15 NRSV.
[33] Cf. Jn 13:27.
[34] Mt 26:48.
[35] Mt 27:3, 5.

[40:8] *All my enemies would whisper against me.*

None of them was speaking against me with confidence. And, therefore, you find the Jews seeking how they might seize him on the sly, and they were whispering to Judas, and he was whispering to them, for he did not shout while entering the synagogue, "What will you give me if I betray him to you?"[36] Those ones themselves, in fact, did not come by day to arrest him. Therefore, Jesus himself says this, "In the daytime I teach" in the synagogue, and now "you have come as though against a robber."[37]

[40:9] *They were contriving a word of transgression against me.*

They used to read the Scriptures "every Sabbath,"[38] in order to learn the things of the law. And though it was necessary for those who read with the law to know who is the one prophesied and attested by the Scriptures, on the contrary, *they contrived a word of transgression against me*, saying, "It is only by Beelzebul that this fellow casts out the demons."[39] "If this man were from God, he would not break the Sabbath."[40] "Are we not right in saying that you are a Samaritan and have a demon?"[41] This is the word of transgression, which they were contriving against him.

And it is possible, since also at the registers of the judge the word *contrived* is often understood, they contrived words before Pilate against him.

[40:9] *Surely the one who lies down will not also arise, will he?*

Now, he himself says: since they surrounded me with death, I was lying down, for in the Scriptures the word "lying down" sometimes signifies death. Even sleep is called "lying down," and the copulation of a man with a woman is called "lying down." Furthermore, death is called "lying down" in Scripture because of the expectation of resurrection, for in the very same way that the one who lies down, if he suffers nothing contrary to nature, may be raised up, so also the one who dies will be raised up. So indeed it is said, "We will all lie down,"[42] and, "I do not want you to be uninformed about those who have fallen asleep,"[43] that is, about the dead. The Greeks in fact say this too.

[40:10] *For even the man of my peace, upon whom I hoped.*

I hoped here means "I was confident" about the man. For the Gospel also made mention of this, that this "man of my peace lifted his heel."[44] For I was saying that it also speaks about him in the Fifty-Fourth Psalm: "But it is you, my man of equal soul with me." "If my enemy had reproached me, I could have borne it, and if he who hates me bragged against me, I could have hidden from him. But it is you, my man of equal soul with me"[45]—we understand this word in the case of one who is likeminded, and again "the wife in your bosom"[46] is of equal soul with you—"my leader and my protector."[47] I had you as a leader, not as my sovereign but as my leader, as one who runs before me.

And here: *The man of my peace, upon whom I hoped.* It is nothing wondrous if you whispered against me and contrived a word of transgression against me, especially if *the man*

---

[36]Mt 26:15 NRSV.
[37]Cf. Mt 26:55.
[38]Acts 13:27.
[39]Cf. Mt 12:24 NRSV.
[40]Cf. Jn 9:16.
[41]Jn 8:48 NRSV.
[42]Cf. 1 Cor 15:51.
[43]1 Thess 4:13.
[44]Cf. Ps 41:9 (40:10); Jn 13:18.
[45]Ps 55:12-13 (54:13-14).
[46]Deut 13:6 NETS.
[47]Ps 55:13 (54:14).

of my peace has become your leader in this wickedness. Therefore, "he lifted his heel," not his head, "against me."[48]

[40:10] *He who eats my bread made great treachery against me.*

The man of my peace, upon whom I hoped, "has lifted his heel against me," he wished to kick me. [The so-called treachery] is a reprehensible trick. Jacob also is called one who deals treacherously, for he supplanted Esau when [he obstructed the elder brother] from the blessing by deceit. To attack someone deceitfully is called a "treachery." Someone [who dresses in rags, tricks another], in order to receive his garment. And the one who acts deceptively to cause the death of someone [makes great treachery against him.]

[40:11] *But as for you, O Lord, have mercy on me and raise me up, and I will repay them.* [295]

Set me free from the evils and the treachery of the wicked word that they devised against them. These things, again, are said in a more human way about Jesus as Man.

But as for you, O Lord, have mercy, and I will repay them. I will be their judge. The one who rises up to repay and to judge, as he finds their dispositions, repays. Many, after receiving proof of their oppression or seeing that the one whom they once condemned himself is going to judge them, according to the passage, "They will look on the one whom they have pierced,"[49] come under blame and know how their recompense awaits them.

[40:12] *By this I knew that you have delighted in me.*

This is the knowledge and proof that I am desired by you, for by this those will know me. The phrase *by this I knew* does not attribute so much to his own knowledge, but rather, "Those who are mine will know by this."

Question: After they are condemned, they will know him?

All who received an awareness of his majesty were either his enemies earlier or disciples.

[40:12] *Because my enemy will never rejoice over me,*

when I am shown to be desired by you, when I arise and am known, because I am in accordance with your will.

It is possible to understand both Judas and the devil who acted on him: in order that they might rejoice, they surrounded him with death; after he rises again they do not rejoice, but rather they are exposed to shame and they assume fear after they behold the one whom they pierced.

[40:13] *But you supported me because of my innocence.*

For I did not know, even if I have become sin,[50] even if I have become a curse,[51] I was not shown to be a curse because of previous sin but in order that I might break the curse and bestow a blessing. And just as he has become sin, in order that he might make those for whose sake he has become sin into the righteousness of God, so also he has become a curse, not in order that he should be dominated by the curse. In this very way, then, he has become a curse for the sake of blessing, sin

---

[48] Jn 13:18.
[49] Jn 19:37; cf. Zech 12:10.

[50] Cf. 2 Cor 5:21.
[51] Cf. Gal 3:13.

for the sake of righteousness: he assumed death because of life.

Innocence, then, often means "naivete," and sometimes it means absolute purity from sin. And when it says, "The innocent believes every word,"[52] and, "Bad company corrupts kind morals,"[53] it is speaking of the kind morals that are superficial. And innocence is also called the perfect virtue, of which it says, "The innocent and upright were attaching themselves to me."[54]

[40:13] *And you secured me before you forever.*

I did not fall into ruin, then, not even for a brief moment; I was innocent before I met with enemies, yet I remained innocent, for *you secured me forever.* Not simply this, then, but *before you.* Now, not everyone who is secured is secured before God, but the one who possesses perfect security: "And he who establishes you with us in Christ,"[55] while you, then, attest to my innocence.

[40:14] *Blessed be the Lord, the God of Israel, from everlasting to everlasting. May it be; may it be.*

The God of Israel, which possesses a mind that sees God, is *blessed*. I ascribe grace and victory to him, not to our own power, for even if I am innocent, yet I assign everything not to my innocence but to the cooperation of God.

The phrase *May it be; may it be* the other interpreters translate as "Amen." Now, the word *Amen* is sometimes understood in place of an oath, for when it says, "Truly, I say to you," Matthew and Luke write the very same word, and Matthew says, "Amen, amen, I say to you," while Luke says, "Truly I say to you." And certainly in the Scriptures it is said, "Behold!" indeed "the handmaiden of the Lord; may it be to me according to your word."[56] And it is also said by those who translate the Hebrew words that it indicates that which is trustworthy. [296]

---

[52] Prov 14:15 NETS.
[53] 1 Cor 15:33.
[54] Ps 25:21 (24:21).
[55] 2 Cor 1:21.

[56] Lk 1:38.

PSALM 41 [42]

[41:1] *In view of the goal. A psalm for understanding, by the sons of Korah.*

The sons of Korah were three temple singers. And their names are recorded in Exodus[1] and in the Chronicles.[2] These, just as some receive one soul and one heart because of faith,[3] so these also, because of the Spirit who associated with them, bestowing the gift of song, received one spirit; because of this they utter the verses of the psalm in unison.

This psalm, however, is not one that is filled with mysteries. For this reason, it has been written "for understanding." So indeed we said in the Thirty-First Psalm, that it is "of David's understanding," because it contained mysteries and riddles. Here also, then, many riddles lie buried. Therefore, there is need of understanding for the one who encounters such psalms that are entitled in this way. And just as it is necessary "to give attention to the public reading of divinely inspired Scripture,"[4] not only to the inscription of the Scriptures but also to "all" of it,[5] so also these ought to be recited and heard with understanding.

And since the word *understanding*, in addition to the obvious meaning, also indicates something else in the passage, "And understanding is good for all those who practice it,"[6] here the understanding that happens and is practiced is moral virtue, for this in particular determines the character of men. He says, therefore, that this psalm ought not to be said by the voice alone, but is also to be understood, and one must practice the deeds that are appropriate to it in accordance with the other meaning of the word *understanding*, of which Paul also speaks. Writing about the service and ministry that it is toward the saints, he says, "May God grant you understanding in all things,"[7] for he does not call "understanding" the knowledge of things that are comparable and incomparable, but practical virtue, for who is understanding in this way other than the one who successfully accomplished and established his own character?

Question: Does this apply both to those who speak and those who listen?

It applies to the one who teaches temperately about temperance and himself possesses the virtue of temperance, which those instructed by him also possess. Indeed, for this reason the true teacher, especially the true teacher of ethics, instructs in order that those who listen might become such as the speaker is.

[41:2] *In the same way that the deer yearns after the springs of waters, so my soul yearns after you, O God.*

It is said that this animal, the deer, is destructive of serpents. And when it kills the serpents, it becomes very thirsty by their poison and longs to find a spring of water, in order that its thirst might be quenched and that it might see

---

[1] Ex 6:24.
[2] 1 Chron 6:9.
[3] Cf. Acts 4:32.
[4] Cf. 1 Tim 4:13; 2 Tim 3:16.
[5] Cf. 2 Tim 3:16.
[6] Prov 1:7 NETS (LXX).
[7] 2 Tim 2:7.

its own reflection, for it is said that the serpents, which are torn in pieces by this animal when they are shaken, fill the face of the deer as if with blood and other things, and it goes away to look into a mirror, in order that it might wash from itself the filth that attached to it because of the destruction of the serpents.

And another thing is also said about the same animal. When, they say, it grows old and loses its hair, it eats a serpent and is made young again. The eating of serpents makes it young again.

Question: Certain kinds of serpents?
Of the whole species or genus of all the venomous serpents.

And this animal also, when its horns fall off because of old age, crouches down somewhere hidden, until the horns appear spontaneously and become hard, for it is exposed to traps when it has no horns, for they are its weapons and its means of defense. When they travel in the woods, then, their horns are caught, and in this way they are detached. For this reason such a proverb also appears: "Woe to deer who have no horns!"[8] And this proverb hints as follows: woe to a man who is helpless, who does not have enough power to help himself.

Therefore, the other meaning is shown [297] here. By saying, *In the same way that the deer yearns after the springs of waters, so my soul yearns after you, O God*, he likened longing for God to the longing of the deer for springs, for God is also a spring, and his word is a spring: "You have forsaken the spring of wisdom."[9] "Because with you is life's fountain."[10] And again, God says, "They forsook me, fountain of living water."[11] And the Holy Spirit is a spring, when indeed all the gifts flow from him and have their beginning from him.

In the same way, then, that the perceptible deer longs for the springs of waters, so our soul, when it becomes a deer and is destructive of those that harm it, longs for you, O God. Those who are "ready to punish every disobedience,"[12] these are the deer that kill the serpents of unrighteousness. And those who received "authority to tread on snakes and scorpions"[13] are deer.

And these deer also pursue the heights: just as the springs of waters, so also the heights, for "the high mountains are for the deer."[14] And again the same says, "He who establishes my feet as a deer,"[15] in order that by being equipped they seek intelligible things.

And since I often said that intelligible things seem to be one thing and another according to one conception and another, even though they are the same thing in substance, the springs of water that the spiritual deer seeks are also high mountains. Insofar as they are given in an elevated way and from above, they are heights, and insofar as they give drink and produce rivers in those who have drunk them, they are called springs.

Now, one must also call the serpents pleasures in an ethical sense, for pleasure is multiform. And "they are swayed by all kinds of pleasures and desires."[16] He is speaking about wicked women whom the heterodox take captive.

These multiform deer, then, do not yearn to seek God, they do not seek one pleasure. However, our Savior and Lord himself is one desire. And as he is called wisdom, truth, light, and righteousness, so also desire. For instance, the bride in the Song of Songs, asking about the bridegroom, about where she can find him, the guards whom she asked say, "What is your beloved more than any other

---

[8] Cf. Aristotle, *History of Animals* 611a, 25-27.
[9] Baruch 3:12 NETS.
[10] Ps 36:9 (35:10 NETS).
[11] Jer 2:13 NETS.
[12] 2 Cor 10:6 NRSV.
[13] Lk 10:19 NRSV.
[14] Ps 104:18 (103:18).
[15] Ps 18:33 (17:34 LES2).
[16] 2 Tim 3:6.

beloved, O fair one among women?"[17] Tell us how yours is different from the many beloveds! And she says, "My lover is radiant and ruddy,"[18] he is not one, he is man and God. Then, expounding his praises, she says at the end, "His throat is sweetness, he is altogether desire."[19] His word is sweet. You know that some desired things are not complete but have something unpleasant intermingled with them: for example, the drinking of sweet wine has something desirable. However, when it is taken to the point of satiety, it produces drunkenness and is not wholly an object of desire. Again, the sun, when it is seen, is sweet. However, when its flame assails one, it has something unpleasant.

Therefore, nothing relating to the word about the bridegroom is unpleasant; he is wholly an object of desire, he is wholly love, according to the one who said, "My love has been crucified."[20] However, the loves for other things have something painful intermingled with them.

Therefore, just as he is "altogether desire," so also he is wholly love, and for this reason my soul, which is destructive of serpents, like the deer, yearns for God. Therefore, when you see a soul overtaken by various pleasures, by many wicked thoughts, like the deer it removes the old age of vice, the old man, and it dresses itself in the new man instead of it,[21] whether you want to understand it as a proverb or literally.

"Let the doe and the foal of your graces consort with you."[22] **[298]** Let the word be about a woman. The woman is a "doe," in contrast to a man, when she destroys the pleasures laid by the hunters. And again she is also a "foal of graces," for to be a foal she ought be young in being temperate and in graces, the virtues, in order that the graces advance in it, for these virtues are frequently called in Scripture "a crown of graces,"[23] a crown of virtues. According to the conceptions of his prizes he is a multitude of graces: being light, truth, and righteousness. He does not have multiplicity in his substance but in his operations and desires.

[41:3] *My soul thirsted for God, who is strong and living.*

"To thirst" frequently means to possess love. So indeed in another psalm it says, "O God, my God, early I approach you; my soul thirsted for you,"[24] for the one who yearns for something and asks to receive it is thirsty for it.

For God, then, *who is living.* As the divine men, who are wholly moved by the Spirit and elevated to theology always say, "The Lord lives,"[25] so Elisha said, "As the Lord lives and your soul lives."[26] Your soul lives in this way, just as the one in whom you participate lives; but you indeed, as one who partakes of him, live in this way.

It is good to look at a certain passage, which the Arians interpret badly: "Just as the living Father sent me, and I live because of the Father."[27] And I took an example: as when someone may say, "As my rational father, I also am rational, and as my father is a living creature, I too am a living creature." Since, then, my Father is alive, I too am alive because of him, because I am the Son of the living one. So too man is said to be a living creature because of his father, since he is the son of a living creature.

---

[17]Song 5:9.
[18]Song 5:10.
[19]Song 5:16.
[20]Ignatius, *To the Romans* 7.2-3.
[21]Cf. Col 3:9-10.
[22]Prov 5:19.

[23]Cf. Prov 1:9; 4:9.
[24]Ps 63:1 (62:2 NETS).
[25]Ps 18:46 (17:47).
[26]2 Kings 2:2, 4, 6.
[27]Jn 6:57 NRSV.

Lectures on Psalm 41 [41:3]

[41:3] *When shall I come and appear before God's face?*

Men who are still in life thirst for God like the deer thirsts for springs of waters. And they say that their desire is not checked until this moment, for they are still far away from God, in a certain sense, in habit and disposition, not in place. And nothing is far away from God in a spatial sense, for "he fills heaven and earth."[28] Therefore the one who proceeds toward him says, "Where should I go from your Spirit, and where should I flee from your face? If I ascend into heaven, you are there; if I descend to Hades, you are present."[29] Those, therefore, who received a vision in this life of the age to come thirst intensely for God, as they see themselves far away, since indeed they are still loaded with the wickedness of the world, and the weight of the world and its corruption.

And there is this also, since in the festivals of the Hebrews it was a custom for them all to appear three times in this year, for "three times a year every male among you shall appear before me," and "he shall not appear before me empty,"[30] no one who is empty will appear before him. Since, then, this one also desires the springs of water, he prays to be filled in order that he should come and appear before the face of God, no longer being empty.

Question: So is he asking a question?
At times [he inquires of no one else, but he talks to himself:] "At what time, then, will I obtain the perfect good, in order that appearing before the face [of God I might no longer be empty of the] graces given by him?"

[41:4] *My tears became my bread day and night.*

He is saying the following: since I knew that I myself was still deprived of the face of God, [being devoid of virtue, I produced] a lament that contributes to the acquisition of virtue, which from pain and.... In this sense indeed it is said, "Those who sow in tears will reap with rejoicing. Going out, they would go and they would weep, carrying their seed. When they come, they will approach with rejoicing, carrying their sheaves."[31] They sow in tears, with sweat, the seeds of virtue, sowing the things of the Spirit. [299] Therefore, when they will reap, they no longer travail, for they have obtained the end of their effort. And when "going out, we go," "we wept because we were taking our seeds." When we still made progress, after sowing the crop we received the fulfillment of its fruit. And when we went with rejoicing, we carried sheaves, no longer seeds.

These tears, then, become the nourishment of the one who yearns to see God and to be visited by him. Therefore he says, *My tears became my bread day and night*. I do not weep superficially, nor only in pleasant circumstances, so that I sometimes spend time in luxury and sometimes in the weeping of repentance, but also in misfortunes, for misfortunes are called "night." "You will feed us with the bread of tears and you will give me tears to drink in good measure."[32] It is necessary to produce the tears of repentance measuredly, in order for bread and water to appear. And at last some other things that follow the labor will come into existence, the harvest produced by the tears.

[41:4] *While it was said to me day after day, "Where is your God?"*

For this reason I was producing so many tears that they became food for me, because I heard them saying to me, "Where is your God?" This both Sennacherib and the Rabshakeh have said: "Where is your God? And you then, O

---

[28] Jer 23:24.
[29] Ps 139:7-8 (138:7-8).
[30] Deut 16:16.

[31] Ps 126:5-6 (125:5-6).
[32] Ps 80:5 (79:6).

Israelite, where is your God, in order that he might rescue you?"[33]

Therefore, the tears became food for me, but "in measure" and I drank and ate them, for I knew that something productive of joy succeeds the tears and their pain.

[41:5] *These things I remembered, and I poured out my soul upon me.*

When I came into recollection and remembrance of these who speak reproaches, of these enemies of mine, I did not depart outside, I did not pour out my soul outside, but *I poured it out upon me*. This is like it: "I was troubled and did not speak,"[34] and what Paul says, "But we felt within ourselves the condemnation of death, so that we would not rely upon ourselves."[35] Indeed, this is also said about Job, for first it says, "Job did not sin at all,"[36] and then, "with his lips."[37]

Here he calls the "soul" the thought. And when he says, "receiving the outcome for those who believe, the salvation of souls,"[38] he calls the same essences that animate bodies in this way. And when he says, "Having purified our souls by obedience to the truth,"[39] he is speaking of thoughts. So indeed they are accustomed to speaking also of men "with good souls." "But as for you, my man of equal soul":[40] he indicates the equal thought and disposition.

[41:5] *Because I shall proceed to a place of a marvelous tent, as far as the house of God.*

We frequently mentioned that the perfection of the virtues is the house of God, while a tent is progress, for the house of those who progress and travel from place to place is the tent. Indeed, when [they served God in the wilderness,] they were serving him in the tent that gives evidence, for [it was called] "the tent of witness." [And the witness] is praiseworthy. We frequently call the words of God, for example, "witness," [both what it witnessed] and what is made known.

Passing then through the wilderness, [they made use of a "tent of witness" at that time, in order that] they should serve God there, send up prayers, fulfill their sacrifices . . . from there they have God moving to the head. But when they arrived in the Holy Land . . . to exist, and the men themselves no longer had tents but houses, [indicating completion, then also] the service of God was no longer in a tent but in a house. When the corruptible body obtains its goal, there is no longer a need of tents. When "God becomes all in all"[41] [at the end, then there are no longer [300] irrational animals,] lest he become irrational among the irrational beings; there are no corruptible bodies, lest he become corruptible among the corruptible, but he becomes "all in all." And he does not become "in all" in a spatial sense, but by being partaken of, neither does a body participate in him, nor an irrational animal, nor—how much more so!—something lifeless.

And to say *marvelous* is also good. Since this tent is divine, it is worthy of wonder. The progressions toward the great goals, becoming goals for other progressions, are beyond goals and have something marvelous, so that both tent and house are the same, progress and goal.

[41:5] *With a sound of rejoicing and thanksgiving, the noise of those who are feasting.*

Then he says: not by chance, nor with ordinary circumstance, does my passage take place, but *with a sound of rejoicing and thanksgiving.*

---

[33]Cf. 2 Kings 18:34; Is 36:19.
[34]Ps 77:4 (76:5 NETS).
[35]2 Cor 1:9.
[36]Job 1:22 NETS.
[37]Job 2:10.
[38]1 Pet 1:9.
[39]1 Pet 1:22.
[40]Ps 55:13 (54:14).
[41]1 Cor 15:28.

There is no lament, when the passage and haste toward the house of God takes place, but rejoicing. "Abraham," for example, "rejoiced" in this way "that he might see my day; he saw it and was glad."[42] And he saw the day of the Lord, after he arrived at his house, at the perfect faith.

The word *exomologēseōs* means two things in the Scriptures, not to mention also a third meaning. The declaration for sins it calls "confession," as when it says, "Come together to confess [*exomologēsai*] your sins."[43] This then is set down in Barnabas, in his epistle: "Come together to confess your sins." And again, "Confess your sins one to another."[44] "My sin I made known to you, and my lawlessness I did not cover. I said, 'I will declare my lawlessness against myself to the Lord.'"[45] He confesses when he weeps over and laments his former sins.

And it also indicates "thanksgiving," as when the Savior says, "I thank you [*exomologēsomai*], Father, Lord of heaven and earth, because you have hidden the divine things from the wise and understanding, and revealed them to infants."[46] He is not thanking the Father for this, for "divine things" being hidden "from the wise and understanding," but for the revelation of them to infants, while those ones thought that they knew them. And these are those who believed from the nations, both the wise and the intelligent, from whom the divine things are hidden, and those of the circumcision are the ones [to whom the prophet Jeremiah] shouted the following: "How will you say, 'We are wise, and the law of the Lord is with us'? A false pen has become of no use to scribes. Wise were put to shame and they blamed them, because they have discarded the word of the Lord."[47] Since they themselves discarded it, Scripture has become useless to them. For by the . . . it has become. And it is said that when the Scriptures were receiving their beginning, they [wrote] them with little ropes. [When books were invented,] again they began to make it with the stylus. And since what is written in the books . . . they thought, so that they own these different writing implements.

"The wise were ashamed," therefore, "and terrified, because they have discarded the word of the Lord. What wisdom is in them?"[48] For how is it possible for them to be wise who discarded the word of the Lord?

"Thanksgiving," therefore, is indicated by the word *exomologēseōs*. And, "We will acknowledge you, O God, all we peoples will acknowledge you. I will tell of your wondrous deeds, when I have an opportunity."[49] He who confesses during a narrative of wondrous deeds [301] is not admitting to his own sins. And again, "I will acknowledge you, O Lord, with my whole heart; I will tell of all your wonderful deeds. I will be glad and will rejoice in you."[50] And [again it indicates the declaration of sins.] And third, the following meaning is meant: often harmony, and the virtue of suitability [is called *exomologēsis*, as when it says,] "With acknowledgment and splendor you are clothed."[51] Nothing in you is [discordant. Well suited is the garment] of virtue, which relates to your splendor. And [again in the Psalms it is said,] "Acknowledgment and beauty are before him."[52] Here again it signifies harmony [and virtue. The word *exomologēseōs*] you do not understand here as the declaration of sins, [nor as the well-attuned virtue that is associated] with harmony.

---

[42]Jn 8:56.
[43]Epistle of Barnabas 19.12.
[44]Jas 5:16 NRSV.
[45]Ps 32:5 (31:5 NETS).
[46]Mt 11:25.
[47]Cf. Jer 8:8-9 NETS.
[48]Cf. Jer 8:9 NETS.
[49]Cf. Ps 75:1-2 (74:2-3); 67:3, 5 (66:4, 6).
[50]Ps 9:1-2 (9:2-3 NETS).
[51]Ps 104:1 (103:1 NETS).
[52]Ps 96:6 (95:6 NETS).

The noise of those who are feasting is as follows: [their shouting is not to confess] with a resounding voice, but this shouting of theirs is to confess [with intensified thought.] "The tents of the righteous are a sound of rejoicing and thanksgiving";[53] among those who progress there is "a sound of rejoicing and thanksgiving," for they were ridding themselves of vice. And it is also possible that the phrase "in the tents of the righteous" means ["in the bodies of the righteous." Then they rejoice,] when they "punish them and bring them into subjection,"[54] when they become temples. . . .

[41:6] *Why are you deeply grieved, O my soul, and why are you throwing me into confusion?*

[The soul is continually in grief and confusion] until someone arrives at the house of God. But as for you, O my soul, after remembering [these things, those who speak reproaches] and say, "Where is your God?"[55] do not be deeply grieved, do not throw me into confusion, be . . .

You can also understand angels as those "who are feasting," [marking a festival according to the passage,] "But you have come to Mount Zion and to the city of the living God, the heavenly Jerusalem, and to innumerable angels in festal gathering."[56]

Why are you deeply grieved and why are you throwing me into confusion? You have the one who helps you at the ready. As when you say to one who suffers and is sick . . . , "Why did you despair of health? See, the physician is here!"

[41:6] *Hope in God, because I shall acknowledge him: the deliverance of my face and my God.*

God is present: expect to be liberated by him from grief and confusion. And then he is liberated from these, when he receives the end of the things that cause him grief, when . . . ; for he eliminates the confusion, he eliminates the grief.

The deliverance of my face. [Face here means "the inner man."] In relation to this passage, "The eyes of the wise man are in his head,"[57] we were saying that in the [same face, when we understand it in relation to what is perceptible,] both the intelligent and the unintelligent have eyes.

The deliverance [*of my face and my God.* If] it is spoken about a "face" [in a human way] within Scripture, as is frequently said, we do not [understand it of the perceptible face.] "May the Lord lift up his face upon you and give you peace";[58] for [God does not possess a perceptible face. And again it says,] "May the Lord make his face shine and bless you."[59] Here the face that [shines and blesses is God the Word.] And he is also called the "image of the invisible God,"[60] the "exact imprint of his very being,"[61] for which reason the one who sees him sees the Father.[62] Salvation and blessing follow [immediately] when this face is lifted up . . . he becomes without confusion.

Question: The face?

The face that man lifted up, man [who is created "in the image and likeness,"[63] the right grasp of God,] is like God's face; it is described. . . . I also once explained that according to a second interpretation. . . . **[302]** He calls the Son the appearance of the Father, an appearance like an exact imprint of him or an appearance that is about . . . they establish ideas within the soul.

You, then, are *the deliverance of my face.* [However, the face that] has been created ["in

---

[53]Ps 118:15 (117:15).
[54]Cf. 1 Cor 9:27.
[55]Ps 42:3 (41:4).
[56]Heb 12:22 NRSV.
[57]Eccles 2:14.
[58]Num 6:26 NETS.
[59]Cf. Num 6:25.
[60]Col 1:15.
[61]Heb 1:3.
[62]Cf. Jn 14:9.
[63]Gen 1:26.

the image and likeness"[64]] is not the face of the body but is that of which it is said, "And all of us, [with unveiled faces, see the glory of the Lord as though reflected in a mirror"[65]]; for he is not saying the following, that without a veil, [having] the face of the body, "we see the glory of the Lord as though reflected in a mirror." The face of the inner man is covered because of ignorance and sin; it is made manifest [and illuminated because of wisdom, for it is said], "A man's wisdom will illuminate his face."[66] This luminous face . . . does not have the veil of ignorance, it does not have the covering of vice, but a clear one [that reflects the "glory of the Lord" as though in a mirror.] You are the *deliverance* [of this] *face*, [then], O God.

[41:7] *My soul was troubled by myself.*

[It was frequently said that this] kind of trouble [is a forepassion.] And this was also said, when "I poured out," he says, "my soul upon myself," [that since I did not pour out my soul] externally, to them I did not appear to have been troubled. The one who is troubled in [thoughts and does nothing but] limits the trouble to these, he is troubled by himself.

[41:7] *Therefore, I shall remember you from the land of Jordan and Hermon.*

Since my soul has been troubled, even if the trouble [has come] against myself, [yet since it has been wholly troubled], I am in need of the bath of cleansing, I have need of baptism.

Therefore, I remembered you [from the land of Jordan and Hermon. Hermon] is translated as "the way of a lamp" or as "anathema." He is saying the following: [when I am] this [high] mountain, [being exalted by light], acting in an exalted way, having my mind elevated, [I will remember you from Hermon. The way that is] illumined makes the traveler proceed straightforwardly; [it does] not [make him stumble. And *from the Jordan.*] Jordan is translated as "their descent." It is possible that this is the [the descent of the Savior, for he did not] descend [for his own sake], but he descended for theirs, as a most excellent teacher [condescends to his disciples.]

[41:7-8] *From a small mountain, deep calls to deep at the sound of your cataracts.*

[The Savior, who became man], is [a small mountain], and he is visible to all, for "in the last days, the mountain of the Lord will be manifest, [prepared on the tops of the mountains, and it shall be elevated beyond the hills. And peoples shall hasten to it, and many nations shall come and say: 'Come, let us go up] to the mountain of the Lord.'"[67] Even if [he was diminished] both for us and for the creation, [yet he possesses something exalted] in comparison with us. And I say: the Word of God, God the Word ["was in the beginning with God."[68] He was with God, then,] and he comes to each of the prophets, for "it called them 'gods' to whom the Word of God came."[69] "The word of the Lord came to me, saying."[70] If, then, [the Word of God] comes to those who are deified, [he comes in part, since] they do not receive the whole power, the whole participation. [He comes to those who partake of him, while he was with] God. The Word has not become with God. [He has his] antecedent [essence with God, for] "the Word was [in the beginning with] God."[71] The Word was not of a different essence than he was. And then "the Word [was with God, and the

---

[64]Gen 1:26.
[65]2 Cor 3:18.
[66]Eccles 8:1.
[67]Cf. Mic 4:1-2; Is 2:2-3 NETS.
[68]Jn 1:2 NRSV.
[69]Jn 10:35.
[70]Cf. Zech 4:8; 6:9; etc.
[71]Cf. Jn 1:1.

Word was God,"[72] since he was God from God and] eternal light from eternal light.[73]

Therefore, from this *small mountain deep calls to deep at the sound of your cataracts*. Listen: in the Eighteenth Psalm it is said, "Day to day spews forth speech, and night to night proclaims knowledge."[74] With the "day" [is bound the Word that spews forth from day to day.] The Word of God, when it is luminous, [**303**] shining, and revealing, spews forth by a kind of harmony [from day to day. The clear] and luminous things we understand from such days, while the deep and [dark things we understand from the night; for] the deep [indicates] darkness and night. "He reveals deep things out of darkness."[75] [The darkness out of which he reveals] is not this darkness, but from that darkness that "he made as his concealment."[76] When we wish to clarify [an unclear expression, for example, we often] discover another unclear one, which is [easier to understand and not wholly unclear to the] student, and from that one we "proclaim knowledge": from night [to night we proclaim knowledge. So] we also understand here, since "the judgments" of God "are a great deep"[77] [—obscurity and incomprehensibility] are indicated [by this word—] for it was said, "The deep like a garment is his clothing"[78]—we make known profundity from profundity, deep things from what is deep. And since not all [deep things] have [the same incomprehensibility, the same] depth, [we make known] things that are wholly deep from what is not intensely deep. [This] sound of the calling of one depth to another depth [comes] from the [*cataracts*, which are the deepest thoughts about God,] those that cascade from above, from him.

And it is also possible [to understand the cataracts in this way: cataracts] are in a certain way the prophets and apostles who pour down and [administer spiritual rain to us.] This *deep calls to deep*. [Does not the teaching of Jesus, being a deep], because it rushes down [from above] and remains unclear, arrive at the sound [of cataracts? And these people, of whom I spoke, attempt] to interpret the depth of his teaching in a way and [to make known deep from deep to their student.] At that time, then, *deep calls to deep* in the [mode of harmony *at the sound of the cataracts*, when these] clarify it by way of teaching.

Now, there are "things that are cannot be told, which man may not utter," for the one who was caught up "into paradise" speaks of them.[79] Indeed, they are words, [since they have the necessity of being true or false]; and the word *words* is equivocal. Then in particular they are called "words," [when they possess thoughts. At times there is a thought] in the soul which does not involve truth or falsity, and at times [by necessity the thought involves either of these."][80]

---

[72]Cf. Jn 1:1.
[73]A reference to the Nicene Creed.
[74]Ps 19:2 (18:3).
[75]Job 12:22.
[76]Ps 18:11 (17:12).
[77]Ps 36:6 (35:7).
[78]Ps 104:6 (103:6 NETS).

[79]Cf. 2 Cor 12:4.
[80]Aristotle, *On Interpretation* 16a9-11.

PSALM 42 [43]

[42:1] *A psalm for David. Vindicate me, O God, and defend my cause from an unholy nation!*

This psalm can be recited [from the person] of the Savior. It lies [at number forty-two, which is six sevens. It possesses] what is sacred and full of virtue in both ways. How the number six [is perfect] was already mentioned. [The number seven is also incorruptible] and is like a virgin, motherless and fatherless, for the number seven [can neither generate nor be generated. A virgin] is that one who does not generate; a virgin is incorruptible.

For this reason, it was often said in our contemplations that we do not look at the six units but at the nature of the number. [And it is perfect.] We say [that the world] has come into existence [in six days] not because God needs time [for this. "And God said, 'Let it be!'"[1] And] the work [overtakes] the word. He willed and those things existed at the same moment. [For it also says this] very thing [in the Psalms: "All that you wanted to do,] you did."[2] His willing is sufficient for existence. [In the same way we also understand the number seven] with respect to virtue, analogy, and harmony. [This was said, that "the number seven does not generate any of the numbers that are within the decade [304], nor is it generated by any of the numbers within the decade."][3]

The number forty-two stands here, then. For this reason also in the genealogy [from Abraham until Christ all] the successions were forty-two, for it was necessary that the one who was begotten from the virgin and became a perfect [man be conceived without] pleasure. Now, every conception comes about with pleasure being joined to it. As Saul.... From "Abraham until David" there are in fact "fourteen generations," and "from David to the deportation to Babylon," there are fourteen successions. And since he needed the number fourteen [because of the similarity of the sevens and because] of the mystery, he removed three generations. And again, "from the deportation to Babylon to the Christ,"[4] fourteen generations are not found, but only twelve. And if [you exclude] Jesus himself, [three generations are lacking from the number forty-two.] For somewhere he reduced the number because of its multitude, and somewhere else [he added names to it. And because of the] similarity of the sevens, [not because of the similarity of the names,] the lack of the three names took place. In the succession, however, he names "Uzziah."[5] [The name "Uzziah"] appears to be similar [to "Okuziah";] indeed, some regard this to be an error in the Gospel, but the conclusion of the [syllogism shows that it is not an] error but a study of the wise man, in order to preserve the [mystical nature] of the numbers.

Vindicate me, O God, and defend my cause from an unholy nation! He calls an *unholy nation* [the people of the Jews, before he heard, "Ah, sinful] nation, people full of sins!"[6]

---

[1] Cf. Gen 1:3.
[2] Ps 115:3 (113:11).
[3] Philo, *Allegorical Interpretation* 1.15.
[4] Mt 1:17.
[5] Mt 1:8-9.
[6] Is 1:4 NETS.

Therefore, since it was set against him [unjustly, he desires that his case be defended and] that he be vindicated from this nation, for they have no reason why they should bring a charge against him. [Without a doubt, all the charges that they produce] are charges against themselves. They say, "This man is not from God, for he does not observe the sabbath."[7] [However, what is] observing the Sabbath? On the Sabbath is it not right to raise the dead? [Is it a "work of service"[8] and a work that is done with toil] to lead one "blind from birth" into sight?[9] [Indeed, when someone does] an honorable [deed, he does not transgress the Sabbath!] Again when they say, "He casts out demons by Beelzebul, the ruler of the demons,"[10] when they say this they confess that he casts out completely; for they were not able to say that those who were not [at all demonized were] cleansed [from demons] by his rebuke against the demons. "Are we not right in saying that you are a Samaritan and have a demon?"[11] He was a Samaritan in the sense of being a keeper.[12]

He who asks of god that judgment [come to him in keeping with his purity possesses great] confidence. He calls on the one "who knows the hearts of all"[13] and [prays] for him [to defend his cause, for he did not know] sin, nor did he commit it, nor did he have deceit in [his] mouth.[14]

"From an unholy nation," then. And we were saying at that time that often, when he is reproving a multitude, it is found [sometimes that he reproves the Jews as his betrayers] and sometimes Judas, when we cited from the 108th [Psalm. The phrase, "O God, do not pass over my praise in silence,] because a sinner's mouth and a deceiver's mouth were opened against me,"[15] he speaks concerning one person. "They spoke against me with a deceitful tongue."[16] "Because if an enemy had reproached me, I could have borne it. But it is you, O man of soul like mine."[17] And after a few words, "Let death come upon them!"[18] [The Jews instigated Judas] to betray him. And he has become, as it were, a commander and a cause [305] of the betrayal. And for this reason sometimes he reproaches him and sometimes the [Hebrews. Therefore he wishes to be vindicated by God] and to be defended from the unholy nation. And he calls him deceitful as well, because . . . he betrayed the benefactor and teacher.

[42:1] *From a deceitful and unjust man deliver me.*

[He does not pray about] not being betrayed and dying, for often in the previous psalms, [it was said that being delivered means not submitting oneself] to the plots of those who conspire against one. Indeed, we were saying that the [martyrs who were cooked in a cauldron during a time of persecution,] who were handed over to the flame, were delivered, since they did not deny. Others, however, [even though they did not suffer, were not delivered, since they sacrificed.] So we also explained what is in the Gospel: "Deliver us from the evil one" and "Lead us not into temptation."[19]

[42:2] *Because you, O my God, are my support, why did you reject me?*

You are [my support and my God.] Indeed, you have what is said [about the Savior], "But he

---

[7]Jn 9:16 NRSV.
[8]Cf. Ex 12:16.
[9]Cf. Jn 9:1.
[10]Lk 11:15 NRSV.
[11]Jn 8:48 NRSV.
[12]The etymology of Samaritan as "keeper" is found in Origen, *Commentary on John* 20:35.
[13]Acts 1:24.
[14]Cf. 2 Cor 5:21; 1 Pet 2:22.

[15]Cf. Ps 109:1-2 (108:1-2 NETS).
[16]Ps 109:2 (108:2 NETS).
[17]Ps 55:12-13 (54:13-14).
[18]Ps 55:15 (54:16 NETS).
[19]Mt 6:13.

lives by the power of God."[20] You are, therefore, *my God* [and *my support*. And that these things did not pertain to God] is clear. That one, however, because he was mutable, had need of support....

But if he will say these things in reference to God the Word, he is declaring in this way: "Since you are king and [God, for this reason I am king and God." In this way] we also explained the passage, "I live because of the Father."[21] "Since [my] Father lives, [for this reason I live." And I used such] an example: "For this reason I am rational, since my father is rational, and for this reason I am an animate being, since my father is an animate being."

If, then, you are my support, *why did you reject me?* Tell me the cause [of the rejection, for I am not the unholy] nation, nor the unjust and deceitful man. Make known, therefore, *why* [*you rejected me*, in order that when I enter into death] I should plunder it, in order that when I become a curse I should bestow a blessing [in its place.[22] They believed, however, that he was condemned as an unjust man, that] he was condemned as a sinner.

[42:2] *And why do I go about sullenly while my enemy oppresses me?*

The Jews who believed in him knew the reason why [he has been rejected and goes about sullenly, not indeed for any other reason] than that he might be made manifest to the others who surrounded him with afflictions.

[42:3] *Send forth your light and your truth.*

"I have come as light into the world."[23] The man Jesus [prays that these things be sent forth to them, not] to him. Now, God the Word is light and truth, for he himself says, "I am [the light of the world,"[24] "I have come as light into the world,"[25] and, "He was the true light."[26]

Send forth, then, *your light and* [*your truth. For when your light is sent forth*] *and your truth becomes evident*, then also the reason [why I have been rejected and go about sullenly] will be known, even that the man who was benefited by me, [since he is one of the Twelve whom I chose,] wars against me unjustly, wages war against me.

The light and the truth therefore are not two things [in essence, for both are the Son of God.] He is light, when by shining he illuminates the soul and [the mind, and he is truth, when he destroys illusion] and falsehood or when he replaces the shadow of the law.

[He did not desire that these things be sent forth for himself—for he always] had light and truth, for he was his temple—but [for others.]

Question: So the reason why he has been rejected was made manifest through the signs?

He did not desire for himself, but for them, [that the cause of his rejection be shown. Light] and truth [work] so that they see clearly why he has been rejected.

[42:3] *These led me and brought me to your holy mountain.*

Your light and your truth [led me to the highest doctrine of the Trinity. In] another sense again God the Word is called a "holy mountain," for "the mountain of the Lord will be manifest. [306] 'Come, let us go up to the mountain of the Lord,'"[27] and, "Who will ascend to the mountain of the Lord?"[28] This mountain is being spoken of. When light does not lead . . . he receives, unless one is illumined by it, one cannot receive a conception of it,

---

[20]2 Cor 13:4.
[21]Jn 6:57 NRSV.
[22]Cf. Gal 3:13-14.
[23]Jn 12:46 NRSV.
[24]Jn 8:12 NRSV.
[25]Jn 12:46 NRSV.
[26]Jn 1:9.
[27]Mic 4:1-2; Is 2:2-3.
[28]Ps 24:3 (23:3).

[one cannot approach the truth from] the shadow, one cannot go to this holy mountain. And [this mountain, God the Word,] is called *holy* because it sanctifies those who approach it.

But if it is said about the Man, then he [is] also the *holy* [*mountain*] itself, for he has dwelling within himself as within a temple the one who became wisdom, righteousness, and sanctification.[29]

Question: Does the man Jesus say, "They led me"?

I said that when he speaks from the person of the Man, he wills for these things to be sent forth for them, for he is always led by light and truth. And when we understand [in a higher sense, we say that] he says this [one account of his body.] Since those who believe are his members and his body,[30] they were guided [into the *holy mountain*, when] they received [participation in the light] and truth of God; he himself also says [that he was led by them into the holy mountain.] *Send forth* [*your light and your truth,*] therefore, in order that men, or the rational [essences] in general, might be illumined, for [they] *lead me*. So we can say: these are my body, when. . . .

[42:3] *And into your tents.*

Since someone [ascends by many progressions] into the holy mountain, [the many] progressions are indicated by "tents." *Lead me,* [then, *into your tents.*] And the tents [that are mentioned] in the plural [can] indicate the different abodes that are with the Father.[31] [Lead me there, then, in order that] those who follow me will arrive there, not that I might come there, but in order that . . .

[42:4] *And I will enter in to the altar of God, to God who makes my youth glad.*

Now, this altar, to which someone enters in, is esoteric. [*I will enter in*, therefore, *to the*] *altar*, from which one of the seraphim took an ember.[32] And [again in the Apocalypse of John] an altar [is found] in heaven, "and the souls of those who had been beheaded because of the testimony of Jesus" are within it.[33] The word shows, however, that "those who had been beheaded because of the testimony of Jesus" [were martyrs in their life on the earth], for they were as victims near the altar. Not everyone can [be beside the altar,] but "the one who has been beheaded because of the testimony."

Therefore this altar is esoteric. [That which was built] in imitation of the other altar [was not esoteric], for all the vessels that were in the tent, those useful in fulfilling the sacred rituals, [Moses] has made "according to the pattern that was shown" him "on the mountain."[34] [That is the one, on which] a sacrifice of praise [is offered] and on which the sacrifice of righteousness is placed; for "offer to God a sacrifice of praise,"[35] "sacrifice a sacrifice of righteousness."[36]

I will enter in, therefore, *to the altar of God*, and then, *to God who makes my youth glad*. For the one who turns away from the shadow of the law and the external [altar and sacrifices, about which the] word comes, "What to me is the multitude of your sacrifices? I am full,"[37] enters [into the altar of God. Therefore everyone who becomes] "a priest according to the order of Melchizedek"[38] will say, "*I will enter* [*into the altar of God*," in order that I

---

[29]Cf. 1 Cor 1:30.
[30]Cf. 1 Cor 12:27.
[31]Cf. Jn 14:2.

[32]Cf. Is 6:6.
[33]Cf. Rev 6:9; 20:4.
[34]Ex 25:40.
[35]Ps 50:14 (49:14 NETS).
[36]Ps 4:5 (4:6 NETS).
[37]Cf. Is 1:11 NETS.
[38]Cf. Ps 110:4 (109:4).

might offer sacrifices] that are better than those that are visible [when I come there.] Therefore, *I will enter in* [from the external altar and from] perceptible [sacrifices,] from the things that are according to the letter, [307] *into the altar of God.* The one who transcends the "oldness of the letter,"[39] knowing that which replaces the shadow of the law and the Old Testament, will say these things.

[42:4] *I will acknowledge you, O God, on the kithara.*

Since I will enter into your altar, having my youth present because of the "newness of the Spirit,"[40] for this reason *I will acknowledge you* with thanksgiving *on the kithara.* Now, I have frequently said that the kithara signifies practical virtue or the body, which is struck by the soul that is adorned with music.

Here *exomologēsis* signifies thanksgiving, for it belongs to one who has obtained his requests. He prayed that the reason for his rejection and for his going about sullenly would be known; he prayed that light and truth would be sent to him, since they led him; he prayed to enter into the altar of God and to receive an experience of the tents and of the holy mountain. Since therefore he has come to experience these good requests, when God has given them to him, even though God has not obtained them for him, for this reason he acknowledges him with thanksgiving, striking both the senses, which are the strings of the kithara, and the various thoughts or members. For when each of the members is attuned to virtue, a string has been put under tension, so that it might be struck melodiously by the plectrum of the truth.

[42:5] *Why are you deeply grieved, O my soul, and why are you throwing me into confusion? Hope in God, for I shall acknowledge him.*

He asked for certain things to be present for him, and while he was still speaking God consented,[41] and consequently even before he received he was so disposed in trust as though he had already received them. Therefore he arouses his own soul and says, *"Why are you deeply grieved, O my soul?"* Since I have decided to acknowledge him, hope in him, expect that the gifts of thanksgiving will be present for you. And the word *exomologēsis* here signifies thanksgiving.

[42:5] *The deliverance of my face, my God.*

You are the deliverance of that which is truly my face. Now, the light is the deliverance of the inner man, of which it says, "A man's wisdom will illuminate his face."[42] And again the saint says that one is to have "the eyes of his heart illumined"[43] and "with unveiled face to see the glory of the Lord as though reflected in a mirror."[44] When the face is reflected by the suitable, divine glory, and it is also illuminated by wisdom, then God is my salvation. Let others, after being delivered from sickness, say, "The physician is my salvation," and let another, after being delivered from a violent wave and tempest, say, "The helmsman is my salvation."

---

[39]Cf. Rom 7:6.
[40]Cf. Rom 7:6.
[41]Cf. Is 58:9.
[42]Eccles 8:1.
[43]Eph 1:18.
[44]2 Cor 3:18.

PSALM 43 [44]

[43:1] *For the goal. A psalm by the sons of Kore for the purpose of wisdom.*

About the goal [it was often said that the] final object of appetency is that for the sake of which all other things [are, while it exists] on account of no other, [since] it is [the most perfect good]. The one who understands the goal knows also [the things before this] that are efficient causes of the goal. And as long as [someone has not arrived at the goal], a continual transformation accomplished by means of progressions [must take place, so that he arrives at the point where there is no longer any end to reach,] except for the object of his appetency that already is. Therefore, one who is wise must be [one who knows the goal . . .] **[308]**

[43:2] *O God, we have heard with our ears, our fathers have taught us.*

"With our own ears," say the saints, "we have heard the words of God." Besides the common sense of hearing, there is an additional hearing with ears when someone is capable of hearing words that relate to knowledge. The physician has a physician's ear when he listens to words relating to medicine, but another person does not have this ear. The one who is able to say, "The instruction of the Lord opens my ears,"[1] is not speaking about the sensible sense of hearing but about the ability to listen to the words of God relating to knowledge.

In this way, then, must one understand the phrase *with our ears*, and this is not superfluous because the verse does not intend to signify the ear that simply exists but the associated sense. And notice how the saint says, "The instruction of the Lord opens my ears." He says, "The Lord gives me a tongue of instruction, so that I know when I must speak a word. He appointed me early in the morning, he gave me a listening ear, and the instruction of the Lord opens my ears."[2] The ear that is given in addition is one that is concerned with knowledge; it hears words in a way that is befitting to God. And whenever this is given, his instruction finally opens the ears. This given, other sense of hearing, which relates to knowledge and hears in a way befitting to God, is the sense that is capable of saying, "I heard inexpressible words,"[3] for this is not for everyone to say, but for one who receives the additional sense of hearing from God. The Savior had these things in mind when he said, "Let him who has ears to hear listen!"[4] Not everyone has ears that hear the words of Jesus that are veiled, the words related by means of parables. For this reason Porphyry was deranged in this matter as well.

O God, we have heard with our ears, with ears that are proper to us, not with those that are common to the unreasoning animals, but with those that are attuned to the words [of God] that relate to knowledge.

Even in the case of sensible languages it has this meaning: the Egyptian hears with ears

---

[1] Is 50:5 NETS.
[2] Is 50:4-5.
[3] 2 Cor 12:4.
[4] Mt 11:15.

that are proper to Egyptians; he listens with his own ear.

Question: Are we then to take "listening" here in the sense of the hearing that relates to knowledge?

Those who are concerned with teaching assume the character of all, a "people full of sins,"[5] for it is not as though each person were full of the same sins, for sins are both contrary and incompatible. For example, the same man cannot possess cowardice and rashness together, but the people taken as a whole can have both of these. And [again, regarding] things that are able to coexist, even if they do not coexist together because of their multitude, when I say that the whole city possesses wisdom, not everyone has the same wisdom, for it is impossible for everyone to have what is right. It is possible, however, to have—so to speak—disobediences.

Our fathers have taught us.

They are our *fathers* in accordance with their teaching. The speakers of these words are wise. As wise men, then, they are begotten from them, not as humans, for many wise men are born from those who are unwise, and many unwise men are born from the wise.

[43:2] *[A work that you did] in their days, in the days of old.*

In their days, which are now old, [you have accomplished every work, which] our fathers have recounted to us. And that it is necessary to understand the hearing in relation to knowledge, [we will show] what happened in days long ago, for example in the book of Exodus. It was impossible to learn that the exodus took place in Egypt without those who taught it, without those who compiled this history . . . for by means of every figure [it is necessary] to say all [the things that took place], lest someone should come along and say [that it did not happen] or should take it [to mean something completely different.]

In the days of old, therefore, means "in the first days." And what is this, to hear [that God transferred the people, whom he sent to Egypt, from being worse people] and in an inferior land to being saints and in the [good land. This is the work] that took place ["in the early days."] And this was by no means [309] indicated beforehand, but it is said in order that the following might be contemplated by it: God transferred men from the region around the earth into the high heavens.

When he says "a work," then, he does not mean "one" in a numerical sense, but he says "a" in the sense of a kind and type of work. By their illumination—for since we understand the fathers to be wise, we say, "in the days," in the days when they were illuminated by the true Light, the Sun of Righteousness—by the illumination of their life a work took place that they did not begrudge sharing with us. The Scripture said and mentioned what the work is: seven nations he destroyed from the place that was later called the Holy Land. Our fathers were planted when they were led by God into that region. Moses, for example, prays, dealing again in the mystical sense, "Leading them in, you planted them on the mountain of your inheritance, the sanctuary, O Lord, that your hands prepared."[6] Observe that no one who lives and listens in a superficial way is able to enter into the holy mountain. The crowds, therefore, who heard in parables, being on the outside, did not enter into the holy mountain, where the parables were made plain. Therefore it is necessary first of all for someone to be led in, and then in this way to be planted.

---

[5] Is 1:4 NETS.

[6] Ex 15:17.

[43:3] *Your hand destroyed the nations, but you planted them.*

This took place not in [the ancient days] of God. He was Ancient of Days already, and we do not say that he was in days of old, but he was Ancient of Days because he was before days, before all time, and it is one and the same for him to be Ancient of Days and to be before the ages, as was said, "He who is before the ages."[7]

Your hand, then, *destroyed the nations*, means "your corrective power."

The angels who administer the corrections can also be called God's "hands," just as we refer to the hand of a king and of course are not signifying the limb of his body by these words. Job also was saying of God's corrective power—rather the devil himself was saying— "Send forth your hand."[8]

He says this, then: *"Your hand"*—either meaning corrective power, or the performance of hard labors, or your administrating power— *"destroyed nations."* Receive the destruction of the nations in an elevated sense to refer to the death of men, insofar as he makes them lose the life in which, as the nations, they were strangers from God. *But you planted* our fathers. [And the nations] are destroyed from the vice that they perform, for their vice was their country and city.

And those are planted by nothing other than your right hand. *Hand* and "right hand" are not the same thing, for the right hand is always a hand, but not every hand is a right hand. Indeed, we are accustomed to saying that things that are done in a praiseworthy way are accomplished by the right hand. [So does it say in the Psalms,] "You held fast my right hand with your hand."[9] The active power of doing good things is the right hand, while the left hand is the opposite. And since the doing of things comes from the disposition and from the faculty of thought called "heart," the wise man is said to have his heart in his right hand, and the fool to have it in his left:[10] so we do not understand these words to indicate places in bodies. The wise man has an intellect that thinks rightly; he has knowledge about [spiritual realities. And a foolish heart] is on the left; it ponders only things that are material. Often "the left hand" is posited in the Scriptures not by way of reproach but by way of diminution, as it says in the Song of Songs, "His left hand is upon my head, and his right hand will embrace me."[11] And concerning [Wisdom it was said, "For length] **[310]** of life and years of life are in your right hand"—where "length" indicates things that are immortal, things that are not brought to an end—"and in your left hand are riches and glory."[12] Now, Wisdom gives riches that are perceptible to the senses. And these gifts from the left hand of Wisdom are not contemptible.

[43:3-4] *You afflicted the peoples and you cast them out. For it was not by their sword that they inherited the land, and their arm did not save them.*

Those whom you cast out, you afflicted and cast out. You brought affliction on them, in order that they might be taught. Often affliction instructs, for here we are speaking of "affliction" that does not come from sin, but the "affliction" that comes from difficult instruction. Since, then, they did not receive the difficult instruction as they should have, they were finally cast out and rejected.

For not by their sword did they inherit the land.

---

[7] Ps 55:19 (54:20).
[8] Job 1:11.
[9] Ps 73:23 (72:23).

[10] Cf. Eccles 10:2.
[11] Song 2:6; 8:3.
[12] Prov 3:16.

In the historical sense, our common fathers, having taken the land from those who were rejected, possessed the land that was taken away from them not by their own war, not by their own power: "for not with their sword, nor did their arm" conquer them, ["but your right hand, your] arm, and the illumination of your face." Where there is illumination, there also is salvation. That, then, by which affliction and rejection comes is simply a hand. So also in one of the psalms it is said about Christ, "And he will place his hand on the sea, and his right hand on the rivers."[13] Where the gale and the brine is, the hand is simply placed against the evil powers, for evil powers are the things that are now signified by the sea.

And "his right hand is on the rivers." Rivers are the prophets, possessing their streams from the Source of Water that "wells up to eternal life."[14] For "he who believes in me, as the Scripture said, out of his belly will flow rivers of living water. And he was saying this about the Spirit whom those who believed in him were about to receive."[15] These rivers, then, "will clap their hands together."[16] And this is the outcome of their harmony. See, then, that the hand is where the sea, the gale, and the brine are.

[43:4] *But your right hand, your arm, and the illumination of your face.*

The *right hand* also has a corresponding *arm*. Not with your own hand or with your own arm did you inherit the land, but the arm of God, his right hand, and the *illumination of* his *face* supplied this to you.

And it relates to a figurative sense in two ways: because not by your own power nor by your own activity were you set free and have you come into the Holy Land. When you receive it in the sense of a more elevated allegory, God's arm, right hand, and the illumination of his face is the Savior. Therefore, you were not ransomed by yourselves, but by this one, and you were transferred from an inferior land into the beautiful one. [Even David] did not conquer because he was prepared, but when God fought together with him, as it says: "So it belongs not to the one who desires nor to the one who hastens, but to God who has mercy."[17]

[43:4-5] *For you were well pleased with them. You are my king and my God.*

[Indeed, you are not only my God,] since you are my creator and the one who brought me into being, but you are also my king, because by [your kingly] providence I rule, [no] longer being entangled "in the cares of life."[18] And you are indeed my God insofar as I am God's creature—and every creature has God as its God—and insofar as I serve in your war, [you are not only my God but also my king.]

[43:5] *You who command deliverances for Jacob.*

[311] To Jacob who supplants vice, because you are his king and God, you command deliverances. And he commands deliverances to the spirits who administer his saving acts, of whom the apostle writes, "Are they not all ministering spirits sent to serve because of those who are going to inherit salvation?"[19] Not in order to secure it and bestow it, but in order to proclaim it beforehand do they hear, "Say to Daughter Zion, 'Behold! Your Savior is coming to you!'"[20]

And the *deliverances of Jacob* could be the specific virtues or the two virtues, the active

---

[13] Ps 89:25 (88:26).
[14] Jn 4:14.
[15] Jn 7:38-39.
[16] Ps 98:8 (97:8).

[17] Rom 9:16.
[18] 2 Tim 2:4.
[19] Heb 1:14.
[20] Is 62:11.

and the contemplative, the vision of the truth and the practice of praiseworthy deeds.

[43:6] *With you we will strike our enemies with horns.*

You see, not by making use of our own horns do we overturn our enemies. But you are our horn and means of defense. Therefore, you have what is said in one of the psalms by all the saints, "And at your good pleasure our horn will be exalted."[21] The horn is not the perceptible one, for again the horn belongs to those who have his defense. Through him they will ward off the harmful things that beset them.

Therefore those who are under you, their king and God, do not possess, it says, any horn other than you. The word in one of the Twelve Prophets accuses some men "who say, 'Did we not have horns in our strength?'"[22] Having horns and having power, we strike the enemies with our horns. For this reason the horns of these people are crushed, for "I will shatter all the horns of the sinner."[23]

Now, it is also possible to receive the horn as a king and a kingdom, as is conveyed in the book of Daniel: "The ten horns are ten kingdoms."[24] Because of this, therefore, having you as king, we have you as horn and *with you we will strike our enemies with horns.*

And in your name, since we have your name on ourselves, *we scorn all who rise up against us,* having your name as an invincible weapon. And it is necessary not simply to have the name. By no means is it the one who calls himself a Christian who has the name of Christ, but the one who is a Christian.

[43:6] *And in your name did we scorn those who arise against us.*

And from this it is shown once again that they have arisen up by their own choice. Such people are not so by nature, nor by nature are some [accused of being "lustful stallions,"[25]] as those who introduce the various natures say.[26]

[43:7] *For not in my bow will I hope, and my sword will not save me.*

Indeed, I do possess a bow and a sword, since I have been equipped with "the whole armor of God,"[27] but I do not hope in these. I do not rest the whole of my expectation in these, [but although I] make use of them, I desire God to become my ally and my foremost combatant, in order that I [may possess] strength [and may be able] to strike against those at whom I aim my darts, and in order that my sword may in the opportune time [strike] my adversaries. And these adversaries are invisible.

Often the spoken [word is called] the "sword" of those who possess it, "who whetted their tongues like a sword,"[28] and the "sons of men, whose [teeth are a weapon and darts,] and their tongue is a sharp sword."[29] And in another place, "His [sword is upon his thigh,"[30] and they not only have swords "in their **[312]** hands" but also on their thighs. And perhaps the words about self-control that mortify "the members that are upon the earth"[31] are swords on the thigh.

Often the things that have to do with production are signified by the name "thigh."

---

[21] Ps 89:17 (88:18).
[22] Amos 6:13 LXX.
[23] Ps 75:10 (74:11 LES2).
[24] Dan 7:24.

[25] Jer 5:8.
[26] This is a clear reference to the Valentinians and the Manichaeans, who introduced different natures of men, corresponding to their spiritual aptitude.
[27] Eph 6:11 NRSV.
[28] Ps 64:3 (63:4 NETS).
[29] Ps 57:4 (56:5).
[30] Song 3:8 LES2.
[31] Col 3:5.

When, for example, it says in Ezekiel, "And every thigh will be moistened with moisture,"[32] this signifies that all are intemperate when they pursue the moistness of pleasures.

[43:8] *For you saved us from those who oppress us.*

Since *you saved us from those who oppress us*, we acknowledged that "with you we will strike our enemies with the horn." For this reason therefore, since this has taken place for us from you, we acknowledged that we must not hope in our bow when we kill with arrows—indeed making use of it, but not as though it were invincible.

[43:8] *And you have put to shame those who hate us.*

Those who *hate* again are different from those who afflict, sometimes in substance and sometimes in conception. Often the same people both afflict and hate, and these are the same in substance.

At times the one who hates is not of such a kind as to be an enemy when he is weak, for even the weak person is able to hate, but he is unable to be an enemy for obvious reasons, for this will damage him. But even if the same people in substance differ only in conception, even if they are one thing and another, God delivers and saves from these, and he *puts* them *to shame*.

[43:9] *In God we will be praised all the day long.*

Among those who are praised, some are praised because of the beauty of their body, others because of their strength. Boxers are praised for their strength, and others for some other skill. Others are praised because of riches, because of their noble birth, but we ourselves will be praised in you. We have no other cause of praise than you, for even if laborious struggles are ours, since we have received them at your hand and "in God we do mighty things,"[33] in you do we have our praise.

Often *the day* signifies the duration of the life of those who are speaking, as it says, "For your sake we are being put to death all day long,"[34] that is, through the whole of life.

[43:9] *And we will confess your name forever.*

Your name bestows great power on us. By it, to be sure, "we scorn" all "who arise against us."[35] For this reason in *your name we will confess forever*.

The word *exomologēseōs* here signifies "thanksgiving." "I will give thanks to you, for you have hidden these things from the wise and the intelligent and have revealed them to infants."[36] Since it is in the dative case, one can say thus, *We will give thanks to your name*, because the name itself has become for us the cause of our salvation. And the following is also possible: *in your name*, which is invoked over us, as when you say, "In your knowledge or in your virtue will I give thanks."

[43:9-10] *Diapsalma. But now you have rejected us and put us to shame and you will not go forth with our powers.*

"[You are my king] and my God." The word acknowledges him to be at the same time king and God, for he is king and God [. . .] of those who draw near to him and approach him. "He commands his deliverances to Jacob." To those who are near [. . .] he commands deliverances and all useful things. About them it says, "In you we will be [313] praised all the day long and we will confess to your name

---

[32]Ezek 7:17 LXX.
[33]Ps 60:12 (59:14).
[34]Ps 44:22 (43:23 NETS).
[35]Ps 44:5 (43:6).
[36]Cf. Mt 11:25 NRSV.

forever," that is, we will give you thanks. And it says, *But now you have rejected and put us to shame and you will not go forth with our powers.* But when you went forth with our powers, in the military sense or with power, with our might, we always accomplished all things. But here everything is opposite for us.

And since I was saying that one should not say the problematic words literally concerning them: Israel, when it strayed, was transferred from Jerusalem into Babylon by way of captivity. And Daniel, those three, Joshua the son of Nun, Ezekiel, and others of the Twelve Prophets were there: Haggai and Zechariah. These were not transferred into Babylon after the fashion of captivity, but because they were participating in helping and healing those who were condemned there. God condemns someone sparingly, that is, he does not allow him to be beyond help. He sends forth his angels and he makes holy men to fall into affliction and captivity not because of their own sins but for the sake of the salvation of others.

They speak, therefore, oppositely about a transformation that took place from good things to difficult things, from being helped and having him as their protector, into their being left in the lurch, but they were abandoned in a particular way, in order that they might become helpers of others, not in order that they might perish but that they might benefit and not leave the sins of those who were condemned to be even greater.

Therefore, *you have now rejected us.* Now, the word *rejected* does not always [carry] a reproach: "Cain went away from the presence of the Lord God."[37] God did not reject him, but by his unconstrained yearning he greeted what was evil, he moved toward vice. Concerning Adam, however, who did not completely fall, it was said that God "drove Adam out,"[38] since he was offering resistance because of the things inside paradise and because he was unwilling to come out. He has been cast out from paradise on account of Eve, his wife, for he transgressed the rule for her sake, for when God asks him, "Who told you?" he replies, "The woman, whom you gave to be with me."[39] He has not said "whom you gave" but "whom you gave to be with me." And this is the intent: I also ... and I thought that, when she was deceived [by the devil,] as she confessed, she was to be cast out of paradise, so I thought to do the same thing with her, in order that I too should be cast out of paradise, for if Adam were not cast out of paradise, the woman would not have reentered paradise.

Not the whole people was saying, "O God, we have heard with our ears, our fathers have taught us," and after a few lines, "but your right hand, your arm ... and the illumination of your face." Not the whole people was saying this. [We] mentioned [earlier] what was said in the letter to the Corinthians, "I give thanks, for in every way you [have been enriched, in speech] and knowledge of every kind."[40] Later again, "Sexual immorality is reported among you."[41] This [was said not] about one people ... in the case of this people there were some who acted in their own way. These, then, "did not spread out their hands to a foreign god."[42]

But now you have rejected and put us to shame.

No one, by sinning, is *put to shame* by God, but by himself. God *puts to shame* in a particular way, when [he allows] one who is not a sinner [to suffer misfortune] with sinners, [314] and the humiliation is useful and brings glory to the one who is made ashamed. He does not have "things hidden for shame," which should be renounced, according to the philosophy of the one who says, "We have renounced

---

[37]Cf. Gen 4:16 NETS.
[38]Gen 3:24 NETS.
[39]Gen 3:11-12 NETS.
[40]Cf. 1 Cor 1:4-5 NRSV.
[41]Cf. 1 Cor 5:1 NRSV.
[42]Ps 44:20 (43:21).

the hidden things of shame, not walking about in wickedness."[43] He who says, "To those outside the law I became as one outside the law,"[44] was not ashamed by it, but the word of Christ compelled and persuaded him.

Question: He who says "I became lawless" is unashamed?

This was said in a way befitting human understanding: no one desired to imitate the wicked.

And you will not go forth with our powers.

Long ago you went forth with our powers; you used to run before us into battles, and we prevailed over those who attacked us. That he did not go forth with our powers signifies the following: by not helping us, you help us. You help us, in order that we might be shown to be athletes, and from that time when we are left alone we may also benefit others, for he did not say, "You brought our powers to an end," but, *You will not go forth with our powers.*

[43:11] *You turned us backward because of our enemies.*

The enemies were behind them. And they are speaking their own praise, for "the sinners were plotting near my back."[45] And in another manner [. . .] the adversaries [do not] offer their backs, they will not grow weak, and they are pursued only by those who are about to overtake them. The Savior therefore strikes the enemies and places his hands on their back, striking them, chasing them off.

These therefore say, "*You turned us backward because of our enemies,*" which phrase—"God turned back"—probably cannot strictly be said about one who by his own choice is turned back and imitates his enemies. That which is brought about by God, however, is good and praiseworthy. Behold! let the companions of Daniel and the other saints who were in Babylon say, "*He turned us backward because of our enemies.*"

[43:11] *And those who hate us were taking spoils for themselves.*

They would not be able to take us under the power of their hand, unless he turned us back in front of them because of something useful. Enemies are also people *who hate*: for when a person is an enemy, this is to hate. We, however, are neither their enemies, nor do we hate them. And for this reason we were far away, for why did your judgment [. . .], O Lord, why did you turn us back because of them, why have you caused us to be with those who are condemned?

Those, then, who previously are in the form of God, when they receive the form of a servant because of pity,[46] such then say: we have come into the region around the earth not because of ourselves but for the sake of others, when you did not go forth with our powers. For formerly you used to go forth with our powers, granting victory to us against our enemies, and preserving us in the country of our fathers where we had arrived. When, therefore, you did not go forth with our powers, we were turned backward because of those who hate us. When those to whom he gave us devastated us, with an evil intention [. . .] And many such things you find in Scripture: out of envy [against Joseph his brothers sold] him in Egypt. For a good purpose, however, the sale **[315]** of that man to Egypt took place. Those brothers did not sell him with this intention. Again Judas betrayed the Savior, and the betrayal became useful in order that "sin of the world"[47] might be taken away. Again, those who crucified him did not crucify him with this intention in mind.

---

[43] 2 Cor 4:2.
[44] 1 Cor 9:21.
[45] Ps 129:3 (128:3).

[46] Cf. Phil 2:6-7.
[47] Jn 1:29.

Those who hate us were taking spoils for themselves, but they did not kill us. And if you say this, it is because they were taking what belongs to us for their own use, and reasonably the things that were handed over and obtained by them have proven timely later on. Therefore they conclude, "All these things happened to us, and we did not forget you."[48]

[43:12] *You have given us like sheep for food.*

Long ago you obviously helped us so that you were our praise all the day long and so that we confessed in your name forever. But why now were we handed over into captivity, though we suffer this not on account of our own vice or impiety? Now, I was saying that those who say this psalm are men such as Daniel was, [. . .] the son of Nave, Ezekiel, Haggai, Zechariah, the three companions, and numerous others. These had not appeared in Babylon because of their own vice. However, in the case of those who were handed over to afflictions, and especially to those in afflictions where the instability of their free will [is involved] because they rejoice in the things by which they were [handed over to] vice, they were sent as physicians with their enemies in order that they might care for them. They present their helping acts, which on the one hand preserve in them the health that is already present, and on the other hand undo sickness and bring health.

They add in addition to the other things that were said also, *"You gave us like sheep for food."* They were handed over as *food* for them; in the manner of lions and wolves they devour us. Nevertheless, when we are devoured, we are not deprived of being sheep: "Israel is a wandering sheep; lions drove him away. The first one, the king of Assyria, devoured him."[49] This signifies something that is done in a praiseworthy manner, when vice does not remain what it is but is dissolved into another quality. One who eats bread, when he sends it down into his stomach, it no longer remains bread. Those, however, who are swallowed and have become the food of enemies were not separated from being sheep.

Often the disciple is said to become the food of the teacher, concerning whom it says, "My food is that someone should do the will of my Father."[50] The Samaritan woman, for example, was a disciple, concerning whom it said, "I have food to eat that you do not know about."[51] [. . .] and again [. . .] to be bread. Bread, however, becomes food. And in a certain sense [. . .]. When therefore the man who preserves that which is in the image and likeness of God becomes a teacher like Jesus, he consumes a wild man by instructing him [and annihilates him, insofar as he is a lion]; **[316]** [then everyone who is devoured] by the teacher and who becomes his food will no longer be a lion. For this reason he is blessed, and he is blessed not because he is a lion but because he has become a man. If, however, at some time a rational man should be devoured because he is moved in his reason by a certain cruel, wild man or by an evil power, he becomes a lion. And such a one is miserable; indeed, "Woe to the man whom the lion eats!" These, therefore, say, *"You have given us as sheep for food."* Though they were eaten, they remained sheep.

[43:12] *And you have scattered us among the nations.*

According to the obvious sense of the expression, they seem to be saying as follows: "We were sown among the nations, we were dispersed in many circumstances." They appear to suffer this only in Babylon and Assyria.

---

[48]Ps 44:17 (43:18).
[49]Jer 50:17 (27:17 NETS).
[50]Cf. Jn 4:34.
[51]Jn 4:32 NRSV.

However, what the passage means is as follows: it is necessary first of all to use the passage from the Gospel, the sowing of these seeds, such as a grain of barley. When they are sown in the earth, they receive this earth into their own being by means of transformation and alteration, for because of the earth they changed, becoming many seeds from one seed: out of the earth they changed into grains. [. . .] the earth that is offered as food, and it forms and transforms it into its own nature.

He calls seeds the saints who say these things: "In you we will be praised and we will confess in your name forever." See! Those who say, "In you we will push our enemies with horns," and the other words, let them also say, "You sowed us among the nations" in the manner of seeds, in order that the nations in a certain way, when we are sown as strangers among them, we might transform into ourselves, and that one of us might become an ear bearing many grains, that many souls might be helped.

And in a different sense those who are helped are sometimes called the children of those who help them, while these are called their fathers, and sometimes they are called "sheep," when those have the post and manner of life of a shepherd. These, then, were let fall like seeds; they assumed into themselves those who were helped by being placed alongside them. The seeds that were let fall transformed the earth. The nations, then, are the earth. And the seeds that were scattered are for the use of others.

Let this also be established more simply: that the Assyrians live in Babylon, and they are not many nations and all nations. Let this also be established in relation to the historical sense.

[43:13] *You have sold your people without a price.*

Without a price have you sold [us, we who are your people]; for when we were led into captivity we were led there not with a price, but we were led by the custom [of captivity], for nothing is less honorable than this. *Without a price*, then, *you sold your people*. [*Without a price*] *have you sold* [us, who are your people], to those who desire to rule over us.

It is also possible to say that that people, for whom [. . .] among foreigners. And since "you sold your people without a price," that is, without taking any repayment, [. . .] them. For they were carried away by their own sins.

It is possible also to understand the phrase "without a price" [. . .] and [. . .]. For this reason we ourselves endured these things that happened to us in captivity [. . .] to be scattered among the nations, in order that you might gather [. . .] himself. God has not carried away such a person, but each by his own sin has carried himself away and has made himself a debtor. In any case that by which the hostile king of souls[52] becomes master over one is called a registration of debts. And it is a registration of debts, which someone composes with his own hands. Therefore, "set this aside,"[53] in order that he might no longer lord it over us by the registration of debts, the one with whom we were involved when we enlisted ourselves to him.

Question: Are they also recorded together with others?

Either we are your people, whom you sold without price—at the time when we were sold—in the manner of captivity, or they are saying this about the people on whose behalf they themselves went into captivity, "*You sold your people without a price.*" And for this reason we endure these things, since for the sake of them you made us take on ourselves the same wretched things with them to help them.

---

[52]That is, the devil.
[53]Col 2:14 NRSV.

[43:13] *And there was no great amount in our fees.*

Often *fees* are given on behalf of some for a reward and a ransom. For example, he says, "Every male that opens the womb is holy."[54] And it says that if a sheep was the firstborn, or an ox, or a goat, when they are delivered one must sacrifice them at the altar. But if it was a firstborn donkey, or some other creature [. . .] the priests [do not offer it], nor is it led to the altar: "You will exchange for a sheep."[55] By a lamb its worth is exchanged and he receives it into the sanctuary.

Therefore he says the following: since they were many [who were purchased without a price,] *there was no great amount in their fees.* Such fees occurred so that [. . .], in this way: since God is the one who gives the fees on their behalf, there is not [. . .] the fees are given for those who are redeemed. By means of a small amount, he is able [. . .] he nurtured great multitudes of men.

And in order that I might speak out of the historical sense [. . .] they were great multitudes of men, and if there had been found there ten righteous men—for as far as this number [. . .] they were being exchanged though there was no multitude in their fees. Therefore none may say [. . .] into Babylon, and though few in number when they were taken into captivity with them [. . .] of themselves, both the people and those ones by means of sin, but the people on the one hand because of their own sins, and they on the other hand because of the sins of others. *And there was no great amount in their fees.* And a few have become sufficient to [. . .] it would have been, if they had repented and had recognized how much they were involved in evil. "Their sins are very great! So when I go down and I shall see whether they are perpetrating according to the outcry concerning them that is coming to me, but if not—that I may know."[56] So great was their sin that it had reached as far as the outcry against their vice and as far as the vehemence [. . .] If, however, I do not find them to be so, but repentant like the Ninevites, I will know them. However, since those who are known by God are not wicked, it says, "The Lord knows those who are his."[57] "Formerly, when you did not know God, you served things beings who are not gods by nature. But now, knowing God, or rather being known by God."[58] When they had known him, then they were known all the more by their benefactor.

[43:14] *You had placed us as an object of reproach to our neighbors.*

In the literal sense, neighbors are those who dwell nearby a city, who are close by, [. . .] since therefore we were led into captivity, *you placed us as an object of reproach to our neighbors.* [. . .] [318] to us. They, however, have not suffered, nor were they dominated by the enemies who rose up against them, but we were.

So also in relation to the mind of the passage, this can be said: when the cross of the Savior has become an object of reproach because of our salvation—for it was said, "He regarded the reproach of Christ to be a greater riches than the treasures of Egypt,"[59]—so also these in a certain way have collided with reproaches, when they were overcome and led into captivity.

It says, "the angels who did not keep their own beginning, but abandoned their proper dwelling," he subjected "in eternal chains."[60] This reproach of the angels is not

---

[54] Cf. Ex 13:12; 34:19.
[55] Ex 13:13 NETS.
[56] Gen 18:20-21 NETS.
[57] 2 Tim 2:19 NRSV.
[58] Gal 4:8-9.
[59] Heb 11:26.
[60] Jude 6.

praiseworthy, because, having obtained their dwelling in heaven and being able to remain companions of God, ever singing his praise, they have come into vice so that they fell from heaven. This reproach is contemptible. See! At all events, the reproach of Christ is not only praiseworthy but is greater than treasures. And if there were no difference between these things, the author of Proverbs would not say, "Do not acquire the reproaches of evil men."[61] When therefore the apostles rejoice and exalt greatly when they are reproached for the sake of Christ, [. . .] when they do something, these reproaches for such things are not good. He himself, becoming a reproach to some, turned the reproach for this into false accusations, which are as though he were not truly reproached at all. In this way, for example, is the statement, "We are without honor, for I think that God exhibited us apostles as the least of all, as men condemned to death."[62] This is not a true reproach, for it does not belong to wicked men but to good men.

Question: In the literal sense?

This is because [. . .] not virtuous things, not pious, and our enemies who approached us were [. . .] and they have not displaced them from their land.

[43:14] *An object of derision and a laughingstock to those who are around us.*

The saints are the ones who say this, [. . .] who came not for their own sake but for the sake of others. And they say, "[. . .] having become, they dominated us and dragged us into their land while those around us hurl reproaches at us, make jokes, and deride us. But the reproach, the derision, and the mockery do not touch us, but those people." As when someone, laughing [. . .], in order that being in relationship with one another, they have children, and [. . .] and that he might enjoy them. They consider, then, those who are deprived of these things to be laughable [. . .]

[43:15] *He has made us into a parable among the nations.*

[. . .] concealed in expression, like should be compared to like. Like [. . .] should become plain, let us see from the Gospel. Jesus likens the kingdom of heaven to the mustard seed, not by saying this, "It is like a mustard seed,"[63] insofar as it is a seed, for this was no longer a likeness but an identification. In favor of [which comparison] is he speaking? The mustard seed has the most modest dimensions among the seeds, [but it has in itself] the power to be able to change and to become such a plant. And the kingdom of heaven therefore, when it reveals the teaching of the Scriptures—so far as the literal sense is concerned—it is something humble and small. Insofar as it was small, he showed it by the mustard seed, because also the gospel message became a plant greater than that of the Greeks. For this reason, then, this parable was spoken.

Therefore, *he made us as a parable among the nations.* If they desire someone among those who were taken into captivity to be a model, they declare to us, "Behold! Those who lived well earlier, [. . .] God, when the right hand of God and the illumination of his face rescued them, they underwent a change into the worst condition." If, therefore, they desire to indicate someone who underwent a change, they cite us.

And *he made us into a parable* not among the [. . .], not in Israel, not among the Hebrew multitude, but *among the nations.* Those who truly are the nations do not know the difference between good and evil, but they consider all things that are pleasant and

---

[61] Prov 3:31 LXX.
[62] 1 Cor 4:9-10.

[63] Mt 13:31.

gratifying to be goods, and the opposites of these things to be evils.

Now, the word *parable* can mean this as well: the rank of the saints has a certain superiority beyond the other ranks of men. For this reason he has made the saints into a parable for them. See! Often men are taken into captivity by their enemies in a different way. One person suffers the loss of the things he has possessed, another has them remaining [. . .] in the winter and the tempest of this life, they have their own [. . .] with corruptible things they fall into ruin.

[43:15] *A wagging of the head among the peoples.*

[The peoples are accustomed] to wag their heads when they see someone changing from success into misfortune, [either because they take malicious pleasure in this] or because they are grieved by it. We have become a wagging of the head among the peoples. All the more vulgar of men may be called "people," who have nothing elevated because they are unwise. These therefore began the *wagging of* their *head* on account of us. We at least, coming to the peoples, to the more vulgar among men, moved their understanding and their head. And their understanding is moved whenever [. . .], whenever he sees the things that are expected to be seen by him.

[43:16] *All day long my humiliation is before me.*

By the phrase *all day long* he means "through my life." The life of man, from birth until death, is sometimes called "one day," and sometimes "one age." So, for example, was it said, "I will never eat meat for the age,"[64] and, "He will be your servant for the age."[65]

I had shame before all this day, in which I endured for the sake of others [. . .] [320]

[43:16] *And the shame of my face has covered me.*

The shame of the inner man has enveloped me. For it did not ruin my appearance, but it covered it. It is possible for a person, by removing the one veil, to present his face naked, illumined, as it is by nature.[66] And, so to speak, when ignorance assails other men, it corrupts their appearance, for they become different from what they were before: from being men they become snakes, wolves, and foxes. The saint, however, even if he does not present his face naked, has it *covered* with *shame*. And it is covered by the putting on of the body, the ignorance that seems to obtain from his incarnation.[67] And whenever a change occurs in his quality—I am not saying that the fox, like Herod,[68] has a veil, but such was his habit and disposition by nature—and whenever someone foolish enters into ignorant things, he has his *face covered*, throwing his ignorance over his face; when a lawless person comes to lawless things, he has his face covered.

[43:17] *From the voice of the one who reproaches me and speaks deceptively.*

He says the following: those who reproach me are also speaking deceptively. Those who speak deceptively, however, strike falsely. Therefore

---

[64]1 Cor 8:13.
[65]Deut 15:17; cf. 1 Sam 27:12.
[66]Cf. 2 Cor 3.
[67]Didymus the Blind believed in the preexistence of souls, and this doctrine starts to become prominent from this moment onward in his exegesis of Ps 44 (43). According to him, souls preexisted their own incarnation, and this incarnation was (largely) the result of the souls' failure to remain in fellowship with God through contemplation and worship. Didymus will grow more and more insistent that this doctrine is the only way to defend divine justice, but his students—judging by their questions in this later part—do not seem entirely convinced.
[68]Cf. Lk 13:32.

he says this: those who are opposed to us [. . .], as it is natural for that which is rational do, but they rather strike falsely. And that they *speak deceptively* [we often say, about those] who say superfluous things.

[43:17] *From the face of the enemy and the persecutor.*

When [*the enemy* and *the persecutor* appeared], I endured all these things. When the enemy and the persecutor appear, [it happens that I suffer shame, that I am] covered by the shame of my face. I do not have these reactions from vice, [I have not forgotten God;] immediately, for example, he added, "All these things came upon us, yet we did not forget you."[69] [. . .] since you no longer go forth with our powers, it came on us that we are turned backwards in the presence of our enemies; it came on us that reproach was given to us by our neighbors, mockery by those who were around us, and that we have humiliation of face, our face being hidden for shame. [From this it is clear] that this is the voice of saints. Many often forget God because of their pleasures, not only because of their unpleasant experiences. It says, for example, "Watch out for yourself, lest when you eat and are full and dwell in good houses [you become overbearing in your heart] and forget the Lord your God."[70] At times, when people come into misfortunes [and they do not put up with them in the right way], they are said to forget God.

[43:18] *All these things came upon us, yet we did not forget you and we did not offend against your covenant.*

[. . .] and Israel was taken captive from Judah in a geographical sense [. . .] and by nature a spatial change of position took place, for he considered [. . .] they did not keep there and toward the laws there [. . .] they were understood to become Babylonian in their soul. [321] Often God prohibited those who remained from living in this way. In order that they might know by experience that what they loved was evil, he deported them into Babylon. With these people, he made in a certain way the saints such as Ezekiel, Zechariah, Haggai, Daniel, and those who were cast into the furnace to be taken into captivity, lest the others be utterly forsaken there, in order that they might be successful, since they were at war.

This is the "Jerusalem above."[71] Those who live according to the divine laws of God inhabit it. If they become rebels to the divine laws, they are transferred into the region around the earth, and this is captivity in the allegorical sense. And again, they are sent together to them here for the sake of help: "There was a man sent from God, whose name was John. He came as a witness to testify to the light."[72] For no other reason did he come other than to bear witness to the light.[73]

Again Jeremiah hears, "Before I formed you in the womb, I knew you, and before you went forth from the womb I consecrated you, I appointed you a prophet to the nations."[74] Before he went forth from the womb he was consecrated and he was appointed a prophet to the nations.

Again, "Just as he chose us in him before the foundation of the world."[75] He calls its genesis

---

[69]Ps 44:17 (43:18).
[70]Cf. Deut 8:11-12, 14.
[71]Cf. Gal 4:26.
[72]Jn 1:6-7 NRSV.
[73]Building on the previous explanatory note, Didymus the Blind believes there were some souls that did not grow indifferent to God in their preexistent state. However, they were sent to earth anyway, incarnated for the sake of others. Although this teaching would appear to compromise the distinctiveness of the Savior, Jesus Christ differs quantitatively from all of them because he was not simply a preexistent soul but was God himself. So his incarnation was an event of an altogether different kind.
[74]Jer 1:5.
[75]Cf. Eph 1:4 NRSV.

"the foundation of the world." And they were chosen before the foundation of the world: Paul and the others around him, and the present election has taken place for them from that time, in order that they might be sent together with those who are occupied with and able to help.

Question: Was Paul speaking in relation to foreknowledge?

Foreknowledge is the vision of things that are to come. In their genus, foreknowledge and knowledge are identical. There is a difference only in time. Take for example: I foreknow that there will be thunder tomorrow. When the thunder arrives at the day's coming, this is knowledge; it is no longer foreknowledge. The knowledge of the thunder does not make such a thing to be, but what kinds of things are, this knowledge obtains. The thing that is known, therefore, makes the knowledge, which does not receive its knowledge from us.

For the sake of an illustration, I am making use of the manner of foreknowledge: one child is born in order to beg, and another in order to live in a house. What kind of just foreknowledge is this, if we receive that these things took place according to foreknowledge? The foreknowledge both justifies and condemns. To foreknow and to know is both to condemn and to justify because of the things that are practiced and the things that are thought. Paul was foreknown in this life as both a betrayer and a persecutor of Christ, as well as an apostle. Were not both of these things foreknown? The foreknowledge therefore made him to have the two things as well. Again, he has not become first an apostle and later a betrayer: this was not foreknown by God. The foreknowledge of God made him at one time an apostle and at another time a betrayer. And surely it is asked, [322] from what in us did he choose the apostles? "Did I not choose you, the twelve?"[76] and, "Those whom he foreknew he also predestined to be conformed to the image of his Son."[77] He is not speaking about their existence but about their being conformed. Foreknowledge does not control existence. God has made; after he has created he knows, for the thing does not make the knowledge of God, for the knowledge of God is eternal. It is received in relation to the things that are to come and it is called "foreknowledge." Indeed, that woman Susanna again says, "He who knew all things before their beginning."[78] The foreknowledge does not make these things or those, but the free will, the things that depend on the will.

I say the following: I foreknow that someone will give birth to males and will have sons. This is not something that depends on the will. Indeed, to become wicked or virtuous, or to have some other habit, these are things that the will must choose. It comes about not from foreknowledge, since God otherwise condemns beforehand and makes righteous beforehand. If he makes righteous beforehand, however, this would belong to his goodness: to justify all.

Again the apostle, being somehow at a loss about Esau and Jacob, says, "What then are we to say to these things? Is there injustice on God's part? By no means!"[79] By doing away with unrighteousness he constrained us to ask how there is not unrighteousness with God. And if it is thus, as those who speak about foreknowledge have it, we find rather that there is unrighteousness with him. "Jacob," he says, "I loved, but Esau I hated."[80] Now, someone is hated in relation to things that are done and in relation to things that are thought. How, then, does foreknowledge have any room? Is unrighteousness to be found with God? But doing away with this, he said, "What then are we to say? Is there injustice on God's

---

[76] Jn 6:70 NRSV.
[77] Rom 8:29 NRSV.
[78] Sus 42.
[79] Cf. Rom 9:14 NRSV.
[80] Rom 9:13 ESV.

part? By no means!" Since there is no unrighteousness with him, let the matter be sought after in a different way, how it has come to pass. Often we have said these things: if we have a correct notion about something, we think about all things appropriately in relation to it, as I was saying about the king.[81]

I was saying the following in accordance with all the manners of captivity: in many unpleasant things [. . .] and being wise in both pleasant and unpleasant things, forgetfulness of God did not happen to them because of this, but then they were grieved, because men exist who are bound by such things, as, for example, concerning prisoners because they are bound in captivity. So at least have some interpreted what runs thus in the 118th Psalm: "Despondency beset me due to sinners."[82] He is dejected when he sees rational men, in the image and likeness of God, having become sinful. And as if a certain father, when he sees his own son and strikes him out of anger and a loss of control, is grieved not because he strikes him but because he has come into such a condition, so also these ones, being noble and knowing that "through many afflictions it is necessary to enter into the kingdom of God,"[83] are by no means wholly immersed in the afflictions. At any rate they say, "We are afflicted in every way, but not crushed."[84] And not to be crushed means to bear afflictions nobly.

Yet we did not offend against your covenant.
Forever the things that are commanded in accordance with your will and [323] in accordance with your judgments endure, and because of this *we did not offend*. When, however, someone says, "Why does someone have many sons, and another is childless; and why is one wealthy and another poor?" he offends against the *covenant* of God. Just as in relation to these covenants that men arrange, if someone wishes to contradict and make war against the things that have been written, he uselessly *offends the covenant*. His injustice seems to be the injustice of the covenant. If someone takes in hand the divinely inspired Scripture in a false sense, as the heterodox do, they offend against the gospel, against the divine Scripture.

[43:19] *And our heart did not withdraw backwards.*

You see that they persevere in conformity with honesty. It *did not withdraw backwards*.
Others have not become as those who have their heart upright, straight, and looking straightforwardly. This happens in the case of us who are unstable and unsteady. Many, after having come into affliction, turned away their thinking so that they grumble against providence.

[43:19] *But you turned our paths from your way.*

He is saying this: we "were running well"[85] on your path before we came down into this condition and manner of life. *You turned our paths from your way*, because you transferred us into another life and a way that corresponds to this life. Nevertheless, even if *you turned our paths*, handing us over into captivity, but even then our paths did not turn aside from your way.

[43:20] *For you humbled us in the place of oppression.*

In accordance with both interpretations of the deportation from Jerusalem into Babylon, receive the phrase *the place of oppression*. Strictly speaking, this is the place around the

---
[81]Cf. PsT 226.10-11.
[82]Ps 119:53 (118:53 NETS).
[83]Acts 14:22.
[84]2 Cor 4:8 NRSV.

[85]Cf. Gal 5:7.

earth, where souls that are burdened with "the body of humiliation"[86] are humbled. The one who is handed over to afflictions is able to bear the captivity and the place of oppression, that is, the land of Assyria or Babylon.

[43:20] *And the shadow of death covered over us.*

Even if the *death* of oppression is laid on us, yet it did not crush us. Its *shadow covered over us.* For example, let a heavy stone be suspended on high. Let someone come under this, but let it not fall on him. And let him see sometimes the shadow of the stone over himself. Now, the shadow of the stone does not accomplish what the stone itself does. God delivers from this very thing. It was said, "The dawn from on high appeared for those who are in darkness and the shadow of death."[87]

[43:21] *If we have forgotten the name of our God and if we spread out our hands to a foreign god.*

At last they are no longer speaking these things to God. The former words he said to God himself, "You turned our paths from your way, you humbled us in the place of oppression." At last they are speaking about God to others who assume that they have come into these things on account of their sins and lawless deeds, and they say, "*If we have forgotten the name of our God and if we spread out our hands to a foreign god,*" **[324]** that is, if we have worshiped a foreign god. One must consider "foreign gods" to be all those that are falsely named "gods" in Scripture, for it was said, "All the gods of the nations are demons."[88] Not to our own belly, not to our wealth, did we stretch out our deeds, allegorically called "hands," not to a foreign god and to the enemies who seem to have overcome us.

[43:22] *God did not seek these things out.*

I was saying that it has been customarily read thus: "Will not God seek these things out?" And I was saying that I read it so: "*God did not seek these things out.*" He is saying the following: do not suppose it to be a small thing to forget the name of God or to stretch out the hands to a foreign god. And *God seeks these things out.*

And you know that some, especially among persecutions, were saying this: that one can do this without doing it with the heart. Many at least perished while saying this, and they were silent about the name of God as if they had forgotten him. This, they say, God does not [see], and he does *not seek out these things.*

Question: Surely then he *does seek these things out?*

The subsequent word of the psalm does not yield this sense.

[43:22] *For he himself knows the hidden things of the heart.*

Let the one who does not know the hidden things of the heart seek first, whether one dealt in this way or in that. For example, if someone, being made wise, may say, "I did not stretch out my hands to a foreign god," I say, "I, who do not know the secret things of the heart, investigate concerning these things." But God does not investigate, for *he knows* these *things.*

And now he is speaking about *the hidden things* that he knows for certain: "Because for your sake we are put to death all the day long; we are regarded as sheep for the slaughter."[89]

---

[86] Phil 3:21.
[87] Lk 1:78-79.
[88] Ps 96:5 (95:5 NETS).

[89] Ps 44:22 (43:23).

[43:23] *Because for your sake we are put to death all the day long; we are regarded as sheep for the slaughter.*

Those who for the sake of God *are put to death all the day long* and have been *regarded as sheep for the slaughter* are not in doubt either that they had forgotten the name of God or had stretched out their hands to a foreign god. For this reason he does not seek out these things in their heart, because they are evident.

We were regarded, then, *as sheep for the slaughter.* Everyone who wishes persecutes us.

And this also is possible: even if some make war against us, yet we so regard ourselves as sheep that are offered as victims, as those that are offered to God for "a pleasing sacrifice."[90] Doubtless also in the Apocalypse of John, "the souls of those who have been beheaded because of the testimony of Jesus"[91] appeared in chorus "under the heavenly altar" of God, as sacrificial offerings, that is, they were approaching that place.

[43:24] *Awake! Why do you sleep, O Lord? Rise up, and do not reject us until the end.*

God seems to sleep whenever he is patient while men oppress his saints and have become haughty against him. Doubtless they send up their prayer, saying, "Raise up your hands against their arrogant deeds until the end,"[92] and, "May the arrogance of those who hate you arise to you forever."[93] God seems to sleep whenever he is patient, whenever he looks past his own who are afflicted.

Rise up and do not reject us until the end.
[325] For even if we have come into captivity and are afflicted in the place of oppression, we men, though we are mortal and changeable, have reverence for you. Let us not be utterly rejected.

Israel was rejected in Babylon, when they began to worship Bel, the image of Nebuchadnezzar,[94] and the other divinities Babylonia had made; he was rejected *until the end*. The companions of Daniel, however, even if they were rejected in a spatial sense, they were not rejected until the end, for they remained in the same piety.[95] Daniel seems to be rejected, but he was not rejected until the end when the lions were bridled and he ascended unharmed.[96]

[43:25-26] *Why do you turn your face and forget our poverty and our affliction? For our soul is humbled into the dust.*

It is the same thing to sleep and to seem to turn away the face. Let the one who delivers and saves us from the wickedness that holds us fast appear!

Why then are *you turning* away? Are you therefore forgetting *our poverty and our affliction?* Because of you we are afflicted; because of you we are poor. You, however, do not forget these people. Someone overcomes in the midst of these things, he receives them even when they are grievous, even if they are unpleasant.

Dust was mentioned because their essence is more bodily. *Our soul*, then, the soul of those who say these things, *was humbled into the dust.* We are clothed with "the body of humiliation,"[97] but we were not humbled by him. As when someone, for example, receives fetters from a certain tyrant, he seems to be humiliated, but he was not humiliated, for he has the same majesty and the same splendor. Because of this we are poor and afflicted, because our soul for a time does not have its

---

[90] Rom 12:1; Phil 4:18.
[91] Rev 6:9.
[92] Ps 74:3 (73:3).
[93] Ps 74:23 (73:23).
[94] Cf. Dan 3:1.
[95] Cf. Dan 3.
[96] Cf. Dan 6.
[97] Phil 3:21.

proper stature manifest, being humbled into the dust and *our belly cleaved to the earth*.[98] He is not saying this about them in truth but about their own members, about their own people.

For the stomach to be humbled into the earth is twofold in meaning: when someone thinks earthly things and seeks the things that are below,[99] he does not produce heavenly offspring, he does not beget rational and pious people, but only what is human, but the soul that says these things becomes a mother.

For our stomach cleaved to the earth. According to the second understanding, the belly that is fed by heavenly bread, which receives heavenly nourishment, cleaved to heaven. As many as eat the flesh of the dragon and use the same food with the serpent, that is, the earth, have their stomach cleaving to the earth. And as it is said in the case of sensible things, "'Food is meant for the stomach and the stomach for food,' and God will destroy both one and the other,"[100] so also when the belly and stomach does not feed on heavenly things, when it does not receive from its divine bridegroom, it has its stomach cleaving to the earth.

[43:27] *Arise, O Lord, help us and deliver us for the sake of your name.*

[326] We pray for your help, lest the afflictions, by lasting too long, should harm our soul, which is changeable. And next, lest they seem to speak by putting trust in their own righteousness, he says, "*Arise, O Lord! Help us and deliver us for the sake of your name.*" We call you by name. For this reason we have come into these grievous troubles, because we are yours, and for the sake of our help you sent us into this misadventure.

---

[98]Ps 44:25 (43:26).
[99]Cf. Col 3:2.
[100]1 Cor 6:13 NRSV.

PSALM 44 [45]

[44:1] *For the end. Concerning those who will be altered. For the sons of Korah. For understanding. An ode about the beloved.*

Alteration is a motion and a certain transformation in quality. Not every motion and transformation is an alteration. For there is a transformation that accords with one's origin. I say, for example, that the egg becomes a bird and the kernel an ear of grain. This motion and transformation is in accordance with the origin. And there is another that comes in accordance with corruption: when the body of man is corrupted and broken down into fluids, worms, and the like, it is not said to be altered but to be corrupted. And there is also another motion and transformation that accords with growth, when there occurs an addition to a previously existing quality. For when I make haste from a lesser to a greater size, I am said to grow and to be diminished when the quality withdraws and becomes less.

Alteration, therefore, is a motion according to a quality, for example, from sickness into health and from health into sickness, from ignorance into knowledge and the reverse, from unbelief into faith.

For the end, then, *concerning those who will be altered*. We have frequently expounded the things that concern the end, that the end that is after all things is the final object of appetency. This psalm, therefore, is *for the end, concerning those who will be altered*. When the alteration reaches such an intensity that it is no longer able to be intensified further, at the end of things, when "God becomes all in all,"[1] it is no longer possible for the quality to be increased.

Every knowledge and every virtue is a quality. One can therefore begin in virtue and progress in this, and it is always possible to add further to what already is. However, when someone possesses the virtue perfectly so that nothing is lacking in him, he is altered into the goal. Similarly, both in the case of knowledge and wisdom, we say the same thing: someone is introduced to wisdom and subject to reproach, since he is capable of sinning; for "rebuke a wise man, and he will love you."[2] No one, however, is reproached when he does not have those things for which he will be reproached. This wise man, who is subjected to reproach because he is newly formed and was just now introduced to wisdom, is able to progress always. However, when he receives wisdom to the extent that it is no longer possible for him to receive [327] an intensification of it, this one is altered into the end.

And here indeed, because they are still loaded with "the body of humiliation,"[3] even though there are many saints, they receive only "from his fullness,"[4] not his fullness, not each from the fullness, but "all from the fullness." And they receive here "the seal of the Spirit,"[5] not the whole Spirit himself, if I may say so. Whenever "the partial" vanishes, and the goal at last arrives,[6] and he appears "face to face,"[7]

---
[1] 1 Cor 15:28.
[2] Prov 9:8.
[3] Phil 3:21.
[4] Jn 1:16.
[5] 2 Cor 1:22.
[6] Cf. 1 Cor 13:10.
[7] 1 Cor 13:12.

and men become like God according to the word, "when he is revealed, we will be like him, for we will see him as he is,"[8] then here is the end of those who will be changed.

And it is good to say *of those who will be altered* and not "of those who were altered." No one is praised for knowledge and virtue, when he has become knowledgeable or virtuous, but when he is knowing; for virtue and knowledge belong to those who are active in them, they have their being in being performed.

For the end, then, *concerning those who will be altered*. Now, we have this blessed, divine, and supernatural alteration from the right hand of the Most High, for it is said of it, "This alteration comes from the right hand of the Most High,"[9] for just as "though he was rich, for our sake he became poor, so that by his poverty we might become rich"[10]—and notice, "though he was rich he became poor for our sake," indeed, when he was altered and appeared. And while remining without the visitation he is the same: he always possesses his being rich. And "he became poor for our sake." When, therefore, by becoming poor for our sake he makes us rich, we are altered in accordance with his wealth and we come to the end when we become rich as he is, as far as this is possible, when we behold "his glory, the glory as of the only-begotten from the Father, full of grace and truth."[11]

"From the fullness," then, the saints receive. No one person receives the fullness, nor do all. So also is the expression meant, "I will pour out from my Spirit."[12] He did not say "my Spirit." For those who bear the Spirit here receive "the seal of the Spirit."[13] And the seal is poured out from the Spirit. The seal, however, is a part of something whole.

For the goal, then, *concerning those who will be altered*. "This alteration," then, "comes from the right hand of the Most High."[14] The right hand of the Most High is immutable and inalterable. It always remains the same and unchanged, for we understand it as nothing other than the Savior. Let us see, then, how it is altered. It condescends in order to instruct, and then we are truly helped, when it condescends. However, when it remains by itself, we ourselves are not helped.

Therefore, he says the following: "Surely, the Lord will not spurn forever or forget to be compassionate?"[15] Again, "Or will he cut off [328] his mercy from generation to generation or will he shut up his compassions?"[16] He says, "And I said, 'Now I have begun,'"[17] when I received knowledge of the right hand in its condescension. "Now I have begun." He has come to the beginning of knowing the truth, to the beginning of knowing the works of providence, the compassions of God, which do what is good.

"I said," therefore, "'Now I have begun.'" He says, "This alteration," which I myself underwent, is "from the right hand of the Most High." This altered me. None of the things that came into being was able to alter me in this way, for all of them are in need of the One who leads them to progress, who perfects them.

And, in accordance with those who speak in public what is more popular, we will say that this is the alteration of the Most High: although he is a blessing he has become a curse,[18] in order to abolish curses and make known those who are blessed. Although he is righteousness, therefore, he has become

---

[8] 1 Jn 3:2 NRSV.
[9] Ps 77:10 (76:11).
[10] 2 Cor 8:9.
[11] Jn 1:14.
[12] Joel 2:28.
[13] 2 Cor 1:22.

[14] Ps 77:10 (76:11).
[15] Cf. Ps 77:7, 9 (76:8, 10 NETS).
[16] Cf. Ps 77:8-9 (76:9-10 NETS).
[17] Ps 77:10 (76:11 NETS).
[18] Cf. Gal 3:13-14.

sin,[19] and such sin as is productive of righteousness. And "in him" we become "the righteousness of God."[20] We do not simply become righteousness but the righteousness of God!

We have frequently said that those who are called by a new name have the name of habits, when they are perfected according to them. So, for example, Paul calls "Love" the one who is perfected in love, as far as is possible in this life, for the word, "Love is not arrogant or rude. It is not ostentatious,"[21] is not said about the virtue of love, the commandment that is greater than all others,[22] but about the one who has it, about the one who has the quality.

The Savior, then, becomes all things for our sake. He becomes flesh, "so that we might become the righteousness of God,"[23] for after beholding "his glory, glory as of the only-begotten,"[24] we do not remain flesh, but we become gods, like those "to whom the Word of God came."[25]

"This," then, is "the alteration" according to both senses, either that one by which we were altered or that one that he endured for our sake, not being changed, not being altered according to the divinity, but according to the economy, according to the inhumanation.

For the end, then, concerning those who will be altered. These who will be altered, who are still in the process of being altered, will arrive at some time at the end of the alteration. For no one begins in order not to be perfected, but in order that after many progressions he might arrive at the very limit of that quality in accordance with which he is changed. And what is the goal other than being deified, in order that he might become all?[26]

Some understand it about the resurrection of the dead, saying that those who are raised have an incorruptible body instead of a corruptible one, a spiritual body instead of a natural one, and a strong and glorious body instead of a weak and inglorious one.[27] However, when Paul spoke he did not say, "And we all will be altered," but "we will be changed," "and the dead will be raised imperishable,"[28] [329] since the body is raised essentially. For it does not become incorporeal instead of a body, but from being such a body such a body undergoes a change in quality. When we understand it so, only in accordance with a quality, it is an alteration. When however, since the corruptible is not the same as the incorruptible, the corruptible becomes incorruptible, it was changed, it was changed in accordance with a transformation. I am not saying that from being a body it has become incorporeal, but it has become an incorruptible body instead of a corruptible body.

Question: But the body remains?

The body remains, even as the soul remains when the sinful soul becomes righteous. And the transformation has occurred in accordance with an alteration. If, therefore, the resurrection takes place in accordance with an alteration, the flesh is again flesh, the corruptible is again corruptible, for I do not call what is corruptible or flesh a quality. Therefore the resurrection occurs in accordance with a change. When, for example, we modify the surface of a vessel that has been made out of terracotta either by means of painting or in some other way, this is altered, for it remains the same. But when, after making a vessel out of clay, we move it toward the fire and it becomes terracotta, this is not an alteration

---

[19] Cf. 2 Cor 5:21.
[20] 2 Cor 5:21 NRSV.
[21] 1 Cor 13:4-5.
[22] Cf. Mk 12:31.
[23] Cf. 2 Cor 5:21 NRSV.
[24] Jn 1:14.
[25] Jn 10:35.

[26] Cf. 1 Cor 15:28.
[27] Cf. 1 Cor 15:42-44.
[28] Cf. 1 Cor 15:51-52.

but a change, not because it was excluded from being made of clay when the terracotta was introduced, but because that vessel has become made of terracotta.

Again sand and saltpeter, when they are prepared by the glass smelters, become glass in appearance, and I am not saying that the sand or the saltpeter was removed, but those same things have become glass. And that this is a change, understand: the saltpeter, when it was saltpeter, was liquefied when the moisture penetrated it, and the glass that has been made from it is not liquefied. Again the sand was scattered, when the moisture penetrated it. But when it becomes glass, it is no longer scattered.

Therefore, I do not call this a change from one substance to another substance, but that it has gone from something that perished to something that became. The saltpeter and the sand perish and become glass. The corruption of these things does not bring them to an end in nonbeing. And the vessel of terracotta, as I said, having been made of terracotta by fire, does not overthrow the clay into nonbeing, and the terracotta does not come from somewhere else. In the same way the bird comes from the egg, for the egg is not cast aside in order that the bird might be introduced. That very thing changes into this; it is no longer truly an egg, for this bird now flies, it has sense perception. But the egg experienced none of these things.

And Paul has made use of the term *seed*: "It is sown in corruption, it is sown in weakness."[29] I say: the seed of the living being, when it is a seed, is not the living creature. But it transforms into the living creature, for after the seed disappears the living creature is born externally from somewhere, but the earlier seed itself being changed into an exterior form, then from an exterior form into an embryo, after being an embryo, having become a living creature, it undergoes birth.

These, then, are changes, not alterations, for no transformation belongs to a quality alone. [**330**] And one can find many such examples. Even Paul himself, making use of seeds, says: the kernel of grain is a kernel before sowing. But when it encounters agriculture after it is sown, it becomes an ear. "But," others say, "but it is grain again." They did not understand that what was said is an example. And often it was said that examples are not homogeneous with what they illustrate, since they would no longer be examples.

Again, what is at this moment a newborn and a child are not the same thing. Nevertheless, the newborn changes into the child, and I am not saying that the child came from somewhere after the newborn came to its end in nonbeing, but the newborn itself changed both in growth and in another quality: it has become a child and advanced in age. And on the one hand, in respect of age the newborn is one thing and the child another, but in respect of the man who advances in age there is no difference, for a single man is subject to being a newborn and to that time of life, and after that time is past, again the man is subject to being a child. And when he changes from being a child into being a youth, again his age has changed. And this is a quality; however, it is an essential quality. And again the newborn always advances in age until it arrives at old age. It changes, therefore, in qualities and in ages, for I said that the ages are essential qualities. But the same man remains.

Even if the body, then, receives an immeasurable transformation in the resurrection, it is a body, not indeed the same body, not the body that was before the transformation. So Paul also was compelled to say that they were different. And he said, "It is sown a physical body, it is raised a spiritual body."[30] He says,

---

[29] 1 Cor 15:42-43.

[30] 1 Cor 15:44 NRSV.

"It is not the spiritual that is first, but the physical, and then the spiritual."[31] And where the first and the next are mentioned, no identity is meant. Nevertheless, however, we do not understand the first and the next as a consequence of a change of essences, but of a change in the same body, since it has become incorruptible instead of corruptible and spiritual instead of physical.

Therefore, change is one thing and alteration is another. The transformation of the soul makes the alteration, I mean the praiseworthy or even the blameworthy alteration, for it is also possible to be altered for the worse, as it was said, "How gold will grow dim; the good silver will be altered!"[32] And it says, "The precious sons of Zion, who were lifted up with gold and silver, how were they reckoned as earthen pots, as the works" of their own "hands!"[33] Allegorical interpretation will explain other things again, for it is said that gold has been transformed into earthen vessels not in a literal sense but in an anagogical sense.

For the end, then, *concerning those who will be altered. For the sons of Korah. For understanding.* And since this superscription and the whole psalm contain hidden mysteries, for this reason there is a need of understanding for the one who recites this ode, for it is *for understanding*. And I was saying this also in relation to the Thirty-First Psalm, since it was spoken with an enigma.

An ode, then, *for the beloved*. This ode of victory has come into being *for the beloved*, [331] for he himself has also become the cause of the change. For I said that "although he was rich, he became poor"[34] in order that he might make us rich, not rich in illusory appearance, not rich in a way that is perceived by the sense, but having "speech and knowledge of every kind."[35] I said that having become a curse, he secured a blessing.[36]

The beloved, therefore, has become the cause of this most excellent alteration. For this reason the ode is dedicated to him, just as the ode of victory is offered up for a general or a king even though it belongs to others who also fought at his side, to his bodyguards and soldiers, yet the crowning achievement of the victory is ascribed to the king or the general.

Question: *"For the beloved"?*

That is, "about" him, for the phrase "for someone" is not always said, "that any opponent may be put to shame, having nothing evil to say about us,"[37] for here the phrase "about us" is not said instead of "advocating for us."

[44:2] *My heart belched out a goodly theme.*

Some understand this psalm to be spoken both from the person of the Father and from the person of the perfect man, the wise man.

You know, however, that the belch of food that was already swallowed produces an aroma, for a belch is nothing other than the exiting of wind from the stomach, which shows the quality of what has been swallowed beforehand. Indeed, when someone has an apple within himself, he has the belch that produces the quality and aroma of an apple. When, therefore, the saint has the "Bread of Life"[38] within himself and the flesh of Jesus, which is "true food,"[39] and the fruits of the "tree of life,"[40] and drink the wine that is harvested from "the true vine,"[41] he has a belch that corresponds to the foods that have been swallowed earlier. The one who is so nourished and belches is meant: "The good person out of

---

[31] 1 Cor 15:46 NRSV.
[32] Lam 4:1 NETS.
[33] Lam 4:2.
[34] 2 Cor 8:9.
[35] 1 Cor 1:5 NRSV.
[36] Cf. Gal 3:13-14.
[37] Titus 2:8.
[38] Jn 6:35, 48.
[39] Jn 6:55.
[40] Gen 2:9; Rev 22:2.
[41] Jn 15:1.

the good treasure of the heart produces good."[42] And since it is about intelligible things, he did not shrink from saying *heart* instead of the treasure of the stomach.

Therefore, the one who is nourished with blessed food and profits from the flesh of Jesus and the "Bread of Life,"[43] the bread of heaven, produces words that correspond to what he has eaten and will say, "*My heart belched out a goodly theme.*" For a time, then, we talk about the man. The sons of Korah, producing hymns with the same understanding and the same spirit,[44] offer them in the singular. As the word, "In the same way that the deer yearns after the springs of waters, so my soul yearns,"[45] so also here they speak as one and in the singular, "*My heart belched.*" However, this is attributed to each of the wise. For when the wise produces these things that he has in his heart and that he has eaten in order to instruct, he *belched out* the *goodly theme.* From which, again, the saying infers that if someone who is not nourished desires to produce a word, it is not a good belch. And again, the one who is nourished with the worst foods has a vicious and evil word of instruction.

[44:2] *I myself speak my works to the king.*

My works are trusted to such a degree, and they bring against me neither condemnation [332] nor accusation. *I speak to the king* himself, to the judge.

[44:2] *My tongue is the pen of the swift-writing scribe.*

My word is signified by the *tongue.* Often you will find *tongue* instead of *word.* As when it says, "The Lord will destroy all deceitful lips and a boastful tongue,"[46] he is speaking of the arrogant word.

[44:3] *You are graceful in beauty beyond the sons of men.*

And the *sons of men,* that is, the wise men of the world and those who profess teaching in whatever way at some time, seem to have *beauty* in their own words. However, the beauty of our word is *beyond the sons of men,* it is a beauty sent by God, it is God-given, it is true wisdom. Therefore, it possesses something greater than the sons of men, who emit from their own heart words and teachings that come together from their own effort and learning.

Listen now: the psalm is understood from the person of the Father. And perhaps all those who interpret it understand it so. The supernatural, the great, and the superior thoughts are made manifest with difficulty, by means of many examples. Often, therefore, when we desire to say that God is one, we speak of innumerable things. We say that nothing combines with him: in him there is no matter and form; he is a unity, he is a oneness, and with difficulty, by means of a multitude of words, we make the thoughts manifest.

However, when I wish to speak about wine, it is sufficient to say "wine," for it is said to those who know what it is, and we signify by means of a word the thought alone. With "earth" it is the same. We have no need of many words.

When, however, we say that God is "earth," because he says, "Surely, I have not become a wilderness to Israel or a dried-out land, have I?"[47] then we use innumerable words in order that we might show how God is called "earth." Again when we say that he is a "source," we do not say only a few words as we do when we

---

[42]Lk 6:45.
[43]Jn 6:35, 48.
[44]Cf. 1 Cor 1:10.
[45]Ps 42:1 (41:2).

[46]Ps 12:3 (11:4).
[47]Cf. Jer 2:31 NETS.

speak about a source that is subject to our senses. About God, however, we say many things: since that which pertains to God and the fullness of his good things does not flow into him from outside and is not furnished to him, but rather he himself is the fullness of good things. Because he is the fullness of the good things, therefore, the fullness of the virtues, he is called "source."

And the generation of the Savior from the Father, then, is not effortlessly understood, nor can it be learned by those who wish, but only by those to whom the revelation of the Father and the Son has come—for just as the Father reveals the Son, so also the Son reveals the Father—there is need of many examples, in order that the relationship of the Son with the Father and his generation might be made clear.

For example, he calls him "the radiance of the light."[48] The radiance does not belong to the light from outside. He is begotten from him. And the light does not exist before the radiance, for the light and its radiance are together. Therefore, when we desire to show that the generation of the Son is eternal, we say that he is eternal radiance of eternal light.

The heterodox, however, do not understand how each of these things is said, and they do not understand them as examples, and they say, "The light [333] is an essence, the radiance is an energy. Isn't the Son therefore the energy of the essence and not the essence?" They do not understand, however, why this was said: in order that one might learn that the Father does not exist before the Son, for the Father is not a light that is subject to our senses, and the Son is not a radiance that is perceptible by the senses. Teaching has come in human terms, in order that we might learn what we do not know from what we know. And we know that light does not exist before radiance.

Again, the Father is called the "source of wisdom," for "you abandoned the source of wisdom."[49] He wishes to show that, just as the water is not foreign from the source, so neither is wisdom foreign from the one who is "only wise,"[50] for he calls the Father "only wise," although he would not have called any of the things that came into being "only wise," for there are many who derive their name from the wisdom that they possess. The Father, however, is not called wise because he derives his name from wisdom, since he would no longer be "only" among those things that partake of wisdom and are called wise from it. But he is called "only wise" because he gushes with wisdom, begetting wisdom, so that it makes no difference whether one calls the "only wise" wisdom or wisdom the "only wise," since he is wise from one who is wise.

Here again, therefore, the word, desiring to show the relationship of the Son with the Father and his generation from him, says that the Father is the source of wisdom and the source of life, for he is also called the source of life: "They forsook me, the source of living water."[51]

And here again, the word, desiring to show that the Savior is not different in essence from the Father, calls him a Word that is belched forth from the heart, for "My heart belched out a good Word." God, however, possesses a heart that is nothing other than himself, for the heart signifies the mind. And he himself is mind. And as it is said that he does not possess immortality as something different from himself and that he has life in himself, which is nothing different from himself, so also he has a heart that is nothing different from himself, for he is mind, and the Son is the offspring of his mind. And the word is the offspring of the mind.

"My heart," then, "belched out a good word." And in order to show that the heart

---

[48] Wis 7:26.
[49] Baruch 3:12 LES2.
[50] Rom 16:27.
[51] Jer 2:13.

which generated and the offspring are good, he called the offspring "good," for it is beyond doubt that when the offspring is good, that which generated it is also good. However, the converse is not observed. What is generated from something good happens not to be good when it suffers change. However, since the Word is immutable and does not change like the others, so also the good out of the heart of the good Father possessed his generation.

Again, since among humans genuine offspring are those produced from the womb, it says again, "From the womb, before the Morning-star, I brought you forth."[52] To generate is proper to the womb, just as it belongs to the hands to make. Whenever, for example, Scripture wishes to present God as the genuine Author and truly as the Creator of creation, it says [334] that the creation is the works of his hands, for "I will observe the heavens, works of your fingers."[53] And since some think that to generate and to create are the same thing, if this were so, it would follow to say, "The heavens are the offspring or my hands," or to say, "Out of the hand I brought you forth." Not that he does not [generate also from his hand], but that these things differ in conception.

The relationship that is from the Father is indeed indicated by all these things. As I was saying a little earlier, that when someone says only one thing in a perceptible way, he called it by its strict name. In the case of God, I say all these things in order that by them all I should make him free from what can be said about God in misconception.

And here, therefore, the heart of the Father generates. And—I am speaking now in the case of what is human—sometimes they are productive of thoughts, and sometimes they receive them from outside through teaching. Therefore, they are not called the fathers of thoughts that they only recite, having become habituated in them. Certainly we call the discoverers of certain kinds of knowledge the fathers of knowledge, and those who learn by others we do not call the fathers of knowledge. They say indeed, for example, that Moses has come the first father of law giving, that he did not receive the laws from another, but he himself was led into this by God.

"My heart," therefore, "belched out a good word." As an offspring from the womb, so also the good word in the heart. And in the case of God, heart and womb are not two different things.

I myself speak my works to the king.

Here a sudden change of person has taken place. The good Word himself, who is generated, being in harmony with the Father, says, "*I myself speak my works to the king.*" For as when we hear, "God said, 'Let there be!'"[54] and "He himself spoke, and they came to be; he commanded, and they were created,"[55] we do not understand these things in a human way, for he did not command and speak what should be done and how it should be done to the Son, who was ignorant of these things, but for our sake, in order that the harmony between the Father and the Son might be shown, because by one will all things have come to be and all things are provided. When it says, "And God said, 'Let there be,'" do you suppose that he makes use of a pronounced word? We were saying that the work outstrips the word, and the word is not earlier in time than the work, but only in conception. If, then, these things are so, how must one understand "speaking"? We do not understand it in the sense of a discursive voice, of a noise that passes from mouth to ear.

In order that what is harmonious might be shown, these things are also said about the Spirit, of whom the Savior said, "He cannot

---

[52] Ps 110:3 (109:3).
[53] Ps 8:3 (8:4 NETS).

[54] Cf. Gen 1:3.
[55] Ps 33:9 (32:9); 148:5.

speak on his own."⁵⁶ The phrase "he cannot" means the following, that without him and the Father, his word or teaching is not handed down. And in the case of the rest, of created things, it often means that someone speaks without God when he does this erroneously. The Holy Spirit, however, has not become separated from the message of the Father; if I may say [335] so, he himself is the message.

I myself say, indeed, *my works to the king*. Next the Savior says, "My tongue is the pen of a swift-writing scribe." My tongue writes infallible laws on the hearts of men, for "I will put my laws in their minds, and write them on their hearts."⁵⁷ And on fleshly, and not stony, hearts God writes by his living Spirit.⁵⁸

And see that the pen of the swift-writing one can be the Holy Spirit. He writes quickly . . . mind, they are: "Once God spoke; these two things I heard."⁵⁹ And in the obvious sense of the word . . . it is. And in two ways I interpreted the saying, "Once God spoke, these two things I heard." And . . . When it is proclaimed about circumcision, the wise hears two things: both about the sensible circumcision, which is according to the commandment, and about the spirit. Once, when God spoke about sacrifice, we again hear these two things: both the sensible circumcision according to the law and the one offered up by the spirit, called "a sacrifice of praise."⁶⁰ And in the case of each commandment it is the same: about the Sabbath when it says, then, "These two things he heard."

And I was speaking of another more exalted sense, which is also difficult for many to understand: when God wishes to command many things, for example, the Decalogue, he does not speak in one command, but . . . all the things were heard by the thought of the listener.

"These two things I heard," in order that you should also understand more than these things. And it is also thus, and it is clear to the many; however, let us observe, a thought is not the same thing as an expression. A thought is the operation of the mind, of which the word is the symbol. "Words that are spoken by the voice are the symbols of what is experienced by the soul."⁶¹ An expression is that which subsists in the imagination of the one who is about to speak, for the thought, which is immaterial and pure, is not [able to put to sound] anything about itself. Something in it does not combine with the things that are combined by the expression, in order that it should be shown. For this reason there is also an expression. And it subsists together in the imagination of the thinker, for which reason I thought. And the imagination in me puts together how it is necessary to interpret the thought.

The images that subsist together from one thought are given substance by the Word of God, and for this reason "I heard two things." And the thought that can interpret to others what is thought belongs among the difficult things.

As then, when once God spoke, someone hears two things according to the two interpretations that have been given, so also God's Scripture is understood not according to a single thought or word. This pen writes spiritually. For this reason he is swift-writing. And in the case of swift-writing men, there is some interval of time, in order that he might combine what is first and what is second. Here, however, there is not any interval, but the swiftness is such that there is no interval in it.

Question: How were you saying that there is a sudden change?

The person of the Father was the speaker of the word, "My heart belched out a good word." And the Father is no longer the speaker of the word: "I myself [336] speak my works to the

---

⁵⁶Cf. Jn 16:13.
⁵⁷Heb 8:10; Jer 31:33.
⁵⁸Cf. 2 Cor 3:3.
⁵⁹Ps 62:11 (61:12 NETS).
⁶⁰Ps 50:14 (49:14); Heb 13:15.

⁶¹Aristotle, *On Interpretation* 16a3-4.

king," but the Son, for I do not understand it as the followers of Eunomius say: "The very person who belched a word says to the king, to the one whom he set up, to the word that was begotten, he speaks of the works, in order that he might know how to speak of them, in order that he might recognize them."

Question: Of what kind are the works?

These that he accomplished by means of the economy. Let one of the works be that he has a word like the swift pen of a writer and of one who writes quickly.

It is also possible that the Man who serves is a pen, and God the Word, who made use of him is the scribe; for by this one he wrote to the world. . . . did they bring an accomplishment? His works have been fulfilled . . . another says these works to him. . . . For this reason he fled from the face of God. And when he was not yet . . . He was in company with him; he announced to him in his company, that he is not to partake of the tree [from which] God wills to preserve [him], because just as [for the purpose of] "guarding and working"[62] paradise for him he made him for himself. Likewise, we do not separate the person who says this from the Word, as when . . . "I discuss," "I announce," "I think," we do not separate all of these from the soul, nor do we separate them all from the body, but the one who is composed of both says what he thinks. This operation, however, belongs to the soul; it is the composite who speaks. And when I say, "I am walking swiftly," or "I am warm," or "I shiver," now the composite is the one who speaks about his own body.

My tongue is like the pen of a swift-writing scribe. You are graceful in beauty beyond the sons of men.

The word of the gospel is beyond all the words that are human. . . . of the Man who was assumed and of the Word of God who assumed, . . . he is a good word and a king.

[44:3] *Grace was poured on your lips.*

This is interpreted by the Gospel according to Luke, for once he entered into the synagogue in Capernaum, "and the scroll of the prophet Isaiah was given to him" in order that it might be read. It said, "And all were amazed at the gracious words that came from his mouth."[63] So his words are so full of grace that they rule over those who listen to them. And it calls "listeners" those who hear with intelligence, not those [who hear] with the ear, for all hear the gospel, both Greeks and Jews . . . but they are not [amazed] at the grace of the words as it is necessary, [having labors from them] . . .

Question: Is there another person here?

Grace was poured on your lips—either the Holy Spirit [337] says this or the writer does. And sometimes the Father speaks as a witness, for often we have said that "lips" signify speech, for "remove unjust lips far away from me."[64]

[44:3] *Therefore God, your God, blessed you forever.*

And this is said about the Man, for to be blessed with a reason does not belong to God the Word. He himself is blessing, the source of blessing. And a reason lies here in the word *therefore* as it does also in the passage, "therefore God, your God, anointed you."[65] However, this being anointed for a reason indicates that the one who has been anointed is virtuous, for because he did righteousness and hated lawlessness he has obtained the chrism.

For this reason he would be blessed forever, since he had a tongue like the pen of a swift-writing one, or rather, of a scribe. It says these things about the Man. And since he has the priesthood and the teaching without

---

[62] Gen 2:15.
[63] Lk 4:22 NRSV.
[64] Cf. Prov 4:24.
[65] Ps 45:7 (44:8 NETS).

succession—for even if heaven and earth pass away, his words remain[66]—he was blessed forever.

[44:4] *Gird your sword on your thigh, O powerful one!*

Often the thigh stands for manly movements. We were saying, for example, that the word in Ezekiel discredits those who have the fluids of intemperance: "And every thigh shall be wetted with moisture,"[67] that is the loin, the members of procreation, are soiled with moisture.

These things surely would not be said about the virtuous. You have, for example, in the Song of Songs what is said by the bridegroom to the bride: "Like a necklace"—since you adorned yourself perfectly with purity, O soul or church, who prepared for no other than the true Bridegroom, God the Word—"are the shapes of your thighs."[68] She has been likened to a necklace, to an adornment around the neck.

And often an adornment around the neck signifies "obedience." It indicates also that the church is obedient. Paul says, "Wives, be subject to your husbands in the same way that the church is subject to Christ."[69] "The shape," then, "of your thighs," which are, as it were, the desires and the appetitive powers, have been shaped in accordance with a fine necklace.

And on the one hand one must understand anagogically, and on the other hand also literally what is said about the intemperate, "Every thigh shall be wetted with moisture." Both the thigh of the soul and the thigh of the body aid intemperance. Because of this, Abraham, when he was sending away the elder of his own house, that divine and wise servant, for the betrothal of Rebekah—I am speaking to the letter—he made him place his hand under the thigh of Abraham, in order that he should conduct the virgin blamelessly and purely, for after arranging his endeavor he was made to swear an oath under the thigh, under the sexual impulse, so to speak, for in this way he conducted the virgin without harm.[70]

Since, then, the Savior received the temple by means of a human birth, he says to him, as to one who is powerful—for he is God the Word—"*Gird your sword upon your thigh, O powerful one.*"

We say therefore: the faithful man, the temperate, the imitator of God, **[338]** is girded around the thigh with the Word of God that cannot be shattered, which is sharpened beyond every two-edged sword,[71] in order to cut away the extraordinary passions, for the one who participates in the pursuit of an honored marriage and keeps the bed uncontaminated[72] has the Word of God as a sword that cuts away. When, therefore, it calls God the Word or the soul that is yoked to him here "powerful," it is speaking of the inhumanation, of the birth from a woman.

Gird yourself, therefore, with this sword, while your graciousness and your beauty remain. Now, beauty and graciousness are sinlessness, when they are predicated of the soul, for he did not know sin.[73]

And when this is about God the Word, it says the following: the beauty of God and the graciousness remain in you after becoming man, for you did not undergo an alteration from being the Word and the Word of God.

And to each of the chaste, at last, it is said: desire beauty and graciousness from the rest of the virtues. Take also prudence, the word that prunes.

Question: What kind of sword should we understand?

As the word that is about prudence, as the word in general, as the word that cuts away.[74]

---

[66]Cf. Mt 24:35; Mk 13:31; Lk 21:33.
[67]Ezek 7:17 LXX.
[68]Song 7:1.
[69]Cf. Eph 5:22-24.
[70]Cf. Gen 24:2-3.
[71]Cf. Prov 5:4; Heb 4:12.
[72]Heb 13:4.
[73]Cf. 2 Cor 5:21.
[74]The manuscript ends abruptly here. Likely the lecture series continued on from this point, but we have no preserved record of it.

General Index

Aaron, 99, 106, 301
Abel, 55, 65, 265
Abraham, 5, 10, 21, 55-56, 65, 67, 81, 83, 107, 109, 136, 172, 180-81, 204, 214, 243, 291, 304, 313, 324, 328, 362
Achish, 177-78
Adam, 27, 80-81, 102, 128, 162, 186, 206, 213, 305, 339
Aetius, 81, 220
Ahab, 140, 174, 218
allegorical sense, xxv, 21, 53, 65, 68, 87, 100, 172, 179, 240-41, 295, 304, 336, 346, 349, 356
anagogical sense, xxiv-xxv, 7, 63, 91, 121, 129, 172, 175, 178, 181, 212, 234, 245, 256, 268, 312, 314, 335, 356, 360, 362
anthropomorphites, 194, 252-53, 325, 359
Apollinarians, xxv, 22, 42, 68, 179, 251, 314
apostles, 57, 72, 82, 84, 87, 90, 94, 146, 150-52, 186, 194, 209, 327, 344
Arians, xx, 37, 220, 255, 321
Aristotle, 72, 291
Bardaisan, 173
Basilides, 160
body, 13, 16, 34-35, 39, 63, 66, 68, 80, 88, 92, 94-95, 98-100, 109, 131, 133-34, 156, 160, 168, 173-74, 183, 192, 195, 198, 203, 208, 212, 222-26, 234, 246, 248, 254, 265, 268-69, 271-72, 274-75, 285, 299-300, 304, 309, 312, 313, 323, 325, 332, 340, 345, 349-50, 352, 354-55, 361
Cain, 65, 80, 161-62, 283, 339
Christ
  appearance or inhumanation of, 2, 4, 22, 34, 45, 58, 66, 68, 72, 74, 78, 98, 112, 125, 136, 138, 142, 152, 158, 160, 171, 178-79, 202-3, 237, 243, 305, 307, 326, 353-54, 362
  body of, 22-23, 25-27, 31, 34-35, 37, 42, 66, 68, 100, 133, 135, 138, 160, 162, 178-79, 206, 219, 240, 242, 300, 304-5, 313, 331, 356-57
  creator, 14, 114, 136, 144, 237-38
  divinity of, 3-4, 7, 29, 38, 42, 44-45, 49, 58, 85, 106, 119, 123, 133-34, 152, 155-56, 158, 179, 187, 203, 212, 244, 291, 303, 321, 325, 326, 330, 353-54, 358, 362
  economy of, 22, 27, 35, 66, 179, 354, 361
  generation of 2, 42, 81, 221, 358-59
  humanity of, 3-5, 10, 24, 26, 29, 32, 34, 38, 41-42, 45, 52, 58, 85, 87, 98, 120, 133-34, 149-50, 152, 155-56, 158, 168, 187, 191, 242, 251, 267, 299-300, 306-8, 314, 317, 321, 330-31, 353, 361-62
  sinlessness of, 15, 24, 28, 35, 38, 40, 151, 153, 168, 202, 204, 213, 220-21, 242, 243, 267, 307, 311, 314, 362
  soul of, 22, 35, 38, 40, 42, 135, 154, 159, 220-22, 243, 251, 300, 304-5, 310, 314
church, 52, 59, 61, 91-92, 118, 128, 140, 154, 173, 175, 179, 190, 198, 242, 247, 250, 254-55, 271, 362
contemplation, xxiii, 81, 100, 102, 132, 152, 165, 186, 209, 218, 237, 240, 307
Daniel, 111, 339, 340-41, 346, 350
David, xxvi, 6-7, 52, 69, 81, 93, 101, 130, 164-65, 177-79, 217, 231, 249, 256, 286, 302, 328
Delilah, 226-27
deification, xxiv, 97, 104, 141, 296, 326, 353-54
Dimoirites, 304
disposition, xxiii, 7, 17, 19, 41, 48-49, 74-75, 80, 82, 87, 90, 115, 123, 126, 137, 145, 150, 157, 163, 180, 186, 191, 218, 227, 232-33, 236, 238, 240, 246, 248, 251, 261-62, 271, 278-79, 282, 284, 299, 303, 306, 309, 317, 322-23, 335-36, 345, 354
docetism, 2, 159-60
Donatists, 167
Egyptians, 82-83, 99, 195-96, 276, 301, 334
Elijah, 23, 165, 174, 181, 218, 221, 256
Elisha, 44, 96, 181, 321
Elymas, 92, 168, 234
Esau, 96, 141, 294, 317, 347
Eunomians, xx, 47-48, 81, 220, 361
Eve, 80-81, 186, 213, 287, 339
Ezekiel, 305, 339, 341, 346
Father, 2-3, 7, 12, 16, 27, 29, 38, 42-44, 49, 81, 112, 119, 127, 131, 133-34, 138, 149, 153-55, 158-59, 161, 171, 178, 182, 188, 192, 196, 202, 205, 211, 228, 230-32, 244, 251, 256, 291, 294, 297, 299, 306, 311, 321, 324-25, 330-31, 341, 356-61
figural sense, 33, 121, 336
final goal, 10, 14, 48, 96-98, 104, 111, 118, 126, 142, 163, 231-32, 238, 245, 261, 302, 323, 333, 352-54
forepassion, xxiii, xxvi, 31, 40-41, 71, 221-22, 262, 274, 296, 300, 314-15, 326
free will, 19, 50, 72, 79, 82, 88-89, 112, 128, 136, 161-62, 193, 194, 199, 233-34, 259-60, 279, 292, 300, 337, 341, 347
Gnosticism, 3
Goliath, 101, 173, 302
Greeks, 52, 62, 158, 167, 204-5, 241, 243, 295, 316, 344, 361
habit, *see* disposition
Haggai, 339, 341, 346
Haman, 80, 214
Heraclitus 130
Hermes Tresmegistus, 82
Herod, 84, 194, 345
historical sense, 7, 20, 27, 36, 130, 172-73, 175, 336, 342-43
Holy Spirit, xxiv, 7, 11, 16, 18, 28-29, 42, 46, 51, 63, 93, 97, 102, 104, 115, 123-24, 128, 130-31, 133, 137, 141, 165, 180-82, 187, 201, 204, 208, 271-72, 282, 289, 295-96, 299, 302, 304, 306, 319-22, 332, 352-53, 359-91

illumination, 12, 21-22, 60, 74, 78, 81, 93-94, 103, 105, 153, 186-87, 243-44, 257, 262, 273, 277, 289-90, 326-27, 330-32, 334, 336, 339, 344-45

imitation, 3, 7, 9, 14, 77, 87, 112, 133-34, 155, 171, 184, 195, 234, 247-48, 254, 259, 261, 263, 277, 331, 340, 362

immutability, xxiii, 1, 48, 101, 104, 119-20, 237, 255, 300, 353, 359

intellect, 13, 27, 32, 59, 63, 78-79, 87, 93, 96, 100, 104, 143-44, 147-78, 153, 171, 175, 186, 214, 240-41, 251-53, 262, 265, 272-73, 275, 277, 292, 309, 335

Isaac, 109, 141, 160, 181

Isaiah, 94, 216, 305

Jacob, 42, 44, 51, 96, 109, 160, 188, 213, 317, 336, 347

Jeremiah, 27, 29, 46, 89, 182, 222, 346

Jericho, 100, 197

Jews, 30, 36, 41-42, 51-52, 61, 63-64, 98, 108, 150-51, 153-54, 167-68, 190, 204-5, 214-15, 222, 245, 247, 256, 266, 276, 281, 286, 300, 306, 314, 316, 328-29, 330, 361

Jezebel, 84, 174, 209

Job, 23, 28-29, 56, 82, 105, 169, 182, 222, 270, 277, 323, 335

John the Baptist, 29, 51, 67, 76, 84, 120-22, 124-25, 133, 165, 224, 346

Joseph, 10, 57, 84, 100, 108, 111, 145, 206, 209, 217, 221, 266, 284, 340

Joshua, 339, 341

Judas, 34, 39, 88, 101, 154-55, 177, 250, 256, 261, 278, 314-17, 329, 340

judgment, 18-19, 24, 110, 123, 136, 151-52, 196, 199, 228, 248, 267-68, 317

Kataphrygians, 302

Korah, 319, 357

literal sense, xxiv-xxv, 10, 14, 21, 27, 36-37, 44, 61-62, 87, 103, 115, 122-24, 129, 172-73, 181, 183, 194-95, 198, 214, 216, 244, 256, 290, 301, 303-5, 339, 343-44, 356, 362

Lot, 206, 224

Manichaeans, 306

Marcion, 160

Mary, Mother of God, 2-3, 5, 7-8, 12, 26-27, 29, 39, 145, 159-60, 190, 304, 309, 328

moral sense, 16, 155, 311, 320

Moses, 20, 81, 90, 122, 124, 167, 173, 177, 195, 216, 220, 234-35, 256, 280-81, 286, 331, 334, 359

mystical sense, 112, 121, 334

Naboth, 84, 94, 209, 217, 263

Nebuchadnezzar, 112, 179, 217, 261, 350

Origen, xxiv

Palladius, xx-xxi

participation, xxiii, 7, 10, 45, 72, 97, 99, 136, 141, 143, 162-63, 169, 181-82, 184, 189-91, 194, 201, 203, 211, 238, 240, 242-44, 258, 271, 293, 321, 323, 326, 331, 358

passion, xxiii, 35, 41, 44, 95, 108, 147, 152, 174, 186, 188, 190, 202, 216, 235, 271, 300, 312, 315, 362

Paul, 32, 88, 121, 128, 165, 167, 204, 215, 217, 224, 231, 241-42, 244, 292, 297, 302, 306, 323, 347, 355

Pelusium, 116

perfection, 22, 41, 48, 53-54, 64, 75, 87-89, 91, 96-97, 102, 104, 117, 120, 128, 133, 142, 146, 164, 172, 176, 185, 188-90, 193, 198-99, 203, 210, 230-31, 238, 242, 246, 252, 254, 261, 279, 289, 297, 306-7, 323-24, 353-54, 356

Pharaoh, 173, 177, 179, 195, 235, 271, 276, 281, 286

Pharisees, 30, 101, 217, 268

philanthropy, 6, 139, 249

Pilate, 315-16

Porphyry, 333

pre-existence, xxv

progress, 21, 28-29, 53-54, 58, 64, 91, 96, 98-102, 120, 128, 161, 169, 172, 173, 182, 188, 198, 203, 210, 238, 252, 289, 293, 306, 322-23, 325, 331, 333, 352-54

Protagoras, 222

providence, 18, 35, 73, 79, 158, 162, 171, 182-83, 195, 210, 235, 239-40, 264, 270, 312, 336, 340, 348, 353, 359

Rebekah, 21, 204, 362

restoration of all things, xxiv, 50, 117, 126, 139, 171, 185, 219-20, 223, 248, 250, 323, 347

Rufinus, xxiii

Sadducees, 2, 30, 217

Samson, 226-27

Samuel, 23, 28, 46, 91, 93

Saul, 23, 93, 101, 106, 177, 181, 286, 328

Socrates, 148

Solomon, 130, 225, 313

Stoics, 50

Susanna, 10, 84, 100, 108, 145, 206, 209-10, 212-13, 216-18, 220-21, 256, 262-63, 284, 286, 307, 347

theology, 184, 212, 219

Timothy, 242, 292

Trinity, 72, 138, 180, 300, 330

Uriah's wife, 101, 103

Valentinus, 160, 173

worthiness of God, 1, 252, 333

Zechariah, 339, 341, 346

Scripture Index

Old Testament

Genesis
1:1, *106, 228, 237*
1:3, *328, 359*
1:26, *16, 17, 20, 157, 159, 167, 169, 170, 195, 220, 241, 325, 326*
1:27, *188*
1:31, *264*
2:1-2, *61*
2:3, *102*
2:7, *169, 300*
2:9, *219, 356*
2:10, *244*
2:15, *102, 361*
2:25, *186*
3:8, *80, 128*
3:11-12, *339*
3:15, *252*
3:22, *219*
3:24, *81, 162, 219, 339*
4:1, *213*
4:7, *283*
4:16, *80, 161, 339*
6:3, *130*
6:11, *142*
11:2, *115, 217*
11:4, *20*
11:6, *115*
11:7, *115*
17:5, *180, 181*
18:9-14, *180*
18:20, *104*
18:20-21, *343*
18:27, *81, 83*
19:17, *206*
21:1-7, *180*
23:4, *12*
23:6, *5, 124, 172*
24:2-3, *204, 362*
25:29, *294*
26:5, *55*
27:33, *141*
28:20-22, *46*
31:32, *213*
32:2, *95*
39:5-12, *108*
39:17-20, *84*
41:37-45, *84*
48:15, *256*
48:16, *188*
49:33, *109*

Exodus
1:21, *103*
3:6, *107*
4:10, *82, 280*
4:11, *280*
5:2, *18*
6:24, *319*
7:12, *99, 301*
8:19, *99*
9:3, *271*
9:15, *271*
9:27, *18*
10:2, *253*
12:11, *57*
12:16, *329*
13:12, *343*
13:13, *343*
14:4, *195*
14:12, *281*
14:13, *281*
14:15, *281*
14:21-22, *124*
14:29, *124*
15:1, *286*
15:2, *139*
15:4, *6, 172*
15:9, *155*
15:10, *235, 273*
15:12, *235*
15:17, *334*
15:18, *4, 123*
16:8, *256*
16:35, *174*
17:11-13, *173*
19:6, *216, 225*
20:12, *11, 107, 192, 290*
21:17, *107*
21:24, *55*
23:1, *199*
23:10-11, *103*
23:14-17, *117*
25:40, *331*
32:6, *89*
32:20, *123*
33:20, *216*
34:19, *343*
34:28, *256*
38:8, *90*

Leviticus
5:17, *248*
5:17-19, *248*
16:29, *117*
16:31, *50*
19:18, *308*
19:36, *55*
23:4-44, *117*
23:27, *117*
25:8-10, *103*
26:23-24, *128*

Numbers
4:3, *102*
6:25, *325*
6:26, *325*
16:22, *228*
27:16, *228*

Deuteronomy
1:31, *159*
4:29, *47*
5:10, *235, 236, 244*
5:11, *64*
6:5, *12, 203*
6:6, *234*
6:7, *234*
7:15, *196*
8:11-12, *346*
8:14, *346*
10:12, *12*
13:6, *214, 316*
15:17, *74, 345*
16:1-17, *117*
16:16, *322*
16:20, *156, 163, 208, 249, 284*
19:19, *210*

23:18, *36*
23:24, *49*
30:6, *91*
30:20, *12, 91*
32:11, *241*
32:16-17, *247*
32:21, *247*
32:30, *172*
32:42, *80, 270*

Joshua
6:20, *100*

Judges
16:6, *227*
16:9, *227*

1 Samuel
3:7, *28*
12:5, *106*
15:33, *23*
16:1, *46*
16:10, *81*
16:13, *93, 302*
17:42, *156*
17:45, *173, 302*
21, *181*
21:10, *177*
21:10-15, *181*
21:13, *178*
21:15, *178*
22:10, *101*
27, *181*
27:3, *181*
27:12, *345*
28:15, *23*
30:24, *102*

2 Samuel
2:4, *93*
5:3, *93*
6:14-22, *132*
22:14, *121*

1 Kings
6, *130*
10:2, *225*

365

17:1, *186*
17:6, *256*
17:10-11, *174*
18:4, *174*
18:12, *174*
19:5-6, *174*
19:10, *81, 221*
19:14, *221*
21:10, *217*
21:13, *84, 263*
21:29, *140, 218*

2 Kings
1:2, *312*
2:2, *321*
2:4, *321*
2:6, *321*
6:15-17, *96*
18:34, *323*
25:2, *161*

1 Chronicles
6:9, *319*
25:1, *286*

2 Chronicles
3, *130*
5:12, *286*

Esther
4:16, *214*
7:9-10, *80*

Job
1:8, *28*
1:11, *18, 335*
1:21, *82, 183*
1:22, *182, 323*
2:3, *28*
2:10, *56, 323*
3:3, *222*
3:8, *223*
5:11, *197*
5:19, *83, 146*
5:21, *217*
6:4, *270*
7:20, *170*
10:8, *169, 171*
10:9, *170, 171, 300*
12:22, *327*
16:9, *218*
19:13, *278*

25:5, *229*
26:7, *62*
31:17-18, *28*
40:16, *204*
41:34, *121*

Psalms
1:1, *89, 207*
1:1-2, *189*
1:2, *108, 115, 234, 307*
1:4, *207*
1:5-6, *151*
2:1, *30, 154*
2:2, *30, 41*
2:4, *253*
2:6, *4*
2:8, *134*
3:2, *152*
3:7, *217, 219*
4, *252, 257, 311*
4:1, *145*
4:2, *157*
4:4, *234*
4:5, *331*
4:6, *105, 186*
5:3, *22, 186*
5:5, *73, 81*
5:6, *24*
5:10, *106*
6:6, *234, 297*
6:7, *79*
6:10, *206*
7:2, *142*
7:9, *88*
7:11, *110*
7:15, *80*
7:16, *27, 214, 252*
8:1, *204*
8:3, *359*
8:9, *204*
9:1-2, *324*
9:15, *80*
10, *53*
10:15, *72, 73, 250*
10:17, *169*
11:2, *94, 253*
11:4, *159*
11:7, *163*
12:3, *156, 357*
12:4, *94*
12:6, *258*
12:7, *251*
13, *300*

13:3, *94, 174*
14:3, *142*
15:2, *168*
15:2-3, *55*
15:5, *55*
16:5, *220*
16:7, *88*
16:9-10, *68*
17:8, *195*
17:11, *275*
18, *286*
18:1, *87, 121, 277, 286*
18:9, *66, 202, 307*
18:11, *239, 327*
18:13, *121*
18:18, *255, 262*
18:33, *320*
18:46, *321*
19:1, *270*
19:2, *327*
19:7, *108, 166, 230*
19:8, *277*
19:11, *230*
19:12, *70, 77, 129*
19:13, *70, 71*
20, *2, 3, 4, 5, 6, 7, 8, 9, 10, 11, 12, 13, 14, 15, 16, 17, 18, 19, 20, 85, 132*
20–21, *1*
20:7, *173*
21, 22, 23, 24, 25, 26, 27, 28, 29, 30, 31, 32, 33, 34, 35, 36, 37, 38, 39, 40, 41, 42, 43, 44, 45, 46, 47, 48, 49, 50, 51, 52, *133*
21:1, *20*
21:7, *17*
22, *54, 55, 56, 57, 58, 59, 60*
22–26, *53*
22:3, *112*
22:5, *25*
22:6, *60*
22:11, *38*
22:16, *31, 68*
22:24, *45*
22:25, *184*
22:28, *50*
22:29, *11, 69*
23, *62, 63, 64, 65, 66, 67, 68*
23:1-2, *240*
23:3, *240*
23:5, *240*

24, *61, 70, 71, 72, 73, 74, 75, 76, 77, 78, 79, 80, 81, 82, 83, 84, 85*
24:1, *61*
24:3, *62, 330*
24:3-4, *230*
24:4, *62*
24:5, *230, 260*
25, *87, 88, 89, 90, 91, 92*
25:5, *261*
25:11, *78*
25:14, *77*
25:15, *91*
25:16, *221*
25:21, *318*
26, *94, 95, 96, 97, 98, 99, 100, 101, 102, 103, 104, 105, 106, 107, 108, 109*
26:8, *132*
26:10–29:2, *108, 117, 245*
27, *111, 112, 113, 114, 115, 116*
27:4, *54*
27:5, *301*
27:12, *73*
27:13, *249*
28, *117, 118, 119, 120, 121, 122, 123, 124, 125, 126, 127, 128, 129*
28:1, *110*
28:4, *113*
29, *131, 132, 133, 134, 135, 136, 137, 138, 139, 140*
29–34, *131*
29:1, *128*
29:3, *120*
29:4, *120*
29:5, *120, 264*
29:6, *43, 122*
29:7, *120*
29:8, *120*
29:9, *120*
29:10, *127, 129*
30, *142, 143, 144, 145, 146, 147, 148, 149, 150, 151, 152, 153, 154, 155, 156, 157, 158, 159, 160, 161, 162, 163*
30:1, *20, 282*
30:3, *111, 300*
30:7, *138, 195*
30:10, *283*
30:11, *283*

Scripture Index

30:12, *218*
31, *165, 166, 167, 168*
31:3–32:13, *168*
31:11, *150*
31:18, *203*
32, *170, 171, 172, 173, 174, 175, 176*
32:1, *73, 151*
32:2, *11*
32:5, *126, 324*
32:5-6, *126, 129*
32:6, *126, 129*
32:10, *215*
33, *178, 179, 180, 181, 182, 183, 184, 185, 186, 187, 188, 189, 190, 191, 192, 193, 194, 195, 196, 197, 198, 199, 200*
33:1, *43, 225*
33:4, *181*
33:6, *181, 182*
33:9, *359*
33:13, *157, 175*
33:16, *6*
34, *202, 203, 204, 205, 206, 207, 208, 209, 210, 211, 212, 213, 214, 215, 216, 217, 218, 219, 220, 221, 222, 223, 224, 225, 226, 227, 228, 229, 230*
34:1, *260*
34:7, *207*
34:9, *157*
34:10, *44, 47, 77, 96, 174, 187, 212*
34:14, *56, 75, 155, 248, 284*
34:15, *9, 73, 78, 174*
34:16, *18*
34:21, *196*
35, *232, 233, 234, 235, 236, 237, 238, 239, 240, 241, 242, 243, 244, 245*
35–39, *231, 248, 258*
35:1, *215*
35:8, *253*
35:10, *37, 149, 168, 272*
35:20, *113, 215*
35:25, *99*
35:28, *286*
36, *247, 248, 249, 250, 251, 252, 253, 254, 255, 256, 257, 258, 259, 260, 261, 262, 263, 264, 265*

36:1, *166*
36:1-3, *108, 117, 245*
36:6, *327*
36:6-7, *157*
36:8, *60*
36:9, *244, 320*
36:10, *244*
37, *267, 268, 269, 270, 271, 272, 273, 274, 275, 276, 277, 278, 279, 280, 281, 282, 283, 284, 285*
37:1, *249, 254*
37:3, *248*
37:4, *190, 298*
37:8, *250, 254*
37:9, *255*
37:11, *255*
37:14, *265*
37:19, *257*
37:21, *284*
37:27, *56, 264*
37:29, *109*
37:34, *109, 260*
38, *287, 288, 289, 290, 291, 292, 293, 294, 295, 296, 297, 298*
38:1, *295*
38:4, *273*
38:5, *289*
38:18, *267, 283*
39, *300, 301, 302, 303, 304, 305, 306, 307, 308, 309, 310*
39:3, *288*
39:4, *298*
39:6, *296*
39:7, *249, 298, 299*
39:12, *11*
40, *312, 313, 314, 315, 316, 317, 318*
40–44, *252, 257, 311*
40:1, *249*
40:2, *92*
40:3, *100*
40:5, *303*
40:6, *22, 299*
40:7, *299*
40:10, *238*
40:14, *304*
41, *320, 321, 322, 323, 324, 325, 326, 327*
41:4, *134, 314*
41:9, *316*

42, *329, 330, 331, 332*
42:1, *357*
42:3, *325*
42:4, *54*
42:5, *40, 221, 272*
42:8, *25*
43, *334, 335, 336, 337, 338, 339, 340, 341, 342, 343, 344, 345, 346, 347, 348, 349, 350, 351*
44, *345, 353, 354, 355, 356, 357, 358, 359, 360, 361, 362*
44:2, *271*
44:3, *18*
44:5, *338*
44:8, *25, 184*
44:17, *341, 346*
44:19, *34, 83, 92*
44:20, *111, 339*
44:22, *74, 230, 338, 349*
44:23, *228*
44:25, *35, 351*
45:3, *203*
45:5, *270*
45:7, *59, 361*
48:10, *204*
48:14, *116*
49:5, *252*
49:12, *169, 269, 291*
49:18-19, *15*
49:20, *169*
50, *101*
50:14, *304, 331, 360*
50:16-17, *227*
50:16-18, *110*
50:21, *110, 227, 297*
51, *101*
51:7, *129*
51:15, *287*
52, *101*
52:3, *224*
52:8, *54*
54:1, *143*
55:6, *241*
55:9, *217*
55:12-13, *316, 329*
55:13, *49, 316, 323*
55:15, *329*
55:19, *335*
55:22, *30*
55:23, *111*
56:8, *297*

57:4, *253, 337*
57:6, *210*
57:7, *261*
58:6, *217*
59:4, *80, 143*
60:9, *161*
60:12, *338*
62:2, *315*
62:11, *360*
63:1, *321*
63:3, *54*
63:5, *51*
63:8, *285*
63:9, *235*
64:3, *337*
65:2, *272*
65:4, *119*
66:4, *13*
66:12, *124*
66:18, *71*
66:19, *71*
68:2, *32, 257*
68:6, *40*
68:17, *245*
68:20, *240*
69:10, *149, 151*
71:6, *86*
71:9, *242*
72:7, *14*
73:1-3, *282*
73:23, *78, 91, 142, 271, 335*
73:23-24, *262*
73:27, *78*
74:3, *350*
74:12, *4*
74:14, *242*
74:23, *350*
75:1, *136*
75:1-2, *324*
75:10, *337*
76:1, *204*
76:4, *236*
77:4, *288, 296, 323*
77:6, *40*
77:7, *353*
77:8-9, *353*
77:9, *353*
77:10, *178, 179, 353*
77:11, *178*
77:13, *179*
77:14, *179*
78:8, *187*
79:8, *187, 308*

80:1, *116*
80:3, *20, 66, 105*
80:5, *123, 322*
80:7, *66*
80:19, *66*
82:2, *212*
82:7, *157, 159*
83:1-3, *110*
83:16-18, *70*
83:17, *71*
83:17-18, *195*
83:18, *71*
84:1, *120*
84:2, *120, 294*
84:4, *97, 120*
84:6, *65*
85:10, *308*
85:11, *142, 163, 307*
86:9, *50*
88:4-5, *242, 300*
88:5, *256*
89:8, *74*
89:17, *337*
89:25, *18, 336*
89:37, *76*
91:4, *94, 310*
91:9-10, *216, 294*
91:16, *289*
92:13, *120*
93:1, *15*
93:2, *169*
93:3, *18*
94:12, *269*
95:1, *131*
96:1, *13*
96:5, *349*
96:6, *324*
98:3, *13, 211*
98:8, *336*
101:4, *39, 213, 215, 279*
101:7, *43*
102:18, *52*
102:22, *50*
102:23-24, *289*
102:26, *13*
103:1, *190, 224, 276*
103:2, *224*
103:5, *8, 96, 109, 190, 214, 241, 276*
103:22, *224*
104:1, *224, 324*
104:5, *62*

104:6, *239, 327*
104:15, *54*
104:18, *320*
104:24, *103*
105:15, *59, 106, 189*
105:37, *87*
106:1, *245*
107:6, *82*
107:13, *146*
108:1, *169*
108:10, *161*
109:1-2, *329*
109:2, *329*
109:2-8, *314*
109:6, *278*
109:12-13, *88*
109:24, *40*
110:1, *7*
110:3, *359*
110:4, *331*
112:2, *65*
112:3, *250*
112:9, *137, 250*
115:1, *76, 119*
115:3, *328*
115:16, *237*
116:11, *141*
116:15, *199*
117:24, *12*
118:6, *44*
118:12, *153*
118:14, *277*
118:15, *325*
118:16-17, *18*
119:32, *55, 112, 143, 207, 260*
119:53, *348*
119:64, *235, 236*
119:96, *64, 97, 142*
119:131, *262*
119:160, *286*
120:5, *11*
120:6-7, *201, 251*
121:1, *79*
124:2-3, *98, 99*
124:7, *80*
126:5, *297*
126:5-6, *322*
127:1, *173*
128:4, *65*
128:5, *65, 109*
129:3, *340*

130:3, *142, 159*
136:6, *62*
136:25, *169, 236, 272*
137:5-6, *34*
139:6, *134*
139:7-8, *322*
141:1, *203*
141:5, *59*
141:6, *99, 301*
141:7, *149*
142:7, *6*
143:2, *228*
143:7, *110*
143:10, *136*
145:13, *4*
147:2-3, *197*
147:3, *198*
149:5-6, *313*

Proverbs
1:7, *165, 319*
1:9, *321*
1:21, *144*
1:24, *182*
1:28, *194*
2:1-2, *44*
2:4-5, *44*
2:5, *152*
3:11-12, *283*
3:12, *283, 294*
3:16, *335*
3:30, *163*
3:31, *150, 209, 293, 344*
4:9, *321*
4:16, *147*
4:17, *241, 242*
4:24, *182, 361*
4:27, *235*
5:4, *362*
5:5, *245*
5:15, *111*
5:19, *321*
5:22, *73, 151, 165, 243, 261*
6:16, *208*
7:1, *128*
7:14, *208*
7:15, *208*
7:21, *286, 287*
7:26, *290*
8:13, *232*
8:22, *7, 37*
9:2, *58, 240, 242*

9:8, *252, 258, 267, 270, 280, 352*
9:9, *252*
10:2, *254, 292*
10:3, *175, 257*
10:6, *65, 260*
10:13, *57, 95*
10:23, *56, 308*
10:26, *258*
11:23, *8, 276*
12:5, *262*
12:18, *253*
13:13, *87*
14:9, *151*
14:15, *10, 75, 318*
15:7, *287*
15:9, *194*
15:12, *280*
15:27, *232*
15:29, *9*
16:12, *127*
16:33, *214*
18:6, *182*
18:9, *259*
18:12, *197*
18:17, *252, 284*
18:21, *161, 287*
19:17, *258*
20:6, *157*
20:9, *69*
20:13, *175, 257*
21:31, *173*
22:17, *199*
23:24, *107*
23:31, *184*
24:7, *252*
26:9, *40, 245*
26:27, *253*
27:19, *170*
31:4, *20*
31:8, *262*

Ecclesiastes
1:2, *291*
1:4, *52*
2:14, *27, 59, 100, 273, 325*
2:19, *292*
7:23-24, *134*
7:29, *167, 220, 269*
8:1, *262, 273, 326, 332*
8:5, *255*
8:8, *91*

10:2, *335*
10:8, *253*
11:2, *180*
11:7, *105*

Song of Solomon
1:3, *204*
1:7, *21*
2:5, *271*
2:6, *335*
3:7, *313*
3:7-8, *313*
3:8, *313, 337*
4:6, *24*
4:7, *138, 255*
4:9, *79*
5:1, *60, 242*
5:9, *321*
5:10, *321*
5:16, *321*
6:10, *198*
7:1, *362*
8:3, *335*
8:5, *255*

Isaiah
1:4, *44, 328, 334*
1:9, *125*
1:10, *216*
1:11, *305, 331*
1:16, *196*
1:16-17, *194*
1:20, *270*
2:2-3, *326, 330*
3:7-10, *216*
5:1, *94*
5:1-14, *216*
5:4-6, *33*
5:6, *237*
5:7, *104*
5:11, *62*
6:1, *216*
6:6, *331*
7:15-16, *28*
8:4, *28, 59*
8:13, *189*
8:18, *134*
9:6, *188*
9:7, *14*
9:12, *99, 219*
9:15, *51*
10:3, *254*
10:13, *264*

10:14, *264*
11:2, *165*
13:10, *14*
14:12, *237*
14:13, *237*
14:13-14, *237*
14:14, *237*
17:13, *105*
22:13, *298*
23:17, *103*
25:8, *38*
26:9, *21*
26:12, *297*
26:17-18, *147, 213, 306*
27:1, *279*
28:5, *10*
28:9-10, *28*
28:10, *29*
29:10, *140*
29:11, *305*
29:12, *305*
29:13, *27*
30:6, *82*
30:15, *62*
30:17, *172*
30:26, *198*
31:2, *56*
33:11, *63*
34:5, *80, 270*
36:19, *323*
37:36, *188*
40:3, *124*
40:4, *279*
40:5, *272*
40:6, *272*
40:9-10, *66*
40:15, *290*
40:31, *241*
42:1, *44*
42:13, *67, 127*
42:14, *110, 227*
43:2, *124*
45:7, *171*
45:8, *235, 237*
45:12, *188*
45:14, *273*
45:17, *93, 212*
46:12, *88, 251, 278*
48:16, *16*
49:16, *144*
50:4-5, *333*
50:5, *304, 333*
50:9, *93*

52:5, *119*
53:5, *202*
53:9, *11, 28*
54:17, *249*
55:6, *185*
55:9, *303*
56:10, *36*
56:11, *36*
58:9, *9, 66, 135, 310, 332*
58:13, *266*
58:14, *109*
59:5-6, *296*
60:19, *13, 186*
61:10, *229*
62:11, *66, 336*
63:1-2, *66*
65:16, *150*
65:20, *180*
66:5, *150, 201*

Jeremiah
1:5, *27, 346*
1:10, *114*
1:14, *297*
2:3, *98*
2:13, *320, 358*
2:24, *295*
2:31, *357*
2:35, *27, 71*
2:37, *27*
3:20, *247*
3:22, *128*
3:25, *205*
5:8, *337*
5:23, *294*
7:17-18, *46*
7:28, *294*
8:4, *131*
8:8-9, *324*
8:9, *324*
8:14, *123*
9:3, *161*
9:4, *192*
9:5, *192*
9:8, *112, 192, 226*
9:18, *79*
10:23, *260*
11:1, *182*
12:2, *88*
12:7-8, *41*
12:8, *41*
13:17, *79*
15:9, *137*

15:17, *89*
16:19, *52, 121*
17:12-13, *299*
17:13, *275*
20:14, *222*
23:24, *322*
31:33, *262, 360*
48:10, *113*
49:8, *235, 275*
50:17, *341*
51:9, *63*
51:51, *186*

Lamentations
1:8, *267*
1:9, *208*
3:38, *264*
3:41, *235*
4:1, *356*
4:2, *291, 356*

Ezekiel
2:6, *33*
2:8, *305*
2:10, *305*
3:3, *305*
7:17, *204, 338, 362*
9:10, *252, 255*
11:19, *88, 251, 271*
11:21, *214*
16:10, *263*
16:44-58, *224*
16:52, *71, 206*
18:4, *131, 314*
18:20, *174*
22:31, *27, 252, 255*
28:12-14, *10*
32:2, *121*
36:22, *119*
36:25-26, *129*

Daniel
3, *350*
3:1, *217, 350*
3:50, *124*
3:86, *49*
6, *350*
6:10, *183*
6:16, *111*
7:24, *337*
9:5, *75*
12:2, *70, 151*

Hosea
3:5, *302*
7:6, *289*
7:13, *260*
7:16, *214*
8:8, *98, 301*
9:2, *109*
9:17, *106, 256*
10:12, *257, 277*
11:6, *123*
12:3-4, *44*
12:8, *298*
13:4, *114*

Joel
2:28, *204, 272, 353*

Amos
3:10, *292*
6:13, *337*
8:3, *33, 257*
8:11, *257*
9:10, *39*

Jonah
1:2, *104, 270*
1:8, *232*
1:9, *232*
3:5-10, *214*

Micah
2:1, *234*
2:7, *1*
2:9, *236*
2:10, *208*
4:1-2, *326, 330*
4:7, *4, 123*
5:2, *2*
5:3, *2*
5:4, *116*
6:8, *169, 261*
7:8, *282*

Nahum
1:8, *126, 127*
1:9, *126*
1:12, *121*

Habakkuk
3:1-2, *296*
3:2, *141*
3:13, *59*

Haggai
1:3, *40*

Zechariah
1:3, *128*
2:4, *188*
2:5, *189*
2:8, *30, 189, 265*
3:1, *278*
4:8, *326*
4:10, *102, 195*
5:7, *54*
6:9, *326*
9:14, *128*
11:1, *122, 264*
11:2, *122, 264*
11:3, *122*
12:4, *173*
12:10, *317*

Malachi
1:4, *114*
3:7, *128*
4:2, *12, 21, 60, 74, 103, 137, 168*

APOCRYPHA

1 Esdras
4:47, *131*

2 Esdras
21:22-23, *286*

Judith
8:29, *170*

Wisdom of Solomon
1:1-2, *47*
1:2, *185*
1:3, *279*
1:13-14, *264*
1:15, *137, 264*
4:9, *11*
4:11, *11*
4:13, *11*
7:26, *358*
9:15, *98, 312*
11:17, *171*
12:10, *110*
13:5, *18, 79, 114, 158, 160, 199*
14:13, *250*
16:21, *256*

Sirach
1:1, *103*
1:26, *74, 132*
1:30, *168*
2:4, *183*
4:21, *206*
6:4, *49*
6:10-12, *278*
9:17, *20*
11:27, *150*
15:9, *43*
18:7, *97*
20:1, *280*
20:5, *288*
20:5-6, *288*
20:6, *288*
21:27, *223*
24:21, *47*
25:11, *44, 77, 96, 152, 157, 174, 188*
27:11, *40, 100, 184, 198, 262*
27:26, *209*
28:25, *287*
50:7, *40*

Baruch
3:12, *320, 358*

Susanna
8-21, *108*
22, *216*
42, *347*
43, *307*
52-59, *218*
60-62, *84*

NEW TESTAMENT

Matthew
1:8-9, *328*
1:16, *26, 160*
1:17, *328*
1:20, *26*
2:23, *78*
3:3, *124*
3:7, *121, 125*
3:9-10, *122*
3:10, *114, 122, 125*
3:11, *124*
3:12, *121*
3:15, *178*
3:17, *120*
4:2, *256*
4:10, *120*
4:23, *135*
5:3, *180, 198*
5:5, *109*
5:6, *47*
5:7, *172*
5:8, *25, 49, 78, 79, 88, 208, 245*
5:9, *226*
5:11-12, *150, 293*
5:14, *32, 119, 186*
5:16, *22, 119, 184, 232*
5:20, *307*
5:25, *213*
5:28, *71*
5:34, *64*
5:37, *64, 193*
5:44, *84*
5:45, *169, 311*
5:48, *64, 133, 230*
6:4, *196*
6:9, *176, 185*
6:9-10, *203, 297*
6:13, *25, 57, 73, 146, 210, 218, 329*
6:19-20, *292*
6:21, *49, 292*
6:24, *78*
6:33, *104*
7:11, *56, 96, 104, 249*
7:15, *233, 289*
7:21, *80, 228, 231, 299*
7:22, *299*
7:23, *299*
7:24, *103, 151*
7:26, *151*
8:2, *306*
8:2-3, *135*
8:3, *313*
8:12, *51, 218, 270*
9:2, *166*
9:6, *166, 188*
10:22, *84, 300*
10:28, *44, 49, 188, 208, 248*
10:32, *211*
10:37, *107*
11:3, *136*

Scripture Index

11:5, *114*
11:15, *333*
11:21, *139, 239*
11:23, *156, 197*
11:25, *324, 338*
11:28, *268, 273*
11:28-29, *266*
11:29, *76, 198, 251, 277*
11:30, *273*
12:2, *268*
12:5, *268*
12:17, *44*
12:24, *316*
12:36, *262*
12:37, *262, 287*
12:50, *80*
13:1-23, *179*
13:8, *235, 269*
13:11, *25, 70, 132*
13:17, *252*
13:23, *235*
13:31, *344*
13:42, *218*
13:47-48, *63, 121*
13:50, *218*
13:52, *61*
16:9, *114*
16:24, *193*
16:28, *92*
18:3, *86*
18:6, *91*
18:6-10, *188*
18:12-13, *236*
18:21, *102*
19:28, *223*
21:31, *51*
21:43, *190*
22:13, *218, 252*
22:21, *162*
22:29, *1*
22:32, *291*
22:43-45, *7*
23:2, *127*
23:35, *65*
23:37, *128, 136, 180, 224*
23:38, *180*
24:3, *11*
24:13, *300*
24:29, *13, 14*
24:35, *109, 168, 248, 250, 362*
24:51, *218*
25:15, *259*

25:16, *259*
25:21, *6*
25:23, *6*
25:24-25, *259*
25:25, *259*
25:26, *259*
25:27-28, *259*
25:30, *218*
25:41, *252*
26:14, *314*
26:15, *88, 315, 316*
26:31, *31*
26:34, *154*
26:37, *221, 300, 314*
26:48, *315*
26:49, *315*
26:52, *80, 253*
26:55, *316*
27:3, *315*
27:5, *315*
27:35, *22*
27:52, *179*
27:52-53, *180*
27:53, *180*
28:6, *38*
28:20, *11*

Mark
1:3, *124*
1:13, *256*
1:15, *165*
1:37, *194*
1:41, *313*
2:9, *312, 313*
3:17, *121*
4:8, *235, 269*
4:20, *235*
6:19-28, *84*
8:19, *114*
8:34, *193*
8:38, *88, 308*
10:29, *107*
12:31, *354*
12:35-37, *7*
13:13, *300*
13:24, *14*
13:31, *109, 168, 248, 362*
14:33, *40, 221, 314*
14:45, *315*
15:24, *22*
15:29, *27*
15:34, *22*

Luke
1:2, *188*
1:15, *28, 29*
1:17, *165*
1:35, *5, 16, 27, 304*
1:38, *318*
1:53, *190*
1:78-79, *349*
2:13, *67*
2:14, *18*
2:35, *39*
3:4, *124*
3:6, *13*
3:7, *121, 125*
3:9, *114, 122, 125*
3:16, *124, 133*
3:17, *121*
4:2, *256*
4:8, *120*
4:13, *41*
4:22, *361*
4:42, *194*
5:8, *126*
5:13, *313*
5:27, *177*
5:29, *177*
6:21, *297*
6:27, *71, 84*
6:35, *259*
6:36, *311*
6:45, *357*
6:46, *201, 228, 299*
7:41, *101*
8:8, *235*
8:14, *33*
8:15, *63*
9:26, *88, 308*
9:62, *206*
10:13, *239*
10:15, *156, 197*
10:17, *42*
10:19, *5, 73, 125, 320*
10:20, *275*
10:30, *197*
11:2, *176, 185, 297*
11:4, *25, 57, 210, 218*
11:13, *104*
11:14, *280*
11:15, *151, 153, 329*
11:51, *65*
12:8, *211*
12:20, *243*
12:31, *104*

13:11, *275*
13:32, *345*
13:34, *128, 224*
13:35, *180*
14:11, *197, 276*
14:25-26, *107*
14:26, *107*
15:17, *224*
16:16, *122*
16:22, *243, 313*
16:22-23, *214*
16:25, *56*
17:10, *91*
17:21, *254*
18:14, *197*
19:10, *131, 279, 306*
20:38, *109*
21:33, *109, 168, 248, 362*
21:34, *63*
22:15, *8*
22:31, *41*
22:33, *154*
23:34, *22*
23:43, *220*
24:32, *289*

John
1:1, *181, 326, 327*
1:2, *326*
1:3, *106*
1:3-4, *137*
1:4, *94*
1:7, *76*
1:9, *330*
1:14, *68, 81, 98, 134, 156, 160, 161, 178, 220, 354*
1:16, *352*
1:17, *163*
1:18, *202*
1:20-22, *120*
1:23, *120, 124*
1:29, *4, 305, 340*
2:19, *112, 242*
2:21, *242*
3:5, *52, 223*
3:13, *160, 237*
3:16, *81*
3:18, *81*
4:14, *54, 175, 257, 336*
4:23, *51*
4:34, *341*
5:6-9, *135*
5:8, *312*

5:11, *312*
5:23, *119*
6:24, *194*
6:31, *147*
6:32, *35*
6:33, *175*
6:35, *143, 175, 190, 219, 240, 257, 356*
6:38, *27, 306*
6:41, *175, 240*
6:47, *12*
6:48, *175, 190, 219, 240, 257, 356*
6:55, *175, 240, 356*
6:57, *2, 153, 321*
6:62, *160*
6:70, *347*
7:38, *18, 63*
7:38-39, *336*
8:12, *94, 119, 330*
8:40, *3, 4*
8:44, *192*
8:48, *151*
8:52, *109*
9:1, *329*
9:16, *24, 153, 316, 329*
10:9, *3*
10:11, *3, 32*
10:14, *152*
10:17-18, *154*
10:18, *39, 242, 243*
10:27, *54, 240*
10:29, *154, 155, 256*
10:30, *7, 133*
10:35, *181, 326, 354*
11:25, *153*
11:26, *137*
12:2, *283*
12:27, *40*
12:46, *330*
13:18, *316, 317*
13:27, *315*
13:30, *155*
14:2, *331*
14:6, *3, 143, 153, 162, 261*
14:9, *134, 244, 325*
14:10, *7*
14:12, *14*
14:23, *112, 131, 133*
15:1, *47, 242*
15:14, *192*
15:15, *192*

15:19, *83*
16:13, *360*
17:3, *12, 244*
17:11, *251*
17:12, *251*
17:14, *83*
17:16, *83*
17:21, *133, 171*
18:5-8, *154*
19:15, *30, 311*
19:23, *36*
19:24, *22*
19:37, *317*
20:35, *329*
21:18-19, *193*

Acts
1:3-4, *67*
1:18, *261*
1:24, *170, 329*
1:25, *250*
2:1, *102*
2:24, *311*
2:29, *179*
2:32, *38*
2:36, *106*
3:14, *49*
3:14-15, *4*
3:15, *5*
4:32, *163, 171, 191, 319*
5:41, *82*
7:59, *143*
7:60, *143*
13:10, *92, 108, 168, 235*
13:22, *69, 231*
13:27, *316*
14:22, *186, 348*
20:35, *172*
21:34-35, *217*
23:6, *217*

Romans
1:1, *165, 231*
1:14, *241*
1:19, *48*
1:20, *79*
1:24, *235*
1:25, *235*
1:26, *235*
2:4, *159*
2:10, *225*
2:12, *166, 233*
2:14, *167, 189*

2:16, *165*
4:9, *167*
5:3, *249*
5:5, *204*
5:10, *149*
5:14, *305*
5:19, *152, 305*
6:5, *199*
6:12, *95*
7, *321*
7:6, *332*
7:14, *108, 234, 282, 295*
7:24, *34, 274*
7:25, *274*
8:7, *94, 234, 271*
8:8, *234, 271*
8:9, *94, 99, 234, 271*
8:15, *42, 123, 128*
8:18, *14*
8:24, *109, 176*
8:29, *42, 86, 347*
8:31, *93*
8:32, *38*
8:33, *93*
8:35, *146, 301*
8:36, *74*
9:13, *347*
9:14, *347*
9:16, *75, 174, 260, 261, 301, 336*
9:21, *153*
10:3, *307*
10:10, *113*
11:3, *81, 221*
11:5, *125, 247*
11:30, *205*
11:30-31, *205*
11:30-32, *247*
11:32, *204, 205*
11:33, *84, 239*
11:33-34, *205*
12:1, *304, 350*
12:6, *176*
12:11, *162*
12:13, *172*
13:12, *21, 96*
13:13, *21*
15:3, *149, 151*
16:18, *10, 75*
16:20, *284*
16:25, *165*
16:27, *358*

1 Corinthians
1:4-5, *339*
1:5, *81, 175, 176, 253, 356*
1:10, *40, 163, 185, 191, 225, 357*
1:18–2:6, *30*
1:24, *5, 67, 74*
1:30, *189, 211, 293, 331*
2:2, *152*
2:6, *46, 53, 58, 225, 241, 242, 306*
2:8, *30, 68*
2:9, *141*
2:10, *141*
2:11, *170*
2:14, *295*
2:16, *25*
3:1, *191*
3:2, *53, 244*
3:3-4, *26, 157, 159*
3:9, *114*
3:11-12, *10*
3:12, *19, 288*
3:16, *97, 111*
3:17, *208, 248*
4:5, *230*
4:8, *5, 124, 172*
4:9-10, *344*
4:15, *32, 88*
4:21, *57, 95*
5:1, *175, 339*
6:7, *201*
6:9, *51, 201*
6:13, *351*
6:17, *69, 163, 191, 244*
6:19, *208*
6:20, *119*
7:1, *83*
7:5, *282*
7:9, *124, 288*
7:23, *138*
7:32, *91*
7:34, *63, 91*
8:13, *74, 116, 141, 345*
9:21, *340*
9:27, *98, 100, 226, 234, 272, 300, 312, 325*
10:4, *301*
10:13, *6*
10:25-26, *61*
10:31, *119*
11:3, *27, 29*
12:3, *70, 137, 201, 299*

12:8-9, *97*
12:15-17, *20*
12:16, *162*
12:21, *162*
12:27, *20, 162, 331*
12:28, *154, 250*
13:3, *299*
13:4-5, 7, *354*
13:4-7, *203*
13:8, *255*
13:9, *47, 98, 190*
13:9-10, *142, 224*
13:10, *190, 352*
13:11, *28, 189*
13:12, *190, 352*
14:20, *86*
14:32, *181*
14:38, *152*
15:23, *179*
15:24, 5, *127*
15:28, *10, 96, 97, 117, 176, 185, 323, 352, 354*
15:32, *298*
15:33, *10, 75, 207, 253, 280, 318*
15:42-43, *355*
15:42-44, *268, 354*
15:44, *355*
15:44-46, *115*
15:46, *268, 356*
15:47-49, *139*
15:49, *275, 292*
15:51, *316*
15:51-52, *354*
15:54, *301*
15:56, *6*
16:9, *58*

2 Corinthians
1:9, *323*
1:21, *318*
1:22, *97, 224, 352, 353*
1:24, *92*
2:11, *221*
3, *345*
3:3, *115, 360*
3:5-6, *133*
3:18, *90, 186, 326, 332*
4:2, *70, 340*
4:4, *303*
4:8, *57, 82, 146, 186, 196, 348*

4:10, *35, 95, 98*
4:18, *255*
5:2, *297*
5:4, *98*
5:5, *224*
5:13, *141, 302*
5:14-15, *38*
5:16, *133, 152, 158, 161*
5:21, *11, 24, 153, 159, 168, 178, 187, 202, 213, 221, 236, 243, 267, 307, 311, 317, 329, 354, 362*
6:16, *73, 131, 247*
7:10, *275, 276, 283, 288, 297*
8:9, *45, 47, 187, 311, 353, 356*
9:9, *137*
10:3, *295*
10:5, *173*
10:6, *125, 320*
11:10, *237, 238*
12:4, *327, 333*
12:20-21, *215*
13:4, 5, 7, *312, 330*
13:8, *94, 108*

Galatians
1:4, *154*
2:20, *150, 153*
3:13, *13, 45, 178, 187, 317*
3:13-14, *153, 202, 330, 353, 356*
3:14, *45*
4:4, *160*
4:5-6, *42*
4:8, *213*
4:8-9, *152, 255, 343*
4:19, *32*
4:22, *181*
4:22-24, *305*
4:25, *181*
4:26, *346*
5:7, *348*
5:15, *219*
5:24, *94*

Ephesians
1:3, *16, 65*
1:4, *346*
1:18, *79, 332*
2:2, *66*

2:6, *269*
2:8, *249*
2:10, *171*
2:12, *125, 187, 212*
2:15, *167, 171*
3:17, *63*
4:14, *207*
4:16, *219*
4:22-24, *290*
4:27, *39, 215, 234, 261, 277, 278, 287*
5:2, *38*
5:8, *22, 119*
5:13, *267, 270, 295*
5:14, *131*
5:18, *241, 242*
5:20, *182*
5:22-24, *362*
5:27, *46, 255*
5:32, *305*
6:11, *251, 337*
6:12, *189, 290*
6:13, *94*
6:15, *263*
6:16, *94, 202, 251, 274*
6:17, *204*

Philippians
1:23, *11, 223, 224*
1:24, *224*
2:6-7, *45, 187, 340*
2:7, *155, 178, 179, 187, 203*
2:8, *41*
2:10-11, *15*
3:6, *307*
3:19, *70, 206, 207, 235*
3:20, *180, 235, 266, 268, 270, 300*
3:20-21, *206*
3:21, *83, 92, 349, 350, 352*
4:1, *10*
4:7, *127*
4:13, *87, 121, 277*
4:18, *28, 350*

Colossians
1:13, *123*
1:15, *152, 155, 244, 303, 325*
1:16, *79, 114, 137*
1:16-17, *144*
1:18, *5, 42*
1:20, *14, 15*

2:14, *342*
2:16, *266*
2:18-19, *219*
2:19, *219*
3:2, *351*
3:5, *8, 35, 193, 337*
3:9-10, *290, 321*
4:1, *55*

1 Thessalonians
2:4, *87*
2:8, *87*
4:13, *316*
5:7, *60*
5:16-18, *183*
5:17, *185*
5:17-18, *193*
5:18, *182*
5:21-22, *194*
5:22, *196*
5:23, *14, 39, 143*

1 Timothy
1:7, *245*
1:19-20, *215*
1:20, *101*
2:4, *193, 266*
3:14-15, *242*
3:15, *132*
3:16, *68*
4:13, *319*
5:24, *24*
5:25, *24*
6:16, *119*
6:17, *16, 292*
6:19, *16*
6:20, *292*

2 Timothy
2:4, *336*
2:7, *165, 312, 319*
2:8, *165*
2:11, *199*
2:19, *255, 343*
2:20, *153*
3:1-2, *256*
3:4, *153*
3:6, *320*
3:16, *305, 319*
4:2, *281*
4:7, *261, 263*
4:7-8, *246*

373

Titus
1:16, *228*
2:8, *193*, *356*
3:5, *260*
3:10, *294*
3:11, *294*

Philemon
13–14, *128*

Hebrews
1:3, *16*, *155*, *187*, *212*, *244*, *291*, *303*, *325*
1:14, *336*
2:9, *14*, *34*, *38*, *179*, *202*
2:10, *5*
2:11, *42*
2:12, *22*
2:12-13, *42*
2:14, *38*, *127*
2:17, *42*
3:1-2, *106*
3:6, *97*, *130*
4:9, *83*, *266*
4:12, *204*, *362*
4:14, *269*
4:15, *220*, *221*
5:9, *155*, *240*, *285*
5:12, *29*, *53*, *58*
5:13, *53*
5:14, *242*
6:1, *53*
7:3, *117*
7:25, *8*, *10*, *11*, *45*
8:10, *360*
10:1, *57*
10:5, *22*, *299*
10:7, *299*
10:16, *262*
10:24, *263*
11:9, *297*
11:13, *297*
11:25, *250*, *255*
11:26, *343*
12:2, *151*, *300*, *307*
12:22, *325*
12:23, *42*
13:4, *210*, *362*
13:7, *263*
13:15, *360*
13:17, *263*

James
1:1, *231*
1:15, *57*, *131*, *174*, *196*, *199*
1:23-24, *90*
1:25, *90*
2:15-16, *259*
2:17, *249*
2:26, *143*
4:8, *69*, *191*, *208*, *227*
5:16, *136*, *324*

1 Peter
1:2, *251*
1:8, *297*
1:9, *323*
1:9-10, *220*
1:18-19, *138*
1:22, *49*, *69*, *323*
1:25, *248*
2:2, *53*
2:5, *53*, *216*
2:9, *216*, *225*
2:11, *99*
2:21, *74*, *168*
2:22, *11*, *15*, *24*, *28*, *38*, *159*, *168*, *243*, *267*, *329*
2:23, *15*
3:18, *5*, *11*, *68*
3:18-19, *135*
4:1, *22*
4:8, *166*
4:14, *209*
5:6, *197*

2 Peter
3:9, *110*, *159*

1 John
1:5, *211*
2:1, *9*, *10*, *45*
2:17, *137*
2:29, *42*, *118*, *252*
3:2, *10*, *48*, *98*, *353*
3:4, *166*, *284*
3:6, *79*
3:9, *118*, *252*
3:14, *260*
3:16, *87*
3:21, *69*, *86*, *186*
4:2, *68*
4:8, *191*, *203*
4:18, *44*, *157*, *158*, *162*, *174*, *188*, *191*
5:1, *42*, *118*
5:18, *118*

Jude
6, *270*, *343*

Revelation
6:9, *331*, *350*
8:13, *297*
12:4, *51*
14:7, *119*
20:4, *331*
22:2, *219*, *356*

ANCIENT CHRISTIAN TEXTS

SERIES EDITORS

Gerald L. Bray

Michael Glerup

Thomas C. Oden†

Ancient Christian Texts is a series of new translations, most of which are presented here in English for the first time. The series provides contemporary readers with the resources they need to study the key writings of the early church for themselves. The texts represented in the series are full-length commentaries or sermon series based on biblical books or extended scriptural passages.

This series extends the ecumenical project begun with the Ancient Christian Commentary on Scripture, promoting a vital link of communication between today's varied Christian traditions and their common ancient ancestors in the faith. On this shared ground, we gather to listen to the pastoral and theological insights of the church's leading theologians during its earliest centuries.

Many readers of the Ancient Christian Commentary on Scripture have wished to read the full-length works from which excerpts were selected. Several of those texts have not been available in English before or have existed only in cumbersome English in isolated libraries. The work begun by Thomas C. Oden and the Institute for Classical Christian Studies to make more of these texts available to the general reading public continues today.

The volumes, though not critical editions, provide notes where needed to acquaint general readers with the necessary background to understand what the ancient authors are saying. Preachers, pastors, students and teachers of Scripture will be refreshed and enriched here by the ancient wisdom of the church.

www.ivpress.com/act

For a list of IVP email newsletters, including information
about our latest ebook releases, please visit

www.ivpress.com/eu1